OUTFOXED AGAIN

Winning for Animals

GW00691564

By
Mike Huskisson

Published by
Animal Welfare Information Service
PO Box 8, Halesworth, Suffolk, IP19 0JL
www.acigawis.org.uk

Outfoxed Again was published by the Animal Welfare Information Service in February 2017.

Other books by the author
Outfoxed
Outfoxed Take Two

ISBN 978-0-9933822-1-5

Printed and bound in Great Britain by Clays Ltd, St Ives plc

DEDICATED TO SUE AND MY FAMILY.

THEIR LOVE, TOLERANCE AND SUPPORT HAVE BEEN
BEYOND EQUAL.

CONTENTS

PREFACE

This is a book about front line animal rights activists. 'Rights' means animals have a right to their lives—and a right to be treated decently and humanely. *Outfoxed Again* is funded by current and former activists and those who care that the view from the front line is seen. Back in the 1980s the key issues of the era, for those concerned with animal welfare, were bloodsports, vivisection and factory farming. Other topics included circuses, the fur trade and zoos.

Today the issues are more global—pollution of the seas, degradation of the environment and global warming. In 1984 we were more parochial. Our concerns of that time have not been resolved; they have just been swamped by wider issues.

Outfoxed Again seeks to explain what activists do and why and how they do it. It also seeks understanding of the motivations of those opponents in the front line. It is far more than an account of their guarded views and explanations as offered in the written word or considered interviews. Here you will read what bloodsports enthusiasts and scientists do and say when they believe they are amongst their own. As such, because times have changed, it is an insight without equal.

Outfoxed Again, the second part of a planned trilogy, is the sequel to *Outfoxed Take Two* (2015) that was a revised and updated version of *Outfoxed* (1983). In the main, animal rights/welfare theories and concepts developed and explained in *Outfoxed Take Two* will not be repeated here. *Outfoxed Take Two* and *Outfoxed Again* are to be regarded as companion volumes.

Outfoxed Take Two detailed the first phase of my campaigning work for animals from the late 1960s through to the end of 1983. That embraced my work as a hunt saboteur operating to thwart fox, deer, hare and otter hunts; my involvement in the 1977 desecration of the grave of legendary and long-dead Huntsman—John Peel— and subsequent jailing for 9 months for helping to push his headstone over; and my deep undercover work from 1981 to 1983 to expose hunting wildlife with dogs.

Outfoxed Take Two included detailed accounts of the reality of fox and hare hunting, hare coursing, the hunting of wild red deer with packs of hounds and mink hunting. It described the birth of the direct action animal rights movement here in the UK. Youngsters realised that signing petitions and lobbying against cruelty were not their only options (important though they are); they could also take swift and effective action to end the cruelty.

This second work is subtitled 'winning for animals' but is of course about winning for our own species as well. In the short term, it gives people real joy to save lives. In the longer term, we inhabit a small fragile planet. If we ever render it impossible for animals to live here with us we will vanish soon after. Furthermore, for the duration of our short lives, we surely impoverish our presence by surrounding ourselves with cruelty.

Outfoxed Again covers my campaigning work with many colleagues from 1984 to 2005. This embraces a time of great change for animal rights campaigners. The lengthy campaigns to abolish the hunting of wildlife with dogs achieved some success with the Hunting Act 2004. That created abolition by word of law—but there has proved to be a world of difference between the letter of the law and any enforcement in the fields. For a variety of reasons at the time of writing (2017) the hunting fraternity can ignore the law with impunity. Their only frustration is they cannot boast about their actions in lurid write-ups of lengthy hunts.

In terms of vivisection there has been little progress. The 1876 Cruelty to Animals Act was replaced by the 1986 Animals (Scientific Procedures) Act but vivisection is still rampant behind closed doors. Yes, we are now less likely to hear of cats and dogs stolen from the streets for vivisection but being purpose-bred is no better for the animal concerned.

Back in 1984 the video camera became available as a weapon for campaigners. These were not the modern tiny cameras where the lens can even be concealed in a button, rather they were large and bulky, taking a full-sized VHS tape. Even so they were a welcome advance over their predecessors, the Super-8 cine film cameras. With a video camera if we could see it we could film it. We could record sounds and with adequate batteries could film for the duration of the tape. Most importantly that tape could be passed direct to a television company for transmission, usually with the safeguard of copying the tape first.

In terms of photography, 1984 was still long before the digital age but we could make use of photographic advances such as automatic exposure metering which made photography faster—an important factor in difficult situations. We still had to cope with using 35mm films. These were 24 or 36 exposure films with film speed (ASA) settings varying from 100 to 800 to start with. Later, 1600 ASA films became available. (The higher the number the easier it was to take photographs in low-light). But, unlike with digital cameras or mobile phones, there was no opportunity to immediately check the image. Films back then were exposed and sent away for processing. That put valuable films at risk; they could be lost in the post, lost by couriers or mishandled by processors. Such films were difficult to load into the camera in a hurry, particularly in pouring rain or with fingers numbed by cold.

I started off using a couple of Nikon F2 cameras—the top professional camera of the day. Later I added the Nikon F3 to my inventory then the Nikon F4. In time the appearance of such professional cameras became hard to explain to hunters so I started to acquire and use top quality compact cameras such as the Contax T2.

1984 pre-dated mobile phones, sat navs for cars and GPS devices. To make a phone call we still had to find a phone box and, as for navigation about the countryside, map reading was an essential skill. To establish location, we needed to be able to read the grid reference from an Ordnance Survey map. During the time frame of this work many welcome technological advances were made providing new opportunities for the investigative campaigner.

All we sought was to show the public what we could see ourselves. That was a whole lot easier in 2005 than it had been in 1984. By 2005 we had the concealed body cameras and remote self-contained cameras. The latter can be concealed in woods. They go to sleep until triggered by a passing person when they wake up, film for a few minutes and then return to sleep mode. We could still only have dreamed of the cameras on drones and cameras on car dashboards available today.

Whilst *Outfoxed Again* reaches back some 33 years into time now, it is largely compiled from contemporaneous notes, diaries and letters and in the latter parts from video and audio recordings made during the investigations. Chapter two (the Royal College of Surgeons) is based on printed articles from the time, my court notes, a booklet that I wrote whilst in prison and prison letters.

For the hunting accounts, I again follow the hunting convention whereby unless or until it is shown otherwise all hunted foxes are male and hunted hares are female. For hunted deer, their sex is obvious—apart from young calves. For mink hunting I followed the fox hunting convention and assumed that a hunted mink is male.

Time has inevitably taken some of the people named hereafter: from our side Richard Course, John Hicks, Kevin Saunders, Alan Clark, Tony Banks and Clifford Pellow to name but six great campaigners. Many from the hunting side have passed on. Some have also changed sides. Some have changed back again, with at least one going in each direction.

When I wrote the text of the original *Outfoxed* back in the summer of 1983 I would never have thought that in the hunting season 2015-16 I would have witnessed exactly the same cruelty to our wildlife—and certainly not more than ten years after the so-called hunting 'ban'.

It is fair to point out that much of what I describe is denied by the hunting world. Hunters damned me as a contemptible criminal and cursed the fact that many from various hunts unwittingly befriended me and guided me to the very core of hunting. Spokesmen for hunting accused me of lying, exaggerating, faking evidence 'in camera' or setting up incidents.

Over the years, hunters perfected a repertoire of excuses to explain away anything untoward that happened in the hunting fields. Confronted with shocking evidence they claimed it never happened or was a trick created in camera or in computer. For many hunters, our videos showing cruelty are mere fabrications.

If anything did happen it was set up or they were not there. If they were there they saw nothing. If they did see anything it was an accident. If it was not an accident, then whoever did it was unknown to the hunt. If they were known, then swift and severe disciplinary action was taken.

Hunters also claimed that my evidence of cruelty amounted to nothing more than isolated examples. My response was to draw the analogy of being confronted with a barrel of apples, many of which we believed to be bad. It was hard for us to extract an apple. By one means or another I have done so and that apple was rotten. When I reached in and pulled out another that too was rotten. I pulled out another and that was rotten. How

7

many apples do we have to pull out before we accept that the whole barrel is rotten?

I stand by my words and images. I have described what I saw and heard. I provoked nothing. I photographed and filmed what I could. I am not a professional writer, nor photographer, nor film maker but I hope that by combining here my abilities at each I can convey some idea as to how animals are really treated in our world. Yes, the hunting described here was some years ago now but at the interface between hound and quarry little has changed.

Mike Huskisson, Suffolk, England. January 2017

ACNOWLEDGEMENTS

So many colleagues have helped me over the years both in the fields and with research. I cannot name everyone, and some prefer not to be named—but you know who you are and I thank you all. For notable help with investigative work over the time-frame of this book I mention, in alphabetical order: Laina Cracknell, Lynne Edwards, Jane Evans, Dave Fox, Mark Glover, Kevin Hill, Terry Hill, Howard Hodges, Janet Jackson, Philip Kiernan, Donna King, Alan Knight, Penny Little, Melody MacDonald, Ed Maynard, Mike Michalak, Roy Parker, Lawrie Payne, Steve Rackett, Daniel Rolke, Ben Stewart, John Tierney, Andrew Tyler, Liz Varney, Les Ward, Andrew Wasley, Dave and Cee Wetton, Jim Wickens and Aideen Yourell.

I should also mention Jim Barrington. Even though he changed sides, without his support and help, a lot of my early successes against hunting would never have happened.

For specific assistance with this text I thank Stephan Bodini, Joe Hashman and Dave Wetton for their great help with proof-reading. If this book has any literary merit that is due to the ability and diligence of my proof readers. They not only corrected spelling, grammar and punctuation they also enhanced the text by suggesting changes for elegance. I have made additions after proof reading so any errors are entirely down to me.

I thank Dave Wetton, Kevin Hill and Joe Hashman for their contributions that clarify incidents they witnessed. I am grateful to many others—people such as Mike Butcher, Philip Kiernan, Dave Fox and Alan Knight—for their help with clarifying facts and naming individuals. I also thank the many supporters of the Animal Cruelty Investigation Group and Animal Welfare Information Service, some sadly no longer with us, whose generous donations and legacies have funded the investigative work described here and have paid for this publication.

I acknowledge the assistance provided by the publications of the various national groups. Of great value were *Cruel Sports*, then *Wildlife Guardian*—magazines of the League Against Cruel Sport (LACS) and *HOWL*—the magazine of the Hunt Saboteurs Association (HSA). I also acknowledge help from *Liberator*—the campaigning newspaper of the British Union for the Abolition of Vivisection (BUAV), and *The*

Campaigner—the magazine of the National Anti-Vivisection Society (NAVS).

I have also made use of many books. In particular (in order of date of publication):-

Caught in the Act (The Feldberg Investigation) 1994. By Melody MacDonald, compiled and edited by Jill Russell.

From Dusk 'til Dawn 2007. By Keith Mann

Save Our Stags 2008. By Ian Pedler

(I recommend all three books to students of these issues)

Finally, this would never have happened without the stalwart support, advice and encouragement of my family to whom I am eternally grateful.

This is not a book about me and what I did for animals. This is primarily about the Animal Cruelty Investigation Group (ACIG) and the Animal Welfare Information Service (AWIS), the field investigators and supporters and funders of these groups and what WE have done for animals. It is also about how we have worked with many from a variety of groups ranging from the South East Animal Liberation League (SEALL) through Advocates for Animals, the BUAV, HSA, British Divers Marine Life Rescue (BDMLR), LACS, Irish Council Against Bloodsports (ICABS) and NAVS to the RSPCA to make our fragile world a better place for all. We have battled callousness and cruelty with compassion and within the law. We have countered violence not like for like, but rather with a steel-edged resolve to do what is right and lawful.

I have been privileged to work for many years with some of the very best individuals and teams of animal activists. We have shown how ordinary people, working alone or together, really can make this world a better place for animals—and consequently for people. They need only be determined and dedicated.

But these are but a few battles won. Horrendous suffering continues. We have only shown what is possible. There is so much still to do.

This book starts in 1984 and ends in 2005. The text is not in strict chronological order. If it were, it would have confused the reader to switch from hare coursing to fox hunting, then to work in a research laboratory, then field work looking for artificial earths followed by work following live export lorries.

So, types of work are grouped together: direct action; undercover work against hunting and in a laboratory; hunt monitoring; investigative work in the countryside; hunt violence; work in Ireland; talks and debates; political work and my role in the Lord Burns Hunting Inquiry; and lastly the final road to political victory.

Ultimately the index holds the key to finding the material within. All the photographs included were taken by the author, unless otherwise indicated.

CHAPTER ONE
Beyond Outfoxed

The original *Outfoxed* was published on December 15th 1983. Early in the New Year of 1984 I resumed my field investigations by checking for artificial earths in fox hunt countries. Saturday January 14th, a colleague and I checked known sites in Worcestershire Foxhounds country. The following day I showed Maureen Lawless, a journalist from the *News of the World*, an artificial earth in an isolated copse in Heythrop Foxhounds country near Sezincote. With the Heythrop due to meet nearby a couple of days later we suspected activity at the site. We found nothing untoward.

On Monday January 16th, I delivered 50 copies of *Outfoxed* to WH Smith's in Swindon. That night I met a hunt saboteur colleague and we again checked the artificial earth site. We were concerned there might be a fox held captive in the underground complex but we found nothing.

We were still concerned that a fox might be put in the earth on the morning of the hunt so the next day with the Heythrop Foxhounds meeting at Bourton my hunt saboteur colleague and I, Maureen Lawless and a photographer from the *News of the World* returned to the site. We agreed that if a fox was imprisoned in the earth we would let him go and I had taken along a toy fox to replace him. The thought of a terrierman lifting the chamber lid to bolt a live fox but instead being confronted by a fabric fox appealed. But we found no live fox. So, we took up a concealed position from whence to record any interaction between the hunters and their artificial earth but they must have found other foxes and gone elsewhere because they came nowhere near us. Heythrop Foxhounds' artificial earths were to figure greatly in my future investigative work.

Saturday February 4th 1984 was eventful. I travelled north to the Yorkshire Television studios in Leeds for the filming of a Jimmy Young programme involving Jack Charlton. I was a minor stooge placed in the audience briefed to ask Jack about his mink hunting days, specifically September 8th 1982 with the Three Counties Minkhounds when I had been undercover within the hunt. Somehow, perhaps in how the question was put to me, poor Jack got the false idea that I was accusing him of throwing a mink live to the hounds. He was set to storm off the stage and 'sort me out' but luckily for me was restrained!

Two weeks later I did more TV work when I met the BBC2 *Oxford Roadshow* team to film me attending the meet of the Heythrop Foxhounds at Eyford Knoll—the former home near Stow-on-the-Wold of legendary Huntsman Captain R.E Wallace. The crew decided that it would make good television to film me 'undercover' within a hunt and then confront them afterwards over my presence. I had told the film crew that I would be with the Heythrop that day. The programme contacted the hunt and secured permission to film—with the hunt demanding £100 from BBC2 for their services. The crew said nothing about their real reason for being there.

The Heythrop hunters then insisted the film crew could only follow the hunt in a supporter's Range Rover. The programme makers resisted this and the compromise was agreed whereby a hunt official would 'guide' the crew. The BBC2 Range Rover would follow a hunt vehicle

I met the film crew at nearby cross-roads before the meet for some preliminary filming away from the hunters. They asked me to wear something to make me stand out from the sea of green hunters for their camera. The best I could find was a bright red scarf. I looked like a Swan Vesta match—hardly the best disguise for an undercover operator.

At the meet the BBC2 crew did a lot of banal filming to hide their real purpose. The hunt had clearly called out their troops to impress them as the field was larger than usual. I was amused to see the immaculately dressed hunters preen themselves for the camera. I attended the meet but had to keep my head down as the Kennel Huntsman, Tony Collins, could have recognised me. Brian Toon from the Masters of Fox Hounds Association was the official brought in to guide the film crew.

Hounds were taken into nearby woods and spoke immediately, streaming away in pursuit of a fox. Finding so quickly was somewhat unusual. Later that day I took time out to pick through the woods but could find nothing suspicious. Half the earths there were blocked, to keep foxes above ground.

I kept in touch with the hunt through the day. As expected they killed nothing. The crew had arranged to interview one Joint Master, Steven Lambert, in the fields afterwards but the hunt went on so long that the light failed. The crew then hastily booked a room in a nearby hotel for the interview and asked me to attend. When Steven Lambert was told of my involvement and doubtless guessed the real purpose for all the filming he at first declined to participate, as did Brian Toon. With some persuasion from the crew they changed their minds. Brian Toon seized the opportunity to bring up my being jailed for pushing over the headstone of John Peel.

In time, I decided to return for a closer look at hare coursing. This ancient pastime was a test of the speed and agility of two dogs against the agility and stamina of a hare. In English coursing there were two main variants. In the first, lines of carefully controlled beaters were put out over the open fields with the aim of driving hares towards a pre-selected field. Care was taken to ensure that only one hare at a time was driven onto the field. On the field, near where the hare was driven in, the Slipper hid holding the two dogs due to run. The hide, known as the shy, could be bales of straw, a canvas and pole construction or it could just be a thick hedge. Two lines of coursers, one line on either side stretched away from the Slipper into the field in a funnel shape. These 'flankers' had the task of keeping fleeing hares in clear line of sight from the Slipper. The Slipper held both dogs in a slip lead. If he judged the hare to be suitable, his task was to give the hare a start of 80 metres upwards and then, if both dogs were sighted on the hare, he released them. The coursing was then adjudicated by a mounted Judge who galloped alongside.

The hare was fast but not as fast as the greyhounds. They quickly caught up and then her only means of escape was to turn sharply. The dogs could not match that agility. They would skid to a halt, get back on line and chase the hare again. Again, she would turn. If the hare could survive for around seven turns her pursuers tired and she could escape.

For the course to be judged the dogs wore bandage collars; one wore red the other white. Hare coursers stressed that no points were awarded for a kill but that was not strictly true. Each course was marked on points with points awarded for pace and for working ability—the ability to course the hare, to press her closely and make her turn. The Judge could award up to three points for the first dog to reach the hare. Whether one dog got the three points depended on the lead that dog had over the other and whether the fleeing hare had veered one way or the other to favour one dog.

Once the hare has been turned then further points are awarded to the dog that makes the hare turn successively. A full point was awarded if the hare was made to turn by more than ninety degrees and half a point was awarded for a turn of less than ninety degrees (called a wrench).

The first dog to reach the hare and make her turn would usually win the course. The second dog up would have to work hard to overturn that lead that could be up to four points. If a dog bounded up, turned the hare and killed her he would win outright. A dog that won after a short course would have a significant advantage over other dogs in later rounds of the event that might have done much more work. Coursing could be gruelling for dog as well as hare and enthusiastic coursers carefully noted the duration of each course to gain an idea as to which dog was likely to win.

Coursers often cheered the death of a hare. They did so for several reasons: the dog that caught and killed the hare usually won and his supporters would cheer; if the hare was killed the coursing would end so neither dog would tire further; they might also cheer to irritate any antis watching. The Cup Final event for hare coursing was the Waterloo Cup held annually on the flat open fields around Great Altcar, north of Liverpool.

Sunday February 19th, I drove north and stayed in a bed and breakfast in Southport ready to attend the running of the 1984 Waterloo Cup the following day. I got up early and arrived at the usual venue for the first day at the Withins at 9:15am. It was immediately obvious that coursing was unlikely as the ground was frosted. A ground inspection at 9:30am confirmed this. The disgruntled crowd were told that there would be further inspections at 10:30am and 11:15am. Both confirmed that the ground was still unsuitable but at the latter inspection the conditions were improving. It was announced that if that continued coursing could start at 1pm.

I estimated a crowd of some 400 to 500 coursers hanging around hoping to see some coursing. In mid-morning, a large contingent of hunt saboteurs arrived to oppose the cruelty. Police escorted them along the road through the lines of coursers. As I stood with the coursers, watching, one saboteur shouted in my direction: *"There's the mole from the League Against Cruel Sports!!"* I took it personally, was mortified and discretely vanished. I drove out, found a phone-box and called the League Against Cruel Sports (LACS) offices to report the coursing was delayed by frost.

I returned to the venue at 12:45pm and encountered hare coursers streaming out; the day had been cancelled. Driving away I found hunt saboteurs and complained about their colleagues identifying me. However the saboteurs were being clever and I was being oversensitive. With all the talk of undercover moles within hunting and coursing they had decided beforehand to identify opponents as moles in this way to set them against each other and it was pure chance that put me in the way of the taunt. I resolved that should the situation be repeated and I was amongst a crowd of hunters when someone shouted, "*There's a bloody anti!*" I would promptly grab some hunter, any hunter and say " *This guy? I've got him.*"

As it turned out, that year the coursers needed little encouragement to fight each other. With plenty to drink and no coursing to watch petty feuds spilled over. In the afternoon, there was a massive brawl at the well-known coursing pub, the *Scarisbrick Arms*, Downholland Cross, involving some 300 coursers. The licencing hours had been extended all afternoon. It seemed that during the merriment Congleton coursers remarked that Stoke City FC was 'shit'. Stoke coursers argued back in typical fashion. One Congleton courser was smashed in the head with a brick, suffered serious injuries and later died. Another was stabbed.

The next morning, I was back at the Withins at 9:30am. On arrival at the venue the police stopped all cars entering and asked the occupants for information regarding the *Scarisbrick* pub brawl. Later in the day I overheard coursers bragging that anyone who knew anything said nothing.

The coursing started at 10:30am. The Withins was a test of speed. The shy, where the Slipper hid, was a canvas hide type construction to the left as you stood watching from the bank side. To the right from that angle was the escape area, the sough, a line of Rhododendron bushes. It was some 400 metres from the shy to the bushes. The Slipper could easily give the hare a start of up to 150 metres here.

As I joined the crowd I could see beaters and hunt saboteurs tangling in distant fields. As well as taking pictures I kept a careful note of the coursing. The second hare coursed was killed. On the fifth course the dog wearing the red collar won. The hare was bowled over and caught. There was a tug-of-war with the live hare being pulled by both dogs. One dog won and ran off with the hare but when that dog was caught and the hare released the hare ran off and escaped! Hares were killed on the sixth and seventh courses and on the tenth—the latter after much struggling. Another hare was killed on the eleventh course. On the thirteenth course the hare escaped but only after a very long and punishing course.

There were 28 courses run before lunch was taken at 2:00pm. There were nine kills, two after much struggling by the hare and two after a tug-of-war. Of the 19 hares that escaped in addition to the one already described escaping after a tug-of-war another was bowled over but still escaped.

Lunch was a 50-minute affair. There were 21 courses in the afternoon. Five hares were killed. On one, the 39th of the day, the hare was killed by a single dog as the other dog ran unsighted. One hare was killed after a tug-of-war; one killed after slipping into a ditch full of water. On the last course of the day the hare was coursed, caught and killed instantly by one dog. Most kills happened early in the day and perhaps to counter this, the hares were given increasingly long starts as the day progressed. A high kill ratio early on was unusual as that was when the press and TV cameras were most likely to be in attendance. It was usually the case that when the media left the slip-length shortened. Hunt saboteurs were most effective when they drove large numbers of hares on to the coursing field—the dogs were not slipped if there was more than one hare on the field, sometimes there were six! Coursing supporters cursed that outcome as the hares that ran through were not rounded up and consequently were lost.

At one point in the afternoon prominent hare courser, Sir Mark Prescott, and an entourage of burly stewards, marched down the bank side urging the coursers to "go and sort the sabs out". The coursers I was with told him, in forthright terms, that they were not interested in sorting out "those twats" whilst the coursing continued and that if he really wanted to recruit such a team they should first stop the coursing.

Despite attempts to encourage coursers to violence most were happy to leave it to the police. This was in sharp contrast to events I had witnessed the previous year when the stewards were clearly restraining the crowd from attacking the saboteurs. The difference is explained by whether the media were present. In the public eye the stewards were well behaved.

Many hares seemed reluctant to run into the escape zone sited at the right-hand end from our viewpoint on the bank. This puzzled coursers around me. Some opined it might be due to poachers shooting from the cover there in previous days. I saw one hare killed when she ran into, and bumped off, the barbed wire lining the field. The stewards raised the bottom strand to try to cure the problem but many coursers feared that raising the wire might harm any dogs pursuing. The day ended after 5pm.

The next morning, Wednesday February 22nd, I was back for the second day of coursing, this time at Lydiate. I arrived at 9:45am and the dogs were in the slips but the first course was not until 10:30am. I stayed to watch ten courses. There was one kill, on the seventh course. It was particularly gruesome. In a desperate attempt to escape, the hare jumped the ditch bordering the coursing field and ran through the line of watching coursers. One dog stopped, but the other continued the chase and caught her in the long grass behind. She was screaming. Handlers rushed forward. I watched as one pulled the struggling hare away from the dog, placed his boot on her head, grabbed her back legs and tugged her body clean away from her head. Having arranged to meet BBC2 in Manchester at 2pm I had to leave early. In any case the light faded as heavy rain swept in. My car was boxed in in the car park and I had to pay a young kid to go and find the owner—it was too risky to ask too much myself as I had to keep away from the likes of Peter Atkinson and Bert Gripton who might have recognized me and were in attendance! Whilst waiting, I learned that hunt saboteurs were spotted on the distant horizon. Sir Mark Prescott immediately organised a gang of sturdy lads and led several car loads to 'sort them out'.

Sometime during the morning Eddie Coulston, an anti-coursing protestor, was just standing watching the coursing from a distance when a hare courser ran up behind him and struck his head violently with the steel base of a shooting stick. Eddie's skull was smashed with fragments of bone driven into his brain. Called to the scene, police assumed Eddie had caused the trouble and frog-marched him from the fields. The officers at first refused to call an ambulance despite the pleas of two qualified nurses. When eventually admitted to hospital Eddie was put in intensive care. His injuries were rated as 'critical' and his wife was warned that it was 'touch and go' whether he would survive. Eddie subsequently spent nearly two weeks in the Neurological Unit of Walton Hospital before making a slow recovery. He suffered life-changing injuries.

After discharge Eddie spoke about his attack: "*Acts of violence such as the one to which I was subjected must not deter us from our aims of achieving total freedom from persecution for all the creatures with whom we share this planet.*" (*Cruel Sports* Number 13—Summer 1984).

I eventually left Lydiate at 1:45pm. As an oversight on the whole event I noted in my diary that whereas the followers of foxhunting were largely geriatric these coursers looked to be mostly aged 15 to 30 and nearly all male. With the coursing being on a weekday I wondered whether it had something to do with the high unemployment rate at the time and watching or even owning running dogs being a cheap form of entertainment.

On March 6th, following his release from hospital, I met Eddie at his home where he was recovering with his family. I was shocked at his injuries. His assailant was Paul Willingale, Secretary of the Mid-Essex Coursing Club and a leading light within hare coursing. He appeared at Preston Crown Court on Wednesday October 31st 1984 and after a three-day trial was convicted of assault. He was sentenced to 12 months' imprisonment, half of which was suspended. Because he only faced 6 months in jail he was released after 4 months. The coursing fraternity rejoiced at his lenient treatment for nearly killing a man.

Not everyone was so happy. The LACS were tipped off he would be released from Norwich prison early Monday March 4th 1985 and would go to the meeting of the Kimberley & Wymondham Coursing Club at Kimberley Green near Norwich, where he had two dogs running. I observed Norwich Prison gates from dawn, saw him released and followed him to the hare coursing venue where he received a hero's welcome. I slipped in amongst the coursers, undercover, and took several pictures. The Judge was Pippa Le Roux and Slipper Bob Blatch. Paul Willingale had *Kowhai Duchess* running in the Fred Bowles Rose Bowl and *Hoovers Tempest* competing in the Barnham Broom Cup.

After the 1984 Waterloo Cup, I returned to the hunting fields the following month. I monitored the meet of the Surrey Union Foxhounds at Forest Green on Saturday March 10th 1984. A group of hunt saboteurs from the Reigate area attended. They were led by the indefatigable Colin Skilton. I started a friendship chain that day that culminated in my marriage the following year and, at time of writing, 32 years of happiness since!

During 1984 I pursued other areas of interest. I supported anti-vivisection campaigns. On Saturday May 12th 1984 I joined the Mobilization for Laboratory Animals march in London from Speaker's

Corner to Trafalgar Square and took photographs from the podium. At the end of that month, on Thursday May 31st, I photographed a noisy and well-attended demonstration against the Fur Trade Dinner at the London Hilton. Sunday June 24th was a busy day. I started at Clapham Common photographing LACS staff and committee members taking part in the London to Brighton cycle ride. I then drove to Guildford station to photograph North Downs HSA activists setting off to walk to Reigate to raise funds for their wildlife protection work. My day ended in Brighton recording the LACS cyclists at the end of their 57-mile ride. They raised £3,000 for the LACS Sanctuary Appeal.

On the evening of Tuesday July 31st 1984 I joined and photographed a protest against the visit of Cross Brothers Circus to Tunbridge Wells. The exploitation of animals in circuses caused deep offence. The venue was the Recreation Ground at Southborough. Demonstrators from groups including Animal Aid, Animal Rights Tonbridge and Tunbridge Wells, Tunbridge Wells Friends of the Earth and the RSPCA attended. Mark Gold, from Animal Aid, was invited in to see the animals—and advised by his guides to take care at night. A 'crowd' of about 40 took their places in a tent that held 400 to 500.

A couple of employees were aggressive towards the protestors. Such circus protests were notorious for the violence from employees. There was something distinctly sinister about being punched by a clown. My good friend, the late Leigh Perkins, was a merchant seaman during the Falklands War. He survived the twin Exocet missile strikes that sunk his ship, the SS *Atlantic Conveyor,* on May 28th 1982 (after being hit on May 25th). Twelve sailors died. Leigh came home uninjured. He later joined a protest outside his local circus; was attacked by circus staff and put in hospital!

August 26th 1984 was memorable. I took my role in the SEALL raid to expose the Royal College of Surgeons (RCS) detailed in the next chapter.

The following year, Saturday January 19th 1985, I supported and photographed the protest march against the Institute of Psychiatry in Camberwell, South East London. Some 1,200 people joined the march organized by the South London Animal Movement. Marchers set off from Jubilee Gardens, passed the House of Commons, then headed for the laboratory where, amongst other experiments, fits were induced in baboons, rats were injected with poison, parts of the brains of monkeys were removed and guinea pigs were exposed to hallucinogenic drugs. (*Liberator* February/March 1985).

The following month I returned to hare coursing for the second day of the Waterloo Cup at Lydiate on February 27th 1985. With my involvement in various court cases I had to keep a low profile.

My time working for the LACS was ending but I still liked to check stag hunts. On Thursday March 14th, I met close friend, John Hicks, the LACS Sanctuaries Manager and we monitored the meet of the Devon and Somerset Staghounds at Haddon Hill. That was spring stag hunting. At the meet, we found no sign of the hunt, so telephoned their kennels. We learned the meet was changed to Wheddon Cross. At about 1pm we decided to move on to look at the Quantock Staghounds who had met at Crowcombe Park Gate. We had one of those cherished 'Get off my land!' incidents where we could order hunt supporters to keep off the recently purchased LACS sanctuary at Alfoxton. We left that hunt at about 3:30pm and returned to the Devon and Somerset Staghounds. They killed at about 4pm. As I was a hunt monitor, rather than undercover observer, I had no opportunity to record anything of the gralloch (the disembowelling of the dead deer and sharing out of slices of liver and other trophies).

I stayed in the West Country and met John Hicks again the following day to monitor the Devon and Somerset Staghounds meet at Bicknor Bridge. I left my car at *The Black Cock* pub and accompanied John in his LACS vehicle. At the meet I photographed supporters. When we went to talk to one Master—Maurice Scott, another Master—Norah Harding warned us the land was private and we should get off. We did. John Goscombe, one of the enthusiastic hunting lads I befriended during my previous undercover work, was there. He told me the boys would love to see me out mink hunting again. The hunt must have killed at about 2pm because soon after that we saw them packing up. It was hard to tell who the hunters hated most—John Hicks or me. It was March 23rd 1985 when I was officially sacked by the LACS for my admitted role in the RCS affair. Two days later, Monday March 25th, I drove to the New Forest to help colleagues monitor the New Forest Buckhounds who hunted Fallow deer. I joined an excellent team of observers including John Hicks, Graham Sirl, Gary Colbourne and Ken James. Again, as an outside observer, rather than undercover with the hunters, I could only photograph from a distance.

The following month I witnessed an incident that should have warned me of the length police were prepared to go to curtail animal rights activism. It was Saturday April 27th 1985—the day of national protests for World Day for Laboratory Animals. I was commissioned by the National Anti-Vivisection Society (NAVS) to photograph their event. NAVS hired a train, christened the Draize Train, to take protestors from Birmingham New Street station to Ledbury for a march to nearby Toxicol laboratories. The focus of the protest was against the Draize Eye Irritancy test.

The NAVS protest was well-attended (about 2000), noisy and peaceful. As a photographer, I joined demonstrators gathered outside the perimeter of Toxicol at the end of the march. Some abuse was exchanged between protesters and staff inside. It was entirely peaceful until I saw a man dressed in typical animal rights clothing pick rocks from a pile of rubble and hurl them at the laboratory windows, smashing some. He encouraged others to join him. When they did, police rushed in and made arrests. I then saw the man who started the stone-throwing pointing out for arrest those activists who had followed his lead! It was a classic case of the agent provocateur. That man, clearly an undercover police officer, then quickly disappeared from the scene.

Autumn 1985 was spent on the Wickham trial. Most of 1986 was consumed by work involved with preparing my defence to the RCS charges and culminated in my imprisonment.

CHAPTER TWO
My work with SEALL. The Royal College of Surgeons are prosecuted, convicted then acquitted.

"Scientists and surgeons who experiment on animals cannot be allowed to remain totally above the laws that apply to other people who have the responsibility of caring for animals." (Margaret Manzoni, speaking for the BUAV, outside Bromley Magistrates Court, February 19th 1985.)

I spent two years from April 1981 working undercover, with some success, to expose the cruelty inherent in bloodsports. I knew there was an equal, if not greater, measure of cruelty lurking out of sight behind the high fences and locked doors that protected vivisection.

Like all animal rights activists I opposed bloodsports, vivisection and factory farming. People often asked which I opposed most and why? My stock answer was that in my opinion animals suffered the greatest pain in vivisection, they suffered in the greatest numbers in factory farming and they suffered for the least reason in bloodsports.

I took the view that in a democracy like ours, where the goal for the campaigner was political change, the campaign against bloodsports had to take priority because for so long as animals could be killed simply for fun any other cruelty inflicted on them would be tolerated. Bloodsports formed the dam of ignorance and callousness that had to be breached before any other humane legislation could be passed. For so long as bloodsports remained legal, any politician faced with public demands to abolish vivisection or factory farming, could easily find refuge by saying that yes, they might be cruel and unnecessary, but surely not so cruel and unnecessary as bloodsports. Accordingly, I made opposing bloodsports my personal priority—but I also had it prominent in my mind that I had to look at exposing vivisection wherever possible.

From 1984, when living in Tonbridge and still working as Press Officer for the LACS I started to switch focus towards vivisection. I did not have to look far. The Royal College of Surgeons (RCS) is an august body with a history dating back to the 14th century. Its formal title, the Royal College of Surgeons of England, was granted by Royal Charter in 1843. The College is a registered charity that exists to advance surgical standards and improve patient care. In 1931, after receiving a gift of £100,000 from Sir Buckston Browne, the RCS built their surgical research centre at Buckston Browne Farm at Downe in Greater London, near the former home of Charles Darwin and not far from Biggin Hill—the famous Battle of Britain fighter station. It was also not far from Tonbridge.

In time a variety of animals were housed at this research centre including dogs, pigs and primates. Such could not be housed on the very doorstep of London without drawing the attention of the large numbers of compassionate people who formed the animal rights movement.

In the autumn of 1983, in response to concerns expressed over the standard of care for the animals held at the farm, animal rights activists undertook observation of the premises. Whilst it was hard to see what took place in the monkey unit it was quickly ascertained that many breeds of dog were held on the site.

Even at that time dogs used for experimental research were almost invariably beagles. A whole industry existed to breed dogs for research, nearly always beagles but occasionally Labradors. Beagles are the experimental animal of choice because they are docile, placid, trusting dogs that will withstand harsh treatment without biting back.

Dogs bred for research have a known pedigree and background. Furthermore, from birth, all that happens to them, the treatments they are given etc. can be recorded. Accordingly, such purpose-bred dogs can be used for very precise experimental work. They are, and always have been, expensive to supply—costing in 1984 around £400 for each beagle.

However, given that some experimental work amounts to little more than practising simple surgery techniques on anaesthetised animals—cut them apart then sew them together again—there was clearly pressure to save money by using other breeds, including mongrels, that are not purpose-bred and are considerably cheaper.

The question of how such dogs were acquired by research laboratories had long taxed animal rights activists and anyone else who cared for dogs. There was historical proof that dogs had been stolen from the streets to supply to laboratories. In a Northern Animal Liberation League (NALL) raid on Sheffield University research laboratory in 1980 several dogs were rescued including a black Labrador, *Blackie*, that was subsequently reunited with his original owner. *Blackie* had been stolen and sold to the University.

Dogs could also be acquired by deception. There were innumerable adverts in local newspapers and newsagent's windows offering pet dogs 'free to a good home'. At that time, it was a simple matter for unscrupulous people to respond to such adverts, claim to offer a good home, take the dog away then sell it either to an intermediary, or directly to a laboratory. The owners of the unwanted pets were often too keen to be rid of their charges to delve too deeply into assurances of 'long-term loving homes'.

Representatives of the research industry tried to claim that some owners would knowingly and happily pass their pets on for research—they would all be anaesthetised and would feel no pain. Many doubted this. If that were true why advertise the dog 'free to a good home' in the first place? Why not sell it direct to the laboratory or their agents themselves?

The RCS obtained dogs for research at Buckston Browne Farm from Animal Pharmaceutical Technology (APT) Consultancy, an animal supplier operating from a private home near Wickham, Hampshire.

The Animal Liberation Front (ALF) moved swiftly to rescue dogs from the RCS. The farm was divided into three units: the main residential building, the monkey unit and the dog unit. On the night of October 1st 1983 an ALF team entered the dog unit and rescued six inmates. Four looked to be ex-racing Greyhounds and the other two appeared, by their behaviour, to be former pets. These dogs were taken away, health-checked by a vet and then homed. The ALF team declined to take an Alsatian that had recently been operated on and was judged too ill to be removed. The relevant day-to-day log kept by the RCS detailed this raid and the need to tighten up security at the farm. Within seven days all these dogs were replaced.

After extensive observation of the laboratory prior to the raid by the ALF, and through the raid, activists confirmed the variety of dogs held at the farm and the primitive, cramped, conditions for the primates. These observations, coupled with facts known to the International Primate Protection League (IPPL), caused great disquiet within the animal rights movement and made further action to gain proof of the plight of the animals held there a certainty.

The primates were marmosets and crab-eating macaques, *Macacca Fascicularis*. Macaques are native to south-east Asia where they live in social groups with females dominant. Their preferred choice of home is the upper tree canopy of tropical rain forests.

At the RCS farm, some 250 macaques were housed, not in lush vegetation, but in metal boxes. They were separated into two groups. Some were for use in experiments. The remainder were in a breeding colony. With wild-caught monkeys so expensive it was clearly viewed as good economics for a hard-pressed charity, such as the RCS, to breed their own. At a time when the use of animals in research was widely questioned it was also good politically to use home bred, rather than wild-caught, stock. But they were still macaques.

Their cages were small metal cubes with each side a mere 3ft 6 inches. They were arranged in tiers separated by trays for the collection of excreta and waste food. The four sides were steel bars and the roof and base aluminium mesh. The cubes were so cramped that an adult monkey standing on the floor could touch all four sides and roof without moving position. Such was their home for years.

Monkeys held for experimentation were kept in isolation but for some breeding monkeys there was marginal improvement. Some cages were joined side to side in communes of two to six cages thus allowing the monkeys to pass from cage to cage and thereby express rudimentary troop behaviour. Monkeys are highly intelligent and inquisitive animals that cannot sit for long in a bare cage without trying to find some means to relieve their excruciating boredom.

Breeding took place in a natural but antisocial way—by placing a suitable male in the same small cage as the female. After the appropriate time the male was removed and the female left to bear and rear her young.

Such a solitary method of procreation and infant rearing conflicted with all their social instincts. In the wild there are many monkeys to help with the nurturing of the young. Also, there is room in the wild for the young to get away from the adults. This natural behaviour is denied within the confines of a cramped steel cage. It was no surprise that some captive-reared monkeys displayed disturbed behavioural traits. Some mothers rejected their young or even attacked them.

The fallibilities of housing monkeys for long periods in such caging had been known for years. The conditions in the primate unit at the RCS research laboratory caused great concern to those devoted to primate welfare—such as the IPPL. Macaques were held for dental research. Their experimental protocol involved them being given a controlled set diet and then being treated with the proposed vaccine to see if it blocked or alleviated the onset of dental caries. There was a control group so that comparison could be made between those given the vaccine and those not given it.

Of course the monkeys, though confined, were still wild animals. They could easily inflict deep bites on handlers. For ease of safe handling the cages had a system known as the 'crush barrier' whereby the front of the cage could be forced towards the back thereby trapping the monkey and holding him/her immobilised so that he/she could be treated safely.

A day-to-day record was kept of the care of the monkeys at Buckston Browne Farm. This detailed any injuries or ailments they suffered, together with any treatments. The keeping of these detailed records, Incident Report forms, was to prove highly significant.

The macaques were named by the RCS staff. The way one macaque, *Mone*, suffered was exposed to the public and thereby highlighted the suffering inflicted on all primates in laboratories around the world. *Mone* was born in the wild in a very close family unit, a cohesive animal society, a very social society where adults take turns at caring for the young. In the natural cycle *Mone* should have grown up to take her own role within her troop but she was denied this. She was trapped and fell into the hands of animal shippers. She may well have been moved from place to place before her final destination—a European research laboratory.

Mone was bought by the RCS on September 2nd 1975. Sometime in 1976 she arrived at Buckston Browne Farm. She was conscripted into their long-running dental research programme. The goal, seemingly, was to enable humans to eat all manner of sweet things and then have periodic vaccinations to stop their teeth rotting. Many felt it wrong that animals should pay with their whole lives so that humans could be careless and carefree. More will be heard about *Mone* later.

South East Animal Liberation League (SEALL) raids

Extremist animal rights actions from the early 1970s onwards could be divided into two main types, both organised and led by intelligent, determined and cunning people. Firstly, the ALF in which small bands of activists entered premises, usually at night, with two goals: firstly, to rescue animals and secondly to damage property to stop further suffering.

Secondly, and later, came the actions of the Animal Liberation Leagues who exploited the latest technology—the video camera—to the full. In their raids, large numbers of activists entered premises, usually in daylight, intent on gathering the maximum amount of information about what happened to animals there whilst at the same time causing the minimum amount of physical damage. Incriminating documents would be seized and photographs and video film taken. Videos would be swiftly passed to the media. The first such action was by the NALL against the Babraham Agricultural Research Centre, near Cambridge in the summer of 1980.

The SEALL, formed in mid-1983, was organised and led by clever and passionate activists. John Beggs, their Press Officer, was at the time studying for a law degree at Brunel University. [He qualified and progressed through the legal ranks to become an eminent QC most noted, curiously, for his brilliance at defending police interests.]

A SEALL raid similar to that by the NALL against Babraham was staged against the Wellcome laboratories in Beckenham, Kent in September 1983. There followed a series of SEALL marches and demonstrations. From early 1984 SEALL commanders took a close interest in the animals held at the RCS. Action was planned with two goals: firstly, to expose the variety of breeds of dogs held at the farm and seek answers as to how those pet dogs were acquired; secondly to expose the conditions in the primate unit.

Activists undertook extensive surveillance of the farm. In the quiet and peace of night the farm was entered and the precise locations of the buildings and means of access to them noted. Distances were measured: from gates to doors, from doors to doors and from buildings to buildings. The presence or absence of locks and alarms was noted. A comprehensive plan of the premises was compiled.

SEALL planners then switched their attentions to the areas surrounding the farm. The locations of nearby houses, road junctions, footpaths and other means of access and escape were recorded. Timings were made of how long it would take activists to leave their vehicles and reach the planned access points to the farm. Similar timings were recorded between the exit points and places where activists could be picked up. Various combinations of routes were measured, compared and evaluated. A plan evolved. Timings were also made of a high-speed drive from nearby police stations to the research farm. These gave the maximum period that activists could safely stay within the farm gathering evidence.

After weeks of close surveillance followed by hours of detailed discussions a plan was confirmed. A team of dedicated activists was recruited from all over the South East of England and assigned tasks. Group leaders were hand-picked and each in turn briefed their group members. There were many separate groups. One was tasked with providing vehicle support; another with gaining access through the perimeter and to the buildings. One group was tasked with photographing the animals; another with taking video film. Another group was assigned to search for documents. A group was asked to recruit supportive journalists to accompany the raid. Finally, there was a general support group tasked with providing assistance wherever needed.

I knew nothing of the detailed pre-planning but subsequent court cases gave me plenty of opportunity to learn. It was anti-vivisection work. Whilst I had been involved in anti-vivisection protests—including direct action such as my rescue of Smoking Beagles from the ICI laboratories in 1975—my main area of concern was working to expose the cruelty inherent in bloodsports. I was busily engaged as the LACS Press Officer.

The LACS are a law-abiding organisation that oppose bloodsports. They are concerned almost entirely with monitoring hunting and political campaigning and are opposed to any direct action that might be construed as illegal. Though SEALL planners knew me to be a competent photographer and I lived nearby, they did not immediately think of me when it came to recruiting activists for one of the photographic groups for this raid. However, I had attended and photographed the SEALL march in Brighton on June 2nd 1984 protesting at the mistreatment of primates at nearby Shamrock Farms.

At a later SEALL meeting in Tonbridge I spoke at length about the need to secure photographic proof of the cruel ways in which animals are treated. I was talking then of the LACS experiences of using an acquired videotape to confirm the cruelty inherent in baiting badgers with dogs, along with my own experiences of exposing bloodsports. In hindsight, clearly some at the meeting felt that I could extend my photographic expertise to cover the dogs and monkeys held at the RCS. On Friday August 24th, I was telephoned at home and asked if I would be available to photograph monkeys the following Sunday. Told I would be working with other journalists, I said I would be pleased to help.

The SEALL raid on the RCS had been scheduled for Sunday August 26th 1984. At the last minute, I was included in the operation. I was told to rendezvous in Biggin Hill at 10:15am on the Sunday. I knew that area well having worked previously at nearby FOAL Farm Animal Sanctuary.

I arrived at the rendezvous armed with my camera and flash equipment. I was picked up by activists and driven towards London until we stopped at a woodland clearing. This was a hive of activity with cars parked all around and people running to and fro with clear purpose. Instructions were shouted. Laden as I was with photographic equipment I was told to join a young activist that I recognised from my days out with local hunt saboteurs—Caroline Dawkins—and board one of two Ford Transit vans. I found the van packed with others laden with an assortment of 35mm and video cameras. Other activists were directed to the second transit van. When both vans were full remaining activists were directed to the fleet of cars.

We soon set off in what I was told was a convoy of two vans and five cars. Huddled in the back of the windowless crowded van it was difficult to tell our direction but I quickly gathered from conversations that our target was the research premises of the RCS at Downe. As a latecomer to the scheme I had not been party to the intensive pre-planning. I was simply told to follow everyone else, photograph any monkeys I saw, damage nothing and afterwards, on exiting the site, to look out for cars displaying green stickers in their windscreens. Drivers of those vehicles had been tasked with picking up Press people.

Whilst the mainstream press was paid, all the activists involved were volunteers. They may have only been doing this for love and for the burning desire to right a wrong—but their actions were fully professional.

Years of working together as hunt saboteurs, protecting our wildlife from violent and aggressive hunters, had made SEALL activists very good indeed.

We arrived at Buckston Browne Farm earlier than planned so drove past the premises, waited in a secluded car park for a few minutes then returned at precisely 11am. The convoy braked sharply to a halt, doors were flung open and everyone disembarked.

Whilst most of our Press party were milling about fiddling with camera equipment, checking settings and that flash leads were connected etc. I noticed another group of activists—many of whom had donned balaclavas—running down a public footpath that led away from the road beside the RCS buildings. As these disappeared our Press party followed; with Caroline Dawkins and I tagging along in their midst.

As we jogged down the footpath I noticed a man innocently tending his adjacent garden. He stood watching us, open-mouthed in astonishment. Things like that did not happen on a Sunday morning in the sleepy backwater that was Downe! I did not linger to watch him but I suspect that he ran inside to phone the police. A report of a group of people running down a footpath in rough clothing and wearing balaclavas would not generate much police interest—a report of them doing so beside an animal research laboratory would induce the maximum police response. The clock was ticking against us.

At the end of the footpath there was a five-barred wooden gate on the right-hand side. Reaching this I could see ahead that many activists had already crossed this into the premises. I watched as they disappeared from sight around various buildings. Everything was quiet.

I paused to check once again that my bulky battery pack was firmly connected to my camera flash unit and the latter to my trusty Nikon F2 camera. With everything in order Caroline and I climbed the gate and followed figures around the building to our left. I had that nervous feeling in the pit of my stomach, as I had on many previous actions with hunt saboteurs. This was trespassing to help animals: like rushing to stop the dig-out of a fox in a wood or running onto a hare coursing field. We put ourselves in harm's way.

We crossed what appeared to be a rubbish tip, ran beside the incinerator where carcasses were burned, then headed towards the sounds of heavy banging coming from one building. We passed some outside wire-mesh runs, up to a door that I noticed was partially open. There were still occasional sounds of banging but the predominant sounds then were of barking. Peering in through the door I was greeted with a sight akin to that in an RSPCA dog home, or indeed at any dog-rescue kennels.

I saw a cocker spaniel, then a sheltie collie, then a Labrador cross, a pure-bred Old English Sheepdog and another Labrador cross. It was a world of difference from the sight that had greeted me when, back in the summer of 1975, in the dead of night, I had opened the kennel unit at ICI's infamous Smoking Beagle laboratory at Alderley Park, Cheshire. On that occasion, I had been confronted by rows of purpose bred beagles all shying away timidly from their cage fronts. Here at the RCS, some nine years later, it was a collection of dogs, as from your local dog show, all rushing to the front of their bars and all clamouring for attention.

Although my mission was to photograph monkeys I could not leave these canines unrecorded. Caroline and I slipped into the building determined to photograph these dogs to try to trace their origins. I wound my film and started photographing through cage fronts.

I soon realised that the kennel bars would intrude into my photographs so, to improve the image quality, when I reached the kennel of the Old English Sheepdog I took one photograph through the bars then opened his kennel door and walked in. This poor dog bounded up to greet me as if I was some long-lost friend. He jumped up with paws to the fore and nuzzled me—a lovely display of affection, but far too close for me to take his photograph. I shouted, "*Down!*" He backed off, bewildered, hesitated, then raised his paw in an offering of friendship again. I took a second photograph of him. He then bounded up to me again and I gave him a good cuddle. I wanted to take him. I wanted to take all the dogs. I wanted to trace their origins and check with their owners that they truly wanted them to be experimented upon and killed in such circumstances. But I knew the law and I could not take any—I could only help them with my pictures.

Sadly, our time was slipping away. We had been advised there would be only ten minutes at the premises from when the first person entered to when the police might arrive. Caroline had left my side and entered the adjacent kennel where she was petting a very friendly elderly Labrador cross. I shooed my own canine friend back, closed his kennel door and moved on to his neighbour. This dog was so friendly and came so close that it was nearly impossible to photograph him. Only with considerable difficulty and some pushing did I succeed.

A shout from outside that the monkeys were in another unit reminded me of my assigned task—to photograph monkeys not dogs—and if I was to achieve that I needed to move on. In other situations, ten minutes can appear interminable, but when you have access to sites seldom seen, time passes all too quickly.

Young Caroline, nearly in tears, was reluctant to leave the dogs. We agreed that she would stay behind to assist others taking photographs whilst I looked for the monkeys. Heading out of the dog unit at one end I passed some rooms with doors ajar. Glancing in each I saw a succession of expensive looking equipment used for experimental work. I paused momentarily to take a photograph in each room as I thought it might help prove the precise nature of the work being carried out. It also proved that none of that equipment was damaged by the SEALL activists.

Darting out of the top door of the unit I ran towards the adjacent building. Ahead I saw many activists streaming back towards the gate over which we had first entered. I wondered whether our time was up and it was time to leave. I headed in their direction and saw people being directed up the side of the monkey unit, next to the footpath. It seemed that people were urgently required so I headed that way. There was a broken window and I could see people inside passing out bundles of papers and documents to a small group huddled outside. Individuals grabbed handfuls of documents and ran back towards the gate. I was pondering how to get into the unit to photograph the monkeys when a small bag containing files of papers was thrust into my hands. I was told to take the papers away as they were important. That was something I was unprepared for.

I had gone to take photographs. Taking documents was another matter. I hesitated and flicked through them. They appeared to be photocopied record sheets containing details of individual macaques. Even a cursory glance showed time and again mention of injuries—an arm trapped, broken or fractured. It immediately struck me that we might have in these documents proof of animals suffering at the RCS. If the few that I had read had shown that, what might the others reveal?

I put the few that I had looked at back in their carrier bag and decided to take them away to have their contents checked. I had no sooner done this than the shout went up that it was time to go. I had failed to secure any images of monkeys but the opportunity had passed. I turned and followed the crowd back towards the gate.

Crossing the gate with many other activists we all turned to the right and ran. We went over a stile and out into an open field. There were many streaming over the field. I looked for anyone I recognised and saw Caroline Dawkins. I ran to her and together we went through a small wood and emerged onto a golf course.

It was 11:15am on a Sunday morning. Suitably attired gentlemen out enjoying their mid-morning round of golf stood open-mouthed and aghast as a motley crew of activists, dressed as for a ramble, strolled over and around their perfectly manicured greens. Leaving this natural baize, we entered another larger wood and then the group split. Those of us in the Press party were sent in one direction, others elsewhere.

I gathered later the plan was for us to meet our pick-up cars on the perimeter road around Biggin Hill airfield but when our guides reached that area it was already being patrolled by police cars. We were bustled back into the safety of the wood and advised to split and scatter. We were told that our pick-up cars would remain patrolling the nearby roads for the next few hours looking to snatch us to safety.

An excellent, if obvious, ploy would be for us to pose as courting couples out for a stroll. Caroline and I joined another 'couple' and we set off, skirting the inner edge of the wood. Selecting a suitably recognisable tree I removed the 35mm film from my camera, placed it in a waterproof carton, and buried it to be collected later. I re-loaded a new film.

We exited the wood behind the school on Jail Lane, Biggin Hill, crossed the games field and were heading for the road when we saw a police transit van laden with officers proceed slowly down the road and stop. We crouched concealed behind some bushes. We may have been hidden from view from officers on the road but we could easily be seen from above. When a helicopter arrived, and hovered over us, we were distinctly uneasy. Given our proximity to a small but busy airport it was no surprise to see a helicopter above but this one was intent on hovering directly over us. We judged it to be a police helicopter.

We split again into two pairs. Caroline and I crawled beneath the cover of dense shrubbery. Battling through, we made our way to an old secluded barn. Within the barn, I could see through gaps in the roof, the helicopter hovering nearly overhead. The police crew would be in close communication with their colleagues on the ground. It would be only a matter of time before police on foot, probably (and ironically) with dogs, would be zeroed in onto our hiding place. We pondered our plight.

The best plan seemed to be to conceal Caroline under the straw with the precious documents and then for me to lead the helicopter and pursuers away on foot. I carefully hid Caroline and prepared to make a break for it when our attendant helicopter suddenly, and noisily, veered away. Clearly the officers on board had seen a more tempting target. It later transpired that aerial police had indeed seen a large party carrying rucksacks crossing nearby fields but when they diverted police resources to pursue these 'activists' they turned out to be an innocent group of scouts out on a camp!

Caroline and I were left alone in the barn thanking our luck. With time to spare I used the self-timer on my camera to take a photograph of us (our version of a 'selfie'). If my film was seized and processed that would be an innocent image. After what we took to be a suitably safe period, and when all was quiet above, we left our sanctuary. We crossed back through the school grounds and headed out onto the road. Minutes later a pick-up car stopped. I recognised the driver—that determined and dedicated activist, Tony Faramus. He was delighted to whisk us away to safety.

[As a young man living in the Channel Islands during World War Two, Tony had opposed the actions of occupying German forces. In consequence, he was captured and transported to Mauthausen and Buchenwald concentration camps. Tony described his experiences in his autobiography *Journey into Darkness*. He died August 4th 1990.]

A short drive through the narrow back lanes took us to the A25. We turned east towards the village of Brasted and stopped in the car park of *The Lamb*. This had been the planned rendezvous for the pick-up cars after the raid but we were by then very late and only a few were there. I said I had documents that appeared to be very damning and should be passed to lawyers. When I showed them around I was advised to take them to the Scientific Advisor for the British Union for the Abolition of Vivisection (BUAV)—Phil Churchward—in London. I said I would be happy to but I needed a lift back to my car.

Caroline Dawkins and I then parted company. I was given a lift to my car with a colleague who then showed me the way to Phil Churchward's house in Forest Hill. With the documents safely in Phil's hands I had other work to attend to. I still had my film with important pictures to recover. It was late in the afternoon when I returned to Biggin Hill, parked in Jail Lane and retraced my steps to the tree where I had buried my film. It was all quiet with no sign of police activity.

That night there was extensive coverage of this SEALL raid on national television news. Video film of the dogs taken during the raid was shown, as were slides of monkeys from the RCS collection that were taken. The following day there was wide reportage of the raid in the national newspapers. Some slides of the monkeys had been given exclusively to the *Daily Mirror* after their reporter promised to give the story good coverage. The *Daily Mirror* proved spineless. They gave the story no coverage at all and handed the slides to the police. Although the slides were stolen it was strange how some media were happy to use them whilst others felt obliged to hand them back to the police.

Between 70 and 80 SEALL activists from all over the South East had taken part in this raid in broad daylight on the fringes of London. A large contingent of police officers had been drafted into the area in hot pursuit of the activists. The police helicopter was quickly on the scene. Not one single activist was arrested.

I personally suspected that, with police officers having the same feelings and consciences as most, when they entered the RCS and found the monkeys and particularly the large numbers of what appeared to be former pet dogs, they were not too interested in arresting those who had tried to help them. That was even more likely given there was little evidence of malicious criminal damage. Some weeks later a couple were questioned by police about their possible involvement in this raid but they were quickly released without charge. In due course, criminal charges were indeed brought as a result of this raid, but not against any animal rights activists— the charges were brought against the RCS!

BUAV take legal action

The BUAV was aware of concerns over the animals held by the RCS. Sight of the documents secured by SEALL confirmed their worst fears. The BUAV was very capable with expert staff and a dedicated Executive Committee. The staff was led by Office Manager Margaret Manzoni. Kim Stallwood was Campaigns Officer. On the Committee were many shining lights for compassion including John Beggs, Marcia Guess, Mandy Journeaux, Steve McIvor and Louise Wall.

The SEALL raid had produced significant documentary evidence of suffering to animals at the RCS. Here are some selections from the evidence printed in the BUAV magazine *Liberator* (October/November 1984):-

"On 12/3/84 Mr Wickham carried out a gall bladder laparoscopy on a male collie cross called Baggins (a reasonably simple operation using an endoscope to examine the gall bladder) within 4 days the dog was killed because of peritonitis. The post mortem revealed that Mr Wickham had failed to close the gall bladder incision properly and the suture clip had come off. Baggins had about one pint of blood/bile stained fluid in the peritoneal cavity and large clots around the peritoneum — the free bile in the peritoneum and haemorrhaging of the peritoneal vessels resulted in peritonitis. On 16/3/84 Baggins was put down, he was very lethargic, vomiting, had diarrhoea, a fast pulse, pale gums and a swollen and tender abdomen.

12/3/84 was a busy day for Mr Wickham who carried out another gall bladder laparoscopy in the afternoon, on a dog called Petal. Petal fared somewhat better than Baggins, her stitches opened slightly on 15/3/84 and on 19th she had a gaping wound with pus exuding from the sutures. The wound was cleaned until Petal was put down at the end of her experimental use (30/3/84). Despite working for an institute claiming to set the highest standards in research and surgery, Mr Wickham is seemingly incapable of closing wounds properly and the basic aseptic techniques to prevent infection."

Could any of this evidence be used to prove breaches of the criminal law? To understand the situation, it is necessary first to comprehend the laws that applied at the time (1984) regarding laboratory animals. Animals actually in the course of experimentation came under the 'protection' of the 1876 Cruelty to Animals Act. So long as the RCS had a valid licence from the Home Office, which they did, they could more or less do as they liked in experiments.

However, for animals not under experimentation, the situation was different. They enjoyed the more discernible protection of the 1911 Protection of Animals Act. The problem was that 'course of experimentation' was wide-ranging and embraced animals being prepared for experiments, undergoing them and recovering from them.

To bring any action for cruelty where the treatment had been carried out under the auspices of the 1876 Act was regarded as a non-starter. Though much of the paperwork detailed the most gruesome experimental work being perpetrated on both dogs and monkeys it was accepted that nothing could be argued in court to be a breach of the law. However, in the case of one named scientist (Mr Wickham) the experimental protocol was so bad that an application was made to the Home Office to revoke his licence to operate.

It was different when it came to possible breaches of the 1911 Act. Sadly, the dogs could not be helped by this as they were all held for a short period before, during and after being experimented on. Their suffering was deemed to come under the 1876 Act. However, the primates were luckier. Whilst the RCS imported monkeys from the wild they had also instituted a programme of breeding their own. Primates held long term in the RCS breeding colony enjoyed the protection of the 1911 Act.

The BUAV consulted solicitor John Mackenzie about possible prosecutions that could be brought against the RCS. After examination of the documentary evidence seized, John saw that charges could be brought based on the incident report sheets, including some I had handled, that detailed day-to-day problems in the management of the monkeys.

One immediate problem with bringing any prosecution under the 1911 Act was that summonses had to be issued within 6 months of the alleged incident. Time was pressing. Tragically many very strong cases were left by the wayside as they had fallen 'out of time' but one case shone out as being a candidate for prosecution. This concerned a female breeding macaque named *Mone*.

Mone, an import from the wild, had entered the RCS colony some 8 years previously in 1976. Rather than being used in the experimental programme she was placed in the breeding colony and her offspring were harvested and used for research. On June 22nd 1984 she was found collapsed in her cage suffering from dehydration. Senior animal technician in charge of the primate house, Bruce Bidewell, administered the routine remedial procedures and in due course *Mone* recovered. He dutifully filled in his incident report and blamed her dehydration on inadequate ventilation in the monkey unit.

From the wording of this report Bruce Bidewell, who had worked at the farm from 1968 after leaving school, was fully aware the unit was prone to overheating and did so regularly in the summer months. He wrote that the optimum temperature for macaques was 68-72°F and yet in his unit they regularly soared to over 90°F. He attributed this to the poor design of the ventilation system.

Mone had clearly suffered in her cage. The RCS were responsible for that suffering. From the wording of Bruce Bidewell's report it was clear that at least two staff members (Bidewell and the person he sent reports to) had been aware for some time of the basic design faults in the ventilation that caused that suffering and yet had done nothing to alleviate it. There appeared to be excellent grounds for prosecuting the RCS under the 1911 Act for causing unnecessary suffering to *Mone*.

John Mackenzie was happy to press ahead with this single prosecution but many incident reports referred to macaques suffering broken or fractured limbs after trapping them in the bars of their cages. Some macaques died whilst trapped. Limb trapping was so frequent that the BUAV felt obliged to at least try to bring prosecutions for cruelty in some of those instances. However, they knew the chances of success with those cases was far less than with that of *Mone*.

There were two reasons. Firstly, by the very nature of the incident it was usually a one-off for the individual monkey. It was harder to prove culpable negligence and it would be easy for the RCS to dismiss it as a simple accident and claim they took as much care to avoid such accidents as any of the many similar institutes housing primates in similar caging. Secondly, some of the four cases selected for prosecution (within the six months time limit) were experimental animals for whom the 1876 Act excused just about any mistreatment.

In November 1984, the BUAV went to Bromley Magistrates Court and asked that the RCS be served with five summonses alleging infringement of the 1911 Act. The Magistrates duly obliged. It was then a matter of gathering all the evidence into a focus for this landmark BUAV prosecution. Even bringing such a case to court was a momentous leap forwards for the animal welfare/rights movement.

The IPPL was approached for help. Their advisor, Cyril Rosen, gave invaluable assistance by explaining the nature of macaque lifestyle in the wild and the precise requirements for keeping them in captivity. However, it was not enough to show that by keeping macaques in small cages the RCS were infringing their basic rights to swing freely in the trees. That was obvious. The prosecution had to show there was a basic set of guidelines for keeping macaques in cages, laid down by recognisable and accepted authorities on primate care that the RCS should have been aware of, that nevertheless they breached.

This was a matter of testing the law. Cyril Rosen's expertise at tracing a path through various published recommendations concerning primate care from organisations around the world proved vital. Cyril also knew about the system of caging used by the RCS, that was designed by Dr Coid, and was aware of its shortcomings and of the alternative improved systems available. Cyril could also give expert evidence as to the suffering endured by the macaques after suffering fractures and dehydration. In this he was helped by an experienced RSPCA vet.

SEALL activists had seized priceless evidence that gave the BUAV a strong case. There were Incident Reports and the annual reports of animal management at Downe. There were X-rays and other items of documentation. On the publicity side, there were graphic colour slides showing primates at the RCS, some with their foreheads tattooed. However, could material acquired during the SEALL raid be entered into a court case as evidence? Would Magistrates accept evidence acquired that way? Would they accept it had even come from the RCS? The burden is always on the prosecution to prove every link of the evidence chain.

Obviously without evidence as to the history of the documents the RCS lawyer could state in court that no connection had been proved between the RCS and those documents and that the magistrates should strike the case out (and they would). The animal rights movement needed to prove how the documents passed from the RCS to the SEALL; from the SEALL to the BUAV and from the BUAV to the court. With no activists arrested on the day there was no-one to hand to easily confirm this.

At this point I should digress slightly. After the RCS raid SEALL activists carried out another raid on a research laboratory. This was in September 1984 against BIOS laboratories, a contract-testing laboratory housing beagles. Then on Sunday October 28th 1984 the SEALL launched perhaps the most audacious series of raids ever launched by the animal rights movement. In precisely coordinated raids, involving dozens of activists, the SEALL invaded three separate premises: another contract testing laboratory—Wickham laboratories; a firm of animal suppliers—APT consultancy; and a dog breeding and boarding kennels—Cottagepatch kennels. The SEALL activists overcame armed and violent resistance to acquire their evidence. Some activists were arrested on the day. In the days that followed police also swept into custody anyone else they thought might have helped in any way, including me.

From the start Hampshire Constabulary hyped the incident; a large team of officers from their vaunted Regional Crime Squad ranged across England, from Coventry to the south coast, raiding numerous homes and premises. Many activists were arrested and accused variously of Conspiracy to Rob, Conspiracy to Assault, Conspiracy to Burgle or Conspiracy to cause Criminal Damage. In scuffles at the sites, when activists were threatened with shotguns, some of the site residents suffered minor abrasions. The media were told by John Duke, the Chief Constable of Hampshire, falsely, that these injuries were 'life-threatening' and if any victims were to die within a year his police would bring murder charges. It was true in law—but hardly likely to happen from minor cuts.

We were all held in the cells at Fareham Police Station. In due course twenty, including me, were charged. When we appeared before the Magistrates the prosecution vigorously opposed our bail and we were remanded into custody. The women were taken to Holloway Prison, the men to nearby Winchester Prison. My girlfriend Sue (we have now been married for 31 years) visited me in prison.

The following week, on Tuesday November 6th, we were again presented before the Magistrates and again the prosecution vigorously opposed our bail. This time though we had a hand-picked team of London solicitors, including the brilliant John Mackenzie, who eloquently and forcefully argued our case. We were released on bail, albeit with strict restrictions. I had to leave my Tonbridge home and live with my parents many miles away. I also had a 12-hour night-time curfew.

In the meantime, police continued their travels around homes in the south-east of England interviewing and questioning activists and their friends and acquaintances. Their openly stated view was that anyone charged, or likely to be charged, faced serious enough charges to 'see them locked away for years'. This sent a shock wave of concern throughout the animal rights movement.

Young Caroline Dawkins, for reasons ultimately known only to herself but possibly based on a combination of the perceived threat from the police, personal anguish over a boyfriend and her youth, consumed a mixture of pills and alcohol that was to cost her life. I was miles away with my parents so knew nothing of her traumas. When I heard the shock news that Caroline was on a life support machine in intensive care at Redhill General Hospital I journeyed to join relatives and friends at her bedside.

I felt utter despair. We had never been anything more than fellow activists but there she lay, a colleague, a comrade, fragile, small and oh so gentle. Her life prolonged only by the rhythmic pulse of the machine. I touched her hair but life had gone from it. The strands felt like the hair of an inanimate doll. All the love of those beside her was not enough to bring her back. Caroline had left us. She had cleared security and was in the departure lounge for heaven.

In time her parents made the inevitable, heart-breaking, decision to turn the machine off. It was December 15th 1984. Caroline Dawkins was just 20 years old when she slipped into the eternal sleep. I was grief stricken then but now, as a father of three children, I can truly understand the full magnitude of the loss her parents suffered.

However tangled and complex her feelings were before she took that overdose, I knew she held the clear certain knowledge that, from the earlier raid on the RCS, we had secured evidence that would see the Royal College of Surgeons damned before a court of law. I had stood helpless and watched the sun set on her life—I would not see the sun set on her dreams for justice for those who could not help themselves.

Royal College of Surgeons prosecuted

Wednesday January 30th 1985 was momentous. The BUAV prosecution of the RCS, alleging five breaches of the 1911 Protection of Animals Act, opened before Bromley Magistrates amid shrouds of secrecy. The Magistrates withheld their names, "*because of trouble in the past*" and addresses of witnesses were scribbled on paper handed to the chairman of the bench.

Five charges of causing unnecessary suffering all related to named macaques. *Frencs*, an experimental animal, was found alive on May 14th 1984, trapped by the arm and released by cutting the surrounding grid. *Drude* was an experimental female found dead on May 17th 1984, hanging from the top of her cage, her arm trapped. *Druw* was another experimental female found dead, hanging from the top of her cage, on June 8th 1984. *Krencs* was a male used for experiments found on June 10th 1984 with his arm trapped in the stainless-steel floor grid. He was released. Finally, *Mone* was a breeding macaque found collapsed and severely dehydrated on June 22nd 1984. *Frencs, Drude, Druw* and *Mone* were all found at 8:30am, probably at the first morning check. One wonders for how long they had suffered. *Krencs* was found at 9:15am. It seems there was no supervision of the monkeys at night lest it disturb them.

I assured John Mackenzie beforehand that, if required, I would give the evidence confirming the documents before the court had been taken from the RCS during the raid. Our second witness in the information chain was Phil Churchward, the BUAV Scientific Adviser. Phil could confirm he had received these documents from me, examined them and handed them to colleagues at the BUAV.

John Mackenzie warned us that by giving this evidence and thereby admitting our involvement in the raid we faced the prospect of being arrested as we left the witness box. I discussed this with Sue. As I already faced serious charges because of the Wickham raids, any further charges coming from the RCS raid could result in me losing my bail. I did not relish the prospect of spending many months on remand in Brixton Prison. I faced a second problem. If I gave evidence admitting my involvement in an animal rights raid, albeit in my own time on a Sunday, and without the knowledge of the League, I would be sacked from my job as Press Officer for the LACS.

The LACS campaign lawfully. At the time they sought the abolition of bloodsports by Act of Parliament. The view of Executive Director, Richard Course, was that if they expected people to respect any law banning bloodsports they should encourage respect for the law as a whole—and certainly demand that of their staff. [Ironically history has shown that the LACS achieved their law banning bloodsports—but the hunters ignored it with impunity.]

There was also the problem for the LACS that hunters delighted in accusing the LACS of involvement in or support for illegal animal rights activity. Whenever such accusations were made the LACS would take action for libel or slander. Were the LACS to do anything other than sack their Press Officer, when he admitted involvement in an animal rights raid, they would have to withdraw from all their active libel actions and never again sue over similar accusations.

Sue and I knew if I gave the evidence there would be consequences for us. Weighing against that were the benefits for our cause. We had near *prima facie* proof that *Mone* and her companions were being mistreated. Even getting the evidence heard in an open court would be a great step forwards. If the BUAV could secure a conviction against such an august and revered institution as the RCS for infringement of the 1911 Protection of Animals Act that would send shock waves throughout the global vivisection community. To the public, animal rights activists would not only be accusing vivisectors of atrocities—they would be proving they occurred.

At the very least a victory could bring legal changes to better protect laboratory animals. Could the RCS even be closed down? Could the very foundations of using animals in research be questioned? The stakes were high. What sealed it for me was the silent blood oath I gave to young Caroline, my companion on the day, as she lay dying. No weakness or cowardice by me would cause this case to fail. Whatever the personal cost I would ensure the public knew the nature of the cruelty that lurks behind locked laboratory doors.

Sue and I discussed it, as did Phil and I. We agreed that if it was essential for our case to proceed I would give the evidence. On day one we arrived at the Magistrates Court in good time. I reminded John Mackenzie that if he could prosecute without my evidence that would be preferable but if my evidence was needed or if it strengthened our case I would give it. As everyone trooped into court Number One Phil and I, as potential witnesses, were directed to sit on hard wooden benches outside.

The morning dragged on. Police officers passing to and from the court took an interest in us seated outside: two animal rights supporters who had not joined colleagues in the public gallery. We must be witnesses. We could not be expert witnesses as they were allowed to sit in the court. We must be witnesses to the facts of the raid. We had already marked ourselves out from the many animal rights people we had chatted with beforehand. I felt the cold cuffs of the law grip on me. I went to the toilet.

It became clear, from conversations overheard, there was a mighty row between John Mackenzie and the defence barrister—Andrew Smith— as to the wording of the summonses. John Mackenzie won that tussle but soon after he emerged from court and told me I would have to give evidence. The case would collapse without it.

As I entered the court and took the stand there was a flurry of activity amongst the police. My evidence was over quickly as I explained exactly what I had done. I was then released from the witness box and allowed to sit in the public gallery at the back to hear the remainder of the case. Phil Churchward, called next to the witness box, gave evidence as to his role.

Our evidence accounted for how the vital documents came to be presented before the court by the BUAV, but would the Magistrates accept this material? Not surprisingly the defence argued that as the evidence had been acquired by unlawful means it should be struck out. John Mackenzie pleaded legal precedent for the view that evidence should be considered solely as that—evidence—and that it could only be struck out if likely to inspire prejudice. As this did not, it should be allowed. The Magistrates retired to consider the matter overnight. There had been speculation that the police might arrest Phil and me as we left the court precincts but although they were there in numbers they made no approach to us.

In the morning, the Chairman of the bench opened proceedings by stating they had considered the admissibility of the documents and decided they should be admitted, but only as pieces of paper; the wording on them would have to be proved by evidence (i.e. from their author Bruce Bidewell).

John Mackenzie called Bruce Bidewell to the witness stand. He was asked if he could recall incidents where monkeys at the farm had become dehydrated or had trapped their limbs in the caging. He agreed that he could remember such incidents in the years he worked at the farm, but not specific dates, nor to which individual monkey. When John offered him his own Incident Reports to refresh his memory the defence objected saying if he could not recall them, they should not be allowed.

John pleaded to the Magistrates that what he proposed doing was no different from allowing a police officer to refresh his memory from his notebook. The bench agreed. Bruce Bidewell recognised his Incident Reports, confirmed their authenticity and by using them gave the court a more detailed account of events. On May 17th 1984 he had noted on one: "*Animals becoming trapped in cages is now fairly common, especially in communes. If and when new cages are bought areas where these incidents can arise should be avoided.*"

After the incident involving *Mone* he noted: "*Ventilation system inadequate. Each year during summer months temperatures in animal areas soar. This year they have regularly been between 85°F and 92°F. They should be 68°F to 72°F.*"

He recommended: "*Overhaul ventilation system. Place intake and extract vents in correct position, i.e. at high and low level. At present they are opposite each other which means there is no circulation whatever.*"

Bruce Bidewell assured the court he chose to work at Downe because of his love for animals. He guessed that was why other staff worked there too: "*I know of no instances where animals were treated cruelly by staff.*"

The court was told about faults in the ventilation system—that two vents that should have been circulating air in the primate house were not working for a time. John Mackenzie said of the living conditions for the macaques at Downe: "*It is inconceivable they should have to live in the type of cages provided at Downe. One gets the picture of lack of consideration for the needs of this or any other breed of animal and makes the RCS guilty of a criminal offence."*

The case was adjourned to Monday February 11th 1985. The next prosecution witness called was a heating and ventilation engineer named Mr Moffet. He confirmed that the ventilation system in the monkey house appeared inadequate and suggested suitable air conditioning systems that could maintain the required temperatures.

The prosecution then called expert witness Cyril Rosen (1927 - 2013) from the IPPL. He gave a detailed account of the natural lifestyle of these macaques, *Maccaca Fascicularis*, their preferred choice of habitat and the temperature ranges in which they lived. He explained the nature of the caging used at the RCS, how it had been perfected in the early 1960s by a Dr Coid. He added that nothing had been done since to improve the caging, despite all the evidence to show the need to cater for the psychological needs of captive macaques. He explained that, by the very design of the caging, limb trapping was inevitable in inquisitive and bored primates. He compared the cages used by the RCS to Victorian slums.

Under cross-examination Cyril stressed his concern for animal welfare: *"I do not consider experimental animals to be disposable test tubes."* When asked about the primates chewing their caging he said: *"Mouthing is common; an animal chewing its way through metal is, in my experience, unique."* John Mackenzie re-examined and drew this observation from Cyril: *"Because animals in experimentation make a considerable sacrifice for humanity they should be given better treatment."*

The next prosecution witness was RSPCA vet Paul Hobson. His evidence was mainly clinical. Shown many X-rays he identified them as showing monkeys with various limb fractures and breaks. He was asked about dehydration, why it occurred, the suffering it was likely to cause and how it could have been avoided. All the incidents referred to in the documents were of monkeys suffering in ways that could have been avoided. Paul stressed that the more an animal's actions are reduced by confinement, the greater the responsibility of owners to provide for the welfare of the animal.

The prosecution ended and the defence took their turn. Their main arguments were firstly that all their housing conformed to published guidelines including from the Universities Federation for Animal Welfare (UFAW) whose handbook was frequently referred to as 'the Bible' for laboratory workers. Secondly, they were closely monitored by the much-lauded Home Office Inspectors, who had never made a single complaint about the RCS.

The first defence witness was Professor Newell Johnson, Head of the Dental Research Unit at the RCS. After listing his many qualifications, he launched into a monologue about how their work was vital for the welfare of mankind. His evidence in chief had little bearing on the case, other than he denied they would knowingly inflict suffering on monkeys.

The cross-examination by John Mackenzie was incisive. He suggested that never mind what was known about the standard of caging and required standards of care when the colony was created in 1963, it was all woefully inadequate by the time of these incidents in June 1984 and known to have been so for years. As head of the unit he should have known what was going wrong and rectified it. At this he became evasive, saying he had not worked for the RCS for long, and he spent most of his time at their London Offices in Lincoln's Inn Fields. Professor Johnson's evasiveness even irritated the Magistrates.

As he claimed their work was so vital he was cross- examined on the point. The experiment was a long-term study to see the effectiveness of a vaccine at reducing or preventing dental caries. The macaques were denied bedding because chewing that could interfere with the dental research. Professor Newell Johnson agreed that, with the monkey's teeth being the focus of the study, it would be best to have the most natural conditions for their teeth. How then could he reconcile that need with the fact that due to sheer frustration and boredom the monkeys regularly chewed through the aluminium mesh of their caging? Surely this variable factor would imperil the validity of the results, particularly as the cages were not all uniform in structure; some had more aluminium than others?

He was questioned as to why more was not spent to improve the conditions for the monkeys, specifically their ventilation. He replied that as a charity they were short of money but, even so, plans were in hand to improve the ventilation. [In contrast, staff accommodation at the farm appeared well maintained.]

The next defence witness was John Eric Cooper, veterinary conservator at the farm. He was directly in charge of the welfare of the animals. In his evidence in chief he described how he had only recently arrived at the farm but, in his time there, he had undertaken numerous measures to improve the welfare of the resident animals. The measure he was most proud of was the instigation of the Incident Report forms. It clearly irritated him that it was these very forms that were used as the basis for the prosecution of his college.

John E. Cooper disputed Bruce Bidewell's comments regarding the optimum temperatures at which macaques should be held, saying they could easily withstand higher temperatures. He told the court that though the ventilation system was not strictly at fault it was nevertheless being overhauled. He voiced his opinion that, as at the time *Mone* was in the enforced company of a male, to be mated, her dehydration was caused by that male preventing her from accessing the water.

He said that her dehydration was comparatively minor; that all the correct remedial measures were taken to assist her recovery and she did swiftly recover. He explained that macaques are a species that very effectively hide their symptoms of dehydration and therefore none of the staff could be blamed for not noticing that she was approaching that state. As to the limb trapping, John E. Cooper regarded that as very unfortunate; but bound to happen with an inquisitive species such as the macaque. He said caging used by the RCS conformed to all the standards laid down in the regulations and was like that used in many similar institutes.

Under cross-examination John E. Cooper was pressed closely as to why *Mone* dehydrated. If males were likely to deprive female companions of access to the single water source why not provide a second water bottle? He replied that an extra bottle would reduce the view into the cages, making his job more difficult. If, as he alleged, the macaque is a species capable of concealing symptoms of distress, why was there not the closest monitoring of their welfare? John Mackenzie put it to him that if they are really that good at hiding their distress perhaps, on that hot June day when *Mone* dehydrated, all her companions were in a similar state of dehydration but had yet to collapse. He appeared never to have considered that possibility.

John Mackenzie tackled him about limb trapping. When he was referred to other Incident Reports and to copies of annual reports from the Downe laboratory that related to incidents earlier than the six months time limit allowed for prosecutions, John E. Cooper conceded that such incidents occurred fairly regularly. He also agreed that a monkey that trapped its limb that way would inevitably suffer.

The matter was raised of a visit to the farm by a Home Office Inspector just four days before *Mone* dehydrated—and on the very day that another macaque named *Rage* died—June 18th 1984. John E. Cooper agreed that that visit had occurred. He explained it was a routine unannounced visit and the Inspector had no recommendations as to any changes in the conditions that should be made. He said he was in close contact with their Home Office Inspector, usually at least once a week. He claimed to have no warning when Inspectors would visit Downe and said they were inspected two or three times a year. Each visit lasted less than half a day and it seems the Inspectors did not even check the Incident Report forms.

John E. Cooper stressed that the RCS was open to genuinely interested visitors and the defence asked the three magistrates to tour Buckston Browne Farm to see the conditions. The prosecution immediately requested to join this. It was agreed that John Mackenzie, expert witness Cyril Rosen and Margaret Manzoni from the BUAV, who brought the prosecution, should accompany the tour. The following morning the entourage arrived at the impressive gates of Buckston Browne Farm. The magistrates and John Mackenzie were allowed in but Cyril Rosen and Margaret Manzoni were barred. Later, back in court, a complaint was raised over that pettiness but the RCS promptly denied they had invited either Cyril or Margaret.

The final defence witness was Miss Mary Branker, a veterinary advisor to Twycross Zoo and one of Britain's top authorities on primates, with more than 30 years' experience. She was a Zoo Inspector, a past President of the British Veterinary Association and a founder of the UFAW.

Introduced to the court as an expert in primate care she described how she had visited Buckston Browne Farm on a spot check as a Home Office Inspector: "*No warning was given of my visit and I found the conditions very satisfactory*." She praised the conditions for the primates: "*If you compare their life in the wild it is probably infinitely more comfortable in laboratory conditions.*" She could not fault the conditions, adding that for macaques physical isolation is alright so long as they can see and hear other monkeys. She declared that that species of monkey did not need exercise to stay healthy. She put the dehydration of *Mone* down to the presence of the male and said that limb trapping, such as was alleged to have occurred, was a regular problem with macaques.

Miss Branker was asked whether conditions could be improved for these macaques. Might furniture put into their cages make their lives more interesting—and lessen the chances of limb trapping caused by boredom? She said that was not necessary.

[No doubt unintentionally, no less a national paper than the *Times* injected a bit of humour into the coverage with this report dated February 16th 1985 of the visit by the magistrates and expert witnesses to the farm: "*After the visit, a zoo inspector, Miss Winifred* [sic] *Branker, told the court that conditions at the farm were good. A dehydrated monkey might have been exhausted by frequent mating.*" A bit of leg-pulling here probably by other journalists passing on supposed 'quotes'!]

The defence made their closing submissions. Their view was that limb trapping occurrences were 'unfortunate accidents' that could have happened anywhere. They stated that some of the animals involved were in the experimental colony and therefore fell outside the protection of the 1911 Act. For *Mone* the defence was that no-one truly knew why she dehydrated. The RCS speculated that it could have been due to an illness or her being deprived of water by her male companion. They regarded it as very unlikely that her dehydration was caused by the raised temperatures and, in any case, they said they had done all they could to help her.

The Magistrates retired to consider their verdict, saying they would return after the weekend. John Mackenzie came and spoke to Phil Churchward and me. If the RCS were convicted of all, or indeed any, of the charges we would be safe from police prosecution. Should they be acquitted on all counts then it was likely we would be arrested and charged with actions connected to the SEALL raid. In my case I would be unlikely to get bail and could expect many months in prison on remand.

I was summoned to the LACS offices and told the inevitable news by my close friend Richard Course. After my admission of involvement in a SEALL raid I was sacked, albeit with an amicable settlement. Sue and I then headed back to her parents in East Anglia for what could well have been our last few days together for some time.

At dawn on the morning of Monday February 18th 1985 we drove away from Norwich heading for Bromley Magistrates Court. I am never usually a pessimist but I carried a toothbrush in my pocket, ready for some months in the cells. A large contingent of animal rights supporters, police officers (both uniformed and plain clothed CID) and the media turned out to witness this landmark judgement. Just before I entered the court I passed my car keys to a close friend.

I sat in court flanked by police. They asked me not to make a fuss if I was arrested. The bench convened and announced their verdict. The Royal College of Surgeons were guilty on count 1. They were guilty of causing unnecessary suffering to *Mone*. The RCS were acquitted of the remaining 4 counts concerning limb trapping. To lose them was a blow, but only slightly lessened the stunning thrill of having proven to a court of law that one of the most prestigious laboratories in the land (and indeed in the world) had inflicted unnecessary suffering on one of their animals.

It was hard to discern who was the more traumatised: the RCS representatives in court or the police officers who so eagerly anticipated arresting me. When it came to the punishment of this august body the most we had expected was that they would be given a conditional discharge. If convicted the Magistrates would give a stern warning to the RCS, warn them to do better in future and leave it at that. But they did far more. The bench imposed a fine of £250 upon the RCS; in effect treating them as common criminals, such as shoplifters. The court was stunned.

The compassionate side left in a state of euphoria and piled into the nearest pub for a well-earned drink to celebrate. My joy was tinged with sadness that Caroline Dawkins was not there with us. I congratulated John Mackenzie and everyone involved in bringing the prosecution. Television, radio and press reporters mingled amongst us seeking quotes.

Interviewed outside the court, Margaret Manzoni for the BUAV said: "*This is just the beginning and we aim to reverse the position where laboratory animals are separated from the rest of the animal kingdom by law.*" She went on to praise the magistrates: "*They went to the farm and saw the horrendous, small wire-mesh cages where socially active primates are jailed for life. There must now be pressure to close this house of death.*" She was damning about the whole research business: "*Scientists and surgeons who experiment on animals cannot be allowed to remain totally above the laws that apply to other people who have the responsibility of caring for animals.*" (*Orpington Comet* February 22nd 1985, front page).

The conviction of the RCS for cruelty was reported on television and radio news and by every national newspaper.

Appeal/Acquittal

At their press conference after conviction the RCS declared their intention to appeal. The Magistrates had patiently listened to days of evidence, and had visited Buckston Browne Farm, so it was not obvious that there were any flaws in the prosecution. However, the prospect of defending this conviction as prosecutors posed a very real financial problem for a small company such as the BUAV.

They had already incurred great expenditure bringing the case thus far. Could the organisation pour yet more money into this struggle? It was agreed by the BUAV Committee to approach the Director of Public Prosecutions (DPP) to ask the Crown to take over the prosecution. The RCS had been proven to have broken the law and the Crown was asked to step in and uphold that verdict. It was suggested that if they declined the BUAV would have to withdraw, leaving the RCS to win by default. It caused some surprise when the DPP agreed (had they declined, the BUAV would of course have found some way to raise the money to continue the case).

The RCS appeal was heard before Judge Jean Graham-Hall sitting with two Magistrates at Croydon Crown Court on July 1st 1985. Appearing for the DPP was Graham Boal and for the defence, Richard Du Cann QC. The evidence heard at the Magistrates court was heard again. The DPP relied on my evidence to sustain the prosecution but I was not called. RCS witnesses were called. One new witness was Professor Bertram Cohen the previous Head of Dental Research at Buckston Browne Farm.

There was a noticeable change in the attitude from the RCS witnesses to their erstwhile colleague Bruce Bidewell. At Bromley, he had been praised. At Croydon, he was damned as someone whose Incident Reports could not be believed as, at the time of writing them, he was leaving the RCS. Richard du Cann QC was heard to curse repeatedly the Incident Report detailing the dehydration of *Mone*, damning it as a "*wretched piece of paper*".

On July 4th, after listening to lengthy submissions, Judge Graham-Hall retired with her colleagues to deliberate. They returned after about an hour and found for the prosecution. The RCS remained convicted of cruelty. However, instead of just refusing the appeal and leaving it at that, she went on to express her view that *Mone* had been deprived of water by her male companion, that the RCS should have foreseen that that could happen and taken steps to avoid any suffering caused by it. *Mone* had been put in a cage for nine days to mate, when the received wisdom was that mating should only take four days. It was also said that macaques could exist for up to four days without water without collapsing.

The bench said that because the implications of these facts were never put together by those in charge of Downe Farm they found that *Mone* was wantonly and unreasonably caused unnecessary suffering. The RCS appeal was refused—but the bench had not allowed the defence to adequately debate the issues of the deprivation of water by the male.

That legal error by Judge Graham-Hall and her colleagues was surprising and convenient, both for the RCS and for the police so fervently hunting me. It guaranteed the RCS would emerge blemish free—and I would one day face a jury. The RCS legal team were outraged (or delighted?) over this error and announced they would appeal again—seeking Judicial Review of the decision.

Our advice was that, on this purely legal technicality, the RCS were probably right. It had nothing to do with the quality of evidence, the nature of it, if *Mone* had suffered, or whether she had been deprived of water by her mate, or had dehydrated for another reason. It was simply that Judge Graham-Hall and colleagues had based their judgement on this factor and not allowed adequate opportunity for it to be debated.

With their appeal refused by the Crown Court the only avenue open to the RCS for further appeal was to apply through the Divisional Court for

Judicial Review. When they did it was quickly perceived by all they would win—and Phil Churchward and I would be back in the legal firing line.

I soon felt legal pressure again. I had proposed to Sue on June 22nd—and she made me the happiest man by accepting. Wednesday July 10th proved interesting. I had driven to London with a SEALL colleague and amongst other work collected our wedding rings and a camera. On our return through south London we were very obviously tracked by a police helicopter that flew above us. Driving through residential areas we knew of its presence by seeing residents in their gardens looking skywards. We thought to lose it by driving into a gypsy site, but that failed. We finally found sanctuary by driving into a tunnel and stopping. Incredibly, the helicopter hovered low, giving the occupants a view up the tunnel. It was anything but discreet following and doubtless designed to send a message.

I continued my animal welfare work. Monday July 15th, I met Dr Robert Sharpe, Scientific Adviser for NAVS and accompanied him on a visit to the University of East Anglia to see a humane scientific research project funded by the NAVS. The animal welfare/rights movement not only condemned and exposed vivisection, they promoted and funded humane alternatives that did not involve animal suffering.

Meanwhile, the police started to build the legal cases against us. Having done little for almost a year there was a flurry of activity. Leading figures at the RCS were interviewed and asked for their account of the day and the events immediately after. In August Scotland Yard approached John Mackenzie seeking to interview Phil and me on a mutually convenient date. Arrangements were made and on August 21st 1985—a week before the first anniversary of the SEALL raid— the two of us, accompanied by a solicitor's clerk, went to that notorious tower building in SW1. Question followed question off a type written sheet. To all the answer from us both was the same: "*I claim my right to remain silent*".

September 7th 1985 was most memorable—Sue and I married. At the end of that month I joined 18 other defendants at Winchester Crown Court for the Wickham conspiracy trial. The trial had been scheduled to start on Wednesday June 12th. That June day I had donned my best three-piece suit and walked into court early, soon after 9am. The police officer on duty at the door doubtless could not conceive that I was a defendant.

I followed two chaps—a smartly dressed black guy and a long-haired fellow who looked to be a biker. 'Biker man' said something to the police officer that elicited this reply: "*Oh, you don't want to worry about that sir, they often call for more jurors than are needed in case some are rejected.*" Clearly he was on the jury panel. The biker then queried the cases to be heard that day. The police officer pointed to the long list of names of the Wickham 19 and cheerfully offered the following reply: "*It is this lot here, but they will be better known to you as the Animal Liberation Front. They are the mob who went in and smashed up those laboratories.*"

In my turn, I quietly pointed out that I was a defendant, asked the way to go and the officer, taken aback, directed me upstairs. I immediately reported what I heard to John Mackenzie who in turn told my barrister, Bernard Phelvin, who raised the matter with Judge Lewis McCreery.

Judge McCreery initially said they would not be jurors as the jurors had not been asked to attend court until noon. There was an adjournment whilst enquiries were made. Judge McCreery returned with 'good news' — the two men who spoke to the police officer had been identified: "*Would you like me to bring them in?*" Bernard Phelvin replied he would be grateful. Two men were brought into court and gave their names. Both said they were not jurors but had an interest in our case. Both said the officer at the door had told them there were three trials that morning and indicated the format of each and what it was about. Judge McCreery sought reassurance from Bernard Phelvin: "*Does that satisfy you?*"

I did not recognise either man as being ones I heard spoken to by the police officer at the door. I passed a note to my counsel to this effect and Bernard told the Judge he was not satisfied.

When the jury panel were brought in I quickly identified the two men I had seen spoken to and passed a note to Bernard Phelvin. Judge McCreery spoke to the identified man: "*You, sir, at the back, when you arrived this morning did you speak to the police officer at the door?*"

The juror in waiting replied, "*Yes, I did.*"

Judge McCreery: "*Did he say something to you about this case; what the substance of it was?*"

Juror in waiting, "*Yes, he did.*"

Judge McCreery: "*I think you had better not serve on the jury. You may be excused.*"

The second juror in waiting was identified, gave the same answer and was likewise excused. A somewhat exasperated Judge McCreery then said to my counsel: "*Mr Phelvin, may we now proceed?*" Bernard replied that as it had happened to those two jurors it may have happened to others to which Judge McCreery retorted: "*I am not going to take it any further. I am not going to interrogate each of these jurors in waiting about anything which may have been said to them before.*"

Counsel for the other defendants joined the fray and asked for the remaining panel of jurors to be questioned further. Judge McCreery reluctantly did so, asking if any had been spoken to by the two who had already admitted being spoken to by the police officer. No-one said those two had spoken to them. Another barrister, Mr Stoppa then intervened suggesting the proper question to the jury panel should be: "*Did the police officer say anything to you about the case?*" Judge McCreery replied: "*One of these days, Mr Stoppa, we are going to start this case.* [Then to the jury] *Did any police officer at the door say anything to any of you about the substance of this case?* [There were mutterings in the affirmative] *Will you hold up your hands?* [numerous hands were raised] *All those who have held up their hands will have to be excused. Would you, all who held up your hands, be good enough to leave the Court.* [Twenty-three jurors left].

Judge McCreery then asked the Clerk of the Court: "*Who is the police officer in question?*"

Judge McCreery thought that was the end of the matter but Mr Stoppa applied to discharge the whole jury panel. Judge McCreery: "*That application is refused.*" Mr Stoppa sought to argue his case in the absence of the remains of the jury and those jurors in waiting left the court. The various barristers rose to agree the point that there must have been some discussions amongst the jurors in waiting about what was said, and the panel should be discharged. It was Trevor Burke who asked for the number who raised their hands and left to be recorded (he had counted them). Some barristers were sharp in their demands.

Mr Grey: "*It cannot be said that the jury in waiting can approach this case with an open mind. If things have been said to them, whether by the police officer direct or have been passed on by the people who have spoken to the police officer, then it cannot be said that this jury is not a tainted jury.*"

Judge McCreery exclaimed: "*Is what?*"

Mr Grey: "*Not a tainted jury.*"

Judge McCreery: "*If I may say so, that is hyperbole, Mr Grey. What you really mean is, it cannot be said that some jurors may not have had something prejudicial said to them. That is the accurate position.*"

After some discussion with the Jury Summoning Officer, Judge McCreery ruled that a police officer on duty at the door to the courts had 'unadvisedly' spoken to potential jurors. Accordingly, the entire jury panel were discharged and the case adjourned. As we left the court I saw the very same officer on duty at the door. He spat words venomously at me: "*That's another one for the dole. I hope you're satisfied.*" I sensed that Hampshire Constabulary did not like me very much.

Speaking with our lawyers afterwards we realised we had to get the jury panel discharged. Potential jurors quickly realised that if they raised their hands to admit being spoken to they would be discharged. Those with malevolence towards us would keep their hands down, hope to be selected for the jury and give us a far from fair hearing. It would have been interesting if Judge McCreery had called the police officer to the witness box, sworn him in and asked him who he had spoken to. John Mackenzie then sought on several grounds to have the trial moved from Winchester but his application was refused.

The second Wickham 19 trial commenced on September 30th 1985 and ended in December 1985 with the acquittal of me and eleven other defendants. The trial intricacies are too lengthy to discuss here. All I would say is that I was with the finest campaigners I have ever met. The whole courtroom experience is one of pure theatre. It is about how you look, how you sound, your body language and your whole demeanour.

Whenever I was asked potential trap questions I was careful to take a sip of water to show to the court that I was confident and rock-solid certain—no shaking in my hand. I looked up Judge McCreery in *Who's Who* and saw he had served in the RAF. Our trial embraced Remembrance Day. I was careful to be the first in that courtroom to wear the poppy. Tiny, tiny gestures but Judge McCreery clearly forgave me for my role in the June fiasco—he was benevolent to me in his summings-up.

Seven colleagues were sadly convicted and on December 4th were jailed for up to three years. They put themselves in harm's way to help animals and paid the price. After the trial John Beggs, Press Officer for SEALL, commented: "*The sentences are not going to stop the resolve of Animal Rights activists in this area to expose the abhorrent business of animal experiments or the trade in stolen pets. The real violence is what is being done to the animals. It is the vivisectionists who should be in the dock.*" (*Hampshire Chronicle* December 6th 1985)

Immediately afterwards I faced a two-day trial on a further serious charge. When police had searched the LACS offices they also searched my car parked there. They summoned me to my car and asked me who owned it. I explained it was a LACS car but mine to drive. An officer put it to me: "*So you take responsibility for anything in the car?*" I of course said, "*Yes.*" They opened the car boot and found a sawn-off shotgun. I was aghast. I recalled how during my previous court case over John Peel, boots that had never been anywhere near Cumbria were found to have soil on their soles that supposedly could only have come from that churchyard in Caldbeck. I felt like I had fallen down a well and had no idea what was at the bottom. The police were triumphant.

I had no idea how the gun got there. My barrister, Bernard Phelvin, made short work of the case in court. As he pointed out to my jury I gave the answer of the innocent man. If I had really known there was a gun in my car boot I would have said anything other than I took responsibility for everything there. Even Judge Lewis McCreery seemed to agree. The jury barely had time for a cup of tea before acquitting me.

However, the police had yet another card to play. It was Friday December 6th; instead of walking free from the dock I was immediately arrested again by two Hampshire CID officers. Police told family and friends I would be taken to London to be questioned over the SEALL raid on the RCS and I could be collected from Orpington Police Station after I was bailed. In fact, I was held in Winchester Police Station until all my colleagues departed, then released on bail to reappear at Orpington Police Station the following Tuesday. Hampshire police had scores to settle.

December 10th 1985, at Orpington Police Station, I was duly charged with three alternative counts relating to the RCS raid: handling stolen documents; receiving stolen documents; and aiding and abetting persons' unknown to steal documents. My legal advisors told me they were minor charges, that I had an excellent chance of being acquitted and even if convicted, I would be unlikely to be jailed. It was nearly 16 months after the original SEALL raid and nearly 11 months after I had admitted in Bromley Magistrates Court my presence on that raid. I was bailed to the same Bromley Magistrates Court on December 17th.

I made a couple of brief court appearances each being adjourned to the succeeding one before committal proceedings were heard by Bromley Magistrates on March 18th 1986. John Mackenzie fought my committal. He

45

argued there was no evidence against me upon which a properly directed jury would convict. My actions had not been dishonest. I had not stolen anything—all the documents I had taken I had returned. It was to no avail. The Magistrates committed me for trial at Croydon Crown Court.

January 23rd 1986 brought a brief hearing before the Divisional Court in London. The RCS sought Judicial Review of their appeal refusal. There was no judgement as the DPP conceded the case. The RCS were duly acquitted on the legal technicality that Judge Graham-Hall, in her summary when refusing their first appeal, had commented on matters which the RCS barrister had not been given opportunity to rebut.

In response, the BUAV organised a peaceful occupation of the RCS offices in London and launched a campaign to free *Mone*. On the evening of Monday January 27th, I spoke at a packed public meeting in Bromley in support of the Free Mone campaign. John Mackenzie and Steve McIvor (BUAV Campaigns Organiser) also spoke. The following Saturday there was a March for Freedom through Bromley, Petts Wood and Orpington as the climax of a nationwide week of action for *Mone*.

The BUAV later served ten further summonses against the RCS relating to the caging and housing of all the macaques held at Buckston Browne Farm. They came to nothing.

The prosecution/conviction/acquittal of the RCS did little to harm the careers of those scientists involved but there were pressures at the time. After the original conviction, John E. Cooper wrote a letter, dated July 18th 1985, to his colleague Professor H.C. Rowsell, the Executive Director of the Canadian Council on Animal Care that included this: "*The past 10 months have been very unpleasant and distressing....As far as I am concerned I have lost nearly a year's work and my enthusiasm has waned considerably....... I wonder whether I shouldn't offer my resignation to the Scientific Advisory Committee of WSPA* [World Society for the Protection of Animals]. *I don't in any way feel responsible for the court actions against the RCS but I don't want WSPA to be embarrassed by my connection with them.*"

The BUAV took other action. They called upon the Home Secretary, Leon Brittan, to revoke the Licence of one scientist, Mr Wickham, who performed experiments on dogs at the RCS. Documents taken by SEALL showed that Mr Wickham caused suffering to the dogs over and above the suffering they would have experienced from the experiments themselves.

The RCS case caused concerns worldwide. This letter from Dr Michael Fox of The Humane Society of the United States was published by the *Veterinary Record*, August 10th 1985:

"*Sir—I was disturbed by the tone of the Comment entitled 'Implications of an unusual case' (VR, July 20, p4) concerning the conviction of the Royal College of Surgeons because one of their monkeys almost died from dehydration.*

It is quite obvious that the animal was placed at risk when put into a cage with a dominant male for breeding purposes since its physical condition was not adequately monitored, if at all, until it collapsed from dehydration.

Should we not question routine laboratory animal husbandry procedures and cage designs that do not permit an animal so confined to have some control over its immediate environment? A small cage or 'rape box' is probably ideal for breeding monkeys, but is it humane?

The Comment raised none of these concerns; only concern for the risk to the veterinary profession of being prosecuted if cases like this were to occur in the future. Since there was not one word of criticism of the Royal College of Surgeons or concern expressed for the monkey, I am left with the impression that interests of the profession come before animals' interests and our professional responsibilities toward them."

Wickham connections

The whole RCS saga was inextricably linked with the so-called Wickham connection. It concerned the supply of animals to the RCS. The RCS held various species for experimental use. They had smaller animals, such as frogs and newts, at their research laboratories in Lincoln's Inn Fields. At Buckston Browne Farm at Downe there were larger animals including macaques, marmosets, dogs, sheep and pigs. Macaques and marmosets were acquired in two ways: bred on site and purchased from Shamrock Farms, the primate supplier based near Brighton.

The RCS dogs were of various breeds including many mongrel types. Where did they come from? Before the SEALL raid animal rights activists were baffled. After it, the explanation was found buried amongst the many piles of documents taken. There were several certificates of supply indicating different breeds of dogs as having been sent to the RCS from APT Consultancy in Hampshire. Further, there was correspondence between the veterinary conservator at the RCS—John E. Cooper—and the head of APT Consultancy, a Dr Walker. Clearly the RCS had complaints about the unhealthy state of some animals received. APT promised to do their best to correct the problem.

Sadly, research laboratories can still use dogs but they are now purpose-bred and usually beagles. Being purpose-bred, their exact age and full medical history is known. Consequently, they are, and always have been, expensive (such a beagle in 1984 cost around £400). It was clear from documentary evidence seized by SEALL from the RCS that their dogs supplied by APT came cut-price; they cost about £70. Their ages were guessed at and almost nothing was known about their medical histories. If little was known about their background where did they come from?

APT Consultancy clearly supplied the RCS with many dogs and may well have supplied dogs to other laboratories as well. One might have expected APT to operate from large premises with many kennels, but in fact it operated from a single small room in a tiny upstairs flat. Around Wickham in Hampshire there were three businesses all dealing with animals and all closely connected. There was Wickham Research Laboratory at Wickham, a contract-testing laboratory. APT Consultancy,

47

located in the nearby village of Mislingford, who were animal suppliers. Finally, there was Cottagepatch kennels in Mislingford, a breeding and boarding kennels for dogs. Two of the directors of Wickham Research Laboratory were Dr David Walker and Dr William Bamber Cartmell; both veterinary surgeons. APT Consultancy was run by Dr Walker. Dr Cartmell was the vet for Cottagepatch kennels.

In court during the Wickham trials Dr Walker agreed that through his APT he supplied dogs for research to the RCS. He agreed he was the only source of non-accredited dogs (i.e. non-purpose bred) for the RCS but when pressed as to where his dogs came from became evasive and Judge Lewis McCreery would not allow further questioning—saying it was not APT Consultancy who were on trial.

In a newspaper interview before the Wickham trials Dr Walker was more forthcoming, saying there was a steady source of supply of dogs for research from members of the public who no longer wanted them. He cited the numbers of dogs given to the likes of Battersea Dogs Home and the RSPCA but subsequently put to sleep when they cannot be homed.

Just how such a random selection of dogs from a variety of breeds and ages could end up at the RCS awaiting experimentation is open to speculation. They could indeed be knowingly given by the public for research, doubtless with the assurance that the dog would be fully anaesthetised and would feel nothing when operated on for vital research. They could have been bought off the public using lines such as: 'If you don't want your dog I will give you £10 for him and he will be used in medical research to help save lives—and he won't feel a thing'. They could be obtained by deception with people answering advertisements offering dogs 'free to a good home', claiming to do that but in fact passing the canine to a laboratory. Finally, they could be stolen off the streets by well organised gangs who then passed the dogs through to research without saying how they acquired them, as happened to *Blackie*.

We tried to trace the former owners of the Old English Sheepdog I had photographed at the RCS, but sadly without success.

CHAPTER THREE
I am prosecuted and jailed. Supporters who help my family form the core of the Animal Cruelty Investigation Group.

Following my committal for trial to Croydon Crown Court, John Mackenzie was happy to be my defending solicitor. I was delighted as he had performed brilliantly securing my bail during the Wickham trials in the face of intense opposition from the police and prosecution. John asked Trevor Burke, one of the excellent team of defence barristers in the Wickham trial, to defend me.

We had several conferences during the spring and summer of 1986 during which my defence strategy was planned. We thought that for me to be convicted a jury would have to be certain I had acted dishonestly—that is dishonest by the general test of public standards. Secondly that I had stolen documents. The prosecution had to show I had the intention to permanently deprive the RCS of those documents.

We felt my defence was on secure ground. How could my behaviour be dishonest? I was a photojournalist on that SEALL raid. Like other journalists present I had not concealed my identity. My pictures had been used by the news media. Whilst I had indeed taken documents away it was only after I saw they contained evidence of criminal mistreatment of animals at the RCS. I immediately handed all those documents on to a body that I knew would use them for prosecution. I believed I had done my public duty. Moreover, I had been happy to go to court and identify the documents I had taken from the RCS.

I spent the summer working with colleagues at NAVS, General Secretary Jan Creamer, Tim Phillips, Juliet Gellatley and Bill Bingham on the origins of AIDS and the potential threat to mankind from using primates in research laboratories [see *Biohazard: The silent threat from Biomedical Research and the creation of AIDS* published 1987 by the NAVS.]

My trial was scheduled for September 22nd 1986—my 33rd birthday—and was moved from Croydon to Maidstone Crown Court. Early in September the indictment came through with one charge amended. Instead of being accused of aiding and abetting persons' unknown to commit burglary I was accused of burglary and theft myself. As before, it was laid with the alternative of two lesser charges.

Trevor Burke saw nothing unusual in that. At the time the charge of 'aiding and abetting' was falling out of use and the Crown preferred that of substantive burglary. However, for me it rang alarm bells. I had been told the original three charges were minor and I would be unlikely to be jailed if convicted. But burglary was different. I could feel the cell door beckoning. By then Sue was seven months pregnant with our first child.

Although dark clouds were looming we did not let this affect our lives. Like any dutiful prospective father, I joined Sue on ante-natal parentcraft classes. Held on Thursday evenings at 7:30pm I helped her with practising her breathing exercises and learned how to help her in the hospital. But we knew that I had a mighty hurdle to clear first and it was likely that Sue would face the pain of delivery alone.

Sunday September 21st 1986 we left Suffolk and drove south to stay with close friends Dave and Cee Wetton near Maidstone. Next morning we were in court early. Firstly, for a conference with Trevor Burke and secondly for me to take up station at the entrance to ensure that there was nothing untoward said by the police officers to potential jurors. I wanted no repeat of the corrupt attempt at jury influencing we had from Hampshire Constabulary at Winchester Crown Court.

Maidstone Crown Court was, in 1986, a modern building. My case was heard in Court 4, a claustrophobic room tucked away on the fourth floor lacking any natural light. The curtain rose on the show at 10am. I stood in the dock at the back, a prison officer by my side. The table immediately in front was occupied by the solicitor's clerk and the police; the table in front of them by the two barristers. The high spot was taken by the Judge—or in my case Recorder. Sue and friends sat in the single row of chairs backed against the wall that formed the 'public gallery' to my left. On my right, there was a double row of benching for the jury.

The jury panel were called in. With the agreement of Trevor Burke and prosecution barrister, Martin Hall-Smith, Recorder Matheson questioned them. Did any have any connections, directly or through family, with the RCS or the vivisection industry? Did any have connections with hunting or with any animal rights organisations or activities? Two raised their hands and were dismissed.

Shortly before noon my trial started. Martin Hall-Smith made the case for the prosecution. The Crown had learned from their misfortunes in the Wickham trials. There they had pitched the case high, making out to the jury that the raids had been attacks of near terrorist proportions, and had found themselves short of evidence to justify the hyperbole. For my case the prosecution was pitched low-key. Just a straight-forward account of what happened and how by my evidence in court I had admitted my involvement. Martin Hall-Smith said that whatever their views on the matter I was guilty of the offences and should be convicted.

Witnesses were called. The first, at 12:20pm was Brian Eaton the Senior Medical Laboratory Scientific Officer—a role he had held for fifteen years. Present during the raid he gave a graphic account of events. He was in his car at the farm when he saw people in his rear-view mirror. Many wore masks. There were loud noises, banging, and thunder-flashes detonating with smoke billowing everywhere. He drew a sketch of the layout that was photocopied and passed to the jury. He described driving around and parking between the two laboratories. He lost all sense of time during the drama. He described seeing a man running to the residential quarters with a sledgehammer raised as if to break a window. Brian Eaton approached this man and warned, "*People live there*" at which the man turned away and went back to his colleagues. Brian then approached this main group but was advised not to approach further so he did not.

Brian Eaton described seeing one raider carrying an air-horn. He sounded it in what appeared to be the signal to leave as he called out, "*Everybody out!!!*" A smoke bomb was thrown in his direction. He was amazed at the large number of people that left the buildings (he estimated 50 to 60) and headed for the field at the back, with the man with the air-horn bringing up the rear.

Brian then entered the Surgical Research Unit over a door that had been knocked flat. He found most doors damaged, papers strewn about, filing cabinets opened and the animals in a distressed state— but none missing. He described his own office as, "*just very untidy.*" He said some junior technicians were on duty that morning. A young girl named Deborah Hoare came out of the Surgical Research Unit and ran towards him in a state of shock. He described her trembling and crying. There was then an hour break for lunch.

Brian Eaton returned to the witness box and was shown a succession of documents. There was much debate as to whether they were originals or photocopies. At 2:30pm Trevor Burke started his cross-examination. We held our breath wondering how far Recorder Duncan Matheson would allow Trevor to go. In similar circumstances at Winchester Crown Court Judge Lewis McCreery had allowed the defence virtually no leeway but here, to our pleasant surprise, Recorder Matheson was more lenient.

The fear for the prosecution in such circumstances is that if the defence is allowed to fully explain to the jury the nature of the horrors that the defendant sought to expose then, whatever the evidence, the jury might acquit in something akin to a 'perverse verdict'. In effect the jurors are saying: 'Well, I would have done the same'. At Winchester Crown Court Judge McCreery had repeated over and over it was not Wickham Laboratories and associated companies who were on trial. Recorder Matheson did the same—stressing it was not the RCS who were on trial.

Questioned by Trevor Burke, Brian Eaton revealed he had worked for the RCS for about eleven years. Their work included surgical research on mice, cats, dogs, monkeys, pigs, rabbits, guinea pigs and sheep. The research was conducted within two buildings. They were licensed premises and the work was exempted under the Cruelty to Animals Act 1876. He said they had never once been prosecuted, reprimanded or had their licence revoked during the many years he had worked there—or indeed previously. He agreed there had been a visit to the farm by Home Office Inspectors on June 18th 1984—the very day that a monkey named *Rage* died of dehydration. He agreed that the RCS had been prosecuted and convicted of cruelty to a monkey named *Mone* and it was confirmed that the conviction had eventually been overturned on appeal.

Brian Eaton declared that John E. Cooper had responsibility for organising the supply of dogs and he checked that those dogs were suitable for experimentation. When Trevor Burke tried to bring photographs into the case the Recorder objected saying: "*I am prepared to give you a considerable amount of latitude as long as it doesn't end up in the Royal College of Surgeons being on trial.*" After some discussion, photographs of a variety of dogs were shown to Brian Eaton. He agreed that none were purpose-bred. They were adult dogs that the RCS purchased. At that time, they only had one supplier—APT consultancy run by Dr David Walker. They paid £70 a dog, a bit more for greyhounds. Purpose bred beagles cost £400 to £500 and as a charity the RCS did not have much money available.

There followed a police witness who described the seizure of documents during a search of my home. At 3:25pm the prosecution called their star witness—David Barker. He was Deputy Clerk to Bromley Magistrates, present for the original prosecution of the RCS. His evidence detailed the basic facts of that case, how I had voluntarily given evidence to Bromley Magistrates and the nature of it. Martin Hall-Smith took him through my original words referring to the official shorthand note taken at the time. This purported to be an exact word for word record but there were discrepancies to be corrected. The most obvious was that I was supposed to have said that I took away 'bills' when I actually said 'files'. Minor in that case but in others it could be more serious. There ensued a detailed debate as to which documents I had identified during the prosecution of the RCS.

Just after 4pm, Trevor Burke cross-examined. David Barker agreed that in the Magistrates Court the Justices were not lawyers; as Deputy Clerk he was the lawyer. Trevor put it to him that: "*If he* (Huskisson) *had not waived his rights and given evidence the Royal College of Surgeons would not have been prosecuted?*" David Barker agreed saying: "*Yes, the documents had to be linked to the farm.*" Trevor Burke sought confirmation before the jury of the 6-month time limit for prosecutions to be brought under the relevant Act and David Barker agreed. Then, when Trevor referred to four other incidents, two of monkeys being found dead and two of monkeys being found hanging with their arms trapped, Recorder Matheson objected.

Trevor Burke explained he was trying to elicit the nature of the work at the laboratory and the possible sources of supply of the animals that were being experimented on. He aimed to show that I had reasonable cause for disquiet at what was going on and therefore my actions in going to the farm in the first place were not those of a dishonest man. Recorder Matheson did not like this questioning and blocked it.

Trevor protested and the jury was sent out so the issue could be discussed by the lawyers. A twenty minute debate raged. Trevor emphasised that an essential element of my defence was showing that I had not been dishonest, had no intention to keep permanently any documents, and that it was vital to bring out the facts about the RCS known to me at the time. My defence hinged on the motives for my actions—unless we could show what drove my actions my defence would collapse. Recorder Matheson pondered, then again blocked that line of questioning, saying it was me in the dock not the RCS. I sensed that cell door swinging shut.

The jury were recalled and with Trevor barred from asking any further pertinent questions of David Barker he was discharged.

Recorder Matheson sent the jury home telling them when they would be required the following morning. After they left, Recorder

Matheson reminded Martin Hall-Smith that burglary could be interpreted as being intent on causing criminal damage and had he thought of applying to amend the indictment? That induced a furious protest from Trevor Burke. He said that having made the Crown aware of the nature of my defence Recorder Matheson now sought to exploit that knowledge by introducing an element to the trial to which my defence would not apply. The question of dishonesty does not apply where criminal damage is concerned, nor does it matter whether or not there is an intention to permanently deprive. Even Martin Hall-Smith appeared unhappy at the turn of events. However, Recorder Matheson was adamant and insistent that the indictment could be amended, even at that late stage. He urged Martin Hall-Smith to consider it and, if he wished, to make the necessary request in the morning. I doubted Recorder Matheson would turn the request down.

Some weeks before, a sympathetic police officer had warned me that I was taking on powerful forces and would have no escape from the Royal College of Surgeons' prosecution. That night we all went for a quiet drink to celebrate my birthday. It was a time for reflection. It then seemed certain Sue would give birth alone and the three of us would spend at least one more Christmas apart.

In court the next morning, in the absence of the jury there was debate about the indictment. Recorder Matheson invited Trevor Burke's view. When Trevor replied, Recorder Matheson said: "*I follow your point, I just don't agree with it.*"

There then followed debates as to the meaning of 'dishonesty'. Recorder Matheson stated there was legal authority that conduct may be reprehensible without being dishonest. He clearly feared a possible perverse verdict here when he added: "*It would not surprise me in the least if the Jury came back shaking their heads saying we take a dim view of this but it is not dishonest.*" He raised the matter of Joint Enterprise and said they should look at everybody's motives, not just mine, and he still thought I should be charged with unlawful damage. The legal debates were furious. Trevor said he would invite a retrial. He had revealed the defence and once he had seen the force of that defence the Judge had amended the attack. Trevor concluded: "*Perhaps I should have kept my mouth shut and left the Crown to prosecute this case unaided.*"

There was a further adjournment then, still in the absence of the jury, Martin Hall-Smith applied to amend the indictment by the addition of a further count of burglary contrary to section 9(a) of the Theft Act with intent to cause unlawful damage to a building and its contents. Recorder Matheson invited Trevor Burke to comment. He did so and sought the discretion of the Recorder to disallow the amendment. Recorder Matheson listened and even admitted: "*I am aware that the initiative for this came from me,*" then ruled the amendment admissible. At 12.25pm the jury was recalled and the whole new indictment read to me again. I again pleaded 'not guilty' to all charges.

Recorder Matheson gave so much help to Martin Hall-Smith that at one point Trevor Burke was moved to say: "*Your Honour is conducting the prosecution's case very much better than prosecution counsel himself — I wish you would do the same for the defence.*" To which the Recorder replied: "*Don't let us get carried away, Mr Burke.*"

The last witness on the morning of Tuesday September 23rd was Professor Newell Johnson from the RCS. I had last seen him in the witness box as a defence witness for the RCS. Abroad on the day of the SEALL raid, he said large numbers of RCS incident report forms were missing afterwards but that many of the stolen documents were produced in court. There was the usual one hour break for lunch soon after 1pm.

At 2.15pm John E. Cooper, the veterinary conservator at the RCS since 1978 was called. He explained how his responsibility was to advise on the health and welfare of the animals kept for research. Based in London he made routine visits to Downe. He had a bleep device and was on hand 24 hours a day to provide a veterinary service for the animals at Downe. He shared the call duty at the RCS with a colleague. On the day of the raid he was away running a course at a zoo in Jersey. He was next at Downe nine days after the raid. When he returned, he found his office at Downe the same as when he left it.

Trevor cross-examined John E. Cooper. Asked about some of the incidents the veterinary conservator said: "*Death isn't suffering, it can be very humane.*" His opinion of a monkey found hanging dead deprived of water was that it was, "*a disturbing incident.*" He said that whilst the monkeys were at the time tattooed with their name across their forehead this no longer happened. Asked about the variety of breeds of dog kept at Downe he said: "*They are of a type identical to dogs kept by members of the public.*" Shown my photograph of the Old English Sheepdog he agreed he was clearly a mature adult, adding he had been at the RCS for some time and their technicians looked after him. Shown the incident report form regarding *Rage* he agreed he had died of dehydration on June 18th 1984. Recorder Matheson then intervened to block further similar questioning.

There followed a debate about such questioning in front of the jury. Trevor was allowed to show John E. Cooper some of the photographs, to which he responded: "*It's like looking at long lost friends.*"

The next witness was Bruce Bidewell. He was employed at the RCS until July 28th 1984 and had worked for the college for about eight years. His job concerned the routine day-to-day running of the animal unit. Shown some photographs he confirmed they were copies of slides he had taken at the college. The x-rays were of incidents that happened to the animals in the unit. He complained that his diary and some slides were still missing.

Some statements were then read from police officers. The prosecution aimed to prove that amongst many documents seized from my home after the Wickham raids were original RCS documents that had not been returned. These were in fact photocopies of RCS documents in one file and amongst a large collection of scientific papers were two articles detailing work carried out at the RCS.

That matter had already been dealt with by my defence when it was raised at my committal stage. John Mackenzie had questioned Bruce Bidewell about them and he confirmed that there was nothing on the papers to identify them as having come from the RCS, no college stamp or similar. Bruce agreed they were available to the public and freely circulated amongst the scientific community. I do a lot of library-based scientific research and take copies of documents, legally, for reference. Little weight was placed on this evidence by either the prosecution or Recorder Matheson.

The prosecution case concluded soon after 3pm on Tuesday September 23rd. I was granted a five minute adjournment to go to the toilet. Then, in the absence of the jury, Trevor Burke submitted I had no case to answer on any of the five counts. Recorder Matheson disagreed on the first four but agreed that the matter of documents and articles taken from my home by Hampshire Constabulary was nonsense. He confirmed he would direct the jury to find me 'not guilty' on that charge. One down, four to go!

It was then time for my defence. There was only me. Soon after 3:30pm Trevor called me to the witness box. To set the scene, and establish my role as a photojournalist, he went over my activities in the animal rights movement as a photographer, my work in Afghanistan in 1980 as a photojournalist and my employment with the LACS as Press Officer from 1981-1985.

A brief résumé of my undercover work to expose bloodsports was given, together with some of the attendant media coverage. That proved to the jury that in August 1984 my reputation as a photographer was known widely in the animal rights movement—and therefore it was no surprise that I was asked to take that role. Further, Trevor showed that my employment by the LACS, an organisation known to be totally law-abiding, meant I would not have been told anything more about the raid than was deemed necessary. Trevor Burke then took me through my account of events leading up to the raid, my role on the day, and the aftermath and finally my giving evidence at Bromley Magistrates Court. This took about an hour after which the court was adjourned for the night.

Wednesday morning started with a fifteen-minute delay caused by the absence of a shorthand writer. In the absence of the jury Martin Hall-Smith asked that they be made aware of my antecedents (as detailed in *Outfoxed* (1983) and *Outfoxed Take Two* (2015)). He claimed that by my saying I was married I was claiming good character to which Recorder Matheson retorted: "*That is not evidence of good character!*" The prosecutor then said that by my saying I had returned the documents I took I was claiming good character. A legal row ensued for nearly an hour.

Trevor pointed out that there had been no imputation of the prosecution witnesses. I never put my character in issue and to raise the matter of the John Peel incident would be very prejudicial. I already had little chance of escape but if the prosecution revealed my conviction for desecrating the grave of a long-dead Huntsman I would have no chance.

Eventually Recorder Matheson found in our favour— blocking any cross-examination as to my character. The jury were recalled and I was cross-examined from 11:40am to 3pm with an hour break for lunch from 1pm.

Martin Hall-Smith could not challenge my credentials as a photojournalist but he sought to show that I must have known far more about the planning of the raid. Gaining little success, he changed tack to the time immediately before the raid when I first met the rest of the party in the woodland clearing. He pressed that I must have realised that something criminal was afoot, that people were going to take and keep large quantities of documents, were going to damage property and that they knew it was wrong because they were equipped with balaclavas to conceal their identity. I maintained I had only been told there was to be a demonstration, had been asked to photograph monkeys not take away documents and that in my opinion if documents were taken they should be photocopied and returned.

Martin Hall-Smith pressed hard that I must have known that damage to property would occur and that I would have been happy to see such damage. I strongly refuted this, making it clear that whilst I certainly would like to see the RCS closed and demolished, it should be done legally. Wanton damage would only tarnish our public image and moreover did nothing to harm the laboratories. They would merely bring in valuers to assess the damage and claim full replacement costs from their insurance.

Unable to show I had any personal desire to steal or smash property Martin Hall-Smith then claimed that, whatever my feelings, I must have known that others that day had the desire to commit such criminal acts, and that I had freely associated myself with them. I had to agree that many documents taken away were not, and never have been, returned. Further, I agreed that property had been damaged but I made it clear that to my knowledge it was only the minimum necessary to gain access. I had personally seen plenty of expensive machinery left untouched. [*Orpington Comet* February 8th 1985 reported that £15,000 damage was caused.]

Martin Hall-Smith then turned to my account of the events. Why did I carry on when I recognised that law-breaking was occurring? I explained that my actions stemmed from when I looked into the open door of that first building, the dog unit, and saw the various breeds housed within. They were pets and I could not believe that any owner would knowingly sell or give them to a laboratory. I thought that by photographing them I would gain vital evidence that might reunite some with their owners.

Martin Hall-Smith asked why then did I not leave immediately after? Why go to the monkey unit? "*Well, I had been asked to photograph the monkeys.*" I was asked if, when by the monkey unit, I really did leaf through documents to assess their content. I confirmed that I did. (Such documents were gold-dust to animal rights activists so of course I flicked through them). He ended by probing the matter of my position within the movement and opined that I must have been involved in the raid planning. I maintained that my connection with the LACS meant I was not generally trusted by other animal rights activists.

Recorder Matheson then questioned me on a couple of minor points. Trevor Burke cleared up a few matters on re-examination and that ended my evidence. There were no further defence witnesses to call. Caroline Dawkins was at peace beyond the reach of the law and to have called Phil Churchward would have exposed him to the risk of prosecution.

It was time for closing speeches. At 3:10pm Martin Hall-Smith went first. His was virtually a repeat of his opening speech with some additions. I must have known more about the raid. I had possibly been involved in the planning, but certainly knew from an early stage that morning that property would be stolen or damaged, yet far from dissenting I had wholeheartedly associated myself with the enterprise. Therefore, I was guilty of burglary on both counts. If the jury thought I was not, then by my own words, I had more or less admitted the third charge, and certainly admitted the fourth.

Trevor Burke's half-hour closing speech in my defence was a masterpiece. He went in hard that I might strike the jury as being foolish, stupid, or pathetic, but surely not as dishonest. He reminded them that I had not had to give my original evidence at Bromley Magistrates Court. Had I not done so I would not have been there facing them from the dock. I gave evidence because of my determination to expose a crime. In that I had been successful albeit that later, sadly, the RCS were acquitted. He stressed my reasons for neither wishing to see documents permanently removed, nor wishing to see property damaged. He emphasised that I was there as a photojournalist. As for Joint Enterprise, he explained that my physical presence alone was never enough to make me party to a crime.

The final speech—the summing up from Recorder Matheson—was left until the following morning, Thursday September 25th. Sue and I left for what we knew would be our last evening together for some considerable time. Trevor had warned that if convicted on either of the first two burglary counts I could expect a sentence of 18 months. If acquitted on the first two counts, but convicted on either of counts three, or four, it would be 9 months. I had already been acquitted on one count, but it was too much to expect to be acquitted on all the remaining four.

On Thursday morning Sue and I were, as usual, in the court precinct early. We strolled along the riverbank to feed the ducks, then had a cup of coffee in the canteen to calm the nerves. Then it was time to head for the fourth-floor court and face the inevitable.

In the absence of the jury, Recorder Matheson said he had typed definitions of the offences to give to the jury. Trevor Burke objected and even Martin Hall-Smith said he had never heard of that being done but Recorder Matheson cited legal precedent. When Trevor found the authority for this in Archbold (the legal bible) he accepted it. Such a move appears to be done to save the jury sending out a stream of notes when deliberating their verdict, but it was unusual and seemed calculated to weigh against me.

The jury were recalled and Recorder Matheson carefully explained that it was for the prosecution to prove my guilt, not for me to prove my innocence. The burden of proof was on the prosecution and the jury had to be certain I was guilty before convicting me. He proceeded to detail the evidence in a calm methodical manner.

One of many strange things about my case was that there were no conflicts of evidence. No disputes over eye-witness evidence, forensic evidence, or answers to police questions. It was a debate as to my frame of mind and motives at the time. Recorder Matheson queried whether I could have been as ignorant as I claimed about the planning and purpose of the SEALL raid, but generally he said little to concern me until he explained the intricacies of the law to the jury.

When he explained the implications of Joint Enterprise I knew I was guaranteed a swift trip to jail. The concept enabled the conviction of individuals for equal participation in a raid even if they personally had done nothing illegal— such as a look-out or a getaway driver for a burglary. He told the jurors to think beyond my own personal level of involvement. They needed to consider whether other raiders had stolen documents (many documents had been taken and not returned) and whether others had damaged property (property clearly had been damaged). If they believed I had knowingly and willingly associated myself with those other raiders I was guilty of the burglary charges.

Recorder Matheson then reviewed the evidence concerning the lesser charges. After that, just before lunch, the jury were sent out to deliberate. When the jury had left Recorder Matheson congratulated Trevor Burke: *"May I say that your closing speech to the jury yesterday was one of the best I've heard."*

I had expected to be remanded in custody to the court cells once the jury were sent out (particularly after a jury direction almost certain to convict me) but no, I was granted bail to the court precinct. [I guess they accepted that as I had voluntarily walked into Bromley Magistrates Court to start with I was unlikely to 'do a runner' there]. We enjoyed a nervous last meal in the top floor restaurant and awaited the relevant announcements on the court public address system.

At 3:30pm we were summoned back to court 4. The jury had been asked to consider 4 charges. These were two burglary counts, 1 and 2. Then, as an alternative, count 3 and as an alternative to that count 4. If their verdict was 'guilty' on either count 1 or 2 they need not consider counts 3 or 4. If it was 'not guilty' on both 1 and 2 then they should consider count 3. If 'guilty' on count 3 they should not consider count 4. Only if it was 'not guilty' on count 3 should they consider count 4 —and if they got to a 'not guilty' on count 4 then a miracle would have happened!

The jury had returned with a question written on a note for the Recorder. After reading it he passed it to the barristers. Trevor glanced at it and indicated the worst to me. They had reached a verdict on count 1, did not need to consider counts 3 and 4 but were undecided on count 2. Should they continue to deliberate? This could only mean that I was guilty on count 1. I looked to Sue and friends in the public gallery and shook my head.

Recorder Matheson explained that another ten minutes would have to elapse before a majority verdict could be brought in so he sent the jury out to carry on with their deliberations. Instead of being bailed to the court precincts I was remanded in custody and taken down to the cells. After the necessary time elapsed I was brought back up to the dock to hear the formal verdicts. I was found guilty unanimously on count 1 (burglary and theft). On count 2 (burglary with intent to cause unlawful damage) I was found guilty by a majority of 10-2.

Recorder Matheson lectured me: "*I don't doubt for a moment that you have deeply held convictions about animals and their use for experiments but this sort of raid is all too prevalent and is an example of the chilling intolerance one finds too often. There are far too many people with strong convictions who believe they are entitled to ride roughshod over other people's rights. I accept without hesitation that you did not physically do any damage or personally steal any documents. That was done by others. If I had thought you were one of the organisers or ringleaders I would have sent you to prison for at least three years.*"

Then, as expected, I was sentenced to 18 months' imprisonment on count 1 and similar, concurrent, on count 2. It was 4pm on Thursday September 25th 1986. Our first child was due in less than three weeks. Sue would face the trials, tribulations and happiness of childbirth on her own.

Sentence

I was taken down to the cell area beneath the court and searched. I met Trevor Burke and thanked him for his sterling efforts. I asked to see Sue to hand my court notes and other items to her. Anticipating the result, I had previously left my car keys with her. I was told a brief visit would be arranged and advised to hand Sue all money in my possession as well. I was then hustled into a small windowless cell to reflect on my situation.

Two thoughts put my circumstances into perspective. Firstly, I thought of Caroline in the confines of her coffin. Secondly, I found that standing in the middle of the floor, unlike the primates I had tried to help, my cell was big—I could not touch all the walls around me nor the ceiling above. Most importantly, I would be released one day, and through a gate, not up the cremation chimney.

After about 15 minutes my heavy door was opened and I was escorted into a small room divided by a line of cubicles. At each a chair was placed facing a wall of reinforced glass. [Years later Sue and I saw similar as tourists in Alcatraz prison, San Francisco Bay].

Sue sat in one cubicle on the other side of the glass. We could see each other, talk, but not touch. I had dropped out of society and the doors had shut to seal me. I was engulfed in the prison system. Our child would be born with his/her father in prison. For the first days, weeks, months and perhaps near year of that infant's life I would be but a distant figure, seen only for the short spans of prison visits. I would miss the joy of bath-times, the gurgles of feeding, the first faltering steps. It was so sad. We talked of momentous things but also of trivia—how to work the boiler timer, where the radiator bleed key was etc.

59

Minutes condensed to seconds and all too soon we were forced to part. I was held in the same cell until about 5pm then brought out to join others. Men like me who were convicted and jailed that day and several still on trial but remanded in custody. We were prepared for our coach trip to Canterbury Prison. Handcuffed in pairs there was an odd number and I ended up cuffed up to a prison officer. Our escort led us to board our coach in the sealed bowels of the court house. The great solid doors slid open and we were driven away. Half an hour later, after negotiating the one-way traffic system in Maidstone on a weekday evening, we were back outside the same court—but on the other side of the road.

Having previously served a 9-month prison sentence for animal rights offences back in 1977-78 (detailed in *Outfoxed* (1983) and *Outfoxed Take Two* (2015)) I knew what to expect. Arriving at Canterbury Prison reception area the sequence was: change into prison clothes; a quick medical check—have you got AIDS? No. Carry on. A quick bath, the opportunity to take a meal if wanted, then up onto the prison wings. The smell of such an old closed prison is the same the nation (probably the world) over; boiled cabbage and body odour.

I was put in cell A3-28—cell number 28 on the third floor of A wing. It was a pleasant surprise to find that not only was I on my own but there was provision for only one other inmate anyway (there were two single beds). Much of my previous time in closed prisons had been spent 3-up— that is with a double bunk bed and a single bed in each cell. The previous occupant had left reading material; a couple of old newspapers. I was delighted to find that I could control my own light; there was a switch on the inside. There was still 'slopping-out' (a bucket for a toilet) but minor luxuries like the ability to control the light were welcomed.

My being in Canterbury Prison, of all prisons, seemed strange. As a child, I had been incarcerated in a boarding school high up St Thomas's Hill in the town. That was from 1965 to 1970. To while away the many hours of boredom I had walked the streets of Canterbury, even on occasion past the prison gates, not knowing that one day I would end up the other side. I had also visited the prison in the late 1970s when I had called in to see animal rights legend, Ronnie Lee, who was on remand facing charges resulting from the rescue of laboratory mice.

Sleep did not come easy that first night. Prisons are noisy and that was only the second night I had spent apart from Sue since our marriage. In the morning, there was the usual long wait to see the prison Governor or his assistant and be told my situation. My prison number was P69140. My EDR (Earliest Date of Release) was September 24th 1987—that was when, provided I behaved myself, I was certain to be released. My Parole date was March 25th 1987. It was another welcome surprise to learn that I was eligible for parole. At the time of my previous sentence only prisoners serving 3 years or more qualified.

Asked if I had any questions I requested to be transferred as soon as possible to a prison near Norwich to be near Sue who, I explained, was expecting in less than three weeks. The officer must have thought "*Your fault sonny for putting her in that position*." But my tale was too long to explain. He assured me he would do his best.

On the prison transfer coach from Maidstone I had raised the matter of a transfer with the officer to whom I was bonded by steel. He said that I would certainly be transferred to a low-security prison, most likely to Camp Hill on the Isle of Wight. A lovely location, but the thought of being stuck there whilst Sue was giving birth in a Norwich hospital, and then nursing a very young infant, filled me with horror. There would be little chance of many or any visits. However, I soon learned there was a regular prison transport from Canterbury to prisons in the Norwich area—Highpoint near Newmarket, Wayland near Thetford and Blundeston near Lowestoft. Any of those would suit us fine.

Cell life in Canterbury prison was a pleasant improvement on my previous experience in Durham prison—and to be honest was better than my time in the public school up the road. Single occupancy did not last long. On my second night, I was joined by a young Irish lad given a 3-year sentence from Maidstone Crown Court for drug smuggling. My cell-mate was one unhappy man and pressing for a retrial. Apparently, a customs officer, a prosecution witness against him, had made an off-the-cuff remark to his barrister indicating they knew the identity of a vital defence witness but had not revealed this in court. If all convicts were believed there would be few guilty men in prison but his case struck me as a cause for concern.

Whilst we still had to cope with the degrading business of the shared cell 'toilet' being a bucket that lurked beneath an ill-fitting lid in one corner, and jugs of water to wash, shave and clean our teeth, the prison officers made efforts to improve standards. I soon learned that if on the last bang-up for the night (at about 6:30pm) you asked the officer slamming your door to be allowed out for a shower he would add you to his list. This was written on the palm of his hand. Then, at some subsequent time that evening, you would be allowed out to use one of the three showers in the recess along the landing. What joy it was to wash away the taint of prison life. Yes, they were scalding hot but better that than freezing cold.

On my first afternoon in prison I had a welcome surprise when Sue visited. I thought that before any visit I would have to go through all the palaver of sending out visiting orders etc. but no. Sue had stayed overnight with Dave and Cee Wetton and for this first visit had simply phoned the prison and been allowed in.

We had been apart for less than 24 hours yet I already felt like the prisoner I was, the caged man. Talking to my dear Sue across the visiting room table was talking across a great legal canyon. Who could say when I would next be allowed to cross to the other side? At such a time when each second is savoured, each touch treasured, half an hour passed so quickly. Little did we know when we parted that when we next met my young son would be on the scene—well, more visibly.

Saturday September 27th I joined other inmates for the evening film show—the video *Death Wish 3*. The following Monday I started prison work, in the mailbag shop. It was dull repetitive work, but a good opportunity to chat with fellow prisoners. That afternoon I learned that I would be transferred to Wayland Prison in Norfolk on the Thursday.

October 2nd 1986 was a good day for our family. I was transferred nearer home in prison transport from Canterbury prison. Our coach left at 7:30am and at 10:45am arrived at the modern, category C prison, Wayland, near Thetford, Norfolk. As we approached the front entrance I recalled months earlier that Sue and I had considered buying a house very close by. Had we done so I doubted whether I would have been granted that transfer.

In Wayland, I was allocated to House 3. I found the luxury of not only having a single cell but also a toilet and wash basin within! The prison was divided into four houses in each of which there were facilities for inmates to play table-tennis, pool, and darts and there were two television rooms. Each house had showers and baths. For the evening association period, that lasted 2½ hours, our cells were opened and we could virtually do as we liked.

On my first afternoon, there was a football match between Wayland Prison and a local police team. Wayland won 6-0 (but the police were a man short). The following morning, I was paraded before the Governor—a young woman, and told the usual about the regime and my sentence.

To my delight Wayland Prison had a wonderful library. This was far more than the moth-eaten collection of books with the last pages torn out that I had found in other prisons. It was a branch of the Norfolk County Library—and books could be ordered from anywhere in the Norfolk system. My time would not be wasted. I could do serious research.

There was a well-equipped gym and excellent sports field. In the evenings, the prison ran a selection of classes. I put my name down for pottery, woodwork and art. I learned that I could apply for Sue to bring in my lever-arch files full of research work for NAVS into the origins of AIDS.

Regarding prison diet, I needed Sue to send in my card proving membership of the Vegan Society to get vegan food. Once that arrived I was given a near endless private supply of soya milk, Vecon vegetable stock (like Marmite), nuts etc. My diet was the envy of many.

Sunday was notable for a rugby match against nearby RAF Watton that our prison team narrowly lost 15-17. Wayland of course always enjoyed home advantage in any games.

Sue's first visit was scheduled for Monday October 13th. I was waiting in the dinner queue at 11:30am. A senior officer tapped me on the shoulder: "*No visit, your wife is in labour and has gone into hospital.*" Friends and supporters outside had pleaded that I be allowed a short day parole to be with Sue for the birth. They offered to pay escort costs for prison staff and to stand thousands of pounds bail for me to be there to see our first child born but it was not allowed. You could get parole from prison for the funeral of a blood relative but not for a birth. I was told that prison officers would tell me the outcome up to 11pm. After that night staff would slip a note under my cell door.

No news next morning. I commenced work in the Tailor's shop making prison clothing but I had barely started before I was excused at 10am for rugby training.

Our son was born late on Tuesday October 14th. I was told the following morning. Sue and I spoke on the phone on the Thursday. I had been in the pottery class for an hour from 6:30pm, had returned to my block and was soaking in the bath when the prison tannoy rang out: "*140 Huskisson to the S.O.'s* [Senior Officer's] *office!!*" I rushed to the office, was handed the telephone, and allowed to chat with Sue—and hear our son gurgling with delight in the background.

In the chapel service the following Sunday the Prison Chaplain was kind enough to ask for a blessing for the three of us. On Thursday October 23rd—nine days after he was born—Sue brought our lad in on a prison visit. I cried with joy to hold them both. I wanted the visit to last for ever. The benefit of being in Norfolk was we could have frequent visits. A week and a day later Sue brought our son in again along with my best man, Alan Knight and his partner, Liz Varney. Alan and Liz had driven miles from their home near Tonbridge—I was fortunate to have such friends.

Whilst it was always difficult parting at the end of visits I was lucky because our son was so young and could not understand the situation. How much harder if he had been, say, 5 or 6 years old and cried out, "*Daddy! Daddy!*" and tried to cling to me at the end of each visit.

On Sunday November 2nd, I played my first competitive rugby game since boarding school days some 16 years before—coming on as a substitute for the last five minutes of the match against nearby Thetford. My contribution was inauspicious. We had been leading before my entrance. Thetford then scored and we lost 13-14. I never handled the ball but managed to make some tackles.

My predicament was made known to animal welfare/rights campaigners across the UK and around the world. The NAVS ran a supportive article in their magazine, *The Campaigner*. My good friend Louise McKenna, one of the founders of Zoo Check (now the Born Free Foundation) generated great support for me amongst compassionate people in Australia.

I received a welcome flood of supportive letters from around the globe. I was truly never alone. I had the enduring love of my family and felt surrounded by friends from all ages, all walks of life and all countries.

In campaigning terms, I was restricted to library research. My only 'direct action' was moving worms stranded on the concrete exercise paths after rain to adjacent grass to spare them being trodden on. One letter of mine at the time notes that we had mice in our cells.

Life at Wayland was punishment for inmates only in the sense of deprivation of liberty. Poor Sue had to cope with the struggles of everyday life whilst I was in what amounted to a closed fitness and creative writing camp and had everything done for me. I was served quality vegan food and did not even have to wash up!

In terms of work I started off in the Tailor's shop where I was shown the intricacies of machine stitching. I was happy to spend my meagre earnings on stamps for replies to friends around the world.

Offered a wide-variety of evening classes I participated in many. They were great opportunities to chat to fellow inmates and the civilian instructors. Soft Toy classes were on Monday evenings. Amongst other items I made a cuddly dolphin for my son. In Woodwork, I made a mobile from cut-out animal shapes to hang from his bedroom ceiling and I constructed a sturdy bird table. [It was indeed sturdy because at time of writing (August 2016) it still stands, albeit with some support, in our garden. That product of my prison labour has fed many generations of birds.] I also attended Pottery classes and created pots for our cacti.

Sometimes evening classes were cancelled, on one occasion because of 'flu amongst the staff. More often they were cancelled because of concerts provided by visitors. My Woodwork class on November 5th 1986 was cancelled for a concert provided by a young girl singer from Norwich accompanied by a comedian. We were not the easiest of audiences but the efforts made by these outsiders to entertain were greatly appreciated.

At weekends, we were shown videos. The selection for Sunday November 16th was *Ladyhawke*. Often popular programmes in the TV rooms, such as *EastEnders*, were watched through a fog of cannabis smoke. I have never taken such drugs in my life and it is somewhat ironic that the only place that I was forcibly exposed to them was inside prison. Drugs were rife and caused many conflicts and fights between prisoners. I guess the drug haze in the television rooms was tolerated by prison staff because at the time it placated and calmed the prisoners.

Wayland prison was well staffed by professional and conscientious officers and I honestly cannot recall any serious conflicts between prisoners and officers—let alone assaults by one against the other. Gym facilities were fabulous. We also had a large playing field. I went jogging, did occasional weight-training and was delighted to train with the prison rugby squad. Wayland played frequent matches against outside opposition. I seldom played but was always pleased to cheer our lads from the side-lines.

Supporters on the outside raised a 'Mike Huskisson Appeal Fund' to help Sue during my incarceration. This was run by my close friends Dave and Cee Wetton and Alun and Joy Davies. When people learned of the sacrifices that my small family had made to help the cause they were generous in their support.

As well as sport and evening classes I read a lot, particularly animal welfare literature and scientific journals. My correspondence with many supporters both in the UK and around the world kept me in touch with animal welfare campaigns on the outside. All the research that I had undertaken for NAVS on the origin of AIDS was coming to fruition.

Tuesday November 25th was eventful. Sue and Huskisson Junior visited along with Jan Creamer and Prince Galitzine from NAVS. Such visits always heightened the sense of separation and loneliness amongst prisoners. There was drama at the end of that visit when two fellow inmates scaled the high fence in a desperate escape bid. There was great commotion. One was pulled back by a prison officer—the other cleared the fence and ran off into the distance! We were all then 'banged-up' in our cells and counted. I heard on one officer's radio that police with dogs were out in Wayland Wood looking for the escapee. He was later caught.

That same day I submitted an application for a radio. Only a basic radio was allowed. It had to be MW/LW only (not FM, presumably to stop any attempt to communicate with people outside). It could only be battery operated, not mains adapted. Sue's efforts to find a suitable radio brought real rewards for me. I could listen to football commentaries—and follow the progress of Norwich City. I had converted from Arsenal to my new local team and had spent many a happy/anguished hour and a half cheering on the Canaries at Carrow Road with my father-in-law.

Tuesday December 2nd, my Mum and Dad visited with Sue and our son. Whilst it was a delight for them to meet their grandson it could and should have been in better circumstances. My Dad had risen through the ranks to become an army officer. He fought through the Second World War. He later became a bank employee and finally a coastguard. That was yet another time he visited his eldest son in prison. I blame my parents—they taught me firstly to truly care and secondly never to expect anyone else to do anything that I was not fully prepared to do myself.

On the afternoon of Sunday December 7th, I played in an 8-a-side rugby practice match. I was scrum-half and during the game cut my left knee on a sharp flint on the pitch. [Some years later when undercover amongst hare-coursers I used to see dogs lacerate their paws badly on the sharp flints littering the surface of East Anglian fields]. I had to leave the pitch, visit the prison doctor and he inserted a stitch to secure the flap of skin. Whilst I was being repaired another player came in with his little finger bent at right-angles. It was either broken or dislocated. He was given a prison escort to the Norfolk and Norwich hospital for X-ray. Another player came in with an injured back. The final victim of the game was another with a bad cut. Playing rugby is a great way of keeping fit.

One problem Sue faced at home was an infestation of mice in our aged house. We sought advice from animal welfare colleagues and found the solution in a set of humane plastic (catch and release) mouse-traps.

My visitors on December 17th were Sue, our son and close friends Alun and Joy Davies who were so effectively running my appeal fund. The animal welfare movement gave me superb support. On that day alone I received 48 cards and letters. It caused problems with fellow inmates when they saw the mail-officer laden with letters—most of which went to me. I explained that I was, in effect, a political prisoner and that most of my letters were from people I had never met. I planned to use the visit to give Sue the mobile I had made for my son in Woodwork classes for his Christmas present. Sadly, it was not in the visiting room, so the one and only first Christmas present I had lovingly constructed for my son could not be given to him.

Just before Christmas there was rumour of a prisoner transfer back to Kent. I hoped to avoid it. I played in the rugby match against Watton Town on Sunday December 21st. We had been leading 6-4 with ten minutes left but then lost two players to injury, had no substitutes, and they scored two minutes from time to win 6-8. I played on the wing and relished not just watching sport but playing it. Curiously the rugby matches in prison lacked the malevolent vindictiveness that permeated my school rugby matches. No blind-side punches at helpless victims there.

I opened the cut in my knee again. To protect it I had requested a knee bandage from the prison hospital but was told the Sports department supplied them. I asked the Sports department and they said that the hospital supplied them. I asked Sue to bring a bandage in on a visit. She did but I was banned from having it. Instead it was placed in my property in reception for me to take on the day of my release. I hoped it would have healed by then.

Friday December 19th brought memories flooding back as I attended the prison Carol service. It was a poignant time with those attending very cognisant of their separation from loved ones. The first reading was Isaiah, Chapter 11 verses 1-9—the very words from ages past, the hopes for a kinder world, that Sue and I requested be read at our wedding but, for some reason, our Reverend read the wrong verses. Here are verses 6-9:

The wolf shall dwell with the lamb,
And the leopard shall lie down with the kid,
And the calf and the lion and the fatling together,
And a little child shall lead them.
The cow and the bear shall feed;
Their young shall lie down together;
And the lion shall eat straw like the ox.
The sucking child shall play over the hole of the asp,
And the weaned child shall put his hand on the adder's den.
They shall not hurt or destroy
in all my holy mountain;
for the earth shall be full of the knowledge of the Lord
as the waters cover the sea.

Tuesday December 23rd, I received a very welcome letter of support from the Honourable Alan Clark MP, a Government Minister at the time. He was a fearless advocate for animal welfare causes and was never afraid to ruffle a few feathers.

Christmas Day was pretty much the usual routine. I got up at 7:30am, shaved and dressed. My door was unlocked at 7:55am with breakfast served a quarter of an hour later. I had cornflakes with added muesli then beans and tomatoes on toast and finally bread with Vecon. At 9:00am I went for a brief walk around the inner fence. It had rained heavily previously but by then was only drizzling. It was dark and gloomy. At 9:45am I attended the hour-long Church of England service in the prison chapel. [This was my second Christmas Day in prison—I was sure it would

66

be my last]. I then had another walk around the fence chatting with mates before returning to my spur (prison wing) at 11:30am for lunch.

I enjoyed a delightful spaghetti/pasta mixture with an assortment of nuts and tomato purée plus roast potatoes, mashed potatoes, carrots and peas followed by a huge chunk of vegan Christmas cake and a vegan mince pie. No-one could fault the prison authorities for trying. I took my meal back to my cell where I was locked up until 2pm. After lunch I watched fellow inmates playing cards. I then enjoyed another stroll around the fence followed by a lengthy soak in the bath, watched some more card games until tea was provided at 4:30pm.

Tea was a tasty salad that included asparagus tips plus a mixture of tinned mushrooms/green and red peppers followed by pear halves for pudding. We were then locked up in our cells from 4:45pm until 6:30pm. I read and wrote letters to supporters. Evening was spent in the television room watching *EastEnders* followed by *Only Fools and Horses*. At 9pm we were banged up for the night. I wrote more letters and enjoyed my special Christmas present to myself—a can of coke bought from the canteen. At 10:30pm I did my exercises, read until 11:30pm then savoured the luxury of flicking my own light out.

In time, I received a letter from my solicitor, John Mackenzie, advising me to withdraw the appeal I had launched as it would not reach the Appeal Court until long after I was discharged. I duly did so. The prison video shown on New Year's Day night was *Back to the Future*.

My first visit in the New Year was planned for January 13th but was cancelled due to snow and delayed until Monday January 19th when Sue came in with our growing infant and her Mum and Dad. Quite what they thought of seeing their son-in-law in prison goodness only knows. They must have thought their daughter had made a fine catch!! In fact, of course, they were very supportive.

Sharing prison visits amongst family, friends and colleagues could be difficult. Visits were short and hardly frequent. The first call for visits was Sue and family but I had also to meet supporters for campaigning reasons. Others wanted to visit me to show support and it was difficult at times to find diplomatic ways of explaining that that was not always possible.

Talking of the bad weather it is often said, rightly, that the families on the outside do the sentence, not the prisoner. Further proof of this was dealing with harsh weather. Whilst Sue waded through deep snowdrifts across open fields to reach our isolated, vacant, house and turn off the water stop-cock I sat reading, wearing only a shirt, my cell so atrociously hot that I had the window open.

I saw the prison optician on January 20th. I planned to see the prison dentist but there was a lengthy wait for his services and I never succeeded.

On February 1st, I was asked if I would take a transfer to the annexe at Norwich prison. That would put me in a category D prison (the lowest security rating) whereas Wayland was category C. I asked for time to think.

Whilst slightly nearer for visiting, the accommodation was in dormitories rather than single cells. That would make it a lot noisier, with the likelihood of being unable to sleep until the last person had turned their radio off. I valued the privacy of my own cell to study and write in. I also appreciated the sporting facilities at Wayland so declined the offer.

February 4th 1987 was a momentous day. Back on November 14th I had filled in my first application for parole. If granted I would be leaving prison after serving six months—on March 25th 1987. If refused I would be leaving, if I behaved myself, on September 25th. Those six months would make a big difference to Sue, our son and me.

I had just returned from work in the Tailor's shop at 4:30pm. The senior officer called me aside; he wanted to see me after tea as he had my parole result. I could not face the nerve-wracking wait until 6pm so pleaded to know. He confirmed that I had a parole date for March but he could not remember which day. I was so delighted and excited that I could hardly eat. After tea, I went straight up to the S.O.'s office and signed the form with my parole date confirmed as March 25th, seven weeks hence. I asked an officer if I could phone the news to Sue but he said they were busy. I went to the usual Woodwork evening class; when that ended at 7:30pm I returned to my house and the S.O. was kind enough to phone Sue the great news.

The clock was now ticking towards my release and new life as a dad and husband. I faced a rush to write letters to supporters around the world and complete my numerous evening class projects before my departure.

Later in the month came a reminder of the emotional perils of imprisonment. My son was taken to hospital with a minor problem of a blocked tear duct. What if it had been more serious? It was for some prisoners. There is the pressing fear that a loved one will face some life-threatening situation. Animal rights activists endure the further fear that a much-loved pet will face similar perils. Activists facing a long sentence know their pets will die without them—they will never see them again, other than in pictures.

My diary notes that my young son was delightful and adorable on his visit on Monday March 9th. Sometimes he could be a bit grouchy. He had no idea what was going on, but that day he was wonderful. The week before, I had finally finished his cuddly dolphin in our soft toy class. A concert in our visits room replaced classes on the Monday night. The evening was enlightened by chaps from Radio Norfolk endeavouring to make a recording of it.

One of many fund-raising activities organised by supporters for my appeal fund was a sponsored walk in Tonbridge on Sunday March 15th 1987. Sue took the leading role with our son. The event was supported by many activists both by their presence and financially.

That same afternoon, I played rugby against Norwich College. I had expected to be brought on as a substitute but in the event played the whole game. Our previous game against these opponents we had won easily but this was different. They led 0-3 at half-time. Early in the second half we scored following a punt forwards and a rush for the ball. I thought I might get there first to score my first try but a Wayland colleague beat me. In the closing minutes of the game we were driving towards their line. Our scrum half whipped the ball out, ran to my side of the pitch and was tackled. He managed to off-load the ball to me. I made a quick jink then was over the line to score! After all my games and practice sessions at Wayland that was my first try. My colleagues were roaring with laughter as when the referee blew his whistle I looked aghast expecting some infringement to be given. There was just time for the conversion then the match ended.

My rugby career spanned from when I was an 11-year-old public schoolboy to being a 33-year-old prisoner of the state. I had scored with what proved to be my last touch of the ball. My teammates at Wayland were muscle machines. I was far from muscular and was delighted to even share the pitch with them. To score was special for me. My diary notes how much I missed being able to celebrate with Sue that minor triumph.

Our videos that weekend were *Out of Africa* on the Saturday and *Jewel of the Nile* on the Sunday. Even though we were in single cells night noise could still be a real problem. I once pleaded with an officer to get a guy some cells away from me to turn his stereo down in the early hours of the morning. I later learned the officers found him fast asleep in his noisy cell! Many must have complained about such noise because soon notices were pinned up in all houses saying that after 10pm prisoners using radios, cassette recorders etc. must do so with headphones or an earplug.

My time inside gave me plenty of time to chat with fellow inmates. With Wayland being a category C prison they were mostly an amiable crowd; all trying to pass their sentences without hassle and get back to loved ones. There were squabbles and some fights, but they were usually caused by rows over drugs and money—problems easy to avoid.

One mate was a muscular Chelsea football fan who certainly had a propensity for, if not convictions for, violence. (Not a bad fella to have on your side in prison!) He delighted in recounting tales of bloody battles between fans of his beloved Chelsea and followers of other teams. He had the humility to admit that not all battles ended in his favour. He told of once picking a fight late one evening with a young Aussie in West London. When he had hit the Aussie with his best punches and the Aussie kept coming he put his hands up saying: "*Okay, I've had enough.*" The Aussie responded: "*Nah mate, you've had enough when I say so....*", and proceeded to knock him from pillar to post, and then some.

Near the end of my stay I was told that as few other inmates were being released on my day I should advise Sue to be waiting at the prison gate at 7:45am instead of the usual 8am. She was to tell the officer at the gate she was meeting me, otherwise I would be put on the prison minibus and taken to nearby Thetford railway station.

For my last prison visit ever, on Thursday March 19th, it was just Sue and me, as it had been on our first visit. On my last Sunday, I watched the valiant Wayland rugby team easily beat Watton Town.

On my last day, I had the usual appointment with the medical officer at 8:00am. That was possibly to check that I was fit and well—and could not make any subsequent claims of abuse. Later in the day I settled up the high finances of prison life. I signed out my last four pots made in the pottery classes. I paid 60p for two cube-shaped pots and £1.05 for four others. At the canteen, I collected my wages—£4.43 less 6p taken for the Common Room fund (so like boarding school!) I used all my wealth to buy chocolate bars to give to the lads on my corridor and to other friends.

I enjoyed my last walk around the perimeter fence; returned my library books, then in the afternoon appeared before the discharge board. I was cleared to go. With joy, I watched the sun set on my last ever day of prison life.

Early on Wednesday March 25th 1987 I walked out of the prison gates to be met by Sue and my best man—Alan Knight. Six months before I had been taken down to the cells below Maidstone court. A man shattered and exhausted by seemingly endless battles to protect animals from the establishment. I walked from Wayland a proud husband, a proud Dad, refreshed, invigorated and with an army of supporters keen to back me and help me win lawfully for animals.

Postscript

The RCS experimented upon dogs to try to make better surgeons and with primates so that we could have better teeth without having to care for them. Animals suffered considerably and intolerably. Using animals seemed to be the easy option when there are other humane alternatives. We can have human health without animal suffering.

Driving makes one of the most complex demands on the human body in terms of eye, brain, hand and feet coordination. It is possible to teach every level of intellect—including some with little intellect at all—how to drive safely without killing anyone, so it is surely possible to teach clever people to operate on humans without needing to practice on live animals.

People often say it is better to try first on an animal, rather than risk a child, and if you oppose vivisection you are the sort that faced with a child and a dog drowning would rescue the dog first. This argument has been put to me at countless debates. My response is that we should seek to avoid suffering wherever possible. Animals differ from humans in countless ways and are best left alone. Once we introduce a gradation of suffering that is justifiable then we enter dangerous realms. If it is okay to sacrifice an animal to help a human, then how long before it becomes okay to sacrifice some humans to help others? There are plenty already who say that experiments should be done on murderers, paedophiles or aborted infants. Many, if not most, if not all, would happily experiment on their neighbour's child to save their own.

We like to see ourselves as heroic and selfless but when the aeroplane catches fire on the runway and there is a scramble for the exit doors history shows that very few are of the 'after you fella' variety. Most will kick and fight their way to life. As for the drowning child and dog scenario, my answer is I would rescue the child first and then go back for the dog. I suspect that those who pose the question would not put themselves at risk to save either—particularly if there was a big sign before the river saying 'No Entry, Trespassers will be Prosecuted'.

Regarding dental health, it is simple. We are given teeth to last a lifetime and with a modicum of basic care they will. If we choose to abuse our teeth through poor diet choice, and poor hygiene standards, why should animals pay the price? It is the same as smoking and excess drinking. The animal kingdom is not an endless reservoir of innocent souls to be exploited to compensate for our ignorance and callousness.

As for the RCS research laboratory at Downe, it is now long gone. It fell into disuse at the end of the 1980s then was closed and boarded up. When driving nearby I would periodically stop to look at the place. I did so in 1997 and spoke to one of the site security guards. He invited me in for a look around. Without any prompting, he told me of dreadful cruelty inflicted on animals held there. He recounted how he and his mates found all sorts of discarded paperwork confirming dreadful experiments performed on animals. I asked to take some pictures of the derelict site and he was happy to allow me. It was he who offered me the memorable line that the only way animals left that place was 'up the incinerator chimney'.

CHAPTER FOUR
Rehabilitation, back to animal welfare work opposing dog fighting and badger digging.

On release from prison my first task was to get back into the role of husband and father. Integral to that was finding some means of earning a living. I now had two prison sentences to declare on my CV. I also had to answer to my parole officer and that lasted until September 1987.

After a short family holiday, I set about applying for jobs. For a time, I worked at a nearby garden centre—a job secured even after declaring my prison record. But it was not long before I returned to animal welfare.

At the time the Government supported business start-up with the Enterprise Allowance Scheme. This helped new businesses with regular support payments for a year. I had been on one scheme before my sentence and resumed it sometime after release. Sue and I then became partners in our small research and photographic business. We are still in business at the time of writing.

I resumed contact with investigative journalists working for the *News of the World*. In 1988 I helped them with investigations into dog fighting and badger abuse. I acted as a contact bridge between the paper and colleagues at the LACS and RSPCA.

At the time the long-banned bloodsport of dog fighting was resurgent. It was Canadian dog-breeder and author Ed Reid who in 1976 started importing and selling American Pit Bull Terriers (APBTs). He also published his book *Canine Gladiators* that detailed dog fighting. Ed Reid was always publicity shy but he admitted his role in the rise of dog fighting in an interview published in *Weekend* February 25th 1989: "*Regrettably, I concede I'm responsible for much of the spread of dog-fighting in the UK.....But the book was supposed to be just a historical study. I'd seen fights between dogs in Mexico where it's legal, and I was horrified by it. The strength of the animals impressed me and I wanted to pass on my findings through the book.*"

The APBT breed is not recognised by the Kennel Club. Ed Reid welcomed this saying: "*They ruin dogs by powdering them up and encouraging breeding only for looks. The English bulldog could take on a 2,000lb bull 100 years ago. Now, it can hardly walk! The pit bull terrier is what the Staffordshire terrier should have been today without being bred into a freak. If it comes to a tussle these pit bulls are the boys.*"

In the interview Ed claimed never to sell a dog if he thought it would be used for fighting and vehemently denied ever being involved in dog fighting in the UK. He expressed contempt for dog fighters: "*The people who do this are a lot of cowardly, gutless little degenerates who couldn't take the punishment they expect their dogs to receive in the pit.*"

In dog fighting two evenly matched dogs are put into combat in a confined area known as a pit. Because the dogs are tough and game the fights are bloody and gory. They continue until one dog declines to 'scratch' i.e. continue to fight.

In late January 1988, I joined an undercover team seeking to infiltrate and expose a dog fight taking place on Sunday January 31st in Dublin. Our undercover man was the immensely courageous Graham Hall. I was assigned to provide back up along with *News of the World* investigative reporter Maureen Lawless and photographer John Snowdon. Sadly, whilst I have the looks and vocal tones ideal for infiltrating hunting and shooting and for getting in amongst vivisectors, my appearance is useless for penetrating gangs of dog fighters and badger diggers. For the latter tasks a muscular tattooed man like Graham Hall was perfect.

That January weekend a mob of dog fighting enthusiasts from across the UK, some 75 in total, headed for the venue, crossing the Irish Sea by ferry. Graham went ahead on the Thursday January 28th. He was deep undercover amongst the dog fighters. He stayed overnight in Liverpool with a lad named Steve and caught the ferry to Dublin the next day. They were met at Dublin by Irish ex-jockey Gary Griffin, one of the top men in Irish dog fighting who put them up for two nights.

I followed on the Saturday with my two colleagues. John drove a 2-litre Alfa Romeo. We caught the 5:15pm Dublin ferry from Holyhead, Anglesey. We had another new gadget in our car—a car phone. En route to Holyhead we tried to use this to call Convoy (the *News of the World* travel agency). We planned to book our car onto the ferry and a second hire car (with Irish number plates) in Dublin. But we could not make contact.

We only just reached the ferry in time—ours was the last car on. The scheduled crossing time was 3½ hours. However, the Irish Sea in winter can be rough and our crossing was severely delayed. We did not dock until 11:15pm. The standard customs check took another 30 minutes. By the time we drove to collect the Toyota Hiace van that we had by then booked, the hire staff had, not surprisingly, gone home.

Because we were on *News of the World* business we had rooms booked in a smart hotel—Jurys, Ballsbridge. We had an indirect means of contacting Graham—through a mutual contact point in the UK. This was where the best laid plans started to go awry. We were told that Graham was in a Council house in Raheen Road near to the *Chasers* pub in Kylemore Avenue—originally dictated to us as Killmore Avenue. Well, the *Chasers* pub is near but not in Kylemore Avenue and Raheen Road is some distance away; it is Raheen Drive and Raheen Park that are nearby. [This is all easy to see in 2016 with the Internet and Google maps, but back in 1988 we had to make do with paper maps and word of mouth].

We urgently needed to hire a second vehicle if we were to establish and maintain unobserved close pursuit of Graham and his colleagues in the morning. Our car with English number plates would certainly stand out—even more so at that time. By then it was 1am and we could find no 24-hour hire car firm. We were still trying to contact local supporters of the Irish Council Against Bloodsports (ICABS) to help us when the staff from the original hire car firm that had been booked to meet us off the ferry contacted us. The girl arrived at our hotel at 2am and started completing the forms but as soon as Maureen gave her occupation as a journalist she said that the insurance for her was too high risk and she would have to decline the hiring. Same story when John said he was a photographer. I might have been okay, but my name was not on the hiring form.

We had to find exactly where Graham was staying. No-one in the hotel had an A-Z of Dublin, nor any equivalent map. When we asked at the hotel about getting to the *Chasers* pub the response was: "*Now, you wouldn't want to be wandering around there at this time.*"

The best solution we could think of was to take advantage of our car. I would call a taxi to the hotel and ask for the street address we had been given. Then John and Maureen would follow my taxi in their car, pick me up and drive me home. All fine in theory but this was now 2:30am, in Dublin in 1988—at the height of the 'troubles'.

My taxi driver double checked that I genuinely wanted to go to the street address I gave. I confirmed it and we set off. In those early hours of Sunday morning there was little traffic. Seated in the back I saw my driver checking his mirror, once, twice then ever more frequently. He started to drive faster and faster and checked his mirror constantly. When he crossed red lights at speed my worry verged on panic. He was clearly trying to lose the person he perceived to be following. What if he succeeded?

John and Maureen dropped from sight. We crossed junction after junction and ended up in a very tough-looking part of town. It was poorly illuminated and, long before the era of sat navs, my driver had problems finding the right street. He stopped by a group of young lads standing on a corner and wound his window down to speak; "*Can you tell us where Kylemore Avenue is?*" One replied, "*Who wants to know?*" My driver growled the unsettling answer: "*The Brit in the back.*" More unsettling was that the destination was just around the corner. I jumped out, paid my driver, gave him a tip and prayed that John had managed to keep track of the hectic route. Mercifully he had and plucked me to safety moments before the lads came to enquire as to my business in their area.

We continued our search for Graham's location and after some driving around found his car parked outside the number of the house he had given us, but in Raheen Park. Another vehicle, belonging to known dog fighters from Newcastle, was parked nearby. We searched for a suitable observation point from where we could watch and follow in the morning. We could not find one. With English number plates on an expensive car we stood out. If anyone became suspicious of our presence the whole operation—and, most worryingly, the safety of Graham, would be jeopardized. We decided to drop back and try again in the morning, hoping that Graham would either contact us or we could find him.

In the morning from our hotel we hired a car from Avis without problem. After confirming that Graham and colleagues had left their base we continued by scouting around suspected factory sites but without success. We returned to our hotel in case there was contact from Graham through our UK intermediary. In time Graham sent a brief message that he was safe, had attended the dog fight and secured excellent evidence.

With another severe gale forecast for the Irish Sea that night, doubts arose as to whether the 11pm ferry would sail. Would the dog fighters catch it or would they wait for the morning sailing? We left our hotel and took up position at 10:30pm in a secure observation point near the B&I offices from where we could observe the boarding of the ferry. We saw known vehicles board the ferry and followed them. The dog fighters piled out and started to exercise one of their dogs on the car deck.

We walked to the ship's bar and encountered many more dog fighters. They were sitting dotted about the lounge in small groups as if they did not know each other. Over the address system the Captain announced that due to the adverse weather the sailing would be delayed by an hour. We took plenty of pictures of each other, careful to catch some of our real targets—the fighters—in the background. Photographing individuals became easier once the ship sailed and some fell asleep.

Graham made surreptitious contact with us. To make it easy to talk safely he booked a cabin and arranged to meet there to update us. He had done brilliantly. The organisers of the dog fight ran a smooth operation. The fight was staged in a factory on an industrial estate on a Sunday morning. To have had a host of cars drive up to such a venue early on a Sunday would have aroused suspicion. Instead the crowd were directed to a nearby pub, the *Halfway House* (where Graham and his gang had enjoyed a drink on the Saturday night), and told to leave their vehicles in the park opposite the pub. From there, at 8am, the dog fighting enthusiasts were collected by a green lorry belonging to a paper company. They stood in the back as they would in the carriage of a crowded underground train—and were charged 5 Irish pounds each.

The lorry was driven for some 5 minutes to the Ballymount Industrial Estate, the shutters of a disused paper warehouse raised, the vehicle driven in, the shutters closed and everyone disembarked. Anyone watching from a distance would have seen nothing unusual. The fights then went on throughout the day with a large audience numbering around 150 on tiered seating lining the makeshift wooden-sided fighting pit. There were children amongst the crowd, some as young as five or six. Much blood was spilled. One dog, belonging to an Irishman named Joe Walsh, had his jaw ripped out. The young children were hoisted on to shoulders so as not to miss any action. There were four fights, one lasting some two hours. Bets ranged from 50 to 1000 Irish pounds cash on the outcome.

Graham Hall mingled amongst the crowd taking pictures surreptitiously whenever he could with his small camera. One guy who was seen taking a camera out was told: "*Put that fucking thing away!!*" Graham told us one owner was so angry when his dog lost that he pulled out a handgun and shot it dead in front of everyone. I had little doubt that if any fighter had realised who Graham was he could have met the same fate. Some from the Dublin mob openly boasted about killing someone and getting away with it; others apparently had recently netted IR£16,000 from an armed robbery on a Post Office. No one could doubt Graham's courage, or his ability to mix freely with some of the most unsavoury animal abusers.

Our ferry docked at Holyhead at 4am on Monday February 1st and we returned home. I was exhausted. Graham stopped off to call in at some of his many Liverpool and North Wales-based dog fighting contacts before he returned to work at dawn on the Tuesday.

Another dog fight was staged in Dublin the following Saturday night. The venue was the dance floor of a small hotel. Graham was again invited to attend but declined as he preferred to try to gain access to a British dog fight—that would be within the range of our judiciary. The problem was that on the English dog fighting scene the audiences were far smaller and only a select few trusted individuals were invited.

Richard Course, Executive Director of the LACS, had wanted to tip-off the Irish police about this scheduled dog fight on February 6th and have the fighters arrested on site. There was a fierce debate as to the wisdom of this. Would the Irish police take the tip-off seriously? We did not know the fight location, could the police find it? We would have to tell them what we knew and how we knew it, and that would imperil Graham, other investigators and dash hopes of any further similar investigations. Why had we not tipped them off about the previous fight? There was an almighty row between Richard Course and senior staff that ultimately led, later that year, to the departure of the former from the League. The Irish police were not told about the second fight.

On February 21st 1988, the *News of the World* printed a large story about this investigation along with pictures taken by Graham. This caused widespread outrage and led to an investigation by the Irish Gardai who quickly identified known IRA gunmen in the crowd. Four dog fighters from Dublin were identified and brought to trial in September 1988 in the first prosecution for dog fighting in Ireland. Graham Hall courageously gave evidence in Dublin District Court, under police protection.

Thomas Woulfe, Joseph Woulfe and Gary Griffin were each imprisoned for 3 months for assisting in a dog fight and for ill-treating dogs. Each defendant had a dog that fought that day in January. Graham described to the court the injuries the dogs suffered: "*The wounds were horrific, the dogs were torn apart. One had half his jaw torn off.*" (*Irish Times* September 27th 1988).

Detective Sergeant Gerry O'Carroll reported searching a warehouse identified by the Dublin Society for the Prevention of Cruelty to Animals and finding more than 200 empty beer cans, empty cigarette packets and discarded food. When he interviewed Thomas Woulfe the defendant showed him a silver trophy his dog had won at the fight. The officer told the court that champion dogs were retired after three bouts and were then worth up to IR£1,000 each when used for breeding.

Mike Butcher, a special investigator from the RSPCA, gave evidence. He told the court he had been investigating dog fighting for six years. Shown photographs of the injured dogs he confirmed they were consistent with dog fighting injuries. As well as jailing the three defendants, District Justice Joseph Plunkett ordered the confiscation of their dogs, fined them IR£100 and ordered each to pay IR£578 for witness expenses. A fourth man was charged—Richard Bernard—but, lacking the courage of the dogs, he fled.

Graham Hall was certainly a colourful character. A man short on words but long on action, he was the spark that could make most things happen and the sort of guy you would want on your side in any conflict. He was constantly pressured by elements within the media to secure stories ever more quickly. When I worked with him we gave him whatever time he needed. In consequence he achieved brilliant results that proved how those addicted to the most brutal bloodsports really behaved.

We spent much time chatting. Graham left school barely able to read or write yet had a streetwise intelligence and cunning hard to match. He struggled to read books but could read people well and was easily able to part a fool from his money. He had a genuine desire to thwart those who sought to abuse the helpless and not only animals. Later he exposed wealthy British paedophiles who travelled to Tunisia to use and abuse children loitering around the beaches ('chicken' as they termed the poor waifs).

The League and *News of the World* were always careful to handle Graham properly. He was paid for the project regardless of results. He was told to only ever be 'a fly on the wall' to record what happened. It could take months of patient work to befriend and expose gangs of animal abusers. Friendship and trust had to be cultivated. Every successful investigation made it harder to secure the next. Some in the media were naïve enough to expect investigators to phone strangers in the week and then watch badger digging on Saturday, cock fighting Saturday evening and dog fighting on the Sunday. The real world was nothing like that.

Just as animal cruelty investigators welcomed the wonderful campaigning opportunities created by the arrival of the video camera so did animal abusers. They are addicted to recording their abuse. They like to relive that abuse over and over again and they delight in sharing their exploits with like-minded colleagues.

Dog fighters, badger diggers and badger baiters sought to record their cruelty. They liked to be able to brag amongst their fellows about the fighting prowess of their dogs. Before video cameras reached our high streets, they had to send cine films away for processing if they sought movie-action cruelty. Even still photographs had to be processed professionally as few abusers could process their films at home. Sending films away exposed abusers to a real risk of being caught. Those who worked in the processing laboratories could easily report the films to the police or the RSPCA. Some animal abusers were caught that way.

The wonder of the video camera for abusers was that nothing had to be processed. The cruelty was recorded in colour and with sound, could be copied at home and could be savoured repeatedly. We soon heard reports of so-called sporting pubs in rural hunting areas staging special after-hours events. Videos of badger digging, badger baiting and dog fighting were shown to audiences of terrier enthusiasts.

An early example was an hour-long recording of badger baiting held near Liverpool in 1984. The tape was acquired by the *Sunday People*. It was a rarity in that it was out and out badger baiting—the badger was confined to a small pit and terriers were set on him one after another and in multiples. It is a nauseating film. The battered and bleeding badger was repeatedly given time to recover before the fight continued. He was killed off-camera. By pausing the very start of the video we saw surrounding scenery, including recognisable power pylons. If we could have found that location, there might have been further evidence leading to the culprits.

LACS Committee Member Michele Harrison and I spent hours walking wasteland 'brownfield' sites around Liverpool trying to find the exact location, but without success. We learned later that the young terrier enthusiast who recorded that cruelty fled to Ireland until the storm of publicity died down. Once six months had elapsed he was safe from prosecution and returned.

If the Dublin dogfight was videoed I never saw it. However, Graham Hall's next achievement was to acquire a copy of a dog fight video filmed by the fighters themselves. The fight was staged on January 21st 1988 in a unit at Meadow Lane Industrial Estate, Ellesmere Port, across the Mersey from Liverpool. The dog fighters themselves recorded the date of their crime on their tape—a tape easily copied.

That Ellesmere Port dog fight was an hour long involving two APBTs, one named *Sykes*, the other *Buck*. The APBT was the classic fighting dog. Imported from the USA from long lines of fighting stock they were conditioned and trained to be fearsome fighting machines—but their aggression was almost invariably only towards their own canine kind. Aficionados admired dogs that because of great muscular strength and aggression could overwhelm an opponent and win easily in the pit but they worshipped dogs that could withstand being battered from corner to corner by an opponent—and then come back to win. Such dogs were referred to as 'dead game'. Supremely loyal they would fight to the death for their master; conversely their master thought so little of them they would happily watch them do that.

In the UK, weak men were attracted to owning strong dogs as if in some way the undoubted courage of their dogs could make up for their own inadequacies. They also picked up and copied the fighting language from generations of dog fighters in the US. Magazines circulated detailing fights (rolls) and enthusing over the prowess of individual dogs and offering pups for sale from select breeding lines.

The APBT was aggressive enough anyway but the dog fighting enthusiasts wreaked havoc in the bloodlines as they sought to make their dogs even crazier in the ring. Inbreeding was carried out specifically in search of the instability that might create an awesome ring fighter. If ever a breed of canine was used and abused to fuel the cruel perversions of man, the APBT was the prime case in point. Other breeds were involved, such as Staffordshire Bull terriers.

I again took the role of link man between the LACS and the *News of the World* for that dog fighting investigation. With the help of the RSPCA we identified three men involved in the Ellesmere Port fight: Michael

78

Brown, Paul Butler and Ken Ryder. Michael Brown was the referee and Paul and Ken owned the dogs. The men had bet each other that their rival's dog would not last an hour in the pit with theirs. As part of our inquiry we had to identify where Ken Ryder lived. We knew his street address on the outskirts of Manchester, but not the house number.

Our solution was to knock on one of the doors and ask. "*'Ere mate, can you help me please, I am looking for Ken Ryder—the lad who breeds the dogs*." We were lucky and were directed to the right house. If we had been unlucky the door might have been answered by a kid who called up the stairs: "*Dad! There are some people here for you!*"

The APBT *Sykes* belonging to Paul Butler was later rescued from his makeshift home—a cut down oil drum in a back yard—by police officers accompanied by my old friend Rorke Garfield and his legendary National Animal Rescue Association (NARA). The RSPCA took care of *Sykes*, including the veterinary treatment for the deep tears to his muzzle suffered during the fight. I saw *Sykes* later and it only took a brief encounter to appreciate his latent power. Another dog, running free, came bounding up to him full of aggression, barks and snarls. *Sykes* neither barked nor growled. He just looked at his potential opponent—and the outwardly aggressive dog soon made haste away. It was *Sykes*'s way of saying: 'Forget all the show stuff—just bring it on.'

The law caught up with the animal abusers when the RSPCA prosecuted. At Northwich Magistrates in October 1988 Paul Butler pleaded guilty to causing dogs to fight. His colleagues fought on. Their trial was heard at Winsford Magistrates Court on Monday November 14th 1988. Ken Ryder denied a charge of causing the dogs to fight and Michael Brown (the referee) denied assisting at the dog fight. Both changed their pleas after excerpts from the video were played to the court—the video evidence was graphic and unanswerable. Nicholas Coleman, prosecuting, told the court: "*The violence, suffering and injuries sustained were quite appalling.*"

Jailing each for the maximum six months and banning each for ten years from keeping a dog, Stipendiary Magistrate David Rowland said the defendants had shown 'callous indifference' to the suffering of dogs. He added: "*They are incapable of realising the utter revulsion that ordinary decent people feel when they see, as we had to see, this video tape.*" (*Liverpool Echo* November 15th 1988) [Tapes such as this along with tapes of badger digging and baiting and cock fighting circulate widely and freely amongst the community of bloodsports enthusiasts.]

At the time of this trial Paul Butler was serving a three-year prison sentence for other offences. Mr Boag speaking for Butler told the court: "*He is genuinely remorseful. But he says there are different standards. You see other types of blood sports on TV which seem to be quite acceptable.*" (*The Scotsman* November 16th 1988) This was a not uncommon justification offered by dog fighters and cock fighters. Both said that in their 'sports' the two opponents were evenly matched, one on one. They contrasted their pastime with what they saw as the atrocious bullying inherent in setting packs of dogs on foxes, hares or deer that enjoyed widespread approval amongst the elite, including royalty.

Graham Hall, the *News of the World*, the LACS and the RSPCA were an effective team for exposing the darkest corners of the bloodsports world—and bringing perpetrators to justice. On May 12th 1988 I drove to Birmingham to meet Graham Hall and Maureen Lawless to discuss future investigative work. We were being inundated with tip-offs and information about the abuse of animals. Some were false—designed to lure investigators into traps; others plausible. There were reports of foxes baited by gangs of yobs and fox cubs moved for hunting. Badgers were reportedly dug out down south and transported up north for baiting. There were allegations of a gang operating stealing fighting breeds of dogs from around the UK and transporting them to Southern Ireland for dog fighting. We received so many allegations of cruelty but where should we start?

For a time, dog fighting in the UK was closed to outsiders. Graham switched his attentions to men with terriers who abused badgers. Such abuse was (and is) almost invariably born out of fox hunting. As a form of entertainment fox hunting depended on the fox being hunted above ground with followers, usually on horseback, sometimes on foot, following behind. Tiring foxes sought sanctuary below ground, usually in a natural fox earth, a rabbit warren, badger sett or perhaps an artificial earth.

Then the Huntsman called his terriermen to either evict or deal with the fox. Hunt terriers would be entered to the sanctuary. The fox might bolt and be hunted again—or might stand and fight in which case he would be dug out and killed. Hunt terriermen were proud of the fighting abilities of their dogs. But it was no real test of courage against a fox—an animal little bigger than a full-grown Tom cat. They viewed it as a better test to pit their terriers against the black and white—the badger. The ultimate test was dog against dog. Whilst it was possible, as I had previously proven, to turn up at a fox hunt and befriend their terriermen an easier and quicker route to their hearts was to follow up their advertisements offering dogs for sale in the sporting press. Such people were all too keen to demonstrate the prowess and fighting abilities of their canines. Meeting them, befriending them, talking their language and being generous with drinks were the routes to uncovering and exposing their pastimes. Graham Hall was expert at that.

At the time, we had a real problem dealing with the rise of badger abuse. It was illegal but so hard to prove. If men were spotted digging at a known badger sett and reported to the police, the culprits would plead their innocence. They claimed they were only after foxes, which was legal; and would not dream of digging for badgers. To support this fairy-tale some gangs were even smart enough to carry dead foxes with them to show to any inquisitive police officer.

Graham Hall was unleashed to infiltrate and expose the badger abusers in a joint investigation by the *News of the World*, the LACS, RSPCA and local badger groups. Graham recruited his friend Tony Reynolds to help. I was tasked with linking the various groups together and providing support. Suspects were identified by the RSPCA and then befriended by

Graham. Two separate gangs of badger diggers were targeted. It was not long before individuals invited Graham out to see their dogs 'at work'.

Sunday November 6th 1988 proved eventful for Graham Hall. He accompanied Clive Reed-Smith, Vincent Newbury and Richard Jones as they dug for a badger in a wood at Marros on the Dyfed coast near Tenby. They had set off at 6:30am and had permission from the farmer to dig on his land. Graham filmed the dig openly for the lads to watch later—they were happy for a video camera to be used as they knew the videotape would not need processing. To gather extra evidence and for his security Graham also wore a recorder with concealed microphone.

The video recorded comments from the diggers. When Graham queried the fearsome biting ability of a cornered badger one terrier enthusiast replied: "*No, I tell you what, hit em with a shovel and hold 'em with that, and they're fucked.*"

As the dig progressed the dogs suffered injuries from the fighting below ground. One digger checked a terrier for wounds and reported cheerfully: "*It's not fucking tears like, it's just holes...*" When the badger was seen, the excitement reached a crescendo: "*The pig's poking his nose out.*" The badger tried to escape. The diggers tried to get him out by pulling the dogs that held him: "*He's trying to get out there the other end....he's chewed already....go on, let him* (a terrier) *pull him out...got hold of him to the side I think...if he's got hold of him tight pull him out...he has....here he comes this side....he's got hold of the head he has.....no, he's got hold of the tail...oh, it's the tail this end....alright son get in there.*" (*Wildlife Guardian* Issue 12, Winter 1989).

The badger made a dash for freedom and escaped down another hole. It was too dark to dig him out again. Far from being dismayed the diggers were philosophical: "*The thing is you see, you let 'em go like that and they're here next time, know what I mean. At the same spot again.*" Badgers were not always so lucky. One digger boasted about a previous dig: "*We had him out, we had about eight terriers on him.*"

The gang returned to Clive Reed-Smith's house to watch Graham's videotape. Graham performed a clever trick. Tapes at the time were full-sized VHS so it was easy to take them out of the camera and put them into a player to watch. But Graham concealed a tape cassette in which he had broken the tape. After the dig, he swapped that for the real one in his camera. When he tried to play the tape from his camera for the diggers to see it failed—there was nothing. Graham cursed his camera for breaking the tape. The diggers were disappointed but forgot about the film. The next they knew about it was when the images hit the media.

The video provided crucial evidence. Beforehand badger diggers had successfully convinced courts they were only ever after foxes and, had they known it was a badger their dogs were battling, would have taken their dogs out. The video proved that when the badger was clearly recognisable, far from packing up and leaving, the diggers were spurred on.

We liaised closely with the RSPCA over these investigations. On Saturday January 21st 1989 I met RSPCA Inspector Roy Gee to brief him about our work. He had been tracking these diggers for years and offered us his assistance. The LACS took out a private prosecution against this gang. The case was heard at Whitland Magistrates Court near Haverfordwest on Friday June 16th 1989. Clive Reed-Smith, Vincent Newbury and Richard Jones all pleaded guilty to digging for a badger in contravention of the Badgers Act 1973. Surprisingly their solicitor told the court that his clients would never again participate in any field sport, legal or otherwise. The Chairman of the Magistrates declared their wish to: "*protect both badgers and people in their locality.*" Each terrierman was fined £400 and ordered to pay £100 towards costs.

Graham moved swiftly and freely amongst gangs of badger diggers. He gained expertise with some that he deployed against others. On November 27th 1988 Graham and Tony accompanied three diggers—Alan Mallet, Philip Williams and a young man identified only as 'Rob'—to a dig at Four Oaks near Newent, Gloucestershire. Williams knew the site well from his many years of doing the terrierwork for the local Ledbury Foxhounds. Graham met Mallet at the entrance to his farm at 5:30am that Sunday morning and Mallet then drove Graham to pick up his colleagues.

At the selected farm (Philip knew the farmer) they checked one badger sett but found no signs of badger. They checked other setts and earths nearby before returning to their first choice and finding their quarry. Graham was again armed with a video camera and concealed recording equipment. [My role was to later transcribe the recordings] In time the badger became visible. When Graham asked to video the badger a digger responded: "*There he is look, the cunt.*"

Philip Williams commented: "*I'm sure this is the cunt we left here last time Alan.*" As it appeared the badger would bolt the diggers prepared to set their dogs on him. Graham cleverly intervened to save the badger. He requested the badger be caught alive so that he could take it home to bait with his dogs. This idea appealed to the diggers.

They netted one exit from the sett. The badger bolted, was caught in the net and clubbed unconscious by Philip Williams swinging his spade. The comatose badger was put in a bag. The Welsh diggers returned home. When Graham and Tony returned to retrieve the badger and release him they found he had swiftly chewed his way out and escaped.

Graham phoned Alan Mallet at home the following evening and recorded his call. Graham pretended he had taken the badger home and set his dogs on him but in the baiting one of his dogs was badly bitten and needed veterinary care. Could Alan Mallet advise? Mallet boasted of his good relationship with a local vet who could help if Mallet paved the way: "*If he knows it's me he'd be alright like; he knows I go after badgers.*" The mercenary motives of this vet were clear: "*It will fucking cost you....it will cost you like 'cos he'll keep his mouth shut like.*" Clearly this vet was experienced and expert at repairing the canine casualties of 'country sports': "*I've taken him dogs down there that have been on the deer......with all their guts ripped open...clamped them together right....you can't even find a scar on either side.*"

These diggers had a lurcher and when Graham queried the ability of such a lightweight dog to deal with a badger Mallet was adamant: "*And the old dog can see him like, she fucking yanks him out then like...she'll fucking rip his fucking head off like.*" Allowing the badger to bolt presented no problem: "*Let them come out of the hole on their own and then let her go...an' I'll tell yer something, that fucking badger won't go nowhere...she'll fucking grab him by the throat right....she'll kill the bastard right....she's fucking mental.*"

The following week Alan Mallet and Philip Williams went badger hunting again. They searched four setts but only at the last, near Mynach, Dyfed, did they find one. However, the light was fading and they were unable to evict the badger.

As before the LACS prosecuted. Graham Hall again courageously gave evidence. In the tiny courtroom, he had to sit very close to the diggers and their friends. The case resulting from the Mynach incident was heard at St. Clears Court House near Carmarthen on Thursday June 8th 1989. Magistrates convicted both Mallet and Williams of attempting to dig for a badger and fined each £500 with £500 costs.

The case of the dig near Newent was heard by Gloucestershire Magistrates on Monday June 19th 1989. Mallet and Williams pleaded not guilty—claiming they were only after foxes. Philip Williams boasted of his active involvement with the Ledbury Foxhounds and that he followed four other fox hunts.

I gave evidence in the afternoon about transcribing conversations from the videotape and in recorded phone conversations. [Such recorded phone calls were not of the much maligned 'phone hacking' variety where C records what A is saying to B. This was A—Graham, recording his own call to the diggers—B.] The Magistrates found Alan Mallet and Philip Williams guilty of digging for, taking and cruelly ill-treating a badger in contravention of the Badgers Act 1973. Each was fined £750 and ordered to pay £650 costs.

With all these court cases and the attendant publicity, the badger diggers largely went to ground. Animal abusers generally became very suspicious of strangers—particularly strangers armed with video cameras. Graham Hall, the *News of the World*, and the LACS carried on probing though. Close attention was paid to advertisements in the hunting magazines offering dogs for sale. They often boasted about the abilities of these terriers. This led in time to the infamous Builth Wells badger abuse case that took place on April 1st 1990.

Graham Hall saw the following advertisement in the *Shooting News*: "*Black Lakeland Terrier, will face any quarry. No time wasters, £100.*" The use of the phrase 'any quarry' suggested the dog had been used in illegal attacks on badgers. Graham phoned the Manchester number of the advertiser—David Shaw—and arranged to meet him near Manchester Airport on Monday March 26th 1990 to discuss buying the dog named *Jock*. Another terrierman—Trevor Limb—joined them. David Shaw offered to prove how good *Jock* was by inviting Graham to join them on a badger hunting expedition in Builth Wells with three local terriermen, Mark White, Darren Leach (a slaughterman) and Shaun Williams.

So it was that Graham met up with five terriermen on Sunday April 1st 1990 to dig badgers from a sett near Builth Wells. One of the Welsh three was armed with a shotgun. Graham asked to film the proceedings and was allowed—but was told not to film the men's faces.

The resultant video was truly horrific. Three badgers were dug out and killed one after another. The *News of the World* published the gruesome details in this report by Maureen Lawless on April 15th 1990:

"Shaw watched with glee as two lurchers and three Jack Russells unearthed the first badger. He reached into the hole, tossed it to the pack and let them tear at its body and legs.

White put in his boot before the men dragged the dogs off. Then as the injured badger tried to crawl away, Leach cold-bloodedly blasted it twice with his 12-bore shotgun. Incredibly, it still took minutes to die after the dogs were released again.

Leach brought the second badger down with a single shot, laughing with his mates as the dogs finished the job.

But he killed the last badger himself—putting his foot on its neck and slowly pushing in his knife eleven times before cutting its throat."

Jim Barrington, the Executive Director of the LACS said: *"It's the most damning piece of evidence we've ever had. We hope it will shock MPs into demanding a change in the law."*

Once again Graham tried to save one of the badgers by asking if he could take it home alive to bait at his place but the other lads refused saying they could always get him another live badger another time.

At the end of the dig the dead badgers were lined up on the grass. The excitement of the kills made them careless. Forgetting the need to hide his face David Shaw happily posed in triumph with badgers and terriers for Graham's camera. Limb and Shaw took two of the dead badgers back to Manchester. They paid a taxidermist £70 to mount one of the heads. Both the bodies were wrapped in foil, cooked and eaten.

Jock, who was badly bitten and lost several teeth fighting with the badgers was later purchased by Graham. He was swiftly provided with veterinary treatment and homed with a caring family. Here is the vet's report about *Jock*: *"This dog was presented with extensive injuries to the face which were ulcerated and infected. The nose was extensively torn and severed from the maxilla, creating a fistula from the nasal chamber to the mouth. This requires extensive and repeated surgery in order to repair it. The incisor teeth were missing and the canines damaged sufficiently to require removal. In my opinion gross unnecessary suffering was caused by these injuries."* Jock clearly paid a heavy price for 'facing any quarry'.

There were three digs for badgers that day. At the second dig, there was Graham, Trevor Limb, David Shaw and Mark White. Once again the badger was dug out and baited but he escaped by running away down a hill. At the third dig with the same team present they could find no badger.

Once again the LACS prosecuted. At the time, no-one could be jailed for cruelty to a badger. So the LACS, as well as charging them with cruelty to badgers under the Badgers Act 1973, also charged them under the Protection of Animals Act 1911 with cruelty to *Jock*. There were several court appearances with the video being shown to magistrates, the key one being at Llandrindod Wells Magistrates on Friday August 24th 1990. Tom Hart prosecuted for the LACS. All five men pleaded guilty to charges of digging, ill-treating and killing badgers and causing unnecessary suffering to a dog. Their case was adjourned for sentencing.

The final act was played out in court at Brecon, Powys, on Monday September 24th 1990. Almost four years before, I had been sent down—now it was the turn of animal abusers. Brecon Magistrates jailed each of the five terriermen for three months. In addition, White, Shaw and Limb were each fined £1000, Leach and Williams were fined £800. Each was also ordered to pay £300 costs and banned from keeping a dog for five years.

The LACS then took the video to Parliament and, supported by the *News of the World*, pleaded with politicians to make offences under badger protection laws imprisonable. Other groups became involved and campaigners up and down the country lobbied their MPs. People power worked. Parliament listened. Under the Protection of Badgers Act 1992 offenders could be jailed for up to six months.

Across the country compassionate people banded together to protect badgers. Badger Groups were set up comprising dedicated and knowledgeable people who gave freely of their time to protect badger setts. The groups were coordinated by the National Federation of Badger Groups which in 2005 became the Badger Trust.

There were intimate links between the bloodsports. Fox hunters who sought more of a test for their terriers took to badger digging and baiting. Badger baiters who wanted even more of a test took to dog fighting. An example was 'country sportsman', James Ellison. In August 1983 James Ellison, Peter Doey and Andrew Cuthbertson were convicted of digging for a badger by Appleby Magistrates. All three pleaded not guilty, claimed they were searching for fox cubs and boasted they had hunted with the North Lancashire and Cumbrian Fell packs. (*Lancashire Evening Post* August 25th 1983)

Nearly six years later James Ellison appeared before Chorley Magistrates, pleaded guilty to one offence of being connected with dog fighting and two offences of causing unnecessary suffering to a dog, and was jailed for three months. Police had raided his home the previous year. They found five APBTs chained individually in his back garden. One, *Mindy*, was found with recent scarring around the head and forelegs. In a letter Ellison said the dog had won a fight in one hour 32 minutes and proved himself 'very game'. Mr James O'Riordan, defending, said Ellison had been around dogs all his life, breeding lurchers, then working terriers and lastly pit bull terriers as pets (*Lancashire Evening Post* March 15th 1989).

CHAPTER FIVE
Undercover work to expose hunting wildlife with hounds and hare coursing.

In the autumn of 1988 I tried my luck at watching hunting again. On Wednesday October 19th, I went to the meet of the Waveney Harriers at the *Duke William*, Metfield in Suffolk. The hunt spent a lot of time drawing around the old World War II US Eighth Airforce airfield. Hunt saboteurs from the Norwich group attended. They were watched by one Police Sergeant.

The hunt saboteurs intervened successfully to save the first hare hunted. When saboteurs called hounds away from the hare the Huntsman stopped his pack and took them away. Sadly, a hare was killed in the early afternoon when she was chopped down in a field of crops on the old airfield site. There were lots of hares about. I just monitored from a distance. ('Chop' is a hunting term that refers to quarry killed without having the opportunity to run far. The quarry may be caught by surprise or make an early mistake. Hunters regret it because it denies them the hunt they yearn for.)

January 1st 1989 was significant. Sue and I started as partners in our Research and Photography business. I began touting for freelance work as a researcher, investigator and photographer with the big animal welfare groups—Animal Aid, the BUAV, the LACS and the NAVS.

There had been yet another debilitating power struggle at the LACS. After a clash over personalities rather than policies my good friend Richard Course was ousted and replaced as Executive Director by my equally good friend, Jim Barrington. The mistake Richard Course made, as I told him years later, was that he worked all hours of the day, took little holiday and exhaustion eventually impaired his judgement.

I met the LACS Executive Committee and they were happy to put work my way—on the strict understanding that I only operated within the law. Their rule was superfluous; with a wife and young child to care for and two prison sentences behind me I was not going to put a foot wrong again.

Working with the LACS I set about easing back into undercover work to expose hunting with hounds and hare coursing. During the remainder of the 1988/89 season my first task was to check whether I could still work undercover. My long-term goal was to find evidence judged missing from my first undercover work in 1981-83. I sought to show the flouting of the 'rules' of hunting was not confined only to West Country hunts. I aimed to expose as flawed the main arguments used to justify the obvious cruelty inherent in hunting and hare coursing.

This mission was aided by the new technology—the video camera. I set about gathering information about how hunting and coursing works in different parts of our country. For *Outfoxed Take Two* I worked mainly in the West Country. For this second project that part of the UK was out of bounds for me—but the rest was fair game.

There was a problem. Hunters and hare coursers travelled great distances to pursue their pastimes. I could always be recognised and would have to be on my guard. It was not that I was very recognisable—I have bland features—it was the combination of being inquisitive, carrying cameras and at the forefront, with the hounds, that would draw attention.

My first work on Monday January 2nd 1989 was to interview residents in Vicarage Lane, Mettingham, near Bungay, Suffolk. Following the Boxing Day meet of the Waveney Harriers at the *Angel Inn* in Lower Olland Street, Bungay, hounds had rioted. In theory, such harriers at the time hunted hares and the occasional fox. In practice, their hounds often ran amok and hunted just about any creature. Two pet rabbits were killed by dogs in Vicarage Lane that day. I interviewed their owners who were both distraught and angry. It was no surprise their children were heartbroken over the slaughter of their pets.

I sent a full report to the LACS and asked the LACS solicitor—Tom Hart—to send 'warning-off' letters to the Waveney Harriers asking them to keep their hounds out of private property in Vicarage Lane.

I love the hares and other wildlife that surround our rural home in Suffolk. To help them I knew I would rapidly have to get back into the deep undercover role. By 1989 I was blessed with a wealth of knowledge about how hunting works. I could use that knowledge, or hide it, to suit the situation. I opted to try my luck locally first.

In my first phase of undercover work, 1981-83, I had little opportunity to see hare coursing. For this second attempt, I was based in East Anglia where hare coursing was popular. At the time, with bloodsports under increasing pressure, the hare coursing fraternity dreamed up a solution. They saw the greyhound racing fraternity as a lucrative source of new supporters. To attract them they offered a valuable prize. This was a nomination place for a dog in the annual Waterloo Cup for ex-racing dogs that were entered into a specific hare coursing event. There was a lot of clamour in the 'sporting press' about this offer.

Behind the scenes greyhound racing and hare coursing were intimately linked. The Greyhound Stud Book was run out of the same offices in Newmarket as the National Coursing Club. I decided to go to a greyhound racing event at my nearby Great Yarmouth track to see what the punters made of these connections.

In the evening of Wednesday January 4th, I went racing. I had hoped to find owners/trainers/supporters of track racing prepared to condemn, on the record, the link between the Greyhound Stud Book and the Coursing Club. Revealingly those I spoke to were involved in, or supported, both. Perhaps it would have been different at a London Stadium.

Interestingly, I spoke to one owner who had two dogs die after a coursing meeting. This apparently was caused by the tendency for the dogs to overexert themselves by continuing pursuit of the hare after the latter left the coursing field. One dog died from a stroke the night of the meeting, the other from a stroke the next day. He also explained that the dogs suffer cuts etc. to their feet due to coursing frequently being arranged over fields littered with sharp flints.

For the Saturday, I looked at a nearby Harrier pack. I chose the Cambridgeshire Harriers meeting at Fulbourn—an area I knew well from teenage years in nearby Abbotsley. This meet was not advertised but I obtained it by telephoning the Hunt Kennels:

"Who are you?"

"My name is Michael Robinson"

"Oh well that is alright then, we have to be careful because the antis try to find out our meets. We are meeting at Fulbourn at 11".

At the time, there had been a spate of thefts of small horseboxes— the type easily hitched to a Land Rover or other 4x4 vehicle and driven off. This was partly fuelled by the unwillingness of the hunting fraternity to obey simple road traffic laws. The tow vehicle and trailer towed should wear the same number plates. There are specific exclusions for farm use but just as laws regarding the farm use of 'red' diesel was often ignored by hunters so was legislation about number plates.

This was later disputed with the claim being made that as long as the trailer could be traced back to the owner via the registration plate, even if the towing vehicle displayed a different registration, that was legal. The LACS asked the Metropolitan Police for clarification and received this reply: *"The law relating to registration marks displayed on vehicles and trailers is contained in the Vehicles (Excise) Act 1971 and the Road Vehicles (Registration and Licensing) Regulations 1971. Under this legislation where one or more trailers are attached to a mechanically propelled vehicle, the owner of the vehicle must ensure that there is displayed on the trailer or rear most trailer the registration mark of the mechanically propelled vehicle."*

To expose this, we looked for and photographed towing combinations where number plates differed. I photographed several at this meet. [I had seen this before and in other situations. On one occasion near London I drove up behind a vehicle towing a horsebox. Nothing caught my eye until I pulled out to overtake and a large grey proboscis came out of the open part and wrapped around the side. Astonished, I dropped back and it was indeed an elephant being transported. As I looked closer I noticed different number plates on the tow and the towed. I pulled off the motorway and found a traffic police officer. I jumped out and reported that I had just seen a stolen elephant proceeding west along the M4. The officer looked at me as if I needed breathalysing. I have no idea of the outcome.]

One curiosity I noted at the Harriers was their hounds were of different sizes. When they found a hare they appeared to run in all directions. When I queried this lack of control with a female car follower, saying that it must put the hounds at risk, she assured me *"These are a world-renowned pack of hounds"*. The hunt packed up at 1:45pm.

My first return to fox hunting was when Sue and I attended the meet of the West Norfolk Foxhounds at Morton Hall near Norwich on Monday January 16th. The meet was not advertised but gained from an HSA colleague. We walked the line of parked hunt vehicles looking for illegal number plate combinations. Then it was just a matter of chatting with some of the hunt supporters, to gain some rudimentary cover, before we left for Norwich. It was a low-key re-introduction to the world of fox hunting. We went to Norwich library and I consulted the Road Traffic Act legislation about number plates.

I also contemplated and made enquiries about concealing a camera in a pair of binoculars. [Unbeknown to me at the time, back in 1967 Raymond Rowley, Chairman of the LACS, had attended and photographed the Waterloo Cup using a camera disguised as a pair of binoculars (see *Outfoxed Take Two* page 10).]

The following day, January 17th, I was back undercover amongst the world of hare coursing. Along with colleagues from Cambridge and Newmarket, Dave Fox and Sarah, I went to the meet of the South of England and Newmarket Coursing Club at La Hogue Farm, Chippenham at 9am. The meeting was advertised. We each paid £5 for an entry card that gave details of all the coursing.

The first event was The Victor Chandler Track Dog Stakes. This was for track dogs that had never been coursing. Sir Mark Prescott put up his Waterloo Cup nomination as prize, these apparently are "like gold dust," to the winner. Because the whole meeting was designed to attract newcomers to coursing from the track racing world we were easily able to blend in with the crowd—all the more so as I could talk knowledgeably about the Greyhound Racing I saw earlier that month at Great Yarmouth.

The winner was a dog named *Wappenbury Whisp*. I took several slides of another dog, *Screwball*, entered for the event. There were no kills until 10:50am when a hare coursed by a dog on either side made an error and was caught. I was back by the loudspeaker car trying to photograph Sir Mark Prescott so missed this. I could only watch as a picker-up wrestled the hare from the dogs, knelt on the ground beside her, and chopped her neck four times.

The very next course, at 10:55am another hare was caught. The two dogs fought over her and she could be heard squealing. She then fell out of the dog's jaws on to the ground and ran off. The dogs pursued but the hare escaped.

At about this time, during one course, a greyhound was over-run by the judge's horse, but was unhurt. It is unclear whether this was due to inexperience on the part of the dog (a Tracker unused to coursing) or over exuberance by the judge.

Coursing then moved to another nearby field where the judge was denied the use of his horse. According to the Judge, Walter Dick, the landowner, "*Doesn't allow horses on his land*". Walter Dick was a top Irish Judge renowned in Irish Coursing circles as the man who one year in the Irish Cup gave the verdict against the lead dog—the first dog to turn the hare. Such a dog nearly always won the course and was so expected to do so that the bookies had even started paying out!!

I stood with the coursing crowd on one side of the field and soon found hares being coursed around my ankles. I took several slides.

The coursers moved to a third field, ran some more courses before stopping for a late lunch at about 2:30pm. I returned to Newmarket with my colleagues to discuss the day's events. We saw no kills other than that at 10:50am, but other hares may have been caught off the field (where a substantial amount of coursing occurred).

Sir Mark Prescott had certainly succeeded in creating a popular event. I estimated 140 cars of supporters in attendance (we took the registration numbers of nearly 100), and the crowd was about 300. This gathering caused a significant blockage on the minor roads when moving from field to field. The Police had been present in force at the start (4 cars) but left when they found no evidence of any anti-coursing protestors.

Sir Mark Prescott was an interesting character. Expelled from Harrow for disruptive behaviour he was just 21 when he took over some historic racing stables in Newmarket and soon became one of the most talented race horse trainers. He was an aficionado of exotic game fowl and was a boxing referee. He produced memorable quotes. Of his successful racing set up he said: "*I have looked at many women in my life, but only one jockey.*"

For a man with an obsessional interest in the bloodlines of horses and coursing dogs he showed a surprising lack of interest in creating his own saying: "*You cannot choose your children, and if I had a son he may well be anti-bloodsports and a ballet dancer. But you can choose your assistant trainers........I want to hand over Heath House to the person who is worthy of it, not because the person is merely related.*" (*Horse and Hound* November 3rd 1994).

Later that January I visited badger digging sites on the England/Wales border and in Wales. Whilst in the area I took the opportunity to visit another fox hunt, the Monmouthshire Foxhounds, meeting at The Pant Farm, near Forest Coal Pit, north of Abergavenny. The meet was not advertised and was difficult to ascertain. I phoned the hunt but no-one would disclose the meet; I met a wall of: "*We've had some problems with antis.*" I used the pseudonym 'Martin Hodgkinson'—a strange choice actually. Usually I preferred using my own Christian name as it is hard to react naturally to being called by a different first name; secondly the surname sounds perilously close to my own.

Eventually on the Saturday morning, after a lot of work to convince her I was genuine, the Hunt Secretary, a Mrs Higgs, revealed the meet. I went and mingled with supporters but as a complete outsider—and at a hunt that seldom sees 'tourist hunters'—it was hard to make progress. I just took the usual stock images and picked up a few names to help future undercover work at other hunts.

I again photographed vehicles towing horseboxes wearing different number plates. As for hunting they soon marked a fox to ground but seemed to do nothing about it. I began to feel distinctly unwelcome so left as I had a meeting arranged with Roy Gee to discuss our badger digging investigations.

I then switched the focus of my undercover work to the Irish equivalent of the Waterloo Cup (the premier hare coursing event in England.) Hare coursing was different in Ireland. Park hare coursing was popular. In that, instead of hares being driven over open fields to the coursing arenas, the arena was fixed and purpose-built. Hares were netted elsewhere and brought to a pen beside the coursing field. From there, hares were driven one at a time down a channel and onto the field. The Slipper gave each hare the approved start before releasing his two dogs.

The hare then ran in a straight line for the escape zone at the far end of the field. If she reached it she escaped and the dogs were balked. It was fine in theory but often the hare made a mistake, turned away from the escape zone and was caught before she could reach it again. Another difference was the quarry was the Irish hare (*Lepus timidus hibernicus*) rather than the Brown hare (*Lepus europaeus*).

For that project I contacted a colleague—Dave Weeks—and we arranged to journey together. On Saturday January 28th 1989 I collected a hire car for the long trip. The following Monday morning I collected Dave Weeks from his home and we drove to Fishguard. We booked our car onto the ferry at 2:15pm and sailed at 3pm. After an uneventful crossing, we arrived at Rosslare, Ireland at 6:30pm. It was my first visit to rural Ireland. It was quiet, peaceful and beautiful—like stepping back into the English countryside of the 1950s.

I found a phone box and called first our Irish contact and then Rosemarie McCarthy from the ICABS to confirm details. We then drove west and booked rooms in Dooley's Hotel, Waterford.

We were up early on Tuesday January 31st and left at 8am to drive to the north-west to Clonmel in County Tipperary. We arrived in the town at 9:20am but the coursing venue— Powerstown Park horse racing track— was difficult to find. I stopped and asked a couple of young lads. They were going there as well, so we gave them a lift and they directed us.

With the hare coursing not due to start until 11am (a laid-back affair, Irish coursing—most English coursing started at 9am) there was hardly anyone at the venue. Such times can be risky for undercover operators; when there are few people about, and a long time to wait, inquisitive opponents can ask awkward questions.

We drove back to Clonmel and walked the town trying to purchase hare coursing memorabilia to enhance our cover as coursing supporters. Surprisingly we found little evidence in the shops that this is the 'Coursing Mecca' of Ireland. We returned to Powerstown Park an hour before the scheduled start. I parked at the venue, tucked my small Olympus 35mm camera in my pocket and we went in, paying IR£5 each.

We saw a collection of sturdy wooden tea-chests. Some piled high, others lined the coursing field. We soon learned that those boxes were highly valued by coursing enthusiasts as bases to stand on for a better view, (claimants even chalked their names on these prized possessions!)

Compared to the primitive facilities at English coursing (even the Waterloo Cup had tents and portaloos) the facilities here befitted a renowned horse racing track. There was a members' grandstand that cost IR£1 extra for entry and another larger grandstand with a high viewing gallery. The bookies' stands were clustered in front of this second grandstand. We counted 24 bookies' pitches that first day.

The first dogs were called to the slips at 10:45am. We joined the crowds packed tightly at the front viewing rails lining the course. The Slipper, wearing a red coat, was in a green shed to the right of the course, in the far corner away from us. Behind him was a small copse holding the captive hares; a fenced channel connected the two. To our left was the escape zone, of hessian sacking on a wooden framework, raised slightly from the ground. On either side of this was an impenetrable barrier of chicken-mesh fencing, with conifer branches interwoven in it. A gate was concealed in this, to the left of the escape zone. Through that the dogs were taken after each course for dope-testing (there was much money at stake, both in terms of prizes and subsequent breeding from winning dogs).

The edge of the coursing field on the other side was lined with chicken-mesh. A small green hut was sited almost directly opposite us. Several men took up station within it. Hare despatchers and the man who waved the red or white flag indicating the winner of the course. To their left, our right across the field from us, and to the right of the slipper, was a single flanker. His job was to scare back any wayward running hare to ensure she took the correct line towards the escape zone.

Just on the coursing field, the other side of our railings and to our extreme left, level with the hessian escape zone, was a small inverted V screen. The owners/trainers of the dogs in the course waited there and dashed onto the field to catch their charges when either the hare was killed or she escaped under the screen.

Coursing started at 11am. The first hare coursed was killed. By then the event was packed. Supporters packed around us, either side and behind me. Consequently I felt it could be distinctly unhealthy to point my camera at the kill. The next course the hare escaped but on the third there was another kill. It was noticeable that though both hares were clearly alive and struggling in the greyhound's jaws, and needed to be despatched, neither squealed in the pitiful plaintive manner so commonly heard at English coursing.

After watching a few more courses I decided it was time to try to record something so took my camera out. We had noticed one or two people with cameras but no-one around us had one and it was stated in the programme "No unauthorised photography permitted". When I showed my camera I expected trouble. I heard people around me muttering about my using a camera and they watched me intently whenever there was a kill. My small camera would have shown little of any kill so I let discretion be the better part of valour and opted to record other parts of the meeting.

It is fair to point out that the large crowd (we estimated about 3,500) was very vocal and at the crucial times they cheered the hare. They cheered if she escaped and on neither day when we attended did we hear them cheer the kill. This was in stark contrast with the unsavoury mob that supported English hare coursing. At every English coursing meeting I attended I heard the kill cheered, admittedly sometimes only by one or two of the more drunken elements. At the Waterloo Cup, I heard substantial numbers, notably on the bank side, cheer with delight each and every kill.

We saw eight hares killed. When I asked people around me how many hares had been killed the previous day their estimates varied between 11 and 20. The *Dublin Star* reported the number killed that Monday as 12.

There was coursing from 11am until 1pm when there was a break for lunch. Coursing resumed at 2pm. As we sat in our car during the lunch break we saw across from us, beside his car and reading a paper, none other than Sir Mark Prescott. After lunch we had tea in the restaurant and found the coursing being shown there on television complete with commentary.

During the lunch interval, I sought permission to take photographs. I was told that I needed to speak to either a member of the Committee or to the Secretary, Jerry Desmond. I found a member of the Committee but his response was: "*We have been caught far too many times by people claiming to take innocent photographs, you must ask Mr Desmond.*" The latter took some convincing. My referring to other coursing I had attended, specifically the day at Newmarket when track dogs were welcomed, helped and he relented. He added that I was not to photograph the kill. I felt more at ease taking pictures in the afternoon from a position near the escape screen. [Jerry Desmond died in 2010]

We left at 3pm to meet Rosemarie McCarthy in Cork and returned to our Waterford hotel about mid-night.

The following morning, Wednesday February 1st, we returned to Clonmel. The coursers had been expecting a demonstration from ICABS supporters and with none the Monday or Tuesday that had to be the day. Mindful of the way the Waterloo Cup organisers have chosen to run off courses early, and even advanced their whole meeting by a day to thwart demonstrations, I thought we should not pay too much heed to the advertised start time of 11:30am. We arrived at 10am to cover the possibility of a last-minute change. Our caution proved unnecessary as the coursing started as scheduled.

We first seized a good spot close to the railings. However, with a crush of supporters around us, it was difficult to take pictures. I was equipped with my Nikon F3 with 80-200 zoom lens. When I had earlier asked Desmond for permission I had only shown him my small Olympus compact camera. It was in fact quite professional but looked amateur. Armed with permission to photograph I deployed my obviously professional equipment. There were just 3 kills that final day; none within effective range of my camera.

The expected demonstration took place outside the main gates in the morning. Many ICABS members and supporters paraded up and down the road in an orderly manner waving banners and placards. I leaned over the wall and took some pictures, and was duly abused by the compassionate side: *"Why don't you go and photograph the bloody coursing?"*

Coursing started at 11:30am and ran until 12:30pm, when there was a half hour break. It then ran until 1:45pm, when there was an hour break for lunch (in such a knock-out competition the winning dogs from each round needed time to recover).

At the break for lunch, in response to the loudspeaker announcement that copies of the video recording would be on public sale, we went to the video transmission lorry and ordered a copy for IR£50. We knew the 'tugs-of-war' in which greyhounds tussled over a live hare would be censored out but it was hard to see how they could cut out scenes of the hare being hit by the dogs, particularly when coursing continued after the hare was initially hit. This proved to be the case.

The five finals started at 2:45pm and continued until 3:15pm. Just before the finals the loudspeaker announcer asked the audience to remember all the coursing fans that had passed away in the previous year and called us to stand for a minute's silence. No sooner were we seated than we were asked to stand again for the Irish National Anthem.

As for the results *Metro Magic* won the Kitty Butler Stakes; *Boston Cha* the T. A. Morris Stakes; *Needham Wonder* the Jack Mullan Champion Stakes; *Redundant Pal* the Patsy Byrne Oaks; and *Donovans Ranger* the main event—the Seamus Mulvaney Derby.

At the end, I had expected Sir Mark Prescott to stay for the presentation of prizes, perhaps to say something in support of coursing from the platform and that would be an opportunity to photograph him. However as soon as the last final was completed he ran past us, an expensive looking cigar hanging from his mouth, clearly determined to reach his car and get out of the park before the rush.

A lorry was drawn into position in the crowd in front of the Grandstands. Jerry Desmond stood on the platform, with the Mayor of Clonmel, the Chairman of the Clonmel Chamber of Commerce, the President of the ICC, and the Chairman of the Executive Committee of the ICC. Everyone was duly thanked. I photographed these ceremonies.

As well as Sir Mark Prescott, we had seen Jonjo O'Neill at the coursing and four members of the Clergy. We left after the last presentation and stayed the night in a hotel in Wexford, near to the ferry. We caught the 9am ferry home on the morning of Thursday February 2nd. On our drive home through Wales we paused to photograph the joint meet of the Pembrokeshire Foxhounds and Gelligaer Foxhounds at *The Duke of Edinburgh* Newgale, near Haverfordwest.

The following Monday, February 6th 1989, I was back coursing in East Anglia with the Swaffham Coursing Club meeting at 8:45am at Bodney Water Tower. Bodney is a tiny Norfolk village north of Thetford (not far from where I spent time at Wayland Prison). The first dogs were due in slips at 9am. With my previous recent history of going greyhound racing at Great Yarmouth, coursing at Newmarket and coursing at Clonmel my cover as a genuine greyhound enthusiast was excellent. I paid £5 for my entry card.

An organiser—a man identified to me as Michael Darnell—stressed the need for everyone to take care when driving the hares onto the coursing field saying: "*We need every hare we can get today.*" That could have been because there was a shortage of hares in the area or because they had a lot of courses to fulfil, or a mixture of both.

The huge army Stanford Training Area was nearby and at various times of the day there were soldiers in full combat gear on exercises all around the field. It was startling seeing lads creeping through the woods in camouflage carrying their weaponry.

The morning hare coursing all took place on the same ploughed field. The beaters close to the Slipper appeared badly organised and hares were driven backwards and forwards before even entering the coursing field. Inevitably some were tired before they had to run for their lives.

There was a large hummock at the bottom of the shy on the Slipper's right side. I moved around and found a position on the blind side of it. From there I took several pictures. There were many kills. At first I used my 80-200mm zoom lens but that did not give enough magnification so I returned to my car for a 500mm mirror lens. That needed lots of light to be hand-held but fortunately it was a bright day. The dogs were slipped from 3 of the 4 sides of this square field. Then we stopped for lunch.

We drove to a new field nearby for afternoon coursing. I took up an excellent position, at the end of the flanking line, with the sun behind and no-one near me. If hares were caught it was likely to happen close by.

All my gut instincts were to run on the field and stop the coursing—as I had tried to do as a young sab years before—but here I knew that my best chance of helping all hares was to record how these were treated this day. Using a powerful combination of 500mm lens and the new 1000 ASA Ektar film I secured some useful images. It was a long day, one of great fun for coursers but great suffering for hares. The coursing eventually ended at 4:30pm.

Two days later, on February 8th, I attended the meet of the Swaffham Coursing Club at Soignee Farm, Westacre, north-west of Swaffham. Another traditionally early start was scheduled. The meet was 8:45am with first dogs in slips at 9am. However, I had driven through dense fog on my journey there and there was dense fog at the meet. Coursing was impossible in such conditions. The dogs needed clear sight of the hare. The Judge needed to see the dogs and the owners needed to be able to retrieve their dogs. It was no surprise that the start was delayed until the fog lifted at 11am. Initially I had a good position on the far side from the main crowd at the end of the flanking line, with the dogs being slipped to my right. There was a kill but it occurred across from me, near the crowd, and was lost from my sight in the mist.

That beat finished and there was a pause in proceedings whilst the beaters were sent out on the opposite side. The position was reversed. I was still across from the crowd but the dogs were then being slipped from my left. I again moved to the end of the flanking line but this time, instead of being isolated, I had a group of three near to me.

There was an old courser, a middle-aged man, and a youngish aggressive looking chap. The old man looked suspicious when I took pictures; he kept looking at me with his binoculars. Far from shying away I walked up to him and asked him where we were on the coursing card (it was easy to lose track of which dogs were running in which event). He asked me who I was, where I lived, the coursing meetings I had attended etc. My cover story was good and he appeared satisfied.

I returned to my position and soon afterwards there was a kill right in front of me. The flankers and trainers all ran up to the dogs. The Judge galloped up. Sadly, there was no way I could have taken photographs and walked out with my film. Even though accepted as a coursing enthusiast photographs of kills had to be taken surreptitiously. Coursing photographers took images of owners posing with dogs, dogs running, hares turning and trophies being presented—they did not photograph hares being ripped, torn and tussled over.

I took more photographs of dogs running and with the mist descending again left at the next break. By chatting to supporters I gathered useful intelligence. A key courser—Nick Reed-Herbert—was identified. He chatted with many coursers of whom Ramony Charmain and July Delamaine were identified to me.

Later in February, the 17th, I visited the East of England Coursing Club. Their meet was at Postland between Crowland and Wisbech in Lincolnshire at 8:30am with first dogs in slips at 9am. That meant an early start from home. The entry card was just £3. The Judges were Bob Burdon and Terry Monaghan; the Slippers Bob Blatch and P. Sagar. We started at the small airfield, on the left, a few miles north of Crowland on the A1073 towards Spalding. The coursing then moved to Rex Sly's farm a few hundred metres to the north. The bulk of the beaters were school children earning money whilst on half-term holiday. The first drive was blank. Three hares driven in by the beaters escaped through the beat line before they could be driven past the hidden Slipper and on to the appointed coursing field.

This was winter and the weather atrocious. Snow flurries were driven horizontally across the field by bitterly cold winds. On the second drive hares were soon found and coursing commenced at 10:10am. The second hare coursed was killed. She could be heard squealing for several minutes. The Picker-up, Rob Bettinson, later told me that Judge Bob Burdon had sworn at the owner/trainer who retrieved the dogs and the hare for not killing the latter more quickly. When I asked this young lad what the problem had been he told me he had difficulty killing the hare as his hands were so cold he could feel nothing.

The beat was sent out to bring in three drives from that position. We then moved nearer the farm, and stopped for lunch. When coursing resumed I again took up a position in the flanking line. A young partridge ran onto the field. With this bird running about coursing was impossible. The other flankers and the Judge tried to scare it away but without success. The Judge then called for someone to pick it up. I ran onto the field and had

Top: North Downs HSA sponsored walk, Guildford to Reigate, June 24th 1984.

Left: protest outside Fur Trade dinner, London, May 31st 1984.

Right: demonstration against Cross Brothers Circus, Tunbridge Wells, July 31st 1984.

Above: SEALL march in Brighton, June 2nd 1984, against Shamrock Farms.

Left: Kim Stallwood addresses the crowd in Trafalgar Square. BUAV rally, May 12th 1985.

Top: Old English sheep-dog held by the Royal College of Surgeons, August 26th 1984.

Left: Caroline Dawkins escaping after the SEALL raid, August 26th 1984.

Bottom: Operating table at the Royal College of Surgeons , Buckston Browne Farm.

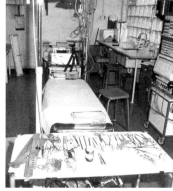

Royal College of Surgeons, Buckston Browne Farm, closed and derelict, July 7th 1990.

Left: SEALL information gatherers at the Royal College of Surgeons (RCS), August 26th 1984.

Bottom: News coverage of the RCS conviction.

Bottom right: Margaret Manzoni from the BUAV interviewed, February 19th 1985. (Pictures from television news).

Top: *Tag* the fox held captive in the shed of the terrierman to the Derwent Foxhounds (picture *News of the World* October 24th 1982).

Left: John Hicks holds *Tag* after his rescue.

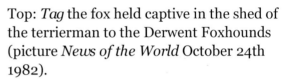

Right: Ellesmere Port dog fight, January 21st 1988. Bottom: Dublin dog fight, January 28th 1988 (pictures Graham Hall/ *News of the World*).

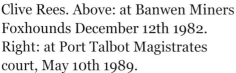

Clive Rees. Above: at Banwen Miners
Foxhounds December 12th 1982.
Right: at Port Talbot Magistrates
court, May 10th 1989.

Below: terriermen from Mr Goschen's Foxhounds play with a live
lactating vixen circa 1987. Colin Didriksen (left), Richard Grogan (right).
(Picture anon. gift)

Kimberley & Wymondham Coursing Club
March 4th 1985. Right: Paul Willingale
watches after release from 6 month jail
sentence for nearly killing an opponent.
Below: Waterloo Cup February 28th 1989.
Below left: Jonjo O'Neill watches the coursing.
Below right: supporter climbs marquee.

Hare catching with the Swaffham Coursing Club. Above: March 11th 1989. Above right: Maureen Lawless and author in undercover role. (Pictures above, Graham Hall/*News of the World*).
Below: Swaffham Coursing Club, March 2nd 1991.

Left: hare nears escape zone.

Irish Park Coursing, Clonmel, February 1st 1989. Below left: Jerry Desmond Secretary of Irish Coursing Club addresses crowd. Bottom: ICABS protesters outside.

National Institute for Medical
Research (NIMR).
Above: Melody MacDonald
with Professor Feldberg.
Below: Professor Feldberg at
home December 7th 1989.

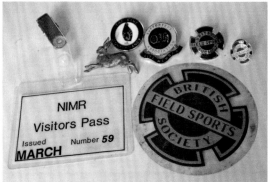

Above: tools of the trade for an undercover investigator.

Right and below: preparing a rabbit at the National Institute for Medical Research, December 21st 1989.

Bottom: burning a rabbit, December 15th 1989.

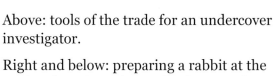

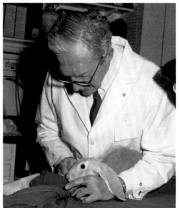

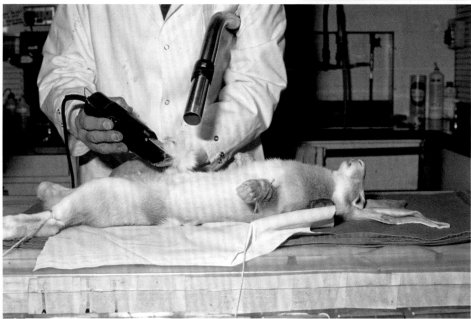

Lamp placed just above the shaved abdomen.

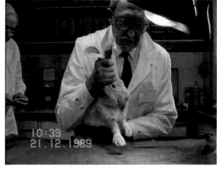

NIMR December 21st 1989.

Left: rabbit gets an injection of Sagatal.

Below left and right: rabbit is cut and kicks and struggles.

Bottom right: Les Ward from Advocates for Animals in the laboratory, April 5th 1990.

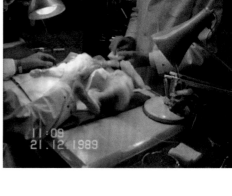

Below left: the end of the experiment, March 30th 1990.

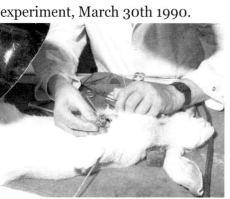

Above: inadequately anaesthetised rabbit reacts to burn. January 10th 1990.

Left: Professor Feldberg enjoys a cup of tea in his laboratory, April 5th 1990.

Right: Professor Feldberg gives an injection of Sagatal. Below: rabbit struggles on operating table, April 23rd 1990.

Bottom: Newsnight, July 1990. Les Ward interviewed. (Pictures from Newsnight broadcast).

Builth Wells badger abuse, April 1st 1990. Three badgers were baited with dogs, shot and stabbed to death. (Video pictures Graham Hall/*News of the World*).

Above: Chris Williamson from LACS watches defendants leave Llandrindod Wells Magistrates Court, July 17th 1990.
Right: Jim Barrington interviewed after the defendants were jailed, Brecon Magistrates Court, September 24th 1990.

Faroe Islands, August 1990.
Top left: blood on quayside from where 50 dolphins were slaughtered. Top: Alan Knight with dolphin head, August 13th 1990. Left: Liz Varney with dolphin heads.

Above: Jim Hayes and Alan Knight with dolphin heads, August 13th 1990. Right: Liz Varney interviewed about the expedition, August 14th 1990.

Faroe Islands, August 1990. Above and left: harvesting and killing salmon. Below: moving salmon, August 8th 1990.

Bottom left and right: the team from British Divers Marine Life Rescue.

just caught it when the dogs were slipped against a hare. I stood still and they coursed all around me.

Afterwards I returned to the flanking line and one of the trainers asked me for the partridge, to stash in his pocket. I refused him. At the end of that drive I took the bird to an adjacent field and released him. A young courser complained to me that he wanted it and told me he would chase it and catch it again. I said that he should leave it alone. The bird clearly belonged to the landowner and it would be bad for the image of coursing for any supporter to be seen wringing the neck of such a bird and stealing it. He left it. After having to stand watching helpless as animals were killed it was nice to intervene and save a life.

The next drive was arranged curiously. Hares were driven in by the beaters over a nearby minor road. I took up position to watch after parking behind owners D. Smith and S. Merrills driving a battered green Escort van.

We then moved to the final drive, one where the coursing field was surrounded by deep ditches. I watched as one hare, closely pressed by the dogs disappeared down into the ditch. She never came out. I thought she had run along the ditch bottom. Rob Bettinson ran past me; the dogs had killed in the ditch bottom at 3:45pm.

I asked Rob Bettinson what happened to the dead hares afterwards. He said they were sold for club funds; he thought for £3 each. I asked to buy the hare killed in the ditch to take home to eat. He said to ask John Balls, the Slip/Field Steward (the man with the loudhailer). I asked the latter and he sold her to me for £2. I judged it good for my cover to do this. I also wanted close-up photographs of the hare.

With the light failing and them needing just three more hares to complete the first running of the 'Airfield Stakes', they did a walk-up course over the last field. In walk-up coursing the hares are not driven in by a line of beaters towards a pre-chosen coursing field. Instead the coursers walk in a long line across a field with the Slipper in the middle, to the fore, holding a pair of dogs by his slip lead. When a hare was put up and ran away she was given the required start before the dogs were slipped. Then it was typical coursing. They found and coursed one hare.

I saw three hares killed from fourteen coursed. During the day, I noticed that the beaters, numbering about forty, mainly school kids, were often driven along the main Crowland to Spalding road from drive to drive. They stood huddled on a cart towed by a tractor. It did not look safe. I left at 4:30pm and stopped off on my way home to photograph the dead hare.

My stay at home was little more than a pit-stop. I left soon after 6am the next morning, Saturday February 18th, to return for the second day of that meeting at Postland. With dogs in the slips at 9am we started off in the same field where we had done walk-up coursing the previous evening. I was at the end of the flanking line, to the Slipper's left, next to Rob Bettinson.

Three out of the first four hares coursed were killed. These hares were killed in front of the flanking line opposite me so I crossed over. Typically, the fourth hare was killed near where I had previously been. With the hares jinking, twisting and turning the best they could to save their lives

I had but two prayers: first that each hare would escape; secondly that if she was to be killed that her death happened within range of my camera. When the public saw the price our wildlife paid for the fun of the few I hoped it would generate anger sufficient to end the pastime.

The fifth hare killed ran into the ditch behind me desperate to escape the closely pursuing dogs. When she never emerged, I guessed she was running the ditch bottom. I ran as fast as I could to the scene with the dogs' owners/trainers in hot pursuit. If I could just grab the dogs I could lawfully and reasonably stop the course and save the hare as, with the hare in the ditch, the judging of the coursing had ended. After that, any owners or trainers would appreciate having their dogs restrained from further fruitless pursuit. I was fast enough to gain a few seconds on my own, out of sight, in the ditch but I was too late to help the hare. One dog was tearing at her lifeless body. I took three pictures before anyone saw me.

Five hares had been killed in the first hour. At 9:30am I had counted about 50 vehicles. There were cars and four-wheel-drive vehicles packed with supporters and there were dog-vans.

In the running of the 'Airfield Stakes' for eight mixed puppies I saw some of the problems faced by a coursing Slipper. He had to settle both dogs side by side, with each dog having clear sight of the hare. Only when both dogs were straining at the leash to pursue the hare could the Slipper release them. But these were inexperienced puppies. One dog had never been in such slips before. He panicked, twisted himself around and became entangled in the harness. The enormously experienced Bob Blatch had to slip them prematurely otherwise they would have fought each other. The puppies were caught and put back in the slips. The owner of the troublesome and nervous dog stayed nearby to calm him.

The coursing entourage moved on to the next drive. I took up my preferred position at the end of the flanking line. Coursing Inspector, Bill Balls, whom I had seen at the Swaffham meeting walked up and stood near me. I asked him what his work entailed. He told me there was a legal requirement for his job. He had to check hares were not too 'balled-up' and they were not heavy with young. Hares became 'balled-up' when they were driven in by the beaters over ploughed or muddy fields. Their feet then became packed with mud ('balled-up') and that severely reduced their manoeuvrability—their ability to turn.

Bill Balls boasted he had the power to stop the coursing if too many hares were being killed. He told me that earlier that morning he had cut open one hare that was very heavy with young. The coursing continued. From that drive a sixth hare was killed.

When the line of beaters came in and the drive ended we all walked off. It was about 11:30am. I was surprised when one of a pair of greyhounds in front of me just collapsed. I took two pictures but then as the trainer struggled to carry the dog I ran and offered help. He thanked me but said he could manage.

A picker up told me he was a very valuable dog that belonged to a Mrs Morton. He added that the dog was an excellent coursing dog, albeit that he only had one lung!

The next drive was a short distance away. The sun appeared, for the first time in two days. I took up my usual position in the flanking line but sensed a degree of suspicion towards me when I unveiled my big Nikon lens. The hares were having a bad day. There was a seventh kill near to me. I used my small Olympus compact camera to photograph the dogs tussling over her. The trainer ran up and killed the hare. I asked him afterwards how to dispatch a hare in such circumstances. He explained that you hold her upside down by her back legs then twist, stretch and wrench her head down, as if to pull it off.

At 1pm we paused for lunch. In the afternoon we moved to an adjacent field but the incoming beat lines and the flankers close to the Slipper were poorly organised. Most hares driven forwards escaped before reaching the 'shy'. Coursing then moved to a nearby small airfield. This was used by a Gliding Club but it was understood that coursing had priority. The eighth and final kill occurred on the airfield, but beyond my vision. For this last drive, I re-joined Rob Bettinson in the flanking line. He confirmed that to kill a hare you dislocated her neck. Many hares killed were not killed by the dogs—but by the first men to reach the scene.

Rob Bettinson unveiled another facet of hare coursing new to me. He said a mate amongst the beaters was organising the capture of hares for the Swaffham Coursing Club the next day—Sunday February 19th. I asked how and he described hares being driven by lines of beaters towards and through hedgelines. The far side of the hedge was netted with long fine purse nets strung across the field. The netting was not taut; if it were the hares would bounce off it. As the hares dodged through the hedge and ran into the field they were entangled in the near-invisible nets and caught. They were extracted one by one, put into small compartments in crates and driven away.

I also learned of problems in the coursing world. Mr Bettinson told me the coursers at that meeting were 'gents', as they had been at the one previous. But, at one before, a whole bunch of 'didicoys' had turned up and had given the Judge abuse. As a picker-up at that meeting he could do nothing right. He was sworn at both for catching their dogs and for not catching them.

The meet cards all warned: "*The committee reserve to themselves the right of refusing admission to the Coursing Ground, or ejecting any person without assigning a reason.*" I wondered how often that was put into effect with anyone other than a group of anti-coursing protestors. I suspected about as often as coursing was stopped for 'balled-up' or pregnant hares. I left at 4:45pm.

The following Monday, February 20th, I left early to attend a joint coursing meeting. The Swaffham Coursing Club and Kimberley & Wymondham Coursing Club met at Kimberley Green, Norfolk at 8:45am with first dogs in slips at 9am. The entry fee was £3 for the meet card, plus £1 for the keeper.

From the meet, we all drove and parked on a hard-standing near to the chosen coursing field close to the B1135. We had a young female Judge— Miss Pippa Le Roux. I had previously noticed her taking photographs from the flanking line at the Swaffham meeting on February 6th. The Slipper was Bob Blatch. Before coursing started I asked Bob about his job. He demonstrated to me how the slip-lead works. With both dogs sighted on the hare and straining at the leash (literally) he could open the two collars simultaneously by pulling on the wire running through the lead to his hand. It was a simple, effective and fair way of releasing both dogs—it is also used in the humane alternative, lure coursing.

At the first drive a Steward with loud-hailer called for volunteers to stand at the end by the shy and stop the traffic if the dogs ran out onto the B1135. No-one moved but I quickly volunteered and it turned out to be a good position. The dogs were being slipped from right in front of me, with the hares driven in across the Kimberley-Coston road. Any kill on the field I could have photographed. Some hares ran out from the coursing field onto adjacent plough and two were killed there.

One owner returned from this field with his dog and carrying the dead hare. I advised him to walk behind the hedge so as not to be visible to the dogs waiting in the slips, i.e. along the B1135. He declined saying antis might see him. I advised him to cross the shy in the interval between courses. He did so and I photographed him.

The slip position changed a couple of times: once to back onto the ploughed field and then to a corner backing onto the B1135. I had little experience of coursing but the latter seemed to me a foolish position as with all the traffic on the road only one hare crossed it to be coursed. When the beat was driving in over the ploughed field a horsebox drove by with horn blaring. Pippa asked me if I thought it was driven by an anti. I said it was either that or a supporter trying to help the beat in a rather dim-witted fashion. I said that as it was a horsebox surely they could not be antis but Pippa replied: *"You'll be surprised, but when I go to Badminton there are a lot of antis there."*

During the break for lunch I chatted to Dave Needham who seemed to be a key figure in the club. He told me how they had successfully caught hares for the club the previous day. To gain an insight and pictures of this aspect of coursing I offered to help. I gave my name and phone number to his wife Jennie. They were clearly short of beaters for such an event. A colleague of his, Don, asked if, as I had a car, I could bring it full of friends to help? I said I would try.

Pippa later told me that she had also been involved in catching hares the previous day. She said they were short of hares at Feltwell.

The coursing moved to a field across from the Coston road where more hares were killed. We then drove on to another nearby field. I initially took up my favourite position in the flanking line that backed onto a ploughed field. However, with the possibility of seeing hares being netted,

I thought it unwise to risk my cover too much by photographing kills so I moved to a position nearer to the Slipper to photograph the Slip. This proved a mistake when a Suffolk Foxhounds supporter approached me and quizzed me as to my support for Field Sports. He had a word with Pippa, and in due course she rode up to me.

"*What film are you using?*"

"*It is colour film.*"

"*Where is your camera?*"

"*Oh, here in my inside pocket.*"

"*Why do you hide it in there?*"

"*It's not hidden, I keep it there to keep the batteries warm, if they get cold they pack up.*"

"*Oh.*"

I sensed she was not convinced.

On one course one dog was unsighted and dropped out but the remaining dog caught and killed the hare, an unusual occurrence. At the end of the day I saw one owner bathing cuts on his dog's feet. I asked how they were caused and he said by the dog making sharp turns over the flints on the ground. He complained that sometimes their claws were torn clean out. Coursing ended at 4pm by which time I had counted six kills.

I returned the next morning, Tuesday February 21st, for the meeting at 8:45am in the car park of Somerleyton Hall, beside the B1074 near Lowestoft. It was held by permission of Lord and Lady Somerleyton. The entry card cost £3 plus £2 collected for the keepers.

The whole atmosphere had changed. The coursers seemed suspicious of my presence. Pippa Le Roux and Dave Needham were near to me and I tried to make conversation about the breeding of the dogs. Pippa then went to her car and took out her camera. She asked a lady with two dogs to pose in front of my car, but it was all too obvious who she was trying to photograph. I sat in the driving seat. I adopted a pose of casual concealment. With sun-visor down and my flat cap shading my eyes I doubted she had much success. However, my cover would not bear much scrutiny—my car number plate was registered to my home.

We drove to the first coursing field. I walked up and confronted Pippa. I asked her if it offended anyone, or if I trod on anyone's toes by taking photographs? Had they a club photographer who photographed owners with their dogs and made a living out of selling?

She replied: "*Oh no, it's nothing like that, it is just that we don't know you and wonder if you are an anti?*"

I feigned astonishment: "*Well really! Are you sure I am not offending anyone? I won't take any pictures if it offends anyone.*"

Pippa, "*Well, have you asked Gordon* (Humphrey, the Hon. Secretary) *for permission?*"

Mike Huskisson, "*No, but I will.*"

Pippa, "*No, I'll ask for you.*"

She did and he said there was no problem with my taking photographs. The defence I always employed when under suspicion was to take a step closer to the person suspicious of me. It was difficult when all you really wanted was to leave but to do that was to admit your guilt. Being bold and stepping towards those who suspected you usually worked.

The first drive was reached via an extremely muddy and rutted drive more suited to a four-wheel-drive vehicle than my car. I stood right by the line of the Slipper. When passing clouds cleared I found the sun in my eyes which was bad for photographs. There was one kill on the field. On that drive, for the first time in that coursing surveillance in England, I saw a hare allowed to escape as she was judged too weak to course. Such 'benevolence' was a fairly frequent occurrence at Clonmel.

When the beat came in we drove to the second field. The hares were coursed over plough and there were several kills on and off the arena. I photographed aged Sandy Mackenzie, a near neighbour of mine, who I had first seen coursing back in the 1970s when I was a hunt saboteur. He walked with a dog and carried a dead hare.

At the end of that drive, when the beat came in, I ran in and photographed the dogs head-on in the slips before their owners could remove them. That made the classic hare coursing picture—the sort a coursing enthusiast would take. I caught the ear of Gordon Humphrey, the elderly Hon. Secretary of the Swaffham Coursing Club, and explained my interest in photographing the dogs and 'country sports'.

For the third drive the beat was sent out on the opposite side and the slip was simply moved to the opposite end of the field. More hares were killed. I noticed and photographed Bill Balls, the Coursing Inspector for the East of England Coursing Club. When that drive finished we all returned to the car park of the stately home for an early lunch. It was a nervous time for me as that is when awkward questions can be asked.

Relief came when at 1pm we set off for the last field for the finals. The Eric Stubbings Cup was won by *Widger Uccello* owned by J. Delahooke and trained by Michael Darnell. The Hartley Hawes Memorial Cup was won by *Rockwell* owned by the famous jockey, Walter Swinburn, and trained by Michael Darnell. *Widget Utrillo* owned by J. Delahooke and trained by Michael Darnell won the Dan Riordan Tankard for puppies. *Bargain Strike* won the Ted Chapman Cup in which there was a track dog running. *El Menaka* owned and trained by Mrs Mackensie won the Swaffham Cup. *Slightly Naughty* won the Swaffham Oaks on a bye and *Brookville Glen* owned and trained by Les Anderson won the Newscombe Cup.

After all these finals, there were still hares in the beat funnel, so two trial events were run. Because they were trials neither dog wore a coloured collar. I photographed a kill on the second trial. We returned to our vehicles and I recorded the noted coursing figure, Michael Darnell, with a dog by his white van. I counted nine kills in total. When the day ended, I drove to Diss to take my film in for processing.

For the Saturday, February 25th, I headed out towards Cambridge for the meet of the Isle of Ely Coursing Club at Balsham. It was the usual early start—meet at 8:45am with first dogs in slips at 9am. The card entry fee was £1.50 with a further £2 collected for the keeper. The meet was along the small lane from Hildersham to Balsham. This was winter. Heavy snow had fallen in the North and West of England the previous night. We started off clear but cold, then showers of freezing rain fell, then it became dry and very cold. Experienced coursers whom I had spoken to at the East of England and Swaffham clubs had scant regard for the Isle of Ely Club. I was warned that organisation was poor, dogs were late in slips, they put out poor beat lines, and had poor flanking lines. When I tried to telephone the Secretary, Frances Clark, for the meet location I found she had the wrong number printed in the National Coursing Club (NCC) list of Secretaries so I obtained the meet from Gordon Humphrey. The coursing took place on land belonging to Lord Vestey and Mr Kiddey.

When I saw Gordon Humphrey standing nearby I asked Frances for permission to take photographs saying: "*I've done it for the Swaffham.*" She replied "*Well if you do it for them you're welcome to take photographs here.*" There was an apprentice Judge—a Dr Low—and an apprentice Slipper in attendance. There were four different slipping positions on the first drive. One hare was killed on the field. I noticed the Judge was static. Although mounted he never galloped alongside to judge the course.

We moved location and a second hare was killed during walk up coursing over plough. Beat lines were then organised to drive in over this ploughed field but it was blank. An absence of hares there was very unexpected. A long pause in proceedings followed whilst they decided what to do next.

Whilst we stood waiting Dave Needham came up and asked me to help with catching hares on March 11th, and to bring friends if possible. I said I would try to get some of my fishing pals along. Dave and Gordon then left. I overheard Gordon asking Dave to drop bundles of sticks off at 'Mark's', and saw them transferring the load.

We moved to course over Lord Vestey's land at about midday. At a suitable opportunity, the club raffle was drawn. A Mr Gill approached me, gave his address and asked me to send him copies of prints I had taken of dogs in the slips at the first drive. I was happy to as it improved my cover. The beaters were taken from drive to drive on a trailer towed by a tractor.

During further walk-up coursing the apprentice Slipper had a go. But he slipped the dogs on a hare that was running, not away from them, but at right angles across them. That hare was never turned before she escaped through a nearby hedge. The Judge had little alternative but to signal 'No Course'. Experienced coursers muttered they had never seen such a thing happen. The beat was then arranged to drive hares through a wood and out onto a grass field. Two hares were killed in that drive. One was caught by a single dog too close to me to photograph. The owner of the losing dog had a swearing row with the Judge over his decision. (Probably one dog had been unsighted when both were slipped. The unsighted dog would then dash about aimlessly and leave the sighted dog to course and catch the hare alone. Dogs should not be slipped unless both were sighted.)

We then drove on to course over a field of standing crops. Four more hares were killed there. I watched as one was caught, escaped from the dogs, was caught again, escaped again, was caught again then killed. The kills were messy. It was clear there were no experienced killers in the flanking lines. A hare is a big animal. All would struggle violently when caught; killing them quickly and cleanly took expertise.

Frances asked me what I intended doing with all my photographs. I told her they were for personal use and for my interest in recording 'country sports'. She said that was alright, they just didn't want them going in magazines as: "*Too many hares are being killed today. Usually we only kill three in a whole meeting.*" Perhaps cheekily for a professed novice like me I added the opinion that she should have some experienced hare dispatchers in the flanking lines. She replied that the problem was that all the good people in that regard were busily engaged holding their dogs.

Hare coursing done by poorly supported clubs was likely to cause suffering to hares beyond that usually expected in the pastime.

We next moved to an adjacent ploughed field where another hare was killed. The club were short of the hares required to run the last three finals and as it was getting dark I left. I had seen nine hares killed in around 21 courses. Some courses were 'byes' where one dog drops out, usually through injury, and the second still must run a course to ensure that all dogs do a similar amount of coursing time. When a club was short of hares, as they were here, they ran two bye dogs together. The course was not judged, as both dogs go through, but running them together saves finding one more hare. One owner was upset after his dog 'won' a paired bye contest against a particular dog but then lost the real course against the same opponent.

I asked experienced coursers why so many hares were killed. They thought the high ratio of hare fatalities was due to the weather and ground conditions causing hares to come onto the field 'balled-up' with mud. Coursing Inspector Bill Balls was present throughout the day but did nothing to remedy this situation.

A week later I returned to that Mecca for the hare coursing world—the Waterloo Cup held annually on those wide-open fields at the Withins and Lydiate, near Formby, north of Liverpool. I had previously attended this event in 1976 and 1977 as a hunt saboteur. I then went in 1983 and 1984 in the undercover role. For 1989 I was undercover but working as a press photographer for the *News of the World*.

The paper was keen to expose the close links between horse racing and hare coursing. During the afternoon of Monday February 27th I left home. After picking up my colleague Janet Taylor we checked into the Clifton Royal Hotel at Southport. With the paper making the booking no expense was spared. The hotel had a heated indoor swimming pool and for the one and only time in my life I had a king-sized waterbed. I found the experience weird—and it was hard to sleep.

Next morning, we were up early. We drove to the Withins for the first day of coursing. The meet was at 9am for a 9:30am start.

It was potentially awkward for me. My posing as a press photographer was risky. Although some years had passed since my days of working on *Outfoxed* I might have been recognised by some of the coursing hierarchy, or by some at the British Field Sports Society (BFSS) as a former LACS employee. I might also have been recognised by East Anglian coursers who knew me as a lowly club follower. I had to take care.

We drove up just before 9:30am, and showed the invitation that Janet had received from Sir Mark Prescott to the Gateman. We were directed to the Press car park. Caroline Yeates from the BFSS came up to us, took our names (I was Martin Woodward), and asked us which paper we were from. She gave us two "PRESS" badges (a card on some string), two Complimentary Meeting Cards, told us when the Press Conference would be (10:30am), and where the hospitality tent was.

We split up to look for Jonjo O'Neill, and any other jockeys present. I saw many people I had been coursing with over the weeks before, Dave Needham etc. I also saw Charles Nodder and Peter Atkinson from the BFSS. Thankfully, if they saw me, they did not recognise me. The coursing was slow to start. When hares arrived they flooded onto the field, too many to course. In time the organisers got it right and drove one hare at a time on the field. Some were killed right in front of the television cameras.

Janet, a practised sleuth, found Jonjo O'Neill and "Ginger" McCain about mid-day in the Nominators' enclosure. That select area was reserved for people with dogs running in the event, and their guests. I looked across and saw a problem for me. Dave Needham and Gordon Humphrey sat in their car just four vehicles away from those I had to photograph.

I tried to sneak a picture of our targets but with little success. It was risky to linger too long, so, after a short while, I took the direct approach and simply asked Jonjo for his picture. He was happy to pose.

That done I walked to the bank side, in amongst the real rough element, to photograph the coursing. When light permitted I used my 500mm mirror lens, otherwise the 80-200 zoom lens. It was, as usual, freezing cold and very windy.

The field was covered with pools of water, so hares and dogs were slipping and sliding about. One hare was killed in the bottom of a water-filled ditch by a single dog. Another was caught by both dogs in a 'tug-of-war'—she was a living rope between the two. One dog won this tussle and ran off with his prize. A chap ran after this dog, caught him and made him drop the hare. This hare promptly ran off but was caught again and killed.

Another hare that was caught by both dogs in the middle of the field was dropped and also ran off, but she escaped. The beat line came in late in the afternoon. It was due to be put out again but by then the light was so gloomy that I had no chance of taking meaningful photographs so we left.

Drink flowed freely at the Waterloo Cup. It greatly entertained the crowd on the bank when drunks in the large marquee firstly climbed the support poles inside it and then climbed up to the top from the outside by holding on to the guy ropes. At one point there were urgent tannoy appeals for the vet—Mr Guilliard. They had problems with dogs falling into the water-filled ditches as they pursued their quarry.

I counted two hares coursed that escaped not at the usual rhododendron end but by running back past the Slipper's hut. This put them right back in the beat-funnel so that they became prime candidates to be coursed again a few minutes later. I counted at least nine kills. At the morning Press Conference Sir Mark Prescott had said that if more than two were killed it would be a bad day. One problem was that during the coursing large numbers of the lout element were walking to and from the bank, behind the rhododendron screen. Movements there might have deterred hares from escaping through the area. Sir Mark had told Janet that those who wanted to watch the dogs coursing would stand near the Slipper, or midway down the field; only those who wanted to watch the kills would stand at the bottom near the rhododendron line. That was precisely where we found Jonjo O'Neill (and the nominators' enclosure).

During breaks we had wandered around the many stalls. Amongst the plethora of country coats, walking sticks and leads we saw stallholders selling prints of dog fighting and cock fighting. We also saw a demonstration against coursing by about 60 hunt saboteurs. They marched up the road closely marshalled by the police. Abusive taunts were exchanged between the two sides. We returned to our hotel. After purchasing swimming trunks, I used the indoor pool. Janet and I then made plans for the next day.

Wednesday March 1st coursing was at the usual venue for the second day—Lydiate. We drove up and again identified ourselves as 'Press' to the Gateman. We were directed to, *"see Barry"*. We chose to ignore that advice and parked amongst the other cars. We then separated. Whilst Janet went to find 'Barry', and hopefully another jockey—Greville Starkey, I joined the rougher element waiting for the coursing.

The dogs were put in slips at 9:30am as usual but it turned 11am before any hare appeared on the field. It was freezing cold and surely cannot have been good for the dogs to be tensed up like a tight spring, ready to go, for so long. Indeed, at about 10:30am the owners took their charges out and walked them up and down to keep them warm.

The first course happened at 11:05am with the hare coming in from our left. She escaped. On the second the terrified hare jumped the ditch in front of our feet and landed right in the crowd, just ten metres to my right. One dog leaped after the hare and caught her. She was killed by the crowd.

On the third course the hare was killed on the field opposite us. For the fourth the hare bounded over the ditch into the area where nominators and people Sir Mark Prescott had labelled 'snobs' were packed on our left. A re-run of the second course, I thought, as both dogs piled in after her. However, there was no sign of the hare. Then a roar went up on my left. The poor hare had clawed and swum her way along the bottom of the water-filled ditch towards us in a desperate effort to escape. A man a few places to my left yanked her out by her back legs and threw her, not towards the car-park behind us so she could escape but back onto the coursing field. Fortunately in the meantime the dogs had been seized by their owners and were unable to continue the pursuit. That determined hare lived to run another day. On the fifth course the hare was killed in the middle of the field, making three hares killed from the first five coursed. The beat then came in. With a considerable delay inevitable, before it went out the other side, and the fact there were no jockeys present, and the danger that if I was recognised by Peter Atkinson or Charles Nodder it would jeopardise future undercover surveillance of hare coursing, we left. It was 1:30pm.

Saturday March 4th brought a return to fox hunting when I attended the meet of the Suffolk Foxhounds at Coney Weston House, Coney Weston. There were hunt saboteurs present throughout the day. I took the role of a casual follower and trailed along taking a few pictures. I returned to the same hunt the following Thursday for their meet at *The Four Horseshoes*, Thornham Magna. It seemed they never found a fox all day and packed up at 2:30pm. I went on to the meet of the Easton Harriers at the nearby *Cherry Tree*, Yaxley. The Huntsman's horse suffered a badly cut leg and the hunt had problems keeping their hounds from the nearby, busy, A140.

Saturday March 11th produced some graphic evidence. I fulfilled my promise to Dave Needham from the Swaffham Coursing Club to 'help' with hare catching. I took along a couple of friends—Maureen Lawless from the *News of the World*—and our ace undercover investigator, Graham Hall. I met Graham and Maureen at nearby Watton at 9:15am and we all drove out to Bodney Water Tower.

There were about 40 beaters. We were each given a flag, shown how to wave it, and organised in beat lines across the fields. We then just walked along chatting to others near us. Hares ran away from us and were tangled up in fine mesh purse nets. The struggling creatures were then pulled from the nets and shoved into small wooden crates. We were told they would be taken away to re-stock other areas short of hares and there would be a hare shoot after our visit, so any hares left would most likely be shot.

I took some pictures but it was no surprise that Graham was the most forceful photographer and secured the best images. At one point he concealed himself in one of the many World War II era concrete pill-boxes dotting the site. From there he photographed hares entangled in the purse net, grabbed by coursers and carried back to be squeezed into small wooden transport crates. One hare was carried held only by the base of her ears. Graham also photographed the wooden crates piled up one on top of another in the back of a Land Rover. There were four drives in total. We left at 3pm. We made a variety of excuses for why we did little to help, such as 'too much to drink the night before'. By our presence alone when so many ostensibly keen coursers did so little to help their club, I felt my cover was secured within the local coursing world.

The LACS had long taken an interest in the hygiene standards at hunt kennels. I was tasked with investigating, so the following week Sue and I drove to the New Forest. Thursday March 15th found me in a position to photograph the New Forest Foxhounds kennels. That was routine surveillance work.

My return to investigative work had gone well. I had achieved success working with the LACS and the *News of the World* but I needed my own group to fund my own projects, to work with other groups and to work in the other areas of our concern such as vivisection and factory farming.

CHAPTER SIX
Creation of the Animal Cruelty Investigation Group (ACIG), investigative work, the National Institute for Medical Research.

"The publicity forced them to take the action which they should have taken much earlier." (MRC Inquiry report, February 1991)

As I returned to more fieldwork I thought to draw on the support that I had received whilst in prison to help me purchase the equipment that I needed. I had kept the names and addresses of those who had kindly supported my Appeal Fund.

I sent a letter to each explaining that I proposed to undertake further investigative work, that I would only do so lawfully, and sought their financial support to pay the expenses of such work. I set up the Animal Cruelty Investigation Group (ACIG) in June 1989 and invited people to join as supporters. My friends and colleagues were enthusiastic and many generously supported my new group. Many of those originals support my work to this day and their donations have paid for this publication.

In the summer of 1989 we had contact from a hunting informant keen to tell us the truth about fox hunting. She clearly had a lifetime of experience and knew what she was talking about. Once again I worked with a journalist colleague—Janet Taylor from the *News of the World.* On Monday July 17th 1989 I drove across country and picked up Janet and a couple of hunt saboteur colleagues. We drove to meet Lady Waechter at her home in Suckley to the west of Worcester. She was Master of the North Ledbury Foxhounds from 1948 to 1989 and had seen a lot of changes during her Mastership. We had a long chat and she was happy to speak on the record, then and other times.

Lady Waechter explained how her kennelman had been suspicious about the behaviour of a fox killed by their hounds and had arranged for the body to be examined by a vet. The vet confirmed the fox had been crippled before being killed by the hounds—his tendons and paws had been cut. Lady Waechter complained to the MFHA about the actions of the terrierman and sent them photographs of the fox. When she judged that the MFHA failed to investigate her accusation properly, and even failed to return her photographs, she approached the LACS (*Wildlife Guardian* 19 Winter 1991/92).

The 1989/90 hunting and coursing season started for me in October. My aim was to develop and extend my contacts within hare coursing and develop some deeper infiltration into fox hunting. Monday October 9th, I drove to the meeting of the Swaffham Coursing Club at Needham, east of Diss. I arrived to find it cancelled due to the ground being so hard.

At the end of that week, Saturday October 14th, I attended the meet of the Waveney Harriers at Cratfield, Suffolk. I had a new weapon in the ACIG armoury to try—a full sized professional Panasonic video camera that took top quality Super VHS tape. I claimed a private interest in recording 'country sports' but no doubt the hunters wondered who I really was.

The following week, Saturday 21st October, I was back with the Waveney Harriers for their meet at Sotterley Park, near Beccles. During the day the Whipper-in rode past and said to me in triumph: "*Hello Mr Huskisson!*" They had noted my number plate the previous week and asked a hunt-friendly police officer who my car belonged to.

That proved an interesting day. Hunt saboteurs from Norwich and Lowestoft were present doing an excellent job protecting our wildlife. Hunters loathed effective saboteurs and often tried to block them in on a road. They did precisely that at one point. A young girl rider thought she would compound the mischief by backing her horse into the anti's car (there was a good prospect of denting the car and if the horse was injured they could accuse the saboteur of driving into the horse).

She manoeuvred her horse with aplomb, dented the car bonnet and the hunters around thought it mighty funny—until the driver got out and was not a hunt saboteur! She was an uninvolved passing motorist and understandably irate. The hunters were mortified and profuse in their apologies. We later saw another rider fall off and later still encountered a riderless horse. It was chaotic. Thankfully there were no kills that I was aware of.

The following Saturday I switched back to undercover surveillance of hare coursing at the meeting of the Isle of Ely Coursing Club at Heath Road, Swaffham Bulbeck, east of Cambridge. I paid £3 for my entry card, £1 for the keeper. I joined the crowd and took slides of the coursing whenever I could.

On Wednesday November 1st, I was back with the Waveney Harriers at *The Duke William*, Metfield. As they knew my identity it was no longer undercover work, more a matter of me monitoring them.

Three days later I was back undercover with the Cambridgeshire Harriers from their meet at Manor Farm, Landbeach. This was a hunt that I had regularly sabotaged as a youngster. I was pleased to see Cambridgeshire hunt saboteurs in attendance again. I then went on to the meet of the Trinity Foot Beagles (the Cambridge University pack) at Cottenham Racecourse. With the Harriers meeting at 11am and the Beagles at 2pm it was common for keen hunters to switch from one to the other.

It was easy to chat to and befriend the young beaglers. For that phase of my undercover work I tended to use different aliases for the different activities, so that if my cover was blown at one it would not end all others. I was 'Michael Robinson', lived near Bury St. Edmunds and worked in the van trade, small deliveries etc. I took plenty of slides and in return they gave me their meet card.

That card was invaluable. It saved phoning the kennels for meets not advertised in the likes of *Horse and Hound*. Such calls could be risky. Kennel staff could ask awkward questions and the worst was if the Huntsman was not there and someone said: "*Oh, give us your number and I will get him to call you back.*"

I turned up the following Tuesday, November 7th to see the Trinity Foot Beagles at Bourn Grange at 1pm. On the way, I called in at Newmarket to meet hunt saboteur colleagues and collect some graphic pictures they took of a kill by that hunt. The hunt spent most of their time on and around the old airfield. I chatted about hunting and their hounds with keen student followers—Simon and Tamara—and took many photographs. There were no kills and the day ended at 4pm.

I was next out with a hunt many miles away. Saturday November 18th I joined Jim Barrington, Executive Director of the LACS, to watch the meet of the Hampshire Hunt at Bentworth near Alton, Hampshire. With Jim regularly on television and in consequence known well by hunters, there was no question of undercover work. We did not identify ourselves—we just watched. Hunt saboteurs from Petersfield HSA were out. We also met LACS colleague Elva Adamson. She was a memorable character when it came to protecting wildlife, wholly dedicated and fun to be with.

There was a car accident at a crossroads during the day. Whether it was caused by hounds on the road or by drivers being distracted whilst watching hounds or hunters I do not know. Despite the best efforts of the hunt saboteurs a fox was killed in the early afternoon. Jim and I watched as a hunt redcoat carried the body from the scene and dumped it in the woods. A terrierman then collected the body and took it away, discreetly wrapped in a blue dustbin bag.

We went on to see the Clinkard Beagles. They had met at nearby Home Farm, South Warnborough at 12:30pm. There were many hunt saboteurs in attendance led by that most determined character and close friend, Aubrey Thomas. I photographed from distance before hunting ended in rapidly descending darkness.

The following Tuesday, November 21st, the weather provided welcome relief for wildlife. I drove to meet the Trinity Foot Beagles at Lambs Cross, Westwick but dense fog caused it to be cancelled.

At the end of that week I was reminded of the perils of opposing bloodsports. I was shopping in a nearby town, pushing my young son in his pushchair when a follower of the Waveney Harriers and Suffolk Foxhounds recognised me. He shouted and swore and assured me that if he ever saw me at either of 'his' hunts again he would batter me. As an intimidating character he had a lot to learn from others I had encountered, but it was deeply unsettling for my young son.

Saturday November 25th was marked by an early start and long drive to attend the East of England Coursing Club at Twenty between Bourne and Spalding in Lincolnshire. The Judge was Terry Monaghan and the Slipper Bob Blatch. I mingled, chatted, watched and photographed.

Two days later, Monday November 27th, I tried for the meeting of the Swaffham Coursing Club at Kimberley but the event was cancelled due to frost the previous afternoon. The hares were lucky because it turned out there was no frost that morning.

The next day I joined the Trinity Foot Beagles for their meet at Punch Farm, Landbeach, north-east of Cambridge. I paid £3 for the 'cap' and had a good chat with the hunt followers. They were again mostly students. Some looked to be alumni. I gave them colour prints of their hunt that I had taken previously at Bourn. Amongst other hunting tales, they told me their hounds had rioted and killed a chicken earlier in the season whilst being walked. There was no kill that day.

Early in December 1989 the focus for my undercover investigative work switched to anti-vivisection work. Thursday December 7th was my first day working with Melody MacDonald to expose the National Institute for Medical Research (NIMR), Mill Hill, London.

This project was instigated by dedicated animal welfare campaigner Melody Macdonald. Horrified after reading scientific papers detailing experimental work with animals at the NIMR by aged Professor Wilhelm Feldberg CBE FRS, she telephoned him and expressed fascination in his research.

Professor Feldberg had for many years been injecting a variety of substances including strychnine, curare, anti-freeze and LSD into the brains of conscious cats and observing them to see the deleterious effects. The effects included vomiting, catalepsy (unconsciousness with rigidity of the body), pilo-erection (hair standing on end), fits, shivering, growling, incontinence and salivation. In 1965 he published an article naming 33 substances which he and colleagues had injected into the brains of conscious cats. He listed the effects on those cats (Feldberg W., Fleischhauer K. "*A new experimental approach to the physiology and pharmacology of the brain*", in *Brit Med Bull* 1965; 21(1):36).

Professor Feldberg was one of the most highly regarded, most experienced, most qualified researchers working anywhere in the world at the time. For the scientific community he was effectively 'God', and the NIMR, where hundreds worked, was heaven—for the researchers. [It is interesting that Captain Ronnie Wallace during his time at the Heythrop Foxhounds was also viewed as 'God' by hunt supporters.]

Flattered by her interest Professor Feldberg invited Melody to his laboratory at the NIMR. She told him that she would like to write his biography. The NIMR, founded by the Medical Research Council (MRC) in 1913, was the largest research establishment of the MRC. Melody witnessed an experiment on a rabbit when she first visited with a journalist on May 18th 1988. She visited again, alone, on July 13th 1988 and saw an experiment on a cat.

Melody then tried to interest the animal welfare/rights movement, and the media, in her ability to gain virtually free access to the laboratory. Her investigations continued. On December 1st 1988 Melody and a journalist went for dinner in London with Professor Feldberg. Throughout early 1989 Melody continually sought assistance with her investigations.

In April 1989, an accident changed the course of the earlier experiments. A table lamp used to illuminate the operating table fell towards the abdomen of an anaesthetised cat. Subsequent tests showed that hyperglycaemia had occurred (the blood sugar level was raised). Feldberg was intrigued and sought to investigate further. Despite it being well known that burns and other traumas raised blood sugar levels the Home Office agreed to the new work and amended Feldberg's Project Licence in September 1989. Professor Feldberg prepared a further application for submission to the MRC for a project grant. He argued that further studies: *"may help us to obtain a clearer understanding of some forms of clinical diabetes."* It was Medical Research.

Meanwhile Melody continued her search for help and eventually in the autumn of 1989 found interest abroad. On November 8th 1989 she took Dr Michael Fox of the Humane Society of the United States (HSUS) into the NIMR. They witnessed an experiment on a tabby cat and Dr Fox took excellent photographs. He later described that experiment as *"crude if not absurd."*

I first learned we had access to the NIMR on November 19th 1989 when Jill Russell, a dedicated anti-vivisection researcher and an ACIG supporter, put Melody in contact with me. Melody telephoned and told me she could get permission from Professor Feldberg any time she liked to watch him experiment at the NIMR. She was certain that as others had accompanied her before there would be no problem with her taking me in as a guest. I could hardly believe what I heard!! No need to creep around and over fences in the dead of night. No need to burst in along with 50 others. I could just stroll in, sign the visitor's book and watch, photograph and maybe even film experiments taking place on higher mammals, rabbits and cats. I seized the opportunity and asked Melody to arrange another laboratory visit as soon as possible. We fixed a provisional date of Friday December 1st but that was delayed nearly a week.

I arranged to meet Melody at her London home around 11:30am on Thursday December 7th 1989. We then planned to drive the short distance to the NIMR in north London. I caught the train from Diss, allowing myself plenty of time. However, the Norwich to London rail line is notoriously unreliable. My train was delayed 1½ hours by a broken rail. It was past noon before I even arrived in London.

I met the glamorous Melody—it was easy to see why Professor Feldberg had been flattered by her interest in his work. Melody drove us to Mill Hill. As we approached the front doors at around 2pm I looked at the security cameras and pinched myself to check that this genuinely was happening. We signed in and awaited our escort to the laboratory.

I was equipped with 35mm cameras and my large, bulky Panasonic AG-450 professional Super VHS camcorder. We met Professor Wilhelm Feldberg and his technician John Stean. Professor Feldberg had worked at the NIMR since 1949. He and John Stean had worked together for some five years. In a long career at the NIMR John Stean had risen to the position of Head Technician. He had retired but was asked to come out of retirement to assist Professor Feldberg.

When we entered the cramped laboratory Professor Feldberg looked to me a Grandad-like figure, elderly and frail but amiable. Melody introduced me as her friend, an Englishman living and working in the US. We explained that Dr Fox had asked for more photographs of the work. We also asked permission to use my video camera saying: "*We would like to take film to demonstrate the nature of animal experimentation in the UK to American students.*"

Professor Feldberg readily agreed saying that we could film and photograph whatever we liked. I placed my big shoulder-mounted video camera on a tripod and left it running. That freed me to take photographs. The burning experiments were carried out on cats and rabbits. The animal selected that day was a cat. Personally, I am more of a dog man than a cat man, but it clutched at my heart to see this poor creature strung out on the operating table.

I was a veteran of the animal rights movement, hardened to seeing animals in appalling circumstances. I was used to mingling with the hunting fraternity, people who by their own admission find the best of their fun seeing animals being ripped apart. I was used to being with men and women who whoop with glee when seeing animals suffer and die. I found myself in awe of Melody a kind, gentle and compassionate person who had the courage to put herself in the front line—in a laboratory to witness a perfectly healthy animal reduced to a bloody mess in the interests of science. At one stage I photographed Melody seated next to Professor Feldberg talking to him right in front of the dying tabby cat.

This was another example of the hard edge of undercover work. Many would be traumatised in such circumstances and run out screaming. Melody loathed the cruelty every bit as much but knew her only chance of stopping such cruelty was by steeling herself and helping to record what happened in the certain knowledge that doing so might end it.

From their detailed notes Feldberg and Stean recounted to us the fate of that cat. First anaesthetised at 9:30am his abdomen was then heated by the simple method of lowering a table lamp to just above the skin. Samples were taken periodically for measuring changes in blood sugar levels. Anyone who recalls replacing an old-fashioned light bulb just after it had blown knows how hot such a bulb became.

We discussed their enthusiasm for experimenting with cats. Professor Feldberg explained he liked working on cats as "*the constituency of the tissue is very much closer to human beings.*" John Stean injected the cautious thought: "*We're just living in hope that cats aren't in charge of heaven.*"

The cat died on the operating table at precisely 3:41pm. [The timings shown on the video recorded that day are out by an hour as the camera was set for British Summer Time and had not been changed] The cat was then dissected and his heart cut out. Finally, the torn body was picked up and dumped in a bag.

Professor Feldberg then invited all three of us for tea. We went to a very pleasant tea room in Mill Hill, Broadway. After all I had witnessed it seemed utterly surreal. I had to let my dietary preferences slip in such company. Professor Feldberg then invited us to his beautiful house nearby. He was an admirable host and delighted in showing us his valuable artwork collection including many pencil drawings.

Melody and I returned to the NIMR at the end of the following week, on Friday December 15th. The previous day I collected some prints of my photographs of the cat experiment to give to Professor Feldberg. My alarm shrieked long before dawn. I drove to Mill Hill and met Melody outside the NIMR at 9:45am. We went in at 10am as arranged, signed in and were met by John Stean who escorted us to the laboratory. That day they were experimenting on a rabbit, a long eared, lop-eared rabbit. I learned that breed was chosen because their long ears had easily accessible veins. I took video film, colour slides and black & white prints.

We arrived in time to see Mr Rabbit in his holding pen. He looked harmless and helpless. He was taken from his holding cage and given his first injection of the anaesthetic pentobarbitone sodium (Sagatal). Once anaesthetised the rabbit was tied, belly up, to the operating table. John Stean then used an electric razor to shave the abdomen of the rabbit, and neatly used a vacuum cleaner to suck the hairs away whilst doing so.

Rather than keep a hand-written log of the events witnessed I relied on the video camera that ran the whole time to provide the evidence and precise timings. The following incidents were recorded:

10:43-10:45: More Sagatal was given. The restrained rabbit jumped as Professor Feldberg attempted to inject Sagatal into a vein in the ear. Professor Feldberg was clearly having difficulty piercing the vein. He remarked: "*Can't see it, that's the trouble.*"

10:49-11:00: The technician, John Stean, attempted to string out the rabbit, to tie him to the operating table. The rabbit, that was supposedly anaesthetised, moved and screamed. More Sagatal was given.

11.09-11.22: They attempted to insert a venous cannula. The rabbit jumped. Eventually, after 13 minutes of efforts, the venous cannula is in place.

12.09-12.10: Questioned concerning legal changes resulting from the Animals (Scientific Procedures) Act 1986 and its effect on his work, Professor Feldberg replied: "*I don't know what the changes were.*"

12.18: I was keen to ascertain whether these scientists liaised with others doing similar work—so that there was no duplication of research effort (and waste of animals' lives). Asked what he knew about others doing similar research Professor Feldberg replied: "*I don't know because I never read other people's papers.*"

It was no surprise that at age 89 Professor Feldberg found this work onerous. At 12:48pm I noted he had fallen asleep at his desk—whilst the rabbit lay on his operating table.

13:21-13:23: The rabbit is burned when the lamp is lowered to just above his shaved abdomen. John Stean comments, "*There is a faint smell of cooking,*" then laughs.

Four thermometers were deployed on or in the rabbit to measure temperatures throughout the experiment. One was inserted into his anus, one in his abdomen, one just below his skin and another measured the temperature on the skin surface.

The temperatures recorded from the living rabbit were: Rectal: 38.8C; Visceral: 41.4C; Subcutaneous: 83.4C; Epidermal: 131.5C.

13:31—13:32: My video camera recorded the visibly scorched abdomen.
14:39: The rabbit was pronounced dead.

I left the NIMR at 3:45pm. I drove home to the company of Sue and our two young children. I was rather shell-shocked after the whole experience of the day. The later MRC inquiry said of that day: "*There was, possibly, a degree of avoidable pain.*"

I knew my evidence was priceless. For all the claims about research with animals being closely scrutinised and carefully managed to ensure the animals never feel any pain on just my second visit to the NIMR, one of our best laboratories, I had seen a rabbit struggling on the operating table and heard that same rabbit squealing in pain. Moreover, I had filmed what I had seen and could prove the cruelty. I knew that more evidence of a similar kind might enable us to stop those experiments. Though fully involved in other undercover work—particularly to expose hare coursing—I knew I had to commit every available resource to my work at the NIMR.

I asked Professor Feldberg if I could return to see more of his work. He invited me to see another experiment planned for the following week on Thursday December 21st. That was the day after the *News of the World* Christmas party that I attended. It meant I was already in London, staying at a hotel. It also meant that I had to be circumspect at the party and lay off the drink as I would need my wits about me the following morning. The one and only time in my life I was invited to a party for a National newspaper and I could barely drink. But I had crucial work to do.

My alarm woke me at 7am and I caught an early underground train to Mill Hill. Melody was unable to accompany me so that was my first visit on my own. I was at the front door of the NIMR at 9:45am and signed in as my usual scrawled Mike Hutchinson. Near to my real name but not exactly it. After my well-publicised involvement in the Smoking Beagles at ICI in 1975 and the Royal College of Surgeons affair in 1984-86 I thought I could hardly use my own name, but I was able later to use it.

It was another burning experiment on a rabbit. I took video film, colour slides and black & white photographs. Again my video camera was placed on a tripod and left to record the whole experiment. The following incidents were recorded:

11:09-11:16: Professor Feldberg used his scalpel to cut into the rabbits' leg to insert a venous cannula. The rabbit moved when cut. Professor Feldberg remarked, "*It is light.*"

He meant that the rabbit was lightly anaesthetised. Instead of giving the rabbit more anaesthetic he carried on using his scalpel. The rabbit moved again. Seeing this John Stean warned: "*I don't think you're going to get away with it Prof.*"

The restrained rabbit struggled furiously and then screamed. The rabbit was then given more Sagatal by injection. [This film sequence was later widely shown on television.]

When the rabbit screamed and struggled John Stean rushed to close the laboratory door. One can ponder why he did that. What is certain is that even with the door shut with my camera running the world at large would soon know what took place within.

11:48-11:50: Something was going wrong. John Stean looked at the rabbit and remarked: "*The belly looks distended Prof.*"

The rabbit lifted its head twice from the operating table. John Stean sees this and comments: "*Probably a bit on the light side Prof... .lifting its head a bit.*"

11:58-12:08: Something was now going seriously wrong. The rabbit was beginning to inflate and was dying. John Stean appeared baffled. He remarked: "*Something must be leaking, it must be.*"

The rabbit died before any experiment could be undertaken. The subsequent MRC inquiry noted the struggles of this rabbit (Report page 13) but made no observation in their findings as to it suffering. I left the NIMR at 12:30pm.

Christmas passed and I spent time in the hunting and coursing fields. In the New Year, 1990, Melody and I decided to take our investigation in a new direction by interviewing Professor Feldberg at his Mill Hill home. It was important to interview him outside the laboratory situation about his work. We had learned from media experts that for us to use our video film of him in his laboratory it would help to get him to sign an official Copyright Release form. Professor Feldberg was keen on this idea and invited us to meet him at his home on Friday January 5th 1990. I met Melody at 1pm in the car park of a nearby café and we interviewed Professor Feldberg at home for a couple of hours from 1:30pm. I had the properly worded release form and Professor Feldberg was pleased to sign it.

I asked to see another experiment and Professor Feldberg invited me back to the NIMR for his next on January 10th. Once again I was alone. I arrived at 9:45am and was met by Professor Feldberg. As he was the most respected and revered scientist in the building and I was his guest there was no question of my credentials being challenged. Scientists grew used to seeing me walk in laden with photographic equipment.

That was another burning experiment on a rabbit. Once again there were problems with administering the anaesthetic and with the rabbit struggling. The angle-poise lamp was first lowered over the abdomen of the anaesthetised rabbit at 14:38pm. Soon afterwards the rabbit kicked so violently in pain that all four thermometers were ejected. Professor Feldberg gave the rabbit more anaesthetic. The lamp was again lowered to just above the shaved abdomen.

I looked at the rabbit and saw part of his intestines were hanging out and were under the lamp. I pointed it out to John Stean and the intestines were pushed back in. The measured visceral temperature rocketed. It was too high to be measured by the scale of their thermometer. This rabbit died soon after 15:30pm. The MRC inquiry report about that day admitted the rabbit, "*probably suffered unnecessarily.*"

With rabbits squealing in pain, Professor Feldberg falling asleep, and the thermometers used unable to record the temperatures inflicted, it was clear that what I witnessed was both cruel and scientifically inept.

I resolved to complete our investigation as soon as possible. I needed to secure more evidence as I knew that mishaps on one or two days could be excused: it was a one-off mistake; Professor Feldberg had a migraine that day etc. I needed to show that, whatever the proclaimed brilliance of his youth, at age 89 Professor Feldberg was incapable of working humanely with animals.

I phoned Professor Feldberg repeatedly with a view to seeing further experiments in February and early March but without success. Some experiments were cancelled because John Stean was off sick. Then Professor Feldberg was away on holiday. At least no animals were dying whilst I was unable to film their suffering.

It was March 30th before I was invited back to the NIMR. On that day they tested the effects of an alpha-adrenergic blocker on the rabbit. There was no heating of the abdomen involved. The MRC inquiry later noted (page 13): "*One incident when a sample of blood is being obtained from the rabbit. It struggles, obviously distressed.*" They found that this rabbit suffered: "*a degree of avoidable pain.*"

Melody and I spent our time away from the laboratory trying to generate interest amongst big anti-vivisection groups in taking this project to completion. My fledgling ACIG had purchased the video camera and other equipment to secure the evidence but we lacked the contacts and political clout to ensure our investigation had the desired effect. We wanted the experiments ended and Professor Feldberg's licence to experiment taken away. If anyone had broken the law, we wanted them prosecuted. I was not being vindictive. I had paid dearly for being on the wrong side of the law and I wanted to put those who illegally abused animals in the dock.

I approached my colleague Les Ward, Director of the Scottish group Advocates for Animals. Les consulted his ruling body and they were happy to buy into our investigation. I spoke to Professor Feldberg and asked if I could bring a friend to see another experiment. Professor Feldberg kindly invited us back to the NIMR on April 5th 1990. During the whole investigation numerous people were taken to see Professor Feldberg at work. He seemed genuinely flattered by their interest.

Les Ward travelled down from Edinburgh. We met at Mill Hill East station at 10am and travelled together to the NIMR. I was equipped with my usual video camera and 35mm camera but I also took a new camera purchased with ACIG funds. That was a Bronica medium format film camera that produced professional results. I knew my open access to a vivisection laboratory could not last and I wanted to secure the best quality evidence. Another rabbit was used and killed, but it was purely a control experiment. There was no heating employed.

I made the long journey north to Edinburgh twice in April to visit Advocates for Animals to discuss the progress of this investigation; once on April 11th and again on April 19th/20th.

I returned to the NIMR for what turned out to be my final visit on Monday April 23rd 1990. Again I was on my own and again a rabbit was used. The following account is taken from the video record:

11:35-11:36: Professor Feldberg told me he was about to insert a tracheal cannula. I looked at the rabbit tied to the operating table and warned Professor Feldberg (using the language of the laboratory I had picked up): "*I think you'll need some more anaesthetic. It's a bit light.*" Professor Feldberg replied: "*Let me have a look.*" He promptly attempted to insert the cannula into the base of the neck of the rabbit. The restrained rabbit jumped. Professor Feldberg used his scalpel four more times. Each time the rabbit jumped. Professor Feldberg commented: "*I think we might get it without difficulty.*"

He then used surgical scissors to cut the rabbit. As he snipped the rabbit moved. As he continued snipping the rabbit constantly squirmed in pain and lifted his head off the table. This continued for some time as the rabbit moved violently.

Professor Feldberg poked his finger into the hole he had cut in the rabbit's neck. He then excised a bit of tissue. He used his scissors again and again the rabbit moved. More tissue was cut away. He snipped again and the rabbit attempted to get up. He snipped again and again following which there was a violent reaction from the rabbit. Professor Feldberg had reached beyond the chest wall and snipped away. The rabbit still moved. As the cannula is eventually tied on the rabbit struggled violently and jumped numerous times.

Later, when we were about to depart for lunch in the nearby staff room, I looked at the rabbit and commented that he had moved. John Stean looked and confirmed my report: "*I think it's a little on the light side possibly Prof.*"

The rabbit then attempted to get up kicking and struggling against the string that held him tight to the operating table. John Stean was alarmed: "*Yes, oh gosh, it's getting up Prof.*"

John Stean held the rabbit down and more Sagatal was injected. In the afternoon, when the lamp was lowered to the burn position, the rabbit again struggled. He died around 14:30pm. I left the NIMR for the last time just over an hour later.

Of these events the MRC report was unequivocal: "*Unnecessary suffering was caused to a rabbit on 23rd April 1990.*"

As a family we often cared for unwanted rabbits. Each had character. Handling rabbits in the laboratory I was struck by the poignancy of it all. As I stroked their fur and rubbed their ears I knew they would never again (if, as purpose-bred, they ever did) feel the earth beneath their feet. They would never chew grass or dandelions, never feel sun (or rain) on their backs. They would die before the day was out. I had risked my cover to save the rabbit that was not operated on, was just a control. I offered to buy him, but was told it was 'not allowed'.

We acquired other damning evidence. I recorded a telephone conversation with John Stean on the evening of Sunday April 29th 1990. John was quick to explain some of the problems of working with Professor Feldberg. Of his grant application John Stean observed: "*He was very naughty about his grant application.....he's a very obstinate man, and if he doesn't want to do something, or if he thinks he's done enough, it's almost impossible to move him with dynamite, you know."*

John went on: *"He is nearly ninety and though he has lost a lot of his mentality..um..he has lost none of his obstinacy."* [Laughs] I answered after joining in the laughter: *"It's like when you were trying to get him to read the papers."* [Scientific papers to see what his colleagues were doing] John answered: *"Oh he won't. Well as I was telling you I was determined he was going to get one, and I started to read it to him and he promptly went off to sleep."*

I had witnessed the reduced mental and physical abilities of Professor Feldberg. Animals suffered as a result. That was no surprise but I was shocked at the callous disregard shown by scientists at the NIMR for the well-being of their colleague. On April 23rd as he sat by his operating table I saw a pool of liquid on the floor beneath his stool. When Professor Feldberg stood up it was clear he had wet himself. The front of his trousers was soaked with strong smelling urine. John Stean confirmed on the telephone: *"I'm afraid he's incontinent."*

That explained why Professor Feldberg was reluctant to go that day to the staff room for lunch; he preferred to take lunch in his laboratory but that was not allowed. John Stean confirmed the episodes of incontinence happened, *"quite a lot."* John explained that on other days Professor Feldberg appeared unaware of his urine soaked trousers and was happy to visit the staff room.

I asked if the problem was the staff toilets were far away or was Professor Feldberg just not aware of urinating? John said toilets were not far away and it was hard to say what the problem was. He explained that when Professor Feldberg had his last bump in his car he gave up driving. John thought that with his incontinence and lack of mobility he might give up working but he was hanging on, *"literally like grim death."* John said many feared that to stop him working would be signing his death warrant.

On that April 23rd Professor Feldberg obeyed the rules and we all went to the staff room for lunch. His colleagues looked at him, sniggered, smelled the urine and walked out. Whilst I loathed him for the cruelty he inflicted on animals I felt for him as a fellow man. I was shocked that no-one had the courage to get him away from that situation. The scientific community gave Professor Feldberg a multitude of awards and honours, but no real care when he needed it.

We talked about their next experiment. They had planned one for the next morning but John told me he had persuaded Professor Feldberg to cancel to concentrate on answering a letter from the Home Office. He thought they might have experiments on the following Wednesday and Thursday. We discussed changes to the lamp and heating arrangements. They were being supplied with smaller rabbits and these were more vulnerable to harm from burning.

John Stean explained he wanted to reduce the temperature: *"We're getting somewhat smaller rabbits and it's possible that you know they're not standing up to it quite the same as the big ones, perhaps their area is relatively larger, but er you know I had another fight with him* [Professor Feldberg] *over that........cos when we did ten minutes at 80 degrees the rabbits didn't survive and er we repeated that and of course now I managed to get him down to five minutes but you see it hasn't survived that...."*

At times John Stean's frustrations with his colleague became evident: *"So you see this is why things are so slow because you know he is so obstinate....... it took me almost a month actually to get him to agree to use diluted anaesthetic because, you know, you've got much more margin of safety if you do it that way.... It's no good my pointing out to him that er..[I interject]..we've done this three times and the animals died every time, he has to come to that conclusion."*

John then elaborated more on their working problems after I asked if they had problems with cats standing up to the heat of the lamp: *"No, well some of them didn't, no, that that is true. But it it is difficult from my point of view because, in fact with this last time he said well let's write the paper together and well he had said that earlier and I said "Well look Prof. I make virtually no contribution to the scientific side of this whatever, I don't think we should" but with this last one I had had sort of a bit more to do with it and I agreed but, you know, one minute he treats you as though you are a sort of co-author, and next minute it's just as though you were, as I say, a junior technician from the fifties."*

I agreed: *"Yes. Yes".*

John Stean continued: *"It's quite incredible. You know he even snatched a pipette out of my hand the other day?"*

Mike Huskisson: *"Really?"*

John Stean: *"And I..I said to him 'Prof. Prof. this is absolutely ridiculous,' because you know we, we were going to take some some blood from the jugular vein, and he cut it and it pooled, and we were anxious to get a sample so that we had some sort of reading, and I seized a Pasteur pipette and started sucking it up, and he snatched it out of my hand, and of course by doing that he spurted. ... all the blood came out of the pipette of course, and I said to him "this is absolutely ridiculous Prof. you know after all these years and you still don't want me to do anything at all" and he said "Oh look here um you know remind me the next day we do an experiment and we'll.... .we'll of course make it different you know."*

I sympathised: *"I know...I mean..I I do feel for you John sometimes it's.."*

John Stean: *"Well no that wasn't, I wasn't sort of trying to gain.. to gain your sympathy for me or anything like that...."*

Mike Huskisson: *"No. . . no it's...."*

John Stean: *"It's just that people coming in as you have, and spending a good part of the day there, must wonder what the hell is (laughs) going on."*

Mike Huskisson: *"Well I can see it, you know, you're sort of saying to Prof. you know, it's.. it's a bit light, or it's light and this, and I mean.. it it's.., when really you'd like just to sort of top it up yourself. But.."*

John Stean: "*Yes. Yes.*"

Mike Huskisson: "*You know, um...*"

John Stean: "*Well I mean from... from my point of view that has been probably the most disappointing part of working with him over this last five years because so many of the sort of wrinkles and things that I've learnt, he won't accept any of them, none of them whatever.*"

Mike Huskisson: "*No*"

John Stean: "*It it is very frustrating, there are certain things that either he he never knew, or I think much more likely, he's simply forgotten, and you know I say them to him day after day after day,*" (laughs)

Mike Huskisson: "*I mean, isn't there anyone else........*"

John Stean: "*...it's just a waste of time it really is.*"

Mike Huskisson: "*And there's no-one else that you could have a word with that might say it to him that might sort of have an effect on him?*"

John Stean: "*No I don't think so..... and the last person in the lab he worked with was Gordon Bisset. They did a number of experiments together, but I think in the end Gordon decided that it, again this is in confidence, that it was just too difficult to work with him, you know.*" [Professor Bisset worked closely with Professor Feldberg for some 25 years.]

I noticed early in our investigation that Professor Feldberg asked Melody on several occasions who she was and what she was doing there.

Our discussion returned to the reply to the Home Office and I queried why they asked Professor Feldberg about recovery experiments:-

John Stean: "*I think they've got themselves a lit.....a little bit muddled up, you know, because er....*"

Mike Huskisson: "*Well it's almost as if they're talking about the earlier work he did isn't it?*"

John Stean: "*Yes. Yes you see they said it because you've got Phentolamine on every item of your licence and you say that the Phentolamine work has stopped but we conclude that all work on living animals has now stopped which is, I don't know how to describe it, (laughs) it's almost naive really. But then of course they are remote from it, aren't they?*"

Mike Huskisson: "*Yes.*"

John Stean: "*They're looking at bits of paper and er so....*"

I was later astonished to learn that Professor Feldberg's incontinence had been a problem for some time. When I referred to the problem of him going to use the staff room in urine soaked trousers John Stean said: "*As I say he um.. other days he's gone up there an an that hasn't prevented him from going up there you know so it's it might have been that time, but he's been up in there so often in that condition that we we've almost sort of got used to seeing him now, so I don't really know what can be done about it, I did speak to Gordon Bisset, because um you know he's not only a Professor of Pharmacology but he's medically qualified..,*"

Mike Huskisson: "*Mm*"

John Stean: "*You know, and er, he wasn't very forthcoming over it really.*" (laughs)

I then speculate about them doing something to help Professor Feldberg and John Stean agrees: "*But, you know, with this incontinence thing I I thought they'd have done something.. .I'm not a medical man but I really thought there were all sorts of devices that could be got...... Mind you on the other hand you see, knowing what Prof. is like, his Doctor may have.. (coughs).. .may have said well, you know, you can have this that and the other and he he may have refused it.*"

There was clearly a problem with Professor Feldberg following advice:-

John Stean: "*You see, I mean, coupled with two or three years ago he was prescribed er hydrotherapy er swimming in warm water and when he did it he he it seemed to do him a lot of good and he had a holiday in the Bahamas where he could swim in warm water and he was much better for it,*"

Mike Huskisson: "*Yes.*"

John Stean: "*But in the end he wasn't prepared to give up the um you know the time. It meant going over to Northwick Park and that sort of thing...*"

Mike Huskisson: "*Yea.*"

John Stean: "*He he just wouldn't, he, we're pretty sure he sort of signed himself off you know, he wouldn't do it.. .said it was a waste of experimental time.*"

Mike Huskisson: "*Very difficult isn't it?*"

John Stean: "*Oh it is quite a diffi. .. .and he is a very charming man, and extremely generous to the point......*"

Mike Huskisson: "*Yes, cert...*"

John Stean: "*He is a difficult man, there's no doubt about that.*"

Mike Huskisson: "*Mm. Well, I'll try and er get in one day before I go back um perhaps, well, I always give him a ring in the evening you know beforehand.*"

I speculated how the situation was allowed to continue:-

Mike Huskisson: "*Well one wonders really how the powers that be sort of. . . you know allow it to continue like that really?*"

John Stean: "*I suppose that the truth of the matter is really.. um.. they should have, they should have stopped it, probably last. . . last Autumn, something like that, you know.*"

Mike Huskisson: "*Yes. Well certainly there's been a change since... just since I've been going in.*"

John Stean: "*Oh yes.*"

Mike Huskisson: "*You know from December to now.*"

John Stean: "*Oh no he, there has been quite a deterioration in the last few months, there's no doubt about that..,*"

Mike Huskisson: "*Yes.*"

John Stean: "*. .I don't know, you can never tell can you but.. I.. if he deteriorated at the same rate I think it's quite on the cards that he won't*" be able to keep on working until September, I think we'll just have to wait and see, you know........I suppose you know what most people think now, apart from the Grants Committee is that now that it's sort of gone on for so long really um.. they just want nature to take its course I suppose..."

I asked about visits by Home Office Inspectors and whether they ever asked John Stean about the work.

Mike Huskisson: "*Well don't the Inspectors the Home Office Inspectors ever ask you, you know when they come round they ever ask anything about, you know, how things are going, or whether....?*"

John Stean: "*Well um this is strange because um the one before this one now er Dr Brouwer got on quite well with him. Prof. was a a much more.. his mind was much more adept.... and much more flexible and er he got on quite well with him er I think this lady now that has taken over um she did oh she did she came out once and he was certainly better than he is at the moment but of course the letters that we have got marked have come from her but...*"

Mike Huskisson: "*I mean does she stay there the whole time or does she just sort of..?*"

John Stean: "*Well, no, when, when they come out they usually have lots of people to see, you know......They don't just come for the one person, but she she spent er a fair bit of time with him but there was an Inspector before Dr Brouwer now he, we saw him oh it must have been at least two years ago and he, er that was when we were doing, regularly doing recovery animals, and he Prof. took him over to see everything and he, you know, cats with the venous cannulas and everything, and he he made a comment that, the Inspector to me afterwards, that Prof. had had great difficulty in getting the needle in the cannula, you know because of his eyesight and I said well he alwa.... he may appear like that.. but I said he always manages you know to cannulate them and so a little strange isn't it you know that this one, sort of three Inspectors ago, not not on his mental ability but on his physical ability, you know cos his eyesight wasn't very good, did notice that, but neither of the other two did an sort of picked that up really.*"

Mike Huskisson: "*But you'd have thou.. you'd have thought as he sort of gets into, you know, that sort of age they'd perhaps come round more regularly and sort of perhaps look more often, wouldn't you? And ask you as well?*"

John Stean: "*Yes.*"

Mike Huskisson: "*Because I mean you're you're the chap that works there with him the whole time.*"

John Stean: "*Yes.*"

Mike Huskisson: "*But er....*"

John Stean: "*Well of course under the old type of system that wouldn't be so, it's only since the new legislation has come in um.. that apparently I have to be a Project Holder but not, don't hold a Personal Licence. Apparently there has.. you know I do have to be a Project Licence Holder.*"

Mike Huskisson: "*Mm. And have they ever asked you about him at all?*"

John Stean: "*No, not really, not really.*"

Mike Huskisson: "*No?*"

John Stean: "*Well of course even though he's clearly in his dotage he he's still very dynamic and he, you may have no..., he's very jealous. You know he doesn't really like people asking me questions about the work.*"

Mike Huskisson: "*Yes.*"

John Stean: "*You know even if he's no longer capable of answering, because he's forgotten or he can't pull his thoughts together but he he you know he clearly resents it.*"

The call ended with me planning to phone on the Tuesday evening with a view to seeing further experiments on the Wednesday or Thursday. I never called as I had by then secured enough evidence to put an end to the experiments—great for the animals and good for Professor Feldberg.

With my work completed I handed the reins over to Les Ward and his colleagues at Advocates for Animals. Les Ward painstakingly viewed the many hours of videotapes, taking detailed notes from each. He compiled a report for Advocates for Animals. The matter was raised at the Animal Procedures Committee meeting on May 3rd 1990. The Home Office immediately revoked the Personal Licences of Professor Feldberg and John Stean. The Project Licence was surrendered to the Home Office. It was less than 5 months after my initial visit to the NIMR.

On May 9th Advocates for Animals publicised the investigation. It was widely reported in the printed media and on television, sometimes with powerful headlines such as: "*Scientist's licence revoked after illegal experiments*" (*The Scotsman* May 10th 1990)

It was no surprise when this caused outrage to the public and consternation to the scientific community. There were demands for the scientists and for the NIMR to be prosecuted, the Home Office inspectors to be sacked and the need for any future use of animals in research to be closely scrutinised by independent experts.

Media coverage brought other facts to light. The *London Standard* May 9th 1990 reported that Home Office Inspectors had made 14 visits to check on Professor Feldberg's work in 1989 alone. That made his laboratory one of the most closely scrutinised and supervised of any in this country. John Stean revealed that incompetence by Professor Feldberg had been detected years before the work ended. Was it a matter of allowing cruelty to continue so long as it remained out of public view?

Professor Feldberg and John Stean believed my video film was to be used as a teaching aid for students in America. Professor Feldberg surely performed his best for my camera. If we had used a hidden camera what incompetence might we then have recorded? Furthermore, just what suffering occurred when we were not there?

Vivisection survives thanks to enforced public ignorance. The public invariably, in one way or another, funds such cruelty, and frequently suffers from the side-effects of inaccurate and haphazard animal studies. Public funding demands public accountability. People have a right to know what happens in research laboratories.

When this investigation was first publicised and my name was associated with it, it was not long before journalists warned me that I was being accused of stealing documents and other items from the laboratory. It was a cheap shot from beleaguered scientists. I had taken nothing other than knowledge.

Melody MacDonald, the instigator of this investigation was intelligent, articulate and photogenic, so she was highly sought after for interview. She spoke at length to the *Sunday Express* on May 13th 1990: *"He was using three perfectly healthy animals a week when I met him — and by the end of the experiments, when they were killed, they were mutilated beyond belief.*

I asked him many times if he liked animals. He didn't really come back to me on that much — I don't think they interest him.

But he does have a peculiar fascination with cats. When the cat was on the operating table, he used to call it 'Her Majesty'. I formed the impression that they are his favourite research tool.

I wondered what effect this kind of work has on the people who do it day after day. I learned very quickly that if I was going to witness an experiment, which I did on my very first visit, you had to curb your natural emotions and be very detached. It was no good bursting into tears or getting over-excited — I wouldn't have learned anything. I had to slot into that part.

But my original thought, which was confirmed by the experience, is that this kind of work is totally archaic in today's world of sophisticated computer technology and biochemical testing.

I think it is very unscientific and can be misleading. It may inhibit progress to focus on animals in this way, blinkering doctors as to the real causes of human illness.

I also believe it is immoral. I don't believe good can come from evil, and vivisection is an evil practice. I don't think God put creatures on this earth to be experimented on — and if we break God's laws, nature eventually shows us the error of our ways with disasters such as mad cow disease.

It is important for everybody to know what is going on. Vivisection won't be abolished in five minutes — but while it is still being practised, we should do all we can to alleviate suffering."

The worldwide scientific community rallied to support Professor Feldberg. The following letter was published by *Nature*, Volume 345 21 June 1990:-

"*Animal experiments*

SIR—We write to protest strongly against the article by Peter Aldhous (**Nature** *345, 190; 1990). We are all former colleagues of Professor Wilhelm Feldberg from soon after he succeeded Sir Lindor Brown as head of the division of physiology and pharmacology at the National institute for Medical Research, formerly directed by Sir Henry Dale. We have* *known and admired the work Feldberg has carried out for nearly 70 years, over 50 of them in this country. We offer no comment about the allegations reported; we have not seen the 'evidence'. We would merely say that it is difficult to believe that a man so kind and gentle, so careful and meticulous over his experiments, could conceivably be guilty of deliberate cruelty to any animal or any human being.*

We object first to the lack of any adverse comment on the behaviour of the two people who offered 'evidence' to the Advocates for Animals. It is indeed typical of Feldberg's kindness and consideration that he was ready to invite them into his laboratory. Nature does in fact refer to "deception" and "pretence"; but it is difficult to imagine a sorrier tale of lies, fraud and deceit than is to be found in the two years' effort of Miss MacDonald and the five months' effort of Mr Huskisson. As to any alleged contravention of the 1986 act, it is perhaps worthy of note that it took them a remarkably long time to obtain, or to report, any 'evidence'.

Our second objection is that there is no Indication in the article of the very great value of the absolutely fundamental contributions made by Feldberg. These have been first in our understanding of allergy, and then in establishing chemical transmission at the adrenal gland, the neuromuscular junction and the ganglionic synapse, and more generally in developing the concept of neurohumoral transmission at synapses and by neurons of central origin. He is held in high regard and affection by the scientific world, recognized among other ways by his Royal Medal and his CBE.

'The only mention in **Nature** *of Feldberg's distinction is in relation to the possibility that it may have exempted him from proper monitoring. The first mention made of him refers to him simply as "an 89-year-old researcher". This is a sad lack of understanding of a lifetime of brilliant pioneering scientific work.*

We would have expected **Nature** *to have given a more balanced account of this most unfortunate incident, to have shown a very much more sympathetic attitude towards a great man of biomedical science, and to have condemned out of hand the disgusting methods used to collect the 'evidence' against him, which disfigure the animal welfare movement.*

W.W. DOUGLAS & J.M.RITCHIE
Department of Pharmacology. Yale University School of Medicine, New Haven, Connecticut 06510 USA
JOHN GRAY
The Laboratory, Citadel Hill, Plymouth PL1 2PB, UK
W.D.M.PATON
13 Staverton Road, Oxford OX2 6XH, UK
PERRY OF WALTON
The Open University in Scotland, 60 Melville Street, Edinburgh EH3 7HF, UK"

There were follow up articles. A feature titled: "*Animal experiments: the sickening truth is revealed*" was printed in *Take a Break* (Issue 35, September 1st 1990). The power of the video camera to bring about change was highlighted in an article titled: "*Camcorder Crusades. Two animal rights campaigners use camcorders to gather evidence*" published in *Camcorder User* November 1990. [Sam LaBudde, whose work highlights the plight of dolphins, was the other animal rights campaigner profiled]

The MRC who funded the NIMR set up an inquiry. I was asked to give evidence and agreed provided that I could record my contribution. The MRC accepted. On Wednesday September 26th 1990 at 2pm I gave evidence at their inquiry in London. That was four years and one day after I was jailed for securing the evidence of cruelty inflicted on animals by the Royal College of Surgeons. The MRC inquiry was no court of law but having been in the dock so often myself I welcomed the opportunity to tell scientific leaders the reality about their mistreatment of animals.

The MRC inquiry published their report on February 4th 1991. In addition to those already mentioned other findings of interest were:

"*Professor Feldberg: When the Professor started his experiments of heating the abdomen of animals, that work was not covered by the project licence. That was a breach of the Act. After the point had been drawn to his attention, he, nevertheless, continued with one or two more experiments. That was a deliberate breach of the Act.* [This related to the burning experiments carried out by Professor Feldberg between mid-1989 and September 19th 1989 when his project licence was amended] *On a number of occasions he failed to maintain an adequate level of anaesthetic. That constituted an inadvertent breach of his personal licence conditions. It also meant that the work was unauthorised by the project licence.*

The Home Office: The Home Secretary failed to weigh adequately the likely benefit of the research against the likely adverse effects on the animals involved, as he is required to do under Section 5(4) (of the 1986 Act). If he had done so, it is reasonably certain that the amendment to the project licence which allowed the heating of animals' abdomen would not have been granted."

That was the summary finding. In the body of the report their criticism of the Home Secretary was sharper. This was on page 21:-

"*In fact, Professor Feldberg's application for a M.R.C. grant for these experiments was not submitted until 1st December 1989. Although a decision was delayed, the project never received M.R.C. approval.*
We find it difficult to understand, in these circumstances, how the Home Secretary could have met the requirements of Section 5(4) when he granted this project licence and its amendment. He is required to weigh the benefit likely to accrue - in our view, negligible - against the likely adverse effects on the animals concerned.
Those effects — certain rather than likely — were extremely adverse. The animals died."

Regarding Home Office Inspectors there was a difference of opinion between the Inquiry team and the Inspectors as to the role of the latter. This was from page 36 of the report:-

"*The Home Secretary has a team of Inspectors who make unannounced visits to various establishments and are in a position to advise the Home Secretary in relation to the various authorities he is empowered to issue, amend, or refuse. We ascertained that these visits to the N.I.M.R. averaged one each month. We also ascertained, that over a comparatively short period, staff changes resulted in three different inspectors being used.*

These Inspectors were involved with the work of Professor Feldberg in various ways. He had held a personal licence or its earlier equivalent for over fifty years.

The Inspectors told us that they did not see their role as being involved in uncovering improper laboratory procedures. Their concern was to ensure that, at each licensed establishment, all the statutory appointments had been made and that proper controls in relation to the use of animals were in operation.

We take a different view having regard to the provisions of Sect 18(2) (c) and (d) of the Act which stipulate the following duties:

c) "to visit places where regulated procedures are carried out for the purpose of determining whether those procedures are authorised by the requisite licences and whether the conditions of those licences are being complied with;

d) to visit designated establishments for the purpose of determining whether the conditions of the certificate in respect of the establishments are being complied with."

The Inquiry team were pointed in their findings:-

"*The Home Office Inspectors failed to comply with their statutory duties when they did not act as promptly and effectively as they should have done when they were becoming increasingly aware of difficulties involving Professor Feldberg. The publicity forced them to take the action which they should have taken much earlier.*"

The MRC Inquiry considered the suitability of using Sagatal as an anaesthetic. They concluded that rabbits are difficult to anaesthetise because there is a very narrow margin between an inadequate dose and a fatal dose. They accepted there were other preferable anaesthetics but Sagatal had been widely used for a long time and was approved by the Home Office.

The MRC Inquiry also considered the question: "*Was the Project Justified?*" The Grants Committee of the MRC considering the project grant application put the application out to three independent experts for their opinion. The following is an extract from page 19 of the report:-

"*Not unusually they were sharply divided in their advice. One regarded it as "of considerable importance" and praised the simplicity of the experiment, a point echoed by a second supporting referee. The third adviser, however, saw the project quite differently. This adviser felt the project indicated ignorance of the mass of work already done on the effect of burns. He dismissed the aims of the work as "of no importance" and catalogued the published work which, he inferred, would simply be* duplicated. These views were carefully considered by the Grants Committee. Having taken into account all factors, eventually, the application was rejected.

In the meantime, the Home Office, which had already granted a project licence in respect of earlier work, had now amended that licence to cover the new project involving the heating of rabbits' abdomen.

This situation, i.e. of rejection by the M.R.C. and approval by the Home Office is not necessarily a paradox. A project could meet the criteria of the Home Office as set out in Section 9 of the Animals (Scientific Procedures) Act and yet be turned down by the M.R.C. simply because its limited funds had to go to other activities.

However, in this case, the rejection by the M.R.C. would appear to have been based on the view that the work would only cover matters already well researched and documented.

The methodology of this project must also be considered. We were able to view the work which was filmed. It had been praised by one assessor for its "simplicity". However, Dr Michael Fox of the Humane Society of the United States, who, at the suggestion of Melody MacDonald, actually visited the Laboratory, described the experiment as "crude if not absurd". Our view is that, applied to the methodology, the word "crude" is not inappropriate."

The MRC report drew this response from the Home Office in Hansard March 11th 1991 in a written answer to a Parliamentary Question:-
"Mrs. Rumbold: The Home Office accepts the Medical Research Council inquiry report's finding that, as a result of a failure by Professor Feldberg and Mr Stean to maintain anaesthesia of sufficient depth, up to four rabbits were caused avoidable suffering.

Primary responsibility for ensuring that procedures regulated by the Animals (Scientific Procedures) Act 1986 are carried out properly at an establishment lies with the holder of the certificate of designation. In the light of the report, officials have discussed with the certificate holder for the National Institute for Medical Research proposals for improving the management, control and monitoring of animals procedures at the institute, which he is now considering. We have also asked the MRC for the evidence of the alleged deliberate breaches of the Act referred to in the report.

As for the two recommendations contained in the report relating to the Home Office, initial proposals have been put to the Animal Procedures Committee about the position of aging licensees and we shall consider what action may be necessary when the committee has completed its consideration of the issues arising from this case.

We do not accept the recommendation in the report for an increase in the number of animal (scientific procedures) inspectors. Although the report suggests that inspectors should be more closely involved in monitoring the treatment of animals during experiments, this is principally the responsibility of personal licensees, who have a duty under the law for the *care of their animals. It would be impractical to expect inspectors to be present whenever animal procedures are carried out."*

The political attack led to legal changes that effectively ended geriatric scientists experimenting on animals in the UK. But there were no prosecutions for the crimes. *Veterinary Record* January 4th 1992:-
"Parliament

No prosecution in Feldberg case

THE Home Office has decided not to refer to the Director of Public Prosecutions the cases involving Professor Wilhelm Feldberg and his technician Mr John Stean at the National Institute of Medical Research. Mrs Angela Rumbold, Minister of State at the Home Office, told the Commons in a written reply on December 10 that it did not consider that there were grounds to justify such a referral.

Mrs Rumbold said that the Home Office had accepted that up to four rabbits had been caused avoidable suffering in experiments at the centre because of the failure by the two men to maintain anaesthesia of sufficient depth (see VR, February 9, 1991, p120).

However, as soon as it was clear that avoidable suffering had been caused to animals, the Home Office had taken action to remove the personal and project licences held by Professor Feldberg and Mr Stean, thus ensuring that they did no further work involving the use of living animals.

While there was prima facie evidence that there had been breaches of the Animals (Scientific Procedures) Act 1986, it was considered that, in the light of all the circumstances of the case, including the effective administrative action already taken, no further purpose would be served by asking the Director of Public Prosecutions to consider prosecution.

Home Office officials had discussed with the certificate holder for the National Institute for Medical Research proposals for improving management, control and monitoring of animal procedures, following the Medical Research Council report on the case. Those improvements had now been implemented and the chief inspector of the Home Office Animals (Scientific Procedures) Inspectorate had written to all certificate holders reminding them of their responsibilities under the 1986 Act.

The Home Secretary had agreed, following the 1990 report of the Animal Procedures Committee, not to grant project licences to those aged over 70 except in exceptional circumstances, and that personal licences should be reviewed when it was known that a holder had retired. Where personal or project licences were held by people over 70, they would be reviewed every 12 months. The revised procedures, agreed by the committee, would be introduced in April 1992."

It seemed they could not prosecute anyone without first charging Professor Feldberg and at 89 he was judged too old to face the rigours of cross-examination. Many judged that if he was capable of experimenting on animals he was capable of justifying his actions to a court. However, the power of the video camera was proven. Without one there would have been no change for the animals and most likely have seen me back in court.

After all the publicity we came under considerable pressure to release the addresses of Professor Feldberg and John Stean. I refused. Their work was over; their experiments were ended; our job was done. As it stood the names Feldberg and the NIMR were a laughing stock, a symbol of incompetence, callousness and casual cruelty. No-one involved in the investigation wanted to see demonstrations outside the homes of Feldberg or Stean that would turn them from villains to victims. I pleaded: "*He is 89 years old. How can any protest against him make him anything other than the victim? It is the animals who are the victims—let's not shift the sympathy from them to him.*" Colleagues saw the sense of this.

There were many criticisms of my investigative work. It was claimed that for all the hours of videotape I recorded only a few minutes showing animals suffering However the camera was set to run throughout the day— it was not just a matter of my picking it up to film when something significant happened. In addition, whilst it was only a few minutes, for the animals suffering that was long enough.

It was also pointed out that my film only showed four occasions when rabbits suffered. I was in the laboratory on just seven days: one day to film a cat being experimented on and six days to film rabbits. There was no heating of the abdomen involved on either March 30th or April 5th. Of the six rabbits that I filmed the MRC Inquiry found there was certainly unnecessary suffering caused to one, probably unnecessary suffering caused to another and possibly avoidable pain caused to two others.

Curiously, the day that caused the most public outrage when shown on television, when the rabbit struggled violently on December 21st, merited no adverse comment from the Inquiry. So, four out of the six rabbits that I filmed suffered adversely. I wonder what happened to the animals I was not there to film?

Critics also questioned why we took so long to conclude our investigations. I first visited the NIMR on December 7th 1989. Thereafter the experiments were sporadic. There were closures over Christmas and the New Year. In February and March there was a lengthy period when John Stean was off with 'flu and another when Professor Feldberg was on holiday. It was not until the incidents filmed on April 23rd 1990 that I felt we had secured the evidence required to end the work, rather than merely protest against it. Ten days later the matter was raised at the Animal Procedures Committee and the experiments ended. It would have been far quicker and infinitely better if the experiments had been ended internally when a Home Office Inspector or fellow scientist first realised they were going woefully wrong but that never happened.

As to any medical benefits coming from it all I asked Professor Feldberg and John Stean if there was any interaction with those suffering from diabetes; whether their experimental work might be guided by clinical feedback but this did not seem to happen. I once jokingly suggested the main finding might be that if you suffered from diabetes you should not take a hot water bottle to bed—and they laughed.

Professor Wilhelm Feldberg died on October 23rd 1993, nearly 3½ years after our investigation put an end to his experimenting with animals. Far from killing him, our ending such work saved many animals from unnecessary suffering, and probably gave him a new lease of life.

In one sense Professor Feldberg was unlucky—or got what he deserved depending on your viewpoint. He could have worked in any of the best laboratories anywhere in the world but he ended up in the NIMR. He spent his dotage amongst so-called friends and colleagues who accepted seeing him walking around in clothing soaked with his own urine. It is hard to imagine any other working environment that could be so callous to any employee let alone such an aged and revered figure. However, the NIMR is a huge employer where animals are killed by the thousands for research—empathy has by definition to be virtually non-existent.

Advocates for Animals quickly produced the campaigning video *Exposed* that showed the key video clips from our investigation. Later the excellent book *Caught in the Act* [Jon Carpenter Publishing ISBN 1-897766-05-x] that detailed the Feldberg investigation by Melody MacDonald was published in 1994. It was compiled and edited by Jill Russell and carried a foreword by Dr Michael Fox.

CHAPTER SEVEN
Other animal welfare issues

The ACIG was created to investigate all forms of cruelty to animals, primarily in the UK, but I envisaged working with colleagues in nearby countries. We took on a variety of projects listed here in alphabetical order.

Faroe Islands expedition

In the summer of 1990 the ACIG was pleased to support LACS, Care for the Wild, and British Divers Marine Life Rescue (BDMLR), in a joint investigation into the killing of whales and dolphins in the Faroe Islands, part of Denmark. I worked with my best man, Alan Knight, Chairman of the BDMLR, his partner Liz Varney, an accomplished photographer and journalist, plus an excellent team from BDMLR.

On Tuesday August 7th I caught the London train then flew from Heathrow to the Faroe Islands via Copenhagen. Alan and Liz had travelled with the advance party. They drove a van towing a fast rigid-inflatable boat (RIB) and caught the ferry from Scrabster near Thurso to Torshavn in the Faroes. They endured a very rough crossing in a Force 9 gale. When I flew in Alan met me at Vagar airport and we caught the ferry back to Vestmanna where the team had hired a house. Alan set up our cover story. We posed as a dive club on a summer holiday to the Faroes. Alan had written to several dive clubs there and his exchange of correspondence with them helped to allay suspicions as to our true intentions.

Early in the morning of Wednesday August 8th, we took our boat out but it was too rough to make a planned visit to check sites on Mykines. In the afternoon we drove out and visited a fish farming enterprise. The value of such a business was made clear when we saw a helicopter being used to ferry fish—in something akin to a large tea urn—from one site to another because of pollution.

Ecological damage is one of the main problems caused by intensive fish farming. Large numbers of fish are confined in the nets. These fish are fed and not all food given is eaten. Food that is eaten comes out the other end. The fish are dosed with chemicals to try to prevent diseases. The fish also suffer in ways not thought—with the nets being shallow the fish cannot dive deep enough to avoid the rays of the sun and are thus prone to getting skin cancer.

We visited sites where whale kills had been reported. We talked to locals but found them suspicious of strangers. At that time, even in August, few tourists visited the Faroes. English people were suspected of being there only to investigate the killing of whales and dolphins.

Other groups had exposed such slaughters as being truly horrific. The idea was to herd a pod of marine mammals into a shallow bay and kill them all. To do that was surprisingly easy—once man had taken advantage of the protective instincts deep in such mammals. With the pod trapped in a bay all they had to do was inflict a deep bleeding wound on one and the others would not leave their stricken colleague. Slaughtering all was then easy. The sea would turn to blood. Disturbing images show young children encouraged to wade about in the gore.

The Faroe Islands in 1990 were awash with money. Their fishing industry was immensely profitable. The whale and dolphin kill was not needed for money or for food—it just seemed a tradition the islanders were determined to maintain, regardless of what outsiders thought.

Friday August 10th was a day for information gathering. We chatted to mariners in the harbours seeking information about whale or dolphin kills. We spent the evening socialising on a docked Danish fisheries protection ship. We repeated our story that we were a group of divers on holiday—and with our fast boat and plenty of diving equipment we certainly looked the part. When we first approached in our RIB they asked us where we came from. Our reply "*The UK*" elicited the amazed response, "*What! In that?*" The Captain of the Navy ship invited us on board for drinks in his cosy boardroom. Much drink was flowing and it was strong liquor. It was impossible to miss a round without appearing antisocial—and we needed to be very sociable. At one point a minor disagreement nearly flared into something more serious but the situation was defused.

We had a local informant. On Saturday August 11th, he told us a pod of 50 North Atlantic white-sided dolphins were killed at Kollafjordur on the island of Streymoy two or three days before. We immediately drove to the site and found pools of blood on the quayside and saw dolphin heads bobbing about on the floor of the bay. It was a distressing sight.

We filmed and photographed what we could but it was not long before our actions attracted the attention of locals. They stormed round and were far from friendly. We protested our innocence but only just escaped. We drove out to the accompaniment of vigorous banging on the sides of our van. For Alan, Liz and I it reminded us of our days as active hunt saboteurs.

We made a film to contrast the stark, memorable beauty of the islands with the horrors inflicted upon their wildlife. On Monday August 13th with the land approach too risky we decided to make full use of our boat and diving equipment to get better film of the dead dolphins at Kollafjordur. Two experienced divers—Alan Knight and John McGuinness—put on full diving kit and armed themselves with underwater cameras. Our plan was to roar into the bay; put our divers in to retrieve and or film the dolphin heads then leave before any locals could get out in boats to stop us.

We looked like a squad from the Special Boat Service. The similarity ended at the looks. We raced in at full speed, stopped and our divers rolled backwards off the sides—in Special Forces style—and promptly stood up. The water was that shallow. We retrieved two torn and bloody dolphin heads; filmed and photographed them and left before any locals could react.

We took our heads elsewhere to record them in more detail. We spent the rest of our trip touring likely bays, chatting with our informant and others to ascertain information about kills. On Thursday August 16th I caught the flight home. I had problems getting my films hand-searched by security rather than passed through what at that time were powerful X-ray machines that many believed could damage films.

Tuesday August 21st, I met Liz Varney, and BDMLR colleagues Ray Gravener (the National Director) and Jim Hayes in London. We tried to interest ITN and other media outlets in our Faroes investigation that proved dolphins were killed as well as whales. Most declined as media interest was elsewhere. The Iraq War had started with the Iraqi Army's invasion of Kuwait on August 2nd.

We secured some media coverage. Next day, August 22nd, the *Daily Star* ran a half page report with pictures taken by Liz. Questions were asked about the legality of the kill at Kollafjordur. We later learned that 12 people involved in that kill, that had taken place without the permission of the local authorities and in an unregistered bay, were prosecuted and each heavily fined.

Alan and Liz carried on with their work to protect marine life. Sunday December 5th 1993 was fascinating. I met them in Lowestoft and accompanied them to check over a ship they were looking to buy. She was purchased and renamed the *Ocean Defender*. On Monday June 13th 1994, I photographed her setting off down the Thames and under Tower Bridge. *Ocean Defender* was used to promote marine conservation and help in the rescue of marine animals after the *Sea Empress* oil spill off Milford Haven in February 1996. Alan became Chief Executive Officer at International Animal Rescue in 1999.

Fox ecology–facts not fiction

When I started campaigning for animals in the late 1960s the RSPCA was heavily infiltrated by fox hunters, factory farmers and other assorted animal abusers. They ensured the RSPCA was vocal for cats and dogs but said little about wildlife or farmed animals. That changed during the 1970s, thanks to campaigning by people like John Bryant and Richard Ryder who supported the RSPCA Reform Group, set up in 1970. The RSPCA returned to its origins—campaigning to alleviate cruelty to all animals.

Colleagues sought to improve the image of the unjustly maligned fox. This native species is an asset in our countryside—a predator of genuine agricultural pests. Yes, vulnerable livestock such as caged hens need to be protected, but that is easily done with suitable netting.

In the early 1980s colleagues Graham and Lyn Cornick at their Hydestile Wildlife Hospital near Godalming, led the way promoting an accurate understanding of wildlife, in particular the fox. I visited Graham and Lyn on Tuesday June 12th 1984 and photographed their rescued foxes. Years later, Tuesday July 9th 1991, Sue and I took two of our children to see the wonderful work done at Hydestile. I photographed *Misty* (see front cover of this book). In the 1990s when Trevor Williams left the LACS staff he set up the Fox Project to foster better understanding of foxes. John Bryant, when he left his League employment, promoted living in harmony with nature and where required the humane deterrence of wildlife, such as foxes, perceived to cause problems in the urban environment.

Welfarists seeking to spread the facts about our relationship with wildlife have faced real problems from opponents spreading fiction. Our media has delighted in fox scare stories. The hunting fraternity accused me of faking photographs and video. Whereas my images are genuine, hunters have been caught using faked photographs. In the autumn of 1994 2500 posters appeared on farmland besides roads showing a fox 'attacking' a chicken with the claim that was a 'country problem' for which foxhunting was the 'country solution'. The LACS exposed the truth in a feature *"Hunters Use Faked Photos In Anti-Fox Campaign"* in *Wildlife Guardian*, Issue 27, Winter 1994. An expert reported the fox looked to be stuffed and the hen-run was hastily erected for the image, as the grass in the run was lush (anyone keeping hens knows they soon degrade grass).

The BFSS angrily denied the LACS allegations. However, the following issue of *Wildlife Guardian* (28) reported that the Frank Lane Picture Agency, which supplied the photograph to the BFSS, admitted to the *Darlington and Stockton Times*: *"It was set up. The fox had been captured and then let out with the chicken behind the wire."* They claimed the photograph was ten years old. Had it been taken within the six months time limit, the League would have considered prosecuting those involved under the 1911 Protection of Animals Act for cruelly terrifying a hen.

Fur Farming

In September 1990 I took ACIG investigative techniques north to a fox fur farm near Halifax. An animal rights group, experts in this field, had contacted the ACIG. They had accumulated a great deal of evidence as to the workings of this fur farm but needed good photographic material to interest the national media. My ACIG was pleased to help.

Saturday September 29th 1990 produced memorable images. I met Chris Aston and a lad named Bob near the farm at Ovenden Wood, Halifax. They showed me the layout and I took photographs and video which enabled the group to interest *The People* newspaper who did their own work and on October 14th 1990 published a centre page spread about the farm. There was editorial comment as well.

The next month whilst working in Scotland with Les Ward we tried to find the mink farm at Penicuik. We located the site and photographed rows of sheds but on closer examination they were all empty. We found a neighbour and asked about the mink farm. We learned it had closed the previous year 'under pressure from animal rights people'.

Mark Glover from Lynx, a leading campaigner opposed to the fur trade, was concerned about a cottage industry of raising chinchillas for their fur that was growing up around Britain. Chinchillas were often offered for sale for breeding in classified advertisements in local papers.

On Saturday May 11th 1991 I caught the train to Nottingham. Mark met me at the station and we visited a garden centre that sold chinchillas as pets. Chinchillas were also raised on a more commercial basis.

The following month, June 7th, I wrote to Fred Duggins, a leading breeder of chinchillas—he had 30 years' experience and was Vice Chairman of the Chinchilla Fur Breeders' Association. I posed as a man looking to expand my business interests and keen to see how his chinchilla business operated from his farm in Clent in the West Midlands. I expressed an interest in purchasing a breeding stock plus cages and ancillary equipment.

Fred sent me a hand-written reply on June 12th. He warned me of the pitfalls in rearing chinchillas and invited me to view his operation. I wrote again at the end of June and fixed to meet in late summer. That was a busy time—it was the height of the Quorn Foxhounds investigation. On Sunday September 22nd 1991, I telephoned Fred and arranged to meet him at his farm at 11am the following morning.

Fred and Joan Duggins lived in splendour. Their farm was high on a hill with a swimming pool in the front patio. The chinchillas were housed in a single wooden building to the side of the main farm house. Fred was welcoming. He described his chinchilla business as a profitable side-line.

He started with chinchillas in 1958. He said they had endured difficult times, sometimes losing up to 40 animals to disease. He reckoned vets charged too much and knew little about chinchillas anyway so to keep the animals profitably you had to be able to do much of that side yourself. He explained that at the time he had 200 breeding females. He was proud of his sophisticated computerised record keeping that detailed breeding, illnesses, show records etc.

Fred sold his pelts through Denmark, and warned me that I would need to buy a licence to do so. I was then taken on a guided tour of their chinchilla house. The house was well ventilated and insulated with temperatures maintained within certain limits. The chinchillas were played Radio 2 day and night to accustom them to noise. Fred warned me of many expenses I would need to meet to keep and breed chinchillas successfully. His animals were housed in individual wire cages with linking tunnels that allowed males to move from cage to cage to mate. The females wore a collar that stopped them using the tunnel.

Some females were with young. Fred was proud of breeding near white chinchillas. The cages were stacked in three tiers. They were cleaned out every week, a job that took a day. There was no smell or any evidence of any illness or disease. The caging appeared small. Each had a piece of wood for the inmate to chew on. Fred was knowledgeable and articulate. He did not try to lure me into buying animals at great expense. He was at pains to stress the time and expense needed to keep them 'properly'.

For chinchillas, value was in their fur. Unless near perfect they lost value. Animals poorly cared for lost value. Care may have been good but the cruelty lay in the deprivation of liberty and consequent denial of their birthright. There was also real concern that garden shed operations would not maintain the high standards required. Wild chinchillas live in colonies in the Andes mountains of South America. Hunting for their fur has driven chinchillas to the point of being critically endangered in the wild.

I secured words and images but the media were not interested unless I also supplied pictures of chinchillas being killed. I might have been able to secure such photographs or video. Fred was open about killing (he broke their necks) and pelting his animals. I could have told him I needed such images to show my employees how to kill and pelt chinchillas. But in moral terms to do so was to cross the line and was never possible. I could never have animals killed simply to make a story. Without images of killing, the media lost interest.

Most fur farming involved mink. On Saturday August 24th 1996 I checked out an old mink farm at Brome in Suffolk. I confirmed it was disused and derelict. Such farming was profitable for some. On Sunday September 1st 1996 I photographed the thriving mink farm belonging to Britain's biggest fur farmer, Mike Cobbledick, at East Youlstone, Devon. It was one of the most fortified sites I ever encountered.

Throughout the 1990s, increasing pressure from groups like Lynx/Respect for Animals, and the Coalition to Abolish the Fur Trade, swung public opinion ever more against the fur trade. Respect for Animals produced particularly memorable posters. Their image of a woman trailing a fur coat leaking blood with the slogan: "*It takes up to 40 dumb animals to make a fur coat. But only one to wear it.*" was unforgettable.

My own slogan: "*Fur coats are worn by beautiful animals and ugly people!*" proved popular on clothing, badges and car stickers.

In August 1997 I spoke at a couple of events against mink farming. The first on Tuesday August 19th was at a public meeting called by the Newcastle Animal Rights Coalition at the Memorial Hall, Ponteland. The second was on Sunday August 31st—the day when we woke to the news that Princess Diana and Dodi Fayed had been killed in a car crash. I met my colleague Lawrie Payne at Maningtree station and we drove to the South Dorset Anti Bloodsport Society demonstration against the mink farm at Child Okeford. I spoke briefly at the meeting outside the farm.

Continuous public pressure from campaigning groups generated the public anger that was translated into political pressure and ultimately political action. Fur farming in England and Wales was banned by the Fur Farming (Prohibition) Act of 2000. Under that all fur farms in England and Wales had to close by January 1st 2003. Although there were no fur farms in Northern Ireland or Scotland both also banned fur farming shortly afterwards. [The fur trade has proved resilient. An article by Richard Conniff, *Back in Fashion*, in *National Geographic* September 2016 revealed the resurgence in wearing fur: "*Fur farms dominate the trade, and production has more than doubled since the 1990s, to about a hundred million skins last year, mostly mink and some fox. Trappers typically add millions of wild beaver, coyote, raccoon, muskrat and other skins. That's besides untold millions of cattle, lambs, rabbits, ostriches, crocodiles, alligators, and caimans harvested for food as well as skins.*"]

Live Exports

Any long-distance trade in live animals causes immense suffering. The shameful export of live calves from the UK to Europe for the veal trade caused deep-felt anger in the mid-1990s.

In 1995 there was rising public outrage over this trade in veal calves. Christopher Barrett-Jolley ran a firm called Phoenix Aviation that flew veal calves out from Baginton airport, near Coventry. Calves were regularly taken to the airport by lorry. Animal rights activists protested at the front line of the trade. On Wednesday February 1st 1995, Jill Phipps, 31, was crushed to death under the wheels of an export truck carrying calves into Coventry Airport. Nearly one hundred police officers were on duty. Ten protesters broke through police lines and attempted to bring the lorry to a halt by sitting on the road. Some tried to chain themselves to it.

Jill and the others assumed that police officers and the lorry driver (Stephen Yates) would respect human life. They were wrong. Police on duty allowed the export lorry to continue making progress despite the clear safety problems. The vehicle was only halted by police once Jill had been crushed beneath the wheels.

An eyewitness commented: "*Jill died after police waved on the lorry carrying the calves despite the fact that protesters were still occupying the road the lorry was to go down. Despite their public claims to the contrary, Warwickshire police were so keen to protect the business of this filthy firm that they had made little effort to ensure the way was clear. Assuming the road to be clear after the police had signalled him to move on, the truck driver moved off at speed, knocking Jill down and crushing her under his wheels.*"

The CPS decided there was not enough evidence to charge Stephen Yates with causing death by dangerous driving, nor even driving without due care and attention. Jill Phipps was a caring compassionate young lady who put herself in harm's way to help those who could not help themselves. She paid with her life. She could do no more. In any protest movement those who lead the way are often hurt.

[On December 5th 2002 Christopher Barrett-Jolley and his brother-in-law, Peter Carine, were each jailed for 20 years after being convicted at Basildon Crown Court of plotting to smuggle £22m worth of cocaine into Southend Airport.]

I thought the ACIG should take a closer look at the trade. On Monday May 8th 1995 I met at Harwich with two colleagues. Janet Taylor, a former journalist and founder of the Farm Animal Sanctuary near Birmingham, is an expert in the care of farm animals. Lawrie Payne, my hunt monitoring colleague, was a fireman and Executive Committee member of the LACS. We planned an expedition to Europe to expose aspects of this trade.

Our primary target was the Dutch end of the trade in calves flown from Coventry to Schiphol airport, Amsterdam. Our secondary target was calves exported by ship through Brightlingsea, Essex to the small Belgian port of Nieuwpoort and beyond.

If both failed, then we would seek to expose the live export trade through the Dover-Calais route and on into France. If nothing else, we expected to be able to have a look at some European slaughterhouses.

We caught the 11:30am ferry from Harwich to the Hook of Holland and then the train to Amsterdam where we checked into a hotel near the station. In the evening we checked out some of the local 'sites'. Aspects of the sex industry were seriously disturbing. I am a broad-minded individual and am happy for fully consenting adults to do whatever they like with each other—but not when it involves children or animals.

After an early start, we left our hotel at 7am and reached Schiphol an hour later. First we collected our hire car. We opted to hire cars rather than take our own because having local number plates they were less noticeable to those we followed. Also, with the steering wheel on the correct side, fast pursuit is easier and safer.

We left our car in the airport park and called the mobile number of our observer at Coventry airport to ascertain whether the calf flight had left. We learned that there was some problem with the flights. The morning dragged on. Eventually the Antonov AN-26 plane, our target, landed at Schiphol soon after 2pm. By then rain and mist had swept in. We had used the morning profitably by reconnoitring the airport and knew that live animals being imported passed through the KLM 'Animal Hotel' for veterinary inspection. We expected the plane to head for this and were surprised when it travelled to a far distant part of the field.

We drove as close as we could to the plane. Nothing seemed to be happening there so we returned to the Animal Hotel. I asked a chap about livestock flights from Coventry but he knew nothing of them. We split up. I stayed in the car park to watch the Animal Hotel whilst Lawrie and Janet drove back to the plane. We met back at the airport viewing terrace at 6pm. Neither team saw anything of note. We were more than a little deflated. Had we missed them? Had the calves ever been on it? It was a long way to go to draw a blank.

We telephoned our UK informant and learned there was little likelihood of any further flights to Schiphol the following morning. Might the flights be going to Rennes in France instead? Who could tell? [Unbeknown to us at the time, the calf flights had been suspended on May 4th and on July 14th 1995 Phoenix Aviation went into liquidation.]

We decided to take our secondary target at least for the next day and aimed to witness the ferry arrival at Nieuwpoort. We set off on the long drive south and stayed overnight at Antwerp along the way.

The next morning, Wednesday May 10th, with time to spare in Antwerp, we took the opportunity for a look around, including in the Cathedral. In late morning, we set off again and arrived in the picturesque coastal port of Nieuwpoort soon after lunch. Well in time to meet the ferry, the *Caroline*, expected between 5:30 and 6:30pm. We did a thorough reconnaissance. Lawrie asked in a Ship's Chandlers and learned that a ship carrying sheep docked at the Fishing Harbour. We checked out where the *Caroline* would dock, where she would be unloaded and the route the livestock-laden lorries would take on departure. We then sat in the early summer sunshine to wait.

The *Caroline* duly arrived at 6:15pm. She chugged into view with her very recognisable engine note. Her captain turned her about in the river—a lengthy procedure as she only just fitted—then docked. A lorry was backed up and the unloading ramp winched into place. We positioned ourselves either side of this ramp. The *Caroline* was loaded with calves, not sheep. Bewildered calves were cajoled from the *Caroline* along the narrow ramp and into the lorry with slaps and whacks from handlers wielding hollow plastic tubing. The driver found difficulty forcing the calves into the confines of the compartments in the lorry. Using his boot he succeeded.

Some calves were reluctant to leave the *Caroline* but the seamen encouraged dawdlers by poking them with a long thin rod and even with the handle of a broom. These young calves looked just a few days old. They were visibly disorientated by the noise and the strange surroundings. They surely missed their mums (few sounds are more pitiful or futile than the moos from a cow for her stolen calf. The dairy industry relies on people remaining deaf to such cries).

A group of Belgian schoolchildren were brought forward to witness the loading. They looked as baffled by it all as the calves were bewildered.

The lorry was loaded in two tiers and it took some time. Eventually, when full, it was driven away to make way for another. We moved to a suitable position to follow and waited. We waited and waited. Nothing happened. Lawrie and I went to see if there was any further unloading of calves from the *Caroline*.

As soon as we were away from our car the lorry driver set off. We ran back and followed at speed. The driver tried slowing at traffic lights. He may have hoped they would change to red and he could cross, but the red would balk us. If that was his plan it failed as there was other traffic about.

He then pulled over on the hard shoulder on the outskirts of the town. It was just after 8pm. We stopped some hundred metres behind. We watched as one of his colleagues, who we had seen helping with the unloading, drove up and spoke to him. We waited. Some twenty minutes passed and we figured that he had called the Police. We had little option but to wait and see.

In time a Police wagon pulled up boxed us in and armed officers emerged. The situation was potentially difficult. None of us spoke the language. We were English in a Dutch hire car with Dutch number plates. There had been many lies told in the UK and world media at the time about 'animal rights terrorism'. We needed to be diplomatic and were.

Lawrie Payne, a fireman, was used to dealing with other emergency services. We asked the officers what the problem was. We were told in no uncertain fashion it was "*not allowed*" to follow livestock lorries.

The officers demanded our passports. We had one full UK passport and two visitors' passports. Both types were fully valid in Belgium but the Police told us that the visitors' passports were "*not in order*". While lengthy negotiations continued the lorry full of UK calves that was our target disappeared into the distance.

We were then taken under close escort back to Nieuwpoort Police Station where our passports were photocopied. In due course the officers agreed that our documents were indeed in order and released us. [I later checked with my MEP and visitors' passports were lawful in Belgium. As for following lorries, that also was lawful, so long as one followed from safe distance and abided by all the traffic laws.]

We found a hotel near Utrecht and the following morning drove back to Amsterdam and resumed our observations from Schiphol airport, but without success. We then learned that the exporter had issued a press release saying the live export flights had been suspended for four weeks to allow for the plane to be serviced.

We returned home but switched our focus to the shipping trade. Thwarted once from our lawful investigative work we were determined to try again. Monday June 5th brought another early start. After waking to my alarm at 4am I left an hour later. I collected Lawrie and we drove to Ramsgate port where we met Janet. We caught the 10:30am Sally Line ferry to Ostend. It was a Belgian Bank Holiday so the hire car office was closed but there was a number to call on the window so we eventually collected a local hire car.

We called our Essex informant and learned there were no sailings of the *Caroline* from Brightlingsea that day. We looked instead for the livestock lairages, believed to be near Lokeren and booked into the Carlton hotel in Gent. After a fruitless search the following morning we found we were in the wrong part of the country so headed back towards Nieuwpoort. On the way, we called in at the small town of Izegem, the site of a notorious slaughterhouse Janet exposed some years before.

We parked nearby and walked to look through the fence. When Janet saw drovers hitting the cattle with sticks I moved for a closer view to try to film the mistreatment. Janet and I were then confronted by a couple of irate slaughterhouse workers. They demanded the films from our cameras. When we refused, they told us they had called the police.

They claimed they had nothing to hide and invited us inside— provided that we put our cameras away. We accepted and were invited into their office where they offered us tea and coffee.

We had nothing to fear from the police and waited to see them. A senior officer arrived and announced that he proposed to seize all our cameras, all our films and hold us in custody until we paid a substantial fine!! I asked what we had done wrong. He explained that in Belgium it was illegal to photograph anyone without their permission. By taking photographs from outside the slaughterhouse we had broken that law. I responded: "*Really? So, if I photograph my children holidaying on your beach I have to ask permission from everyone else in the background? That seems to me to be nonsense.*"

He then made a phone call, "*to the D/A*" he said. Afterwards he offered us a 'deal'. If we just handed over our films he would allow us to leave with our equipment. He assured us that they would process our films and return anything to us that did not relate to the slaughterhouse.

I replied that, on that basis, I was happy to hand over my print film (that contained only a couple of photographs of the outside of the slaughterhouse). I added that I was not prepared to hand over my video tape (it had other material on it and I also needed it for Nieuwpoort).

The police officer became irate and uttered the direst threats. I calmly explained: "*I'm very sorry. I don't believe that I have done anything wrong. If you feel that I have then you have to arrest me but if you do I would like to speak to British consular officials.*"

At that he became even angrier. He cursed British people for coming over and interfering in Belgium and said Belgians never go over to interfere in Britain. His fellow officers and the slaughterhouse workers present nodded in agreement.

I gently reminded him that Belgium had good reason to be grateful to British citizens who in the past had willingly crossed the Channel to 'interfere' as he called it and put right what they believed to be wrong. I reminded him that just down the road at Ypres you could barely take a pace without stepping on soil stained with the blood of British youth given some 80 years ago to help his country. I politely suggested he should not curse British people who he clearly believed 'cared too much'.

"*Pa!*" he retorted, "*That was 80 years ago and is long forgotten!*" I hope he was wrong. [We should never forget the horrendous loss of life in the First World War. On just one day, the first day of the Battle of the Somme, Saturday July 1st 1916, the British Army sustained 57,000 casualties of whom 19,240 were dead. Many more died before that campaign ended. Amongst them my Sue's grandfather, who never held his son, was killed in action and has no known grave—I found his name on the Menin Gate.]

Given the attitude of the senior officer I felt that the conversation was becoming pointless. I asked if we were under arrest. When the officer confirmed that we were not arrested I told them that I proposed to leave and to stop me they would have to arrest me. I knew we had done nothing wrong—we had only taken photographs and film from outside the fence. It was not a restricted site. There were no signs saying 'No Photography'. They let us all go with some parting curses, and we kept all our films.

As we left I apologised to my colleagues for my belligerent attitude. It had worked in that case but I knew that there were plenty of police forces around the world where my words would have elicited nothing but a sharp smack around the head with a truncheon.

Somewhat shaken by the events at Izegem we continued to Nieuwpoort. With the changing tides the ferry was expected any time from the early hours of the morning onwards. In late evening, we took up a discreet surveillance position at the harbour entrance.

We telephoned our observer at Brightlingsea. At 3:45pm on Tuesday June 6th lorries loaded with calves had passed protestors at Brightlingsea. It was confirmed the *Caroline* had sailed at about 5pm so it was a matter of waiting, waiting, waiting. People often imagine investigative animal welfare work as full of excitement and fear, high speed chases and the like. In fact it is mostly about being bored, tired and hungry and deeply upset by the unpleasant if not gruesome sights that we have to record.

We settled down to wait. With three in our car the shift system was ½ hour on watch then 1 hour asleep. At 4am on Wednesday June 7th the *Caroline* sailed into view. We filmed her chugging up the estuary then moved to the quayside. At 5am unloading started. That time we kept well away so as not to alert them to the fact that animal welfarists were about.

We parked in an innocuous position overlooking the exit from the freight area and waited. It was 7am before a pair of lorries laden with calves appeared. As they seemed likely to be heading on a long journey into Holland we followed them. Following any vehicle unobserved is far from easy. Our task was made harder by the fact that we were only in one vehicle ourselves (with two or three pursuit vehicles, you can alternate the ones that follow closely). Heavy rain and consequent spray on the motorways did not help. On the plus side our target vehicles were large, recognisable and unlikely to speed away. We hung well back and allowed the rush hour traffic to intervene.

When the pair of lorries parted company between Brugge and Gent we opted to follow one towing a large trailer. Once we reached the minor roads the driver realised he was being tailed. However, he did not appear too concerned perhaps because we had Belgian number plates. After some cat-and-mouse work, we followed him to a farm near Ruiselede. We filmed him unloading some calves from the rear trailer unit then followed again as he drove off.

The next journey leg was longer. We went through Gent to Antwerp; then north into Holland; past Breda, then north towards Utrecht. We looked with concern at our dwindling fuel gauge. Our target pulled into a service station. Would there be time for us to fill our tank or was he just stopping to make a phone call? No, he was just buying sweets and soon departed. We rejoiced that we declined the option to refuel. Had we done so we could easily have been stranded perhaps with a half-full tank or caught up in the queue to pay.

Onwards ever onwards we drove. We felt for the poor calves rattling about in what was by then a lightly loaded wagon. At another stop I walked up to film the calves in the lorry and ended up chatting with the driver. He asked what I was doing and I explained that we just wanted to film the calves and where they went. He appeared visibly relieved that we had no violent intention towards him and only sought to film. The journey went on.

Past Utrecht we headed west towards Amersfoort and then Apeldoorn. I saw Arnhem nearby on the map. Our fuel gauge was by then showing nearly empty. Our pursuit would be forced to an end soon, one way or another. To our relief our target turned off for Barneveld, a small picturesque town south of the motorway. Through a deluge of rain, we trailed him to a pristine looking veal unit in the small village of Kootwijkerbroek. We opted for the direct approach and walked up to ask if we could film.

The lady in charge spoke English poorly (but still many times better than any of us could speak Dutch!). She was reluctant to allow us to film anything. We explained that we just wanted to show the conditions the calves were going into. We appealed to the driver saying that surely they had nothing to hide. Having already spoken to him we had an element of rapport. He shrugged his shoulders and agreed that we could film. The lady followed that cue.

The ramp of the lorry was lowered and the calves forced down the slope. They were then encouraged on into the unit. Inside, I filmed the tiny frail calves, far from home, forced individually into the small crates with slatted floors and flat featureless sides that would be their 'home' for the next six months. Such a veal crate system was illegal in the UK. Janet extended a hand of compassion to one calf in his cell. Clearly missing his Mum he suckled on her hand.

[In 1987, following a campaign led by Compassion in World Farming, the UK Parliament voted to phase out the veal crate system in Britain. The ban took effect in the UK in 1990. British farmers then had no hesitation sending their calves to be incarcerated in such systems in Europe. Further lobbying by compassionate campaigners then led to the veal crate being banned across the EU in January 2007.]

In due course, we left that veal unit and drove to catch our ferry home. When I eventually returned to my bed it was some 45 hours after leaving the comfort of one in Gent. Back in the UK I booked a film editing studio in Norwich and spent two afternoons putting our *UK Calves* video together. That video, produced in a few days, showed the full price paid by animals for a pint of milk or bar of chocolate. We gave copies to many media outlets and to the major animal welfare groups. I also gave a copy to Essex Police having been assured that it would be shown at the relevant stations of the officers asked to deal with the Brightlingsea demonstrations.

We returned to see the calves some months later. On Wednesday September 20th 1995, following my visit to the Biomedical Primate Research Centre (BPRC), Lawrie Payne and I took the opportunity to travel across Holland to see the veal calves again. It took a fast and faultless drive to leave the BPRC at Den Haag, travel to Kootwijkerbroek, film the calves then return to the Hook of Holland to catch our evening ferry.

Critical to the success of that mission was a swift and smooth operation at the calf unit. When I spoke to a packed public meeting at Brightlingsea on June 29th 1995 about our work I had, as I always did at talks, appealed for help from the audience.

I had specifically asked for anyone capable of translating to and from Dutch. I had two offers of help so I typed a letter of introduction for Lawrie and myself to the Dutch farmers at the veal unit and had it translated. Having that document worked a treat. The farmer was very suspicious and sceptical when he first saw us approaching laden with cameras but when he read our letter he welcomed us in.

We were given freedom to film and photograph whatever we liked. When we had first seen the calves on June 7th they were still small for the size of their crates. They could just about turn around. 3½ months later, they were considerably bigger. Their movement was restricted to a slight shuffle to either side plus a small movement forwards and backwards.

I gazed into their blank unseeing eyes and could not help but contrast my full life over the intervening months with their featureless and boring existence. They were denied their birth-right of a life with their mothers and in open fields.

Our swift drive for the ferry and subsequent journey home was uneventful. We were told that the calves would go for slaughter in December. I had planned to visit the farm again, either on their final day or just before, but problems at the LACS intervened to thwart such plans.

Livestock Markets

Filming effectively at any UK livestock market was all but impossible without a hidden video camera. Whilst we could convince hunters that we wanted to film their pastime for the fun of viewing later, and showing to friends, no-one would want to film animals passing through a livestock auction.

Sunday March 8th 1992 proved fruitful. I met colleagues Alan Knight and Liz Varney. Alan ran a small engineering company and had conceived a plan to conceal a standard video camera in a shoulder bag. The camera would be fixed in the bottom of the bag with a hole cut for the lens and that hole covered in fabric, cut from tights, to conceal the lens. I gave Alan a video camera to work with. We took delivery of that first-generation hidden camera at the end of the following month. It was a clever device that could be turned on and off remotely by pressing something akin to a shutter release cable for a standard 35mm camera. One limitation was that you had to hold the bag head-high to give the lens the required view.

I put the bag camera to use early the following year. I worked with investigative journalist, Andrew Tyler, on a project commissioned by Animal Aid to expose the reality of livestock auctions. On Wednesday January 6th 1993 I left early to meet Andrew at Banbury Livestock Market. Dressed in farming clothing we posed as potential buyers. Andrew had all the knowledge of the correct terminology. However, as in any small rural auction environment, outsiders stood out a mile.

We stayed in Banbury and were at the market the next morning for 7am. There was plenty of action with pigs and sheep being unloaded from lorries but at that early hour it was too dark to film. We returned when there was more light. We filmed pigs being auctioned, dead pigs in pens, sheep in pens and bullocks being driven into the auction ring. The hidden camera worked admirably and enabled us to film many breaches of the Welfare of Animals at Markets Order 1990.

We recorded an employee jabbing beef cattle in the ribs, rapping one across the legs and thrusting his stick up the anus of others. We filmed young calves being prodded around the sales ring by a man with a stick and a pig being moved with a kick to the neck and a knee in the side.

Our investigation extended to other livestock markets. The following week, on January 13th, I drove to Thirsk and met Andrew Tyler again. The next morning, we arrived at Thirsk Livestock Market armed with our hidden camera. The locals were immediately suspicious: "*Who are you? Are you Animal Rights here to cause trouble?*" We explained that we aimed to purchase stock for a new farming enterprise but they appeared unconvinced. We found it most effective to work as a team—whilst Andrew used the camera bag I concealed his actions.

Monday January 25th I met Andrew Tyler again and loaned him the hidden camera to use at Wickham Market Livestock Market. In March 1993 Animal Aid produced an illustrated booklet detailing their investigations titled—*Auctioning Animal Flesh*. Mark Gold, Director of Animal Aid, wrote an excellent foreword demanding that existing legislation protecting farmed animals be better enforced. Beyond that he recommended people consider giving up meat altogether.

Thursday March 18th 1993 was interesting. I accompanied Alan Knight to visit a television exhibition in London and see a demonstration of hidden cameras. We came away impressed and full of ideas.

The following year I helped Les Ward from Advocates for Animals in an investigation into cruelty at Scottish Livestock Markets. Les visited many livestock markets, I helped on some visits. Les met me in Edinburgh on the evening of Monday July 18th 1994 and I stayed at his home. We left early the next morning to attend Peebles Auction. Equipped with concealed video cameras we were prepared to film, but the auction was cancelled due to lack of entries.

We went on to the auction at Castle Douglas where we saw sheep sold. There appeared to be no problems so we drove to Dumfries and filmed cattle auctioned. There was a chap hitting animals to drive them into the auction ring. We ended a long day looking, without success, in Ardrossan and Saltcoats for evidence of horses being imported into Scotland. The next morning Les and I visited the livestock market in Stirling. We arrived early, just after the animals. We walked in for a look around first then returned armed with hidden cameras. Les went to see the sheep auctioned and me the cattle. The SSPCA were there monitoring the auction. We saw some violence towards the animals but not so bad as it had been at Dumfries. People at the auction guessed we were from an animal welfare group.

I returned to Scotland for more investigative work with Les that autumn. Les met me at Edinburgh station on the evening of Sunday November 13th and I stayed with his family again. The next morning we visited Glenfield Auction Mart in Paisley. We divided our resources. I used the camera hidden in a bag. Les was wired for action, a camera lens concealed in his cap and the recorder hidden in his pocket.

We recorded rough treatment of the calves and bullocks. One bullock was so stressed that he jumped over the bars of his pen into the adjacent pen. We stayed at the market for four hours, by which time our camera tapes had run out, and batteries run flat.

The next day we visited John Swain and Sons Auction in Edinburgh. Again I had the camera in the bag and Les the outfit with lens in his cap. There was all the usual rough treatment associated with a livestock market. We saw pigs pulled by their ears and kicked. One pig had overgrown feet, another a malformed ear. We saw a man clout a cow on her nose with a stick.

With hidden cameras we were never certain what the camera filmed, until we checked later. The viewpoint might be obscured or the horizon at an angle. Consequently, my best film was secured late in the day when I leant over a wall and used my standard Hi8 video camera to film the loading of pigs onto a transporter. There was a much kicking and harsh treatment of the pigs until the workers saw me filming when they became gentler.

The next morning Les and I went to the Advocates for Animals office in Edinburgh. I was kitted out with the camera lens concealed in my cap then Les dropped me off at Oliver and Son Auction Mart in Edinburgh. I went in and saw sheep being auctioned—some were lifted up by their fleece. When it ended Les met me and we looked at the skin yard and abattoir but there was little to see. Les then had a visit at his office from his local CID and had to explain why his car number plate had been noted outside the livestock auction the previous day.

Les Ward wrote a detailed account of his investigation published in the Advocates for Animals Annual Pictorial Review 1995. The report found livestock markets "*are places where the main legislation governing the treatment of animals at markets is being breached routinely and where grossly insensitive handling of calves, pigs, sheep, cattle and poultry appears commonplace.*"

The extent of the abuse was detailed: "*The investigation revealed 34 instances where we believe there have been infringements of the regulations governing the treatment and welfare of animals at markets. Copies of the 'Advocates' report, together with the filmed evidence, have been sent to the Minister of Agriculture, the Secretary of State for Scotland, the Farm Animal Welfare Council (FAWC), the Scottish SPCA and the RSPCA.*"

Sir Colin Spedding, Chairman of FAWC commented: "*The level of violence, particularly the beating with sticks was extremely disappointing. It was almost as though people enjoyed using sticks violently. The behaviour of these operators was really in violation of all the Ministry's codes.*" (*The Scotsman*, February 9th 1995.)

New Forest Ponies

For years people complained over the cruelty involved in the round up and sale of ponies from the New Forest. In September 1991 the ACIG was pleased to assist the *News of the World* and the New Forest Animal Protection Group (NFAPG) in an investigation into this trade.

I drove down for the pony round-up at Slade Farm, Pilley on Sunday September 1st armed with video and 35mm cameras. It was like stepping back in time to scenes from the wild-west! Frightened foals had their owners' marks branded on their flanks with red-hot irons. The corralled animals were frightened and powerful and took some subduing. This clearly gave plenty of fun for the humans that participated and watched but caused fear, anguish, and at times pain, for the ponies.

The following Thursday, September 5th, I returned for the Beaulieu Road Horse Sales, again recording scenes with video and 35mm cameras. I worked with a *News of the World* team. The sales started at 10:45am and ended at around 3:30pm. It was blazing hot and the pens were packed. Some ponies were sold for a pittance—and to who knows what fate. There was at least one notorious meat trader present. Another chap was willing to buy a pony from any source from our undercover man.

These sales—and the unknown fate for the ponies—generated widespread concern. Several animal welfare groups were represented at the sale, some unbeknown to each other. Foals were bought by rescue groups, including for Carla Lane, but more than 260 were sold to meat traders.

The *News of the World*, whose representatives saved a mare and her foal by purchasing them, published their feature on the pony sales on September 15th 1991. In an article by Maureen Lawless and Janet Taylor under the headline: "*Save Death Row Ponies Pleads Macca*" Paul McCartney was quoted: "*If you love animals you can't let them be treated like this. Why should our ponies end up as some French family's meal?*" Carla Lane added: "*These pony sales should be stopped. These animals should not be killed to fill a Frenchman's belly.*"

Pet Cemetery

The investigative work of the ACIG spanned many aspects of animal welfare. In the summer of 1994 my colleague Janet Jackson reported a surprising state of affairs at Silvermere Haven Pet cemetery located in Byfleet road Cobham. It was one of the most upmarket pet cemeteries in the country—with fees to match.

The burial fees then for a large dog were: grave £199.75; coffin (optional) £94; standard marble headstone £88.13; standard marble surround £99.88; chippings (optional) £47; engraving on headstone £2.29 per lead infill letter; plus an annual maintenance fee of £23.50. All these charges were VAT inclusive but still amounted to £528.76 with the coffin and the chippings but excluding lead infills and the annual maintenance fee.

For those fees one expected to find everything in order, peaceful and as perfect as possible. I met Janet on June 26th 1994 and we visited the site. Our senses were assailed by the most appalling smell that emanated from a pit around the back of the crematorium full of partially buried carcases.

This death pit posed a real risk to other pets and wildlife. The soil was spongy to walk on, like a well-sprung mattress, from the bloated carcases beneath. Closer investigation revealed the torn limbs and carcases of an assortment of creatures. Exposed fragments of putrid skin, flesh and fur swarmed with flies. Blood and dark body fluids oozed from one rotting animal. The stench was savage, the health hazards obvious. Where did the animals come from? Were they road fatalities? Had they been euthanised by vets, if so with what? Any drugs used would linger in the carcases and posed a risk to any pets or wildlife scavenging from the pit. [A letter in *Veterinary Record* May 15th 1993 p515 reported an incident where a collie bitch on a farm nearly died after scavenging from a calf euthanised with pentobarbitone and buried under 18 inches of earth.]

After gathering proof of the situation I contacted MAFF to ascertain the precise legal situation, which was covered by the Animal By-Products Order 1992. I then alerted the relevant local authorities and the media. On Tuesday July 12th, I took Maureen Lawless from the *News of the World* to visit the site. Saturday July 23rd, I checked the site again and there was still a stinking pit there. A Waste Regulations Officer from Surrey County Council and Environmental Health Officer from Elmbridge Borough Council visited two days later, Monday July 25th 1994. They pre-warned the proprietor Tim Gilbert of their inspection and when they arrived the pit was apparently nearly filled in. Mr Gilbert explained the situation.

In December 1993 his incinerator at the crematorium broke down for a short period. Because he did not believe he had a licence to move the animal bodies Tim Gilbert disposed of the carcases of some 40 animals by burying them together in the pit around the back. He insisted he covered them adequately and claimed that if uncovered it had been done by foxes.

The Council officials took statements from me and other eyewitnesses. They advised me that he had no licence to bury animals in such a location or fashion. Even if he had a licence they were not properly buried. On their instructions, the pit was filled in and the animals within properly and safely buried. I was assured local authorities would monitor the situation closely in future.

Pig swill farm on the Isle of Wight

At the end of May 1990, I worked with experienced journalist Andrew Tyler on a joint ACIG/Animal Aid investigation into pig swill farming on the Isle of Wight. After a meeting at the LACS offices in London on Tuesday May 29th I drove south and caught the 5pm ferry to the Isle of Wight. I met Andrew and we checked into a small B&B hotel.

Andrew had some two years previously worked on Ashley Shirlaw's Isle of Wight swill farm. That was a 500 pig operation with the pigs fed on the binned waste collected from a round that included local holiday camps, restaurants and hospitals in the Newport, Bembridge and Ryde areas. Andrew needed me there with my video camera to complete his investigation. We spent the day of Wednesday May 30th taking photographs and videos at swill farms and then caught the 5pm ferry back to the mainland that evening.

Andrew published his findings in a report entitled "*A business that stinks*" in the *Guardian* June 29th 1990. He described seeing a piglet suffering from meningitis. Of the swill boiling unit on the Shirlaw Farm he reported: "*The stench up close was mesmerising and it seemed incredible that his pigs could be fed such a suppurating mess, thick with its head of fungus and still littered with chunks of crockery and the odd spoon or knife."*

The site was deeply disturbing with dead pigs lying semi-immersed in the syrup of muck whilst their fellows 'played' with a variety of cutlery found in the mire. I found it particularly sad because after my time working at FOAL Farm Animal Rescue centre I knew that if only given the chance pigs are some of the cleanest animals on the farm.

[Andrew told me that during his previous investigation he had gone on the bin round collecting the food waste to feed the pigs. The vehicle emanated a foul smell and the contents looked revolting. A passer-by called to him something like it was funny the pigs had to eat such garbage. Andrew retorted that people ate it as well—when they ate the pigs! There were real concerns at the time about food chains and harm to the public by what was fed or injected into livestock. The Bovine Spongiform Encephalopathy/new variant Creutzfeldt-Jakob Disease (BSE/vCJD) crisis in the UK was created by the greed and ignorance of intensive livestock farmers who fed herbivorous cows with commercial feeds that included protein supplements made from ground and cooked remains from diseased and injured cattle and sheep. BSE was first noticed in cattle in 1986. The epidemic lasted until 1998. More than 180,000 cattle were infected and 4.4 million slaughtered during the eradication programme. In 1998 the BBC reported the cost of BSE to the taxpayer was set to top £4 billion. Many people paid a far higher price. Nearly half a million BSE-infected animals entered the human food chain before controls on high-risk offal were introduced in 1989. Worries grew over the transmission of the disease to people. On May 16th 1990 the Minister of Agriculture, John Gummer, tried to feed a beefburger to his four-year-old daughter to show British beef was safe. She, wisely, refused the burger and he took a large bite himself. Chief Medical Officer, Sir Donald Acheson, said at the time *"Beef can be eaten safely by everyone, both adults and children, including patients in hospital."* But it was not so safe. The disease was transmitted to humans (where it is described as vCJD) by eating contaminated food. In 1996 the UK government was forced to admit the link between BSE and vCJD. By June 2014 vCJD had killed at least 177 people in the UK. On October 4th 2007 the daughter of a friend of John Gummer, Elizabeth Smith, died aged just 23 after a three-year battle with vCJD. Mr Smith said his daughter needed round the clock care as the disease worsened and was unable to walk for the last two years of her life. *"It was remorseless in the way it killed her off,"* he added (*Guardian* October 12th 2007). At the time of writing, the Australian Blood Service declines donations from people who have lived in the UK for six months or more from 1980 to 1996. From May 28th 2002 the US Food and Drug Administration excluded from donation anyone who spent three months in the UK from 1980 to 1996. The only reason the UK National Blood Service does not exclude such people is there would be few left to give blood—and lack of donated blood would be more dangerous for patients than the risk of contracting vCJD.]

Salmon farming—ecological damage and seal shooting

I had for some time been in contact with John Robins from Animal Concern (Scotland) about the problems caused by salmon farming off the Scottish coasts. There were many concerns: the cruelty to the salmon from intensive and unnatural rearing; the ecological damage caused and the shooting of predators, such as seals, by salmon farming interests.

The People, May 21st 1989, printed a photograph, taken by Paul Yoxon, director of the Skye Environmental Centre showing a pregnant seal that had been shot by a Skye salmon farmer. Paul commented: *"This seal was so badly wounded that it didn't suffer for long. But many are left to die in agony over several days. The fish farmers will shoot at any seal on sight if they have lost salmon and they prefer to do this rather than invest in adequate fencing to protect their stock. It's much cheaper and they know there is very little chance of being convicted."*

Following an outbreak of a killer virus the killing of common seals was made illegal by a 1988 amendment to the Conservation of Seals Act but salmon farmers claimed the right to shoot seals owing to a loophole in the law that allowed them to kill predators threatening livestock. At the time it was estimated that some 3,000 seals a year were shot along with thousands of sea birds and otters. The following year, the *Sunday Express*, March 18th 1990, printed an article describing the slaughter of seals by salmon farmers in Scotland. John Robins complained: *"We have been inundated with complaints from the public about the slaughter that is going on."* Unilever, whose subsidiary Marine Harvest was one of the biggest fish-farming concerns, employed two marksmen to shoot predators found near the salmon cages. In March 1990 a Skye couple witnessed the shooting of seals near Unilever's Cairidh Salmon Farm on Loch Ainort. A guard fired six shots, hitting two seals. One got away leaving a trail of blood, the other was caught. Paul Yoxon added to the chorus of outrage: *"It is a disgrace that this is allowed to happen. It is true that seals can cause considerable damage to salmon farms but surely, given the huge profits, methods of keeping them at bay could be employed."*

John Robins asked if I could use ACIG resources to investigate salmon farming on the Isle of Skye. I was pleased to help such a determined campaigner. Sue and I planned to pose as intrepid tourists with our young family. I hired a motor caravan from Great Yarmouth on Saturday June 2nd 1990. We loaded our vehicle and set off at 2:30pm. I drove for nearly 12 hours and parked for the remainder of the night just outside Lochearnhead. It was an exciting adventure for our two infant sons.

In the morning, we drove on to Kyle of Lochalsh and caught the ferry to Skye (this was before the bridge was built) at 12.15pm. We called in to see my friends Paul and Grace Yoxon at the Skye Environmental Centre at Broadford. They showed us around their centre and we saw some of their excellent work to protect local wildlife. We found an offshore seafarm and parked up for the night nearby.

Our alarm sounded at 5:20am on Monday June 4th. Ten minutes later I walked out equipped with cameras and binoculars looking for any signs of activity. There were no sounds of shooting but from 5:45am I filmed men at work on the fish farm pens. I later filmed as the salmon were harvested and the pens sprayed with a powder—possibly food or pesticides.

The seafarms were floating steel pens holding as many as 20,000 salmon per pen, 1.2 million salmon per loch. The feed, the excrement and the chemicals required to keep parasites and diseases at bay all caused severe harm to the local ecology.

We spent the night parked overlooking Loch Caroy near Balmeanach where there was a seafarm with 14 pens. I woke at 5:30am and walked out checking for evidence of shooting. I found nothing. The following day, Wednesday June 6th, I made an early morning visit to the beach at Portnalong. I found an empty cartridge box and used shotgun cartridges. We then went on to photograph the Cairidh seafarm in Loch Ainort. That evening we again met Paul and Grace at their Environmental Centre and they took us to observe otters from the beach at Waterloo. We spent the night near Broadford.

The following morning, we checked the site in Loch Ainort again. I then gave up on the concept of covert observation and tried the open route. I phoned the Cairidh farm and went to the site for an interview with Alastair Strachan. He was very helpful and told me about their operation. When I asked to visit the platforms to see the salmon he said that regretfully would not be possible because of Health and Safety regulations.

That afternoon Sue and I took our young family to visit beautiful Portree. In the evening we returned to the Skye Environmental Centre and I left an ACIG video camera with Paul and Grace Yoxon on loan for their use for wildlife protection. We then drove to see the seafarm at Torrin. I telephoned John Robins to update him on our progress (or lack of it!).

We spent the night at Torrin and woke to a beautiful sunny morning in a fabulous location. We enjoyed a family walk along the shores of Loch Slapin before departing Broadford at 10am and heading home. Along the route we called in at the Marine Harvest Breeding Station at Invergarry. I gave the employees a suitable story and was allowed in to photograph the hatchery. We then drove on and returned home at 2am.

Vivisection
Biomedical Primate Research Centre (BPRC), Holland.

In 1995, the BPRC at Den Haag, Holland was one of two primate research facilities in Europe. It had 116 chimpanzees and over 1000 macaque monkeys housed at the site located in Rijswijk, an industrial area on the outskirts of the city.

In late summer and autumn, working in conjunction with Les Ward and Advocates for Animals, the ACIG undertook an investigation to expose what happened to primates there. The investigation was prompted by the publication in the *Sunday Times*, August 6th 1995, of the following extract from an article under the heading "*Scientists in secret chimp tests abroad*":

"*Government scientists are secretly doing experiments on live chimpanzees abroad in defiance of a strict ban against such research in*

153

Britain. In one test, condemned by animal welfare groups, a chimp has been infected with HIV.

The research is being carried out at a Dutch laboratory that receives more than £800,000 a year from the European Community but keeps 116 chimpanzees in conditions described by British experts as appalling. Some chimps are held in over-crowded steel cages others are locked together in dimly lit rooms."

At the end of the article the director of the BPRC, Professor Jorg Eichberg, said he was tired of *"complaints based on ignorance"* and welcomed visitors to his centre. Such an invitation, almost unheard of in the UK, was too good an opportunity to miss. Les Ward and I agreed to cooperate to secure video film and more still photographs to show how the primates were treated. I telephoned the BPRC at the end of August and learned their 'Open Door' policy was not quite as open as it had sounded.

There had been a lot of requests to visit. They did not have the time to show any member of the public who wanted to walk around. When I convinced them that I had media connections and was looking to publish an article I was asked would I take a 'Heaf test'? A what? I had never heard of this. They explained it was a test to confirm I was TB free as they were concerned that I might pass TB to their primates. I agreed and we fixed a provisional date for my visit.

Getting a Heaf test proved no easy matter. I needed a referral from my Doctor and even then, my local NHS hospital said it would take months to arrange. Offering to pay did not help as my local private clinic had never heard of the test. The problem was only solved with the help of string-pulling from friends and two lengthy car journeys. I received the test report proving I was clear of TB with just a day to spare.

Lawrie Payne and I had a live export investigation to complete. We combined the two investigations and on Tuesday September 19th Lawrie and I caught the 11am ferry sailing from Harwich to the Hook of Holland. On previous foreign excursions when following livestock lorries, we hired cars with the relevant foreign plates. This time there was no need so we used an ACIG car. We docked at 7:35 pm Dutch time and drove into Den Haag to find the BPRC. A busy city at the end of the evening rush traffic, with rain falling and a steering wheel on the wrong side, and no knowledge of Dutch, made things difficult. By the time we found the BPRC we were grateful we opted to search the night before rather than the morning of the visit. We checked into a quiet hotel in a nearby industrial estate.

Next morning we arrived at the BPRC in good time for my 10am interview with Professor Eichberg. It was a somewhat chilling experience for me as I felt I was speaking to a very charming and plausible prison governor. The interview lasted nearly an hour and was full of how they do this and that and intend to do plenty more, to benefit the primates in their care. I wondered how the primates would view their regime from their perspective if they could but talk.

Professor Eichberg had worked for years in primate facilities in the USA. I asked him if he had ever been bitten when handling primates. He told me he had. I pondered how many primate handlers are bitten by their charges. Clearly such intimate contacts pose a real threat to human health— far beyond the mere bite. I was treated with great courtesy and given a guided tour of the BPRC by a staff member fluent in English. My tour lasted until nearly 1pm. Unfortunately, Lawrie had not had the Heaf test so was not allowed in. He had to wait outside in the car.

I was shown hundreds of primates: outdoor colonies, indoor colonies, breeding units, nurseries and primates under experimentation. I kept my video camera running most of the time, took plenty of slides and prints and asked many questions of my guide. Some primates had been in the unit for 25-30 years. As I looked deep into their vacant eyes I could only feel shame at their treatment by their fellow primates—man.

A variety of experiments took place. There was research into malaria, hepatitis, transplantation and AIDS. Further abuse of primates for AIDS research caught my attention as it was scientists giving primates a cocktail of viruses, carcinogenic chemicals and who knows what else that was a likely cause of AIDS in the first place. (See "*Biohazard: The silent threat from Biomedical Research and the creation of AIDS*".) My tour only lasted an hour but images seen will haunt me for considerably longer.

On return I transferred the Hi-8 video to VHS, sent a copy to Les Ward and had my films processed. Numerous questions arose from the video tape. I entered protracted correspondence with the BPRC to clarify matters. The BPRC staff were helpful, open and prompt in their replies. Advocates for Animals then took the investigation forwards.

Toxicol, Ledbury.

We looked at other research establishments. Sometimes concerned locals and politicians were given guided tours to reassure them. In June 1995 I took advantage of one such offer. It proved an interesting day. On Monday June 12th I left home at 5am and drove to meet an ACIG colleague at Ledbury station at 10:30am. We met a local councillor then went to the nearby Toxicol animal research centre for our 11am visit. I used the name 'Mike Davies' with the address of a local ACIG supporter.

Things went well to start with. Peter Elliott and Douglas Brown from Toxicol were genial hosts and showed us an ICI training video first. It was when we were taken to see the animals that things started to go awry.

We were told that for biosecurity reasons we would have to go through an 'air shower'. That meant stripping to underwear and then wearing a company boilersuit. Hmm I thought. I was wired for sound with a small recorder in my pocket and a microphone taped to my body. How was I going to get through with all that unnoticed? We were taken to the changing room and it took a deft movement on my part, coupled with faked shyness, to strip away all my electronics and hide them the only place I could—in the crotch of my underpants! I succeeded without drawing comment. We were taken to see mice in an 80-weeks toxicity test, then a lone rat, the last subject of a telemetry test. We then had to pass through another air shower before being taken to see beagles. Our visit ended at

1:15pm. From its new location, my microphone recorded little. Toxicol later became Quintiles England and at time of writing is Sequani Limited.

Other anti-vivisection work

The ACIG has been pleased to support investigations into laboratories abroad. For instance, in 1994 we made a substantial donation towards the purchase of a video camera for filming in a research centre in Osaka, Japan. Then, in 1997 I gave help and advice to a Swedish animal rights activist who took a job at a high security laboratory in Sweden.

Zoos

In the summer of 1984 I had the pleasure of meeting Louise McKenna—the caring and beautiful daughter of Virginia McKenna and Bill Travers. Louise was the driving force behind the setting up of Zoo Check to oppose the incarceration of animals in zoos.

Many will recall visits to the zoo as children, perhaps with parents, or in school parties. Before colour television it was for many the first opportunity to marvel at the beauty of creation. However, zoos have many problems. For all the efforts at cage enrichment the animals are still confined in what amounts to a prison. [On May 27th 2016 it was reported that an elephant named Hanako, 'Flower Child', died in Inokashira Park Zoo, Tokyo after spending 67 years in captivity. She had been described as the 'loneliest elephant in the world' (*Mail Online* May 27th 2016)]

People oppose zoos for many reasons: the keeping of animals away from their natural environments (and temperatures); the opportunity for the imprisoned animals to be tormented by bored onlookers; the passion for breeding animals as zoo owners realise that baby animals are cute and cuddly and attract the crowds—but what happens to the inevitable surplus of animals? There were real concerns about links between zoos and the vivisection industry. In 1984 Zoo Check had acquired proof of links between London Zoo and vivisection. In 1986 John Hearn, the Director of Science at London Zoo said: "*In an ideal world zoos could supply animals for research and the breeding colonies would be on display.*" (*The New Scientist*, March 27th 1986).

Even the best funded zoos struggle to keep animal housing well-maintained. The struggling zoos find that neglecting the housing is a way to save money. Wars that break out around the world with depressing regularity cause immense suffering to humans. Where there are zoos in war-ravaged towns animals are sometimes simply left to die in their cages.

I offered to help by visiting zoos whenever possible. As my young family grew up they became accustomed to having to pose by caged animals for my cameras. I had found that if I walked up to photograph zoo animals the zoo workers would take an interest in my actions. If my young children posed by the caging I could photograph them—and then zoom past them to photograph the animals behind—without questions being asked.

We made several visits to Colchester Zoo, on April 6th 1989, March 19th 1991, July 17th 1992 and August 20th 1996. Conditions for the animals steadily improved—but in many cases the inmates doubtless remained the same. During our 1991 visit we saw a pair of elephants brought out to perform something akin to circus tricks before an audience.

In June 1997 we took our annual family holiday in Northern Cyprus, the Turkish part of the divided island. It is a gloriously scenic country steeped in history. On the morning of Friday June 13th, we visited the zoo (Hayvanat Bahcesi) at Gazimagusa (formerly Famagusta). It was a thoroughly depressing experience. There was a lone bear in a bare cage; a lone lioness and two primates kept separately in adjacent cages. The bear was pitiful. His nose was pierced with a large ring and from the damage to the nostril it seemed the creature had been exploited as a 'dancing bear'.

As a former prisoner myself I felt real empathy with those creatures. They faced life sentences for no crimes. I could only record their plight then on our return I sent my information to Zoo Check at the Born Free Foundation (BFF) and to the World Society for the Protection of Animals.

Virginia McKenna at the BFF sent their vet, John Knight, to visit the zoo. The outcome was reported in the Spring 1999 issue of *Wildlife Times*, the magazine of the BFF. The bear, named *Pakise*, had been a dancing bear. She still had a ring through her lip and was thought to be blind. *Pakise* was anaesthetised, her ring removed and her eyes examined. Whilst not blind her vision was seriously impaired and her front teeth had been knocked out years before (no wonder that she looked sad in my photograph). She made a good recovery from her operation.

The lioness, named *Sultan*, was operated on to close an abdominal hernia. She also had two small tumours removed and her teeth cleaned. She too made a good recovery. On the advice of John Knight environmental enrichment ideas were introduced for the animals and the BFF and WSPA cooperated to help pay for a proper food supply. I also heard that the Government of the Turkish Republic of Northern Cyprus would provide a new enclosure for the lioness and would help towards the provision of a new bear enclosure. It was also agreed that neither *Pakise* nor *Sultan* would be replaced when they died. No animal should be in a zoo in the first place but as neither animal could be released to the wild that seemed the best option.

Sunday August 17th 1997 I took our daughter to Basildon Zoo to check conditions. We met my former LACS colleague Kevin Flack outside and then conducted a lengthy inspection.

In the summer of 2000 we took our family holiday in Turkey. On Monday June 12th we drove to Izmir and visited the Culture Park and Zoo. Aside from all the usual problems associated with keeping animals in captivity there were two greatly disheartening aspects. Firstly, the presence of dogs as exhibits in cages and secondly, the way visitors could freely tease and torment the animals. ACIG supporters also visited zoos around the world and reported their findings.

CHAPTER EIGHT
More undercover investigations, hunting and hare coursing.

Throughout the NIMR investigation I carried on work to expose bloodsports. Saturday December 9th 1989 found me back with hare coursers for the meet of the Isle of Ely Coursing Club at Swaffham Bulbeck. The usual scheduled start was 9am but more dense fog delayed it by a couple of hours. Even when the fog lifted the visibility was still poor. I saw six kills. One victim was damned by coursing enthusiasts as a 'bad hare'. The Slipper, John Wilby, made a point of explaining to the Coursing Inspector, a Mr Baker, why he slipped the dogs against that hare.

The organisers complained they were not allowed to course over Council owned land. They made up for that inconvenience by putting beaters in over the Council land, driving the hares off it and coursing them nearby. Chatting with supporters I made friends with a lad from Yorkshire named Dave Stansfield. He owned coursing greyhounds and clearly cared for them. His friendship stood me in good stead for future undercover work.

I was embroiled in a lot of undercover work but there was some play. On the evening of Wednesday December 20th Jim Barrington and I met Maureen Lawless and Graham Hall for the *News of the World* Christmas party at Flynn's. The working relationship between LACS and the paper was excellent. We had much to celebrate.

I had an early start on Boxing Day 1989 meeting Jim Barrington at Fleet Services on the M3 at 10:15am. We went to the meet of the Hampshire "HH" Foxhounds at The Butts, Alton. Our main task was to identify an arch-opponent of the LACS—Barry Peachey—amongst the watching crowd of hunt supporters and photograph him. I did so.

[Barry Peachey, Legal Editor of *Shooting News* and a 'Legal Advisor' to the BFSS, issued writs for libel against the LACS and its Wildlife Officer, John Bryant, over an article in *Wildlife Guardian*, Spring 1987. In the article John Bryant claimed that Barry Peachey, who wrote under the pseudonym 'A.G. Fox' in *Shooting News*, had given false and misleading evidence when called as an 'expert witness' by defendants appearing in court charged with badger offences. John also revealed that despite advertising his services as 'the only lawyer exclusively practising in countryside law' Peachey was not a qualified solicitor or barrister. Further, when he was a police constable attached to Basingstoke Police Station in 1982 he had been disciplined for shooting and killing two pet dogs after they had been caught and shut in a barn by a farm manager in Preston Candover. The case was heard at Winchester High Court in the summer of 1992. The LACS employed a brilliant legal team led by Charles Gray QC. I attended for a couple of days. The return to Winchester Court brought back memories for me. During the case, it emerged that as a police officer Barry Peachey was fined for disobedience for publishing an article on police matters in a bloodsports magazine without first clearing it with his superiors. Dr Stephen Harris and Ruth Murray, called as expert witnesses by the LACS, contradicted Peachey's claim that badger diggers would not ordinarily use small dogs such as Border Terriers and would generally have no use for lurchers or nets. The trial started on Tuesday June 2nd 1992 and ended on Monday June 15th. The jury retired to consider their verdicts at 10:40am. Barry Peachey was confident of victory. The jury returned at 3:50pm and found unanimously in favour of the League and John Bryant. Barry was mortified, more so when the court ruled that he had to bear both sides' costs estimated to be between £250,000 and £350,000. The reputations of the LACS and John Bryant were preserved. Barry Peachey later went bankrupt. The following year, on Friday September 10th 1993, Jim Barrington asked me to accompany him to the bankruptcy hearing at Reading County Court to photograph Barry Peachey, but Barry never appeared. I tried again at Reading County Court on Tuesday October 19th 1993, with John Bryant. That day Barry Peachey did show up and was declared bankrupt. *Wildlife Guardian* 27 (Winter 1994) that reported the outcome revealed that Barry Peachey was Whipper-in to the Clinkard Beagles. Used to 'accounting for' hares he was himself accounted for.]

My last undercover work in 1989 was on Saturday December 30th when I joined the East of England Coursing Club meeting at Postland. This was the second day of the club meeting. As usual I mingled amongst the supporters chatting with as many as I could. One of the Flag Stewards gifted me some club gossip. Apparently an owner, who ran his dogs in club events, would be away for a while as he was in prison serving a 15-month jail sentence for pinching turkeys!

The same Steward told me the beaters, of whom there were over 60 that day, were paid £10 a day. He added that they used to have police officers from Skegness and Boston doing the beating but when they asked for too much money the club stopped using them.

One hare killed was singularly unlucky. She was killed in the bottom of a ditch but would have escaped were it not for a third dog getting away from the slips and joining the coursing. Garret 'Garry' Kelly (1950-2014) was doing the Slipping. At the time, he was generally rated as being the best Slipper in coursing but coursing enthusiasts that day assured me his dad, Billy, was better. The day ended at noon.

In the New Year, despite spending days on my investigations at the NIMR, I still found time for work to infiltrate bloodsports.

A key new piece of equipment was delivered to my home on Monday January 8th 1990—a Sony TR55 video camera purchased with ACIG funds. I had a larger and better quality video camera that I had used at the NIMR, but that was obviously professional. I could not use that Panasonic for hunting and coursing work without arousing suspicion. In 1990 I was a proud father of two small children. It was easy and plausible to say my Sony was purchased to film them growing up, and I just put it to extra use to record my hobby.

As I went deeper undercover within the world of hunting and coursing I developed various aliases. For previous undercover work in 1981-83 I used a fixed name and address but for this work I opted for a variety of names. To subscribe to magazines from opponents I used sympathetic friends and colleagues. If I needed material physically posted to me by opponents I had aliases and a Norwich accommodation address.

On many occasions I just turned up at an event and used different names. If hunters or coursers asked me where I lived I would be vague—giving the town only. If they pressed the matter I deployed two lines of defence: firstly, that I was going through a messy divorce and was living in hotels or with friends; secondly, that my business was collapsing and I was again living as a nomad in hotels and bed and breakfasts. Neither reply by me invited further questioning. If pressed hard, I responded in kind by asking my questioners where they lived, and what they did for a living. Most I met were happier to tell me about their lives than enquire about mine.

I considered taking my new camera to the Barbican Cup hare coursing event in East Anglia on Friday January 12th but when I learned Peter Atkinson would be there I chose not to. He would recognise me and it was one thing avoiding people in the crowds at the Waterloo Cup; keeping away from individuals at smaller meetings was harder.

The following Monday, January 12th, I took the new camera to the Swaffham Coursing Club meeting at Kimberley. The video camera proved a fabulous asset but those early ones had glitches that made it difficult for the filming I was doing. The viewfinder image was black and white—fine for filming coursing over grass but a hare running over a ploughed field all but disappeared. I could rotate the eye-piece to view from above but it was still an eye-piece that needed to be looked through, it was not a screen. The biggest problem for filming coursing was it took a few seconds from pressing the start button for the camera to start filming.

Watching hare coursing you sensed, from watching the beaters, when a hare was coming through on to the coursing field. The flankers then kept the hare in front of the Slipper. The Slipper aligned his dogs, sighted them on the hare and only released the dogs if the hare was suitable. If I waited until the dogs were about to be slipped before pressing the start button I missed the start of the course. If I pressed early I could waste film on hares running through but not being coursed. Films may have been 1 or 1½ hours long but there was also battery time to consider. On very cold days, such as were often experienced at coursing, batteries did not last long. Video cameras also did not like rain. Wet cameras often failed and even the slightest raindrops on the lens obscured the film.

I soon learned how to get the best out of my camera in hostile conditions—to shield the camera with a plastic bag, to have a supply of dry tissues for the lens and to keep batteries warm.

My best information learned that day came from chatting with supporters. One leading figure, Bill Balls, told me he had not been to the Waterloo Cup for eight years. He disliked the coursing there as the hares were imported into the area just weeks before the event and seemed disorientated. He boasted how one of his female coursing colleagues punched an anti-coursing woman at an Isle of Ely Coursing Club meeting near Newmarket some eight years before. Violence towards opponents was ingrained and celebrated. There was one kill but I did not see it. I left when the day ended at 2:30pm.

My video camera had another outing when I took it to the Isle of Ely Coursing Club meeting at Queen's Farm, Fulbourn on Saturday January 20th. I chatted at length with the flag man, Stanley Baker, and a Mr Sharman. I was keen to learn the intricacies of hare coursing.

The following Saturday I returned to hunting with hounds to follow the Cambridgeshire Harriers' meet at Ickleton. The map showed that with the M11 and A11 nearby they were likely to have problems from that meet, particularly given that the area was full of hares. So it proved. The Huntsman lost control and hounds rioted. When I saw one heading straight for the M11 I plucked him to safety. Doing so protected both hound and motorway drivers.

I put the dog in my car and searched for the rest of the pack to return him. They had disappeared in pursuit of a hare so I had no option but to take the hound to Royston Police Station as a lost and straying dog. The police hated me—the least welcome creature in their cells was a dog that was not housetrained. I advised them to contact the Cambridgeshire Harriers as he was almost certainly their dog, and get them to collect him.

The following weekend I headed way out west to witness more hare coursing, but in Ireland. Sue accompanied me with our youngest son. We drove to Fishguard on the west coast of Wales and caught the 3pm ferry to Rosslare. We checked into the Wexford Lodge hotel. The following day, Sunday February 4th, I went to the Open Coursing meeting at Ballyclerihan. That was hare coursing much like an English coursing meeting. Mingling in with the crowd I took slides. That evening we stayed at a hotel in Waterford.

Monday morning we drove to the first day of coursing at Clonmel. I carried my new video camera. We took our young lad in his pram. The previous year the weather had been lovely and sunny but in 1990 it was wild, wet and windy. Clonmel coursing was unlike anything found at coursing in the UK. It was staged at a big horse racing venue with grandstands. Whilst Sue sheltered indoors with our lad and watched the coursing in a degree of comfort on TV screens I took a place at the front of the crowd, near the escape zone.

I quickly befriended those around me telling them that I had bought my camera to film our young son as he grew up. I even demonstrated to some near me how the camera worked—such cameras were still a rare sight in those days. The conditions were so wet that the mounted Judge wore a raincoat over his red coat. The escape zone was a screened barrier with the bottom pole set high enough off the ground for the hare to get through but not high enough for the dogs to follow. That did not always work as planned. I saw some dogs slide on their sides under the pole and into the escape zone after the hare.

The rain deluge drenched the ground. Sometimes a dog would lunge at the hare, miss her and roll over and over. I feared for the well-being of the dogs as they tumbled at speed. Other times it seemed impossible for the hare to escape as she twisted and turned beneath the very jaws of the fast-closing dogs, but escape she usually did. Occasionally the hare would be rolled by a dog. Once I heard a watcher nearby shout, "*Come on the hare!!*"

There were hares caught that I filmed but I knew that if I kept my camera on the struggling hare I would be thrown out. Filming anything at Irish coursing from the crowd was risky; filming such a kill was just not possible. Coursing enthusiasts were keen to film and photograph coursing; only opponents filmed what happened after a hare was caught.

The outcome for the hare depended largely on the length of the slip. If given a long start before the dogs were slipped she often reached and disappeared into the escape zone before the dogs even turned her. Then it seemed the Judge awarded the course to the first dog to reach the escape zone. If the slip was short the dogs caught up with the hare well before the escape zone. She then had to twist and turn to save her life.

That meant some dogs did more work than others to win their course. I guess it was easy to criticise the Slipper but he was a man letting two dogs go—they were not released from traps. The hare flashed past him at speed. He could not release his dogs without both being sighted on the hare. If one dog took time to settle and sight the hare she might have run 20 metres further than in the previous course. The variables were endless.

Watching it all it soon occurred to me that if, as I observed, courses could be judged purely on the basis that the winner was the first dog to reach the escape zone then why have the hare at all? Even when the hare was turned, almost invariably, the first dog to reach her won the course.

When the day's coursing finished, I re-joined my small family and we drove back to our hotel in Cork. That evening we met Jim Barrington who had travelled over to join us on our work.

The next morning, Tuesday February 6th, we drove north looking for a meet of the Ward Union Staghounds. The Ward Union hunted the 'carted deer', namely a stag that was chosen from a tame herd living in large fields at the hunt kennels. The stag was released, given a suitable start and then the pack was released to hunt him. The idea was that when the hounds caught up with the deer they bayed him, he was captured and returned to his cart ready to be hunted again another day. It sounded fine in theory but in practice things could and did go wrong—the main problem being that no-one could effectively explain to the stag the nature of this contrived 'game'.

We were interested to see this pastime for our first time. The meet was scheduled for the delightfully named *Dancing Tree* inn near Trim. We arrived to find the meet cancelled due to heavy rain. The stag was doubtless delighted. We returned to stay in Cork then travelled to watch the final day of hare coursing at Clonmel on Wednesday February 7th. The coursing was again run in torrential rain—so heavy that it made it difficult to take photographs and video film. In heavy rain, I could barely see through my glasses. This was the day of the ICABS protest march against hare coursing. Jim and I exited Powerstown Park to film the protest on the road outside. Jim looked a bit furtive wearing dark sunglasses to avoid being recognised, even in the inclement weather.

The ICABS supporters had been inventive with their slogans. I saw: "*Ignorant, Cruel, Cowardly*"; "*Ignorance No Excuse*"; "*Coursing Clergy Disgrace our Church*" [a reference to Priests seen supporting the coursing at Clonmel]; "*State Sponsored Torture*" and "*Protect our Wildlife, They are part of our Heritage*" amongst many others. They were also vocal with a variety of chants including the old favourite:-

What Do We Want? Coursing Out!!
When Do We Want It? Now!!

Jim and I returned to watch the coursing and again took up a position near the escape zone. I watched as one hare ran through without the dogs being slipped. Perhaps a dog was unsighted or, more likely, the Slipper judged the hare weak.

There was a kill on the far side of the escape zone from us. I heard the hare squealing as she struggled. When the finals were run the roars of encouragement from the crowd were noticeably louder. Afterwards I went to film the speeches and presentations made from a sheltered platform. Local bigwigs adorned the stage in their fine regalia, including the Mayor of Clonmel, who thanked everyone for attending.

On leaving, an unfortunate if memorable incident occurred. The car park, an open field, was churned to a quagmire by all the rain. We helped push other cars out and in turn people helped push me out. As drive wheels spun in the wet they threw up a shower of water and mud so you needed to stand wisely to push. A big well-dressed Irish lad came to push my car. Seeing the danger for him I wound my window down and warned him to push from a position clear of the wheels. He replied: "*Oh...don't worry, go on...go on!*" I revved up, dropped the clutch out, my wheels ejected a wall of slime but with the push we got free. In my wing mirror I saw my assistant standing legs apart aghast. Everything left of his belt buckle was clean country clothing, everything to the right was mud! I did warn him. I gestured 'thanks' and drove away. We laughed, but there were opponents more deserving of such misfortune.

We caught the ferry home on the Thursday. On Saturday, February 10th 1990, I was back with a local coursing club, the Isle of Ely, meeting at Fulbourn. Foul weather had accompanied us from Ireland. It was very cold and wet. Just talking about the dogs and coursing I had seen in Ireland boosted my credibility and cover as a coursing enthusiast.

The following Saturday I took my camera to the meet of the Puckeridge & Thurlow Foxhounds at White Barns, Furneaux Pelham. I knew the hunt from my days as a hunt saboteur in the 1970s. I had never visited it before in the undercover role. I tagged along with the crowd of supporters and videoed the hunted fox running. He was later marked to ground in a wood, dug out and killed. Supporters said he sought sanctuary in an artificial earth.

Monday February 19th proved shocking. I visited the Kimberley & Wymondham Coursing Club meeting at stately Somerleyton. Again it was an early start with dogs in slips for 9am. I took my Sony video camera and filmed five kills on the coursing field. On two occasions, the hare squealed in pain and terror. Though coursing was never judged after the hare and dogs left the coursing field, it often continued over adjacent fields and through woods. One hare we knew was caught as we heard her squealing before she was killed in a nearby wood. Supporters and owners asked me to film their dogs running and I was happy to do so. In return I learned a lot of hare coursing gossip.

I was told about the top jockey, Greville Starkey (1939-2010), who had a dog that won an event at Newmarket but was stolen before he could be given the cup. The dog was later recovered from a car park in Surrey. I learned that leading racehorse trainer Luca Cumani's wife was interested in the running dogs.

I returned to the Puckeridge & Thurlow Foxhounds for their meet at Patmore Heath on Saturday February 24th. Hunt saboteurs were in the area doing their best to protect wildlife. At one point I saw a stray hound in amongst chickens on land near Farnham Green. The chickens were startled but otherwise unharmed.

The following week I spent days undercover at the Waterloo Cup with my colleague Janet Jackson, a very generous supporter of the ACIG. The first day, Wednesday February 28th, started in a near blizzard. Janet and I made our way to the bank side and joined the massed throng of hard-core coursing supporters from around the country. It was no place for a gentle and compassionate soul like Janet but she steeled herself to the sights she would see and the raucous enthusiasm for cruelty. We huddled behind a golfing umbrella seeking sanctuary from the driven snow.

I took along my Sony video camera and recorded graphic footage of hares caught and tussled over alive. The nature of the crowd around us became evident when a hare was caught and someone commented: "*Nice kill that weren't it.*" Janet proved a great help. Tracking coursing through the narrow black and white view provided by the viewfinder I sometimes lost sight of the hare—she then put me right. When snow turned to torrential rain she held the umbrella to protect the camera. Without her, filming would have been all but impossible.

We saw the anti-coursing protest march escorted by police. There were murmurs to the effect of 'let them come over here and we'll deal with them'. We noticed that many hares, instead of heading for their usual escape zone, the rhododendron bushes at the opposite end to the Slipper, were circling back towards the Slipper and back towards the beat funnel from whence they came. This produced some very long and punishing courses. Along with the expected enthusiasm for kills I also heard some shouting of, "*Go on Hare!!*" when a hare twisted and turned for her life.

Plenty of curses were directed at the Slipper, Gary Kelly, and the line of flankers on either side in front of him. A hare would be driven onto the field; Gary would advance from his hide with the two dogs but not slip them. This would earn abuse. "*What a wanker!!*" and later "*You fucking knob head!!*" Such abuse was usually born of ignorance. A more knowledgeable courser explained to his uncouth colleagues: "*If the hare's not straight he can't slip them, end of story.*" The dogs could only be slipped if the hare was strong, both dogs were sighted on her and she had not swung sharply to the right or left. That was never easy in the best of conditions let alone in torrential rain or a near blizzard.

Later, clouds of red smoke drifted over the escape zone end of the coursing field. We took that to be from a hunt saboteur's smoke flare. The abuse directed at the Slipper continued throughout: "*Come on Kelly, get yer act together, wanker!*" Flankers who failed to keep the hares straight were damned as "*Dickheads!*" The many kids who bunked a day off school to join this crowd learned much about abuse and intolerance.

Ditches at the field edges seemed to cause real problems. Some hares went into the ditch and ran the sides, others jumped the ditches, some dogs jumped and some fell in causing themselves injury. There was raucous laughter around us whenever something went wrong such as a dog going unsighted after being slipped (he lost sight of the hare, perhaps after being distracted, and would just stop). More amusement was caused when a hare ran into the escape zone then amazingly declined such safety and returned to the coursing field. She ran the gauntlet of being in close proximity to the bank side crowd.

The only amusement for Janet and I was when we saw a tiny mouse running on the slope of the bank amongst all the sturdy boots and kit of the packed coursers. Had any of the coursers seen him he would have been a mere stamp from oblivion but their attention was elsewhere and he carried on his merry existence unmolested.

It was a day for all weathers. At one point we actually saw sun. Then rain returned. The attitudes in the crowd were just as variable. Kills were cheered but there were also shouts of encouragement for the hare. We saw one hare hit by the jaws of a dog which then rolled. She got up and carried on twisting and turning. With both dogs closing on her and the escape zone a long way away she seemed certain to die. Again and again the dogs lunged to grab her but at the last instant she turned away. She could easily have turned from one dog into the jaws of the other but she always managed to slip by. Gradually she worked her way towards the escape zone. When she reached it, and disappeared into the safety of the cover spontaneous applause broke out from the crowd.

When there was a break for lunch, some coursers headed back to their cars, others gathered around a burger van that drew up behind the bank. The bank itself was littered with rubbish including discarded cans of Carlsberg Special. Drink flowed freely—perhaps to keep the numbing cold at bay. Some coursers were so drunk they could barely walk.

After lunch there was a kill where we could hear the hare squealing with pain. Another time the hare was hit at speed, rolled, but got up and ran away. She escaped but I sensed Janet wincing as she feared for that hare. The bank side for the Waterloo Cup was no place to be if you had any real empathy. Late in the afternoon another blizzard swept in. The visibility was so poor that Gary must have felt obliged to give his dogs a short slip (whilst the hare was still in sight). The hare was killed. The day ended with us stuck in a mighty queue to exit the snow-covered car park.

It was easier to film coursing on the second day, at Lydiate, where the crowd was stationed closer to the field. The first course I filmed ended in a kill. On the third course there was a kill very close to us.

For the second drive the Slipper was positioned on our right side. The coursing field was still wet and slippery. When one black dog lunged for the hare and missed the dog ended up injured and had to be carried from the field. After one kill there was a tussle between the dogs over the hare. *Sam the Man* won the tussle and ran off with his prize. It took time for pickers-up to catch him.

We returned to our Wigan hotel. Next morning, Friday March 2nd, we returned for the Finals at the Withins. We took up our favoured position on the bank side. One hare was killed after an unusually punishing course. *Magellas Bimbo* won the Waterloo Purse; *Linton Hyflyer* the Waterloo Plate and *Sam the Man* the Waterloo Cup, killing the hare in the final. Whichever dog won, the hares lost far too often. We stayed to photograph the presentations of the prizes.

I returned home late on the Friday evening for an early start the following morning to join the meeting of the Isle of Ely Coursing Club at Balsham. I met Dave Stansfield again and filmed his dog, *No Exit*, winning the President's Cup. His friendship stood me in good stead. I also chatted with Arthur Kimberley from the Oxfordshire Coursing Club. He invited me to see his club—one I had sabotaged back in the 1970s—but I never took him up on his offer.

The next morning, I was back in the Cambridge area meeting Dave Fox and other hunt saboteurs who showed me artificial earths they had found. The following week, on Tuesday March 6th, I attended my last hare coursing meeting that season when I joined the Swaffham Coursing Club meeting again at Somerleyton. At the meet we were warned hunt saboteurs were expected but as it turned out we saw no sign of any. That day I used 35mm cameras only. There were numerous kills. To try to complete the event they continued until 5pm but even then, had to divide instead of running the final ('divide' means that the finalists shared the prize). That was the second day of a two-day meeting. On the first day, at Saham Toney, shortage of hares put them behind in running through their card. I also heard a dog named *Slightly Naughty* broke a leg and had to be put down.

When I asked coursers about problems hares faced in the wild I was told many die from Gramoxone (Paraquat) poisoning. Farmers sprayed the herbicide on their fields; hares got it on their paws and licked it off.

Saturday March 10th I visited another hunt, the Cambridgeshire Foxhounds, I had last seen as a young hunt saboteur. It was originally advertised as a Cambridgeshire Harriers meet. I took slides at the meet at Elsworth Lodge before moving on to follow the Puckeridge & Thurlow Foxhounds from nearby Elmdon Bury. I merely mingled with supporters, watched and followed. The only thing of note was finding a large pheasant release pen in a wood (factory farmed pheasants are placed there as an intermediate stage prior to being released to be shot).

The following Saturday, March 17th, I looked at the East Essex Foxhounds meeting at Greenstead Green. Again I mingled with and chatted to hunt supporters. They gleefully recounted an incident a couple of seasons before when their colleagues at the Grafton Foxhounds had ambushed and battered hunt saboteurs. As ever, wherever the fox went, hounds followed. I saw hounds running over a prestigious golf course—to the consternation of golfers trying to enjoy their sport.

The next week foxes won two bouts with hunters due to unforeseen circumstances. I drove on Saturday March 24th to the East Essex Foxhounds' meet at Toppesfield but they cancelled due to hard ground. I went on to the secondary target the Essex Foxhounds meeting at Matching Green but was told they cancelled due to the 'crops coming up'. My tertiary target, the Puckeridge & Thurlow Foxhounds meeting at Dewes Green I could find no sign of. That completed my undercover investigations into hunting and coursing in the 1989/90 season. I had made progress against hare coursing and laid foundations for future work to expose hunting.

In the spring and summer months, as already described, I undertook other investigative work for the ACIG to expose vivisection, salmon farming in Scotland and the killing of marine mammals in the Faroe Islands. In July I added to our armoury of photographic equipment by purchasing a top of the range Nikon F4S with ACIG funds.

For the 1990/91 season, I determined to get closer to fox hunting. My first venture into undercover work that season was to look at cub hunting. As described in *Outfoxed Take Two*, cub hunting was the prelude to the fox hunting season that trained the new entry of hounds to hunt foxes, and taught fox cubs to fear hounds. Hounds and foxes were not always the bitter opponents that people think.

This was a letter from a hunter published in *Hounds* magazine:-
"*Memorable Day With Hounds*
Sir, Two years ago we went cub hunting in Northumberland with the West Percy Foxhounds. It was, by nine o'clock, a beautiful sunny morning, about a dozen of us were standing on a road, leaning against a wall, looking over a grass field towards a covert where hounds were. Suddenly out of the covert we saw a fox cub coming towards us at a steady trot, and heard a rather feeble cry, which emanated from a young puppy - who resolutely followed the cub. We all stood motionless. The puppy came within a yard of the cub - who turned round - snarled and raised a foot. The puppy sat down and scratched his ear and the cub resumed its trot towards us and the wall. Following the cub for several yards, the puppy stopped and looked back where he had come. He seemed undecided whether to hunt on or return to the pack. He looked again at the retreating cub and then galloped back to the covert. We shall never forget the lovely sight of these two young animals eyeing each other with curiosity. The cub, on reaching the wall ran along it until he came to a gate through which he passed, crossed the road and entered another cover."
(*Hounds* magazine. Volume 5, No. 1. November 1988. Page 37)

[This letter highlighted the difference between hunt and anti-hunt. The fox hunter regarded it as a 'lovely sight', one they doubtless hoped to see again. The conservationist viewed it as pitiful that creatures clearly not natural enemies are trained and exhorted to tear into each other.]

I attended the cub hunting meet of the Essex Foxhounds at Rookham Hall, Abbess Roding at 8am, Saturday October 13th 1990. Hunt saboteurs endeavoured to protect wildlife. I mingled and chatted with hunt supporters. I photographed the terriermen walking away from one small copse with one carrying a dead fox. The day ended after about three hours.

I returned to the same hunt the following week for their meet on Wednesday October 17th at Wimbish (Lower Green). I chatted to the Huntsman, George Milton, a mild-mannered, affable fellow. He said he started his hunting career with the Devon and Somerset Staghounds—a pack where I spent much time working undercover nearly a decade before.

I soon learned the intricacies of my new Nikon F4S. Equipped with autofocus it was a major step up in ease of use—I no longer had to look through the viewfinder and twist the lens to focus. However, I found the system could be fooled. A fox bolted from a covert and ran across the open grass field. A hunt servant galloped to head him off. He cracked his whip towards the creature to scare him back towards the hounds. I turned my F4S on this scene but there was early morning mist and my camera hunted backwards and forwards seeking focus. I switched to manual mode to secure images.

One fox was killed in a covert early on. I chatted freely with hunt supporters. They boasted their hunt had killed 7 brace of foxes (14) up until that date. I saw and photographed a young child astride a pony—it was not only young hounds and young foxes that were being introduced to fox hunting. I stayed with the hunt until noon when they packed up.

I returned to the Essex Foxhounds for their meet at Good Easter on Saturday October 20th. The starts were gradually getting later. That was an 8:30am meet. It was a very foggy start. I was informed that hounds killed one fox but that occurred out of my sight. My most memorable images were of horses and hounds in a ford.

The following week I looked at the Waveney Harriers from their meet at *The Duke William*, Metfield. That hunt knew me so I only monitored their activities. I took pictures of hounds and riders assembled at the meet. One rider, in turn, took video film of me. That was a foolish risk I took! As they knew me I should have left them alone. Their film of me working in my full 'hunting gear' could easily have been copied and circulated throughout the hunting world—and thus ended any future undercover work by me.

They were irritated by my presence and directed verbal and physical abuse at me. Shouts of, "*Dug any graves up lately?*" were followed by one lady rider who backed her horse into me. Knowing a horse can kill with a kick I asked her to refrain, and moved to one side. She manoeuvred her horse and carried on backing into me. I saw a police car parked nearby with a couple of officers watching this scene. I walked over and complained to one, PC512, about the rider barging her horse into me and requested he tell her to stop. He smiled and said neither he nor his colleague had seen anything.

I carried on observing the hunt as they hunted the many hares that reside on the nearby disused airfield. Then at 2pm I drove to Halesworth Police Station intending to complain about wilful blindness by two Suffolk officers. The station, a large, modern, multi-storey building, was shut.

On the Saturday, October 27th, I slipped back into the undercover role at the meet of the Essex Foxhounds at Roxwell. I was keen to try out some new very fast film—Ektar 1000ASA—that allowed you to take pictures in low light and pictures at a very fast shutter speed in good light.

I photographed hunted foxes fleeing from hounds and witnessed the curious sight of drain rods used to evict an exhausted fox from sanctuary. Hounds had marked the fox to ground in a road drain on the bend of a fairly busy minor road. The enthusiastic terrier crew were summoned and went to work. The hunt moved on leaving the terriermen to deal with the fox. They netted one end of the drain and inserted drain rods into the other. Sure enough, the terrified fox bolted, but hit the net at such speed that he burst through it, shook himself free, and ran off. With hounds elsewhere he made good his escape. The terriermen cursed.

The hunt exacted revenge on the vulpine race when they killed a fox near Skreens Park at around 11am.

The following Saturday, November 3rd, I returned to hare coursing when I attended the Isle of Ely coursing club meeting at Swaffham Bulbeck. I was keen to fully understand hare coursing. The arguments over hare coursing differed from those over hunting with hounds. Hare coursing was seldom defended as a means of controlling hares. The main advocate for hare coursing was the articulate and forceful Newmarket Horse Trainer, Sir Mark Prescott. He delighted in his reputation as a fearsome pugilist and man with an eye for the ladies. Given his love for combat sports even his own side nicknamed him 'the Bloody Baronet'.

Hare coursers deployed numerous defences. They claimed that coursing enthusiasts looked after the hares on their land for coursing and thereby saved them from being killed by shooting or by farm chemicals. As for actual coursing, they claimed few hares were killed. Only weak hares were killed and any caught were killed instantly by the 'nip to the back of the neck'. Easy claims to make and they sounded good on television or in debates but honestly they were far from the truth.

At the time of this investigative work hares were killed by a wide variety of means. They were shot for 'sport' and 'pest' control. They were killed by accidents on our roads and they were killed for 'sport' legally by hunting with packs of hounds and by hare coursing. Hare coursing was the organised club variety done with greyhounds or lurchers. There were also individuals coursing on land with permission. Then there was illegal coursing—illegal purely because it involved trespass.

There was cross-over between these pastimes. People who shot hares also enjoyed hunting or coursing them. The link between legal and illegal hare coursing was intimate. Few illegal hare coursers ever coursed illegally without at least watching legal coursing first—often from the bank side at the Waterloo Cup. It became a real problem for the legal clubs that sighthound enthusiasts paid the few pounds for an entry card, attended and watched the event, saw where hares came from and went to and returned later to mop them up with out-of-hours and illegal coursing.

Hares suffered the most during legal hunting and coursing. Only in those pastimes was the intention to inflict the maximum suffering on the hare. Everyone else tried to kill hares as quickly and cleanly as possible. Men who hunted hares 'for the pot' wanted the hare dead and in the bag quickly. They gained nothing from subjecting their victim to a lengthy chase, a chase that risked losing the quarry. Illegal coursers aimed to be on the land for the least time possible; every extra minute increased their chance of capture. Conversely, pack hounds were bred not to overmatch their quarry—an hour to ninety minutes was the ideal hunting time for a pack of hounds. In hare coursing the hare was given a start so as to produce the most exciting course to watch and judge.

There was no fairy tale world where hares were kept for coursing and only for coursing. No lands where hares not killed by coursing were neither shot nor hunted by hounds but instead grew old on the fields and died of old age. Old hares would never be killed by coursing because we were assured that the Slipper would never slip his dogs against a hare he judged 'unsuitable', and a pensioner hare was certainly unsuitable.

That Saturday with the Isle of Ely club I tried out the new 1000ASA film and also took black and white prints. It seemed seven hares were killed, some by the lurcher lads who retrieved them after the dogs caught them in woodland adjacent to the coursing field. During the day, I chatted with Nick Low, a keen supporter, about Saluki Coursing.

The following Saturday, November 10th, I returned to the Essex Foxhounds for their meet at Old Barn, Great Canfield. Foxes won as my diary records it was a blank day with poor scenting conditions. I ingratiated myself with hunt supporters though by showing them photographs I had taken at previous meets. This was long before the advent of smartphones. Now everyone photographs anything. In 1990 people were still genuinely interested in quality images of themselves pursuing their chosen pastimes.

The following Saturday, November 17th, was an interesting day. Again I joined the Essex Foxhounds who met at Chalks Green, Leaden Roding. It was a day of murky, wet weather. I took the usual stock shots of the riders. At one point I saw the hunt Chairman, Paul Dixey, grubbing around in a ditch. I stopped to see what he was doing. He was collecting discarded road litter, bottles, cans etc. I stopped to help him and we chatted about the hunt, the hounds and the terrierwork. When I commented about the enthusiasm of the terriermen he remarked that in his view they were, "*a law unto themselves.*" I took that as a hint of something untoward.

Whereas at Great Canfield there had been poor scenting conditions the day with the Essex Foxhounds at Great Sampford on Wednesday November 21st was the exact opposite. It was, as hunters described, a 'screaming scent'. With plenty of foxes about it would, in the absence of hunt saboteurs, take luck for all to survive. One was hunted at a very sharp pace over an airfield. Following in the line of supporters' vehicles I noted the hunt at 40mph on my speedometer. They lost the fox when he found sanctuary in a ditch near the village. That fast hunt was punishing on the horses: I saw one horse with a broken shoe; another with a cut above one hoof. I gave some of my photographs to the Huntsman, George Milton.

The hunt packed up at 3pm. Before they finished I chatted with the Field Master seeking opportunities locally to see and photograph shooting. He gave me a recommendation to a man named Ron, a gamekeeper at the nearby Spains Hall, a shooting estate owned by the Ruggles-Brise family for 250 years. A personal introduction from the Essex Foxhounds was my perfect entry ticket to see the world of shooting.

I accelerated my undercover work. After the Waveney Harriers follower filmed me I knew it could all end at any time and I had to get what evidence I could, whilst I could.

Saturday November 24th proved interesting. I joined the Isle of Ely coursing club for their meeting, once more at Swaffham Bulbeck. I noticed my long-standing ACIG supporter and fellow investigator, Mike Michalak, there with his daughter. Tensions within the coursing world surfaced when there was a blazing row between one keen courser, a man named Nye, and a club steward.

As I slipped deeper undercover within the world of bloodsports I realised the need for an accommodation address. You can only get away for so long with being vague about where you live. On Friday November 30th I bought an accommodation address in Norwich. I could use many personas—but had one address.

The next morning, December 1st, I returned to the Essex Foxhounds for their meet at Stagden Cross. At the meet I spoke to a chap introduced to me as a very keen supporter named Nick Herbert. Nick was a slight, insignificant character, brimming with anger. He appeared to be liked by fellow hunters only for his wealth.

[Nicholas Le Quesne "Nick" Herbert was a celebrity within hunting. He went to Magdalene College, Cambridge where he read law and land economy. He was a Joint Master of the Trinity Foot Beagles (the Cambridge University pack) from 1984-1985. In 1987 he formed the Newmarket Beagles together with Francis Burkitt, Mark Melvin, Roddy Edwards and James Shand. The pack was registered with the Association of Masters of Harriers and Beagles (AMHB) for the 1987-88 season. *Baily's Hunting Directory* 1997-1998 listed the pack as having 20 couple of beagles "*the property of Mr Nick Herbert*". Nick Herbert was Huntsman of these beagles from 1987 and Joint Master from 1989. In 1990 he was appointed Director of Public Affairs at the BFSS, a post he held for six years. In 2005 he was elected MP for the West Sussex seat of Arundel and South Downs. When David Cameron took power in 2010 he appointed Nick Herbert the Minister of State for Police and Criminal Justice—a position he held for two years.]

When I learned there were two vans full of hunt saboteurs out protecting wildlife and substantial numbers of police officers I had to leave. I knew police would check car number plates and when they realised who I was would tell the hunters. I moved on to follow the Trinity Foot Beagles who met at the quaintly named Twenty Pence Bridge, Cottenham at 2pm. I paid my 'cap' of £3 and watched hunting on a cold and misty afternoon. I photographed one fleeing hare and chatted with the student supporters.

ACIG supporters were keen to carry out undercover work themselves. My colleague Janet Jackson photographed a hare coursing meeting on December 5th. She secured some excellent images confirming the cruelty inherent in coursing.

I returned to the Essex Foxhounds on December 8th for their meet at Woolards Ash near Hatfield Broad Oak. Heavy snow was forecast. At the meet I was introduced to Guy Ruggles-Brise by a female Master. He was most welcoming and I arranged to photograph his Spains Hall shoot on Jan 5th at 9am.

I gave enlargements of my photographs to a lady introduced to me as Doreen Cooke, the soon to be Secretary of the Essex Hunt Supporters Club. I was Michael Robinson. I gave her my Norwich address and she told me she would send a Meet Card. She advised me to take my photographs to their Tramps Ball in January. Supporters told me her family sold VW's.

The meet venue at Woolards Ash had beagles in kennels. I photographed them later being walked by a lady who told me they were the Newmarket Beagles. Supporters identified the meet as the home of Martin Herbert, (Nick's dad), who rode with the hunt that day.

On my way to the meet I noticed the terrierman's Land Rover parked in a farm nearby and pondered why. Then I saw a young terrierman emerging from woodland adjacent to Woolards Ash just before the meet. I learned to be observant over events at the perimeter of any hunt.

Their first draw was at Canfield Hart north of the meet. I stood to the south with Mr Ruggles-Brise. I then moved around to the north on the B183. Hounds were silent but then screamed away in full cry. So, they had stumbled upon some creature, probably a fox but possibly a deer.

They crossed the B183 to the west heading for Hatfield Park, the field in full galloping pursuit. I drove north on the B183, west on the A120, then south on the first turning to be west of Hatfield Park. I saw deer coming over first and stopped to photograph them, then headed further south to where I heard hounds. I was joined by other car followers. A supporter to whom I had spoken numerous times before asked me what was happening. I said the Huntsman was casting hounds. He said words to the effect that they should catch that one as it was right in front of them. Laughing, he added *"Here's your fox, go catch him!"* I knew I would have to get very close to a hunt to fully understand it.

Hounds were cast backwards and forwards again and again, far more often than usual but without success. They then had a run circling around to the south-west. Much later in the day near Row Wood I stood with supporters as more snow fell. I was with Guy Ruggles-Brise and a young lad, Ian with his girlfriend. Ian spoke quietly to Guy about a previous incident, near the end of a day. Hounds had marked at a road-side drain. He (the fox) was in it, and they did something that caused concern to watching foot followers. I could only guess at what.

When blizzard conditions swept in soon after 3pm I left and endured a difficult journey home. Before I left the supporters made a point of inviting me to the meet the following Saturday, December 15th, at Kelvedon Hall, the home of Paul Channon MP (1935-2007). I was asked to photograph the meet at that stately home.

I foolishly neglected to check the meet location and assumed that Kelvedon Hall would be in Kelvedon. In fact, it is in Kelvedon Hatch, more than 25 miles away! That was before the days of easily checking such things on the Internet so I should have asked—it is elementary for an investigator to know where to go. After going to Kelvedon by the time I reached Kelvedon Hall the meet was long over. I missed photographing high-ranking Conservative MP Paul Channon handing out drinks to hunt riders but I did find and follow the hunt.

The following Monday, December 17th, I was back amongst hare coursers, attending the meet of the South of England and Newmarket Coursing Club at Valley Farm, Balsham, near the A11. When I arrived for the 9am start I thought I saw a man who lived just a few houses from me in our small village. He would have recognised me as an anti, so I huddled ever deeper into my pro-bloodsports camouflage. I was also on the look-out for Peter Atkinson.

We were transported in the beaters wagon to the coursing site and instructed to use a foot-dip as a precaution against spreading rhizomania (sugar beet madness), rife in East Anglia at that time.

Amongst the supporters I noticed well-known hare coursing photographer Lt. Colonel Ted Walsh with his huge telephoto lens costing some £2500. Other fieldsports photographers were there sporting large lenses. I chatted with country sports celebrity Tony Harvey in the main crowd. In time I meandered over towards the photographers. I enthused over their telephoto lenses and one kindly offered to let me try his 400mm lens and monopod combination on my Nikon camera. I used that to photograph a kill.

I saw Peter Atkinson standing near the Slipper on the opposite flank line. So long as I could see where he was I felt safe. I also saw Sir Mark Prescott. BFSS members from Suffolk and Cambridgeshire had been invited to attend to see what hare coursing was about—few turned up. I heard Charlie Blanning explaining what was happening to a newcomer. They discussed the curse of poaching and in Charlie's opinion the best poacher's dog was a Saluki/Greyhound cross (Tony Harvey disagreed. He doubted it would retrieve quarry to hand).

Tony told me that he went out with the Anglia Lurcher Owner's Club and that he ran dogs with them. When I enquired how their meetings worked he invited me to see at their next on January 9th.

When, at noon, there was a break in the coursing I returned to the sanctuary of my car to avoid bumping into Peter Atkinson. For the second drive, I stood near the Judge in the main crowd. I photographed a hare caught and killed by a bye dog running on his own. I had never seen such a single dog pick-up before. Judge Ronnie Mills reckoned she must have been a poor hare.

On one drive a hare ran onto the field. Too weak to be coursed, she was reluctant to leave—but had to be driven off for coursing to continue. Nick Reed-Herbert (died April 7th 2016) caused amusement to all by running on to the field to chase her away. Even then she was slow to clear the area. Ronnie Mills later opined that she had been coursed before.

I left after the lunch break as I needed to avoid an encounter with Peter Atkinson, and the light was failing. It had been a bitterly cold day.

Four days later, December 21st, I joined the East of England Coursing Club for their meet at Postland at 8:30am. Delayed by traffic changes on the A47, I arrived late just in time to witness the fifth hare coursed being killed. This happened close to Charlie Blanning. I heard the hare squealing in her death throes. Benefitting from professional advice from Ted Walsh I had upgraded my camera equipment. I could not afford the 400mm lens but my ACIG invested in a monopod to produce better results with current equipment.

I steadied my camera on my new monopod and photographed using fast 1600 ASA film. There was a kill on the opposite side of the coursing field. The consensus was hares were handicapped by their feet being balled up with mud as the surrounding fields were very sticky. That reduced their manoeuvrability and increased the likelihood that they would be killed.

In due course we drove to the site of the next drive. There the hares were very slow coming on to the coursing field. The light was also poor making photography difficult. I recognised Dave Stansfield who asked me to take pictures for him. Coursers were cursing because the beat appeared poorly organised. This was due to the beaters, in the main, being school kids who larked about a lot. That was good news for the hares—many escaped at the corners just before being driven onto the field.

I chatted with Charlie Blanning learning the intricacies and intimacies of hare coursing and was with him late in the afternoon as the light failed at about 3:20pm. He spoke a report of each course into his dictaphone. I left at 3:40pm.

Boxing Day 1990 we courted the media. I drove down to meet Jim Barrington and his wife, Ursula. Television companies had asked the LACS where they would be on Boxing Day for the traditional interviews about the cruelties of killing wildlife for fun at Christmas. We chose to attend the Surrey Union Foxhounds meeting at Pewley Downs, Guildford. It lashed down with rain but Jim interviewed with his usual passion and eloquence. We then drove on to the West Kent Foxhounds who met at Kemsing but could find no sign of them.

It was a busy end to the month. Saturday December 29th I joined the Essex Foxhounds for their meet at *The Green Man*, Mill End Green, north of Great Dunmow. They marked a fox to ground and tried to dig him out but could find no sign of him. Mr Fox could have fooled hounds by looking in the hole and then running on; or perhaps there were tunnels in the earth complex that gave him sanctuary beyond the reach of the terriermen. I chatted with supporters, including one who followed the De Burgh and North Essex Bassethounds. By then I was so trusted by the Essex Foxhounds that I was invited by the Masters to their hunt seminar.

Two days later, Monday December 31st, I was back with hare coursing when I joined the Swaffham Club meeting at Little Massingham, near to the Royal estate at Sandringham, where Sue and I spent the first week of our honeymoon.

This was the first time the club had met at that venue and there must have been teething problems as the organisation appeared bad. I was with John Balls. He told me they were asked to drive hares across a field then instructed not to. No-one seemed to know what was going on. They did walk-up coursing over one field then driven coursing with the Slipper sited at the narrow end of a field of long stubble. Hares were driven in but veered to the sides resulting in some short and awkward slips.

As often happened coursing continued off the coursing field. I photographed one hare killed in such manner. They only had one field to course on and four drives towards it. The hares were in short supply but due to bad flanking many escaped out the sides before they could be forced onto the coursing arena.

I discussed the obvious problems with a knowledgeable Irish coursing supporter from the Oxfordshire Coursing Club. He diagnosed that the young Slipper, Nigel Williams, allowed himself to be told what to do, when indubitably, he should have taken charge.

From the last drive two hares coursed were both killed; one, right in front of a family with their daughter on her first visit to hare coursing. The Mum, the wife of a keen trainer whom I had seen many times, said loudly she wanted to complain about the Slipper. She shielded her daughter's eyes from the kill and declared the hare dead—even though she could clearly be heard squealing and seen struggling! They were so short of hares the last two finals could not be run.

*****

1991 dawned and proved to be the most important year in all my many years of undercover investigations into bloodsports. On New Year's Day, I was up before 5am and drove through icy conditions to meet Janet Jackson at her home south-west of London. We then drove on in Janet's Suzuki Vitara to the Alresford Coursing Club meeting at St Mary Bourne.

I sought out and spoke to the Club Secretary, Sally Merison, and asked her permission to take pictures, she said "*Fine*". The coursing was over a sloping field of short stubble. To gain better coverage Janet took a position on one side, high up the hill, me on the opposite side.

I recognised one trainer, a man named Lavender, from the Swaffham meeting the previous day. He asked me to photograph his dog running in the red collar. After release from the slips the white-collared dog led then promptly won by seizing the hare. I photographed the resulting tug-of-war and kill that happened right in the middle.

Sally approached me and we chatted about coursing. She appeared happy with my presence—and my coursing credentials. She explained they coursed hares down wind as they did not like running into it.

The beat was put out again for the same field. Janet told me that several hares were killed high up the hill. Some kills were noticeably protracted. One dog would win a tug-of-war and run off with the live, squealing and struggling hare. Over the large fields it then took pickers-up time to catch the triumphant dog and release and kill the hare.

Coursing stopped for lunch after which we drove in convoy to a new venue. The coursers walked-up the field of stubble first. It held six hares, four of which were coursed. Normal coursing then resumed with the Slipper stationary and concealed. Again we divided resources with Janet one side, me the other. Dogs were badly cut coursing over that field. I saw a man named Bushnell whose dog had an obvious leg injury.

Right at the end of the event one dog collapsed during the course. The Judge thought he had broken a leg. A courser drove his Shogun on to the field and picked up the dog. They announced his leg was smashed so he would be put down. The last two finals were not run out as the owners withdrew their dogs because of the adverse conditions. Not only were there an abundance of razor sharp flints littering the fields but also the short sharp stubble was cutting the dog's paws and legs.

On the Saturday, January 5th, I switched away from the hunting and coursing fields to look at shooting on the invitation of Guy Ruggles-Brise. That work will be described later.

The next day, Sunday January 6th, I availed myself of my personal invitation to the Essex Foxhounds' hunt seminar held at 2pm at Sarah Green's stables in Great Sampford. My credentials as a bona fide 'hunt supporter' were complete. There I was, a former LACS Press Officer, by any account the man most hated by the world of hunting, right at the heart of a hunt event.

The great and good from the Essex Foxhounds were there including Chris Thorogood, a Joint Master, Pat Harrington, another Joint Master, Rob Appleton, a vet, and Henry Marriage, introduced as a hunting farmer. Chris Thorogood explained the purpose of cub hunting was to teach hounds to hunt and to cull foxes. They aimed to split up the litters of cubs so that the strong cubs would give good hunting later in the season. He said that good cub hunting made for good hunting the rest of the season.

Chris said the hunt had lost two hounds on the roads so urged followers to watch out for the hounds. Though the terrierman was unable to attend we heard about terrierwork. If a fox was marked to ground and they wanted to kill him then he was bolted into a net and shot. If they wanted to run him to produce a hunt, then the fox was bolted and hounds held 200 metres back.

We heard about the hounds and horn calls from the Huntsman, George Milton and David. To call for terriers when a fox was hunted to ground there were four blows on the hunting horn—three short and one long. If hounds were leaving the covert there were three blows—two short and one long. We learned about the requirements for puppy walkers. It was all very informative. The best thing for me was that following my participation I was fully trusted.

The following week I completed my profile as a 'hunt supporter' by all but emptying the ACIG bank account to purchase a second-hand Land Rover Defender 90. In that vehicle, decorated with the appropriate hunt stickers, and me wearing full Barbour kit and a flat cap who could doubt that I was anything but a genuine hunt follower?

Wednesday January 8th heralded observation of another cruel pastime. I followed up the personal invitation from Tony Harvey and attended the meet of the Anglia Lurcher Owner's Club at Shirley Hall, Ashley, near Newmarket. It was the traditional early start for hare coursing—8:45am with dogs in slips for a 9am start.

I met Tony Harvey with his son and two lurchers. I paid my visitor's 'cap' of £2 and was introduced to the organiser, Karen. This was walk-up coursing over wide open fields. There were similarities and differences with greyhound coursing. The Slipper wore not a red coat but ordinary country clothing. There was a Judge who did wear a red coat, like in greyhound coursing, but here he was not mounted. It seemed that equipped with a pair of binoculars he walked to the highest point on the ground and judged the course from there.

For the hares there were real problems. Although given a similar start, the lurchers were smart and had far more endurance than greyhounds. In greyhound coursing if the hare could survive a few turns the pursuing dogs would tire and she escaped. With lurchers I was told that a good Saluki/Greyhound cross could kill his hare some two miles from the start point.

With being a close friend of Tony Harvey, and my credentials gained from the world of coursing, the supporters had no problems with me taking plenty of photographs. Indeed, some were positively keen to pose with their dogs.

The following week I joined a LACS expedition for undercover work in the Republic of Ireland. On Monday January 14th 1991, I caught the train to London and then to Holyhead to catch the ferry to Ireland. I was with LACS Executive Director Jim Barrington and Sanctuaries Manager John Hicks. We drove to meet colleagues from the ICABS at Mullingar and stayed at the nearby Bloomfield House Hotel.

We planned to visit the Ward Union Staghounds on Tuesday January 15th but learned their meet was cancelled due to frost. It was bitterly cold with patches of snow. As a secondary target, we chose the Ormond Foxhounds meeting near Birr in County Offaly. The hunters were all in the bar and we wandered in to join them. Jim Barrington was excellent in such situations and soon ingratiated himself. John Hicks had a problem. He was also a smooth and confident talker but as LACS Sanctuaries Manager he had recently been interviewed on television and some hunters recognised him! We made a discreet exit and could only follow the hunt from distance thereafter.

The next day we drove to Cork to meet more ICABS colleagues. We stayed nearby and followed the Waterford Foxhounds the next day from their meet at Durrow at 11:30am. We had the very knowledgeable campaigner John Tierney with us. With his help, we found the hunt in the afternoon. We observed and discussed hunting with the terriermen. That evening we returned to the Bloomfield House Hotel ready for another attempt to follow the Ward Union the next morning.

Friday January 18th, in company with Aideen Yourell from ICABS, we attended the meet of these elusive staghounds at Naul, County Dublin. On arrival we noticed the small green deer cart parked at the roadside. It had two compartments with a red deer in each—one to hunt and one as a spare. The deer were stags with their antlers removed.

Jim strode forward and unleashed his area of expertise by befriending the hunt supporters in the pub. He was good at doing that (too good as it turned out). He gave them all kinds of blarney about how we were English hunt followers keen to see hunting in Ireland. He spoke at length with the Hunt Master and gained his permission to take film and photographs. We needed nothing more. I was armed with my small Sony video camera.

We watched the stag unboxed at 1:30pm. He set off into the distant green yonder. In time the hounds were brought forward and when they hit his scent they screamed away in hot pursuit, with the mounted followers trailing behind. We followed the best we could along the narrow Irish lanes. I was impressed by the knowledge and determination displayed by Aideen.

We learned from other followers that at one point the pack split with some hounds rioting after a hare. In West Country stag hunting the hunted deer could be identified by his antlers—but here they were cut off. It was no surprise when hounds changed deer and set off after an outlier (a deer previously released by the hunt but now living wild). The deer released that day then in turn became an outlier. No deer was caught and the day ended at around 3:30pm.

Aside from the cruelty inflicted upon the hunted deer we felt for the 'spare' deer bumped around in the small cart in the wake of the hunt in case he was needed. At some points we saw the hounds milling around the cart holding that deer and wondered what the poor creature made of it all.

Such stag hunting was hard to justify; with no 'pest control' argument to be made it was purely using and exploiting a magnificent animal for entertainment.

The following morning we caught the 8:45am ferry home from Holyhead. A week later I was back out with hare coursing taking our Land Rover to the meet of the Isle of Ely Coursing Club at Queens Farm, Fulbourn. I then switched focus back to foxhunting. On February 2nd I took the Land Rover out for the first time with the Essex Foxhounds from their meet at *The Duck Inn*, Newney Green. The terriermen laughed at the road tyres I had on my vehicle and were sceptical as to whether they would be of any use off-road.

The following week heavy snow fell. Thursday February 7th was plagued with travel problems. I had made a routine train journey to the LACS offices at Union Street, London. My journey home was considerably delayed by the weather. I expected no problems driving to our rural home in the Land Rover but then encountered cars abandoned in the snow. The adjacent fields looked to be docile fields of snow but I knew there were deep ditches lurking beneath the white carpet—so embarked on a wide detour.

With no hunting on February 9th due to the weather I was next out with the Essex Foxhounds for their meet at Chalks Green on Saturday February 16th. With deep snow lingering that was a day for what hunters described as 'footing' in the snow. No horses, just hunting on foot. My Land Rover proved an excellent tool for such work. The snow-covered fields made an excellent photographic background for the hounds and the red coats of the hunt staff.

At the meet I photographed the terrierman Steve with his terriers. With us all on foot we were all equal and it was easy for me to keep up. When we did need to drive off-road keen supporter, Richard, kindly gave me a lift in his suitably tyred Range Rover.

A fox was hunted and killed in a roadside ditch. Spurts of warm red blood against the snow seemed particularly poignant. The Huntsman, George Milton, grabbed hold of the dead fox's body and set about working his hounds up into a frenzy of excitement. He shook it in front of their noses, then dragged it along the road in front of them.

I then received a phone call that set me off on the most important undercover bloodsports investigation of my whole career.

CHAPTER NINE
Quorn Foxhounds investigation 1991

"What has hunting to fear, after last week's "revelation" on cine film, widely shown on ITN television news bulletins? The answer is nothing — provided that organised hunting with hounds sticks faithfully to its own codes of conduct." (Editor and hunting correspondent, 'Foxford', (Quorn hunt supporter Michael Clayton), *Horse and Hound* August 12th 1983.)

From the very inception of the ACIG in June 1989 I pleaded for supporters to be our eyes and ears in the countryside. I wanted people to be like sponges to soak up any rumour or hints about misdemeanours in our countryside and send them our way.

For some months in late 1990 and early 1991 I received reports of incidents taking place at the Leicestershire-based Quorn hunt that were not in accordance with the rules of the Masters of Foxhounds Association. This involved the handling and release of foxes to produce a hunt. It was apparently being done to keep the pack sharp and thereby provide good sport for the 'glamour' visitors such as Prince Charles who hunted regularly with this pack. The Quorn were said to be the favourite hunt for our future King.

The sources were three from within the hunt, one of whom had since left, and several from observers living locally, including Joanna Woolliscroft, the wife of that great rarity—a compassionate vet. In February 1991 I received another plea to look closely at the Quorn Foxhounds.

I consulted with the LACS and with their backing set out to infiltrate the hunt to try to prove what was being alleged. One of the first difficulties was of the sheer distance of Quorn meets from my home, some four hours' driving. I could get away with telling Quorn supporters that I had attended one of their meets out of desire to see the 'cream of the Shire packs' in action but I could hardly pose as a regular follower travelling such large distances. Accordingly, I assumed the identity 'Michael Roberts', with an address in nearby Huntingdon, a locality I knew well from my youth.

I had excellent ACIG colleagues living in or near Quorn country and arranged to work with one—Ed Maynard a professional photographer. Ed had already gained the status of a trusted follower of the Quorn. On Tuesday February 19th 1991, along with Ed, I attended my first meet of the Quorn foxhounds in the undercover role. The meet was at *The Royal Oak*, Osgathorpe between Loughborough and Ashby de-la-Zouch. It was delayed an hour because of frost. There were still patches of snow on the ground. I used my green ACIG Land Rover, Ed drove his blue Land Rover.

At the meet I took plenty of typical supporter photographs, including of their revered Huntsman, Michael Farrin. When the hunt set off I trailed behind. In the early afternoon hounds hunted a fox and marked him to ground in an earth under bracken on a gentle slope near Whitwick. The earth was a considerable distance from the road and most car followers stayed in their vehicles, chatting, eating, and awaiting events. I knew I would see little from the road so foot-slogged it over the fields to the scene.

To my left I could see the digging party hard at work in the bracken. I knew none of them and knew I would rapidly need to gain some plausible cover if I was to approach and photograph them. I saw a hunt servant exercising his horse whilst he waited in a grass field adjacent to the snow-flecked bracken. I approached and enquired, in naive fashion, what was going on.

He explained the fox had run to ground, that terriers were down, and Michael Farrin was holding hounds in check up in the rocks. I remarked that the whole scene was picturesque and took some photographs. "*It's a shame,*" I said to the Whipper-in, "*if I was nearer the digging party I could get a lovely picture of Michael with the hounds. Can I go over to the earth?*" "*Certainly,*" the whip replied.

That gave me the entry ticket I required. I set off through the bracken to the earth. When I arrived, the earth was surrounded by a group of four men and two children. The men looked at me questioningly and suspiciously. I lifted my camera and reassured them, "*Oh the whip said to come over here to get better pictures of the fox bolting, and the hounds up in the rocks.*"

They seemed happy. I took pictures of the scene and was crouching down to photograph a terrierman working at the tunnel entrance when one of his colleagues shouted at me, "*Get back! Get back!*" and gesticulated the required direction. I complied moving quickly to my left.

In an instant the digger standing at the entrance to the hole whipped out what I at first thought was a terrier. In fact it was the fox held by the back leg. He threw the struggling creature down into the bracken and the whole team started holloaing and whooping with glee. The lead hound, a matter of metres away, set off and the rest of the pack soon followed in headlong pursuit down the slope.

I snapped off photographs as rapidly as possible. The fox ran about 30 metres to the right, swung 30 metres to the left then was overwhelmed and ripped open.

The attention of the terriermen then focussed back to the earth. Their terriers bayed, indicating the presence of a second fox. The hounds were regrouped back at the rocks and everyone returned to waiting mode. This time I was careful to ensure that I was in a better position to record events. I told the men I had never seen a fox bolt from close to and would like to take a photograph. I was directed to a suitable point and advised to be ready with my camera. Soon the fox dashed from the hole and away.

Because he had come out of his own accord that fox was better orientated, made more ground on the hounds, and was soon out of the field of bracken and away. That was excellent for the riders. They rapidly disappeared into the distance in galloping pursuit.

Some of the digging party headed back for their cars. I left in the company of a pair of diggers and their two children. They headed back through the bracken towards their Land Rover parked on grass near where

I had first spoken to the hunt servant.

On the way, their terriers found the remains of the fox and started to worry it. The men rolled the torn carcase over with their feet. Examining the body, they remarked with glee that it had been a vixen. One reached into the shattered stomach and pulled out a string of entrails. "*Pregnant too!*" he said "*Look at the nodules of the young.*" Sure enough the tiny foetuses could be seen within. I stepped back to photograph. "*Why photograph that?*" they queried. "*Oh! I was only photographing the terrier at the fox,*" I explained, thankful that a terrier had entered the scene.

I left their company and returned to my vehicle. It transpired that the hounds pursuing the bolted fox were soon at fault and he escaped. I followed the hunt until at about 4pm they packed up. I met Ed to discuss what happened then was left with a long drive home.

I had ample time to reflect on what I had witnessed. They had handled the pregnant vixen and released her for further hunting. That was a clear breach of the MFHA rules. They had done that in full view of me, a complete stranger to them, and furthermore in the certain awareness that I was using a camera. Clearly they were not only breaking their own rules they were brazen about it. It was no wonder that tip-offs had come our way. I knew I had to keep following that hunt and that if I did I would one day gain damning proof of how they behaved.

The following Tuesday, February 26th, I attended the Quorn meet at Ulverscroft Lodge. The Quorn met four days each week but the Monday and Friday meets were notable for being attended by Prince Charles. Whilst it was likely that more bending of the rules might occur in order to produce sport for His Royal Highness I knew that I had to beware of his attendant Royal Protection Group. I might fool the hunting brigade into believing I was a genuine hunt supporter but not so Special Branch who would doubtless check my vehicle number plate and reveal the truth.

This was another interesting day. There was the usual frantic chase to start with then in time the hounds marked in a wood not far from the meet. I took it they had hunted an exhausted fox to ground. I waited at the road expecting the fox to be quickly bolted as this was the view held by nearby supporters. When after a few minutes nothing happened, I walked up the grass slope to see what was happening. I was too late. Frantic whoops and holloas confirmed the fox had bolted and the hounds and riders set off in hot pursuit. I ignored the chase and continued into the wood to locate and photograph the earth.

I was somewhat taken aback to find that it was a purpose-built artificial earth constructed in typical fashion from concrete pipes. The terriermen were still there packing up the various tools of their trade. Another terrierman arrived on the scene and asked if the fox had been marked to ground. "*No,*" said one, "*we held him there overnight.*" Clearly the terriermen had at the appropriate time for the hunt simply gone to the artificial earth, unblocked the entrances, shoved a terrier in and—hey presto!—produced a fox for the riders. The 'mark' I had heard had been nothing more than excited hounds held in check near the artificial earth.

I cursed that I had been too late to photograph the fox bolting. "*Last week when he did bolt he disappeared into the bracken. This week I was just a minute too late*," I complained. "*Oh, if only you'd said you were coming we'd have held him up in the pipe for you,*" was their reply. To their minds having held him overnight in the artificial earth holding him a few more minutes would have mattered little. Before we left the wood, the diggers blocked the entrances to that artificial earth.

I returned to my vehicle and opted to trail after terriermen Dave and Bob in their blue Renault van. Surprisingly hounds soon lost that fox. I drove around following other supporters then a short time later saw the same digging party huddled around an earth complex adjacent to a minor but nevertheless busy road.

I recognised Dave, Bob, Graham and Brian. There was no sign of hunt riders or hounds. I parked and walked to see what they were doing. The terrier named *Bess* was to ground and Dave was using the locator to track her movements. Some holes were stopped; some were being excavated. I photographed proceedings. Whenever a vehicle passed the men ducked down, hiding from view behind the low fence. Not knowing why, I followed suit, but then queried the reason. I was told it was an old badger sett and that if the public saw the hunt digging at it they might misinterpret things. For the same reason, Bob had been advised to move his van he had parked on the road beside this sett.

Clearly there was a fox about as the terriers were baying. Suddenly one digger exclaimed that he was so close to the fox he could grab it. "*Anyone got a sack?!*" another shouted. The replies were all negative including my own. Everyone looked downcast. They considered holding the fox trapped in the sett whilst the hounds were summoned to the scene. They set about doing this but then opted to bolt him. I was advised that to photograph him bolting I should stand by a certain tree watching one exit. I did but the fox did not oblige and bolted from another exit obscured by dense cover. The men carefully blocked up all the entrances to the earth and then drove off to see if the hunt was in the vicinity. They were not nearby, so that fox escaped.

I followed the hunt by following Dave and Bob's van. We caught up with hounds in Swithland Wood just after they had killed. Michael Farrin brought the shattered carcase out, threw it to his hounds and blew the kill. As the hounds worried the carcase Bob walked in amongst them and asked me to take his photograph with them; I was pleased to oblige. I again cursed the fact that I had missed photographing the fox running. My digger friends advised me not to worry as they had another fox ready in the nearby wood. The three of us hung about as they expected Michael Farrin to bring his hounds back for this victim.

They were disappointed though. As some farmers were moving sheep in the field adjacent to the wood, Bob said it would be bad to let the farmers see what was going on. They left their fox and, somewhat reluctantly, left the area.

We returned to our vehicles, searched for and found the hunt. Again we went in on foot as the hounds were drawing a wood. Dave and Bob described which line the fox would take. They had *Bess* with them and I photographed her as she stood on the wall waiting expectantly. The wood was, as hunters describe, well-foxed. When a fox bolted on the far side from us, riders who saw him, holloaed like mad. "*Fools*" agreed Dave and Bob, "*that's not the hunted one.*"

As expected the hunted fox bolted on our side and Dave and Bob holloaed like mad. One red-coated Master rode up in furious mood and swore at us for holloaing one fox when the pack had already set off after another.

We mumbled our humble apologies. When he was out of earshot Dave and Bob muttered that he had only proved his own "*bloody ignorance*" as he could not tell the hunted fox from a fresh one and had effectively allowed the pack to change foxes thereby ruining a good hunt. Later the pack split into utter chaos and the day ended at about 4pm.

My next day with the Quorn was a bye-day the following week, on Wednesday March 6th. The hunt met at West Leake Manor north of Loughborough. I was fully kitted out with cameras and recording equipment and prepared for events to occur as they had the previous week. There were two dig-outs but no sign of any foxes. Afterwards I met Ed Maynard and showed slides to him and local ACIG colleagues, Christine Harris and Joanna Woolliscroft. That was my last day with the Quorn that season.

The next hunting season, 1991/92, started with early morning cub hunting in late summer. My four hour drive to normal 11am meets had been hard enough but getting to early morning cub hunting meets was really arduous; even more so with three infants at home under the age of five.

Tuesday September 17th 1991, I left at the crack of dawn for the Quorn meet at Kinoulton, south east of Nottingham, at 7am. I repeated my tale that I was a supporter from Huntingdon. From the meet hounds were taken to draw scrubland around the disused Grantham Canal but that was blank. They were then taken to draw woodland east of the A46 where they had more success. I took my small Sony video camera out and filmed some of the holding up. However, I missed filming a fox killed in a stick pile by the terriermen, an incident I only learned of afterwards.

The hunt proceeded to more woodland to the south and I joined supporters standing at one corner. I noticed one supporter named Mick Gill, who drove a Suzuki Vitara, was also using a video camera. To gain cover and have a better chance of using mine to good effect I stood near him and chatted to gain his confidence.

Mick was extremely friendly, welcoming, and enthusiastic about recording the hunting on video. My close proximity to him was just the job for giving me good cover. I told Mick and others that I had a very young family and had purchased my video camera to film them growing up. Using my camera to record hunting was just an extra side-line.

The wood was held up by supporters mounted, on foot, and in vehicles. The hounds bustled about in the wood, sometimes in cry sometimes not. Clearly there were foxes about. Supporters around us reckoned at least a brace.

A cub broke cover but was chased back by hunters. "*Did you get him?*" asked Mick. "*Just a glimpse of him,*" I replied. Later, as hounds crashed towards us through the undergrowth Mick called a warning, "*Coming this way!*" The fox bolted out into the open but was chased back by raucous shouts and screams from supporters.

"*Now, you must have had him,*" said Mick to me. I confirmed I had. As I knew the fox would only be in the open for a matter of seconds I had taken the precaution of leaving my video camera running all the time. [Those early cameras would slip into a 'sleep' mode and take a second or two to 'wake up' for the tape to run and record after the record button was pressed] Mick bore out the wisdom of this with this advice about cameras: "*If you're running you see you've got a chance, haven't you?*"

Another cub broke cover but ran back. There followed protracted hunting within the wood the progress of which could only be judged by sounds as we could see nothing. Foxes darted out and nipped back in. Whenever they were in the open they were greeted by coarse shouts: "*Aye aye Charlie! Aye, aye!*" Then, by way of variation: "*Brr! Brr! Brrrr!*" This was all guttural, Neolithic and clearly very successful at intimidating a small wild animal.

Hounds sounded to be running excitedly. A whip rode up to our corner. "*Have they killed?*" enquired a supporter near me. No-one seemed to know. The whip dismounted and asked me to hold his horse whilst he went to see. I would rather have followed him into the wood but could hardly refuse so was left on the outside. Holding the horse for the whipper-in gave me cover without equal.

Hounds had killed. Michael Farrin brought the remains out into the field. With hounds and supporters around him he cut the brush off, threw the remaining carcase to his hounds, and tossed the brush to one side. I walked forward to video hounds with their prize.

The hunt carried on. They drew one covert from whence it appeared two foxes escaped the surrounding ring of riders. We advanced to a much thicker covert. The dense low cover enabled cubs to run virtually unseen around supporters' ankles. Chris Doherty, the young kennelman, pressed forward to help with his terrier in his arms.

"*There's a brace gone out of this end.*" muttered one supporter near me. Clearly it was all haphazard. Michael Farrin dismounted and waded through the undergrowth doing the best he could. I noticed a fox escaping over the surrounding plough. I said nothing of course and to the best of my knowledge none was killed in that wood.

The hounds were taken on and drew a small copse and then a small area of uncut ground with no apparent success. Then it was on again to another draw. I caught up to find the hunt in full cry in a field of crops.

Frantic cries from supporters of, "*Aye Charlie! Aye Charlie!*" confirmed a fox was in difficulty.

Through my viewfinder I searched for the victim fleeing ahead of hounds but with the limitations of the black and white monitor it was hard to make out the fox. Back and forwards I panned but too late. The fox was headed by a mob of shouting terriermen led by Dave Chapman. A matter of metres from them he was overwhelmed by the pack and killed. I filmed the scene the best I could.

The hounds were cast through the crop again and a second fox bolted on the far side. A whooping and a screaming erupted as the supporters tried to head him back. But the fox would have none of it. With hounds close enough to effectively be coursing him he pressed onwards. He broke through the screen of supporters and was away. The riders set off in galloping pursuit. I assumed he escaped, because Michael Farrin soon brought his hounds back to draw the crop for a third time but there was no quarry left.

We went on to finish the day at a perfectly constructed fox trap. There was a large field from which most of the crop had been harvested. Near the middle was a small length of standing crop. This was completely surrounded by riders, foot followers and supporters in an assortment of four-wheel-drive vehicles. Everyone waited expectantly as Michael Farrin drew hounds through the 'cover'. I ran to try to film the inevitable.

A fox dashed out in my direction closely pursued by the pack. A straight speed test ensued. Fresh fox versus a reasonably fresh pack and the fox won, just. The pack was stopped from continuing the chase and brought back to draw the 'cover' again. Again there was nothing left. A day that had seen three kills appeared to end there. At 11am I embarked upon my long journey home, stopping off in a layby to catch up on sleep.

I returned to the Quorn four days later, on Saturday September 21st, for their meet from Langley Priory, Diseworth south of the East Midlands Airport. I teamed up with my colleague, Ed Maynard, but we worked separately. So far as the hunters were aware we never knew each other—but we watched each other's backs. The meet was scheduled for 7am but was delayed half an hour. The hounds were first put in to draw woodlands around ponds at the meet. They ran with gusto and enthusiasm but without (for them) success. Proceedings then moved to a wood to the south west. Riders and followers surrounded this and the pack was put in. It was soon clear foxes were in residence.

I joined supporters at a ditch leading away from one corner. I had observed them heading a fleeing fox back along this ditch and expected that fox to try again but I was wrong. Unseen by me a fox was killed. Hounds then gave voice again. I concentrated on the ditch but there was no sign of any further fox. Holloaing and shouting from distant supporters confirmed he had broken cover on the far side.

I walked around the wood and tracked along the side of a hedgerow to where I saw a group of terriermen huddled around an earth. Other supporters came to watch. One Joint Master, Barry Hercock, rode up and told us to move away from the hole—out into the field. He was quite clear that they "*want to have a hunt.*" I presumed he wanted to ensure that everyone was well clear from the hole so the fox could bolt in the usual manner.

As we strode across the plough I saw and videoed kennelman Chris Doherty swinging the remains of a dead fox. I ended up standing isolated in an open field, positioned about 80 metres from the hole with riders and foot-followers not far away all intently watching the proceedings. I could see Ed Maynard watching from across the field. I knew he would have his Nikon camera ready.

I started to video the dig out. There were three men at the hole taking turns to dig, another six watching from the hedge-line close by. Michael Farrin held his hounds in check on our side of the field. Suddenly the pack overwhelmed by the excitement of it all rioted and ran over to the hole. Michael Farrin rode over and called them back.

A fourth man joined the digging party at the hole. A rider went over to speak to them. I wondered if he asked how long it might take or whether he warned them I was filming. In case it was the latter I lowered the camera from my eye to my chest, swivelled the viewfinder to the upright position and continued filming. As the hole was in open view of us all I expected to record good film of the fox bolting, my only worry was that the battery power might not last for what could be a long dig. I had to keep the camera running because I knew the fox would not hang around to pose and if I turned my camera off there would not be time for recording to start in the second or two he remained visible.

The minutes dragged on. I observed proceedings through my viewfinder. When Chris Doherty and another man stood back I suspected something was about to happen. A terriermen I recognised as Alan Betts was at the earth. The fourth terrierman stood up and moved back to the left. He appeared to be holding something with tension on it. String, rope, or whip thong? I could not see what. He let go of this. Alan Betts then pulled the fox out by the scruff of the neck into full open view, reached forward and let him go ever so gently into the hedgerow.

They all stood up and called the hounds over. "*Tally-ho! Tally-ho! Whoop! Whoop!*"

The pack unleashed by Michael Farrin charged in. The bewildered fox nipped through the hedge. I thought he would be away but no. There were riders on the other side. Either they never heard Barry Hercock's plea to create a hunt or they ignored him. Whatever, instead of letting that fox run they reacted in the traditional cub hunting manner and headed him back towards the pack. Within the hedge he ran up it for some length then was overwhelmed by the pack and dismembered.

It all seemed both singularly pointless and a clear breach of the Masters of Foxhounds Association rules. In his diatribe eight years before against my investigative work, leading Quorn follower, Michael Clayton, had made it clear: "*If a fox is run to ground it is often left, but if it is decided to kill it in the interests of local fox control, it must be despatched in the earth with a gun. Only the dead carcase may then be given to hounds to break up."* (*Horse and Hound* August 12th 1983)

I wondered whether any foot-followers or riders, who knew the rules and must have seen what occurred, would complain. I walked over to where the hounds were worrying the remains with my camera running. I recognised the big terrierman Bob from the end of the previous season.

"Hi there....he didn't go very far did he?" I commented. *"No,"* he agreed. *"I thought he'd do a run,"* I speculated, seeking to discuss the matter but Bob changed the topic asking: *"Did I see you here last year?"* When I said yes he asked, *"Did you do that photo for me?"* That was the picture of him as he stood amongst the hounds after the kill at Swithland Wood on February 26th.

I might not have lured him into discussing the fox release that morning but clearly I still had good cover within the hunt.

We moved off across the fields and hounds were put into other woods. I was determined to try to record more about the release of the fox. As the supporters lined up to hold up the covert I saw Barry Hercock in position on his horse. I could hardly march up and film him as I questioned him so I just sidled up holding my camera in a casual manner but with it running.

"They didn't give them a run on the one they dug out. I thought they were going to give them a run down there?" I enquired.

"We were. We tried to, but it went through the hedge and then came back again.......That's what we wanted to do...try to get a hunt. Didn't want to kill it." was his explanation.

I tried to push the point further: *"Yea. It's a shame 'cos it would have been nice that."* Barry Hercock agreed: *"Yea, that's what we were trying to do. It ran down the side of the hedge, stopped, turned round and ran back into the hounds.....don't know whether it was trying to get back into the hole again."*

I could not enquire further without arousing suspicion so I returned to watching the covert. Again there were plenty of foxes. I was unable to do any more videoing as the batteries finally ran flat leaving me to use the back-up system of still cameras. That a fox was killed there was confirmed when on walking round I saw and photographed a terrier puppy encouraged to worry the carcase as some kind of training routine.

We moved on to draw other coverts and ended up at a tiny strip of woodland that seemed full of foxes. Riders and foot-followers lined up and the hounds were entered to the copse. The air was immediately full of gleeful shouts: *"Aye aye Charlie! Tally-Ho! Tally-Ho!"*

As young cubs popped out desperately seeking sanctuary supporters swung their boots at them. There were six cubs in the litter; three died within the wood; three escaped to provide fun another day.

The hunt ended by drawing a potato field that surprisingly was blank then packed up at about 11:15am. I had a rather fraught journey home. My eye had seen dramatic scenes—but had my camera recorded them? I confirmed by playing my tape back in camera that Alan Betts had handled and released the live fox but it looked somewhat indistinct in black and white. How would it look in colour on television? Thankfully it was adequate and confirmed what had happened. I knew that would take some explaining by the hunters.

My securing such revealing film that proved the reality of hunting inevitably time-limited my undercover work. We could never sit on such film for long. All fox hunting was cruel but it was clear the Quorn Foxhounds treated foxes with great contempt. We had a duty to stop unnecessary cruelty as soon as possible.

Further, what if Michael Farrin resigned, moved or the Hunt Mastership changed? Regime changes like that would allow hunting authorities to excuse the actions by saying words to the effect that nowadays, everything's changed. For greatest impact, we had to release my film to the media soon. My future as an undercover operator, certainly within the Quorn Foxhounds, was henceforth severely limited.

I resolved to gather as much evidence as I could from the Quorn before my story was exposed. Whilst it was easy to pass myself off as a once-a-week casual supporter by going more often I inevitably drew more attention. Who is he? Where does he live? Why is he not a member of the Supporter's Club? Why does he take all those pictures and film? What does he do for a living? The questions were endless and obvious. Thankfully few if any were asked. There really are some hunters for whom following hounds four, five or even six days a week is no problem.

After the drama of Saturday September 21st, I was next out with the Quorn for their meet the following Thursday 26th. This was scheduled at Frank Salt's Farm near Ashby-de-la-Zouch but on arrival I could find no sign of any hunt there. I called the hunt stable's number and the Huntsman's number but surprisingly no-one who answered had any idea where they were. In desperation, I called Ed Maynard. He advised me to try Old Parks Farm near Smisby, to the north of Ashby-de-la-Zouch.

It was good advice. They met at a mushroom farm there but had moved on by the time I arrived. I caught up with them on National Trust land at Calke Abbey. Hounds were in a dense wood and riders and foot-followers used the rides within to keep in touch. The only thing of interest was when hounds rioted after deer.

I heard the pack in full cry and saw deer cross the ride just metres in front of me. The pack followed soon after. When Michael Farrin rode up I warned him his hounds appeared to be rioting after deer. He did not seem unduly worried. He never stopped the pack. From later discussions with supporters I learned that he believed there to be a fox running as well. Whatever, neither fox nor deer was killed in the wood. The morning ended after hounds drew through crops around Staunton Harold.

Two days later, on Saturday September 28th, I was back for the Quorn meet at 7:30am at Whatton House, near Hathern, north of Loughborough on the A6. That was the home of Lord Crawshaw a former Chairman of the hunt. From the meet, we crossed the ominously busy A6 to the first draw, a small covert. The covert was held up by many riders, terriermen, foot-followers, and supporters in vehicles. I saw Alan Betts amongst the crowd. A verbal warning was quickly passed around that (because it was a Saturday) antis were out as well.

A fox quickly bolted. He defied all efforts by hunt followers to head him back and made off towards the comparative safety of the A6. I moved towards a supporter I recognised and started chatting. Innocuously at first but I soon raised the topic of the fox that was released for hunting the previous Saturday. He recalled the incident and laughed but would not elaborate. I sensed that such an event was just one of those things and not something to talk too much about.

Michael Farrin rode up and down with his hounds. Clearly there was at least one other fox about. This was confirmed by the usual shouts of: "*Aye aye Charlie!! Tally-Ho! Tally-Ho!*" as supporters viewed him. That fox seemed to escape. Soon afterwards we all crossed back over the A6 to woodland near Slade farm. The wood was surrounded by plough and I joined other supporters standing on this to watch proceedings.

The first to flee were hares that dashed along the edge of the covert. Then there was that familiar cry from supporters, "*Aye Charlie! There he is!*" Some of the many schoolchildren watching joined in vociferously. At one point the fox crossed the plough right in front of Michael Farrin and nipped back into the covert. The hounds piled in after him but it appeared that he too escaped.

The hunters became increasingly frustrated at this inconclusive hunting. They moved to the west to a covert near the M1. This was thick, dense and looked to be purpose-made to provide sport. It was tightly held up by riders interspersed with foot-followers. There seemed to be foxes everywhere judging by the cacophony of sounds. Holloas, hounds, horn blowing, the supporters banging sticks on the ground and the fence posts; it was all riotous fun for hunters. As vehicles on the adjacent M1 thundered by and jets from nearby East Midlands Airport roared overhead I heard a few representatives of the geriatric hunting brigade reminiscing nostalgically about the 'good old days' before such modern traffic. When Lord Crawshaw turned up on his All-Terrain Vehicle to admire the events it confirmed that those old days were truly dead, gone and buried.

For all the shouting and enthusiasm, the hunting there appeared singularly unsuccessful. The next move was further afield. I had a long walk back to my car then a drive south down the A6. I found hounds drawing flat marshlands near the River Soar. It was very picturesque but I witnessed nothing of note and the day ended at 11:30am. I drove around to meet Ed Maynard at the home of Graham and Joanna Woolliscroft to show them my recent video. They were all delighted at the progress made to expose how the Quorn Foxhounds operated.

I stepped up my efforts to gather rapidly as much evidence as possible. I routinely left home at 4am. The following Tuesday, October 1st, I attended the Quorn meet at Cropston north of Leicester. It became difficult to explain to hunters how I was out so often yet no-one knew much about me. Proceedings commenced with a draw in crops south of the meet.

That field was blank. We then moved to the north past Cropston reservoir towards Swithland wood. I and all the supporters expected something to happen at this location. I strolled across the fields to the position I had taken up earlier in the year and joined Dave Chapman, Neville Fitchett and others. A fox dashed across the opening between two segments of woodland. "*That makes three,*" muttered one supporter.

I chatted with my hunting chums and tried to elicit if there was an artificial earth in the wood. They merely agreed there were 'earths' there. I sensed I was asking too many questions and that hunt supporters were becoming defensive in my presence. Undercover work needs time to develop properly. Always filming and asking questions was bound to arouse the suspicion of even the most slow-witted hunt supporter but I had no choice—the time clock on my work at the Quorn was expiring fast.

Hounds next drew, without success, a couple of pieces of woodland back towards the minor road south of Swithland before they disappeared at speed. I next found them on the golf course near Roecliffe Manor south of Woodhouse Eaves. As I crossed to follow them I had to beware of low flying, high-velocity golf balls. More so as I suspected they would be driven with some venom by golfers irate at having their genuine sport disrupted. There were many people about. From a distance, it was hard to distinguish who was playing golf and who was following the hunt. I battled through woodland towards sounds of hounds.

When I paused in one thick covert to listen to who was doing what and where they were, I had a magical encounter. The hunted fox came tip-toeing up to me and passed by me. I prepared my camera but there was no sign of hounds following. I remained still and quiet allowing that fox to escape but I then had a problem. If I did nothing the hounds might well come through on his line and hunt him. If I then came out of the wood and was seen by supporters they would doubtless grill me as to why I had not holloaed when I must have seen the fox.

I had to help that fox. My hunt saboteur instincts kicked in and I opted to move sharply to my left and at a suitable distance away from the true line of the fox I holloaed like mad. Within the dense confines of the wood I could always argue to any hunter who might query my actions that I had seen a fox and if it was not the hunted fox at least I could claim that I honestly thought it was. It was also good for my cover to holloa like mad as if genuinely trying to help.

The pros and cons for my actions were debatable but mattered little as the hunt never came to my holloa anyway! I continued to follow and found hounds in the grounds of Roecliffe Manor. Supporters were gleefully expectant as they believed they had a fox trapped in a small area of fenced-in cover near the Manor. Hounds swarmed in hot and close pursuit but without success. Again and again they combed the area but they neither found the fox nor marked him to any hidden hole. One supporter found it incredible, "*You wouldn't believe that twenty couple of hounds could miss one fox!*" he exclaimed. But miss him they did. The hunt then moved north.

Hounds found a fox and hunted him. There was a dig-out but there appeared to be no kill.

The 7:30am meet at Frisby, west of Melton Mowbray near the A607, at the end of the week on Friday October 4th proved interesting. From the meet hounds were taken to draw a small covert to the north, between the minor road and the railway line from Melton Mowbray to Leicester. I saw my friend Mick Gill, the video man, and we chatted. I overheard him talking to other supporters about someone being bitten there previously.

It is unlikely a hunt supporter would be bitten by a hound. It is possible whilst helping at a dig they could be bitten by a terrier. It is also possible that at a dig they could be bitten by a fox. That drew my interest.

Tagging onto the conversation I said: "*What, he was bitten trying to pull the fox out instead of leaving the terriers to do it?*" As we strolled along Mick answered: "*Well, we got two in the hole.....and apparently he put his hand in.....and his hand got bit...had to go and get a jab.*" I could not elicit any more but it seemed to be more proof that live foxes were handled at the Quorn.

Hounds were put into covert and immediately there was evidence of an abundance of foxes. Guttural shouts of: "*Aye aye Charlie! Aye aye Charlie!*" ruptured the still morning air. Hunt followers moved smartly to ring the covert and close the trap. When foxes darted out of the wood, endeavouring to escape, they were swiftly chased back in towards the hounds by a dawn chorus of cries.

"*Should get some good film here,*" Mick enthused. How prophetic those words were. One fox broke cover, ran the gauntlet of supporters and escaped towards the railway line. Realising that much was likely to happen I loaded a new video tape to ensure that I had plenty of tape available. I had one problem with filming: the succession of early morning starts coupled with the need to help Sue attend to our young daughter at all hours of the night had taken a toll on my health. It did little harm coughing and spluttering when using still cameras but such sounds ruined the soundtrack of a video camera.

I moved position from one corner of the wood to the side parallel with the railway line. A fox tried to escape up the hedge-line towards the railway but was chased back. Supporters were joyous. "*We've caught one already!*" one told me. I moved towards the hedge-line, then back. The hounds were rampaging up and down the wood. I saw Michael Farrin get off his horse and go into the wood on foot to help them.

A cub then ran from the wood, taking the familiar route up the hedge-line towards the railway. Supporters shouted to scare him back. With the full pack behind him in the wood he seemed determined not to return and carried on. A red-coated hunt servant on horseback tried to head him back, helped by a female supporter. Still the fox pressed forward. Eventually, at the last instant he turned and was chased back down the side of the hedge into the wood.

I cursed that I had moved away from the hedge saying to one supporter: "*I should have stayed here shouldn't I?*" He replied, "*If you'd*

Above: salmon farming in Scotland. Top: Isle of Skye, June 1990.
Above: Invergarry Salmon Farm, June 8th 1990.

Below: fox fur farm near Halifax, September 29th 1990.
Bottom right: the author photographs a captive fox.

Waveney Harriers at Metfield, October 24th 1990. Right: hunt supporter films me. Wide circulation of that video could have ended my undercover work.

Above: death of a hare, Alresford Coursing Club, January 1st 1991. The hare is caught and subjected to a tug-of-war.

Undercover with the Essex Foxhounds.

Above: Huntsman George Milton leads the hunt, October 17th 1990. Right: Hunt seminar, January 6th 1991. George Milton and Essex Hunt Masters explain hunting theory.

Above: 'Footing it' in the snow, February 16th 1991.

Below: death in the snow. Fox is killed in ditch. George Milton taunts hounds with dead fox, and drags the body down the road.

Above: Ward Union Staghounds, Ireland, January 18th 1991. Deer cart at meet, the release of one deer and 'spare' deer in cart.

Left: Tony Gregory TD addresses ICABS Conference, October 17th 1992.

Right: fox in a box at Vine and Craven Foxhounds kennels, November 1991. (Picture anon. gift).

The box was empty when we visited.

Below: Vale of Aylesbury Foxhounds, January 4th 1992. Huntsmen flail at horse stranded over gate. Below right: hunters placate irate motorists.

Kent and Sussex Minkhounds, March 30th 1991.
Right: the daffodils prove the early start to the
mink hunting season.

Kent and Sussex Minkhounds, April
13th 1991. Above: mink (arrowed) at
bay.

Bottom right: hunt supporter lashes
with stick at floundering mink.

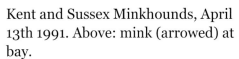

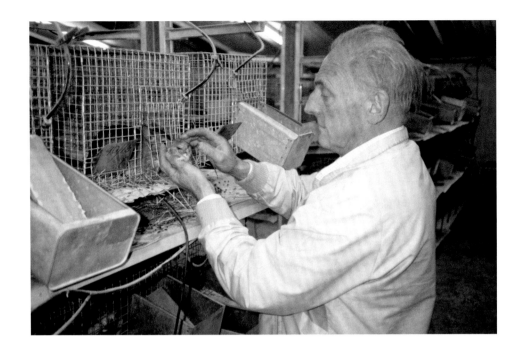

Breeding Chinchillas for the fur trade.

Fred Duggins at his farm, September 23rd 1991.

Tiverton Staghounds, October 27th 1990. Above: fleeing stag runs past hunt supporters.

Below left: stag runs away over the hill. Below right: after the kill hunt supporters gather round for the trophies to be taken.
(All photographs by ACIG investigator Mr X).

Quorn Foxhounds. Top: foxes
(arrowed) flee from earth
after dig-out. Above: terrier
strives to get at dead pregnant
vixen, February 19th 1991.

Right: fox on the run,
February 26th 1991.

Quorn Foxhounds, September 21st 1991. Above: Ed Maynard photographs a fleeing fox. Below: the sequence that exposed the truth. A fox is dug out on left of picture whilst Michael Farrin waits with hounds on right. Bottom right: fox is pulled out and released.

Quorn Foxhounds (from video). Above: a cub is bolted, October 4th 1991. Below: a cub is hunted, marked to ground and dug out. 4 minutes and 29 seconds after he was first held the fox was shot. His body was thrown to the hounds, October 8th 1991.

Puckeridge and Thurlow Foxhounds, November 23rd 1991.

Fox is killed by hounds in front of a home (top left). Instead of taking the body away the Whipper-in flaunts the torn carcase in front of hunt saboteurs. This causes a scuffle as they try to retrieve the body.

Shooting at Spains Hall, Essex. Above: January 5th 1991.

Below: January 12th 1991. Below right: I am in the wagon with the guns.

Above: Banbury livestock market with Andrew Tyler, January 1993.
Left: calf (arrowed) is pushed over, January 6th 1993. Right: dead pig
in pen, January 7th 1993. Below: hides and skins investigation.

Above and left: Patrick Martin shows
me around his Bicester with
Whaddon Chase Foxhounds kennels,
July 18th 1992. Below left: carcasses
at Heythrop Foxhounds kennels,
February 20th 1993. Below right:
hides bought by TV company,
February 19th 1993.

Above left: Essex Foxhounds stewards close footpath. Hunt ends up hiding in a farm, January 23rd 1993. Below: Essex Foxhounds stewards close footpath to hunt saboteurs, September 25th 1993.

After young hunt saboteur, Tom Worby, was killed at the Cambridgeshire Foxhounds, hunt saboteurs reacted peacefully and professionally.

Left: Press conference, Cambridge, April 10th 1993.

Below left: Dave Fox addresses rally against hunt violence, Cambridge, April 10th 1993.

Work to expose live exports.
Above: Lawrie Payne (left) and Janet Taylor (right) look for calf flight, Schiphol airport, May 9th 1995.

Nieuwpoort, Belgium, May 10th 1995.

The *Caroline* arrived and was unloaded. Bewildered calves were driven up the ramp and into the lorry.

Below: we tried to follow the livestock lorry but were stopped by the police.

Left: Janet Taylor photographs slaughterhouse at Izegem, June 6th 1995.

Below: calves unloaded and pushed into veal crates, June 7th 1995.

Left and below: when we returned to the same unit on September 20th 1995 the calves had grown and barely fitted into each crate.

stood there you could have shook hands with him.....kept coming up this dyke as brazen faced as you like."

Again and again foxes tried to break cover and escape but each time were chased back into the wood by raucous shouts from supporters. Whether these were different foxes or the same ones trying repeatedly was hard to say. Frequently a train passed by. I feared we were a little too close for comfort to what was clearly a busy line. Across the country hounds were all too often killed when they hunted live quarry over railway lines. They could be struck by trains or electrocuted.

Hounds hunted up and down the wood. Eventually a cub was marked to ground in an earth just inside the wood, near the corner where I first stood. I strode over and observed proceedings. Michael Farrin was confident they not only had one fox trapped beneath ground there was also a second fox in the wood at the other end. The digging party went to work with enthusiasm. Michael led his hounds out into the middle of the field and held them waiting patiently. Not patiently enough though. The sounds of digging generated too much excitement for their canine minds—on one occasion they broke away and rushed over to help. The whipper in drove them back.

Terriermen clustered around the holes all keen to get involved and help. More spades were brought to the scene. Hounds kept trickling forwards only to be driven back. There was much chatting, fun and hilarity amongst the watching throng waiting so expectantly. There would be no escape for that fox.

One lad working at the entrance to the earth called out: *"Just go and tell him we've seen it at the end of the hole."* Kennelman, Chris Doherty, wearing his blue boiler-suit arrived to lend a hand. Mick Gill, the video man, stood beside me filming. When a bulky supporter inadvertently blocked our view, Mick complained sarcastically: *"Thanks George I can see a lot now!"* Duly chastened George moved. That was one benefit of my being beside the well-trusted hunt videoman. I could never have asked or expected George to move.

Something excited the hounds again and they all crashed over to pile into the holes. It was easy to see how terriers, particularly fox coloured ones, could be bitten in such circumstances. The whip drove the pack back to Michael Farrin. About 10 seconds later the digger at the mouth of the earth leaned back and indicated to the watching crowd that the fox was about to emerge.

He was a truly pitiful sight. His head squeezed out of the hole and the small, wet, bedraggled body followed. He was a young cub. Shaking himself he ran pathetically, trying to flee. The Quorn pack was unleashed in hot pursuit through the wood. I thought he could never escape.

The terriermen suspected there were more foxes in the earth and set about rooting around to see what they could find. I commented that the fox that fled was not very big. Supporters near me agreed. One said: *"He was only a little one....he won't go very bloody far."*

A fox was then observed nipping out from the covert on to the grass and running back towards us before taking shelter in the trees with hounds not far behind. This was a much bigger fox than the one bolted.

Hounds milled about in the wood for some time then a change in tone of their barking indicated they had killed. That fox was killed within the wood on the side where I first stood. I lingered with supporters on the outside wondering what would happen. Hounds were taken to draw the next wood.

A terrierman then walked out of the first wood carrying the bloodied carcase of a large fox. This confirmed our suspicions that hounds were not after the cub we had seen bolted. The consensus view of those around me was that this must have been the vixen. Perhaps she had given her life to save her cub?

Hunting moved to a small covert to the southwest. Along the way to the new site I chatted with supporters to see if I could elicit any more information about the pulling out of foxes from earths by hand.

"*I was surprised when they said the guy was going to pull it out though......*" I ventured.

"*Pardon?*" answered the supporter nearest me.

"*I was surprised when they said someone was going to pull it out, wouldn't he get bloody bitten doing that?*" I pressed.

My new hunting colleague was pleased to explain: "*Well no...not if they do it the right way. There's a technique to pulling foxes out. When you've been bitten three times you learn it!*"

"*Yea, you get hold of the arse end I should think isn't it?*" I responded.

That was precisely the discussion I sought. My video camera was hanging apparently innocuously from the strap around my neck but I kept it running. Although it filmed the ground it acted as a perfect recorder.

My contact warned of possible dangers: "*Put your hand along its head and it puts its head up and it gets you in the fucking mouth.*"

Another supporter chipped in with some expert advice: "*Grab it by the brush...slide hand right up its back to start of its neck and hang on like bloody hell then!*" This drew a burst of laughter from followers around us.

Another experienced supporter offered the following with a visual demonstration: "*You know what my...know what my dad always did...always used to put his hand underneath...take 'em like that mate.*" Clearly I was amongst hunting folk with much family experience of handling live foxes for 'sporting' purposes.

Another supporter expanded on the theme. "*I was up the Fells last year and I seen a bloke pick one out with its...with its one ear.*"

"*Yea?*" I replied somewhat incredulously.

This Quorn supporter was in full reminiscent flow. "*And it never got him....lifted it out here like that.....dropped it...*" he said gesticulating.

The discussion evolved: "*It depends how you catch them, my dad used to go up his stomach and go up that way....*"

"I'd have said bugger that mate. The bottom jaw's shorter than the top jaw, they can get you quicker.."

I tried to elicit which pack in the Fells the supporter had been with when he saw the fox dropped but to no avail. It may have been at a small unofficial pack. I learned only that there were six official Fell packs, that it was all on foot, was wonderful, but it was difficult to get to the top of the hills. Then his attention was distracted and I could not bring him back to the topic without arousing undue suspicion.

Hounds were put into the covert and we all lined up on the outside with Michael Farrin on horseback. A watching herd of cattle mooed appreciatively. Hounds spoke excitedly. There was a short burst of crashing through the undergrowth before hounds killed on the south side of the wood. I moved to the edge and filmed Michael Farrin in with his pack encouraging them to worry the carcase. Mick Gill walked right into the wood to film up close. I considered joining him but decided it would be simply too provocative and might attract too many unanswerable questions. So I hung back. I secured film of Michael retrieving the brush from his victim. I did wonder at his obsession for doing this. He seemed so keen to take the brush each time as if it was a novelty but he must have accumulated thousands over his career.

The hunt then moved to the south, crossed the minor road and headed for the A607. Crossing this they hunted an area to the south and quickly found. A brisk chase ensued which ended far too abruptly for the hunters' liking. The fox was struck a glancing blow by a vehicle when crossing the busy road, then caught and killed by the hounds.

I next caught up with the pack drawing a small but fairly thick covert to the south of the A607. I was right in amongst the tangled vegetation with the supporters. From hound sounds, there was plenty of action somewhere but none near us. Proceedings then moved to a nearby well known hunt covert. Supporters told me it was owned by Ulrica Murray-Smith, a former Quorn Joint Master. I was told that as her gamekeeper fed foxes bountifully we were bound to see good 'sport'.

My informants were right. Foxes popped out of the wood left, right and centre. The hounds ran round and round in circles in the covert, usually in full cry, but no effort was made to pursue the many foxes that left. That morning ended with the hunt drawing the fields back towards their kennels at Kirby Bellars.

That was the Friday. The weekend I spent in Dublin talking to the Irish Council Against Bloodsports about the value of undercover work (without mentioning our successes against the Quorn of course). Two days later on the Tuesday, October 8th, I was back with the Quorn for their meet at Hook Hill Wood, near Shepshed at 8am. I had seen the hounds in and near this wood from their meet at Osgathorpe earlier in the year.

That cub hunting morning proved momentous. Michael Farrin was not hunting hounds. He was away on holiday, shooting deer in Scotland with former Quorn Joint Master, James Teacher (1937-2003). In his absence Jimmy Boyle, the first Whipper-in, was Huntsman.

Hounds first drew the wood. From hounds' sounds there seemed to be plenty of foxes in residence but Jimmy appeared unable to do much with them. Watching supporters were typically critical—commenting that Michael would have done this but never that.

The hunt moved on from the wood to fields of crops, again with no apparent success. Two events brightened the morning for foot followers. Firstly, they found a stream packed with fresh watercress. They waded in and pulled out great tufts. Some were eaten there and then, others stashed in carrier bags for later. Neville Fitchett was clearly proficient at the art of such foraging whilst hunting. He advised me to look out for moss, mushrooms, and anything else that could be scavenged from the countryside.

The second source of entertainment was a lady rider trying to remount her horse. Would he stand still? No. Around and round he went as she struggled to get her leg up and over. Had she been younger there would doubtless have been a rush to give her a hand, but she was old and haughty and it entertained the lads to watch her struggles. This provoked her to fury and she started clubbing the animal with her crop. It was no surprise that far from calming her horse and helping the situation that violence caused further problems. Her ladyship did not appreciate being reduced to a laughing stock before the foot-sloggers.

The hunt drifted on in somewhat haphazard fashion and ended up in mid-morning drawing a small copse near the B5324 by Belton. A terrier lad nudged me and advised me to expect some fun. There was certainly a fox in residence. Hounds spoke immediately. The fox tried to escape by running up the ditch but followers chased him back shouting, "*Aye! Aye!*"

I took a position in the line of supporters surrounding the wood. Brian stood to my right, holding his terrier under one arm and bashing the undergrowth with his stick. On my other side Graham stood holding his terrier. The hounds were in the copse. They bayed then went quiet, bayed then went quiet. The hounds were cast through the copse and soon marked a fox to ground by some fallen, rotting trees, at one corner. The terriermen rushed into the copse and congregated at the scene.

I joined them and filmed events. Alan Betts, Chris Doherty and Dave Chapman took charge of the digging operations. Others present were Brian, Neville, Graham and about 10 more. Many held terriers. One terrier was put to ground and soon could be heard battling with the fox.

Digging commenced. As I filmed my camera flashed in warning that the attached battery had nearly expired, so I changed it. The lady Master rode up and instructed the terriermen to get the gun. One left the scene and collected it from a hunt servant. The gun was given to Chris Doherty. Whilst excavations continued hounds were held some 50 metres away in the open field.

After much digging Alan Betts reached into the hole and grabbed hold of the fox's brush. The terrier, deeper in the hole, was battling with the other end. It was akin to an underground dogfight. At one point the fox tried desperately to escape from the hole but was forced back in by Alan Betts,

Chris Doherty, and Dave Chapman, some of whom leant on the spade that pinioned the trapped animal.

They could not shoot the fox immediately for fear of hitting the terrier that was grappling with the fox head to head. To facilitate a shot safe for the terrier, the roof of the earth was dug back to expose more and more fox.

When Alan leaned forward to shoot, the terrierman next to me tapped me and told me not to film the scene. I tilted my camera down, as if obeying, but continued to film. I was determined the public would see the reality of the end of a hunt. Somewhat bizarrely I saw one terriermen put his fingers in his ears as the fox was about to be shot.

Exactly 4 minutes and 29 seconds passed between when the fox was first grabbed and held by Alan Betts and when he shot the fox. Add to that the lengthy dig to reach the fox, and the hunt to force him to ground, and it is clear there were no 'instant kills' when foxes were hunted, dug out and killed—which was how most foxes were killed in fox hunting.

After the shot the fox carcass was pulled out by Alan Betts, the hounds called up, and the dead fox was given to them to tussle over. In time Jimmy Boyle stepped in and cut the brush from the shattered body. Often the head of the dead fox, the mask, is taken as a trophy but in this case the skull was so hideously disfigured from the assaults as to make it not worth having. One terrierman joked: "*Look—a pop-eyed fox!!*"

Recording this dig out with a video camera enabled me to give the following exact timeline for that kill:-

11:12:02. Chris Doherty was given the gun and put it in his right pocket.
11:21:45. Alan Betts said he had got the fox. He held him by the brush.
11:23:29. Chris Doherty reached for the gun in his pocket.
11:23:48. Chris Doherty placed the gun on the ground.
11:23:54. Gun was seen on the ground in front of Dave Chapman.
11:24:06. Chris Doherty reached into the hole to the left of Alan Betts.
11:24:13. Alan Betts picked gun up, crossed arms with Dave Chapman and put the gun back on the ground at 11:24:15.
11:24:25. Chris Doherty came back from the left side of Alan Betts.
11:24:52 Someone called, "*Alan!*"
11:24:53. Alan Betts replied, "*What?*"
Interest centred on something on the ground, presumably the gun. Chris Doherty leaned down into the hole with a stick in his hand at this time.
11:24:55. Someone called a warning about the gun, "*It's loaded Alan.*"
11:24:57. Alan Betts held gun in his right hand.
11:25:08. Alan Betts tried to put gun in his right-hand pocket. Someone warned him, "*It's loaded Alan.*"
11:25:10. Alan Betts looked at the gun and said, "*It ain't cocked.*"
11:25:20. Gun disappeared from view. It was last seen by the right-hand pocket of Alan Betts.
11:25:23. Gun was on the ground, put there by Alan Betts.
11:26:09. Alan Betts had gun in his right hand.
11:26:14. Alan Betts shot the fox.

With this new evidence gathered we knew my undercover project could not last much longer. We had to put these powerful images into the public domain. I upgraded to 'maximum effort' mode and resolved to attend every hunt I could—even though doing so would likely blow my own cover— no casual hunt follower would attend so many meets.

At the time, we had family health problems. We were all stricken with a virulent and highly contagious sickness and diarrhoea bug. I attended the Quorn meet at Barkby Halt, near Beeby on Friday October 11th. It was a misty start and there were few foxes about. I learned from other supporters that Barry Hercock had suffered a bad fall some days previously. He smashed his leg when his horse fell on him. Two foxes were hunted away from South Croxton and in ensuing hunts two riders suffered falls and were taken to hospital. The day ended at noon and I returned home feeling decidedly queasy.

I was up most of the night with violent sickness and diarrhoea. It was unpleasant and exhausting. My alarm sounded at 4:30am the next morning and I left for the Quorn meet at Garners Gorse, Thrussington at 8am. They caution that if you have bad diarrhoea you should abstain from blowing the trumpet—I guessed the same would apply to blowing a hunting horn, or riding over jumps. I mingled and chatted with riders and foot-followers as usual.

I followed as best I could. There was no kill that I observed. My last day with the Quorn during that investigation was the following Tuesday, October 15th, when I attended their 8am meet at Wysall Brook, north of Wymeswold, off the A6006. They drew hedge-lines first. A fox was marked in a stick-pile but I was told that with no terriers to hand they decided to leave him.

Late in the morning hounds hunted a fox through a small piggery and into a covert north of the disused airfield near Wymeswold. That fox was singularly unlucky. He evaded most hounds but was caught when he crossed a path at the edge of the covert and was snapped up by straggling hounds that happened to be passing.

Hearing enthusiastic hound yelps, I ran around the corner to the scene and filmed hounds ragging the body of the fox. The terriermen, Dave Chapman, Brian Adcock and others at the scene warned me not to film so I tilted my camera up but kept it running to record the sounds. I was told that if I was seen filming, or indeed if the Masters had seen me filming the previous week, I would have been 'sent home'!

The hunt then moved on towards an old airfield and in time hunted a fox to ground in a high place. I struggled through the undergrowth and reached the scene with the terriermen but immediately sensed they were suspicious of my presence with a camera. I was informed initially they had a brace to ground. One bolted and was killed. I was then told there was no sign of the second fox. My presence with camera might have saved his life. I knew my work in the field with the Quorn was over.

My investigations took a new tack. I gathered further evidence by making recorded phone calls. That evening I telephoned Michael Farrin at the Quorn hunt kennels. I sought his opinion on the release of a fox for further hunting filmed on September 21st. I could not ask him outright so pretended I was editing together a film for use by the hunt. I queried first my problems filming the kill that morning.

Mike Huskisson: "*When the hounds caught today and...er..they were ragging the fox I was told by some of the other terrier lads not to film that at all and if I did I'd..sort of..be sent home.*"

Michael Farrin: "*Yes.*"

Mike Huskisson: "*I was wondering what the problem was about that..um..because..you know..Mick Gill has always..sort of, you know, done that and I was just following his lead so to speak.*"

Michael Farrin: "*Well, we don't like it being done too much because, you know..in case it ever got into the wrong hands, which I'm sure it won't.*"

Mike Huskisson: "*Right.*"

Michael Farrin: "*Um..because...you know, we've got to be very careful these days as well you know.*"

Mike Huskisson: "*You see, I said to some of the other lads, well, you know, with a video camera that's fine, you haven't got any problem like that. Sometimes if you're taking still pictures and you take them into Boots to be processed you never know who sees them and..you know..they might get a bit upset and do some extra copies and all that sort of thing.*"

Michael Farrin: "*Yes.*"

Mike Huskisson: "*But I tend to think, you know, a video camera is a lot safer.*"

I spoke about creating a film for the hunt for Boxing Day. I needed Michael Farrin to speak about the release of the fox that was dug out at the Langley Priory meet. He gave me more than I could have hoped for.

Mike Huskisson: "*You see the only bit I've actually got of the hounds catching a fox themselves was that day back at er.... Langley Priory, cubbing, you know back in September.*"

Michael Farrin: "*Yes.*"

Mike Huskisson: "*When um when.. .when old Bettsy [Alan Betts] pulled the fox out and put him in the hedge and the hounds came over and caught him there.*"

Michael Farrin: "*Yea, I know.*"

Mike Huskisson: "*But I... er.. you know I was wondering whether to include that because you can see him handling it you see.*"

Michael Farrin: "*Yea, well, I wouldn't include that if you. .if....if you don't mind, you know.*"

Mike Huskisson: "*No?*"

Michael Farrin: "*No, I shouldn't do that, you know. It's alright, I mean we do handle them like that you know and just let them go but um... I wouldn't like to see it on film, to be honest.*"

Mike Huskisson: "*Right....*"

I telephoned Michael Farrin again the next evening, Wednesday October 16th, and again recorded the call. I was keen to elicit further information about how to handle a live fox for hunting without getting bitten. Here is the relevant excerpt:-

Mike Huskisson: *"I...I... cut out that bit um..of um...where Bettsy* [Alan Betts] *pulls the fox out."*

Michael Farrin: *"That's good of you. Thank you."*

Mike Huskisson: *"It just appears now...the fox looks like it was bolted..um.."*

Michael Farrin: *"Yea."*

Mike Huskisson: *"Because you first..first see him sort of disappearing into the hedge."*

Michael Farrin: *"Yea."*

Mike Huskisson: *"And er...and that's that."*

Michael Farrin: *"Oh, great yea."*

Mike Huskisson: *"But...how on earth do they do it without getting bitten?"*

Michael Farrin: *"Well....you know....it's one knowing their job isn't it? Mm?"*

Mike Huskisson: *"Is it? I mean er...."*

Michael Farrin: *"I mean if you can get a fox at the back of.....the scruff of the neck you know....the back of the neck....on top of the neck.....you know you're alright then, close to his ears, he won't turn round and bite you. But you've just got to know your.....what you're doing."*

Mike Huskisson: *"Oh!...rather them than me because..."*

Michael Farrin: *"Well, I wouldn't advise everybody to do it by any means."*

Mike Huskisson: *"No...no...doesn't look all that..er..safe for your hands."*

Michael Farrin: *"No way."*

Mike Huskisson: *"No."*

During our conversation Michael Farrin elaborated more on the serious injury that Barry Hercock suffered saying: *"I've never seen a man in so much pain as he was."* We also discussed the hunt tally of cubs killed. In the previous season, they had killed 50 brace; that season up until the day of our call they had killed 45 brace.

I then worked with LACS colleagues to release the results to the media. The investigation, the video and stills taken from the video were all strong. Against that I knew the hunting side would find out that I was the undercover operative and I carried all the baggage of my previous imprisonments. But nothing I did in 1977 or 1984 impinged on what I filmed at the Quorn Foxhounds in 1991.

The media were captivated—even more so with the Royal connection. The *Mail on Sunday* led the way with a full-page article on page 3 on October 27th 1991 under the headline: *The Royal hunt's kill.* Hunters learned that all the positive publicity the presence of Prince Charles attracted for their pastime was more than matched by media interest in damning revelations about any hunt he blessed by his presence. The Quorn was his favourite hunt. Jim Barrington was quoted: *"This video is the strongest evidence yet that the code of conduct governing hunting is a sham. It is a breach of the rules of the Masters of Foxhounds Association, the sport's governing body."*

Michael Farrin sounded almost plaintive when he explained what happened: "*We gave the fox a chance to escape but he ran back through the hedge and the hounds got him.*"

Barry Hercock added: "*Our general policy is not to dig foxes. But I was told it would only take a minute in this case.*"

The story was also reported at length, with clips from the videos, on television news bulletins. Curiously my perception at the time was that the clip showing the tiny bedraggled cub evicted from the safety of his earth on October 4th generated the most public outrage—yet that was routine cub hunting.

Nothing in our media release was claimed to be illegal. At the time, we were not aware of any illegality. One incident appeared to be a breach of the MFHA rules. The whole package though amounted to graphic proof of the cruelty inherent in fox hunting—and raised the question that if the best hunt in the country, one basking in Royal approval, behaved like that what on earth did other hunts get up to?

Aspiring new recruits to any compassionate cause often ask if individuals really can make a difference. They certainly can. My short clips of 8mm video film were shown on television around the world. Stills from the videos were printed in many papers. This generated massive debate about how we treat animals in the modern world—in particular the suffering heaped upon them purely for entertainment. The video camera had come of age as the tool of choice for campaigners seeking to educate a sceptical public about the realities of the mistreatment of animals.

A copy of the video was shown to the MFHA. Their spokesman, Brian Toon, said: "*They can decide whether or not the rules have been breached and what action should be taken.*"

The following day other media joined the hunting of the Quorn. The *Daily Star* blazoned across its front page the plea to Prince Charles: "*Pack it in, Sir! Barbaric foxhunt video for Charles.*" and ran the following: "*Fox-hunting Prince Charles was under pressure last night to break his silence and condemn the sickening "sport". He was sent the most shocking video ever made of the cruel country pursuit.*"

Jim Barrington was again quoted: "*It is a total disgrace that the heir to the throne is involved in this despicable practice. It is not a sport—it is a bloody, drawn-out business in which a terrified animal is brutalised to death.*"

Inside, the *Daily Star* revealed their problems trying to elicit some response from Alan Betts. Alan was reported to be in hiding at his girlfriend's house in Leicester. His dad, Henry Betts, threatened *Daily Star* photographer Iain Lynn with a 5ft broom handle and chased him along a road. Then he hurled the pole at Lynn after screaming: "*Clear off from here and just leave us all alone.*" Henry Betts later spoke more rationally about the video: *I was there at the time and saw nothing wrong with what Alan did. He played it by the rules and doesn't deserve all this hassle.*"

My ACIG and the LACS received a flood of new support. In the first seven days, the League registered almost 2,000 new members and supporters. There were also many abusive and hate-mail letters received by the League. Jim Barrington, surveying a pile of such letters, commented: *"We can always judge the success of a campaign by the amount of foul language we get in anonymous letters from the hunters. In this case it is clearly our most successful campaign ever!"*

The hunting world tried to identify the undercover operative—the hunt mole. *Horse and Hound,* November 7th, devoted more than three pages to the Quorn story (the Editor, Michael Clayton, rode with the Quorn). Of my identity, he wrote: *"Who was the spy "mole"? Fair haired, moustached, bespectacled, wearing a cap and a Barbour coat, driving a red car, possibly a Volkswagen Golf. Claimed to be very keen on hunting, and so friendly. Called himself Mike Roberts. The country blokes involved in the terrier work are friendly —perhaps not street-wise suspicious—they accepted his offer to take pictures for their supporters' club. He aimed his camera at anything and everything; no one minded."*

In fact Michael Clayton only had to look at a back issue of his own magazine to find the answer. The man he damned as a *"creepy little spy"* back in August 1983, whose photograph he printed, was the 'Mike Roberts'. Furthermore, the Waveney Harriers, amongst many hunts, could have told them who I was.

Public pressure rose dramatically for the abolition of hunting wildlife with dogs. The videos proved there were few quick kills in fox hunting and often the killing of the fox was delayed to provide entertainment. In the short term, questions were asked as to what the Quorn Foxhounds were going to do to remedy the situation. Would Michael Farrin and the terriermen be sacked? Would the hunt Masters be sacked? Would the MFHA rules be better enforced, or changed to stop further similar events?

Two days after our media release, on Tuesday October 29th, the Quorn Hunt Committee held an emergency meeting lasting over four hours. At that meeting the four Joint Masters of the hunt and the Hunt Chairman, Lord Crawshaw, all offered their resignation. The next morning Committee Member Rad Thomas spoke to the media saying: *"The Committee examined the evidence and admits a degree of culpability to the allegations made. The Committee of the Quorn Hunt attaches the highest priority to the correction of the undesirable situation that has arisen, and therefore proposes to take the following steps with immediate effect: The Quorn Hunt will enact its own strict code of practice, the primary function of which will be the elimination of unnecessary suffering associated with any limited use of terriers or digging."* The final two paragraphs contained what Michael Clayton (*Horse and Hound* November 7th 1991) described as the bombshell announcement: *" The Committee of the Quorn Hunt will meet again this week and until they have concluded their deliberations the senior Masters, Mr Joss Hanbury and Mr Barry Hercock, have been suspended."*

During the night of Friday November 1st there was a second emergency meeting of the Quorn Hunt Committee. The following morning it was announced that the resignation of all four Joint Masters and Lord Crawshaw had been accepted. Capt. Fred Barker, a previous Joint Master accepted the invitation to take over as sole Master and David Samworth was appointed Hunt Chairman. The public perception was that a new regime was installed to sort out the many problems at the Quorn.

Further tip-offs from within the Quorn suggested that something illegal had happened. One of the first public indications was found in the following report in *Horse and Hound* November 7th 1991 under the caption "*Police check firearms licence.*

REPORTS THAT the Quorn terrierman was using a pistol without a firearms certificate in the controversial video shots shown on TV were being denied earlier this week. Hunt sources said it was in fact a humane killer, and no firearms certificate regulations had been contravened, However, Leicestershire police had investigated the reports, and had temporarily taken away firearms from the Hunt kennels near Melton Mowbray while checks were being made on current certificates which are held by Hunt staff."

It was also reported in the same issue that the National Trust had banned the Quorn from hunting over 200 acres at Calke Abbey and a further 80 acres at Ulverscroft, Charnwood Forest. The National Trust did so because the hunting licence issued to the Quorn was in the name of Barry Hercock and became invalid when he resigned. The Quorn could reapply for the licence but were warned that before it would be issued a full report was required by the National Trust head office.

Thursday November 14th was significant. The Committee of the Masters of Foxhounds Association held their inquiry into the Quorn affair. The four Joint Masters who resigned—Joss Hanbury, Barry Hercock, Mrs Di Turner, and Alastair Macdonald-Buchanan—gave evidence, as did Lord Crawshaw and Michael Farrin.

In his 1993 book *Foxhunting in Paradise* Michael Clayton described the verdict and penalties as, "*the stiffest ever handed out by the Association in its one hundred and eight years.*" The two senior Joint Masters, Joss Hanbury and Barry Hercock, were expelled from the MFHA for four years; the two junior Joint Masters, Mrs Di Turner and Alastair Macdonald-Buchanan, were expelled until the start of the next hunting season, in May 1992.

The MFHA Committee decided that the four Joint Masters had breached MFHA rules one and five. Rule one stated: "*Foxhunting as a sport is the hunting of the fox in his wild and natural state with a pack of hounds. No pack of which the Master or representative is a member of this Association will be allowed to hunt a fox in any way that is inconsistent with this precept.*" Rule five stated that members of the MFHA had to bind themselves to abide by its rules and instructions. The MFHA released a statement saying: "*The Committee found that a fox had been handled in such a way that it should have been destroyed and not hunted further.*"

For many this appeared to be typical hunt 'justice'. Severe action was taken against some Joint Masters not even present on the day of the offence while no sanction at all was imposed on Michael Farrin the Huntsman who was present, in charge, and in clear sight of the offence. However, it seemed the MFHA had no sanctions they could impose on hunt staff whose actions were deemed to be the responsibility of the Masters. Furthermore, as a close personal friend of Prince Charles, it may have been that Michael Farrin was regarded as 'untouchable'.

Hunting authorities recognised they not only had to correct what had gone wrong at the Quorn—they also aimed to ensure it did not happen again. The following year the Quorn affair resulted in what Michael Clayton described as the most profound changes in MFHA rules. Radical alterations to the MFHA rules were announced in September 1992. A new rule was specific regarding the digging out of a hunted fox: *"....when a hunted fox is run to ground in a natural earth, there shall be no digging other than for the purpose of humanely destroying the fox..............a fox which has been handled must be humanely destroyed immediately and under no circumstances hunted."*

New rules also tackled the subject of bolting. Hunts were allowed to bolt a fresh fox and could also bolt a hunted fox that had taken refuge in any man-made structure, such as drains, artificial earths, stick piles, straw bales and the like and from rocks and other places where digging was impossible. Rules also stated that bolting the fox should only happen when hounds were far enough away to be out of sight of the place of refuge and out of earshot of the digging operations. Finally, a bolted fox: *"must be given a fair and sporting chance of escape before hounds are laid on."*

The MFHA also issued a Code of Good Hunting Practice which amongst other requirements asked Masters to limit the involvement of volunteer terriermen and supporters at terrier work. Hunters dressed this up as a safety issue given the use of firearms in digging out but many felt it was primarily directed at keeping unknown individuals who might be armed with cameras away from the most sensitive aspect of fox hunting.

With the Royal connection, the Quorn investigation generated great press interest. My diary notes that by November 7th the story, and developments in it, had been covered for 12 consecutive days in one or more of the national newspapers.

The LACS considered possible illegal use of firearms during the digging out and shooting of the fox on October 8th. Chris Doherty had a licence for the firearm used but Alan Betts did not and Alan Betts shot the fox. It was a pure legal technicality but, like driving a car without insurance, one on which the police and Crown Prosecution Service (CPS) might have been expected to act.

Monday November 4th 1991 I drove to Loughborough police station for a meeting with Sergeant Deas to discuss our Quorn evidence. From 11am until 3pm I gave a statement and showed and explained our videos. When other police officers heard that videos were being shown they rushed in, expecting to see pornography. Well, they were disgusting and explicit, but not the films they sought.

It was nice to be in a police station on the offensive for animals rather than on the defensive but it was to no avail. In an ominous foretelling of what would happen when hunting itself was banned the CPS declined to prosecute. It was left to the LACS to pick up the legal reins and enforce the law. Of course I had to give evidence and thereby revealed my identity.

Tuesday August 25th 1992 I drove north and stayed at the Bardon Hall hotel near Coalville. I went for a meal with Graham and Joanna Woolliscroft, Jim Barrington, Ed Maynard and the LACS solicitor—Tom Hart. In the morning, we drove to Loughborough Magistrates Court for the case that started at 10am. By curious coincidence it was August 26th, eight years to the day after the SEALL raid on the Royal College of Surgeons.

As a witness, I had to sit outside for the first half hour before being called to give evidence. I was in the witness box until 1pm. My video recording of the incident on October 8th 1991 was shown to the court and I described exactly what happened.

Under cross-examination by the defence I admitted using several aliases for my undercover work and that I had been jailed twice for animal rights activity. Robert Anderson put it to me: "*You are totally committed to the abolition of everything; hunting, shooting and fishing, are you not?*"

I replied: "*I am committed to finding out the truth about these so-called sports and bringing it to the attention of the British public.*" (*Daily Telegraph* August 27th 1992)

Chris Doherty, a Quorn kennelman for three years, denied the gun was loaded when he placed it on the ground and said that, as he did not have a clear shot himself, he passed the pistol to Alan Betts to use. He claimed Alan Betts only had the loaded gun for five seconds.

Alan Betts, in turn, told the court he had been hunting with the Quorn for ten years. He claimed he did not know he needed a firearms certificate to use the gun.

The Magistrates returned with their verdict just before 5pm. Chris Doherty was convicted of failing to comply with a condition of his firearms certificate that the weapon should be kept in a secure place. He was fined £150. Alan Betts was convicted of possessing a firearm without a firearms certificate and was fined £100.

I was delighted to be involved in enforcing the law against hunters. In the media scrum outside court Jim Barrington rejoiced in the LACS' role: "*It was totally right to bring the case, because terriermen in other hunts are probably doing this all the time. It is a shot across their bows that this sort of activity has got to stop. If it doesn't we will prosecute again when we have the evidence. The law is the law. They broke the law of the land and they had to be prosecuted. The Crown Prosecution Service had a different set of criteria to us and decided not to charge them, but it did not deflect from the facts of the case. The purpose of the League is to bring to the notice of the general public what goes on in the hunting world.*"

Brian Toon, spokesman for the MFHA replied: "*We are quite used to the League Against Cruel Sports using any means it considers appropriate against us. In the League's view no stick is too small to try to beat hunting. Although all hunt masters and employees will take notice of the judgment, I simply do not believe it is true that terriermen in other hunts are acting illegally, as the League has alleged."* (*Daily Telegraph* August 27th 1992).

It subsequently transpired the LACS were two months too late issuing the summons to Chris Doherty. Purely on that legal technicality, in March 1993, Leicester Crown Court allowed Chris Doherty's appeal against conviction. He was acquitted.

With my identity revealed the hunting side had a field day digging up my past. *Horse and Hound* September 3rd 1992 ran a half page report of the court case accompanied by a photograph of me. The *Daily Telegraph* August 27th reported that I had desecrated the grave of Robert Peel in Cumbria. At least *Horse and Hound* got the right Peel—John Peel but then the Editor of *Horse and Hound*, Michael Clayton, in his later book *Foxhunting in Paradise* referred to my *"desecrating the grave of the great Lakeland huntsman Tom* [sic] *Peel"*.

Following the Quorn investigation and before the court case resulting from it I returned to undercover work. I soon learned from other hunters that however aggrieved Quorn followers felt by their public humiliation, supporters of other packs were delighted to see them knocked off their haughty high horses. Arrogance often inspires contempt so it was no surprise we were tipped off about their excesses.

Hunt supporters were well practised at dealing with bad publicity— usually after violence against hunt saboteurs or violence against the public when hounds riot and cause mayhem and havoc. They usually denied anything occurred and if there was film of events then that film was faked. Any miscreant was either unknown to the hunt or if they were known they acted purely on their own authority. Faced with undercover investigations hunters would claim the investigator faked evidence, provoked it or set it up.

I repeat here what I made clear in *Outfoxed Take Two*. I was never anything more than an observant fly on the wall of hunting. I faked nothing and always took the animal's side. I discarded many good filming opportunities to help an animal escape.

Following the Quorn affair, the hunting side made certain allegations that need to be corrected. *Shooting News*, May 29-4 June 1992, printed this footnote to a reader's letter: *"We understand that the League Against Cruel Sports investigator involved in the filming incident did not claim that the fox was thrown to the hounds. It is generally accepted that the video tape was edited in camera.*

Also, the safety aspect was raised. It would have been difficult to shoot a fox with so many people around the earth and it was suggested that the presence of the cameraman, who was at one time in the potential line of fire, made this more difficult."

The allegation that my film was 'edited' in camera and thereby in some way faked gained strength over the years; perhaps because it became a last refuge for hunters unwilling to admit the truth of what happened. I still occasionally meet hunters who mock me for 'faking' my film of the Quorn. When I respond that, if that were the case, why did the MFHA expel the four Joint Masters of the Quorn, they have no answer.

On occasion, to preserve battery power, or save videotape, I switched my camera off. Things happened that were not recorded, but everything I filmed did happen, was genuine and had not been altered in any way. A soundtrack of commentary to explain events was added to the LACS campaigning video but would anyone expect otherwise? The original video-8 tape has always been offered to anyone who cares to check.

The allegation I interfered in the dig by being in the 'potential line of fire' is nonsense and only mentioned to demonstrate the problems we have dealing with hunters. Alan Betts had to reach into the mouth of the earth to shoot the fox he was holding. I was standing well back with other terriermen. I was never and could never have been in the' line of fire'.

Many learned observers noted the link in style between the NIMR investigation and that at the Quorn. The *Independent* did so in their leader column on November 14th 1991.

The great campaigner, Lord Houghton of Sowerby (1898-1996) also did, as the following record (from *Hansard* November 27th 1991) of his comments regarding the Animal Procedures Committee shows:

"*Perhaps an independent viewpoint on what that body does would be beneficial: otherwise, we are in for more undercover work. After all, such undercover work apparently plays an important part in the disturbance that exists in the public's mind as to the use of animals without their knowledge. The trouble in the Quorn hunt was made known through undercover work. Feldberg's work was made known through undercover work. There are other undercover jobs in progress now because people are determined to find out the truth. It is better to set up a safeguard within the system than to leave the growing 'M15 for animals' to find out.*"

CHAPTER TEN
Undercover work during and after the Quorn investigation. The creation of the Animal Welfare Information Service (AWIS).

Chapter eight ended with my visit to the Essex Foxhounds on February 16th 1991. I then became involved in the Quorn investigation but alongside that I carried on with undercover work elsewhere.

February 26th 1991 was a busy day. Following my work with the Quorn hunt from their Ulverscroft Lodge meet, I travelled north for the Waterloo Cup with my ACIG companion Janet Jackson. The following morning, we were up early to attend the first day of the Waterloo Cup at the Withins. We took up our favoured position in amongst ordinary supporters on the bank side. We watched 64 courses during the day. No hares were killed from the first 14 coursed. It was noticeable that the early hares coursed ran for the safety of the end with the rhododendron bushes, later hares turned back towards the Slipper and the beat funnel. One hare was coursed, caught and killed by three dogs.

The next morning, Thursday February 28th, we attended the second day at Lydiate. Whilst Janet took slides and prints I used my video camera. Sadly, we saw many kills, including one hare killed by a single dog running. Another hare had a miraculous escape when she ran from the coursing field into the baying crowd and even escaped their clutches. They completed all but seven courses on the morning drive.

Whilst hares fled for their lives to entertain the crowd some amongst that crowd were too drunk to even notice, let alone appreciate the finer points of coursing. Behind us in the grass a couple of men rolled about semi-conscious due to alcohol intoxication. One clutched a near empty bottle of whisky. The day ended at 2:30pm and we returned home.

Two days later, Saturday March 2nd, I joined the Swaffham Coursing Club for a hare catching expedition at Lodge Farm, Hilborough at 9:30am. We were introduced to the headkeeper, Gerald, and his underkeeper, Miles. We were informed that hares not caught would likely be shot soon afterwards—as there was a hare shoot scheduled. I was given a flag to wave and wandered around the fields taking photographs.

Eighteen hares were caught in the purse netting, extracted and packed into boxes. They were then driven away. We were told that some were sold to an Italian shooting syndicate. I saw many of the stalwarts from the Swaffham Coursing Club helping.

The following Saturday, March 9th, I was back with the Essex Foxhounds for their meet at *The White Horse* inn, Pleshey. My diary notes nothing of any great significance and they packed up at 3pm.

The following Wednesday I was back with the same hunt for their meet at Matching Hall. It was a hot and sunny day. The meet produced a curious slide of a horse 'laughing'. I ingratiated myself further with the terriermen by giving a photograph of the day when they footed in the snow (February 16th) to Steve.

Foxes found the day less amusing when two were killed. The Huntsman told me the first was unceremoniously chopped when the hounds sprang upon him as he sunbathed on the sunny bank of a ditch. The second was put up from the wood at Rookham Hall and killed in the moat of a nearby house. One supporter told me the hunt had killed 32 or 33 brace up until then.

A week later, Saturday March 16th, I visited the Essex Foxhounds again but by then was perhaps becoming too familiar. They met at Chalks Green. With my Land Rover I was used to going wherever the terriermen went. During the day there was a fast circular hunt. Steve and the terrier crew went to drive down one track but Steve cautioned me: "*Don't follow me down the track.*" It could have been nothing more sinister than the landowner did not want anyone other than official hunt vehicles on his land; but it made me think. A change in direction seemed wise.

At the end of the following week I drove to the West Country and attended the meet of the Tiverton Staghounds at Firebeacon at Cove on Saturday March 23rd. It was spring stag hunting. After previous undercover work at that hunt I declined to attend the meet that was some 1½ miles south-east of Cove. I found the hunt at around 11:20am in the area of Hone Hill. I could only follow from a distance. I spent most of my time patrolling the riverbank and driving from bridge to bridge. At one point, I chatted with a young woman out with a child in a push-chair. I was dressed in full hunting kit and asked her if she knew where the hunt was. She replied: "*Glad I haven't heard them, I don't agree with it at all.*"

I would have loved to reveal my true sympathies but could only mutter, "*Oh*" and moved on. I spoke to one supporter whose horse had thrown a shoe and was going home. He told me hounds were still running and were down Stoodleigh way. I drove around for some time—ending up at Chain Bridge—where many deer are killed but with no sight or sound of anything I left at 6pm. It proved how much easier it was to monitor a hunt when you are fully accepted as a hunt supporter.

I stayed in the area and attended the Quantock Staghounds hunt from Over Stowey on Monday March 25th. Again I avoided the meet and caught up with them at 'Great Bear' at 11:40am. At one point I drove to Holford Combe, parked and walked to the high ground. I observed hounds running towards Beacon Hill before they disappeared from sight about 1:45pm. Anticipating a circular hunt I waited and waited. A couple of riders came by heading home. One told me that the hunt had gone towards the deer park at West Quantoxhead but would likely head back my way, skirting by the LACS sanctuary land. They did. I gambled and ran down into Lady's Edge—a mistake as I only had to climb back up which exhausted me. I saw the pack held up whilst the hunt staff whistled for the remainder. The pack surged on towards Holford Combe and I expected them to bring the stag to bay at the bottom but he ran up the far hill. I gambled he would come back towards me. I heard hounds come back into earshot and then a gunshot just over the hill from me at 3:20pm. The hunt had killed just north of Woodlands Hill. I could not go to the gralloch.

During a day with the Essex Foxhounds over Christmas 1990 I had met and chatted with Michael Errey, the Master of the Kent and Sussex Minkhounds. I asked about mink hunting and he invited me down to see his hounds. Keen to take him up on his offer I telephoned him and he gave me their meet on Saturday March 30th 1991 at *The White Hart,* Claygate, east of Tonbridge. So it was that I returned to undercover work amongst mink hunters—but I nearly fell at the first hurdle.

I arrived early to find an old man with recognisable features (a big nose) parked outside the pub. We chatted and he told me of his following the Devon and Cornwall Minkhounds years before. I remembered him and feared he might remember me. His name was Kimball. He reminisced about otter hunting days—how he was given an otter pad at the end of a hunt in 1917; how a woman took her otter hounds to kill a semi-tame otter after the man who cared for the otter had warned them off his land. When hunters arrived at noon they promptly disappeared into the pub.

I waited outside. In time the hunters emerged and we set off in convoy and parked by a bridge over the River Teise. The hounds were taken into a nearby field. I wandered over towards the hounds in company with several hunters including a young Whipper-in named Richard. I was told his mum ran the Hunt Supporters' Club. The Huntsman was Stuart Cole. I learned that one Whipper-in was a man named Dave from the Old Surrey and Burstow Foxhounds. There seemed to be a crowd of terriermen—about a dozen in all.

The hunt drew the river down to the railway line then back again. Hounds seemed to catch a scent at one point but there were no real signs of any mink about. When we crossed the bridge where our cars were parked there was immediate action. Hounds marked at a tree on the riverbank. A terrierman named Tony took charge. He waded into the river and said that he could smell mink. Soon afterwards a mink bolted. One hound grabbed hold of the mink but quickly dropped him. The mink was soon lost from sight in the fast murky water. That mink was counted as a 'probable' kill.

Hounds then marked again at a tree upstream. Protracted digging out operations followed. A terrierman the others nicknamed 'Doughnut' waded into the river carrying a terrier. For all the digging, there was no further sign of the mink. Eventually the hunt moved on, leaving the terriermen behind. A long walk along the riverbank followed. We reached a point where the river divided and, soon after, the terriers found a scent by a small bridge. A terrierman reported to Michael Errey that he thought it was a fox and asked permission to kill him. Michael said no. As the landowner was not there and they had no means to ask him what he wanted done they left the fox. Supporters later told me that a young terrier was put into the place where hounds marked—and came out bitten by what was assumed to be a fox.

We returned to the river junction and then drew on and on. We were all under instruction to keep off the bank by a caravan site, and most did. At one point we encountered a fisherman. As I conversed with him hounds burst into cry as they found a mink on the opposite bank. By then it was about 5pm. Much enthusiastic holloaing from supporters followed. Hounds marked this mink to a hollow in the base of a tree. The mink was soon bolted then promptly ripped in half. Hounds scrapped over the remains. 'Doughnut' grabbed a handful of flesh and fur and other supporters joked that he was trying to 'sex' the mink. I was told that was the second mink they caught that season—the first being when Michael Errey had hunted hounds on March 2nd. We carried on to where some vans were parked. The hunt finished at 6:15pm. We were all given a lift back to our cars. I was invited to enjoy tea and biscuits with the rest of the hunt but declined as I had a pre-arranged meeting with my friends Alan Knight and Liz Varney.

Monday April 8th was a day for a surveillance effort at what amounted to just about maximum range for a day trip. I left home at 6:30am for the meet of the Quantock Staghounds at Firebeacon, Little Quantock at 11am. I reached the Holford area at noon and established mobile phone contact with John Hicks, the LACS Sanctuaries Manager. I took some video of the hunted stag running with the hounds some five minutes behind. John and I worked as a team but despite our best efforts neither of us was on hand to see the deer killed at 2:30pm on the tree line by the A39 near Kilve. I then gave a talk in the evening to a support group in Yeovil before returning home at 3am.

Saturday April 13th produced a scare for my undercover work. I returned to the Kent and Sussex Minkhounds for their meet at that well-known hunting venue—*The Cricketers*, Berwick, between Polegate and Lewes. I arrived at 12:15pm in time to photograph hounds in their van. Most hunt supporters were tanking up in the pub. I had hoped not to see Mr Kimball again but he was waiting outside the meet.

Seated in his car he beckoned me over and asked where I came from. I said Norwich. He replied that was a long way to travel to see a hunt. I responded that it was not really as I had visited friends in Tunbridge Wells and was only driving on from there. He then said: "*I don't know if I should tell you but nine years ago, when I followed the Devon and Cornwall Minkhounds we had a chap come out with us for two seasons taking pictures. He looked just like you! He was the same height, the same build, wore glasses and a cap like you do and was well spoken. He stopped following us, then later we saw all these pictures in the Press. The Huntsman had a dead mink on his pole. This chap—his name was Huskisson—said the mink was alive. It was all lies. He is the most vicious of antis. He was locked up soon after for planning some kind of raid.*"

Rumbled I feared—but I knew I had to face him down. I exclaimed: "*What a bastard—you mean he pretended to be a hunter but all the time he was an anti! I have been told I look like John Cleese but never that I look like a bloody anti! What a bastard!*" He seemed satisfied by my indignation.

I wanted to drive away and leave them but knew that to do so would be to admit my real identity and I had other important work to undertake, particularly at the Quorn. I just had to stay with them.

The hunt moved off at about 12:45pm. We drove in convoy through to Alfriston, parked in a farm and set off. Later, as I took pictures of hounds in the water I could hear Mr Kimball telling other hunt supporters as he pointed to me: "*Yes, that Huskisson looked just like him there.*" Not surprisingly these followers responded, "*Is he an anti?*" gesturing towards me. Thankfully Mr Kimball vouched for me: "*Oh no, he's alright but Huskisson looked just like him.*" I was used as a live identikit for a notorious anti—it was slightly unsettling.

By a river bridge the hounds became excited. It seemed there was a mink in the undergrowth. Then he sought sanctuary in a tree. Supporters shook the tree, dislodged him and he fell into the water. Hounds snapped at him and appeared to injure him. It was murky and fast-flowing tidal water. The mink surfaced and by paddling madly was able to hold station against the flow. For a time, he found some sanctuary on the water's edge, on the far side from me, but the hounds soon closed in and snapped at the small creature. He took to the water again and I photographed one hound a matter of inches behind him, under the bridge.

The mink dived then surfaced again. Bitten again he dived and was carried downstream. He surfaced and the hounds and hunters were closing in. One hunter waded waist deep in the water. He lashed with his stick at the mink swimming on the surface. The mink seemed to be hit. He dived and was never seen again.

Most hunt observers presumed the mink was dead (if not dead he was certainly badly injured). Mr Kimball opined that the mink was alive. This prompted the hunters to resume their search but when that again proved fruitless they moved on.

I chatted with Huntsman, Michael Errey. He told me they killed 2½ brace of mink there the previous season. He said that they preferred to meet there early in the season to avoid the tourists.

We drew on with few sounds of speaking from the hounds. At one point, we supporters had to squeeze through some tunnels. I banged my head on the roof of one and, momentarily stunned, I thought that I had been truly recognised and hit! Thankfully it was only an error of height judgement on my part.

When hounds marked at a hole by a weir great excitement ensued. The terriermen went to work with gusto and the terriers were summoned. When a live eel was found in a mink's holt they assumed the mink was close by. Extensive digging operations followed but of the mink there was no sign.

I tried to save the eel. I asked to photograph him then hoped to flick him back into the water. The terrierman monikered 'Doughnut' moved the eel to a good position for my camera but when I took my picture another terrierman beheaded the eel with one swift blow from his spade.

We then drew an area at the back of Drusillas Zoo Park. The draw extended to the railway line on the Cuckmere River. We stopped at the second farm visited—by the pipe tunnels—and enjoyed tea and cakes. Mrs Errey kindly then gave me a lift back to the start where we had left our cars. I noticed in her car that at the back of the sun visor there was a list of the registration numbers of vehicles belonging to antis. I left with everyone else at about 5:30pm. I had stuck it to the end and thereby maintained my cover but with the Quorn investigation showing so much promise I knew I could not risk another visit to that hunt.

Thursday April 18th 1991 was long and eventful. I caught the train to London and met Jim Barrington at the LACS offices. Jim had arranged a meeting with another hunting informant and fearing that he might be walking into a trap wanted me along in support. Jim drove us to Newport for the rendezvous in a pub. The idea was for me to stay in his car and if there was any sign of trouble—such as the appearance of a van load of hunt thugs—call the police with my mobile phone. Jim walked in for his meeting with Clifford Pellow (1943-2016), the former Huntsman of the Tredegar Farmers' Foxhounds, at 2pm. I waited outside. And waited. It was 9pm before Jim staggered out. Everything was well. Clifford Pellow proved to be one of the best informants recruited from the hunting side and it seemed that he and Jim both tried manfully to drink each other under the table. We booked into the Westgate Hotel, Newport.

Jim and I met Clifford again on Thursday August 29th at Griffin Lodge, Rudry Common. We chatted from 10am to 1:30pm about his many issues with hunting. Clifford told us about how fox hunting really worked. On Friday November 8th 1991 the LACS arranged a press conference for Clifford Pellow at the House of Commons at which he told MPs and our nation the truth about fox hunting. I heard details of the conference on the noon news bulletin on my local Radio Broadland. The LACS then commissioned Andrew Tyler to write the story of Clifford Pellow in the small booklet, *A Brush With Conscience. Why a Huntsman Abandoned His Sport*, published in 1997. This was the introduction:

"For more than two decades, Clifford Pellow served as a professional Huntsman with several packs of fox hounds in England and Wales. The last eight years of his hunting career were spent with the Tredegar Farmers' Fox Hounds in South Wales. Always a stickler for the rules, Mr Pellow became more and more outraged at the abuse of foxes ordered by his Hunt Master in breach of hunting codes of conduct, until, unable to stomach it any longer, he protested. As a result he lost his job.

He took his complaints to the Masters of Fox Hounds Association, which held a mockery of an 'enquiry', and finally 'exonerated' the Hunt Master, Mr Howard Jones.

In November 1991, Clifford Pellow, at the invitation of the League Against Cruel Sports, attended a Press Conference in the House of Commons, where he described to the media and several Members of Parliament, several incidents during which foxes were abused in contradiction of the rules of the Masters of Fox Hounds Association during his career as professional Huntsman for the Tredegar Farmers' Fox Hounds.

Mr Howard Jones, Master of that Hunt, who was publicly accused by Mr Pellow of being responsible for these abuses, launched a libel action against Mr Pellow. The case came to court on 24th November

1994 in Cardiff Crown Court. In his defence Mr Pellow called hunt supporters as witnesses to verify his allegations.

On 1st December, after a six-day hearing, the jury cleared Mr Pellow of libel. The court ordered Hunt Master Mr Jones to pay all the costs of the case - estimated to be almost £100,000. Mr Jones, however, continues as Master of the Hunt with the blessing of the Masters of Fox Hounds Association.

Award winning journalist Andrew Tyler was commissioned by the League Against Cruel Sports to interview Mr Pellow and write the compelling story of a man whose burning conscience caused him to turn his back on a sport which had enthused him from childhood, and in which he had risen to the top, but whose governing body pathetically failed him when he complained of horrific cruelty in breach of their own much-vaunted codes of conduct.

Clifford Pellow has since carved out a new living unconnected with bloodsports and is a member of the League Against Cruel Sports. The League and its active members now benefit from his advice and unique knowledge and experience. He now looks back on his hunting days with new eyes and can no longer justify the continuing existence of the 'sport' he once loved - even if conducted in accordance with the rules. However, it is possible that he would still number amongst hunting's leading professionals today, had his less conscientious superiors supported him in upholding the standards they publicly and piously proclaim in defence of fox hunting."

And these were some of the opening paragraphs:
"When, in 1985, he took a job with a Welsh hunt - the Tredegar - that played slack with the rules, the remnants of his pride disintegrated.
'I was getting very bitter, if you like, about the things that I saw. It wasn't what I'd been brought up to. It wasn't the hunting that I knew, the sport that I had enjoyed, once loved and defended.'
In advance of hunting days, he says, foxes were caught in traps, put into sacks and, after being dragged across a couple of fields to get up a good scent, released for the hounds to slaughter. Bad sport. In one incident, a milkchurn rather than a sack was used. In another, the terrified fox bolted from the bag into a farm where he fell into a manure pit. The farmer's son shot him.
What made matters worse for Pellow was that, from the start of his career, he'd always been a man of starchy correctness, a disciplinarian who'd once been fired for inflexibility. Now, here he was playing his own part in the travesties. "I was as guilty as everyone else. Sickened by it, but guilty".
He remembers one fox, caught and handed over by a local farmer, who was kept for a week in a 40 gallon bone bin, where he was sustained on liver and water. "I remember looking in on him on the Friday, looking at this beautiful creature, which he was, and thinking; Tomorrow this time you'll be a thing of the past, ripped to pieces. Seventeen-and-a- half couple of hounds will be biting at you, each hound with 32 teeth."

'And before that there's the fear as you're grabbed by the tongs and stuck in the sack.'

'I've held a fox many times by the scruff and brush and felt how petrified they get; their hearts banging away like hell; farting and excreting and peeing every time the hounds speak. And I'm the person giving him three seconds to live. I am responsible for it. Absolutely ghastly....'"

Returning to the spring of 1991, on Sunday April 21st, I met Jim again at his home and we both drove to do undercover work at the BFSS South East terrier show at Detling. We looked for terriers and lurchers bearing battle scars.

The following month, on Wednesday May 15th I went out with a new pack of mink hounds for me when I joined the Northamptonshire Minkhounds for their meet at Brook End Farm, Hail Weston. To limit damage caused by my generating suspicions at other hunts I used a new alias—Mike Turnbull. I spoke to a hunter named Ivan Wilmore. I did not see much hunting as they seemed to pack up at 1:45pm; however, I was with them long enough to be given their meet for the following Saturday which was at Collyweston. I had other work to do that day so passed the details to colleagues in the HSA. The hunt was sabotaged—with the saboteurs pretending to follow hunters to the meet to hide that they already knew its location.

Cub hunting in the 1991/92 season was spent entirely with the Quorn Foxhounds. After that successful investigation we concealed my identity and I returned to undercover work elsewhere. In the immediate aftermath of course, with so many of my film clips being widely shown, it was difficult for any investigator to use a video camera at a hunt. Even the most slow-witted hunt supporter was suspicious of such equipment.

Saturday November 2nd I attended the meet of the Bicester with Whaddon Chase Foxhounds at Stratton Audley. I judged they were so sensitive to cameras that I made it a matter of observation only. I chatted with hunt supporters but never took my cameras out.

The following Saturday, November 9th, I joined the Puckeridge & Thurlow Foxhounds for their meet at Brent Pelham. I used our Land Rover and played the role of casual supporter, taking the usual stock photographs at the meet. They hunted a fox and marked him to ground in a pipe. I had no sooner approached the scene than they chose to give him best (they left him). No one said why. If it was my presence as a stranger that unnerved them then we had found a form of hunt sabotage and saving lives that we could only have dreamed of when I was sabotaging that same hunt as a young man back in the 1970s.

On Saturday November 16th I returned to the Bicester with Whaddon Chase Foxhounds for their meet at Chipping Warden. Again, I was just a casual car follower. I conversed with supporters and riders and photographed events. I saw a fox crossing a road but was too slow to picture him. That hunt at the time was notorious for hunting to the very last glimmer of light. I eventually left at 4:15pm in near darkness.

After the Quorn publicity, the LACS received all manner of tip-offs about other hunts. Some information was true, some outdated some false. Wednesday November 20th augured well. The League had been sent photographs of a caged fox in the garage of Mark Wheeler, Kennel Huntsman for the Vine and Craven Foxhounds. The pictures showed his Land Rover parked in front of the garage. The League liaised with the *Mail on Sunday*. I caught the early train to London, met Jim Barrington at the LACS offices and we drove to meet a *Mail on Sunday* reporter and photographer at Fleet services on the M3. We proceeded in convoy to the hunt kennels where we confronted Mark Wheeler about the allegations. The same cage was there but did not contain a fox. Mark showed us around the kennels, denied any knowledge of there being any fox and said the cage was used to store dog biscuits. He refused to allow the reporters to take away a handful of the straw in the cage. I took video film of the encounter then, using more new technology, used a Sony Walkman video player to immediately show the recording to my colleagues.

A hunt spokesman and the MFHA later claimed the fox had been 'planted' in the garage to discredit the hunt. Jim Barrington ridiculed that suggestion: *"The hunt is suggesting that someone strolled into the Huntsman's garage right next to his house, with a fox under their arm in broad daylight with the presence of the Land Rover indicating that someone was home—and then conveniently found a metal container with straw in the bottom and a metal grill over the top. Then, the hunt suggests, that unknown person took a photograph, took the fox out and strolled away with it—again in broad daylight. I don't believe a word of it!"* (*Wildlife Guardian*, 19 Winter 1991/92)

Three days later, Saturday, November 23rd, I secured memorable images of the end of a fox hunt. I had returned to the Puckeridge & Thurlow Foxhounds for their meet at Langley Lower Green. I took my Land Rover and mingled with supporters at the meet. I took stock images with a small compact camera. Followers revealed the planned draws were Meesden then Scales Park. Hounds were initially put in south west of New Farm.

There was a Land Rover full of hunt saboteurs in attendance. They were keen. I watched as all but one followed the hunt on foot across the fields. I drove around through Meesden to a bend in the road at Lower Green and parked near other hunt followers. Hounds drew through coverts towards us then hit a line heading back through Meesden. Supporters turned their cars to follow. I did likewise, trailing behind.

We then stopped in Meesden by a telephone box. Hounds were by then in full cry. When I saw a supporter frantically waving his cap I jumped out of my Land Rover and ran forwards, taking my camera and preparing it. I heard hounds snarling from around a house on my right, and angry residents shouting: *"Get your bloody hounds out of here!"* It was just after noon.

As I advanced I saw some hounds fighting over an object on the grass just a matter of metres in front of a pink-washed house, opposite the telephone box. A red-coat galloped up, left his horse with a foot follower, and rushed to the scene. I thought hounds had killed a cat (as did some other car followers on the scene) but the red-coat pulled up the carcase of a fox from the mêlée.

With no video camera, I could only take still photographs. The young red-coat then walked back to the road swinging the body. Car followers offered to smuggle the body away in their vehicles but he declined the opportunity to defuse what was clearly a situation with real potential for conflict and took it onto the grass on the other side.

At first he held the dead fox in the ditch but then he took it out to allow hounds to rag and rip the carcase. Soon some hunt saboteurs turned up. They tried to wrestle the body away from the hounds. The red-coat tussled with them over the body. I stood with hunt supporters and photographed the struggle.

More hunt saboteurs arrived and the red-coat started to get the worse of things. Some mounted riders called on the car followers who were standing watching to help their man; no-one moved. That was probably because they had seen the hunt servant provoke the trouble. A young woman rode up. She screamed at the watching car followers to help but still no-one moved. Fearlessly, she dismounted and rushed to join the fray. Another red-coat then rode over to the fracas and was a bit free with using his horse and whip as weapons.

A farm pick-up then arrived with some terrier lads. They rushed over and the fox was regained by the hunt. The Whipper-in then did what he declined to do earlier and placed the carcase in the boot of a supporters' car. Throughout I heard other hunt supporters exchanging abuse with residents from the pink-washed house and others from nearby houses who were also clearly anti-hunt. Supporters identified the owners of the pink-washed house to me by name and told me they were known antis.

Though the front gardens were not fenced it was clear the fox had been killed on a front lawn belonging to opponents of hunting. I gathered hounds had also trespassed in their back garden. The distraught lady owner shouted that luckily she had put her cat indoors. She was right.

Besides being fatal for the fox it was a public relations disaster that was entirely the creation of the hunt, not that many hunters worried. When the hunt moved on to the next draw I mingled amongst supporters. They laughed as they recalled events and said Capt. Barclay (the Master) would have fun apologising for all the mayhem. Followers also told me the small area where the fracas with saboteurs took place was a conservation area banned to horses. I returned to photograph signs confirming this.

The fracas in the village had lasted some 15 minutes but no police arrived to deal with it. Clearly the police were called though because later in the afternoon no less than half a dozen police cars turned up.

I noticed in the early afternoon, whilst they hunted in Scales Park, a hound was injured in some way. I saw him pulled from the pack and given a lift away in the back of a Range Rover. At about 3pm, near Anstey, I saw hounds riot. They had been running on a fox—I heard supporters ahead holloaing the presence of the quarry. Then some of the pack broke away to chase a couple of deer and headed towards the B1368. They were clearly gaining on the deer so I drove in pursuit to try to stop the hounds. I noticed other car followers declined to leave their parked positions.

The B1368 was busy and cars were passing as the deer tried to cross. For a moment I feared there had been an accident but fortunately the deer were headed by traffic and turned south towards Hare Street. A red-coat galloped frantically to head hounds off and stop their riot.

Only one hound crossed the minor road south of Lincoln Hill, the remaining hounds stopped. I parked beside this road and saw to my left the red-coat and another rider catch up with the miscreant hounds in the middle of the field. The clearly enraged red-coat dismounted, left his horse with the other rider, and grabbed one hound. He clubbed him about the head with the butt of his whip. The poor hound yelped and cowed.

The red-coat administered a severe beating to the dog—a 'sterning' in hunting parlance. He held the dog by the tail so he could not escape as he punished him. People often ask why hounds, that are such gentle and lovable dogs, look so cowed and timid when hunt staff shout at them. Anyone with real experience of hunting knows the answer.

The hound that had crossed the road after the deer was recalled. There appeared to be another couple of hounds running as well but supporters with powerful binoculars identified those 'hounds' as an Alsatian and a Labrador, presumed to come from a nearby farm. The hunt ended after drawing in near darkness near Great Hormead. When they eventually packed up I too left.

I spent a time giving talks to ACIG supporters and for LACS and doing media interviews about undercover work but I was determined to carry on with undercover work. Saturday December 7th found me heading for the meet of the East Essex Foxhounds at Rivenhall Park. I was driving merrily along near Ipswich when suddenly, with a mighty bang accompanied by ominous clouds of smoke, my Land Rover engine blew up. I had a four hour wait at the roadside before being towed back to Norwich. The engine was a complete write-off but thankfully it was under warranty, just, so was replaced free of charge.

Local hunts were cancelled the following Saturday due to fog and frost but on Saturday December 21st I, at the second time of trying, attended the meet of the Essex Foxhounds at Kelvedon Hall, Kelvedon Hatch, the stately home of Conservative MP, Paul Channon. I photographed him playing the genial host by serving the traditional stirrup cup to hunt riders.

The following week, on Christmas Eve, I returned to the same hunt for their meet at Brick Barns, Chignall St James. Supporters told me it was the home of the Master, Chris Thorogood. He certainly enjoyed full police protection. At the meet, I counted six police squad cars plus a transit van packed with officers from the police support group. In homage to Christmas some riders sported tinsel on their horse's tails. The police entourage followed the hunt for over an hour. With no evidence of any hunt saboteurs in attendance they then left. I followed the hunt and in the early afternoon just missed photographing a kill in a ditch.

For Boxing Day 1991 I met Jim Barrington and Ursula at their London home and we drove on to join my good friends Dave and Cee Wetton at the meet of the Southdown and Eridge Foxhounds at Tunbridge Wells. That was purely monitoring and hunt sabotage rather than any attempt at undercover work. When we saw hounds riot after sheep we tried to stop them and I photographed the miscreant hounds.

That was the Thursday. Saturday December 28th found me back fully undercover with the Essex Foxhounds for their meet at *Green Man*, Mill End Green. From my perspective, it was a quiet hunting day but I greatly enhanced my hunting credentials. The terrierman's Land Rover became bogged in deep mud. He had proper off-road tyres on his vehicle whereas the tyres on my Land Rover were primarily road tyres (with a shallow tread). I had no chance whatsoever of being able to pull his vehicle out with mine but it did wonders for my cover just offering to try. I drove as near as I could to his but it was too muddy—but Steve appreciated my efforts. Eventually the landowner's tractor was brought to the scene and that had the pulling power to extract the Land Rover.

*****

For New Year's Day 1992, as I had the year before, I attended the meet of the Alresford Coursing Club at Breach Farm, St Mary Bourne. I left home at 6:15am and drove south to meet my stalwart ACIG supporter—Janet Jackson. The meet was slightly later (perhaps acknowledging the celebrations the night before). It was at 9:30am with dogs in slips at 10am. There was one exceptionally bad kill. The poor hare screamed in pain and terror for more than 2 minutes before a picker-up retrieved her and killed her. When I saw Peter Atkinson drive up I knew that we would have to be careful. I could be recognised but not Janet but, if she was seen with me, her cover would be blown as well. We opted to leave at the break for lunch.

Preserving my ability to perform undercover work was wise. The coursing had been on the Wednesday. Three days later, Saturday January 4th 1992, I met the LACS Treasurer, Howard Hodges at his home and together we attended the meet of the Vale of Aylesbury Foxhounds near Chesham. It proved to be another revealing day.

The hunt set off and we followed from distance. We were both dressed up in full hunting kit—Howard looked the picture of a genuine hunt follower. At about 12:30 pm we chanced upon an extraordinary scene at a gate to a field from a road near the meet. The hunt riders had jumped this gate into the field to pursue the hunt but for some reason one horse—*Max*, a seven-year-old gelding—had ended up straddling the gate. His back legs were off the ground and he was stuck. There were two red-coats struggling to free the horse; one on the field side, one on the road side.

Our immediate response on seeing the horse trapped like that was to offer to help free him by dismantling the gate. As we saw it, we needed somehow to lower the height of the top rail of the gate. If *Max* could gain purchase from his rear legs on the ground, he could kick himself free. Our offer was refused.

With our help not wanted I stood well back and gathered evidence of the incident. After the Quorn business hunt followers were still sensitive about video cameras so I was only equipped with a 35mm still camera.

The red-coats appeared rapidly to lose their tempers with the horse. At the rear, on the road side and nearest my camera, Gordon Middleton wearing a top hat, cracked his long hunting whip at the rear of the horse. At the front, Joint Master of the hunt and owner of the horse, Alan Hill, urged stricken *Max* on. Alan Hill's wife, Trelawney, the rider of the horse, had dismounted as soon as he became stuck.

This all took place beside a busy road. Red-coated gentlemen lashing at and cussing a stranded animal was not a pretty sight. It was not long before motorists slowed and stopped. Some shouted advice, others condemned the hunters for their actions. One couple stopped and the driver got out offering help. Trelawney Hill's response was terse.

We had seen the hunt fence mender and I suggested we get him to help but the hunters at the scene were adamant they could resolve the problem. The fence mender could easily have removed the top rail of the gate, allowed *Max* to clear it, and then replaced the top rail. Eventually after a lot of whip cracking, shouting, tugging and heaving, *Max*'s struggles caused the gate to tilt. That lowered the height of the top bar. With his back legs then on the ground *Max* kicked clear of the fence and escaped. Trelawney remounted and carried on after the hunt.

Howard and I followed as well. Hounds later killed a fox which supporters described to us as being mangy and already covered in blood, probably from a road accident.

I later liaised with the LACS and the RSPCA to see the hunters prosecuted. We felt the hunters had simply lost their tempers with *Max*— even more so because he was stuck in a very public place. The RSPCA took the case to court. I of course had to give evidence. On Monday February 22nd 1993 I arrived at Amersham Magistrates Court for 9:45am. I was called to give my evidence first.

I told the magistrates where I was on January 4th 1992. I confirmed I took a series of photographs and identified prints taken from those photographs. In cross-examination, the defence brought out my previous criminal record and challenged my claim that the horse had been whipped. I was asked why no photograph showed the thong of the whip on the horse's back. I retorted that a whip cracked over an animal would only be in contact with the skin for a fraction of a second and that it would be a rare still photograph indeed to capture that instant. I pointed out that if only I had used a video camera the issue would never have been debated.

The case was adjourned, then on March 5th 1993 Gordon Middleton (who used the whip) was convicted of cruelly terrifying *Max*. Alan Hill was convicted of permitting *Max* to be terrified. Both were conditionally discharged for one year and each was ordered to pay £750 towards the RSPCA's costs.

March 20th 1993 proved informative. I met Howard Hodges and we monitored the Vale of Aylesbury Foxhounds from their meet near Tring. There were other LACS monitors out and hunt saboteurs. We sought to photograph Gordon Middleton. When I asked some young girl riders if he was out that day they sniggered then said, "*Oh, Mr Whippy - he's over there.*"

'Mr Whippy' and Alan Hill then appealed against conviction. Their Appeal was heard at Aylesbury Crown Court on July 12th 1993. I attended the hearing. Sadly, errors had been made in the gathering of the statements. Accordingly, on July 15th Judge John Slack (1930-2012) upheld their appeal and quashed their convictions.

Returning to 1992, on Wednesday January 8th I took our Land Rover to the meet of the Essex Foxhounds at Great Sampford. I had for some time sensed that my undercover credentials were wearing a bit thin. Hunters questioned me more closely—who was I, where did I live, what job did I do? I noticed hunt riders were never interrogated to that degree and thought that if I learned to ride it might open new opportunities for undercover work.

My plan was first learn to ride. Second, ride to hounds by booking a hireling horse for hunting. Third, feign injury that precluded riding again, but follow the same hunt on foot, with the excellent cover having ridden with them would provide.

From astride a horse it was hard to see, let alone film any of the real cruelty that occurred in the hunting field, but riding to hounds seemed to offer an unchallenged ticket to the heart of hunting. All a fine idea in theory but given that the only mount I had ever sat astride was a donkey in the Troodos mountains of Cyprus when I was a young child—and then I was singularly incompetent and got stuck in a steep place—it was fraught with difficulty.

I sought out local riding stables offering tuition to novices and booked a lesson. Thursday January 9th marked the inauguration of my equestrian career. I drove to riding stables near Great Yarmouth. Once again I had to use a new alias—Mike Frost. The horse world is notably tight knit. My surname is uncommon and I feared that if I proved memorably inept word might soon drift to the ears of hunters that a new guy named Huskisson was making a fool of himself learning to ride.

I read a lot of hunting literature. Before I set off for my first lesson I read an old Arab saying: "*The grave of the horseman is always open.*" When I first sat in the saddle my first thought was how high up I felt. My second thought was, 'where are the handle-bars'. I love cycling and on horseback I greatly missed the feel of anything in front of me to hold on to, and brace against. That first lesson I was led around an indoor arena on a leading rein. I felt real trepidation and severely doubted I could ever ride to hounds.

On Wednesday January 15th, I used our Land Rover to follow the Essex Foxhounds from their meet at Radwinter. The following afternoon I had my second riding lesson—and first experience riding in an open paddock.

Saturday January 18th, I met Howard Hodges and together we paid another visit to the Vale of Aylesbury Foxhounds who met at Lower Farm, Denton. I managed to photograph the hunted fox running. We saw some digging out. Two foxes were killed—one by the hounds and the other was shot in the earth after a dig-out. I then drove on down to Devon.

Monday January 20th found me with the Quantock Staghounds from their meet at Lydeard Hill car park. That was hind hunting. It proved to be another memorable day. I arrived soon after the hunt set off and saw the hind hunted from near the car park to West Bagborough. The pack then split with some hunting on towards Triscombe Stone.

I was near the front and saw supporters looking over what at first I thought was a slope or hill. When I approached closer and peered over I saw the hunted hind standing on what she clearly felt was a safe position—a small ledge on the steep edge of a deep quarry. I first saw her at about 12:15pm.

Hounds could not reach the hind. Hunters could not reach her. Frustrated, they all moved on but one hunter was left on guard watching the hind. I spoke to him and he told me that he was left to watch the deer and call hounds back if she managed to climb out.

Hind hunting in late January means inevitably the hinds are heavily pregnant. That hind was in real danger and I had to help her. Had she emerged quickly I planned to repeat the tactic I used many years before as a hunt saboteur and volunteer to drive off to summon the hunt—but never find them. But she stayed on her ledge. When she was still there at 1:45pm I had to try something else, even if it risked blowing my cover as a 'hunt supporter'.

I returned to my vehicle and used my mobile phone to call the LACS offices and spoke to Jim Barrington. He alerted the RSPCA and then the media. We felt our best chance of saving that deer was to make her predicament public. I ended up running a press event in the Quantock Hills. At 4:15pm I showed a photographer from the *Western Morning News* the location of the deer. Fifteen minutes later I did the same for a BBC cameraman. I then left the area for a rendezvous with a motorcycle courier from HTV to whom I passed my video-8 tape.

Tragically that story ended fatally. The hind could not get out the way she had gone in and, despite the best efforts of RSPCA rescuers who tried to reach her, she slipped and fell to her death. Her unborn calf died with her. Hunters sneered that it was our side that caused her death—forgetting it was they who hunted her into the quarry in the first place and they who had planned to hunt her further and kill her should she emerge.

My few seconds of video were widely shown on television. The ability to get hunting scenes on television the evening of the day they were filmed was a reminder of the real advances made in media terms since the first phase of my undercover work in 1981-83.

Thursday January 23rd was the day of my first riding lesson where I was free of the leading rein. It being my third lesson I was certainly no 'natural'.

Saturday February 1st became a dual-purpose day. I met Howard Hodges again and we went to the meet of the Vale of Aylesbury Foxhounds at Buckland Common near Tring. It was misty and we left the hunt at 2pm when denser fog descended. We looked for, and found, artificial earths.

The following week I attended the meet of the West Norfolk Foxhounds at Wells Green near Great Dunham on Wednesday February 5th. Hunt saboteurs found the meet and phoned the location to me. I drove up and chatted freely with hunt supporters. I needed to prepare the ground for a planned visit to that hunt the following week with Howard Smith from the *Mail on Sunday*. I told hunt followers I had recently moved to the area and lived near Swaffham.

There was another foggy meet when I went to the Essex Foxhounds at Matching Green on Saturday February 8th. Dense fog on the journey made me late. There was no sign of horseboxes, car followers or anyone akin to a hunter at the meet. I eventually found them at High Roding and was told by another follower there had been a late change to the meet to celebrate the 80+ birthday of a good hunt supporter. The stalwart never saw much hunting though that day. It was stirrup cups and nothing more. They packed up at 12:15pm. Ironically the fog cleared at 1pm.

The following week, Wednesday February 12th, I did a joint undercover operation with the *Mail on Sunday*. I met their reporter, Howard Smith, at the Post House Hotel, Norwich and drove him in my Land Rover to the meet of the West Norfolk Foxhounds at Ken Hill, Snettisham. I took slides at the meet and we chatted with supporters.

Clearly hunt saboteurs were expected. We heard the Huntsman urging a tough looking gamekeeper and a bunch of lads to deal with any saboteurs: "*a fiver for a broken bone, double that if you put them in hospital.*" That might all have been regarded as mere banter were it not for what we witnessed later.

Hunt saboteurs had congregated on a footpath by a railway line in the early afternoon. They were not doing anything and no words were exchanged. One hunt supporter, who had earlier been encouraged to violence, strode up. Without provocation or warning he punched a young saboteur full in the face, knocking him to the ground. The assailant ruefully rubbed the knuckles of his fist.

Whilst saboteurs aided their stricken colleague the hunter went to bask in the adulation of his colleagues. As for hunting we saw a few foxes hunted. We left at 3:30pm and I dropped Howard back at his hotel. That same evening I gave a talk about my work to Animal Concern Bedford. Followers of the Oakley Foxhounds turned up. It was remarkable that I was still able to carry on with undercover work at that time.

The *Mail on Sunday* wanted to report about the undercover man who exposed the world of hunting—chiefly the Quorn Foxhounds. On Friday February 14th they met me at home, took photographs, then I with my whole family drove to stay at the Post House Hotel near Northampton (courtesy of the paper). The plan was for me to be seen attending a hunt in the undercover role. They wanted me to be recognisable for pictures so loaned me a fancy new item of countrywear.

Next morning I turned up with my media entourage for the meet of the Pytchley Foxhounds at Teeton Hall, Hollowell. I was briefed to stand with my back to the camera watching the meet. Howard Smith and photographer Lynn Hilton did the rest. We then returned to the Post House for a further interview. My children enjoyed a swim in the hotel's pool before we returned home.

The *Mail on Sunday* duly ran a 1½ page spread about my work under the heading: "*The spy in the hunt*" and the sub-heading: "*Double life of a cunning campaigner who chose to run with the hounds*". It risked my future work within hunts but that work was ending soon—given what my local Waveney Harriers knew about me it was a miracle it had lasted that long—and a lengthy write-up in a national paper was a worthwhile trade.

The following week, Wednesday February 19th, I took my Land Rover to the meet of the Essex Farmers' and Union Foxhounds at *The White Horse*, Mundon. I chatted with George Milton, the affable Huntsman of the Essex Foxhounds. He told me about the prowess of his good friend Richard Down—Huntsman of the Quantock Staghounds.

I followed the hunt with other supporters. At one point a passing car slowed and two anti-hunt women directed a tirade of abuse at me and other hunters. It did wonders for my cover. Even better was when I gave George Milton a lift. We discussed hunting, hunting people, hounds and horses. Any hunter that doubted my credentials would have been reassured by seeing such a renowned Huntsman as George seated in my vehicle!

Saturday February 22nd found me at the Enfield Chace Foxhounds meet at Offley Grange near Luton. It was a cold and windy day. I photographed a fox chopped by hounds in a wood in the early afternoon.

Two days later, Monday February 24th, when I joined the Essex Foxhounds for their meet at Boarded Barns, Shelley I learned that my cover with George Milton and his Essex Foxhounds was not so good after all. I tried to be scrupulous about clearing vehicles of anything that indicated my true allegiance but had I made an error and left something that George saw when I gave him a lift? Maybe I made a verbal error. Perhaps I was too concerned for the welfare of horses and hounds to be fully plausible as a real hunt supporter? Had I confused my aliases?

Whatever the reason, I was grilled at the meet by the Master, Pat Harrington. Who was I? Where did I live? etc. I deployed my usual tale. I was Michael Robinson, lived near Haverhill, had two kids and was self-employed. Then I went on the offensive: Why all the questions? How can they ever expect to recruit new supporters when followers are questioned so closely? Had I done something wrong?

I knew my time undercover was nearly up. A fox was hunted into a drain by the road at Fyfield, bolted and killed.

Later in the week I returned to safer ground. Wednesday February 26th I met Ed Maynard at Graham and Joanna Woolliscroft's house near Leicester and we drove north to stay at the Grand Hotel, Wigan. Far enough away from the Waterloo Cup venue to render an encounter with hare coursers unlikely.

The next morning we left early to attend the second day of the Waterloo Cup at Lydiate. We took our position just as a dog named *Evening Mail* killed a hare in the ditch on our side. Ed used his trusty Nikon equipment; I a new Canovision Hi8 video camera with an excellent lens. We witnessed nine other kills, eight on the far side and one, the last one, near us. As usual supporters cheered when hares were caught.

That morning started misty then heavy rain fell. Drink was liberally consumed. One supporter was so drunk he just lay in the grass. Hares ran for their lives and died to entertain such people—if he saw anything at all it was only the sky. There were plenty of hares and the day ended at 1:15pm. I dropped Ed back at his home.

The next afternoon I left with my family on the long drive to catch the Portsmouth ferry to the Isle of Wight. We booked into a hotel in Freshwater. The next morning, I went to the meet of the Isle of Wight Foxhounds at Downers Farm, Chale Green. The previous year the Huntsman, Stephen Clifton, had been convicted of digging for badgers and we wanted to see if he was still involved with the hunt. There were many hunt saboteurs and police officers at the hunt. When a hunt rider questioned me I told her I was from Chelmsford and followed the Essex Foxhounds. I recognised and photographed Stephen Clifton at the meet.

With the hunt underway I chatted with other hunt followers but it was clear they were suspicious of me. One fox was hunted and marked to ground but left. A brace of foxes was then found in a rubbish tip. One was eventually put out, hunted and killed in front of—and despite the best efforts of—hunt saboteurs. I left in late afternoon when the questioning of me became too intense.

I persevered with riding lessons but Thursday March 5th raised more doubts. I had my usual 3pm lesson. My diary records I cantered on a horse named *Happy* for the first time. I had problems keeping my balance when turning at a canter, and with keeping the reins the same length. Would I ever be able to ride to hounds? Riding to hounds is certainly easier for those who, if not born in the saddle, were most likely conceived near it.

For Saturday March 7th, I joined the East Essex Foxhounds for their meet at Tattersalls, Sible Hedingham. There were three transit vans full of hunt saboteurs out plus LACS Committee Member, Lawrie Payne who was monitoring. Three terriermen driving a maroon coloured Daihatsu pulled up beside me and asked me where I was from and which hunt I followed. I said that I lived in Haverhill and followed the Essex Foxhounds. They invited me to join a 'dust up' with the saboteurs.

With several police officers present, there was no violence. At one point the hunt were in a wood near Toppesfield. I overheard a police officer say to hunt saboteurs: "*They have no permission to be in there so you can do what you like.*" I passed that snippet on to hunt followers with the consequences I expected, some went berserk, ranting at the police officers. For once it enabled police officers to see hunters as we know them to be. The day ended at 4pm with no kill so far as I knew.

Wednesday March 11th proved a quiet day. I joined the Essex Farmers' and Union Foxhounds for their meet at *The Bullocks*, Stow Maries. The only fox found was in a wood by North Fambridge. He escaped on a day that was both windy and dry.

Saturday March 14th found me looking for the East Essex Foxhounds from a meet advertised as being at Greenstead Green. There was no sign of any hunting. A rider pulled up, late as his vehicle had broken down. When he asked locals about the hunt they opined that they had met the previous day. I loaned him my mobile phone to call the hunt kennels. They had time to tell him they were not meeting that day then my battery ran flat.

I went on to the meet of the Essex Foxhounds at Chalks Green. There were three transit vans packed with hunt saboteurs out protecting the wildlife and many police officers in attendance. When the Master, Pat Harrington, saw me she rode up and called out a tad sarcastically: "*Morning Mr Robinson!!*" Several foxes were hunted but intervention by saboteurs saved them.

We received a tip-off about foxes being bred and held for hunting at the Old Schmerley factory site at Newdigate, Surrey. I had checked this with Jim Barrington and Ursula on March 8th but we had found no sign. We received a more detailed tip-off so I liaised with the *Mail on Sunday* again. Friday March 20th gave another early start. I left home before 3am to meet Howard Smith and Lynn Hilton at Holmwood Station at 5:30am.

We went to the Schmerley factory site and methodically checked every building but there was no sign of any foxes. There was however a pen with a half-eaten chicken inside. Perhaps a fox or foxes had been held there? We went on to a nearby hunt site and found a hand-written note stabbed to the wooden door warning hunt saboteurs: "*to fuck right off*". I returned home for 6pm exhausted.

The next morning, I joined the Essex Farmers' and Union Foxhounds for their meet at *The Three Compasses*, West Hanningfield. There were plenty of hunt saboteurs in attendance. It was very windy and the hounds chopped a fox early on behind the old church. I asked the Huntsman if the wind had played a part and he agreed: "*He can't have heard us coming.*" Hunt followers itched to get hold of the saboteurs but the presence of police officers prevented any trouble.

When I attended the meet of the Puckeridge & Thurlow Foxhounds at Brent Pelham on Saturday March 28th I was recognised. I photographed hunt staff and other riders at the meet. The hunt set off and we proceeded to the first draw at Whitebarns. A Land Rover approached and stopped beside my vehicle. The sour-faced driver wound his window down and shouted: "*Mike Huskisson I believe! We have nothing to hide but this is my land and I don't want you ploughing it up, so get out!! I don't want you telling any more of your lies.*" I drove off the field and followed from the roads. The effective and experienced West London hunt saboteurs were present. They soon split the pack over many miles. That phase of my undercover work, at least in East Anglia, appeared over.

I carried on with riding lessons through the summer. June 23rd was notable because I progressed to jumping for the first time; September 1st for a 1 hour hack about the countryside.

The following day, Wednesday September 2nd 1992, I had my first meeting with one of our best hare coursing informants. Starting the previous month he had telephoned John Bryant and me numerous times seeking to pass on information about hare coursing and the netting of hares by hare coursers.

I fixed to meet him in a layby on a busy road many miles from London. Ed Maynard came along to guard my back from distance. The informant sat in my passenger seat with his colleague behind me. He showed me photographs and his phone book and it was clear that he knew a great deal about hare coursing. He offered to tell us about the netting and movement of hares for the Waterloo Cup in return for financial help with expenses. He was awash with knowledge and keen to share it. A leading figure within hare coursing he was disgruntled by the evident class prejudices within the coursing world.

As he put it the ordinary working man was welcome to give money to coursing; welcome to beat fields for hares, to net and move hares; welcome to beat up any hunt saboteurs who tried to intervene; but as for running his dogs in any major events such as the Waterloo Cup, well, that was a different story.

It was foolish for the coursing fraternity to irritate such a person. He explained the intricacies of the netting and movement of hares for hare coursing. This played a vital role in ensuring enough hares were available for the big meetings. He told me how hare coursing worked, who did what, who the key figures were, who thought they were key but effectively contributed little. I learned about the many disputes within coursing and a great deal of gossip as well.

He was also well-connected in hunting circles and told me that Peter Atkinson from the BFSS had complained that after the Quorn publicity in 1991 he was given a 'right bollocking' by Prince Charles. We chatted for 4½ hours and arranged another meeting at his home.

For my riding lesson on September 22nd I rode a very calm horse named *Swoppit* and did more jumping. The tuition yard had very small fences and a nice deep surface to land on which was just as well. On one of several occasions when horse and I parted company and I ended up flat on my back the girls watching guffawed with laughter (my frailty in the saddle often drew an expectant audience). I knew why when I stood up, looked behind and saw I had left an imprint of a portly old man on the soft ground.

With my undercover work at hunts in East Anglia largely over I switched to simply observing hunting and undercover fieldwork. When I went to the Essex Foxhounds cub hunting meet at Old Barn, Great Canfield at 7:30am on Saturday October 3rd it was to join Lawrie Payne and monitor the hunt. It was very wet near the meet and the hunt moved to Canfield Hart. There were many hunt saboteurs in attendance and many police officers—including some flying their helicopter.

Lawrie and I both dressed in country gear. That we could easily be mistaken for hunt supporters was proven when a woman approached us, told us she followed the Essex Farmers' and Union Foxhounds and that she knew who all the antis were if we needed the details for our hunt records.

For a time I followed hunts and drifted from monitoring to undercover work as it suited. On October 10th following the meet of the Thurlow Foxhounds at Great Bradley at 8:30am I openly took video film of them from my car. They reciprocated.

Two weeks later, October 24th, at the cub hunting meet of the Essex Foxhounds at Roxwell I observed keen hunt follower Nick Herbert organising the hunt stewards. I was told that Nick Herbert was an architect of the hunt stewarding idea.

Near the end of the month, Tuesday October 27th, I had another meeting with our hare coursing informant. That day Jim Barrington accompanied me. I met Jim at some busy motorway services at noon then we drove to meet our source of knowledge (he subsequently provided us with a great deal of precious information).

My riding lesson on Thursday October 29th was revealing. I started on *Swoppit* then was changed to a horse named *Dutchy* (*Dutch Gamble*). I was shown a new horse named *Maddy* in the stables and told that *Maddy* had been ridden by the Whipper-in to the North Norfolk Harriers the previous Saturday. That hunt connection confirmed how wise I was to use an alias—even if it meant I always had to pay for lessons in cash.

On Saturday December 12th I met Howard Hodges and we monitored the meet of the Bicester with Whaddon Chase Foxhounds at Stewkley. Our interest was drawn by them hunting close to copses that we knew contained artificial earths. Late in the afternoon I saw a follower named 'Ginger' Dover. As a young hunt saboteur, I learned to be wary of his notoriously short temper and propensity for rage.

I exploited every possible opportunity for undercover work. Boxing Day, Saturday December 26th, drew me to the meet of the Easton Harriers at *The Volunteer*, Saxstead. I was laden with cameras and pretended to be working for a Norwich photographic agency. At that time hunters boasted how many followed hunting on Boxing Day. I told hunters I had been told to expect (and photograph) a crowd of around 3,000,

When I feigned disappointment there were so few there, hunters assured me they had seen 3,000 attending on previous years. In fact there were no more than 500 there that day—a fact confirmed by the attending Police Sergeant.

Monday December 28th 1992 proved the gullibility of some hunters. I was far from home observing the Southdown and Eridge Foxhounds at Cowden Farm, Five Ashes, Sussex. I photographed the meet. When I asked a lady follower what time they planned to set off she queried: "*Who are you?*" I answered, "*Paul Watkins*," and she responded "*Oh, that's alright.*"

A Master named Evans claimed to recognise me as 'a man from *Horse and Hound*'. His horse promptly trod on my foot. The hunt ended up drawing land around Crowborough. I saw a fox running that had an injured front leg. That fox was not hunted but when I commented to hunters about the injured fox they told me they had killed four foxes with injured feet recently. Such injuries were probably caused by snares or traps set by gamekeepers.

I had another riding lesson on the last day of the year. Again I was aboard *Dutchy* and my diary records that it was a good lesson with plenty of different manoeuvres. Soon I would have to put the little riding expertise I had gained into practice.

*****

1993 started off with undercover work with Andrew Tyler to expose cruelty at livestock markets. In the hunting fields my monitoring work became a matter of recording the violence that hunters showed towards hunt saboteurs as much as towards wildlife.

January 16th 1993 provided an example of routine vandalism by hunt supporters. I met Howard Hodges and we monitored the Bicester with Whaddon Chase Foxhounds from their meet at Stewkley. Hunt saboteurs were out as well. We watched a fox seek sanctuary in Christmas Gorse. Two thirds of the pack promptly rioted away in pursuit of a Muntjac deer, one third set off after the fox. There was no sign of any Huntsman in sight. Hunt supporters smashed the windscreen of a hunt saboteur's car.

A week later, on Saturday January 23rd, I joined other LACS monitors to observe the meet of the Essex Foxhounds at *The Butchers Arms*, North End. This was the day that culminated in the notorious Stagden Cross incident that will be described later.

The end of the month, January 30th, Howard Hodges and I monitored the meet of the Enfield Chace Foxhounds from Ganwick Farm near Barnet. The day was memorable for two reasons: firstly, the close proximity of hounds to the busy M25 and secondly the sight of an eleven-year-old lad proudly wearing a hunter's red coat.

Saturday February 13th proved an interesting monitoring day. Hunts caused mayhem on footpaths. Those precious rights of way could be blocked by hunt stewards and damaged by hunt horses ridden along them. Councils became concerned that if footpaths were deeply pitted by horse's hooves in wet weather, and not re-instated, then Councils could be held liable should the public subsequently slip and injure themselves.

That Saturday I met Kim Smith and Berni, Rights of Way Officers from Suffolk County Council. The Council had received numerous complaints of footpaths being damaged by horses. We monitored the Suffolk Foxhounds meeting at West Lodge, Bradfield St. George.

I had warned my new colleagues that if the hunt had stewards out and they suspected us of being anti-hunt they might block us from the footpath. Kim Smith smiled and told me she had been five years in the

Metropolitan Police and no hunt steward would keep her from walking a footpath. There were no hunt stewards to try. Thick fog delayed the start. They then hunted for an hour in Link Wood before deciding to pack up, ironically just as the mist cleared.

I returned to monitor the Suffolk Foxhounds from their meet at Chadacre Park on Saturday March 13th. The police were out in force at the meet. Hunt supporters soon identified me and a supporter with a video camera filmed me. During the day, I saw that a rider had been thrown from his horse. I stopped and went to his assistance, prepared to use my mobile phone if required, but he was unhurt and declined any help.

The hunt marked a fox to ground in a pipe near Aveley Wood. He bolted of his own accord. When he returned the supporters holloaed like mad and he went away again. I did not know whether that fox was caught. The hunt packed up at 4:45pm and hunters gave me a parting V-sign.

At the end of March, I drove to the West Country planning to join LACS colleagues to monitor the Devon and Somerset Staghounds. It was Friday March 26th 1993. As I proceeded west along the new North Devon Link road at about 5pm I saw three young lads die.

It was an accident out of nothing. There was little traffic in my lane but a queue of cars coming down the hill towards us. There was a middle lane that at the time could be used for overtaking by either side. Suddenly from amongst oncoming traffic a Vauxhall Corsa swerved out and across our lane. I saw the front seat passenger clutching the grasp handle above him in terror.

The car smacked head-on into the steel crash barrier on our left that shielded a steep drop. It then bounced back into our lane and the car in front of me, despite braking with full force, could do nothing but smash into the side of the Corsa. It was a high-speed impact.

I braked to a halt metres short of the wreckage. My first thought was to grab my mobile phone, which few had in those days, and call the emergency services. Thankfully I could describe where I was—again at that time they did not have the modern ability to locate the position of mobile phones.

Other motorists had stopped to help and after making the call I rushed to see what I could do. I chiefly remember silence and the stench of petrol. The passenger door of the Corsa had been driven in to the point of the gear lever. The impact on the car in front of me had pushed the engine block to a point under the driver's legs. No-one was screaming in pain nor even moaning. There was just silence.

The driver of the Corsa had his head slumped out of the door window that had smashed in the impact. I felt for his pulse. His arm and wrist were warm but there was no pulse. Blood dripped from his ears. I felt helpless and traumatised. I had seen too many animals die but never my own species. Police later told me the lads had suffered catastrophic injuries. No-one could have done anything to save them

Because of my call police, firemen and ambulances reached the scene quickly. Firemen struggled to extract the driver of the Ford Cortina in front of me. I was given a drip bottle to hold for him—and it was good to feel I could do something else to help.

I had cameras to hand and had considered taking them out. Standing back and recording such a scene seemed distasteful, plus I was so used to getting abuse and threats from hunters at the time of a kill that I feared a similar result from other motorists. I was too shocked to handle further aggression so filmed nothing. At a later interview the police officer cursed the fact that I had not filmed the scene. He told me they were searching for witnesses, particularly of the driving before the accident, and too many motorists had simply driven off afterwards and could not be traced. Video film of the scene would have been of real help.

Three young builders in the Corsa died. They were returning to Yeovil after the working week. It seemed the driver pulled out to overtake then, at the last moment, realized there was already another driver overtaking. When he swerved back he lost control and the rest I witnessed. It was a genuine accident that impressed on me the need to not only look in my mirror when overtaking but over my right shoulder as well. It is a message that I am keen to pass on. Death stalks us all the time and can be but a moment's inattention away.

We are shaped by our experiences. I have seen two of my three children born (I was in prison for our first). I have seen three young men die. I have seen more animals than I can count killed without reason. I view all life as precious, something to be cherished and lived to the full. Where we hold it in our power to give quality of life to others we should give as we expect for ourselves—or better.

The next morning, March 27th, I joined Kevin Hill to monitor the Devon and Somerset Staghounds from their meet at *The Sportsman's Inn*, Sandyway. At the end, I filmed the exhausted stag in water near Cloud Farm but we missed seeing the final kill by a minute or two.

The 1993/94 season started with a 5:30am alarm call on September 8th to monitor the Essex and Suffolk Foxhounds meet at Baylham Hall near Needham Market. Three days later, Saturday September 11th, I met Lawrie Payne and we monitored the same hunt from their meet at Norman's Farm, Ardleigh. There were many hunt saboteurs and police in attendance. I took useful pictures of the hunt 'holding-up' a covert—surrounding a wood with riders and foot followers to keep cubs within (the hunting world was denying to the Advertising Standards Authority that they still did that).

The following week, September 18th, Lawrie Payne and I again worked together to monitor the Essex Foxhounds. They met at Furness Farm, Margaretting. Hunt stewards were deployed but, following the legal settlement described in a later section, they allowed us to use the footpaths.

We returned to the same hunt the following Saturday for their meet at Chalk's Green—a meet I knew well from undercover work with the hunt. Hunt saboteurs were out and we saw the iniquity of hunt stewards allowing LACS monitors to use the footpaths, but not hunt saboteurs. After there was a kill in some rough stubble the Huntsman, David Gatfield, saw me approaching the area and shouted: *"Here's the phantom grave-digger!!"*

My diary for the day includes mention of a young girl named Lynn Sawyer. Lawrie and I had noticed her trailing around the roads watching the hunt. She was not an anti. She clearly knew a lot about hunting but did not appear to be fully integrated with the hunters either. She looked to be a lone observer. We chatted with her and found her knowledgeable and friendly.

The following month the LACS office deployed a team of monitors. It was Saturday October 16th when the Essex Foxhounds met at Barnston. I met Lawrie Payne at Maningtree railway station at 7:30am and we went on to meet Jane Springford and Rebecca Yates from the office. It was important that people working for the League knew what hunting was about. Again, hunt stewards allowed us all to use the footpaths.

The following week I adopted a different form of undercover work. It was not a matter of posing as a hunt supporter to infiltrate a hunt. Instead, I found a hidden position observing a known site to see what the hunters did. It was Saturday October 23rd 1993 and I was interested in the 8am meet of the Suffolk Foxhounds at Rattlesden airfield.

Rattlesden was built for the American Eighth Airforce in 1942. The 447th Bomb Group flew B-17s from there for much of the war. I knew of an artificial earth built by hunt supporters in nearby Thorpe Wood and wanted to see what hunters would do when cub hunting near it. I took up a concealed position. There were sounds of hunting all around me but hounds did not pass the artificial earth until 11am. I filmed them but when the fox dashed by I missed filming him because he was lost in the trees before my camera started.

The next day I enjoyed that rarity of taking my whole family to monitor a hunt. We could do so because it was a humane hunt and I could film and photograph without being subjected to abuse and aggression. We went to the noon meet of the East Anglian Bloodhounds at Tannington Hall near Framlingham.

They hunted a smelly sock that was taken by a runner who set off and was given a 15 minutes' start. They hunted two lines during a day that ended at 3pm. I gathered proof that riders could enjoy a gallop in our countryside without cruelty.

On Saturday October 30th Lawrie Payne and I were joined by LACS employee Michelle Bryan to monitor the Essex Foxhounds meeting at Chaureth Hall, Broxted. There were plenty of footpaths we could use and Essex police were very helpful—telling us where the hunt was going and what they were doing. We also deployed another successful tactic.

For some time when monitoring hunts, we had noticed that passing members of the public had no idea what we were doing. Sometimes, we were mistaken for hunt supporters and received verbal abuse. Lawrie and I suggested that we displayed prominently on our cars magnetic signs with "League Against Cruel Sports" in large letters. (The signs had to be magnetic so they could be removed when parked where we did not want our true allegiance displayed.)

We soon found we had to carry a stock of leaflets as we were often stopped by locals delighted to see us in action against the hunt and keen to know how they could help. That morning, a chap out walking his two dogs saw our mobile advertising and welcomed us to his area.

The following month I was back monitoring alone when I attended the meet of the Suffolk Foxhounds at Felsham House, Felsham on Saturday November 20th. This was near to Rattlesden Airfield and the hunt soon caused chaos on that airfield. The airfield was being used at the time by a gliding club and planes tugging gliders were taking off; planes and gliders were landing.

The gliding enthusiasts were enjoying a lot of fun—until the hunters butted their way in. Had a fox run across the runway and the hounds followed in close pursuit it might have been more understandable. But it seemed that it was just a case of the shortest way from one draw to another was to cross the end of the runway so the riders did that.

I watched the hunt from a road at one end of the runway. I discussed the behaviour of the hunt with the gliding enthusiasts. They were astonished at the arrogance and ignorance displayed by the hunters. 'Just stop your sport whilst we get on with ours' seemed to be their attitude. One gliding controller said to me in exasperation: "*Do they not realise that when a glider is committed to land he has to land. He cannot just rev his engine up and go around again. These idiots are putting themselves, their horses and our pilots in grave danger crossing the runway like that.*"

I explained that many hunt supporters find a real problem in considering the interests of anyone other than themselves. Verbals were exchanged between the gliding club and the hunters and then the latter saw me with my cameras.

I was about the last person they wanted to see in such circumstances. I was given a lot of hassle. Hunt followers in two cars and a four-wheel-drive vehicle tried to block me in to stop me monitoring the hunt. When I squeezed by and drove along the road their intimidation intensified. They first drove close up to the rear bumper of my VW Golf, then swerved out to overtake.

The car overtaking me weaved towards me dangerously, so I accelerated. He then accelerated hard and swerved towards me. I feared being rammed off the road. Trying to severely injure or even kill me merely because I had filmed the hunt displaying contempt for others seemed rather excessive. I sped away, called '999' and ended up giving a statement to Hadleigh Police. Later, I wrote to the Home Secretary, Michael Howard, to complain about the behavior of those hunt supporters.

Saturday November 27th, Lawrie Payne and I enjoyed another interesting day monitoring the Essex Foxhounds from their meet at Stagden Cross. The LACS had been sent confidential documents about BFSS plans for hunt stewarding and we took care to ask the Hunt Chairman, Paul Dixey, about their content. The hunt had a new Whipper-in out replacing David Veasey. Changes in hunt staff in mid-season are unusual and we wondered what the original had done wrong. No-one in the hunt would say. I filmed hounds rioting and trespassing. One girl rider commented, "*Good to see you out!*" We gave her a LACS leaflet which she appreciated. Late in the day

233

we offered a lift to Lynn Sawyer who seemed to have walked miles. She too was grateful for our kindness.

Lawrie Payne and I did a Friday meet on December 10th when we monitored the East Essex Foxhounds meeting at Stambourne. It was quiet at first then hounds rioted and ran around houses and into a garden. The hounds then killed a fox near Ridgewell. There was only a short hunt so we judged the fox was probably headed by hunt supporters. I photographed the terrierman bagging up the remains and taking them away.

Hounds then rioted after two deer near Ridgewell. Deer are reckoned to leave a sweet scent few hounds can resist hunting. A hound riot gave us the excuse to revert to old hunt sabotage tactics. We effectively intervened and stopped the hounds. When the female Whipper-in rode by to gather the miscreant pack I called out that they owed us a drink. She did not agree and insisted they had been hunting fox. We had seen and recorded hounds hunting deer.

With such evidence, many formed the view that given that few hunt followers could tell if their hounds were hunting fox or deer why not discard the live quarry altogether and hunt the humane alternative? A humane scent dragged at speed and with a cunning that mimics that of live quarry was the obvious replacement for cruelty.

Christmas Eve 1993 I monitored the East Essex Foxhounds meeting at *The Crown*, Messing. It was a very wet day and with three Transit vans full of hunt saboteurs out with attendant police officers the hunt were forced to a closure around 2pm.

Monday December 27th was visually memorable. Instead of their usual protest at a Boxing Day meet, the LACS unveiled their eye-catching 'Beauty and the Beast' poster campaign depicting a fox and a red-coated huntsman. Tony Banks MP spoke very well at the London event that was attended by Nick Herbert and Peter Voute from the BFSS.

The last day of the year, Friday December 31st, Lawrie Payne and I monitored the East Essex Foxhounds from their meet at Dynes Hall Gates near Halstead. It was another very wet day. At one point they hunted a fox into a wood where Lawrie and I were. We could not help the fox by sabotage tactics but just our presence with video cameras ready to record anything that happened unsettled the hunt.

When Lawrie went ahead to keep up with the action a young girl rider, mistaking me for a hunt supporter, asked me if there was a fox about. I confirmed there was. Hunt Master, Guy Lyster, rode up and saw us chatting. Clearly irritated he snapped: "*He is evil. He dug up the Duke of Beaufort.*" I corrected him, I had pushed over the headstone of John Peel— and no-one was 'dug-up' in that incident. The female rider merely responded, "*He sounds interesting.*" It maddened some hunters when some of their followers did not hate me as they did. The hunt finished at 1pm, and ended the day looking for a missing hound.

*****

1994 saw a gradual switch away from hunt monitoring work to concentrate more on undercover fieldwork such as finding and photographing artificial earths. Nevertheless, on Monday January 3rd 1994 I returned to the East Essex Foxhounds. They met at Shalford Green. I collected Lawrie Payne from Maningtree Station and then we met Jane Springford at *The Saling Oak* pub.

At the meet the hunters were friendly—even more so when Lawrie helped a girl rider who needed adjustments to the red tail bandage on her horse. We enquired after the hound that went missing the previous Friday and learned the miscreant had still not been found. Hunt saboteurs were out including the indomitable Linda from Halstead.

Hounds were put in to draw a wood south of the meet that contained an artificial earth. We later checked that earth and it stank of fox but there was no sign of any interference with the earth by hunt supporters. It was another day of heavy rain. Lawrie, Jane and I ended up soaked after we stood lining a busy B-road to protect hounds that were in an adjacent covert. The hunt finished around 1:30pm.

The following Saturday, January 8th, when we monitored the Suffolk Foxhounds meeting at Hardwick Game Farm, near Bury St. Edmunds, hunt supporters were far from friendly. A heavyweight driving a red Lada welcomed us with verbal abuse and two-fingered gestures. We were filmed by a hunter with a video camera driving a Range Rover. The day was foggy. On the look-out for hunters riding footpaths we stopped when we saw some on a footpath by Chevington Church. Perhaps they had overdone the stirrup cups because they stopped to relieve themselves. We helped two riders by holding their horses whilst they did so.

Lawrie complained to the Master, Phil Simmonds, about their supporters trying to ram me off the road that day near Rattlesden airfield. He claimed to know nothing about the incident.

Thursday January 20th found me in the support role. I helped in some different monitoring when we looked at the South of England Coursing Club meeting at Spike Hall, Six Mile Bottom near Newmarket. Because of the early start I stayed the night before at a nearby Travelodge and met Jim Barrington, Ed Maynard, and John and Suzanne Campbell. John Campbell, a veterinary surgeon, sadly died in 2010.

Whilst the undercover team, including Ed, John and Suzanne went in for close observation, Jim and I circled on the outside providing back up and prepared to record anything untoward seen outside the coursing fields. Whilst on surveillance my Mother called my mobile phone with the news that my Grandmother had died that morning.

Two days later I met Lawrie Payne and his fellow LACS Committee members Laina Cracknell and Donna King for more monitoring. We started off watching a shoot near East Bergholt then monitored the meet of the Essex and Suffolk Foxhounds at Hill Farm, Lawford. At the meet, I gave Huntsman, Stephen Swann, a nice photograph of himself with his hounds taken at a previous meet at Little Bentley. He appreciated the gesture. I emphasised that with no live quarry involved I could share his interest in hound work.

When I saw a young hunt saboteur named Robin following the hunt on a bicycle, it reminded me of my own youth. The hunt went south towards Little Bromley and Great Bromley but nothing much seemed to happen until just before lunch when a fox went away from woods north of the B1029 and east of Newhouse. There followed a frantic dash north towards Burnt Heath with hunt followers left far behind. Hounds streamed into a farm and garden disturbing horses in a nearby paddock. When most hunt staff caught up I saw a Whipper-in extracting hounds from a barn. There was no kill so far as we knew.

Later that day we saw another shoot underway. Hunt riders rode to us and advised us to go and monitor the shoot instead as, in the view of the hunters, shooting inflicted far more cruelty on wildlife.

On Saturday January 29th 1994 I ventured west rather than south. I joined Steve Watson and an excellent team of LACS monitors, all wearing bright reflective tabards, to monitor the joint meet of the Cambridgeshire and Oakley Foxhounds at Manor Farm, Waresley. There was quite a crowd out as many hunt saboteurs attended along with hunt stewards. [Young hunt saboteur, Tom Worby, died after being run over by the Cambridgeshire Foxhounds' hound van driven by Huntsman, Tony Ball, near Waresley on April 3rd the year before.]

When the hunt set off and the saboteurs went into the woods the hunt stewards did not appear to bother them. The stewards recognized me. When John Boddington, husband of a Cambridgeshire Hunt Master, rode up and asked me where the hunt was, a steward warned him I was 'Huskisson'. He replied, "*One of those fucking antis.*" The hunts ended the day boasting they had killed but we did not see it.

Monday January 31st was a day for long-haul monitoring. After a 4:30am alarm I collected Lawrie Payne from Maningtree Station then we picked up Jane Springford and Rebecca Yates from Brentwood and went to the meet of the New Forest Buckhounds at Belle Vue Farm, Frogham, Fordingbridge at 10:45am. We walked in on foot with Frankie Horan and others from the New Forest Animal Protection Group (NFAPG). Hounds hunted a buck but when he went on land the hunt were banned from they had to return. After that they only put up does. The day ended at 2:15pm. I marveled at the ability of monitors like Joe Hashman and Peter White to run all day with those hounds.

We always sought to involve others in hunt monitoring work taking the view that as many as possible should be involved in watching over our wildlife. The LACS Open Days held annually at their West Country sanctuaries were excellent recruiting places. The Open Days were the perfect opportunity for supporters and staff to meet each other and learn how to work as teams to protect wildlife. League staff also gave guided tours of the sanctuaries so the members could marvel at the wide range of species protected by them.

When Lawrie Payne and I monitored the Suffolk Foxhounds from their meet at Kentwell Hall, Long Melford on Saturday February 5th we did so with Glen, who lived nearby, and Lilian who had travelled much further.

It was a sunny day with excellent scenting conditions. We saw a lone straggling hound nearly cause an accident on the A134.

The following Saturday, February 12th, I met Howard Hodges to monitor the Oakley Foxhounds from their meet at Wootton near Bedford. From the start hounds were put into a tiny copse and a fox bolted almost immediately. Protracted hunting ended when a fox was headed back into a wood by hunt supporters.

Police stopped me for a vehicle check on my Land Rover. Howard knew the Police Wildlife Liaison Officer and had a good chat with him. With the Land Rover, we followed the hunt along some rough tracks. That incensed hunt followers. At one point an irritated elderly gentleman ordered me to turn my engine off so he could better hear hounds. I obliged but, as soon as I did, he swore at me, so I turned the engine back on.

Hunt supporters also blocked the track. When I bumped up onto the verge to drive around them they complained to the police that I had driven over crops. The police were not impressed by the hunt followers' behavior and told us with delight there was no kill so far as they knew.

I could return to undercover work so long as I travelled further afield. Saturday February 19th 1994 found Lawrie Payne and me way up north, undercover, at the meet of the Ullswater Foxhounds at Middale Farm, Longsleddale at 9:30am. We travelled up the night before and stayed with LACS supporters nearby.

Dressed in full hunting gear we were both accepted as genuine hunt supporters. Hounds were taken over Wadshowe Bridge to West Side Fell. We kept to the road and observed the hunt working their way north towards Sadgill up the high tops. Hounds then hunted towards Goat Scar at great speed, far ahead of their Huntsman.

With the Land Rover, we could drive up rough tracks in the following column of hunt supporters. Cars belonging to hunt supporters were recognizable because they sported CB aerials. We chatted with hunt followers seeking snippets of information. A couple of old boys assured us there were fox holes on our right-hand side the fleeing fox would head for.

More worryingly for wildlife, we noticed groups of young lads armed with terriers and lurchers, seated waiting high on the fell sides. We suspected they were hanging around waiting to mop up any foxes that came their way. The hunted fox checked, then headed west. After a long wait, we followed supporters and drove north as far as we could. It was bitterly cold. As we drove higher the track was littered with patches of snow, as well as large boulders. It soon became impassable even for a Land Rover.

Giving up, we drove around to Haweswater and encountered the somewhat comical sight of the Huntsman and his Whipper-in watching hounds through binoculars as they worked the far side of the reservoir. It seemed to be radio-controlled hunting as he used his CB radio to speak to other supporters, presumably nearer the hounds, instructing them what to do. We left the area at 3:15pm when light faded.

Friday February 25th was spent with a great LACS team. I monitored the East Essex Foxhounds from their meet at Penny Pot near

Halstead along with Lawrie Payne, Laina Cracknell and Donna King. Late in the afternoon we saw a fox in Great Monks Wood being hunted by a lone hound. The rest of the pack was in hot pursuit of a herd of deer. As we dressed in country clothes and my Land Rover bore no anti-hunt or pro wildlife stickers we were often mistaken for hunt supporters. At one point the terrierman, O'Shea Jnr, son of the Huntsman, stopped us to ask where the hunt was.

Saturday March 5th was interesting. I met Lawrie Payne and Michelle Bryan and we went to the meet of the Essex Foxhounds at *The White Horse*, Pleshey. We saw Lynn Sawyer at the meet. She told us she was having a meeting with Jim Barrington at the LACS offices on Thursday March 10th to discuss violence from hunt stewards.

There were many hunt saboteurs out and plenty of police officers. Hunt stewards blocked the footpaths to hunt saboteurs but allowed us on. Recognising one of the main stewards, James Purser, Lawrie Payne said as he walked by, "*Good morning Mr Purser.*" That elicited the response, "*Go fuck yourself!!*" Hunt Chairman Paul Dixey and the Whipper-in proceeded to bait me over the John Peel incident.

Hunt supporters became ever more irritable. On Thursday March 10th Lawrie Payne and I observed the Thurlow Foxhounds meeting at Barham Hall, Linton near Cambridge. I had a CB radio system installed in my Land Rover and we used that for the first time.

Hunt supporters photographed us and tried to order us off a footpath at Bartlow. It seemed ironic. The Vestey family owned great swathes of land around there and yet they seemed to begrudge allowing the public to walk up a narrow footpath. We saw plenty of hunting around known artificial earth sites at Horseheath.

At one point, we parked on the verge beside the busy A604 and watched the hunt over nearby fields. I heard the blaring of a lorry horn and a prolonged squeal of brakes. A hound had crossed the road near a bridge and the lorry braked and swerved violently to avoid hitting and killing him. Rubber tyre tracks were etched across the road.

A young Whipper-in ran across and I criticized the hunters for putting their hounds near the main road. I said there could have been a nasty accident and the hound could easily have been killed. He replied: "*Shame...save shooting it.*" I was astonished at his callousness and responded sarcastically: "*What a charming man you are.*" That drew the boast: "*That's what the ladies think Mr Huskisson....that's because I've a big cock!*" Later another red-coated gentleman tried to order us off a footpath near Castle Farm. When we declined to leave, they abandoned whatever they had planned to do.

Much time had passed since I started riding lessons and I knew I had to put my very limited riding expertise to use. Friday March 18th 1994 I went for a refresher riding lesson at Caldecott Hall, near Great Yarmouth. They say that once you have learned to ride a bike you can always ride a bike. I found that for me the same did not apply to horse riding. I rode a horse named *Dillon* and was distinctly nervous.

Driving for the lesson I stopped off to buy a second-hand black hunting jacket, hunting shirt and stock. I asked about tying the stock and was told the instructions were easy to follow. Hmmm. In the shop, I recognised a follower of the Waveney Harriers, but thankfully was not recognised in return.

Saturday March 19th was spent monitoring the Essex Foxhounds meeting at Hatfield Broad Oak. I picked up Lawrie Payne and we collected Laina Cracknell and Donna King. Finally, we were joined by our good friend and excellent field investigator—Kevin Chapple. We greeted the new Whipper-in, Nick Wilson, by name. He seemed sulky that we knew his identity. There were no hunt saboteurs about. Joint Master, Pat Harrington, put that down to the anti-racism march in London. Late in the day we encountered the Whipper-in looking for two missing hounds near Canfield Hart. We searched and found one for him.

When I looked at the ease and confidence with which those hunt riders crossed country at speed I wondered if I would ever be able to do anything the least bit similar. But I had invested too much time and money in riding lessons not to try. I scanned advertisements for hirelings linked to hunting days. There were many hunting areas that I had to avoid. The New Forest seemed feasible but there was one chap there I would have to watch out for. Paul Woodhouse had been Kennel Huntsman at the New Forest Foxhounds since 1992.

Back in 1982 I accompanied Richard Course, the LACS Executive Director, to interview Paul Woodhouse. Paul switched sides and spoke out publicly about the cruelty at the heart of hunting. I photographed Paul for that story and he could have recognised me—even with a hunting hat to obscure my features I had to take care.

[Paul Woodhouse's article about foxhunting in the *News of the World* October 24th 1982 is in the Appendix. He told us about *Tag*, a crippled wild fox held for eight years in a shed belonging to Fred Jackson, terrierman for the Derwent Foxhounds. *Tag* was liberated in a dawn raid byy activists and left at the LACS HQ in London where I photographed him. Paul Woodhouse said: "*That fox was baited by young terriers as part of their training. I was determined to end its terrible ordeal.*" Fred Jackson explained about *Tag*: "*I keep four terriers and they've played with it, but the fox enjoyed it. I never let them fight it. Its front legs were bad when it was given to me as a cub. My kids wanted it as a pet, and we called it Tag.*" He added: "*These bloody do-gooders don't understand us country folk and our ways.*" Paul later switched back to the hunting side and was rehabilitated in the hunting world. In March 2001 he was jailed for eight weeks after punching a passing motorist in the face.]

I booked a hireling to ride with the New Forest Foxhounds. On Monday March 21st 1994 I drove south to stay with an ACIG colleague near the New Forest. The hunt was meeting on Tuesday March 22nd at Moonhills Car Park, Beaulieu. That morning I struggled to hide my novice nature. Even tying the hunting stock baffled me—I ended up using safety pins to make it look vaguely correct.

I was due there at 10:30am to rendezvous with my hireling from Flanders Farm. Arriving slightly late I quickly helped tack up then climbed aboard my mount named *Flintstone*. Part of the deal was that the stables would supply a guide for the day—a young girl named Emma—who was riding *Fiasco*. I was told the guide was necessary to help show me around the Forest but I suspected that it was more to do with safeguarding the interests of their horse, which seemed a good idea.

It was raining at the meet but I took out my small camera and photographed the view of a hunt from astride a horse. I also passed my camera to watching foot followers and asked them to photograph Emma and myself. I immediately detected the change in attitude to me, a complete stranger, but on horseback.

Instead of the usual grilling given to newcomers: *Who are you? Who do you hunt with? Where are you from?* etc; here it was nothing more than *Good morning sir* and other affable greetings. Whatever they may really think (and I do know) the foot soldiers certainly gave the appearance of being in awe and admiration of the cavalry.

We set off and I will readily admit that I have seldom been so scared. Even facing a battering from bully boys at the Border Counties Otterhounds, back in 1976, seemed better. We went into woodland first that was steep and muddy. The worst was crossing narrow wooden bridges that seemed to clutch at my knees and threaten a swift ejection to the rear of the saddle. As a child in Cyprus I recalled the family tale of a family friend who had been partially decapitated by not ducking low enough when riding at speed under overhanging branches. It did little for my confidence. I clung to my dear *Flintstone* and prayed that if there was an open grave for a horseman that day it did not have my name on it.

We just hacked about watching as the hounds cast and found nothing. I thought "*What if they do hit a scent and go away in full cry?*" Gulp. Another rider explained their choice of draw: "*We do it to keep the keeper happy but seldom find anything.*" We then went back onto moorland but again found nothing. Some riders started apologising to me, a newcomer, for the lack of action. I expressed the view that it was fine and that I was just happy to be out hacking in the Forest.

I was fascinated by the changed attitude towards me. Just because I was astride a horse the terrier lads were holding gates open for me, doffing their caps and generally acting subserviently. Under their breath I knew they might well be muttering something like: 'Poncy git, can barely ride a horse,' but whatever, the main thing was that no-one even thought of challenging my credentials as a hunt supporter. I had proven my theory that using a horse was a wonderful way to gain access to a hunt.

A senior figure within the hunt, Pat Hudson, gave me her tatty meet card and said I could have a discount when I next went out with them. I promised to take her up on her kind offer (but have yet to do so). I never saw Paul Woodhouse face to face and have no idea if he was even out that day. Whenever a hunt servant came near me I glanced down, adjusted my clothing, my boots or had some other reason not to be looking at him.

Hounds were taken to try in Hartford Heath then over to North Gate. They found at 1:45pm and went away at what appeared to me to be a great speed. The hunt criss-crossed over the B3056 and one hound had a near miss amongst traffic.

I was happy plodding along at the back but *Flintstone* was not so keen at being left behind. At one point the busy road separated us from the bulk of the riders. *Flintstone* was caught up in all the equine excitement and I knew who the real boss in our pairing was—and it wasn't me. I have witnessed countless hunts where riders pack up early so, when we were near Penerley Farm, and I was confident that I had achieved my goal, I suggested to Emma that we pack up and hack home. We did so at about 2:30pm.

Back at the meet I felt uncomfortable dismounting and handing *Flintstone* over to Emma to take away, untack and take care of. I felt that I should be doing more to help and the whole scenario smacked a tad too much of a boss and servant relationship for my liking.

It seemed the hunt packed up soon after I did. I never rode to hounds again. I had achieved one of my goals. I could afterwards say I had followed hounds on foot, on a bicycle and on a motorbike. I had followed hounds in a car, in a Land Rover and even in the terrierman's Land Rover. I had even followed hounds from astride a horse. In debates the hunting side had mocked me saying I knew little about hunting as I had never ridden to hounds. Such mockery ended in the New Forest.

My plans to use my riding to hounds as a spring-board for deeper undercover work within a hunt faded when the focus of my undercover and monitoring work changed. They vanished after Jim Barrington switched sides in 1995 as he took with him knowledge of my ideas.

Back in 1994 I continued with monitoring and fieldwork. Sunday April 17th 1994 provided variety that strained my physical resources to the limit. I joined colleagues Lawrie Payne and Jane Springford to run the London Marathon. Lawrie and Jane raised funds for the LACS. I raised funds for my ACIG and for our local primary school.

I ran in a fox costume—something I appreciated when the weather was so cold and blustery for the start. I inadvertently almost created chaos at the beginning. People asked who I was raising funds for. When I explained it was to stop wildlife being forced to run for their lives I gave a toot on my hunting horn to clarify the threat and many mistook my horn for the start signal and surged forwards!!

Lawrie, a fit fireman, completed the course in an excellent time. Jane also completed the course in a good time. As for me, being far from fit, I laboured round and ended up finishing in a time of 6 hours 3 minutes. My fox costume took a battering and the erect tail drew many ribald comments. It was all a lot of fun for serious causes.

On the last day of the month, Saturday April 30th, I helped monitor the Devon and Somerset Staghounds meet at Comers Gate. We all met at the LACS offices at St. Nicholas Priory beforehand. At the time the LACS had a great team of dedicated volunteers helping with monitoring West Country hunting. These included Steve and Val Honey, Anne and Ian

Farthing, Grant Palmer, Arminel Scott and Richard Genge. They all, time and again, put themselves in harm's way and faced down aggression and threats from hunters to record the mistreatment of our wildlife.

On that final day of the 1993/94 hunting season the League had many monitors and rangers out and we were well-equipped. We had cellphones, personal mobile radios (PMRs) and a CB system that allowed us to monitor similar transmissions from hunt supporters.

Over the wide expanses of Exmoor, with the combination of open moorland and narrow combes, it was essential to know where the hunters were and where they were heading. Hunt followers used their CBs to communicate every movement of the hunt. By listening in, but not transmitting ourselves, we harvested that knowledge. We communicated with PMRs and if they failed used cellphones. The latter could also be used to call emergency services. I also had a professional scanner that could pick up a wide variety of radio transmissions.

When we set off I joined Kevin Hill in his Subaru. He had a near unequalled knowledge of Exmoor, the runs the deer might take, and the locations of the LACS sanctuaries.

During the day, I met a couple of the lads that I knew from days with the Essex Foxhounds. In particular I chatted with George Milton who had been Huntsman at the Essex when I was following them undercover. We had a mutual respect for each other's viewpoint.

The hunted stag was killed near Yeo Mill at around 4:20pm. Kevin and I were caught up in hunt traffic jams so saw little of the end. Two of our cars were nearer the scene. Our day ended, as it usually did, with a thorough and honest debrief. We all made mistakes—me more than most—so it was important not to criticise errors but rather learn from them. We sought constantly to improve our fieldwork.

Saturday June 18th 1994 was significant for an attempt by me to return to undercover observation of mink hunting. The League had been tipped off that the Border Counties Minkhounds were hunting by invitation at Aynho on the River Cherwell, near Clifton.

The plan was that I would just be in the area, dressed in country gear, and innocently stumble upon them. I saw them at their meet and watched them set off towards Banbury. An elderly hunt supporter told me the hounds were hunting. I was sceptical and went south to a bridge near Somerton to await their inevitable return. I called up my colleague Roy Parker and he joined me. We waited and we waited.

In time hunt supporters drove by, stopped and wound their window down. One called to me asking if I was a fisherman. When I said no he asked, "*Are you LACS?*" I said, "*No.*" He replied: "*You are, 'cos you are talking to Master Parker, and he is.*" I asked if they wanted to talk to Roy and received the reply, "*No! He's a wanker!*" They then drove off. We then learned there were some 80 hunt saboteurs in the area also searching for the hunt. That explained why the hunt vanished.

On Saturday July 30th after receiving a tip-off from Jim Barrington about a mink hunt meeting at *The Swan*, Bluntisham, Cambridgeshire at

9:30am I scoured the area but found nothing. It was easy for hunt supporters to phone in anonymous tip-offs that sent us running all over the country. For all that we still urged colleagues, if they heard rumours of a hunt meeting, to let us know. I would rather have five fruitless searches than ignore one rumour that turned out to be real.

August 20th found Lawrie Payne and me driving to check a report of hare catching at Foulness, Essex. However, we were not allowed on the island as it is Ministry of Defence land, so could only watch from a distance—and saw nothing. On our return, we stumbled upon a fishing competition taking place on a lake near Ardleigh so stopped to take photographs.

Watching the fishermen reminded me of the observation that fishing is a contest between two creatures. One has a brain the size of a grapefruit, the other the size of a chaff of wheat; both have similar intellect. Even though the fish were caught and returned there was evident cruelty in the catching and handling—and it was clear from fish remains nearby that some did not survive the experience.

My 1994/95 hunting season started with a visit to monitor the Devon and Somerset Staghounds meeting at Winsford Hill on Thursday August 25th. In those days there was a great team of LACS monitors including Kevin Hill, Graham Sirl and Howard Hodges.

I accompanied Graham Sirl to start with. They hunted a magnificent large stag that soon went to water at Badgers Holt. He then proceeded down to Chilly Bridge. I took some video film but when I tried to take still photographs the local BFSS official, Richard Walton, blocked my view. It is a sure sign that something is amiss in any public pastime that you are barred from photographing.

The exhausted stag so nearly made it to the safety of the LACS sanctuary at Baronsdown but at the last he swung right-handed and headed towards Hele Bridge and Dulverton. I filmed the magnificent mature stag pushing his way out of a hedge onto a road into a crowd of hunt supporters in a desperate and ultimately futile attempt to escape. He was killed soon after near Marsh Bridge.

Two days later, when the Devon and Somerset Staghounds met at Alderman's Barrow, I accompanied Kevin Hill. It was a day of moorland hunting and we saw little. The stag was killed around 4pm at Woolhanger. The day was memorable for the fact that at the meet the Joint Master, Maurice Scott, rode up to me and asked for a copy of *Outfoxed*. He told me stag hunters had no complaints about its contents. He was only surprised that I took all the hunting photographs, including the one of the stag under the bridge at Dunster.

My first cub hunting observation that season was on Saturday September 24th when I went to the Essex Foxhounds meeting at Furness Hall, Margaretting at 7am. There were hunt saboteurs out along with fellow monitor Kevin Chapple.

There was a lot of violence from hunt supporters towards the saboteurs. Hunt saboteurs made effective use of a device they call a 'Gizmo'.

That played back, loudly, a recording of hounds in cry. It was very attractive to other hounds as like any pack animals they liked to join in.

The 'Gizmo' had to be used with care so that hounds were not drawn into danger such as over busy roads. When used properly it could pull hounds away from their quarry. It could also break them out of a riot, and draw them from danger such as away from roads and railway lines and away from places where they should not be, such as private gardens.

Hunters hated losing control of their hounds and often lost control of their tempers. Hunt supporters forced their way into the saboteur's van, smashed the Gizmo and punched any saboteurs that resisted.

Two days later, on the Monday, I went to the meet of the New Forest Buckhounds at Ashley Walk Car Park at 7:30am after staying with a colleague nearby the night before. I met Ken James and colleagues from the NFAPG and a film crew from BBC Southern Eye.

Wearing full hunting gear, I donned a pair of sunglasses as disguise and wondered down to the meet to chat to supporters. I was accepted as a genuine follower—even wearing shades at that unearthly hour! The day amounted to a long walk in the forest with Ken James and the film crew. They filmed hounds running at Fritham Bridge before the day ended in late morning with no kill.

The following month Lawrie Payne and I took an excursion to the West Country to monitor stag hunting. We drove down on Monday October 10th. As we arrived at St. Nicholas Priory we learned that the hunted stag was swimming Wimbleball Lake for the second time. The Devon and Somerset Staghounds had met at Haddon. We raced to the scene but heard over the radio the stag had been shot.

The next morning, we joined the LACS team to monitor the same hunt meeting at Five Cross Ways. Late in the day with the hunt about to pack up Lawrie and I opted to search north from Tarr Steps along the footpath beside the River Barle. After a mile or so we discerned faint sounds of a whistle ahead and the cry of hounds.

That was evidence that hunt supporters had a deer in sight. We quickened our pace. The whistling became ever more frantic. We ran forwards and at the same time alerted fellow monitors by radio. I saw a commotion and heard splashing in the river to our right. A man in a red hunt jacket wrestled with a deer in the water. Hounds bayed and snarled as they tried to get at the terrified animal.

I raised my video camera to the scene through the undergrowth but for a second or so the autofocus blurred the scene as it hunted for focus through the intervening bushes. I saw the red-coat tug at the deer's ears and try to fend the hounds off at the same time.

The victim was a hind, not the target quarry at that time. The situation changed immediately. Instead of having to film the cruelty in routine hunting there was clearly an urgent need to intervene to help alleviate suffering. That became the first priority; any film obtained was of secondary importance.

I waded into the river to help the young hunt servant keep the hounds back from the deer. He was keen to demonstrate to me that the hind's predicament was nothing to do with the hunt. He turned her round to show me a gaping gunshot wound the size of a fist in her shoulder.

Her foreleg flapped uselessly. As we stumbled on the treacherously slippery river bed she twisted out of his grip and struggled downstream. For all his frantic whistling no hunt supporters had arrived to help. This was a world away from the rhetoric and posturing from the two sides. Here were two anti-hunt activists and one hunter striving together to save one hind from a gruesome fate—had we not been there the hounds, though few in number, would have eventually killed her themselves.

I asked the hunter how we could help. He requested we turn our video cameras off but I explained that we could not. Film not only provided evidence of any mistreatment of the deer it also protected Lawrie and me from any subsequent allegation that the hunt might make (they did later complain to Lawrie that by moving to the riverbank to help he had left the footpath).

The hind had clearly been grievously injured by a shooter. It would be an act of mercy to put her out of her misery—the only mercy she would experience at the hands of man. The Whipper-in asked us to radio our monitors and get them to find a hunter with a gun to come to the scene.

We obliged and we waited. At such times with suffering occurring before your eyes seconds seem like minutes. I feared that with hunters already heading home our colleagues would have difficulty finding anyone with a gun. I suggested there must be a farm nearby where I could seek assistance. The Whipper-in agreed that to be a good plan. He gave me the directions to a farm up and over the hill and I set off.

By leaving the scene I discarded any chance of my being able to film the hind being shot. Such film was rare indeed and would be valuable to our cause but in many years of investigative work I have always adhered to one maxim—that we act first to alleviate suffering, filming comes second.

In soaking wet clothes, I set off up the hillside battling through a dense mat of vegetation. As light faded I quickly became disorientated and, to my intense frustration, was unable to help. LACS hunt monitors on the road found some hunters and they went rapidly to the scene where the hind waited to die.

Lawrie Payne prepared to film the end but the hunters threatened they would not put the hind out of her misery until he agreed not to film them. It was extraordinary. In countless debates stag hunters assured the public that at the end of the hunt with the deer at bay the deer was swiftly and humanely killed with a single shot.

This was the ideal situation for them to prove that claim on camera. There were only a few hounds present, very few supporters, so no reason to panic or rush the shot. The hind could barely move, yet they still insisted the kill should not be filmed.

To prevent any more suffering Lawrie agreed to their demands. The deer was killed with one shot. Her suffering was over. Darkness had fallen by the time Kevin and Lawrie found me.

We proved how monitoring could save lives the following month when Lawrie Payne and I teamed up with Karen Willcox to monitor the meet of the Essex Foxhounds at Matching Green on Monday November 7th. The second fox to be hunted went away from near an old airfield and sought sanctuary in a drain beside a road. The hunters were all set to deal with him until we arrived on the scene. Our presence with video cameras deterred them and they left him.

Later that month we had another interesting day monitoring. It was Tuesday November 22nd. I met the indomitable trio of LACS Committee members—Lawrie Payne, Laina Cracknell and Donna King and we went to the East Essex Foxhounds meet at Stambourne. It was a foggy day. When Donna saw a rider with an injured horse we offered help. Two foxes were found, one of which was killed. The day ended early at 1:45pm. Hunters told us that was because the horse ridden by the female Whipper-in had gone lame. The most interesting revelation was when hunters complained that one of their horseboxes was stolen from near the meet.

If only the hunting world had taken heed of our warnings that they should obey the law and ensure that when a horsebox is towed the tow vehicle and horsebox wear the same number plate. At that meet the thief had clearly driven up, found an unattended horsebox, unhitched it from the owner's vehicle, hitched it to his own and driven off. It was such a common sight to see unpaired number plates that the thief was confident his mismatch would not stand out.

We had by that time found many artificial earths, particularly in country hunted by the Thurlow Foxhounds. On Thursday November 24th Lawrie and I seized the opportunity to combine monitoring and fieldwork. The Thurlow Foxhounds met at Manor Farm, Horseheath. There are numerous artificial earths nearby.

We chose one site. Lawrie took up a concealed position on the footpath whilst I hid in the wood in dense cover overlooking the artificial earth, the entrances to which had been stopped by a hunt supporter. We wanted to record what, if anything, the hunters did at the site.

Nothing happened for a while. Then I heard sounds of the hunt around the wood. Just after noon the first hounds came through. They soon found me in my hiding place and rushed up and stuck their big, wet, inquisitive noses in my face, tails wagging. I knew they would neither be aggressive nor bark but I feared that if they took too much interest in me they would betray my location. I shooed them away. Next the Huntsman came into sight on foot.

He looked at the artificial earth and walked on. When the hunt moved on to draw elsewhere we left and went to check the condition of another artificial earth in nearby Balsham Wood. Both its entrances were also stopped. Heading away from Balsham Wood back towards the meet, soon after 2pm, we encountered a road block on the minor road south-east of the wood.

We were astonished. Rough-looking 'country sports' enthusiasts stopped motorists from passing whilst they indulged in hare coursing. We had had to overcome hunt stewards who blocked public footpaths so that fox hunters could play in peace and there we encountered hare coursers who blocked the highway to indulge in their pastime. I hoped our police would give us more help against coursers than they did against hunters.

I looked at the coursers. None looked to be from any of the recognised coursing clubs that operated there. We backed off to a safe distance and I phoned the police on a 999 call. I told the operator there was a large gang of illegal hare coursers by the Chalk Pits near Balsham.

The police responded quickly. I drove back to the area and directed a police officer to the site. We found other police officers trying to catch an abandoned greyhound. I later learned that at the first sight of the police the coursers ran away abandoning their dogs already out running.

When I phoned Cambridgeshire police that night to learn the outcome I was told that the hare coursers were part of a big gambling syndicate and had taken video film of their event. When the police arrived, the coursers scattered, driving their four-wheel-drive vehicles at speed over the fields. I was told that when the police pursued them the chase became ever more dangerous as the coursers crunched through hedges desperate to escape. The police gave up the chase when it became clear there was a real danger to passing members of the public, police officers and the coursers themselves. No-one was arrested.

The police officer told me he was not prepared to risk lives to save hares. That was a perfectly reasonable view. The Cambridgeshire officer then added that anyway, once the coursers had left his county it was not his problem. That made it sound too much like the Wild West for my liking—'chase the villains across the border and we can forget about them'. [Thankfully East Anglian police forces now cooperate across county borders to combat hare coursing.]

Saturday December 3rd found me down in the West Country again. I met Kevin Hill and we monitored the meet of the Devon and Somerset Staghounds from Tarr Steps Post. We feared they had killed a hind early on at Willingford Bridge but it seemed hounds lost her scent on the water. Instead of going downstream, as the hunters thought, she had gone upstream.

The day was enlightened by a car rally taking place in the same location. Brightly numbered vintage cars became intermingled with hunt followers and it all became rather confusing. Richard Walton was his usual officious self. We always took care not to block any roads or delay any other motorist. When we parked on the grass verge Richard told us we were on private property and should move. We argued we were on Council property and stayed.

The hunted hind was very nearly killed at Zeal Brake around 3:30pm. Kevin and I had seen her crossing a stream. We later saw her jump down onto the road but she was exhausted. She slipped, got up, and then slipped again. Rising again she summoned her strength and made a mighty leap to clear a railed fence that lined the road. That she only just made it was borne out by the hairs she left on the top rail. Just as she vanished into the distance the hunters arrived in force. They saw Kevin with his camera and left that hind.

I spent the day in Kent the following Saturday, December 10th. After an early start, I collected Lawrie at Maningtree and we drove to rendezvous with Jim Barrington and a large contingent of LACS monitors at Ashford Railway Station at 10am. We went to the meet of the Ashford Valley Foxhounds at High Halden but found they had cancelled.

Steve Watson, dressed like a good 'country sports' enthusiast, saw a hunt follower entering a nearby shop and asked him if any other hunts were meeting nearby. The chap kindly told Steve the Wye College Beagles were meeting at Botolph's Bridge near Folkestone.

We reached there at noon and asked in the pub where hounds were. Learning they had moved to a nearby lane we followed and found hounds running through a field of crops. The police were at the scene—which usually indicated hunt saboteurs were present. However, on that occasion someone else may have called officers. When an irate landowner roared up in his Land Rover we braced for trouble but his anger was directed purely at the hunters.

The landowner complained bitterly that the hunt had been banned from his land. There was one trespass by hunters around 12:30pm and another about an hour and a half later. Soon after that the hunt packed up without, it seemed, any kill. We took care to chat to the landowner, take his details and offer our help.

The beaglers seemed almost honoured to have Jim Barrington, the Executive Director of the LACS, monitoring their hunt. At end of day they kindly offered to share their sandwiches and cake with the LACS monitors.

A couple of days later Jim telephoned to say the landowner, a Mr Frith, had formally, in writing, banned the Wye College Beagles and East Kent Foxhounds from his land. We arranged to meet Mr Frith the next day to give him copies of the video of the hunt trespass. On Tuesday December 13th Jim and I duly met Mr Frith at his farm. We explained the work the LACS did, not only to end hunting, but also to curtail the mayhem and havoc that hunters caused in our countryside.

The LACS was very much the farmers' and landowners' friend. It was just one of many efforts that we made to win the hearts and minds of the rural community. We returned to the League office in London to draw the LACS Christmas raffle. That evening I enjoyed a drink with Jim Barrington, Joanna Woolliscroft and Janet Jackson.

A week later, Tuesday December 20th, Lawrie Payne and I monitored the Suffolk Foxhounds meeting at Shimpling. Not much happened until late in the day when we saw hunt riders crossing the busy A134. The traffic was hurtling by and there was a clear and obvious danger. Initially I grabbed my video camera to record the foolishness of the manoeuvre but it was so reckless that our first duty was to avert the danger by slowing the traffic, which we did.

The next day, December 21st, we made another effort at monitoring hare coursing. I collected young field investigator Miles Cooper from Oxford and we drove west to stay at a hotel at Westbury-sub-Mendip. We met Suzanne and John Campbell nearby.

In the morning, Thursday December 22nd, we took a picked team to see the Yeovil & Sherborne Coursing Club meeting at Kingweston, south of Glastonbury. The renowned biologist, Stephen Harris, joined us. I guided the party to the venue where Miles took over as I would be recognised. I monitored events from a distance, met the team afterwards and dropped Miles back in Oxford on my way home.

Boxing Day, December 26th, took me back to Leicestershire. I met Jim Barrington and Joanna Woolliscroft at the closed Six Hills Hotel and we went to the meet of the Quorn Foxhounds at nearby Saxelbye Park. Jim gave the usual Boxing Day interview to a BBC film crew. If any of my erstwhile colleagues at the Quorn recognised me they did not say anything.

For the last day of the year, Saturday December 31st, I had another early start. After collecting Lawrie from Maningtree at 7:30am we drove south to meet Jim Barrington, Kevin Saunders, Kevin Flack and the Ashford LACS monitors at Ashford station at 9:50am. We then monitored the meet of the East Kent Foxhounds at *The Black Bull*, Newchurch. We were intent on protecting Mr Frith's land to the east from any hunt trespass. Police were at the meet in force. When Jim tried politely to explain our role to hunt officials they refused even to talk to him. It was a lack of courtesy that surprised the police.

A fox was hunted and marked to ground in a badger sett near Pickney Bush Farm in mid-afternoon. He was left. Hounds caused a bit of chaos by getting in amongst sheep on exiting that field.

*****

1995 was to prove to be a memorable year—for good and bad reasons. Wednesday January 4th was a busy day. I collected Lawrie Payne from Maningtree and we met Jim Barrington and Joanna Woolliscroft in Chelmsford. Lawrie photographed a thought provoking LACS exhibition in the library. We all then drove to monitor the joint meet of the Essex Farmers' and Union and West Street, Tickham Foxhounds at *The Bell*, South Woodham Ferrers. Finding it cancelled due to snow, Lawrie and I took Jim and Joanna to Horseheath to see the artificial earth that became a badger sett.

We found more evidence of hunt supporters feeding foxes there with dead chickens dumped nearby. Lawrie also found the main badger sett. Jim then had to rush back for a Sky TV interview. I made the mistake of talking to Jim about the New Year's Eve party he attended—a party he had not told Joanna about.

A colleague telephoned on Saturday January 14th and reported the Essex Foxhounds had spent 4½ hours digging out a fox. That sounded like a far from 'instant' kill.

On Friday January 20th I met Lawrie again and we monitored the South of England Coursing Club meeting at Spike Hall, Six Mile Bottom, Cambridgeshire. We walked along a footpath that went right by the venue—to the consternation of the beaters. They ran the three finals right in front of us. Thankfully all the hares escaped.

Around that time my LACS work changed. Every Saturday I manned what we termed a hunt monitoring hotline so that League monitors across the country could report any incidents they witnessed. I then gave advice and help and alerted the police and/or media as necessary.

There was a strange occurrence on Wednesday January 25th. Lawrie Payne and I gave a talk about our work to the Norwich LACS Support Group. Nothing strange there but what was odd was that Jim Barrington and Joanna Woolliscroft made a 3½ hour journey each way to attend our ½ hour talk.

I saw a blossoming romance that could only end in unhappiness for many I liked. Jim Barrington, a handsome, witty and funny man, was certainly attractive to women. When that natural charm was coupled with the power of running a compassionate organisation he became almost irresistible. Fine for singles but people here were bound to be hurt.

I had always known the pairing as Jim Barrington and Ursula Sitko and in the mid-1980s they married. Ursula was clever, compassionate and stunningly attractive. When she was afflicted with a chronic debilitating illness she could have expected better from the man she had loved and supported for years. In turn Joanna Woolliscroft was caring, attractive and married to that great rarity, a compassionate vet. They had an adorable young son.

My diary records that on Monday March 20th when I visited the LACS offices Jim had the look of a man under siege. It transpired that Ursula's mother had died whilst Jim and Joanna were away on holiday in Wales.

During another visit to the office, Tuesday March 28th, Jim was in another foul mood, rowing with Graham Sirl over rent paid for St Nicholas Priory. I found it hard to sympathise as Jim struggled with the self-imposed burden of choosing between Joanna and Ursula. I liked all involved yet inevitably one or more would be hurt. Once again LACS work was affected by affairs of the heart. It seemed incongruous that whilst League monitors faced abuse and aggression and hunt saboteurs were being punched, kicked and even killed, and they were all volunteers, there was Jim, a man paid well to progress our cause and he was distracted by which of his many female admirers to choose.

Another day Graham Woolliscroft telephoned me with the embarrassing question of asking where Joanna was. I may have been expert at telling tales to hunters but maintaining deceptions amongst close friends was not to my liking. It became clear that Jim's behaviour was causing great dissent amongst the LACS office staff. He lost their respect and support as 1995 progressed.

The hunting fraternity heard of these ructions and their response was clever and cunning. Instead of mocking Jim for his personal predicament they wooed him. They later reaped a stunning reward.

Back in the hunting fields monitoring work continued. On Monday January 30th 1995 Lawrie Payne and I combined some fieldwork. We checked artificial earths and watched the Thurlow Foxhounds from their meet at Hobbles Green. The cheerless soul driving a Lada Niva was abusive as usual. Other hunt supporters, who mistook us for hunt followers, agreed he was a very rude man! Whilst driving home I had another run-in with illegal hare coursers being chased by police near Swaffham Bulbeck.

Saturday March 4th was notable for minor mischief making by me. I had taken my Land Rover to monitor the Essex and Suffolk Foxhounds meet at Erwarton. There was no sign of any hunters. The lady publican informed me the hunt had cancelled due to frost (of which there was no sign then). I looked, as always, like a genuine hunt follower. When I encountered two other cars full of hunt supporters also looking for the hunt I told them they had cancelled. When they asked why I explained they were too depressed over the previous day's vote to go out (John McFall's Bill to ban hunting passed in the Commons the day before by a vote of 253-0)!

Nine days later other hunters made clear their view on any attempt to ban hunting. Lawrie Payne and I had gone to the meet of the Essex Foxhounds at Bois Hall, Navestock. There we learned the hunt had cancelled. We called the hunt kennels and an answermachine tape informed us the meet had changed to Margaretting. We caught up with them about midday. The Master, Pat Harrington, was in a bad mood.

Apparently, the Essex had been sent home at 1:30pm the previous Saturday after their supporters fought first with locals and then with hunt saboteurs. We walked up a footpath and were in time to film a fox fleeing through a wood near a badger sett, the hounds close behind. We waited for the fox to return but he never did.

On returning to my Land Rover at 3pm I found the two nearside tyres deflated. The side walls had been cut with a sharp implement such as a knife or a screwdriver. We called the police to report the damage. I could have changed one tyre, but not two, so had to call out the RAC.

Passing hunt supporters gloated over our predicament but unsurprisingly denied all knowledge as to who could have done such a thing. It was some three hours before we eventually left for home.

That sort of criminal damage was often inflicted upon hunt saboteurs' vehicles at different hunts up and down the country. Enraged hunt supporters taking it out on hunt saboteurs who tried directly to stop their cruelty and save lives was one thing. When maddened hunters inflicted the same upon League monitors it proved hunters were aware that political campaigners were getting closer to banning their pastimes.

At the end of the week, Friday March 17th, Lawrie and I were back in the fields. We went to the meet of the New Forest Buckhounds at *The Green Dragon*, Brook near Cadnam. We joined colleagues from Wildlife Action and the NFAPG. I went in on foot several times. I saw hunt bully boys trailing after Joe Hashman and Peter White but as the latter two had film crews from BBC and Meridian Television with them there was no trouble. There was no kill either.

Later in the month, on Saturday March 25th, I monitored the other form of deer hunting. I met Kevin Hill and the LACS monitors to observe the Tiverton Staghounds meeting at Cobbacombe Cross. They spent a lot of time hunting beside the A396, in the River Exe and to the east of the river. On one occasion, we saw hounds close behind some deer.

As hounds ran up and down the busy A396 and crossed the road, motorists braked and swerved to avoid the canines. One hound was tragically hit and killed. We stayed to help the young girl motorist. She was understandably upset but we reassured here there was little anyone could have done to avoid a hound dashing out of the undergrowth. We helped her to phone the AA. The only contribution from hunters was to grab the body of their dead hound and depart smartly.

Wednesday April 19th proved an interesting day in the League offices in London. There had been a flood and many precious negatives and photographs were spoiled by water. Jane Evans, the LACS Representative from Leicester, kindly volunteered to take them home and save any she could. Then my great colleague Kim Stallwood, a campaigner from the BUAV/RCS days, but at the time based in the USA, turned up with a party of American visitors. He was taking them on a guided tour of the animal rights/welfare groups in the UK. I enjoyed the opportunity to converse with enthusiastic supporters and explain some of our work.

In April 1995, I created the Animal Welfare Information Service (AWIS) as the educational arm of the ACIG. My idea was that the ACIG should carry out the investigations—and then the AWIS spread the facts uncovered far and wide. I appealed to my ACIG supporters for hep. Many saw the value of such educational work and were keen to help.

The 1995/96 hunting season started with a 4am alarm on Saturday September 9th. I met Lawrie Payne and Laina Cracknell and we went to the meet of the Essex and Suffolk Foxhounds at Normans Farm, Ardleigh at 6:30am. Hunt saboteurs were out in force as were police—about 50 officers in more than six vehicles. The police helicopter also circled overhead for about three hours from the meet. One fox was killed on the edge of a field of rhubarb. A second fox from that field luckily escaped through the farm, another escaped from a tiny copse. Saboteurs struggled to take any control over the hounds as their new Huntsman, David Trotman, seemed to have better control than his predecessor, Stephen Swann.

I had another early start on Saturday September 16th. I met Lawrie Payne and Rebecca Yates at Scole at 6am. We monitored the West Norfolk Foxhounds meet at Hall Farm, Gressenhall at 7am. There was a big field of about 50 riders. It was a slow start to a slow morning. The only curiosity occurred just as we were about to leave when we found them holding up a small covert by a church.

The terriermen drove off as we arrived, which aroused our suspicions. Then a woman rider blocked me from walking up the road beside the covert. The fox bolted and escaped across the fields. As the pack pursued they split. We last saw the Huntsman, Ian Higgs, trying to gather his hounds together.

The following Saturday I returned, alone, to the same hunt for their meet at the Vinery, Elmham Park. The hunt spent a lot of time in the park. A female rider called out to me: "*Are you with us or against us today?*" to which I replied enigmatically, "*I can be anything you like.*" Hunt followers tried to photograph me. Hounds seemed in cry a lot but I never saw a fox.

The day had ended when I watched a group of riders cantering over an open field of stubble. One horse stumbled and the young girl fell off. I rushed to help and after checking she had hurt nothing but her pride offered her mum a lift in my Land Rover to collect her horsebox.

She gladly accepted but, as we drove, I warned her to expect some curious looks from her hunting colleagues as she sat next to me—the hated anti. Most who saw us looked utterly puzzled.

Events of Wednesday September 27th 1995 must remain shrouded in mystery. I had a productive meeting in the Tesco's car park at Blandford Forum with one of our deep undercover investigators. This courageous person had long worked right at the heart of hunting—in hunt kennels, and was highly regarded. The information supplied about hunting and the hunting mindset was priceless. We agreed to push the project forwards.

Two days later I was back in Essex, at the break of dawn, with Lawrie Payne for the meet of the East Essex Foxhounds at Garlands, Tollesbury at 7am. A cub was killed in a wood on the south side of the road. Guy Lyster and his wife rode up late for the meet. They asked us where the hunt was and we told them.

Friday October 6th found Lawrie and me back with the same hunt for their meet at Little Renters Farm, Tolleshunt Major. Part of our mission was to protect a nearby farm. They had donkeys and had experienced problems from the hunt before. We saw an old fox bolt from the first wood drawn. Despite their best efforts supporters could not head him back.

At the second draw some foxes that bolted were headed back. Lawrie also saw a cat bolt from the area. When we saw a fox circle back into the draw I told a hunt follower not to holloa him as it would confuse the hounds. He saw me dressed in hunting gear and probably took me to be a genuine and knowledgeable hunt follower. Whatever, he obeyed.

Lawrie and I switched to the Essex and Suffolk Foxhounds on Tuesday October 10th. They met at Lamb Farm, St. Osyth. Huntsman, David Trotman, had broken his ribs the previous Saturday so the Master, James Buckle, hunted hounds. When we saw hounds riot after deer on the second to last draw I stopped them and explained to James what I had done.

Later that afternoon I learned that Jim Barrington had sacked the LACS Press Officer, Kevin Saunders and Financial Assistant, Michelle Bryan. Both were hard working campaigners. Matters were coming to a head.

On Thursday October 19th Lawrie and I monitored the Thurlow Foxhounds meet at Chilton Street at 7:30am. As soon as we arrived the hunters called the police—and two police cars raced to the scene. We explained what we were doing and the officers were happy. When a large stag was put out from a wood near Hundon half the pack rioted after him. Later two more deer were evicted from the last wood drawn and a couple and a half of hounds rioted after them. Hounds ran all over the place.

I next journeyed west to join with the LACS team to monitor the Devon and Somerset Staghounds meeting at Comers Gate on Saturday October 21st. They killed the stag at 1:50pm at Marsh Bridge. We were near but not near enough as we were enmeshed in the throng of hunt supporters and hunt traffic. We went on to the Tiverton Staghounds who had met at Firebeacon. They killed the hunted stag in a stream to the west of Clayhanger at 5:30pm. We were waiting by a bridge but the hunters stopped the stag from reaching us. He died out of our sight.

My situation working with the LACS became untenable. The November 1995 issue of *The Field* was on the news-stands in October. In it there was an article *"Should Terriers Stay With The Hunt?"* by Rebecca Austin that included an interview with Jim Barrington. It was an outstanding coup for the hunting fraternity. Here are some extracts: -

"James Barrington, executive director of the League Against Cruel Sports (LACS) describes terrier work as the grim, raw underbelly of the hunting world and believes it puts hunting in jeopardy: *"I regard it as a degenerate and disgusting activity."* he says. *"If there was no terrier work and foxes were given best, the League would feel less antagonistic towards hunting. It would have a new lease of life and a longer future than present.""*

That raised eyebrows. Terrierwork was certainly cruel but anyone who had seen a dead-beat fox at the end of a gruelling hunt knew there was cruelty in routine hunting as well. It could all be avoided by a conversion to drag hunting. The interview went from bad to worse from our viewpoint. Here was the last paragraph:-

"But will Barrington stick to his word? He says his opinion has changed over the years. *"Banning fox-hunting is not the same as banning badger-baiting. I don't want to see tens of thousands of respectable fox-hunting people classified as a disaffected class. There may be a disreputable underclass involved in hunting, and there are certainly many arrogant people on both sides, but fox-hunting has culture, tradition and there are many pillars of society involved in the sport.""*

Jim Barrington had spent much of that year discussing with myself and others the many problems in his personal life but he never once mentioned that he doubted the direction and focus of the LACS campaigns. Near the end Jim commented to me, with exasperation, that the hunters treated him with far more respect than he received from his office colleagues. I was saddened to hear that but tried to explain that people were concerned that he had lost his previous focus on driving the LACS forwards.

As for the comments, in my view, fox hunters could regain their lost respectability by not killing wildlife for fun. They viewed themselves as "pillars of society" but, for so long as they delighted in killing wildlife for fun, few agreed.

Tuesday October 24th 1995 marked the end for me of another LACS chapter. I wrote to Jim informing him with regret I could no longer work with the LACS given the direction in which he was leading it. That was a difficult decision for me. Sue and I had a very young family and I was cutting myself off from a major source of employment. With my record, it would be all but impossible for me to work elsewhere but I honestly could not put my name to the kind of appeasement with the hunters Jim envisaged.

I yearn for a time when there is no animosity in our countryside. I always offered to run the drag line for any hunt in such a way that few of those following would know they were hunting a man and not an animal. There will be a humane future but the hunting of wildlife to exhaustion was in my view non-negotiable. I could never stand and watch people hunt fox, deer, hare or mink. Wildlife should not pay the price of peace.

I had no problem with Jim claiming to have changed his mind—but had real problems with him dragging the LACS with him. He could have taken time out to sort out his personal problems. Janet Jackson, who was another besotted with him, had already offered to back him with some of her immense wealth (her father was an outstanding automotive engineer, and a supporter of the HSA).

I returned to monitoring work relying on the support of my own small ACIG and the AWIS. I also tried to broker some lasting peace deal within the LACS. On Thursday November 2nd I took a call from a reporter from the West Country Press Agency. He had been tipped off about problems within the League. That was the start of a media hunt aimed at breaking the LACS.

When reporters asked why Jim had changed his mind I responded that was a question for him, not me. When they asked whether the numbers of senior LACS Committee members and staff who supported Jim indicated there was a major policy split in the League, I opined that it was more a matter of personal issues rather than policy, and those who supported Jim did so out of personal friendship.

Reports of ructions within the LACS were printed in the national media on Friday November 3rd. The hunting fraternity loved it. On the evening of Sunday November 5th, the LACS Chairman, Iain Blake-Lawson telephoned me at home. He suggested we meet Jim so the three of us could try to resolve the situation. It was the right idea and might have worked months before but by November 1995 it was sadly too late.

Wednesday November 8th was another monitoring day. I followed the Essex and Suffolk Foxhounds meeting at Kings Farm. There were many riders and followers. One fox was killed near cow sheds on the marshes.

My evening, Monday November 13th, was spent fielding a 1½ hour phone call from Jim Barrington. He was combative—none of the problems were of his making and he was contemptuous of many of his colleagues, particularly John Bryant and Graham Sirl.

Late in November, Friday 24th, I travelled north to talk and work. I met LACS and ACIG supporter Elaine Milbourn and gave a talk in Carlisle Assembly rooms about the ACIG. It was nice to be in Carlisle and not be in the dock of its Crown Court.

The next morning Elaine and I left early for undercover work. Elaine had written countless pungent letters to the Cumbrian media exposing the truth about hunting and was well known in her locality for her views. Neither of us should have been able to get away with any undercover work but we went to the meet of the Ullswater Foxhounds at *The Kings Head*, Stainton.

At the meet, we spoke to a chap identified as John Allan, a Committee member. We told him we were interested in watching the hounds and he invited us to follow. John told us about problems the hunt had with a deer park and stressed the need for supporters to screen it if hounds went near. We drove away from the meet in the convoy of hunt cars to the Hutton area. We parked and walked in with hunt followers. We saw two foxes, attracted no doubt by the dead sheep lying about. One hunt supporter praised the fact the gorse was left as it provided a good sanctuary for foxes.

In time a hunted fox was marked to ground. Elaine and I could not approach too close but he was dug out and killed. The hunt proceeded and we followed by car until the day ended around 3:30pm. After all the troubles in the LACS head office it was refreshing for me to be back in the front line with people I knew I could fully trust.

Saturday December 9th found me back with the West Country team when I joined LACS monitors to observe the Devon and Somerset Staghounds hind hunting from their meet at Simonsbath. I accompanied Kevin Hill, Richard Genge and Grant Palmer. The hunt drew first near Warren Farm. The day then alternated between there and Cloud Farm.

Late in the afternoon, with hounds closing in on a tiring hind, Kevin Hill and I ran about three-quarters of a mile along a frozen track (I fell over twice) to reach the scene. We missed that kill near Cloud Farm by around a minute. It was 4:15pm, just before darkness fell.

The problems at the LACS drew the fascination of the national media. The end was widely reported. BBC Radio 4 news at lunchtime on Thursday December 14th 1995 announced that Jim Barrington had resigned. Commentators up and down the country rushed to speculate as to the reasons. However inevitable it caused me great sadness. Jim was a close friend whom I had known, trusted and worked with for many years. Fall-out from the rows cost me a lot of other friendships.

Boxing Day, December 26th was a good day for wildlife. I met Lawrie and Amanda Payne to monitor the Essex and Suffolk Foxhounds meet at Hadleigh. A hard frost gifted a welcome victory to the foxes as there was no real hunting. It was just a hound parade for the public before hounds were walked back to kennels. I chatted with Huntsman, David Trotman.

*****

In 1996 it was clear that not all the hunting fraternity would welcome Jim Barrington with open arms. The magazine for the terrier enthusiast, *Earth Dog-Running Dog* ran this mocking piece in their February issue:-

"JAMES BARRINGTON, one time head of the League Against Cruel Sports found himself set upon by his ex-associates with all the ferocity of a terrier savaging a rat when he was forced to resign from his post as Executive Director. Furious League supporters accused him of using the societies funds to make phone calls to a woman friend while she was holidaying in the Gambia. The bills are said to have amounted to £190 but Mr. Barrington said that he had paid all the money back. Married Mr. Barrington denied that Joanna Woolliscroft was his mistress saying that she was 'his partner' and complaining that 'people in the league were trying to make trouble for him'. A friend of Mr. Barrington said that he was having difficulty choosing between Mrs. Woolliscroft and his wife, Ursula. The league's executive committee voted to appoint accountants to examine Barrington's expenses during his last two years in charge and he has since repaid some money."

[All financial disputes between Jim Barrington and the LACS were resolved. Jim was given a £20,000 pay off plus his company car.]

A later editorial in *Earth Dog-Running Dog* (April 1996) expressed concern at reports in the *Sunday Express* April 14th 1996 of the creation of Wildlife Network by Jim Barrington to broker some kind of peace between pro and anti-hunters:-

"The plain fact is that this is simply a matter of James Barrington attempting to keep himself in the public eye by creating a new job for himself. He has failed dismally with the LACS having been unceremoniously dumped by his former colleagues and he now seeks to infiltrate the ranks of his former opponents, not by admitting he was wrong, oh no, only partly wrong. Most hunters are good people, he now admits, it's just the terrier and lurcher men who are scum.
Our advice to the BFSS is simply this. If a rattlesnake crawls into the office, stamp on it before it does any harm."

Janet Jackson funded Wildlife Network to the tune of hundreds of thousands of pounds.

My first monitoring work in 1996 was on Saturday February 17th when I joined the West Country LACS team to monitor the Tiverton Staghounds meeting at Brayford Mill. I again accompanied Kevin Hill, Richard Genge and Grant Palmer. The hunt spent a lot of time around the new North Devon Link road at Filleigh viaduct. We saw two hinds running but think they lost the hunted deer at Reepham. The Tiverton ended at 4:15pm. Right at the end of the day we glimpsed the rarely sighted North Devon Beagles.

Friday March 29th was a forest day. I met colleagues from Wildlife Action and the NFAPG to monitor the New Forest Buckhounds meeting at *The Queens Head*, Burley. Our side staged a street demonstration and held a collection outside the pub which irritated the hunters. Later in the day a couple of notorious hunt characters threatened Joe Hashman so I helped Kevin and Carole Hill ensure that Joe was never alone.

From the meet the hunt found deer around a golf course almost immediately. The buck was killed at 1:35pm only about 200m from where I was standing in the forest with Carole Hill. We had been waiting by a river, expecting him to return in our direction, but he never made it.

The following day, Saturday March 30th 1996, I attended the LACS Committee meeting in London. After extensive questioning, I was invited to resume my consultancy work.

I was delighted to return to work with the League on much the same conditions. The priority was that I should not break the law. That was easy for me. When I asked about being properly employed as a part-time staff member I was told that it was better all round, given my record, for me to be kept on a consultancy—at 'arm's length'.

In time the question arose of how to deal with checking out tip-offs—such as foxes held in barns—that necessitated a closer inspection of premises. I would not break the law. I would look but I would never break any lock or door. The LACS agreed to pay me if I checked premises out and found something and pay me if I found nothing. However, if when checking a site, I was caught then I was doing it solely for my ACIG—it was nothing to do with the LACS.

That one-sided relationship is common in the real world. Get us the information and we will thank you; try but fail, publicly, and we will disown you. From my perspective, I was happy to attempt the job and have an organisation prepared to pay even if I found nothing. Some wealthy animal welfare groups would pay nothing until you produced results.

I agreed to the terms offered by the LACS on the understanding that the LACS Committee agreed that whilst it might suit all involved for our working relationship to be 'at arm's length', they accepted that, in terms of job security, I was effectively an employee. However, Committee members and senior staff change. A new intake can, and do, conveniently forget unwritten agreements.

I officially resumed working for the LACS on April 1st 1996. Graham Sirl, based on Exmoor, was the new Chief Officer and Kevin Saunders returned as Press Officer. The League was back in proper campaigning mode. At the end of April, I joined the LACS team in the West Country to monitor the Devon and Somerset Staghounds at Comers Gate on Saturday 27th.

There was a strange and rather disturbing ending. My diary notes that at exactly 2:37pm the hunted stag just lay down. Hounds were held back and a rider moved forward and shot the deer. Unusually the hounds did not appear excited at all. We returned to the office at St Nicholas Priory for the usual end of day debrief and to analyse videos taken of previous hunts.

The focus of my work then shifted away from hunt monitoring towards investigative work into the use of artificial earths and other measures taken to encourage foxes for hunts. Occasional monitoring during

258

the 1996/97 hunting season started on Saturday August 31st when I joined the West Country team to monitor the Devon and Somerset Staghounds meeting at Alderman's Barrow.

I again accompanied Kevin Hill, Richard Genge and Grant Palmer. We saw the hunted stag with hounds in close pursuit on National Trust land at Castle Combe south of Lynton/Lynmouth at 2:30pm. The stag escaped downstream towards Watersmeet. We saw Elizabeth Bradshaw, Professor Bateson's research assistant, monitoring the hunt as part of the enquiry into stag hunting by the National Trust.

Whilst a few hunt followers were friendly, most ignored us and some brimmed with hostility. One pulled up in his car and called to me: "*If I see you at the Tiverton* (stag) *hunt I will kill you!*" Such threats might be dismissed as mere bluster but these were country folk, many of whom were armed, some with stalking rifles capable of killing deer at considerable distances. [The Tiverton Staghounds were notorious for violence. In May 2012 John Norrish, 68, their Huntsman since 1995, was jailed for four years for raping a 33-year-old married mother at the hunt ball in July 2011. As described in *Outfoxed Take Two* I had encountered John when he was Whipper-in to the Dulverton West Foxhounds in the early 1980s. He delighted in killing wildlife. *Hounds* (Winter 1999) published a two-page eulogy to him. It opened with a description of how he was taken in his pram to follow the Tiverton Foxhounds. It ended with this: "*For John Norrish it is obviously a matter of respect for both his hounds and the deer and the people who understand and support the hunt.*" Clearly a different concept of 'respect' to that held by most]

In September 1996, I monitored locally. The Dunston Harriers met at Poplars Farm, Wreningham, Norfolk on Saturday September 14th. I was told the meet would be between 7:30 and 8:30am and was there from 7:45am. With no sign of any hunt I waited. An hour later I saw a couple of riders who told me the meet was actually at 9:30am.

I started off in the undercover role, posing as a hunt supporter. They quickly killed a hare in the first field drawn; she evidently made a fatal error. I saw a second hare hunted. The Master rode up and asked if she had crossed the road. I said (truthfully) I had not seen.

Later I saw the hunt gathered around a tree in a field. A footpath led to the scene. I strode up armed with cameras. Hounds had marked a fox to ground. When I aimed my camera, the Huntsman asked who I was and where I was from. With it too local for any attempt at undercover work I said I was Mike Huskisson from the League Against Cruel Sports.

They laughed, left the fox, left the scene and packed up soon after. I lingered to ensure no terriermen returned, then left. It struck me as perfect hunt sabotage.

The Dunston Harriers developed a perfect response to my presence when they met three days later at East Harling. I observed them drawing over the fields for about half an hour then they gathered in a huddle, rode off and vanished. With five riders, two hunt staff and no followers they could simply have hid in a copse until I left the area.

On Saturday September 28th Lawrie Payne drove up from Essex and we monitored the Dunston Harriers meet at the Limes, North Lopham, between Diss and Thetford. Hunt saboteurs also attended including Norma Dinnie-Weall with her vastly experienced Essex crew. Three Norfolk police officers in a Land Rover and car did their best to maintain order.

With an abundance of hares, it was clear the saboteurs would struggle to save every life. At least two hares were killed. The police made three arrests of saboteurs but were decent and released them without charge at day's end.

I returned to the Dunston Harriers on Saturday October 5th. They met at Longwood House, Topcroft, near Bungay, but I could find no sign of them. I asked the farmer and he told me they changed meets. He claimed ignorance as to the new meet. He said police had warned him to look out for 'hippies'!

I drove about but when I could not find them went on to observe the Waveney Harriers meeting at North Boundary Farm, Yoxford, Suffolk. I was a bit late but soon found them. As I photographed them riding along a drive I ran into a volley of outrage and abuse. I was dressed, as usual, in hunting gear and the irate landowner was berating the hunt for trespassing over his land—and he mistook me for a prized prat from the hunt.

When I explained whose side I was on and what I was doing he became very amenable and outlined the many problems he had with hunters trespassing over his land. He was a genuine conservationist who loved all our wildlife and did not want to see hares killed simply for fun, and certainly not hares that resided on his land.

The following Saturday, October 12th, Lawrie and I went to the Essex and Suffolk Foxhounds meeting at Horsley Cross. There were few foxes about; some appeared to be hiding in drains. We overheard hunt followers complaining about lads shooting and using lurchers in the area the night before. We noticed two lads with lurchers following the hunt. The lurcher is one of the most effective fox-killing machines.

I had another interesting day with the Waveney Harriers on Saturday October 19th. They met at Raveningham Hall. At the meet the Master saw me and promptly called the police using his mobile phone. He then warned mounted followers not to ride along footpaths.

When the hunt moved off I was balked by a hunt supporter driving at crawling pace to hold me up. The rest of the hunt followers were held up behind me. The road was then completely blocked to me. When the police arrived, I complained about that behaviour. The officer assured me he had already spoken to the Master.

There were plenty of hares about. For all his warnings against riding footpaths I later saw the Master leading the mounted field along one. It was a rare sight to see a rider thrown by a horse. That day I saw one hapless girl ejected twice—the plucky lass ended up in a ditch.

I was involved in a different form of monitoring on Saturday October 26th when I worked with a farmer to keep the Belvoir Foxhounds off his land. Some years before the farmer had had the temerity to ban that hunt from his land. Hunt supporters then waged a nasty war against his farm causing all manner of criminal damage to his property and harm to his livestock.

The hunt met at Long Clawson and I spent the whole day helping the farmer. Hounds came nearby on three occasions but never trespassed, that we saw.

Early the following month, Saturday November 2nd, I returned to the Lake District for further undercover work with my colleague Elaine Milbourn. We went to the meet of the Ullswater Foxhounds at Denny Hill, Bampton. Again, we were both welcomed as genuine hunt followers. At the meet, as usual, they sold raffle tickets to raise funds for the hunt.

I could hardly decline to buy a strip of tickets but such raffles were ones I hoped never to win. Not all were drawn immediately, so you were invited to write your phone number on the back of the ticket stub. I could not give my own number so gave some random number. That could lead to awkwardness if I returned to the same hunt later to be met by something like: 'Here you won a prize in our raffle but the person we phoned had never heard of you!!'

I was pleased they drew the raffle there and then—and delighted when I won a bottle of sparkling wine! If only they had known they were giving a prize to me out of all their opponents. There was much discussion at the meet amongst followers about the reasons for their revered Huntsman, Dennis Barrow, leaving. The consensus was that he did not like the excesses of the lads with terriers and lurchers who trailed along behind the hunt and could not be stopped.

Hunting all took place around Haweswater Reservoir. When the hounds marked to ground in the afternoon on the far side from us we left and went to look for the large artificial earth complex near Millbeck.

The following Saturday I was back in Essex joining Lawrie Payne, Rebecca Yates and five other monitors to observe the East Essex Foxhounds meeting at Shalford Green. We all observed the 2 minutes' silence that was called for at the meet for Remembrance Day.

During the day Lawrie overheard riders saying they had a hound 'stuck in a pipe' near Panfield Church. It could have been a field drain, an artificial earth or a complete ruse but we had to go and check. We could find nothing. There were four hunt saboteurs out and we saw them save two foxes by the B1053.

Saturday November 16th proved memorable when I ran into real aggression whilst monitoring. I had looked for hare coursing but found shooting, (the encounter is described in the 'Shooting investigations' section).

I returned to the New Forest on Friday November 22nd. I joined colleagues from Wildlife Action and the NFAPG to monitor the meet of the Buckhounds at Clay Hill Car Park, Burley. When I walked in to the meet one witty rider shouted: "*Are you looking for a job as a grave digger?*"

I accompanied Ken James and Frankie Horan. We were told that during November the hunt could only hunt young bucks and they had a young buck harboured. There was a good keeper, Alan Hobbs, who stopped them hunting an older buck. It was a wet day. Joe Hashman and Rachel White teamed up with us some of the time.

The hunt gave up in mid-afternoon with no kill. After a debrief I journeyed on to the Isle of Wight. I joined a great band of LACS members to monitor the Isle of Wight Foxhounds meet at *The White Hart*, Havenstreet. Our side staged a road-side demonstration against the hunt that drew much support from passing locals. Helen and Karen accompanied me. We stayed with the hunt all day but never saw a fox.

On Saturday November 30th I did find the Isle of Ely Coursing Club meet at Heath Road, Swaffham Bulbeck. I just parked up off the road and watched them all day. I was neither questioned nor abused, they just ignored me. It poured with rain. The beat was put out four times with the finals being run after lunch.

My last monitoring effort in 1996 was to join a large LACS protest at the Essex Farmers' and Union Foxhounds meet in Maldon on Boxing Day, December 26th. We had around 200 supporters in the town—slightly outnumbering the hunters. It was another Boxing Day when the LACS called the tune as to which hunt would be televised.

The media would call the League Press Office beforehand to ascertain our plans. Wherever the League staged a protest television cameras would follow. In bitterly cold weather, with the ground hard with frost, the hunt only had a couple of draws before they packed up.

*****

Following the threat of terminal violence from a Tiverton Staghounds supporter early that season I just had to visit that hunt. If we ever allowed them to drive us away by such intimidation, we might as well give up. I attended, alone, their meet at Creacombe Cross, Devon on Saturday January 18th 1997. I parked at the meet and watched.

To make it easy for the hunt to identify me, when the person collecting the cap for the day tapped on my window, I declined to pay, saying I was there to monitor the hunt. To be honest I was glad that the chap threatening to kill me did not appear—yet another dead anti would not make much in terms of headlines.

The hunted hind was not so lucky. She was killed at Tidderson around 3:15pm. During the day the hunt lost 1½ couple of hounds.

I learned a harsh lesson near the end of the season. It was Saturday March 15th and I had met Lawrie Payne and LACS colleagues to monitor the Essex Foxhounds meeting at *The White Horse*, Pleshey. At the meet, I was subjected to the usual taunts and abuse from the Hunt Chairman, Paul Dixey, about my grave digging past.

Hunt saboteurs were also out. At one point Lawrie and I saw a small isolated group of hunt saboteurs out in an open field being attacked by hunt riders. The riders were charging at them flailing with their whips and crops. The bullying violence sickened me.

I passed my camera to Lawrie and asked him not to film anything. I strode down the footpath towards the scene. I had always preached the need to avoid any confrontation and tried to do so but witnessing violent thugs assaulting young kids was too much.

The riders broke away towards me on the footpath. I called out to the Huntsman, David Gatfield, and told him he was a gutless coward. He went mad and spurred his horse towards me. I had believed that if you stood still in such circumstances the rider would find it hard to urge his horse to hit you as the horse was reluctant to impact his chest. Yes, the rider could kick you and flail at you but the horse would not hit you.

Hmmm. I learned the truth when Gatfield barged his horse into me and his Whipper-in used his horse to knock me flying backwards into the ditch. Extricating myself from the brambles and nettles I said that he was still a gutless coward. I was given a second dose of the medicine. As I again picked myself out of the ditch the hunt rode away.

Although bruised and with minor cuts from the brambles I made no complaints. I accepted that, by telling him what I thought, I had provoked him. I resolved though to take measures to learn self-defence (and spent many years after training at karate, kung fu and kick-boxing).

The following Friday I planned to meet Lawrie Payne to monitor the East Essex Foxhounds meeting at Paul's Hall, Belchamp St. Paul. I was late because whilst driving I experienced a sudden deflation in a front tyre on my Land Rover. Thankfully I could stop safely. It was anything but a usual puncture. In fact, all four tyres had been tampered with in such a way as to cause a sudden and potentially catastrophic deflation. When I complained to the police they reckoned it had been done by an expert with malicious intent. That evening I took my first karate class.

Sue and I had to review my work. I was a husband and a father and had to moderate the risks that I took. With the election of a Labour Government and the abolition of hunting on the agenda the hunters were being whipped into an increasing frenzy of aggression and violence.

My first sight of a hunt in the 1997/98 season was on Saturday October 25th 1997 when I returned to monitor the Belvoir Foxhounds meeting at Long Clawson, north west of Melton Mowbray. Once again I was helping a local farmer protect his land. Again, we saw no hunt trespass.

Saturday November 1st brought long distance monitoring when Lawrie Payne and I drove north to Boothby Graffoe in Lincolnshire for the meet of the Blankney Foxhounds. We had received a tip-off from hunters in the area that they were using bagged foxes. We posed as hunt supporters and followed some likely lads around all day but saw nothing untoward. It was, for us, a blank day at the Blankney.

There were several explanations. The tip-off might have been malicious with one hunt trying to cause trouble for its neighbour. It could have been accurate but they had plenty of foxes near that meet so did not need any released. The release might have happened out of our sight. We might have been recognised—but that was unlikely as hunt followers usually cannot refrain from hurling abuse. It may just have been that we were strangers/newcomers so everything was done by the rules in our presence. Who knows?

Beagle meets were hard to find but the hunting world leaked information. Wednesday November 12th was fraught. Lawrie Payne and I monitored the Stour Valley Beagles meeting at New Hall Farm, Mistley, Essex. It was a lovely sunny day but with plenty of hares running about we feared for our wildlife. Sure enough a hare was killed when she was chopped down late in the afternoon.

We returned to the same hunt the following month for their meet at Wix on Wednesday December 3rd. The supporters were most disgruntled when they realised we would be watching them again. We saw some typical hare hunting. The first hare hunted circled left-handed and was lost. The second to last hare hunted escaped when we saw the hounds setting off in full cry running her heel-line.

That was an easy mistake for hounds to make. An observer might see a hare cross a field from left to right, go through a hedge-line into another field and cross over to the right and out of sight. The hounds are cast down the hedge-line and pick up the scent but instead of following the hare to where she is running to they follow her heel-line to where she has come from. Genuine hunt followers would call to the hunt staff to put the hounds right; we of course were happy to see them stay at fault, and the hare escape.

Boxing Day, December 26th, was the usual LACS inspired media circus in Maldon for the meet of the Essex Farmers' and Union Foxhounds. It was lively but not as bad as the year before. The news media conducted their usual interviews.

Last meet of the year for 1997 was when Lawrie and I monitored the Thurlow Foxhounds meeting at Withersfield Hall. Hunt saboteurs were out and it turned into a strange day. The pack was split all over the place. There are plenty of deer in the Thurlow country and hounds just love the scent of deer so it was no surprise when groups of hounds set off in different directions. It became so confused that hunt supporters repeatedly asked us where their hounds were.

One of the red coats leaned down from his saddle and asked me: "*Will I see you at our shoot again?*" I took that to be a reference to my attendance at the Six Mile Bottom shoot the previous month (described later in the 'Shooting investigations' section) and confirmed the intimate linkage between the various pastimes.

*****

My first monitoring in 1998 was when I made the long trip to Salisbury Plain on Wednesday January 14th. We had reports of strange events at the Royal Artillery Foxhounds so I went to their meet at the Officer's Mess, Tidworth. I mingled with supporters, chatted with the riders and followed but saw nothing untoward.

An uncle had for many years ridden with the Royal Artillery Foxhounds. He was an accomplished horseman and a Gunner all his life. We would exchange banter about the merits or otherwise of hunting. I have no doubt that he endured a lot of ribbing over the behaviour of his relative after the John Peel incident. He was though as tough as teak. He had fought the Japanese the length of Burma and would not have stood too much nonsense from fellows who frequented the hunting fields. The Quorn revelations shocked and dismayed him.

Curiously, one rider that day expressed doubts about the success of the forthcoming Countryside March in London on March 1st. He thought the organisers were foolish to have planned only a march with no rally at the end and that numbers would be reduced. From his perspective, he was wrong to be so pessimistic.

I returned to the West Country and joined Graham Sirl and Jill Nield to monitor the Tiverton Staghounds meeting near King's Nympton on Saturday April 18th. It was spring stag hunting and turned out to be a long uneventful day. We did not see hounds running until 4pm. Soon afterwards we saw them being stopped from rioting after Roe deer. The hunt seemed to pack up with no kill around 6pm.

My 1998/99 hunting season started with a return to the West Country. Sadly, there had been more ructions that had broken up the excellent LACS monitoring team there. I drove to St. Nicholas Priory on Saturday September 5th and met Graham and Jill. We then monitored the Devon and Somerset Staghounds meet at Blackmoor Gate. I accompanied Graham Sirl. It was a day of mist, rain and wind and the hunt spent most of the time in the Chains to Barbrook area down in the combes, out of sight. It seemed to end around 6pm with an unknown outcome. I missed the presence of Kevin Hill who had an immense knowledge of Exmoor, the runs of the deer and an uncanny ability to sense where the hunt would go. Luckily for our cause Kevin soon found similar work at the International Fund for Animal Welfare (IFAW).

Saturday November 7th marked a return to familiar ground. I monitored the Isle of Ely Coursing Club meeting at Heath Road, Swaffham Bulbeck. I could only watch and film from a safe position alongside a nearby road. I counted about 30 coursers and supporters and some 20 beaters. Unusually there seemed to be a scarcity of hares.

The focus of hunt monitoring then shifted slightly as we tried to correlate the behaviour of fox hunts with the known locations of artificial earths. Thursday November 19th provided an example. I visited the Thurlow Foxhounds meeting at Weston Woods. I observed them hunting two woods where I knew they had artificial earths, then my car broke down.

With the abolition of hunting on the political agenda we knew we had to focus on bringing the hidden sides of hunting more into public view. Most were aware of the cruelty involved in hunting an animal to death. Many thought, wrongly, it was a price that had to be paid to control animal pests, and furthermore that hunting was the most humane way.

We set about proving the efforts that hunts up and down the country made to encourage foxes. With small hunts, such as the Thurlow Foxhounds it is likely that as a result of supporters building artificial earths for foxes to breed in, log and stick piles for foxes to lay up in and by putting out food and water for foxes they were responsible for putting more foxes into the countryside than they killed by hunting. The facts could only be proven by diligent fieldwork that will be described later.

In many ways monitoring became something we did to reassure hunters we were still about. If we vanished from sight they would wonder what we were up to and start looking for us.

Boxing Day, December 26th, found me at what was fast becoming the traditional Christmas media event—the meet of the Essex Farmers' and Union Foxhounds at Maldon. Local MP, and former LACS colleague, Angela Smith, was on hand to give quotes to the journalists. That year, for the first time, the police had installed crash barriers to control the crowds. Once again the anti-hunt outnumbered hunt supporters. There was a minor scuffle between the two sides as the meet ended.

At year end, Thursday December 31st, I monitored the Essex and Suffolk Foxhounds meet at Fridaywood, south of Colchester. Much of the hunting was over Ministry of Defence (MOD) land. I met Norma Dinnie-Weall and her dedicated band of hunt saboteurs.

A strange event was when a lady walking her dog told me of a dead fox being found in a car park there. As for the hunting the MOD police gave the usual grief to the hunt saboteurs. When I found smashed gates to a bridge along a bridleway I reported the damage to the police. It could have been an accident, but more likely resulted from rage by a frustrated rider.

*****

My first monitoring in the New Year was on Saturday January 30th 1999 when I met Lawrie Payne to monitor the Essex Foxhounds meeting at Bedfords, Good Easter. We were joined by LACS Committee members Laina Cracknell and Donna King and LACS monitors Karen and Kevin. We demonstrated our work to Jane, a radio reporter from BBC World Service.

One fox was hunted, marked to ground and killed at Bayleys. When another fox was marked to ground nearby our presence with four video cameras trained on the scene, and one BBC journalist watching, dissuaded the hunters from any further terrierwork. The fox was left.

On Saturday March 13th 1999 I watched the Waveney Harriers from their meet at Somerleyton Hall near Lowestoft. Unbeknown to me at that time I would be at the same hunt in the same location nearly six years later for their first meet after the 2004 Hunting Act took effect.

Whilst still in the 20th century I filmed the hounds putting up a hare and then later saw her returning for a drink after her exertions.

The following Wednesday, March 17th, I joined a team of eight LACS monitors including Richard and June Guest, Chris Owen, Roy Dowsett and Jane Evans to watch the Wheatland Foxhounds meeting at the Croft, Morville, near Bridgnorth, Shropshire. We were told bagged foxes were to be used. To cover a greater area, we divided into four teams of two. I accompanied Jane Evans and we staked out Oxleasow Rough. It was unclear whether the tip-off was a hoax or hunters saw us there but nothing untoward happened.

We took all tip-offs seriously but particularly so with that hunt. Years ago, a cockfight was staged at the Wheatland hunt kennels. It was

Sunday June 16th 1985 when police and RSPCA officers, acting upon a tip-off that cockfighting was taking place, raided the hunt kennels during a hunt fête attended by some 2000 country sports enthusiasts from all over the country. At first sight of the authorities the men who had been forcing courageous birds to fight to the death all ran away. Eight were caught including the leader of the gang, professional Kennel Huntsman for the Wheatland Foxhounds, Terry Richmond. After the raid Wheatland Joint Master, Richard Milner, said, "*It had nothing to do with the hunt.*" It was later revealed that a cockfighting syndicate had operated at the hunt kennels for four years. Six cocks were found dead on the day of the raid. Twenty one birds were still alive, some injured.

Terry Richmond was sacked from his job and evicted from his tied cottage by another Joint Master, Captain John Foster JP. However, investigations by the LACS revealed that Captain Foster had then quietly installed Terry Richmond in a farmhouse he owned nearby. The League Executive Director at the time, Richard Course, commented: "*It would appear that the sacking and eviction of the ringleader of the cockfighting gang was nothing more than a cosmetic exercise to exonerate Hunt Masters and officials from any involvement. It is beyond belief that any intelligent Hunt Master could be unaware of a cockfighting syndicate thriving under his nose for four years.*"

The subsequent court case was heard by Bridgnorth magistrates on August 19th 1985. There were eight defendants: Terry Richmond; Peter Davies; James Glaister; Mervyn Humphrey; George Meakin; Robert Pinches; Charles Taylor and Michael Theckston. All admitted ill-treating animals, assisting at a cockfight, using premises for cockfighting and possessing cockfighting equipment. Each was fined £1000 and ordered to pay £160 costs.

Terry Richmond was swiftly offered another post in hunt service and in 1987 became Huntsman at the West Somerset Vale Foxhounds.

Phil Drabble commented on this case in an article in *The Field*, September 7th 1985: "*At a recent case at Bridgnorth, Shropshire, eight men were convicted of cock-fighting and fined a total of £5,750. The main* ['main' is a technical term for a cockfighting event] *took place on the premises of the Wheatland Hunt at an open day, ostensibly organised for the Hunt terrier show. Presumably this normal gathering of country folk was infiltrated by the sort of urban element involved in recent dog-fighting and badger-baiting cases. It should be the responsibility of Masters of Hounds to take personal control of conduct on such days, otherwise respectable rural sportsmen will inevitably be judged by the company they keep.*"

That was a naïve comment. There was no infiltration by urban folk. It was simply some 'respectable rural sportsmen' demonstrating their concept of respect.

Saturday April 17th 1999 was a momentous day. I drove my family down to Margate and met the LACS Press Officer, Ben Stewart. We interviewed the indomitable Gwen Barter for an article in *Wildlife*

Guardian. Gwen Barter had courageously monitored, protested and opposed bloodsports for many years. Even in old age she still bombarded the media with perceptive letters highlighting the cruelty behind the glamorous façade of hunting. Almost single-handedly, by direct action, she put an end to carted stag hunting in England. She had generously supported my ACIG for many years and it was a real privilege to meet her.

The following Monday, April 19th, I visited the LACS offices in Union Street for my first meeting with their new Executive Director, Douglas Batchelor. Douglas had the appearance of a benevolent bank manager. At first I doubted he could solve the many deep-seated problems at the heart of the running of the League but he proved me wrong.

He was an excellent Captain of the League ship. He sorted out the problems, returned the League to a steady course, guided her through the choppy seas inevitable around the final passage of the Hunting Act and was at the helm to secure that final triumph. He was also a nice guy who had regard for the history of the LACS, saw the immense value in undercover work and backed the investigation unit to the hilt.

Acquiring meet lists for hunts or fixture lists for hare coursing clubs was vital to our monitoring work. I had a network of supporters across the country who worked at getting hunt meet lists. It fell to me to try for the coursing fixture list. September 22nd 1999 I drove to Newmarket and the National Coursing Club at Clocktower Mews. Funnily enough I saw the Secretary, Charlie Blanning, whom I recognised from my undercover work amongst coursers. He did not recognise me and I was given the fixture list without any problems.

My monitoring work got off to a curious start in the 1999/2000 season because to start with I largely ignored what the hunt was up to. I was looking for faeces! We were concerned at the spread of disease across farmland by hounds and I needed to collect faeces samples. The hounds would routinely defecate as soon as unboxed at the meet.

I attended cub hunting meets of the Thurlow Foxhounds on September 30th and October 7th for that purpose. I was armed with the proper collection kit as supplied by a veterinary surgeon.

I then had several attempts to do the same at Dunston Harriers meets on October 12th; 16th and 19th. The Dunston Harriers meeting at Hardingham Hall, Norfolk, on October 19th was another memorable day. I used a new Sony Digital video camera for the first time. I had bought it the day before for over £1000 with ACIG funds. We used many types of video camera: VHS, video-8, hi-8, Digital 8 and mini-DV.

The significant event however was recorded with a still camera. I photographed a perfect example of hunt sabotage. There had been three hunt saboteurs out, one of whom was my good friend Tim Nickerson. A pleasant and caring young man, he had a nose for where the action was—and was usually in the thick of it.

I had photographed as hounds pressed a hare across an open field. The terrified and tiring hare ran straight towards me as I stood on the verge of a minor road. I stood still and she dashed by me with hounds close behind. As she ran away from me down the road I saw Tim Nickerson at the back of his car parked on the grass verge. The hare headed towards him.

Tim understood the situation. He allowed the hare to pass him by then stepped out into the road and stopped the hounds. He did so using voice and hands but without violence. The hounds were checked and the hare escaped. Because no hunters saw what happened there was no violence, no confrontation and no aggression, just one grateful hare.

I spoke to the Hunt Master who told me his farm was between New and Old Buckenham. Even though he knew my identity he invited me to join them for drinks at the Dunston Harriers opening meet the following Saturday. I courteously declined.

At month's end, I drove west to see the Oxford Draghounds meet at *The Queens Head*, Long Marston on Saturday October 31st. I sought more evidence to confirm that drag hunting was fun, popular and operated without causing mayhem and havoc and without killing anything.

The start was delayed when the quad bike used to pull the drag broke down. It struck me as the drag hunting equivalent of a blank wood for fox hunters. When we got underway I was pleased to give a lift to an eventer named Mike, whose partner Kate was riding. Lots of people had lots of fun, humanely.

I returned to that hunt for their meet at *The Bull & Butcher*, Akeley near Buckingham on Sunday December 12th. I used the name Michael Wallace. It was a wet and muddy day but again there were numbers out enjoying the ride. I chatted with Joint Master, David Skinner.

In 1999 Boxing Day hunts met on Monday December 27th. We had been tipped off that something untoward would happen after the meet of the Quorn Foxhounds at Saxelbye Park, Melton Mowbray. I hid in the crowds and just loosely followed, neither in the full undercover role nor as a monitor. I had an identifiable suspect to shadow but nothing of significance happened. Again, the tip-off may have been a hoax or something could have happened out of my sight (it would not take long). There was a dig-out late in the day but they appeared not to get the fox.

On the last day of the century I drove to Leicestershire to meet the farmer who suffered repeated attacks on his farm because he had the temerity to ban the local hunt from his land. He showed me straw contaminated with the toxic insecticide Mevinphos left on his land.

*****

My first event in the new millennium was some accidental monitoring. Out with my family on Monday January 3rd 2000 we stumbled upon illegal hare coursers on fields at Colegate End near Pulham Market in the early afternoon. I called police on a 999 as there was a real danger to passing motorists on the busy A140. Norfolk constabulary responded quickly and we left them to deal with the coursers.

There is always something new to learn in the hunting fields. Thursday January 13th provided an example when I monitored the Thurlow Foxhounds from their meet at Hill Farm, Stradishall, Suffolk. After lunch I saw what I took to be a kill. Through binoculars I saw dismounted riders and terriermen huddled at a ditch near Highpoint prison on the A143.

When they left, I ventured to the scene to ascertain what had happened. It seemed hounds had marked a fox to a field drain that opened into the ditch. It had been very wet so it must have been an exhausted fox to seek sanctuary in a partially flooded drain. The hunters had blocked the exit from the drain with logs and packed mud. The effect was to create a death-trap likely to drown any fox within.

I unblocked the drain, released a surge of water, and left the scene so the fox could leave without hindrance. Had the fox died there it would have been anything but an 'instant kill'.

Most of the rest of that season was taken up with accompanying the Lord Burns Hunting Inquiry team on their visits to hunting and hare coursing (described later). On Monday March 13th I watched the Thurlow Foxhounds from their meet at Manor Farm, Horseheath to compare hunting then with hunting when the Inquiry team visited on Monday February 21st. To be fair I found little difference worth noting.

Monitoring thereafter changed as investigative fieldwork became more important. I occasionally looked at a hunt, just to reassure them that we were still about, but most of our work was done far from sight.

In the 2000/2001 season, I monitored the Thurlow Foxhounds meet from Great Wratting hall on Thursday November 16th. When the hunt spent time near Barnardiston Hall School I observed in case there was any hound riot over the playing fields. Hounds were put in to draw right behind the school but, surprisingly, there was nothing to interest them.

In December 2000 the hare coursing world staged the largest ever hare coursing event—Greyhound 2000—near Newmarket. Organised by Sir Mark Prescott it was effectively a last hurrah for coursing, a 128-dog stake (the Waterloo Cup was a 64-dog stake). The coursing fraternity promoted the event with gusto. Anglia television asked to interview me for my views on the event. I obliged and met the film crew in the car park of Toys R Us at Ipswich on Wednesday November 22nd. I was interviewed on a nearby grass verge.

Sunday December 10th was a day for memorable images when I photographed the demonstration in Newmarket against Greyhound 2000. There was a protestor dressed in a superb, large, hare suit and many others with pertinent placards. That protest received great support from the passing public.

The next morning, I monitored the first day of Greyhound 2000 at Six Mile Bottom. I had vivid memories of encounters with Richard Clarke in that area. The hare coursers were at Spike Hall, north of the footpath. When I walked the footpath and stopped to film the hare coursing the event security politely told me I could not stand still on a footpath and had to keep moving. Then hunt saboteurs arrived accompanied by police and the latter assured me I could stay still on the footpath.

I had a good view of the coursing and watched as hares were driven alongside a maize belt by the beat and then funnelled on to the coursing field by a lot of wire netting. I saw six hares killed. I took video film and photographs and filmed one courageous protester arrested as she tried to help a hare struggling in the jaws of a dog. [When she was later charged with aggravated trespass I sent her my video that showed both her arrest and the shocking cruelty inflicted on the hare. After her case was dismissed she wrote to thank me: "*The video was most helpful and was shown at the trial. The police video only showed me being arrested and not the hare struggling in the dog's mouth!.......The only woman Magistrate looked visibly distressed when she watched your video!*"]

I returned to Six Mile Bottom on Wednesday December 13th but the coursing was being held elsewhere. The following morning I found them back at Spike Hall, Six Mile Bottom. Coursing had moved to the east of the site they used on the Monday. Again, I observed from a footpath. The day ended with Deerhound coursing and Saluki coursing. The final was not run because a competing dog was injured.

I spoke to three hare coursers who were ejected from the event. They revealed that in the Millennium Cup alone 29 hares were killed from 126 coursed. The organiser's figures were that 23 hares were killed out of 133 coursed over the four days of the event (*The Observer* January 7th 2001). The discrepancy may be explained by the fact that the crowd often see hares killed after being coursed off the coursing field and such kills may not be witnessed by those interested only in coursing on the field.

As had become usual I spent Boxing Day that year, December 26th 2000, at the LACS protest against the Essex Farmers' and Union Foxhounds at Maldon. I collected Lawrie Payne on the way and met Angela and Nigel Smith, David Coulthread, Iain Blake-Lawson and many others from the League there. I also chatted with a reporter, Stephen Milne, from CBS.

*****

2001 started with another sharp reminder of the frailty of life. On Monday January 8th I took our daughter to our usual local Black Belt Academy karate class. On her journey home one of the black belt instructors, a woman with a young family, was killed in a road accident on the A140. It was another young life snuffed out in an instant through no fault of hers.

There was a new intake of staff at the LACS. Andrew Wasley, a great investigator, worked in the Press Office. Mike Hobday took over from David Coulthread as Head of Public Affairs. I first met Mike when I visited the LACS offices on Wednesday January 31st 2001. The LACS had gathered an experienced team for the final push towards abolition.

Wednesday February 21st brought back memories when I made a brief return to undercover work. I joined the meet of the Per Ardua Beagles at 1:30pm at The Old Barn, Clint Lane, Navenby, Lincolnshire. As can be guessed by their name these were the RAF beagles. I used the alias Steve Williams and, dressed appropriately, was welcomed by hunt followers.

As mentioned earlier I preferred to use my own Christian name for undercover work—it was easier to respond to someone calling it—but I had used it so often that I feared word was passed around the hunting world to beware of any bloke with a camera calling himself Mike!

During my drive north there had been much talk about foot and mouth disease on the radio. I knew immediately that it would put a stop to hunting. There is nothing better than a pack of hounds for spreading disease about our countryside. Hounds push and probe into every nook and cranny, defecate and urinate, and a few days later do exactly the same on farms on the other side of the county.

Given the radio reports I expected the meet to be cancelled but it went ahead. The main concern amongst hunt followers was that they would be able to finish their season before being stopped by foot and mouth restrictions. For one young hare it was irrelevant—she was chopped by the pack at 2:30pm. One of the hunt staff told me she was a leveret. I lost contact with the hunt at 4pm and then had a one hour walk back to my car.

The following day, Thursday February 22nd, it was duly announced that hunting was suspended due to the outbreak of foot and mouth. That suspension lasted until December 17th.

We checked whether hunters obeyed the foot and mouth restrictions. On Saturday September 29th we put a combined team of ACIG, LACS and IFAW monitors out at dawn covertly to watch the Seavington Foxhounds from their kennels near Ilminster, Somerset. I was with Peter White and Andrew from the League accompanied Steve Honey. They did nothing more than routine hound exercise.

We suspected illegal hare coursers would pay scant regard to foot and mouth regulations. It was no surprise when on a routine patrol of known coursing sites on Sunday October 7th I stumbled upon illegal coursers at Burwell, near Newmarket, in the early afternoon. I called the police (who responded swiftly). I recorded the coursers then spent time, without success, trying to ascertain who the landowner was to warn him.

In fact the landowners in that area knew all about the menace of illegal hare coursing. To try to deter them they dug trenches and barricaded gateways to render their fields inaccessible.

Two weeks later I was on another patrol in the same area in pouring rain. I had checked Balsham and Dullingham and was parked watching the very likely site of Heath Road, Swaffham Bulbeck when car loads of coursers passed me. I was in country gear in my Land Rover so perhaps they mistook me for the gamekeeper. For whatever reason, they gesticulated towards me and mocked me as they passed.

I alerted the police and pursued the coursers. I then found an abandoned greyhound dodging amongst the cars on the busy road. I used my bulky vehicle to slow traffic protecting both dog and motorists. When police officers reached the scene, we struggled to catch the dog. Usually a coursing dog is a sucker for a cap thrown to the road, and some kindly words, but that one was too frightened.

A fortnight later I had another run in with illegal hare coursers. I found them around noon on Sunday November 4th at Heath Road, Burwell. The lads were experienced 'country sports enthusiasts'. They knew the area well, knew where the hares were and which landowners they could mess about. They excelled at striking quickly, getting their dogs on the land, rattling the hares about, killing some, and disappearing before any police who were called could do anything effective.

Hunting lost no time getting underway as soon as foot and mouth restrictions were lifted. On Tuesday December 18th 2001 I monitored the Suffolk Foxhounds meet at Rattlesden Airfield. Nearby Thorpe Wood contained at least three artificial earths that I knew of. Hunt followers were anything but delighted to see me, but at least they did not try to kill me as they had before. Matters were improving.

A Suffolk Police four-wheel-drive appeared at the meet with prominently displayed 'Hare Coursing Patrol' stickers decorating the rear windows. I discussed at length with Police Sergeant Cooper our joint work to combat illegal hare coursers. Seeing the two of us conversing merrily did little to enhance the tempers of watching hunt followers.

At the meet, everyone present—hunt followers, riders, monitor and police officer participated in the disinfection process. Boots, hooves and tyres were liberally doused. When the hunt got underway they soon put a fox up. He was later marked to ground and, I presumed, killed.

My Boxing Day for 2001 was a far cry from my usual excursion to the LACS event at Maldon, Essex. After extensive investigative work with colleagues from the League and by using state of the art surveillance cameras we had uncovered all sorts of behaviour from hunt supporters around the use of artificial earths.

As will be described later we had paid close attention to the Heythrop Foxhounds and had found dead calves dumped to feed foxes around an artificial earth site near Chipping Norton. On December 26th 2001 I left home at 7am for undercover and investigative monitoring of the meet of the Heythrop Foxhounds at Chipping Norton.

The plan was for me to take up a covert surveillance position within the wood, long before the meet, and see what happened. It was an operation where if it all went pear-shaped and I was found and battered then it was all down to me and nothing to do with the LACS.

The sharp frost on the ground warned me as to what I faced. I hid up for over five hours in freezing conditions. I heard riders outside the small copse and heard their intimate chats. I filmed hounds in the wood, with one taking the chance to chew at the dead calf, but nothing else of significance happened.

When I judged the hunt to have finished for the day I lumbered out from cover and promptly bumped into riders on the road returning home. They say that surveillance work entails hours of watching for a few minutes of action; it certainly did that day.

*****

Monitoring work in 2002 started with a bang, almost literally. After investigative fieldwork with my LACS colleagues we drove to monitor the Heythrop Foxhounds meet at Stow-on-the-Wold on New Year's Day. There had been a rock-hard frost overnight. We no sooner arrived before the ignition warning light illuminated and there was a strong smell of burning.

I parked my stricken Land Rover near the meet. I waited with one colleague whilst the other went in for deep undercover work amongst the hunters. He looked and sounded just like one of them and did the job perfectly. Parked with the bonnet up, a succession of passing hunt supporters stopped and kindly offered help. Shielding our faces (not unreasonable given the cold) we declined their generosity and were grateful that neither of us was recognised. Our colleague returned to say there would be no hunting that day because of the frost, just a short ride.

We tried to drive on again but then the fan belt broke and I had to call the RAC. The final diagnosis was seized alternator bearings and the alternator was replaced.

Saturday January 19th 2002 produced another inadvertent encounter with illegal hare coursers locally. I had collected my Land Rover after servicing. On my drive home I saw coursers near a local village. I returned home, called the police, collected cameras then returned to the scene with my son for assistance. I chatted at length with the policeman who arrived quickly but the coursers had vanished.

January 26th was memorable for another attempt at combined operations in Heythrop Foxhounds country. Whilst one from the LACS team went in for more undercover work as a hunt supporter his colleague and I undertook investigative work and provided back-up in case needed. It was a day of lashing rain and all were thoroughly soaked. Mr Undercover made significant progress within the hunt. Cheerfully enduring such severe weather doubtless marked him out as a stalwart follower.

The intelligence war between the hunt and the anti-hunt raged at that time. We were bombarded with 'tip-offs'. Some were genuine, many were hoaxes and some were aimed at drawing us into a trap.

Monday January 28th was a routine day at the LACS offices until an informant contacted us with tales about artificial earths, foxes held captive by hunters and foxes being fed by hunters. We arranged to meet the gentleman the following Saturday at an address he gave near Towcester. I checked out some of the hunting details he provided, and they were confirmed, but was he the man he claimed to be?

On Saturday February 2nd, a League colleague and I parked near the address and knocked on the door at the appointed time. The lady who answered had never heard of the man we sought. At that moment a strange car with two male occupants drove slowly by us. We tried ringing the mobile numbers we had been given by our informant; all rang but switched to answerphone. Was it just hunters having a laugh at our expense? Was it something more sinister? I had often been photographed and filmed by hunters so they would be more interested in my colleague.

Sunday February 10th 2002 was significant. Whilst on routine patrol for illegal hare coursers I secured valuable film. I first encountered coursers walking the fields at Heath Road, Swaffham Bulbeck at 12:30pm. I then drove around to Heath Road, Burwell and saw them again walking the fields. I circled to the middle of the Heath Roads, the one at Swaffham Prior. When the coursers came into view I filmed them with my camera mounted on a tripod. At that time such coursers still tried the defence that they were innocently walking the fields with their dogs and when a hare popped up the dogs struggled and escaped from their leads or collars. It sounded implausible but there was little proof to the contrary—until my film.

I recorded coursers walking the fields as in walk-up coursing. A hare started to run. One courser sighted his dog on that hare then released the dog to chase her. That was proof of intentional coursing.

I then got a bit carried away with filming and drove on down the cul-de-sac that was Heath Road seeking another filming site. I met a red four-wheel-drive full of coursers hurtling towards me. They did not look friendly so I pulled a swift, combat, two-point turn (reverse first on full lock) and raced away to safety. I called the police when safe to do so.

A few days later I gave a copy of my film to a Suffolk Police Officer. On Wednesday May 15th 2002 part was used in a presentation by Suffolk Police Federation to a thousand police officers at the Police Federation Annual Conference in Bournemouth. It was subsequently used in police training videos about illegal hare coursing. I was delighted to work so closely with our police.

Saturday February 16th was interesting. We staged another combined operation against the Heythrop Foxhounds meeting at Sezincote. Whilst one from the LACS team and I shadowed from distance and monitored their proximity to known artificial earths another went in undercover and mingled with the supporters, gaining useful intelligence.

I spent Sunday February 24th on hare coursing related patrols. Initially I searched likely sites for hares being caught for the Waterloo Cup. I checked Bodney, Saham Toney, Hilborough and Six Mile Bottom, all without success. Informants later reported that hares for the coursing event were caught earlier at Holkham Hall, Norfolk.

I then went looking for illegal hare coursers and sure enough found them, once again, at Heath Road, Swaffham Prior, between Cambridge and Newmarket. I called police on a 999 and stayed in the area to assist officers. I learned that at last Suffolk and Cambridgeshire constabularies were collaborating in a joint operation against hare coursing. No longer would the county borders mark the point of safety for fleeing coursers. The police even had the use of their force helicopter—an expensive machine that I was used to seeing being deployed to protect hunters from hunt saboteurs. It gave real joy to see it used for the benefit of wildlife.

The landowner bordering Heath Road was one who had dug ditches and put machinery barricades in place to bar entry to his fields by illegal hare coursers.

March 11th proved memorable when I again returned briefly to undercover work. A League colleague and I teamed up with a professional photographer named Alec to attend the meet of the Royal Agricultural College Beagles at Park Farm, Shipton Moyne. We posed as journalists and photographers and were accepted on that basis by the hunt followers who welcomed our presence.

One leading follower, Nigel Dallas, whose father was a prominent figure in the Duke of Beaufort's Foxhounds, chatted at length. He gifted me a wealth of information about local hunting activities. I kept my video camera running. It acted as a perfect recorder. I commented about how far behind their quarry hounds were.

Mike Huskisson: "*They seemed a long way behind this hare...I mean..I thought, I mean it's a long way...do they ever catch him?*"

Nigel Dallas: "*Sometimes yea.*"

Mike Huskisson: "*Yea.*"

Nigel Dallas: "*We got one on...sometimes you don't really know if they have, you find out later...or..or..just sheer chance. Sometimes you..if you've got a good scent...if it's very windy you you might chop an old tired hare.*"

Mike Huskisson: "*Right.*" My informant clarified how the hounds soon move on to another hare, leaving it unclear whether or not they had killed.

Nigel Dallas: "*But sometimes they won't hang because if there's a lot of hares and a fresh one gets up they'll sort of leave the the dead hare and off they'll go.*"

Mike Huskisson: "*Oh right so you don't know.*"

Nigel Dallas: "*So you don't always know. Sometimes someone just comes across it.*"

This discussion confirmed the haphazard nature of bloodsports. Often the media portrayed it as an exact science and believed without question hunter's claims for precise numbers of quarry chased and caught. In fact, they frequently had little clue as to what hounds did. Hare hunters often had little idea how many hares were killed each year. This was particularly true with leverets. Furthermore, blood on hounds could easily come from their killing rabbits stricken with myxomatosis (an utterly unpleasant gift to nature from farmers and scientists).

Mike Huskisson: "*How many do they catch in a season then?*"

Nigel Dallas: "*Never really know. Could..could be sort of um 5, 10 brace.*"

I later tried to ascertain whether hares caused much of a problem.

Mike Huskisson: "*Are they much of a pest then here the hares?*"

Nigel Dallas: "*Not a lot, not when there's not too many. I think like anything if it's in numbers...I mean up here there's not a lot of seed but I mean..they..a bit ..trees could be damaged and here they've got lots of trees but the deer are more of a problem with trees.*"

Mike Huskisson: "*Right.*"

Nigel Dallas: "*They're a pest cos they strip the bark off them that's why they have all the fencing around..*"

Mike Huskisson: "*Oh yea, all the guards.*"

So, hares were not much of a problem. Deer were potentially more trouble but that was solved by putting guards around the trees. I was also able to gather useful information about the Duke of Beaufort's Foxhounds, the local horse racing industry, vets and others.

Thursday May 23rd 2002 was a sad day. I learned that my erstwhile colleague, Miles Cooper, had defected to our opponents. Jim Barrington called a press conference at the House of Commons to announce Miles had joined the Middle Way Group. There were plenty coming our way but they brought real information that we could use and had no wish for publicity.

In late September, I accompanied the LACS investigative team far north. On Friday September 27th we caught the train to Edinburgh, checked into a hotel and collected a hire car. We rose before dawn the next morning to kennel-watch the Duke of Buccleuch's Foxhounds at Eildon Hall. Nothing much happened either there or when we looked for the Jed Forest Foxhounds. We did more fieldwork in the afternoon.

The following day we completed some very useful investigative work exposing hidden aspects of the shooting industry. On the Monday, September 30th, we did more dawn kennel-watching followed by fieldwork before returning home. I learned that police had called Sue to ask why a car, hired in my name, was parked near a hunt kennels in Scotland! I phoned Selkirk police station and explained who I was and what I was seeking near the kennels. The officer was happy with my explanation and stressed that if we uncovered anything illegal we should contact them.

The following month, Tuesday October 22nd, I worked with Ryan Parry, a reporter from the *Daily Mirror*, responding to a tip-off that foxes were being held in a barn for hunting. I met Ryan and his photographer at Whissendine, Rutland. We walked a footpath to take a closer look at the farm in question. My view was that if foxes were being held we would smell them from some distance.

We walked, looked, sniffed and observed with binoculars but there was no sign of any foxes. That pushed the responsibility to me to make the definitive check. The *Daily Mirror* team was clear they could not trespass for a closer look. However, if 'someone' could look, and if they found and photographed captive foxes, the *Daily Mirror* would run the story.

The LACS were just the same. They could only be involved at arm's length. If it was all a trap and there were a bunch of terriermen waiting in the barn to beat the hell out of any intruder, then it was nothing to do with either the paper or the League. Years before I had been shot at when I encountered an unpleasant welcoming party on one such night excursion. There is nothing like pellets whistling over the head to focus the mind.

I proceeded with caution. The layout was such that if I left my car anywhere nearby at night it would be suspicious. The recent Scottish incident had proven how sensitive hunts were to unknown cars. The best solution was for me to be dropped off near the target and then my driver to back off to a safe location and pick me up after we liaised by mobile phone. I needed someone sensible with courage and a cool head to persevere should any crisis develop. I recruited an ACIG and LACS colleague.

She dropped me off in the early hours of the morning. After waiting some minutes for my vision to become accustomed to the dark I moved in.

I encountered some initial technical problems that were overcome with fieldcraft. In time and with care, without breaking or harming anything I checked thoroughly and there were no foxes on the premises. I exited, called my colleague and was whisked away. It was another example of mundane investigative work beyond the front lines.

We started to acquire new hidden camera equipment. On Wednesday November 13th 2002 I met Mike Hobday and Andrew Wasley at the LACS offices and tested out new video equipment with the camera lens completely concealed in clothing. Such a 'body camera' enabled undercover investigators to film hunting (or any other abuse) without anyone knowing.

December 22nd proved frustrating. I had another fruitless search following up another tip-off about foxes in a different part of the country. It was all too easy to phone in an anonymous accusation of foxes being held for hunting.

Early in the month I had my first opportunity to practice with more new video camera equipment that gave us a significant advantage in our quest to catch hunt supporters at artificial earths. It was the Remote Surveillance System (RSS) that will be discussed further in the artificial earth section. It encouraged us to switch away from hunt monitoring work.

*****

Friday February 14th 2003 was an interesting day. I received a phone call from my local police officer informing me there was a rough looking crowd of hare coursers in my area. They were from an Essex coursing club I had never heard of. However, I was not to worry about them as they had permission from the landowner to course hares over his land.

I drove out to the area. I could not find the hare coursers but did find the landowner, a nice chap whom I had known for years. I asked why he gave such lads permission to course over his land. He explained, succinctly, the reality of life in the countryside.

They asked permission to course over his land and he refused. They told him they would course there anyway but if he gave them permission they would only course when and where he was happy for them to do so. And the real bonus was that if he granted them permission they would keep illegal coursers away. On that basis alone he gave them permission.

He confided to me that he yearned for the day when all coursing was banned so that he and other farmers could not be intimidated in that way (no-one could demand the right to stage a cock fight or dog fight in a farmer's barn). He did not like hare coursing and did not want hare coursing on his land but felt forced to accommodate it. Some other farmers, faced with similar pressures, just shot their hares to remove the attraction for the coursers.

On Sunday March 2nd, I met journalist Danny Penman at Diss railway station and we searched for illegal hare coursers in the Burwell area. We were keen to chat to some of the hare coursing fraternity to see if they were legal or illegal and ascertain something about their motivations. I knew many drove long distances to pursue their pastime.

When we visited the prime site of Heath Road, Swaffham Bulbeck around lunchtime we saw hares running and then three lads with five lurchers held on leads. We walked up the edge of the copse and conversed with them. They were not too keen to indulge in lengthy conversations but did claim that the farmers did not worry about their trespassing so long as they kept off crops.

When we tried to observe them discreetly we lost them. In that area, there are large fields and those on the fields can disappear from view. Whilst driving from one viewpoint to another they can vanish from sight completely. The lads were not the fearsome ogres the media portrayed. They looked to me to be just like the lads I saw at many a legal coursing club, or on the bank side at the Waterloo Cup. Not the brightest but knowledgeable about their dogs and the ways of the hare.

My 2003/2004 hunting season started with some inadvertent undercover monitoring work. I spent a few days in Wales on investigative work into the shooting industry with LACS colleagues. Tuesday September 30th found us on the A470 near Commins Coch, Powys, and we stumbled upon a gun pack. In trying to follow them we went to an adjacent valley and promptly ran into another whose supporters identified the hunt as the Plas Machynlleth Foxhounds.

That was the gun pack I had observed with the Lord Burns Hunting Inquiry some three years before so I knew to keep my head down. They took us to be genuine hunt followers and were very friendly. We made the friendships and contacts that enabled another LACS colleague to later achieve a major undercover success with that hunt.

Wednesday October 15th 2003 heralded a return to the West Country. I joined a LACS colleague and photographer Alec to monitor the meet of the Dulverton West Foxhounds at West Farm, Braunton Burrows, near Barnstaple. That was another hunt I knew well from a previous encounter. We had been told there was a nature reserve there where the hunt regularly marked hunted foxes to ground and dug them out. With open public access to the nature reserve we expected to be able to watch anything that happened.

We found no sign of the hunt. Their web site advertised their meet as being there but *Horse and Hound* reported the meet as being at Whiddon. Taking the last resort, we phoned the hunt kennels, gave them some plausible tale and the meet was confirmed as at West Farm. We eventually found the hunt at Whiddon Moor but with no public access there we could only monitor from great distance and saw little.

Sunday November 23rd found me back at Diss station. I collected Danny Penman and we drove to the Cambridge-Newmarket area for more investigative work into illegal hare coursing. We met and chatted with police officers on patrol at Heath Road, Swaffham Prior. Officers caught illegal coursers on two subsequent occasions in that same location that same day. No wonder it was regarded as a 'hot spot' for coursing.

To try to add some more depth to our investigation we drove to some nearby gypsy sites and sought to buy a coursing dog. We hoped that some owner might boast about the prowess of his dogs. We tried first a site at Reach. Our plan was doomed to fail. I look and sound like a poncy git in glasses and Danny is gentle and soft-spoken. Not exactly coursing enthusiast material!

Perhaps they took us to be mugs to be easily parted from our money. We were directed to another site the other side of Burwell where we were offered a 14-month old lurcher puppy. We chatted briefly but declined the purchase and left. I had a more local run-in with the coursing brethren on Saturday November 29th. A local informant called to report hare coursers were trespassing on fields near my home. I grabbed my cameras and mobile phone and drove to the scene. I saw a couple of cars, one an estate car containing men and dogs, the other a saloon with men who looked to be judging. I called police on a 999.

I then saw a man from the estate car slip a dog against a hare and I could only watch as the hare was coursed and killed. The coursers fled when they saw me with a video camera. I drove around the site and found, filmed and photographed, the dead hare. She was still warm. I waited for Suffolk police at the scene but they never appeared. I took the dead hare to our vets for post mortem, then collected her body later and buried her.

A week later I took one of my sons on a routine patrol against hare coursing. We soon spotted a vehicle known to belong to coursers. With a passenger to help I could drive in pursuit whilst my son phoned 999. We saw another vehicle parked beside the field being coursed and phoned that registration number through to the police. The controller advised us not to worry about that one. We observed the coursers for a while but when they saw my camera they fled at speed. I followed but when their speed increased and they drove increasingly erratically, to the point of overtaking on a blind bend, I gave up in the interests of safety.

Further contact with Suffolk police revealed it was PC Mark Bryant, off-duty, who was in the civilian car monitoring the coursing. He called me that evening and told me the four hare coursers we spotted were caught nearby later that morning. Mark Bryant was a curious officer. A former gamekeeper he loathed hare coursers but seemed to like fox and hare hunters. I delighted in demonstrating to my son, at first hand, how we worked with police to enforce wildlife protection law.

There was an amusing incident on Thursday December 18th 2003. I drove to Pershore, Worcestershire and met LACS colleagues to undertake investigative work in Croome and West Warwickshire Foxhounds country. We met at the bar of *The Boot* inn, Flyford Favell. As we discussed plans we overheard an elderly gentleman propping up the bar who talked knowledgeably about hunting. We were in country kit so gravitated towards him. He announced himself to be a Mr Cure, a former Master of the nearby Worcestershire Foxhounds. We listened in fake awe as he recounted hunting tales.

A colleague whispered a warning to him, "*They might be antis,*" but Mr Cure mocked the notion, said we were fine and boasted, "*I can spot any antis.*" For hunters drink and knowledge make a dangerous combination.

He proceeded to give us very useful information about the Croome and West Warwickshire Foxhounds which saved us much footwork. He also provided his phone number should we require any future hunt meets.

*****

In the New Year, 2004, most of my work was investigative fieldwork. My first monitoring was on Tuesday February 24th when I accompanied an impressive team to monitor the first day of the Waterloo Cup. We met in the Tesco car park near Great Altcar. There was my ACIG, LACS, IFAW, the RSPCA and Members of Parliament. It was all a far cry from my first visit in 1976 when I had run on to the field as a young hunt saboteur to try and save hares. Twenty eight years later I had the same ambition but a different approach.

I met Colin Pickthall MP, Ian Cawsey MP, Mike Hobday from the LACS, Corinne Evans, Rebecca, Lucy and Liam, plus there were IFAW and RSPCA staff. My role was to help interpret what happened on the coursing field. I accompanied Ian Cawsey MP. It was, as so often at the Waterloo Cup, a bitterly cold day. We observed many courses and it was no real surprise that hares were given notably long slips. We saw one kill. IFAW hired a plane to fly around the coursing field towing an apt banner.

Saturday May 15th 2004 was memorable. I had what, unbeknown to me at the time, was my last day of monitoring before hunting was banned. I had been tipped off by a hunt informant about a joint meet of the Eastern Counties Minkhounds and North Norfolk Minkhounds at Priors Croft, Withersdale Street, Suffolk. I knew that was, at the time, the home of a notoriously volatile follower of the Waveney Harriers so expected a lively welcome.

To hide the real source of our information I faked stumbling upon the hunt by accident. They were aggressive from the start. I was told not to step on the grass, not to photograph properties without permission etc. The problem for the hunters was they had chosen to hunt in an area frequented by otters and criss-crossed with footpaths. I called the nearby Otter Trust to warn them of the presence of a mink hunt. I then walked the footpaths armed with cameras and proceeded to shout warnings to the hunters firstly to keep their hounds away from otters as they were protected by law and secondly not to trespass. The hunters bristled with anger towards me and there were numerous mentions of my criminal past. When up close some blocked the view of my camera with their hand, head, or by peering right into the lens; but there was no direct attack on me. When the hunt reached Mendham Bridge over the river Waveney around 3pm they appeared to pack up. With the hunt ended and them facing a long walk back to their meet I offered a lift to the more elderly and frail looking but they declined. I later learned they claimed to have killed a mink when out of my sight.

*****

On Saturday February 19th 2005 I monitored the meet of the Waveney Harriers at Somerleyton Hall. It was the first day of hunting after the Hunting Act 2004 took effect. That event, and subsequent ones, is the subject of a future book.

CHAPTER ELEVEN
Investigators expose the truth about hunting

Throughout the history of hunting its opponents have sought to expose the truth about the pastime. Initially this was done by written word or verbal account. Use of film camera followed and then the video camera. Many dedicated campaigners have secured key pieces of evidence. Some prefer not to be named to protect their ongoing work. Simply by watching hunting, valuable information has been secured. For years a highly effective undercover investigator—Mrs Z—followed hunts in and around Cheshire and fed back a stream of useful information about hunts, the policing of hunts and the interaction between police and hunt saboteurs.

Janet Jackson carried out courageous undercover work at the Alresford Coursing Club, the New Forest Foxhounds and the West Wales Minkhounds in the early 1990s. Posing as a supporter she secured valuable photographs.

Other investigative colleagues have recorded some truly shocking video evidence, in the most trying circumstances. Here is a small selection.

Buck hunting

That was the hunting of fallow deer bucks with a pack of hounds in the New Forest. It was the filming of fox hunting and buck hunting in the New Forest by Wildlife Action and the New Forest Animal Protection Group (NFAPG) that proved devastating to local hunting. Filming was done in the face of great hostility from hunters by many different people including Joe Hashman, Peter White, Rachel White, Frankie Horan, Ken James, Daphne Ricketts, Gary and Jane Colbourne, Graham Sirl, Jill Nield, Denise Creed, Ron White and Doug Coombes. These were caring people, of all ages and from all walks of life, united in the belief that wildlife deserved protection from gratuitous cruelty.

My ACIG was pleased to give a substantial grant to Wildlife Action to help with the purchase of a video camera. Buck hunting had continued in the New Forest for some 900 years. It did not last long once people arrived on the scene armed with video cameras and showed the public how deer were mistreated. There were numerous incidents recorded.

On September 15th 1995 members of Wildlife Action courageously filmed the killing of a fallow deer buck by the New Forest Buckhounds (NFBH) despite efforts by the hunters to block the view of the cameraman.

Two months later, November 13th 1995, members of the same group were on hand again to film another kill. Right from the meet the hunters were aggressive. A rider blocked Joe Hashman's view and commented: "*Somebody bought you a camera did they?*" My colleagues courageously followed the hunt closely and reached the scene just after the buck was shot. Our cameraman exclaimed, "*Bastards!*" which elicited the mocking reply from the Huntsman: "*Oh it's you cunt......too late ain't yer.*"

As the buck was held by the antlers Joe noticed movement and commented, "*It's still alive.*" The Huntsman shot the buck a second time, in the back of the head. Joe and Peter then filmed as the dead buck, still twitching, was dragged away through the forest.

Hunt monitors filmed several incidents in 1995 and 1996. They filmed hunters standing on an exhausted buck's neck as it lay in a river. Film of hounds attacking a live deer caused the hunt's licence to be suspended for a day. Film in 1996 of hounds attacking another deer caused a three day licence suspension. That same season an incident where the 14-year-old son of a Forest Keeper pushed the head of a buck underwater before holding it for the Huntsman to shoot was filmed. The graphic nature of the videos secured by Wildlife Action and NFAPG monitors in the most difficult of circumstances outraged the public.

Fallow deer are the most gentle and harmless of creatures yet they were subjected to appalling cruelty for entertainment. Deer populations could be controlled humanely using contraceptive methods. Where deer had to be killed, shooting by professional marksmen was the most humane method. Killing deer with hounds was cruel by design and cruel by calculation. The hounds used were bred not for the speed that might have produced a swift conclusion, but rather for the stamina that guaranteed the lengthy hunts supporters sought.

The NFBH operated exclusively on Forestry Commission land and needed a licence to do so. In June 1997, the hunt applied to the Forestry Commission for a renewal of their licence. In July, they asked the Verderers Court for help to get their licence. When it appeared that they would be unlikely to get a licence the NFBH announced at the end of July 1997 that 'with regret' they would not hunt fallow bucks the next season.

The hunters said they would disband and claimed their decision was made because of the 'increasing demands upon the forest made by the urbanisation of its fringes and millions of visitors each year'.

Ken James, from the NFAPG commented: "*The Hunt's excuses are simply a load of old nonsense, as usual. The fact is that they had no choice. They had been forced into a position where deer hunting was impossible as they were highly unlikely to receive a licence.*"

The New Forest Buckhounds caused a final burst of public outrage when they chose to shoot six of their hounds rather than home them either with a leading member of the hunt who wanted to use them for drag hunting or with local residents who offered homes to the hounds. Peter Barfoot, the Hunt Chairman, declared it was, "*kinder for them to be shot.*"

Fox hunting

Saturday October 9th 1993 was memorable for horrific images. At Ocknell's Inclosure in the New Forest monitors Frankie Horan, Denise Creed and Ron White from the NFAPG videoed the end of a hunt by the New Forest Foxhounds. The exhausted fox had sought sanctuary in a flooded drain. Hunt terriermen trapped the fox by blocking one end of the drain with a spade, the other with a net. The drain was twelve inches in diameter and had water flowing through it.

A small terrier named *Tosh* was put into one end of the drain to fight with the fox, head to head. The video camera recorded the timings. After seventeen minutes the soaking wet *Tosh* backed out of the pipe, pulling the fox with it. The two animals had their jaws locked. A hunt servant then stood on the live fox whilst another hunt supporter attempted to prise the terrier's jaws open. When that failed, a gun was produced and the fox was shot in the head. The terrier was removed and carried away, vomiting bile and water. It was anything but an 'instant kill'.

The LACS launched a private prosecution against the three terriermen involved: Keith Colbert, Jeffrey Colbert and John Fleming. In August 1994 Lymington Magistrates considered three charges of cruelty brought under the 1911 Protection of Animals Act. That Act only applied to domestic and captive animals; wild animals had been deliberately excluded to allow hunting to continue.

The case hinged on whether the fox trapped in the drain was 'captive' in the legal sense. The Act stated that 'captive animal' meant any animal which was in captivity, or confinement, or which was maimed, pinioned, or subjected to any appliance or contrivance for the purpose of hindering or preventing its escape from captivity or confinement.

Monday August 15th, I attended the court case to photograph the defendants outside. The magistrates viewed the video evidence, deliberated, adjourned the case and returned on Wednesday September 14th. They decided the fox could not be considered 'captive' and acquitted the terriermen of all charges involving both fox and terrier. An outraged Ken James from the NFAPG commented: "*as the law stands you could do whatever you like to a fox. You could even cover it in petrol and set it alight, the law could do nothing to stop you.*"

A delighted Brian Toon from the Masters of Foxhounds Association (MFHA) said the case showed that, "*when professional hunt terriermen dig to a fox they do it with proper professionalism and with due regard for the fox and terrier. They acted responsibly at all times.*"

Alastair Jackson from the BFSS was not so supportive. He regretted that the League, "*were able to bring this unfortunate video which should never have happened, it was a distressing scene and I think we're all agreed on that.*" When he went on to claim that the New Forest Foxhounds played an important role in keeping the fox population under control Jim Barrington, Executive Director of the LACS, retorted: "*There are few scientists that would agree that fox hunting plays any role in controlling the fox population. The fox can hardly be a pest in the New Forest—they don't tend to eat trees!*"

Reporting the verdict, on the evening of September 14th, millions of television viewers across southern England saw extracts from the shocking video. It had a powerful impact—even more so because the graphic cruelty had been judged perfectly legal. When the same hunt chased another fox into a similar drain in September 1994, and more hunt monitors were ready to film, the hunt chose to move on and left the fox.

The LACS appealed against the verdict and the appeal was heard by the Divisional Court on Monday November 10th 1997. By then Jim Barrington had switched sides. The Divisional Court dismissed the appeal holding that, applying *Rowley v Murphy* [1964] 2 QB 43, the fox was not a 'captive animal' within the meaning of s 15 (c) of the 1911 Act, mere confinement not being sufficient, and was therefore outside the protection of that Act. [The Rowley v Murphy case cited was between Raymond Rowley for the LACS and Colonel Murphy for the Devon and Somerset Staghounds. It followed a stag hunt on August 30th 1962 when a hunted stag ran into Timberscombe village, slipped and became wedged under a furniture van. The stag was dragged out and taken to the yard of the village hall where his throat was slit by Colonel Murphy, Master of the hunt. The League prosecuted Colonel Murphy under the 1911 Protection of Animals Act saying that as the stag was captive he enjoyed the protection of that Act. On March 28th 1963 Minehead Magistrates dismissed the charges saying that the wild stag was not a captive animal. It was only temporarily unable to get away. The High Court was asked to rule and on November 14th 1963 upheld the Magistrates' decision. Lord Parker, Chief Justice, said, "*a mere temporary inability to get away did not amount to a state of captivity, so here something more than mere captivity, some period of time during which acts of dominion are exercised over the animal, is necessary before the animal can be said to be in a state of captivity*." Not surprisingly, compassionate people asked how long—30 minutes, 3 hours?]

Wednesday February 8th 1995 proved how little some hunters care for their hounds. Wildlife Action monitors Joe Hashman and Peter White filmed mayhem, pain and death caused by a pack of foxhounds during routine hunting. Their film, taken mainly from a railway bridge, showed the Blackmore and Sparkford Vale Foxhounds hunting around a railway for a considerable time.

The Huntsman encouraged his hounds to search for foxes in brambles along the railway embankment. A fox was flushed from cover and crossed the track near the cameraman. Hounds later find a fox and give chase. That fox ran along the middle of the railway tracks towards the camera. As a train descended upon them, horn blaring, the fox jinked to one side. Sadly, one hound, nose down on the fox's scent, was run over and had its leg cut off. When Peter White filmed this fatally injured hound, hunters had the audacity to blame the monitors for the hound being there. Joe Hashman supplied this graphic account:-

"*On 8 February 1995 I was with my colleague Peter White, attending a meet of the Blackmore & Sparkford Vale Hunt a couple of miles north-east of Yeovil. Peter and I found ourselves standing on a railway bridge between Trent and Marston Magna. It was a bleak, grey day. Most of the mounted field and quite a few car followers were on the lane with us but we had pole position actually on the bridge with a decent view northwards.*

Peter and I both had a video camera running. We were recording the dismounted Huntsman and his Whipper-In either side of the railway and hounds between them, searching amongst the parallel thorny embankments for a fox. Hounds continually criss-crossed the single track railway, sometimes singly, in pairs and as a pack. Peter and I just filmed and, possibly because attention was focussed on the hunt and we appeared to be doing nothing disruptive, nobody tried to obstruct us.

We are both experienced in the ways of foxhunting and clearly the Huntsman was encouraging his hounds to draw the railway scrub for a fox. And quarry was afoot. We viewed foxes quite close beneath us, trying to steal away discreetly.

We kept our cameras recording and filmed this scenario for many, many minutes. Then, in the distance, saw the headlight of a train coming down the line towards everything. Huntsman and Whipper-In were still on foot, hounds continued to run across the tracks with their noses to the ground, oblivious. A few hounds were on the railway as the train ploughed through them and carried on its passage under the bridge and onwards. We could see, through our camera viewfinders, the body of a hound which had clearly been hit.

Without hesitation, Peter ran through a gate to get closer. I stayed put and kept filming. Next time I saw Peter, seconds later, he was at the scene. His close up footage of the hound shows it alive, panting but with body rigid, laying in between the rails with a leg completely severed. Terriermen types were quickly on top of the accident too. The hound was carried away and undoubtedly destroyed. Peter kind of vanished. He had a knack for being in the right place at the right time, in the thick of it yet undetected. Next thing I knew he was back next to me, cool as a cucumber. We realised that we'd evidenced something important so returned to my house to replay our footage through a television screen.

It was only whilst reviewing the films that we saw what happened in the moments just before the hound was run over; as the train approached a fox jumped onto the railway and ran right down the middle of the tracks ahead of the train. Hounds being hounds, all they are interested in is following their quarry and this they do. The fox, meanwhile, jinked out of the danger zone and (hopefully) made good his escape in the confusion of the chaos he left behind."

Joe Hashman carried out more excellent work in 1996. Acting on information supplied by Mrs Y and LACS colleagues in Cheshire he sought to acquire film of hounds being shot to make room for the new entry of puppies. Hounds that had hunted were killed long before the end of their natural lives, when they were judged too old to keep up with their colleagues. Foxhounds were lucky if they lasted five hunting seasons in the pack. Some were even killed as puppies when they were regarded as unsuitable to start hunting.

Joe judged it likely there would be a turnover of hounds in the week prior to the Opening Meet so embarked on a three-day surveillance project against the Cheshire Foxhounds at the end of October. It was Wednesday October 30th 1996 when, after hiding in the wood for hours, Joe filmed from concealment as a hound was taken to a secluded place by the kennelman and shot in the head. The hound was one of two shot that day, both were thrown into a metal bin. The hunt later claimed both dogs were sick. Across the whole of the UK, in the routine course of hunting, thousands of hounds were killed each year by hunt staff.

Peter White recorded more horrific video on Saturday November 27th 1999 when eight hounds from the New Forest Foxhounds were electrocuted after trespassing onto the main Bournemouth to Waterloo line near Brockenhurst. Hounds had pursued a fox up and down the line for a considerable time beforehand. Shortly after 1pm a train from East Croydon travelling at around 70mph ploughed into the burning bodies on the track. Torn remnants of hounds were stuck under the front of the train.

Stag hunting

The hunting fraternity have always been very reluctant to let observers show the rest of the world what hunters get up to. That was particularly true with stag hunting on and around Exmoor and the Quantock hills. As long ago as September 1930 the LACS magazine, *Cruel Sports* (LACS was at the time the League for the Prohibition of Cruel Sports) reported the Secretary of the League attending the first bye-meet of the Devon and Somerset Staghounds at North Molton. He saw the 'rouse' of the stag and the magazine reported: "*One visitor, who took several photographs of the "rouse," was later accosted by a stag-hunter, who* **"hoped that they were not intended for the newspapers.**""

After undercover filming by Raymond Rowley, Chairman of the LACS and by other League supporters, and my work in the early 1980s, it became even harder to film hunting. For me any return to work undercover in the West Country was all but impossible. Others have come forward to help, some of whom prefer to remain unidentified. One such investigator, Mr X, undertook excellent work in the West Country in the autumn of 1990. He knew little about stag hunting but was enthusiastic, determined and smart. I told him what to expect, what to look for, and the ACIG armed him with an effective camera. Mr X went to the meet of the West Country based Lawrence Clarke Buckhounds on Saturday October 6th 1990. It was a wild, wet and windy day and nothing much happened. Mr X then followed meets of the Tiverton Staghounds that month. After the meet at *The Portsmouth Arms* on the A377 on Saturday October 27th 1990, by good judgement, he was in the right place to photograph the hunted deer up close. Here is his report of that day:

"*Meeting of the Tiverton Staghounds on Sat. 27/10/90.*

The meeting was held at The Portsmouth Arms *pub on the A377. The weather conditions were good through most of the day, though it rained on and off in the afternoon. The meet was very well attended with 50+ cars and a number of families with children. There were 14 riders and 2 red coats. One stag was killed at the end of the day, 3:30pm.*

The hunt started at 11.30am. Followers in cars were reminded by the spokeswoman for the hunt to keep out of wooded areas to avoid disturbing pheasants. We were also asked to help stop the stag from

287

running into areas they could not go into but apart from that not to stop the stag. The initial draw took place in the wooded area near Hacknell. Followers fanned out into the back lanes to act as spotters. Two stags were soon flushed from this covert and headed towards Northcote Manor followed by the hunt. I moved to an area of high ground by Northcote Manor and learned that the hunt was following a stag that was in the woods near Kingford. The stag though doubled back and crossed the open ground to Upcott. By this time supporters in cars were in this area and the stag was forced into the valley below my position followed by the hounds. From my position on the rim of the valley I saw the stag break cover 300 yards away, he was though forced back into the wood by a large party of followers.

However, with the hounds behind him, he was forced from cover near me and a number of photos were taken as he broke through our lines and headed back towards The Portsmouth Arms *with the hounds following. There followed a quiet period in which it was thought the stag had crossed the river. At 1:30pm though he was once again flushed out of cover near Hacknell and headed towards Hill Farm. The hunt then moved from Hill Farm to Kings Hill, then Churchlands to Bircham. At all times the followers in cars were essential, showing where the stag had crossed the road and stopping him if they could.*

From Bircham the stag moved between Cleave and Golland with supporters moving ahead to stop him entering Ash Wood. He then moved from Horsford Cross towards Horridge where there is a large deer farm.

All roads surrounding this area were soon ringed by the supporters. I positioned myself at Dunsham then Chittlehampton. Little could be seen from here though so I continued down towards the river Tarr intending to complete the circle and come back to Ashreigney to see if anyone had any information. While doing this I was informed that the hunt had killed near the road above Horridge. I was informed by a lady that the stag had become entangled in the wire of a deer farm and been shot by the owner. I found the dead stag in a field surrounded by supporters. The guts were fed to the dogs. Slots taken along with other trophies and then the carcase was loaded into a pick-up and driven away. The hunt spokeswoman told me not to take photos and there was some hostility to my presence, though none of it open."

Once again we were getting pictures and information from the very heart of hunting. Kevin Hill did brilliant and courageous work exposing hunting in the West Country. He also started by working undercover for the LACS, then, when his identity was exposed, continued to work as a monitor. When he left the LACS, he worked for IFAW. Here are some of the highlights of his work.

In 1992 Kevin worked undercover posing as a hunt supporter. On October 26th 1992, during autumn stag hunting, he followed the Tiverton Staghounds. At the end of the hunt the exhausted stag sought sanctuary on the patio of a private house and was shot. Kevin filmed the final moments. He said of the incident: *"The Tiverton Staghounds brought the stag to bay in North Devon on the patio of a property where the owners were out. Inside the patio was the owner's dog that I could hear responding to the hounds outside. After a while I observed a hunter with a gun to the right of the deer. The deer was shot and swiftly taken away to a field for the 'carve-up' where I came under pressure as to who I was. Much later after my undercover period came to an end we visited the property and showed the owner the film. He had no idea the stag had been shot on his patio."*

Kevin was a highly successful undercover operator. Both mild-mannered and brave he was usually in the right place at the right time. When Somerset County councillors were deliberating over banning stag hunting on land the council owned on the Quantock Hills, Kevin Hill's accounts of stag hunting proved memorable. Here are extracts from his diary of hunt observations supplied to councillors:-

*"I saw a stag lay down beside a small moorland stream, his head flat on the ground through the traumas of the day. I'm sure his sight was impaired as he looked sadly at a hundred or so people and numerous cars, all within fifty yards. He did not want to run any more but was forced on when the hounds pressed ever nearer. It was that time of day when all knew a "kill" would take place. It's a strange sickening feeling, there is a common tension, as if the adrenalin exuded by ghoulish followers, frantic in their attempts to be part of the slaughter, evaporates into the surrounding atmosphere, poisoning the air. Comments abound, "**He'll go up the hill just one more time but he'll be back down**". The hunter was right, he did go up the hill just once more until his legs could carry him no further. His only option was down, down through the mounted field, riders trying to head him off over, or rather through, fences towards a gully at the bottom. He was trapped, there was nowhere to go. He was shot, dragged by his antlers out from the gully and taken away to a favourite carving field. At least his tiredness, pain and mental torture were over."*

*****

*"A stag became tangled in undergrowth. He was jumped upon by as many men as could get their hands on him. Any correct behaviour towards animals was a million miles away. In their lust for "hands-on" cruelty I wasn't noticed taking photographs. Their faces reflecting the delight and pleasure they were obviously experiencing as they awaited the gun, would they have a story to tell their mates in the coming days! After what seemed an age the stag was shot in the back of the head, he slumped to the ground. Amazingly he stood up again, a shout went up, "**Let him walk!**" So they did, up a slope towards the Land Rover which would later be the bearer of his corpse. His legs moving erratically, his head bowed, his back arched, he was crushed to the ground. He was shot again and no time was lost in cutting his throat. No living creature deserves to die like this."*

(Quoted in *Wildlife Guardian* Issue 26 Autumn 1993)

When no longer able to work undercover Kevin carried on observing, filming and photographing hunting as a hunt monitor. Hunters knew who he was, what he was doing, and the vehicle he drove. They hated his presence.

Thursday September 29th 1994 proved the power of a brave man armed only with a video camera. Kevin monitored the Devon and Somerset Staghounds during autumn stag hunting. The hunt met at West Molland. By day's end Kevin recorded probably the most damning piece of film that confirmed the savage nature of stag hunting—and had a black eye and bruising as a result.

At the end of the hunt the exhausted stag sought sanctuary from hounds in the beautiful River Barle near Dulverton, Somerset. Hunters shot the stag at least four times with a shotgun but each time failed to kill the deer. Even the heavily weighted pellets bounced off the thick skull of the proud animal. The wounded and terrified stag struggled on. Finally, hunt followers wrestled the stag over by his antlers and held him underwater until he died.

In the face of great adversity Kevin Hill filmed the shocking incident. Hunters repeatedly blocked his view, jostled and punched him. In a final attempt to stop him revealing the truth about stag hunting to the outside world they smeared mud over the lens of his camera.

Kevin's film reveals the cunning of the hunters as well as their callousness. To justify and excuse their own aggression and violence towards him they falsely accused Kevin. Their ludicrous accusations made them look foolish. Kevin was there on his own whereas the hunters were gathered around him in a large mob.

The shocking film was widely shown on television. The LACS passed a copy to the British Deer Society who demanded an immediate inquiry by the Masters of Deer Hounds Association. The subsequent inquiry, chaired by BFSS Vice-Chairman Lord Mancroft, slapped a five week ban on the Devon and Somerset Staghounds saying the kill was botched because of unruly behaviour by hunt supporters. Lord Mancroft added that the stag had been eventually killed with a humane killer and not drowned.

Kevin was unable to film the final kill as his lens was covered with mud and his arms were twisted behind his back. However, he did not hear, and his camera microphone did not record, any sound of a humane killer fired. Attempts by hunters to blame Kevin Hill were widely ridiculed; his film proved he was never at any time anywhere near the two gunmen trying to kill the deer. Rosie Pocock the local BFSS representative commented on Good Morning Television that the stag was dealt with "*efficiently*" and observed that it was "*unfortunate that the stag took six minutes to die.*" (*Wildlife Guardian* issue 30 Winter 1994/95)

The outcome of the incident was reported thus in *Horse and Hound*, October 20th 1994: "*The Devon and Somerset Staghounds was banned from hunting for five weeks, until midnight November 18, in an unprecedented decision by the sport's governing body after a committee of inquiry last Friday.*
The committee viewed a video showing repeated failed attempts to kill with a shotgun a stag brought to bay by hounds in the River Barle.

Eventually the quarry was despatched with a humane killer. The committee decided that the incident brought the sport into disrepute. Hunt staff attempting to kill the stag swiftly were impeded by unruly behaviour of foot followers, it was alleged.............
Some footfollowers waded into the river and prevented the two marksmen getting a clear shot. The first shot hit the stag, but it did not die; it began to move up and down the river, and survived a second shot, with two other shots missing the deer. Eventually, the huntsman, Donald Summersgill, and two Hunt followers went into the river, held the deer and despatched it with a humane killer. Altogether the incident took about six minutes."

In autumn stag hunting the following year, Kevin Hill and Peter White, monitoring the Quantock Staghounds for the LACS, secured yet more horrific footage. It was Tuesday August 29th 1995, in what the stag hunters described as a 'pre-meet', stag hunting's equivalent to cub hunting in fox hunting. The hunt met at 6:30am.

By 7:20am Kevin and Peter had already filmed the stag running hard and exhausted, his tongue hanging out and foaming from his mouth. After heading towards Nether Stowey the stag turned and headed back into the hills. At 8am he was seen and filmed running the course of a stream near Great Wood Camp heading towards Adscombe Farm. The hounds were a mere 40m or so behind.

The stag left the stream, crossed a field and ran behind Adscombe Farm. Hounds and hunters closed in. The exhausted stag ended up with wire tangled around his antlers. After running hard to reach the scene Kevin filmed as the stag ran down a shallow slope with the hounds close behind him. The stag stumbled, then ran on with the hounds snapping at him. Supporters tried to block Kevin's view. The stag then fell and rolled over into a small stream where he was engulfed by the hounds. As hounds bit at the helpless stag hunt riders and car followers rushed to the scene. After approximately twenty seconds, with the hounds all around, the stag was shot dead with what was believed to be a humane killer.

This proved the reality of stag hunting—that it often ended in mayhem and cruelty. The truth was in stark contrast to the claims from the BFSS as proclaimed in their leaflet 'No hunting - No deer': *"The stag will stand at bay either on a steep slope, in a thicket or in water....Hounds instinctively know to keep their distance. It is then that the deer can be dispatched instantly at close range, by a member of the hunt staff carrying a special gun."*

Commenting on the film Graham Sirl, the LACS Head of West Country Operations, said: *"The fear and suffering that this beautiful prime specimen went through this morning can only be imagined. But the notion that this so-called 'sport' is a humane way to cull deer is clearly quite ridiculous. This new evidence shows once again how barbaric stag hunting really is and will surely convince the National Trust to ban the activity from their own land at least."*

The following year Kevin Hill was again on hand to record further appalling suffering inflicted upon a red deer stag. It was during spring stag hunting by the Quantock staghounds in April 1996. Kevin Hill monitored the hunt for the League Against Cruel Sports. After a 3-hour hunt over 15 miles the exhausted stag lay down in gorse bushes on National Trust land.

Kevin filmed as the Hunt Master, Bill Fewings, crept up on the deer and shot him. But the deer was not killed. Severely injured the stag ran off. It was subsequently revealed that his lower jaw was smashed. Hunt riders and followers enjoyed a further 14 minutes of hunting this crippled deer before he was shot and killed at close range with a pistol.

Mal Treharne, spokesman for the BFSS, was unapologetic: *"Everything was done according to the book....Nothing untoward happened. I would not think the deer suffered."*

There was something about stag hunting that seemed to make some supporters lose all control around the time of the kill. Even self-styled pillars of society could be afflicted. Here is a report from the *Daily Mail* August 19th 1997:

"Daily Telegraph editor Charles Moore, 40, (pictured) will have winced on opening his sister paper, the Sunday Telegraph, this weekend. His friend Adam Nicolson, 39, stirs bad memories with an article about fox-hunting, whose headline speaks of a 'howling pack of natural born killers'. Mr Nicolson once wrote, also in the Sunday Telegraph, about spending a day stag-hunting. After the kill, his host, 'wailing and screaming.........like a banshee' had scooped up a 'soup-bowl of blood' in his hands and smeared it into Mr Nicolson's hair with 'a manic delight'. Mr Nicolson, horrified, concluded that this 'chaotic, ugly primitivism could only be the sign of something degenerate', Suave Old Etonian Mr Moore was mortified when it emerged that he was the unnamed banshee." [Charles Moore is the biographer of Margaret Thatcher]

Other animal welfare campaigners recognised the power of the video camera and were involved in monitoring hunting to expose the inherent cruelty. Yet more singularly damning film of stag hunting was taken in 1999 by members of the New Forest Animal Protection Group (NFAPG) working in the West Country.

Their films of the Devon and Somerset Staghounds killing a spring stag on April 3rd 1999 were taken by several different camera people including Frankie Horan, Ken James and Daphne Ricketts. The stag was cornered in a small thicket beside the road near the notorious killing zone of Marsh Bridge. As the hounds closed in to attack the deer and the stag struggled to defend himself hunt followers packed around and did their best to block or stop the filming to keep the savage cruelty from being seen by the outside world.

Bloodsports are the only sports where supporters shield the end results from public view. It was like not being able to see the goal scored, the wicket taken or the knock-out punch landed. If the end of a fox, stag or hare hunt had been filmed, reviewed and analysed as in other sports these pastimes would have been banned long ago.

CHAPTER TWELVE
Other investigations into bloodsports

Hunt informants

Some of the most devastating information about hunting has been leaked by hunters themselves. One classic example occurred in the spring of 1987. A friend of Colin Didriksen, a terriermen to the now defunct Mr Goschen's Foxhounds, gave two colour negative strips of film to the LACS.

The pair had fallen out over personal issues and the informant wanted the LACS to know, and tell the world, how Colin treated foxes. The negatives provided damning images. There were eight pictures: three of a family nature; five of fox hunting. Some showed Colin Didriksen and his terrierman friend, Richard Grogan, posed for the cameraman.

They laughed as they held a terrified and lactating vixen aloft by her ears. Colin pointed to her swollen teats. The LACS were told her cubs were slaughtered. She was released for later hunting. The images proved how fox hunters used and abused foxes as mere toys. Whereas the public were shocked at the evident delight in cruelty many fox hunters were perplexed as to what all the fuss was about.

Cruelty to hounds

Hunt hounds have a tough life. In the routine course of hunting thousands are killed each year. Some are killed as puppies when they develop faults judged to render them unsuitable for hunting. In the past some puppies were killed simply for being the wrong colour—for example any puppy bearing a fleck of white would not be accepted into a 'black-and-tan' pack.

Most hounds are killed long before the end of their natural lives when they become too old to keep up with the rest of the pack. Hounds may also suffer from pure neglect. In May 1989, I had the pleasure of attending a court case where I was not the defendant. I drove to Port Talbot, Neath on Tuesday May 9th and met my LACS colleague John Bryant. We witnessed the trial of Clive Rees, a revered hunting enthusiast, who with a colleague was prosecuted by the RSPCA for cruelty to hounds. The trial started the next day, ran for two days, and was adjourned to May 18th.

The following day, Friday May 19th, at the end of the four-day trial before Port Talbot Magistrates, ex-MFH (Banwen Miners) and ex-MBH (South Wales Basset Hounds), Clive Rees was convicted of causing unnecessary suffering to four basset hound bitches. Joint defendant, Stephen Cashmore, was convicted of the same charge.

Magistrates heard that Solicitor Rees had arranged for the bassets to be exported to the USA as a gift to his friend Mr James Sharnberg, Master of the Pennsylvania based Androssan Beagles. Part of the arrangement for export was that defendant Cashmore was to deliver the hounds to a boarding kennels close to Gatwick Airport prior to their trans-atlantic journey.

However, on arrival at the kennels, a kennel-maid and the kennel owner were shocked to see the condition of the hounds. The RSPCA were immediately informed on the request of the local vet. In court the vet, Mr Hilbury, described the condition of the hounds as one of "*total neglect*" and added that it was the worst case of neglect he had witnessed in 26 years of practice.

Answering a question from a defence solicitor as to his bloodsports bias, Mr Hilbury said that for many years he had been the vet to the Hampshire Hunt and at the time worked for the Eton College Beagles.

The hounds, *Lotto*, *Spot*, *Bell* and *Bramble*, were all described as "*totally emaciated*". They were covered in layers of faeces and sores. The act of walking was very painful for them as their feet were raw because of prolonged contact with urine soaked bedding. Their ribs, pelvis and shoulder bones were all clearly visible. One bitch suffered from an infected and fetid vagina whilst another had pus exuding from an ear infection.

In summing up the vet said that the hounds were "*clinically starved*". In his defence Clive Rees claimed he had made arrangements with his mother's lodger, Cashmore, to look after the hounds but Cashmore denied any such arrangement had been made. Clive Rees and Stephen Cashmore were both found guilty and fined £750 and £500 respectively. Rees was further ordered to pay £1050 towards prosecution costs, whilst Cashmore was ordered to pay £100. The prosecution applied for an order disqualifying both men from keeping dogs in future but the Magistrates declined this.

*****

The 1991 Quorn investigation generated a huge amount of publicity. Many within the ranks of hunting realised that the ACIG and LACS were professional and discreet organisations that sought any information about wrongdoings within the hunting world. We were inundated with tip-offs ranging from foxes being reared for hunting to affairs of the bedroom nature amongst the hunt hierarchy.

Hides and skins

When one informant proposed an investigation into the hide and skin trade conducted at hunt kennels it was a whole new line of enquiry. I knew hunt kennels dealt with fallen livestock to feed their hounds but the extent and nature of the trade, and the 'side business' astonished me.

Our informant was a former professional Huntsman who had fallen out with his Masters—by no means an uncommon event. What was different for 'Steve' (not his real name) was that unlike other Huntsmen who had no other means of employment and usually ended up returning to hunting begging for their jobs back, he had another very profitable business. He owed no allegiance to hunting and sought nothing other than some revenge for the many wrongs inflicted upon him.

Steve telephoned the LACS offices and I arranged to meet him. We agreed Saturday May 2nd 1992 in a public place in Guildford at 1pm. He was a pleasant young man with a smooth, easy-going and confident manner. He asked me what I knew about the flesh trade in hunt kennels. I said only that hunts ingratiated themselves with farmers by offering to dispose of fallen livestock and that they used the resulting meat to feed their hounds. In return farmers allowed hunts onto their land.

Steve asked what I thought happened to the hides and skins cut from the dead animals? I answered they were sold as a perk and that like a barman or a waitress taking a tip that income would be unlikely to be declared for tax. But, I had no idea as to the extent of the trade. He told me huge numbers were sold and that professional Huntsmen at many hunts were involved in a neat tax fiddle that raked in thousands of pounds but could easily be exposed.

Steve explained at length how the trade worked. Nearly every hunt operated a service to their local farmers whereby they collected livestock casualties. These were animals such as cows, sheep, and horses that had either died from accidental causes or had to be put down. Sometimes the animal was still alive at the farm and the Huntsman, or his staff, killed it. On occasion, as with Jersey bull calves, there was nothing wrong with the animal other than that it was unwanted and had no commercial value.

There was a steady intake of livestock casualties into hunt kennels, as high as 50 cows a week at some. The meat was fed to the hounds, the offal disposed of to the processing industry and the hides and skins were sold to merchants. We knew some trade existed—but never the full extent of it.

Steve assured me that back in 1992 some Huntsmen boasted of earning £2000 per month cash that way! That equates to more than £3,750 per month in 2016, or £45,000 a year. Further, it was purely cash with no tax involved. Steve said Huntsmen were known for turning up at car dealerships with a suitcase full of banknotes to buy an expensive car.

It was easy to see why being a Huntsman was so attractive. In the first place, it was the supreme position within the hunting world and as such the young (and occasionally old) women fawned over them so the Huntsman had his choice. Secondly they were awash with cash.

Clearly if Steve was right and some Huntsmen truly were not paying tax on this trade and such a fraud was widely practised then the Inland Revenue and ultimately the tax payers lost out significantly.

I told Steve it was fascinating but how could we prove it? He advised me to set up a bogus company involved in the hide and skin trade. Then I should telephone Huntsmen around the country seeking to do business, and record our conversations. I laughed and said that I was a complete stranger to these men. I knew nothing about how the trade worked. Would they talk openly to me and more pertinently, would they really admit they dodged paying tax? I had fooled many a Huntsman but surely no-one would be daft enough to reveal such details to a stranger?

Steve assured me many were greedy and stupid and could be caught. He said that yes they were on their guard against a variety of people—hunt saboteurs; undercover operatives and irate husbands but they would never suspect an approach from this direction. He showed me paperwork from the trade in hides and skins. He taught me the terminology to use. He was cunning—he advised not to ask for all their trade, just that they put a few hides and skins to one side for our driver to collect to start with. He even gave me an audio cassette of conversations he had recorded with Huntsman as a training aid.

I spoke with Jim Barrington and other colleagues at the LACS and they were delighted to pursue this new attack on hunting. Later that month I did library research to familiarise myself with the trade and the key players in the business.

I then set to work. I made up a fictitious company and identities and set about telephoning hunt kennels using numbers listed in Bailey's Hunting Directory. It was nerve-wracking. If I made an error early on word would quickly be passed from kennel to kennel, warning there was a bogus company at work. I could wreck our project before it ever started.

I quickly found just how inaccurate entries in that Directory were. Some numbers were unobtainable. Others were answered by irate people whose telephone numbers were listed in error and were fed up with answering queries as to hunt meets that had nothing to do with them.

When I did get through to the hunt the Huntsman was often busy with the hounds, was just about to leave (the hunt employment year runs from May 1st) or was on holiday. Obviously, I could not leave my number for him to call me back. Often it took half a dozen calls before I spoke to the man himself. Steve cautioned me to speak only to the Huntsman or his family as the nature and value of the trade was usually kept secret from the other staff. It was also nearly always kept secret from the hunt Masters.

When we talked, I would tell the Huntsman that my company was new to the business and that we were prepared to pay an excellent price for hides and skins. Moreover, I stressed that we aimed to provide a reliable collection service and could provide other services he might require such as the delivery of salt to preserve the skins.

I sensed that many Huntsmen, used to having to doff their hats to all and sundry in the hunting field, were pleased to be spoken to as an equal and consequently readily engaged in conversation. Gradually I would turn the conversation round to their relationship with the Inland Revenue. As Steve advised I would suggest that we just had to be in tune on the tax business. I would put it to the Huntsman that, if he declared all his trade for tax, then so would we; if he did not declare anything for tax then neither would we—so what did he do? Then it usually came out whether they claimed to declare all their skin income for tax, some of their income or none of it.

My telephone conversations were all recorded by me and the tapes duplicated for security. In total 133 Huntsmen were interviewed over the phone. Whether they told the truth only they know but their answers were freely given. From that number 66 said that they declared nothing or only part of their income to the Inland Revenue. Virtually all of those insisted on being paid in cash. Another 21 Huntsmen said that at the time they were paid in cash or wished to be paid cash. Of those seeking to be paid in cash 7 were amongst the 25 in total who stated they declared all their income. A further 16 Huntsmen either gave unclear answers or did not wish to change their skin merchant. The final 12 Huntsmen said they did not collect fallen stock or did not deal in hides and skins.

As examples of the interviews David Evans, Huntsman of the Old Surrey and Burstow Foxhounds said he only accepted cash and that in the 'good times' he was earning £2,000 a month from the skin income.

David Allibone, Huntsman of the Taunton Vale Harriers, admitted that he did not declare his income from skins and said he used another name, such as 'Moore' whenever he had "*any surplus I don't want anyone to know about.*"

Jeremy Whaley, Master and Huntsman of the Chiddingfold, Leconfield and Cowdray Foxhounds boasted he ran one of the biggest knacker trades in his area. He admitted he did not declare his skin income and that he preferred cash by registered post adding: "*Obviously from a tax point of view we don't want to get caught out that way.*"

Barry Todhunter, Huntsman of the Blencathra Foxhounds in the heart of the Lakeland Fells explained his own avoidance of tax: "*I don't declare. We never have declared. I don't think anyone does.*" When called, he complained that he had endured a 'bad two months' with only 95 skins to sell. That would still have netted him more than £500.

As for the elite shire packs Neil Coleman, Huntsman of the Cottesmore Foxhounds said that he declared half his skin income. Michael Farrin, Huntsman of the Quorn Foxhounds said that he only declared part of his income from skins adding: "*The money is paid in cash when the driver comes.*"

As to the student packs George Haynes, Kennel Huntsman at the Royal Agricultural College Beagles, said that he did not declare his income. Over at Cambridge University the Kennel Huntsman of the Trinity Foot Beagles, J. Calder, admitted that he did not declare the income from his skin trade and dealt in cash only.

Other highlights from the many hours of recordings were the Huntsman who told me he had not filled in a tax form for years and who believed the Revenue did not know about him. They soon did.

Another Huntsman gleefully told me of the different name he used to elude the tax man. Many told me we could only do business if I kept what I paid them secret from their Masters (perhaps they feared their Masters would reduce their wages when they appreciated the true value of this 'skin' perk).

There was subterfuge both within hunts and between hunts. One Huntsman, after we chatted for a while, told me he sent his skin collection wagon into the country of his neighbouring hunt and that he would only do business if I was discreet as to the amounts I collected from him.

With the phone calls made we realised that we needed some visual evidence for the story as well. We needed pictures of the flesh house at a hunt kennels and the hides and skins. July 1st ushered in the next stage. I called Steve to discuss how we might advance our investigation. He offered to be my guide for a visit to a hunt kennels. I queried whether any

Huntsman would be gullible enough to show strangers his kennels. He suggested we meet Patrick Martin, Huntsman at the Bicester with Whaddon Chase Foxhounds. I had met Patrick years before during previous undercover work when he was a Whipper-in at the Berkeley Foxhounds. I doubted he would remember me. Saturday July 18th 1992 I met Steve at Stratton Audley and we drove to the nearby hunt kennels for our arranged meeting.

Steve used the alias that he was Jeremy from *Country Ways Magazine* in Canada. He was interested in seeing the hounds and how the kennels worked. As he had been a Huntsman himself he knew all the language and chatted with Patrick as if they were best of buddies. I called myself Simon and told Patrick that Jeremy was staying with me in Oxford and had asked me to accompany him to take photographs.

Patrick could not have been more helpful. He gave us a guided tour of his kennels and I photographed some hides and skins. There were only a few—there may have been a collection a few days before.

I recorded many hours of conversations with Huntsmen the length and breadth of Britain, the key parts of which I transcribed. We appreciated we had a better chance of catching any villains if my evidence was passed to the Inland Revenue and they were given time to pursue enquiries before it appeared in the media. On Thursday June 25th I took the train to London to visit the LACS offices. I then called the Inland Revenue investigations team to discuss our findings. That was a day when events conspired to cause travel chaos in London. An IRA briefcase bomb exploded under a car in Coleman Street. That caused a police officer to be treated for shock and the closure of Southwark, London and Tower bridges. Jim Barrington dropped me off to catch the 8:30pm train from Liverpool Street but a factory fire damaged the railway track at Stratford. We had to get the bus to Ilford, then a train to Shenfield and another train home. I reached bed at 2am.

Diligent work with the Inland Revenue led to considerable delay in the publicity. During that time, we carried out further related investigative work. As part of this I liaised with Carlton Television and the makers of their Beam and Da Silva investigative programme. The idea was to buy some skins from a Huntsman. We chose Jeremy Whaley at the Chiddingfold, Leconfield and Cowdray Foxhounds.

Friday February 19th 1993 brought another early start. My alarm sounded at 3:45am. I caught the 5:22am train from Diss to London and was at the offices of Chrysalis Television for 7:30am. We drove to the hunt kennels. We had arranged with Jeremy to be there for 10am but the TV crew had problems getting their hidden camera to work, then the reporter—Roger Beam—forgot his microphone.

When we eventually arrived, nearly an hour late, I was to use the alias Mark Garvey and Roger was to be John Longhurst. We strode up and Roger promptly introduced himself to Jeremy as Roger Beam! That error caused great amusement to his colleagues monitoring from nearby. I who made many blunders was consoled to see that even professionals could make errors.

We bought four cow hides for £15 each and drove them round to Janet Jackson's home to film and photograph. Janet then disposed of them with some decorum.

With the release of the story imminent I was keen to have another attempt at recording hides and skins at a hunt kennels. We decided to make use of the fact that we had a long-term informant embedded in the Heythrop Foxhounds. Their kennels are at Chipping Norton. I called Ed Maynard and once again he kindly offered to help.

Our plan was to visit the kennels when there was no-one about, wander around, find and photograph any piles of hides and skins. The key element was to ensure there was no-one there. We chose a hunting day— Saturday February 20th. I called our informant at 9am to check all the staff were going hunting but was told one horse might be lame. If that was confirmed after trotting up and the chap did not hunt, we could not go.

I met Ed Maynard at a Little Chef restaurant near Chipping Norton; then called our informant at 1:20pm. Everything was well. There was no-one in the kennel area. We drove down, found the flesh-house with piles of skins and dead animals strewn about. It was a bloody site. I hastily took video film and photographs and we left. As a precaution, I had a sack of pony nuts in the boot of my car. If anyone had challenged us I would have said something like: 'Hi there mate, my daughter's pony died recently and this is just a bag of his food that we had left over that we thought you might like. I was just dropping it off as a gift'.

The LACS sent out a briefing document to their Representatives late in February 1993 alerting them to the story. Then on February 28th 1993 the *Sunday Times* published the first exposé of our investigation. The LACS followed this with a Press Release that was widely picked up.

Hunters reacted with both horror and outrage. They viewed it as disgraceful and unsporting that anyone should condemn hunting on any grounds other than cruelty! They viewed my behaviour as odious and downright 'sneaky'.

Conversely I viewed it as fair to attack bloodsports using any lawful means and if at the same time we protected the interests of taxpayers then so much the better. The money Huntsmen cheated from taxpayers to spend on sports cars would be better invested in hospitals and schools.

It was curiously fitting to catch hunters in that way. For years, they had condemned the likes of hunt saboteurs as 'scroungers' and 'dole fiddlers'. Our investigation exposed many in the hunting fraternity as tax fiddlers who together over the years cost our nation millions of pounds. Hunting had, in effect, been subsidised by tax payers for years. The Inland Revenue set about recovering what they could from the vast amounts owed to them in the past. Perhaps more importantly they stopped the fiddle being practised in the future. The hunters again became the hunted.

The investigation extended into other fields far beyond the obvious tax evasion. With most of the hunt kennels involved in trading animal skins the question arose as to whether they were all licensed, as they should be, for such trading by their local authorities.

What about the health risks of feeding raw meat from what were often diseased animals to hounds? Particularly given that those hounds would then be hunting, and defecating, on farms from one end of the hunt country to the other. At the time of the investigation there were some 20,000 hounds kept in Britain for hunting foxes, deer, hares and mink. Virtually all of them were fed on raw meat and offal from farm casualties.

Hounds ingested the tapeworm *Taenia Hydatigena* from the raw meat and then defecated the tapeworm eggs back onto pastures whilst hunting. Sheep, particularly lambs, then ingested the eggs whilst grazing and became re-infected with the tapeworms that caused cysts that damaged the animals' livers. A report in *Veterinary Record* revealed that in one single abattoir lambs' livers were so badly damaged by tapeworms that the majority were rejected for human consumption, representing in that single abattoir an annual loss of £25,000 at 1984 prices.

Another investigation published in *Veterinary Record* concluded: "*Taenia Hydatigena causes very high rates of liver condemnation and it is probable that, nationally, it is now the major cause of lesions and losses in lambs' livers.*"

The Meat and Livestock Commission stated: "*About a fifth of lambs slaughtered in Great Britain are infected with cysts. This loss is caused solely by tape-worms in dogs and is avoidable.....Never feed raw meat, offal or sheep heads; feed only cooked meat....Working dogs and hounds are the main reservoir of dog tapeworms affecting sheep; foxes and pet dogs much less so.*"

The Agricultural Development and Advisory Service (ADAS) a department of the Ministry of Agriculture, Fisheries and Food (MAFF) pointed out the dangers of *Hydatidosis* to both human and animal health: "*Eggs laid by the tapeworm are passed in the faeces of the dog and this may contaminate herbage consumed by cattle and sheep or vegetables intended for human consumption.*"

An egg ingested by livestock or humans hatched in the intestine of the new host. It eventually ended up in the liver where it formed a cyst. Cysts could also form in the lungs, bones and even the brain. ADAS warned: "*...on average 12 persons die each year from hydatidosis. In addition several hundred persons have to undergo surgical operations for the removal of the cysts.*"

A letter to LACS from MAFF dated February 17th 1987 stated: "*Undoubtedly hounds, or hunting dogs, are also sources of tapeworm infection.....studies by the Ministry's veterinary officers have demonstrated that hounds are frequently infected with a variety of tapeworms, including Taenia Hydatigena and they may contaminate pastures over which they roam.*"

Although it was known at the time that it was safer to boil or sterilise all meat before feeding it to hounds the Government refused to order all hunts to feed only cooked meat.

Another concern was what was going wrong in UK farming that such large numbers of animals had to be disposed of in this way? Was the discreet nature of that disposal valuable or even essential for farmers?

My ACIG and the LACS produced a detailed report entitled *Skinned* that detailed this investigation. Hunting folk never had much regard for me but thereafter I was even less welcome in the hunting fields.

Thanks to highly effective political campaigning led by Angela Smith for the LACS the matter was taken up in Parliament. This Early Day Motion number 1938 "*Report On The Abuses By Huntsmen*" was tabled on May 4th 1993:

"*That this House congratulates the League Against Cruel Sports and the Animal Cruelty Investigation Group on producing their report called* Skinned, *on the largely untaxed multi-million pound trade in animals' skins carried out by most of Britain's red-coated huntsmen, is further alarmed by the health risk involved in feeding raw casualty meat to the hounds; and calls on the Government to initiate an enquiry into the whole issue as a first step to introducing legislation to end hunting with dogs.*"

Artificial earths and hunts encouraging foxes

The existence of artificial earths is concrete proof that fox hunting is not, and never has been, about the reduction of fox numbers but all about the production of foxes for hunters to play with in our countryside.

Artificial earths are homes built by hunt supporters for foxes to live and breed in. They were usually coupled with the management of woodland to benefit foxes and often with the provision by hunt supporters of food and water for the foxes. Artificial earths are found in most parts of England, from lowland shires to upland sheep-rearing areas. That their existence has been tolerated by the farming community is proof that, whatever may be claimed publicly, farmers know that foxes pose no significant threat to their animal production industries.

Artificial earths have always been closely associated with hunting. *Baily's Hunting Directory* was a bible for fox hunters. In the very first volume—published in 1897—the following was written about the reason and need for these man-made homes:-

"*The artificial earth is now-a-days very often the accompaniment of the artificial covert, and we think it is just as well to make an earth in every new covert, if only in the hope that wild foxes may take to it in years to come. Artificial earths, however, are almost invariably made in order that they may form a home for hand-reared cubs, and though they are a horrible thing in themselves, there is undoubtedly a necessity for them in these days, where the fox is much interfered with in many districts, and would disappear altogether if he were not carefully cherished. It amounts to this, then, that it is wise to remove and hand-rear such cubs as will not be allowed to live if left where they were bred, and that being the case it is of course right to give the matter one's best attention, in this case by imitating nature as nearly as possible. And writing of imitating nature what natural earth can compare with the elaborately planned artificial* one that is now made? The wild fox lies up in a drain, in a rabbit-hole, or amongst the rocks, while the hand-reared cub has his "mansion replete with every modern sanitary convenience."" (Baily's Fox-Hunting Directory. 1897-8 [Vol. 1] 1897. Page 16)

It has also been known for years that artificial earths should be carefully built and care taken with the feeding of foxes. The following advice is from a hunting book written before World War Two:-

"It should be borne in mind that an artificial earth is frequently the means of introducing mange into a country; that it provides a golden opportunity for a gamekeeper to turn down a bag-fox, for a dishonest huntsman to "doctor" a fox, and for poachers to steal one.
The diagram gives details of a satisfactory type of artificial earth. [Plan drawing shown]
Having built the earth it is necessary to persuade foxes to use it, and the best way of doing this is to turn a litter of cubs into it and to leave them there until the earth smells thoroughly "foxy"~say for a month. It will be necessary to arrange a wire run for the cubs to exercise themselves, and to see that they are fed and watered daily. On no account must they be fed on meat, other than rabbits, rats, or birds. "Butcher's meat" is very likely to introduce mange. For this reason, too, they should not be kept in the earth a moment longer than necessary....Should there be a natural earth in the immediate neighbourhood it should be destroyed, so that the foxes which would normally use it may be attracted to the artificial earth....If absolute quiet is observed a fox may often be bolted from an artificial earth if a strong electric torch is flashed up one pipe. This method is especially useful if it is thought that there are two foxes in the earth, for a sharp man can put down the grating as soon as the first is clear of the mouth; two hunts may then be scored from the one earth." (To Hunt the Fox. David Brock. Master of the Thurles and Kilshane Foxhounds sometime Master of the East Sussex. 1937. Pages 58-60)

Curiously many fox hunters saw a threat to their 'sport' from artificial earths making fox hunting just too artificial. Here is an extract from a book published in 1955:-

"I have been asked to say a few words about the upkeep of artificial fox-earths and coverts, which serve as a **reservoir** of foxes in those districts which would otherwise be insufficiently "foxed" to show consistent sport. I should like to say that the creation of man-made fox-earths borders too closely upon the "artificial" to suit me, for, although it is a comparatively simple matter to see to it that there are always foxes in them, it is nearly always necessary to bolt them in order to get a hunt. With too many artificial earths in a country, hounds get used to having foxes bolted for them and simply go to a holloa when once they are afoot. Very soon they get so used to having half their work done for them that they will not draw regular coverts well when it is necessary for them to do so. Moreover, such procedure comes perilously close to the evil practice of hunting a "bag-man."" (Fox Hunting chapter by A. Henry Higginson in

302

Youth in the Saddle, edited by Lt.-Col. W.E. Lyon. 1955. Page 126. [A.H. Higginson was Master, Cattistock Foxhounds from 1930-1939])

Artificial earths had to be carefully constructed. Here from 1965 a reader of *The Field* asks for advice over their construction:-

"An artificial earth

I should be grateful for help over the making of an artificial fox-earth, please. -A.V. (Staffordshire)

A fox needs a space about 1ft. 3in. cube, but it can be larger. You can either dig a hole in a bank, or create a bank enclosing a cavity. Another way is to create a cavity with cordwood covered with sods, or use logs and earth. Indeed, any cavity with a bare earth floor, no matter how enclosed, will serve. It is said that a fox prefers only one entrance to the earth, but it is often found that if a second entrance is not provided (that is, an exit), the fox makes one." (Reader's enquiry, *The Field*, November 29th, 1965)

With passing years hunting folk became ever more defensive over the role of artificial earths. They greatly objected to any suggestion that hunt supporters built artificial earths to encourage foxes to breed. However, the Duke of Beaufort, the greatest expert on fox hunting, explained in his 1980 book that artificial earths were for breeding:-

"In countries where earths are scarce it is sometimes found necessary to make artificial earths, to provide somewhere for local foxes to have their cubs: in other words, for breeding purposes. Another advantage of artificial earths is that in grass countries where the coverts tend to be small and scattered it is useful to have snug earths judiciously placed at regular intervals, thus persuading foxes to take a good line. An additional advantage is that if an artificial earth is left open, it will only take a few minutes to bolt a fox. Also if it is a blank day, one knows where to go with some certainty of finding a fox.........In this book I only wish to touch on the subject, and to tell you what my grandfather had to say.

He felt that artificial earths should be primarily intended as breeding establishments, and so among the chief points to be borne in mind should be the aspect, position, soil, drainage and materials used for their construction." (*Fox-Hunting*. The Duke of Beaufort. 1980. Page 141)

The existence of artificial earths even in the Fell hunting areas of the Lake District was confirmed by the following extract from an article in a 1993 edition of *Hounds* magazine. This was brought to my attention by a Cumbrian hunt saboteur:-

"Barry drew again down Lansdale Fell, found, and hunted over to Mill Beck, marking to ground in "Porter's Parlour".

Now I would have attempted the short climb to where they were digging, but a very interesting Mr John Gregg came and spoke to me and told me the history of "Porters Parlour". It is the largest man-made borran ever known, built about 30 years ago by Ronnie Porter. A maze of pipes and entrances exists..........The fox in Porters Parlour was accounted for, making a total of four foxes that day. On returning to the kennels, they were a terrier short, so went back to Porters Parlour, where a terrier was heard baying. It was then dug to, and the fifth fox of the day was added to the tally."

(Article by The Gaffer, "*Spring Hunting In the Cumbrian Fells*" *Hounds* magazine. Vol. 10 No. 1. November 1993. Page 28. [Refers to meet of the Blencathra Foxhounds, a Fell pack, Huntsman Barry Todhunter])

Increased media interest in the use by fox hunters of artificial earths forced hunters to admit just how common they were:-

"......*there are artificial earths in almost every hunting county in England.*" (Jeffrey Olstead, BFSS spokesman for Cumberland Foxhounds, in the *Sunday News & Star*, Carlisle. 17/3/1996)

During the fieldwork described in *Outfoxed Take Two* I had found some artificial earths, particularly in the country of the Heythrop Foxhounds. However, in this second phase of my investigative work I was determined to uncover more and confirm how widespread they are across England and Wales.

As mentioned earlier, in January 1984 I returned to the Heythrop site and found it active and in use. As a young hunt saboteur, I had stumbled upon artificial earths in Cambridgeshire Foxhounds country. On Sunday March 4th 1990 I drove to Cambridge and met Dave Fox, the organizer of the Cambridge HSA. He kindly showed me more local artificial earths.

From the creation of the ACIG I had encouraged supporters to be our eyes and ears in the countryside. We asked supporters to walk the footpaths in the woods and fields around them and report anything suspicious to us. We asked people to be alert to village gossip as to who was doing what, and where, in the countryside near them.

In May 1990 our supporter, Mike Michalak, who lived near Cambridge, telephoned to report artificial earths near Newmarket that he and his wife Ingrid had found during rural rambles. Sunday May 20th proved to be auspicious. I met Mike and he guided me to artificial earths in country in the Cambridge-Newmarket area hunted by the Thurlow Foxhounds. That was the start of an investigative project that lasted years and eventually uncovered the encouragement of foxes on an almost industrial scale.

For our investigative work, I copied the attitudes adopted by hunters to trespass. Hunt supporters take the view that they can go anywhere they like until someone tells them otherwise. If anyone told me I was trespassing I exited by the quickest route. I sometimes encountered artificial earths during hunt observations—as when the Quorn Foxhounds met at Ulverscroft Lodge on January 26th 1991.

Colleagues up and down the country put in many hours of routine, unpaid, investigative work looking for artificial earths. One such stalwart was Essex based Kevin Chapple. On Sunday May 26th 1991 I met Kevin and he showed me four artificial earth sites in the Chelmsford area. My good friend Chris Owen had previously shown me artificial earths in Cheshire. Roy Parker showed me some near Banbury. I also worked with Howard Hodges, the LACS Treasurer, to find artificial earths in the Luton-Aylesbury area.

Three days later, Wednesday May 29th, I accompanied Jim Barrington to the Isle of Wight. We went for the court case the next morning of the former Huntsman of the Isle of Wight Foxhounds, Steve Clifton and his terrierman, James Butcher, facing badger abuse charges. Newport Magistrates convicted them and they were fined £500 with £500 costs.

We had received a tip-off about an artificial earth near the hunt kennels. The next morning, May 31st, Jim and I crept around the wood at the back of the hunt kennels and eventually found the site.

Often our work crossed over between campaigns. An example was Sunday June 9th 1991 when I met Mike Michalak and he showed me a site where illegal snares were set and then artificial earths in two different woods in Thurlow Foxhounds country. We closed the illegal snares then reported them to the police (see 'Shooting investigations' later).

With investigative work, it was not uncommon to have blank days. One such was Tuesday June 11th when I met Jim Barrington and we drove to Quorn Foxhounds country. We met Graham and Joanna Woolliscroft and Ed Maynard and searched for artificial earths and badgers' setts in the pouring rain but found little.

Norwich HSA identified artificial earth locations in Norfolk. On Wednesday June 19th I found and photographed two artificial earths in country hunted by the West Norfolk Foxhounds. We received tip-offs from many sources. One sent me to look for artificial earths in Fitzwilliam (Milton) Foxhounds country on Saturday June 29th. I found and recorded one. I spent autumn 1991 embroiled in the Quorn Foxhounds investigation.

*****

In 1992 I resumed looking for artificial earths. Sometimes there were clues as to their location. Sunday January 12th provided an example. I met Howard Hodges and amongst other investigative work we looked for artificial earths in country hunted by the Bicester with Whaddon Chase Foxhounds. After studying the Ordnance Survey map we checked woodlands and found and recorded one earth. The clue was on the map where the wood was identified as 'fox covert'! We later learned that that wood was owned by the hunt. I subsequently found numerous artificial earths in that area working with Howard. Often we linked searching for earths with monitoring a nearby hunt.

Saturday June 13th 1992 took me back to familiar ground. I resumed fieldwork in Thurlow Foxhounds country checking for artificial earths. Besides searching for new sites, I checked known ones for any changes.

*****

New Year's Day 1993 found Howard Hodges and me crawling around woods in Vale of Aylesbury Foxhounds country looking for artificial earths. We found one with not a fox in residence, but a badger. Later that year, Saturday June 26th, I checked a large artificial earth in Thurlow Foxhounds country, in Balsham Wood, and found evidence of food for foxes dumped near both pipe entrances. There was also a trough of water nearby.

It was important to check known artificial earth sites before and/or after hunts met nearby. An example was Thursday October 21st 1993 when

I checked the artificial earths in Thorpe Wood near where the Suffolk Foxhounds would meet the following Saturday. I noted no interference with the earths.

*****

In 1994 we stepped up investigative work searching for artificial earths in country hunted by the Thurlow Foxhounds. Saturday March 12th was significant. That day I found a big new site in a wood, near the Horseheath Point-to Point course, owned by Edmund Vestey, Joint Master of the Thurlow Foxhounds. We also started to look for stick or log piles. These were sites built by hunt supporters to create safe places for foxes to lay up in—and where foxes might be found on hunting days.

We found artificial earths of different types. The common theme was a central chamber with two entrances. The chamber could be built of blocks, bricks or timber and covered with a lid of concrete or corrugated iron. The tunnels were usually a pipe of concrete or glazed pipe; or they could be a tunnel of concrete blocks.

Because of their remote location artificial earths would have cost a considerable sum in time and money to construct. At some of the sites we found evidence of food being put out for foxes, dead chickens and the like, and in some locations we found water butts provided (and regularly topped up). Hunters had for generations appreciated that there were perils associated with feeding foxes. The following was written in the very first edition of Baily's published in 1897:-

"The method of building the horseshoe drain is not of great consequence, we think; stone flags, bricks or pipes, all answer the purpose, but perhaps the flags are best and cleanest, and least likely to generate mange. When the cubs are brought there they must be well looked after and fed, for in all probability they will have left their mother before she had taught them to look after themselves, and at first they are quite unable to find their own food. Rabbits, rats, beetles and birds of every description suit them best, but too much raw horse-flesh often causes mange, which is, with the exception of barbed wire, the greatest curse any hunt can have to face, and we mention this because, if the cubs are located within easy distance of the kennels, the man in charge, in order to save trouble, often secures his supplies from the feeder, and thus the cubs get surfeited with horse-flesh at a time when they are better suited by milder food. Besides which, too, horse-flesh causes the cubs to shirk hunting on their own account, and foxes who get into these bad habits always become pottering, ringing beggars, and often die the moment the food supply is stopped." (*Baily's Fox-Hunting Directory*. 1897-8 [Vol. 1] Pub. Vinton & Co. Ltd. 1897. Page 17)

Sunday April 10th 1994 was productive. I met Mike Michalak again and he showed me a well-constructed stick pile in a wood near Shudy Camps, in Thurlow hunt country. Days of patient and methodical investigative work followed. On June 11th 1994 we found more evidence of food for foxes being dumped near the entrances to the artificial earth in

306

Balsham Wood. I returned a few days later to take quality video film of the site—using a Hi-8 camera mounted on a tripod.

I also aimed to record artificial earths in other parts of the country. One such excursion occurred Sunday June 16th 1994 when I drove south to meet Marian Lanham. She guided me to see an artificial earth in country hunted by the Southdown & Eridge Foxhounds.

Thursday June 30th 1994 I met my colleague, Lawrie Payne, and together we undertook fieldwork in Thurlow Foxhounds country. We found an ancient stick pile in Wadgell's Wood, near the hunt kennels. There were remains of pheasants and chickens dumped nearby. Lawrie was my trusty companion for a great deal of fieldwork thereafter. As already mentioned, he was a professional fireman. The many days of monitoring and investigative work that he did with me were in his free time and as a volunteer.

On Saturday July 16th 1994 I checked a known artificial earth near the Harcamlow Way, east of Linton, near Cambridge in Thurlow hunt country and found chicken remains dumped nearby plus a filled water trough for the foxes. I found more freshly dead chickens dumped there when I checked the site the following month on Monday August 22nd. When I checked the site the following week, on Tuesday August 30th all the chickens dumped the previous Monday had been taken. Local foxes evidently made full use of this food supply.

Saturday September 17th I drove west and met Roy Parker. He guided me to the site of a strange looking artificial earth complex in country hunted by the Bicester with Whaddon Chase Foxhounds.

Regular checking of known sites alerted us to any changes. On Sunday November 6th, I visited the artificial earth in Balsham Wood, Thurlow country. One entrance was blocked with a purpose-made steel grid; the other entrance was blocked with sticks. The artificial earth with entrances of building blocks in the wood by the Harcamlow Way had both entrances sealed with breeze blocks. In addition, the entrance to the earth site through the thick scrub had been cut back to enable easier access.

Fieldwork was integrated with monitoring work. On Monday November 28th Lawrie Payne and I checked known artificial earth sites in Thurlow country. The one in Balsham Wood was blocked again. The one in the copse by the Harcamlow Way was blocked as it had been when I hid up in the wood for hunt monitoring the previous Thursday. On searching that site Lawrie Payne found clear evidence that badgers had taken over the artificial earth complex.

In fact it was more likely a re-occupation than a taking over. To save time the hunt supporter who built the artificial earth probably built it into the remains of a disused badger sett. Local badgers then found a nicely refurbished tunnel complex and reclaimed it. However, whilst hunt supporters could do as they liked with artificial earths if badgers took up residence they became badger setts and enjoyed the legal protection afforded to badgers. Blocking a badger sett with breeze blocks was illegal.

I telephoned the LACS and spoke to my colleague, the wildlife expert John Bryant. He advised to call the police which I did. When I phoned the Cambridgeshire Police Wildlife Liaison Officer I just got an answerphone so I called the local police station. We then waited on the footpath for the police officer and when he arrived guided him to the site. With his authority to confirm that no harm was done we then unblocked the entrances, allowing badgers full access again.

There was extensive follow-up work. Thursday December 1st demonstrated the expertise we had available. I met Lawrie Payne and renowned badger expert, Chris Ferris, and together we visited the site of the artificial earth that had become a badger sett. Chris examined the area closely and found even more evidence of it being an active badger sett.

We then drove to Linton Police Station and gave statements. Nothing came of it. Police later told me that when they asked the Thurlow Foxhounds who their terriermen were the hunt exercised their right to remain silent. As I had also on previous occasions exercised that same right I could hardly complain.

*****

1995 brought more intensive fieldwork in Thurlow Foxhounds country. Thursday January 12th Lawrie Payne and I checked the artificial earth/badger sett near the Harcamlow Way and found a fresh pile of dead chickens to replace the ones we had found dumped on January 4th whilst hunt monitoring. In those early years, we did not have the remote surveillance cameras that were to be developed later. Lawrie and I spent many an uncomfortable hour seated out in woodlands watching artificial earths hoping to film events of interest.

We uncovered plenty of unpleasant sights. One such was Monday January 30th when Lawrie and I found another artificial earth in a small wood near Shudy Camps in Thurlow Foxhounds country. Nearby was an enormous, foul smelling, fetid heap of rotting dead birds, including at least three moorhens. It was a side of the pastime of shooting birds for fun that is seldom seen.

During Sunday February 19th 1995 Lawrie and I hid in the wood for 3 hours hoping to see either a fox using the stick pile or anyone dumping more dead birds. We filmed nothing—proving what a bonus it was when we acquired cameras that we could leave on site that recorded anything that happened in daylight. Usually Lawrie and I worked together, sometimes we worked separately.

Lawrie was on his own on Monday February 27th when he found artificial earth number 17 in Thurlow Foxhounds country. It was in a small copse known as College Grove near Carlton Green and sited next to a disused military building.

In conjunction with our investigative work in the fields we supplied the media with details of our findings. Wednesday March 1st 1995 was notable because *Today* published a report about the activities of the Thurlow Foxhounds. We were concerned about the health hazards caused by the dumping of dead poultry in the woods to feed foxes. On Saturday

March 18th 1995 I wrote to the Environmental Health department at South Cambridgeshire District Council to complain about the issue.

We found some strange sights in the woods, one example of which occurred on Thursday April 6th 1995. Whilst on our usual investigative work in Thurlow country Lawrie Payne found artificial earth number 21 in Norney Plantation. Nearby was a bender with evidence of a person living there.

A couple of months later, Saturday June 10th, Lawrie Payne and I found that another artificial earth was actually in use as a badger sett. This was artificial earth number 20 in Abbacy Wood, first found on April 1st that year. Stick pile number 9 was located nearby.

Monday June 12th was a busy day. After a guided tour of Toxicol Laboratory near Ledbury in the morning I met Jim Barrington. We drove to see and photograph a new artificial earth complex in a newly planted copse in Duke of Beaufort's Foxhounds country near Malmesbury. We were guided around the extensive site by a local supporter.

The following Friday Lawrie and I returned to the site in Abbacy Wood and took up a hidden observation position to try and film badgers using the artificial earth. We were there from 6:30pm. After an hour of being attacked by a variety of biting insects the only creature found was ourselves when the gamekeeper's dog, an Alsatian, came bounding up to Lawrie. The dog was friendlier than his owner, a cheerless soul named Raymond.

He ordered us to leave the land and we set off to do so. He sent his assistant ahead, for what we knew not. When we reached the road, we encountered Paddy Bell from the Thurlow Foxhounds waiting with a camera. Paddy photographed us and when I returned the compliment by turning my video camera on him, Raymond knocked it to one side.

The LACS later received a complaint from the BFSS that Lawrie and I had been abusive and threatening to the gamekeeper. They overlooked the fact that though my camera was hanging from the strap around my neck and pointing at the ground it was running during the whole encounter. The recording proved who was giving out abuse and threats—and it was neither Lawrie nor I.

Thwarted in that attack our opponents then threatened legal proceedings accusing Lawrie Payne and me of causing criminal damage to the grass belonging to the Thurlow Estates that we walked over. The LACS solicitor replied offering £50 each for Lawrie and me in compensation for any damage we may have caused. If the hunt wanted to take it further our words were to the effect, "*See you in court*". We heard no more.

Tuesday July 18th marked another long-haul investigation. I made a 580 mile round trip to photograph an artificial earth in Rodden Bushes, in Cattistock Foxhounds country. I searched for another and when I could not find it assumed it had been dug out by the hunt. Experience showed that if hunt supporters regarded an artificial earth as being in an unsuitable site they would readily move it.

Sunday August 27th, another long expedition, proved memorable. I met LACS Committee Member, Peter Ponting, at *The Hare and Hounds*, Westonbirt, Gloucestershire in the early afternoon. We were guided by a local informant to see an artificial earth site nearby, another in country hunted by the Duke of Beaufort's Foxhounds.

The best constructed and probably most expensive artificial earth I knew of was shown to me on Wednesday October 4th 1995. I drove to meet local hunt monitor and field investigator, Penny Little, at *The Star*, Stanton St. John, Oxfordshire at noon. We then met local informants who showed us the site of a new artificial earth under construction in woodland behind the kennels of the Christchurch and Farley Hill Beagles (the Oxford University pack). That was country hunted by the Vale of Aylesbury Foxhounds.

The earth was a veritable bunker for foxes. The lid to the chamber was of carefully crafted steel. A great deal of thought, time and money had been devoted to creating that home for foxes to live and breed in.

*****

We constantly fed the results of our investigative work exposing the use of artificial earths to the media. On Tuesday April 30th 1996 I met a film crew from Anglia TV at the Little Chef, Fiveways, near Cambridge. It was an area I knew well. Some twenty years before I had bought my first car from a garage there.

We drove to Balsham and the crew filmed an interview with me on the roadside verge about the multitude of artificial earths, stick and log piles in that locality. I then accompanied them to a television studio in Cambridge where they sent a copy of my Hi-8 video of artificial earths 'down the line' to studios in Norwich. A short feature was shown on local television that evening.

Thursday May 9th was a day for revisiting a known site. I returned to Quorn Foxhounds country to photograph the artificial earth near Ulverscroft, Leicestershire I first found when undercover amongst that hunt. That was the first of several visits to Quorn country to check on efforts made by hunt supporters to encourage foxes.

However, the Thurlow Foxhounds remained our main focus for investigations into fox breeding. In the early afternoon of Sunday May 19th Mike Michalak phoned to say he and Ingrid had found yet another artificial earth in Thurlow country. I met them at Ashdon and they guided me to the site in a nearby wood.

It was impressive. The tunnels and entrances were built from concrete building blocks. The two entrances were spaced 23m apart. Each entrance had its shape reinforced with steelwork. Both entrances smelled strongly of fox. Within the wood some 40m away from one of the entrances was a large pheasant release pen. That was artificial earth number 25 in Thurlow Foxhounds country.

Foxes were certainly making good use of these homes so carefully constructed by Thurlow Foxhounds supporters. When on Sunday May 26th I found artificial earth number 26 in a wood near Weston Green a fox left the earth just as I arrived. I hid up in the wood for an hour hoping to film him return but he was too wary—or I was too smelly.

The artificial earths seemed to have a life cycle. They would be built and retained. Some would be removed, some moved, some smashed up. We put the latter down to terriermen breaking the structure up to extract a fox on a hunting day.

On Thursday June 20th I met Mike Michalak again and we checked Over Wood for artificial earths. The artificial earth there, first found in January 1992, was found to have been broken up.

Friday July 5th 1996 put to the test my resolve to only ever behave lawfully. I had set out to undertake more investigative fieldwork in Thurlow Foxhounds country. As I passed through Dullingham I saw a cluster of people watching smoke rising from a house.

I stopped and asked about the situation. I was told a fire in a shed had spread to a house and that a passing lorry driver had already called the fire brigade. I asked if the residents of the house were in the watching crowd; they were not. I asked where the residents were and no-one seemed sure.

We could see smoke and flames starting to billow out of the roof. I banged on the front door. There was no answer. I tried the door and it was unsurprisingly locked. I asked those watching if they were sure there was no-one in the house. No one knew.

I said that I had to be sure. I went and karate kicked the front door open. I called and shouted and checked all ground floor rooms and there was no-one. I likewise checked the upstairs rooms, which had started to fill with smoke and again there was no-one.

There might have been a grandma asleep in her chair. There might have been a pet cat or dog or even a budgie in a cage. I could not leave any creature in a house that might soon turn into an inferno. When the fire brigade arrived, I lingered to take film and photographs.

I had in mind that I had very publicly smashed in a fancy front door. I had already served two jail sentences for causing less criminal damage than that. I had no idea but what if the owner turned out to be a prominent hunt supporter? Would I be accused of causing the damage deliberately? Would I be accused of stealing documents from the house?

I gave my name and address to the firemen, showed them my car and invited them to note the registration number. I told them they could give my details to the homeowner so if he wanted to take up the matter of my wrecking his front door I would be happy to explain. I heard no more.

Friday October 4th, I checked the artificial earth near the Harcamlow Way that had become a badger sett and found the entrances stopped with tightly packed straw.

Early the following month we confirmed the location of one of the most significant artificial earths. The article in *Hounds* magazine three years previously about 'Porter's Parlour' in Blencathra Foxhounds country near Millbeck stuck in my mind. On Saturday November 2nd 1996 after undercover monitoring of the Ullswater Foxhounds with Elaine Milbourn we looked for 'Porter's Parlour', the "*largest man-made borran ever known*." Guided by the description generously provided by our opponents we found what we took to be one entrance to the huge complex before the light failed. The following morning, we returned to the area and met Paul Tillsley who worked undercover amongst the Fell packs.

The three of us then searched for more of this celebrated fox production site. The weather was hostile with pouring rain (not uncommon there!) but we found one brick built chamber and four entrance holes to the complex. A lot of time and money had clearly been invested in producing foxes for the Blencathra Foxhounds to hunt.

*****

We received a steady stream of tip-offs alleging hunts were holding foxes for hunting. Some were genuine, some hoaxes, some may have been genuine but circumstances changed. Each had to be investigated. On the night of January 31st/February 1st 1997 Lawrie Payne and I checked one such report in country hunted by the Heythrop Foxhounds. Several hours of patient probing and surveillance forced us to conclude there were no foxes on the site at the time of our visit, but they may have been held there before. We still had much to learn about fox hunting. It took technological advances in equipment before we made further progress.

Some artificial earths were carefully constructed to make fine, appealing, homes for foxes. Some in Thurlow Foxhounds country were homes with style. On Monday April 14th 1997 Mike Michalak phoned me with the location of an artificial earth he had found the previous day. On Wednesday April 16th, I visited the site in Hollybud Wood near Denston. Artificial earth number 29 was a work of remarkable beauty; the entrances had been landscaped to blend in with the countryside. As with all hunting though it was only a glamorous façade—it had been built for foxes to breed in to be killed for fun.

At the end of the month I returned to Cumbria. I met Elaine Milbourn near Keswick on Saturday April 26th and we paid a return visit to 'Porter's Parlour'. With more time, and better weather, we located more entrances. We measured distances between entrances and drew up a rough map of the area. It was truly an extensive fox-production facility.

The following day Elaine and I looked for more artificial earths and also death pits. We found a death pit on Priests Crag near Watermillock in Ullswater Foxhounds country. When sheep and lambs died from neglect up on the open Fells their bodies were usually just thrown into these open pits. The expectation was that foxes and other scavengers would dispose of the bodies and they did. With man-made homes to live and breed in and a good supply of carrion to gorge on the Lakeland foxes thrived.

As part of our efforts to interest the media in our investigative work exposing artificial earths, on Monday June 30th, I met Roger Cork from the television programme *World in Action*. I showed him one of the artificial earths in Thurlow country.

Wednesday July 9th 1997—the day before the Countryside Rally in Hyde Park—proved significant when I found artificial earth number 31 in

Thurlow Foxhounds country. It was beside a pond in Ditton Park Wood, near Ditton Green. Sheep grazed just a few fields from the wood. Unbeknown to me then that would be the last artificial earth we would find in Thurlow country. There may be many more but we know of 31 sites.

We also found 16 stick or log piles in country hunted by the Thurlow Foxhounds, the last being found on May 14th 1997. In addition, we recorded 7 sites where hunt supporters had left out food for foxes. Given that the Thurlow Foxhounds hunted over one of the smallest hunt countries in the UK this amounted to some of the most intensive efforts at fox encouragement.

It seemed likely that the Thurlow Foxhounds put more foxes into the countryside than they took out by killing. That is not to say in any way that they were beneficial to foxes—the foxes bred in artificial earths and fed by man were far from wild and often far from healthy.

We carried on checking Thurlow sites but also looked for artificial earths in other hunt countries. We encountered some truly unpleasant sights; an example of which being what we discovered on Saturday July 26th 1997 when I met Lawrie Payne and we undertook investigative work in country hunted by the Essex and Suffolk Foxhounds. In one wood, we found a pheasant release pen with numerous rotting fox carcases nailed to a nearby tree. Over the years I found so many dead animals dumped or displayed in our countryside that I became very sensitive to the sweet smell of death and decay.

Many woods were akin to butcher's shops. That was the truth behind the glamorous façade—it was a far cry from the 'chocolate box' image of hunting and shooting.

There was more media interest in the sterling efforts made by Thurlow Foxhounds supporters to encourage foxes. On Wednesday September 10th, I met Mark Watts, a *Sunday Times* reporter, at Balsham. We chatted and I showed him my map with all the sites known to us marked. I then took him to two artificial earths and one large stick pile.

The following week, on Thursday September 18th, I met Penny Little and Bea Bradley and they guided me to see an artificial earth in Caldwell Copse, near Chalgrove. That was country hunted by the Vale of Aylesbury Foxhounds. I went on to talk about the anti-vivisection work conducted by the ACIG at a packed public meeting called by the Save the Hillgrove Cats campaign at the Corn Exchange, Witney.

Investigative work on Sunday November 30th produced a useful result. I had gone to Thorpe Wood in Suffolk Foxhounds country looking for any signs of fox feeding at the artificial earth there. I found no food dumped but did find a newly built artificial earth nearby. On closer inspection of the area it looked as if hunt supporters had dug out an old poorly sited artificial earth and moved it to a new more favourable location. One of the standard defences deployed by hunt supporters, when the issue of artificial earths was raised, was that they were all old and built decades before. That was one built very recently indeed.

Sunday December 7th marked a reversal of roles when I met Mike and Ingrid Michalak at Rattlesden Airfield and showed them that brand new artificial earth in nearby Thorpe Wood. Usually they were meeting me to guide me to earths they had found.

*****

For 1998 the focus of my investigative work searching for artificial earths switched to the Quorn Foxhounds. I felt our job was done in Thurlow hunt country. It made little difference whether the 31 artificial earths already found there grew to 35 or 39. The Thurlow was only a small hunt easily dismissed by the media. The Quorn, for all that their reputation had taken a battering in the early 1990s, was still a major hunt.

Before looking in Leicestershire in early March 1998 I drove west to meet erstwhile BUAV colleagues Margaret Manzoni and Paddy Broughton in Powys. On Thursday March 5th Margaret guided me to an area where the local Fox Destruction Society had enjoyed a day's fun some weeks previous. I looked without success for artificial earths or anything similar but did find a dead fox dumped by a disused badger sett.

My work in Quorn hunt country got underway on Saturday May 2nd. I drove to the site of the known artificial earth near Ulverscroft. There were no signs of any more activity there since my previous visit. As the area smelled of fox I hid up and kept the site under observation for some 2½ hours hoping to film a fox visiting.

I saw no fox but witnessed natural life and death when a weasel caught a mouse. I then checked for artificial earths in a well-known Quorn covert, Thorpe Trussels, near Thorpe Satchville. It is a 13-acre wood owned by the Quorn in their Friday country. At an entrance path is a memorial plaque on a stone proclaiming: "*In memory of the late Lt. Col. Bouskell-Wade of Beeby Manor who left this covert to the Quorn Hunt July 1973.*"

Battling through dense entangled undergrowth my nose was assailed by a foul smell. There was something nasty in the wood. I followed the fumes and found the carcasses of two dead adult sheep. There was no artificial earth but the meat was clearly left there by hunt supporters to attract and feed foxes. I returned to check the same area on Tuesday May 12th. Some woodland clearance had been carried out in the foul-smelling covert. The sheep carcasses were as putrid as expected after ten more days of rotting.

At the end of the month, Saturday May 30th, I checked Thorpe Trussels again. The sheep had rotted further. I went on to check another well-known Quorn wood—Cream Gorse Covert. As usual with such investigative work I parked near a footpath sign some distance away and walked down the road to the site. I climbed a gate and walked along a track into the wood. I was intrigued to hear sounds of construction work, digging and chopping. I crept nearer but feared that if the men had any terriers with them I could be caught and that would end any further work in that area. I backed off, left the scene, and planned another visit.

I returned to Leicestershire on Wednesday June 3rd. First I checked a site between Garthorpe and Stonesby where fox rearing had been reported nearly 30 years before. The named building had been demolished. I then returned to check Cream Gorse Covert and found what had been constructed the previous Saturday.

An area of woodland had been carefully cleared. In the clearing was a newly installed, but strange, artificial earth. There was no central chamber. It was just pipework in the shape of a rectangle with one long side removed. Because there was no chamber it was not built for foxes to live and breed in. It was more of a temporary shelter for foxes. It looked to be the site that a terrierman might check on a hunting day and if there was a fox within hold it there in case it was required by the hunt.

When I returned three days later, on Saturday June 6th, to better record the site I had one of those, thankfully rare, awkward experiences. At the time, I was driving some 50,000 miles a year for ACIG and AWIS work. I expected the occasional car breakdown. What was unfortunate was that the radiator on my Volvo burst when I was close to Cream Gorse Covert. I had to coast as far away as possible then call the RAC. After a long wait, I was recovered and returned home.

Later that month my investigative work switched again, to the country hunted by the Sinnington Foxhounds. Here it is necessary to explain some context. By 1998 the world of hunting knew that anti-hunt investigators were highly professional and very discreet. Hunt informants knew they could pass information to us without us running to the media to reveal story and source. We heard a lot. We were told about feuding within hunts and between hunts. We were told the real reasons why some Masters and Huntsmen suddenly left their positions.

It all built a picture of corrupt regimes built on callousness and selfishness. The sexual tittle-tattle was interesting but it was reports of mistreatment of wildlife that motivated us to action. A familiar sequence developed. A keen supporter would witness something untoward within their hunt. They would complain to the Hunt Secretary who denied it happened or laughed it off. When it continued, or happened again the supporter would complain to higher hunting authorities. They would then be told to shut up—or face an action for libel or slander. At that point many sadly walked away but some took it further and contacted our side.

Early in 1998 we heard reports of events involving fox cubs in Sinnington Foxhounds country in North Yorkshire. It was Sunday April 5th 1998 when I drove north and met colleagues Tommy and Debbie Woodward. We then met our hunting informant 'Y' at Pickering.

'Y' carefully explained that the Sinnington Foxhounds were making extensive use of artificial earths and had even reared cubs confined in one the previous season. The cubs' home was an artificial earth with a cage structure built on. They were then provided with food and water before being released into the covert for hunting at a later date. We were told the cubs were orphans supplied to the hunt by gamekeepers.

It seemed a significant step beyond the usual usage of artificial earths by hunt supporters. Most hunters build nice cosy well-sited artificial earths in the hope that local foxes will naturally take up residence. The

315

Sinnington case was an example of taking it one stage further and putting the cubs there—and keeping them there.

We accepted that sometimes well-meaning gamekeepers or 'pest controllers' were keen to give orphan cubs a chance. 'Pest controllers' called in by urban householders to deal with foxes judged to be troublesome might capture cubs (or adult foxes) alive and say to the householder something like: "*Shall I kill the cubs or release them?*" Many householders only wanted to see the foxes gone, not killed, so could be happy for them to be released. Hunts could acquire foxes in many ways.

'Y' took us to see the covert in question–Muscoates Whin; pointed out its close proximity to the hunt kennels; showed us his photographs of the site taken the previous season and told us about other sites. We asked 'Y' to let us know if there was any similar activity in 1998.

On Friday June 19th 'Y' reported that cubs had been introduced into the caged artificial earth and were being fed. Tommy Woodward, being local, dealt with the initial surveillance, and called on help from colleagues Chris Owen and Janet Smart. Two days later, Sunday June 21st, Tommy spent the whole day from 6am to 10pm in a concealed surveillance position at the site but saw nothing. No cubs and no sign of anyone tending them.

The next day I visited the LACS offices in London. We weighed up the possible scenarios at the Sinnington earth. Whoever fed the cubs might not visit them every day. He might only visit two or three times a week. He could visit at any time from dawn to dusk—which at that time of year was a long day. [Later, when we had motion-triggered stick cameras, such a surveillance operation would have been easier, but in 1998 we had to hide up. We had to be close enough to film events through the thick undergrowth but not close enough to be seen or heard by the terrierman, or more likely, by any terrier he might have. It was not an easy call.]

We opted to proceed stage by stage. The first was to prove there were foxes in the earth. I left London on the evening of Monday June 22nd and was in North Yorkshire for 2am the following morning. I was then up at 6am the following morning and Debbie dropped Tommy and me off near Muscoates Whin (so we did not have to leave a car nearby that might draw attention). There was rain to start with. We were prepared for another lengthy surveillance.

We found a freshly dead lamb dumped near the earth and a freshly dead Rhode Island Red hen inserted up one of the pipe entrances to the earth. Had we just missed the terrierman visiting?

As we pulled the dead hen out from one end of the earth to photograph it a cub exited into the cage at the other end. The cub looked in a shocking state, wet and bedraggled. Our plans changed. We are animal welfare campaigners. We cannot leave any animal suffering in a pitiful state simply to get better film.

We searched out the central chamber to ascertain the state inside. After some difficult clearing away of mud we lifted the lid and were confronted with a foul smelling muddy pit. Artificial earths are supposed to be warm and dry; this one was anything but. We realised there was a second cub in the earth and both were in similarly poor condition.

I filmed and photographed both cubs. We knew we had to get them out quickly to have them properly cared for. In late morning I called the LACS office and then the RSPCA. The wood was privately owned by the Sinnington Foxhounds. The RSPCA could not simply march up and release the cubs, they could only do so after liaison with the hunt.

Two cubs were retrieved from the earth, given veterinary treatment and later released in an area where there was no hunting. My video film was released to the media and shown widely. It rightly caused widespread outrage. Given that the main justification given for fox hunting was the need to reduce the fox population why nurture, feed and water fox cubs? When the main threat from foxes is supposed to be to lambs and chickens why feed fox cubs destined for release lamb and chicken?

[In the past some hunters were open about their movement of foxes, or their caring for 'rescued' foxes. Back in 1960 the *Sunday Express* carried the following report:

"Earl saves cubs-then frees them to be hunted
Sunday Express Reporter
The sixth Earl of Yarborough, joint master of the Brocklesby Hunt, sat in his red and white library at Brocklesby Hall, near Grimsby, and spoke to me of the fox cubs the hunt has cared for and set free. The 67-year-old earl said: "I agree they will be hunted later in the season. But not until they are big boys. We will steer the pack away from them until late in the season. We saved these cubs. There were ten of them. The vixens had been poisoned and rather than let the cubs starve they were dug up just over the boundaries of the hunting area and brought here. We have not imported foxes merely to hunt them. That would be terrible-just like cheating at cards. Some of them were too young to be released right away. They were weaned by my men. When they are hunted they will have a chance-which is more than they had before we rescued them. All we have done is perfectly humane."
The hunt, which meets twice weekly, was called off six weeks before the end of last season because of a mysterious epidemic which cut down the fox population.
Lord Yarborough, a Deputy-Lieutenant of Lincolnshire and a magistrate-his family motto is "The love of country prevails"-went on:-
"Naturally we hope to see some foxes about this season, but I can assure you these foxes were not imported just to be hunted."
'I am keen'
"Of course I am keen on hunting. I have been keen on the sport all my life. I cannot do so much of it now. I am getting older, you know. The spirit is willing but the flesh is weak."
The cubs were brought to Brocklesby by Lord Yarborough's gamekeeper, Mr. Edgar Lidgett and huntsman Mr. Ronald Harvey.
Forty-six-year-old Mr. Lidgett, who lives in the village of Great Limber said: "We brought them over in the spring. They have all been released

now in the woods but we still put the food out for them-chickens and rabbits and things. I suppose this is a bit unusual, especially as they will be killed in the hunt. But they will provide some good sport for his lordship."

'Better chance'

The hunt's joint secretary Mr. Bertie Garner, said: "I don't know anything at all about this. I have not heard of it."

A previous secretary, farmer Mr. James Davey, said: "It is one of those things we don't talk about-or we will have the R.S.P.C.A. and all down on us."

Said the joint master of the hunt, Mr. Mark Patrick: "These cubs stand a much better chance than if they had been left to starve."

An R.S.P.C.A. spokesman said: "We feel strongly that fox cubs should NOT be weaned purely to be hunted.""

The *Sunday Express*. London. August 21st 1960. [The 6th Earl of Yarborough was Master of the Brocklesby from 1948-66. J.E.M. Patrick was Master from 1954-62]]

It is clear hunters acquired foxes from a variety of sources. The Wolverhampton *Express & Star*, July 29th 1983, carried a report of a row over allegations of the Albrighton Woodland Foxhounds 'importing' foxes from nearby towns including Birmingham, for hunting. Mr Churton Pauli, Master of the Albrighton Woodland Hunt denied that his members specifically took foxes out of towns for hunting purposes:

"We occasionally get calls from people on building sites or from their homes saying they have foxes scavenging around and don't know what to do with them…. We have released some into the country, but there are plenty of foxes around, and we would not go into towns looking for them."

Some years after finding the cubs I again checked the Sinnington site at Muscoates Whin with League colleagues. It was on Friday April 5th 2002. We could find no sign of the site where the cubs had been held. It was either destroyed or buried under cut branches. We did find and record the remains of the second artificial earth in the wood. We also found the carcase of a dead deer dumped at one corner of the wood.

The Sinnington story proved the extent of media interest in debunking hunters' myths. On Sunday July 5th 1998, I returned to check Thorpe Wood in Suffolk Foxhounds country. There was no change in the re-sited artificial earth but another brand new artificial earth had been built about 50m to the west of the original, on the other side of a small track. The area smelled strongly of fox. It was the height of summer and a full water butt had been helpfully provided by hunt supporters who nurtured foxes in that wood.

I found more evidence of the great care that hunt supporters take over their constructions on Saturday August 1st when I returned to Cream Gorse Covert. Some tree stumps had been laid over one entrance, perhaps to make it look more 'natural'. I then checked Thorpe Trussels covert (last

318

visited on May 30th) and found the remains of a third dead sheep dumped in the wood. I judged it to have been there at least a month.

Saturday August 15th 1998 was another memorable day in terms of investigative work in Quorn Foxhounds country. I first checked the pipe construction in Cream Gorse Covert. There was no change since my previous visit. I drove on to check the well-known Quorn covert at Gartree Hill. There was the ominous odour of death when I first entered the covert. I combed patiently through the undergrowth and found one source for that smell at the edge of the wood—a freshly dead sheep. The blood was red on the torn carcase and ribs exposed.

I walked further along the tracks in the covert looking for any artificial earths. Along one path I found an empty cardboard box. I walked on and found another. It seemed like casual littering. I then found more empty boxes, similar in type. It was not until I found a freshly dumped box that still had its contents that I realized what purpose they served. That box contained bacon rinds. It was yet another type of foodstuff dumped in the wood by hunt supporters to attract foxes.

At the end of the month, Monday August 31st I returned to Thurlow Foxhounds country to check known sites. The artificial earth by the Harcamlow Way that had become a badger sett showed evidence of very recent badger activity, scratching on nearby trees, badger latrine etc.

The following month, Saturday September 12th, I returned to Quorn hunt country. I checked the site in Cream Gorse Covert and found evidence of disturbance around both pipe entrances since my previous visit. I then visited a local landowner who recounted the many problems that she had experienced with the Quorn Foxhounds. On my drive home my Volvo 440 broke down yet again. I had another recovery experience from the RAC, that time with alternator failure. Long range investigative work was punishing on vehicle and man.

I made another long trip on Saturday December 12th when I drove to meet Wendy, a field investigator near Port Talbot. She took me to see the site of a large cage trap for catching foxes alive. It was in an area used by game shooting enthusiasts. A fox had previously been found there and released by activists. There was no fox in the trap when I visited.

Our suspicion was that some gamekeepers, instead of killing foxes, caught them alive and passed them to their friends in the fox hunting world. It explained the Sinnington cubs and would certainly explain some of the reports we received from hunt monitors and hunt saboteurs of disorientated foxes being hunted.

*****

On Saturday January 2nd 1999 I checked the site in Cream Gorse Covert again but found no change since my previous visit. I called in and found Janet Jackson at home. Besotted with Jim Barrington she had followed him when he left the LACS and supported his new venture, Wildlife Network, financially to the tune of hundreds of thousands of pounds. When her money ran out he moved ever closer to the hunting fraternity. We had a 1½ hour chat and I left feeling truly sorry for her; she had never lessened her opposition to the cruelty of hunting.

The following month, Saturday February 6th, I did investigative fieldwork with Central Television. I met one of our deep undercover operatives in Wootton Wawen Warwickshire, country hunted by the Croome and West Warwickshire Foxhounds. We then met reporter Pam Thompson and a film crew from Central TV. We maintained discreet observation on the hunt terriermen then left to look for an artificial earth in nearby Peopleton Rough. We found one that we judged to be old. I later spent a lot of time with LACS colleagues searching for more artificial earths in that locality.

We reacted to reports from colleagues up and down the country. Saturday March 20th was another lengthy trip. I met Graham Sirl and Jill Nield at Durrington, Wiltshire at noon. We met Carol, a local investigator, who guided us to find an artificial earth in Jugg's Wood, south of Froxfield, that was hunted by the Tedworth Foxhounds.

I returned to Quorn country on Saturday May 1st and met a supporter interested in the investigative side of our work. We checked some of the known sites. In Cream Gorse Covert there was no change in the pipe construction. There was likewise no change at Thorpe Trussels but we made a significant find at Gartree Hill Covert.

We found two freshly dumped dead lambs left there by hunt supporters to feed the foxes. I estimated that one, found by the gate, had been left there only that morning as there were fresh tyre tracks nearby. Plus, there was still blood trickling from the eye socket of the lamb. For my colleague it was a swift introduction to the unpleasant sights investigators could uncover in woods 'cared for' by hunt supporters.

I kept in mind the need to check the artificial earths in Thurlow country. Saturday June 5th I visited Trundley Wood where I knew there were at least two artificial earths, one stick pile, one fox feeding site and three pheasant release pens. The wood had been put forward by the Thurlow Foxhounds to the MFHA Conservation Award scheme.

My visit proved interesting. There had been extensive renovation work undertaken on one of the old artificial earths. One entrance had been replaced with a brand new entrance of concrete pipe. The central chamber had been dug out, renovated and replaced. Hunt supporters had gone to great effort and expense to make the site welcoming for foxes. Their efforts were rewarded. On a nearby ride I saw and filmed a vixen and her cubs playing in the summer sunshine. They were the picture of innocence.

Later that month, Wednesday June 16th, I had the pleasure of undertaking fieldwork with my great colleagues, Kevin Hill and Peter White, who at that time were working for IFAW. We met at Tetbury for investigative work looking for artificial earths in country hunted by the Duke of Beaufort's Foxhounds. A local informer guided us to the site I had previously seen with Jim Barrington on June 12th 1995. Kevin, Peter and I then found another artificial earth in the site of an old quarry near Westonbirt.

Three days later, Saturday June 19th, I was back in Thurlow country. I checked artificial earth number 19, located in Black Grove Plantation and found there had been recent disturbance to the central chamber. Nearby was a gamekeeper's gibbet line decorated with bodies of dead squirrels and weasels.

Back in the same hunt country on Wednesday July 21st I visited the wood by the Harcamlow Way where an artificial earth had become a badger sett. I found that logging work had obscured one of the entrances to the earth/sett. The badger sett had been all but destroyed and was then inactive.

Friday August 13th 1999 proved highly informative. I saw a demonstration of newly developed hidden video equipment that would change the nature of our investigative work to protect our countryside. I met Kevin Hill and Peter White at Tetbury soon after midday. We then met technical expert, Martin. I was taken to see an old artificial earth in Allen Grove, then a new one in Alderton Grove and a fox feeding site at the latter. Martin then demonstrated how covert surveillance video recording might enable us to prove who tended these sites. The equipment he demonstrated came with a hefty price tag—£4,000—but the film it could secure would be priceless.

Saturday August 21st I returned to Quorn country. There was no change in Thorpe Trussels wood. At Cream Gorse Covert it was clear that there had been some cutting back of the brush around the pipe construction.

I periodically checked known sites during the autumn of 1999 but there were no changes observed. The new millennium was to bring more changes at the LACS staff. The excellent Paul Tillsley started working for the League in January. Having done undercover work amongst the Fell packs in the mid-1990s he knew all about the intricacies of hunting.

Late in the year Ben Stewart left and continued his dedicated work elsewhere. He was replaced by Andrew Wasley, a young man with a proven record both of caring for animals and putting himself in harm's way to achieve results. At that time, I was usually called in to give an illustrated talk to new staff members outlining the history of successful campaigning by the LACS. I gave such a talk to new League recruits on Wednesday November 1st.

Andrew Wasley worked full time for the League investigations unit. Others worked as required as well—people such as Jim Wickens, Rob Hughes, Terry Hill and Rachel White. Together they made a great team. They will hereafter be mainly referred to as the LACS team.

Douglas Batchelor not only assembled an excellent investigations squad at the LACS, he also ensured that they were properly equipped with the latest surveillance camera systems. Douglas unleashed his investigative unit upon the countryside with the brief to prove how integral and widespread artificial earths were to fox hunting. The goal was to shatter the myth that fox hunting had anything to do with fox control and everything to do with encouraging foxes for hunting.

Other campaigning groups took on similar work. An example was Sunday July 2nd 2000 when I met Kevin Hill and Peter White from the IFAW investigative team in Thurlow Foxhounds country to check anonymous reports of fox cubs being held for hunting. We combed the location named. Though we found no sign of anything untoward I was delighted to see animal welfare groups cooperating.

Sunday August 6th I made a routine check of sites in Thurlow Foxhounds country and found the remains of what I took to be a long-dead sheep dumped just a few feet from the central chamber of artificial earth number 31 in Ditton Park Wood. When I checked the site more closely later that month, on August 17th, I found what I took to be deer hairs in the remains.

I checked the Quorn sites again on Sunday September 10th 2000. I found the remains of another sheep, that looked to be a few months old, dumped for the foxes in Gartree Hill Covert.

Technological advances allowed new filming opportunities. With early video cameras to film in poor light you needed to attach a video light. That was bulky and made filming up the pipe of an artificial earth difficult. The development of the 'nightshot' facility on domestic video cameras allowed filming in darkness. The result may have been a ghostly black and white but was nevertheless very useful.

*****

Sunday January 21st 2001 found me back looking at known sites in Thurlow Foxhounds country. There was snow on the ground. Artificial earth number 31 in Ditton Park Wood smelled strongly of fox, as did artificial earth number 3 in Balsham Wood. At both sites, I filmed using the 'nightshot' system on my new Sony video camera.

Curiously, when I returned to the Ditton Park Wood earth the following Wednesday, January 24th, there was no smell of fox around the earth. The next day I had lengthy discussions with Andrew Wasley about a variety of investigative projects.

I called in at the LACS offices on Wednesday January 31st and helped colleagues with setting up and operating the new surveillance camera system for use in the fields. When I checked the artificial earth in Ditton Park Wood on Sunday February 18th I met a group of ramblers enjoying a walk through the wood. It was owned by the Forestry Commission England and seemed a strange choice of location for an artificial earth.

With the suspension of hunting on February 22nd due to foot and mouth disease the countryside virtually closed for investigative field work. In time restrictions eased and some footpaths were opened, provided that precautionary measures were followed. When I checked the Thurlow country on Wednesday May 9th I found some footpaths open, some shut and some could be used with caution.

On Wednesday July 4th, I had a meeting at the LACS offices with Mike Hobday and Andrew Wasley regarding investigative projects that could be undertaken as the countryside opened up after foot and mouth restrictions eased. Next weekend, Saturday July 7th, I checked the artificial earth site in Peopleton Rough in Croome country and found some evidence of feeding of the foxes nearby.

Friday July 13th 2001 marked the start of detailed investigations by the ACIG and the LACS into artificial earths in the country hunted by the Croome and West Warwickshire Foxhounds. I met one of the LACS investigations team at Worcester Shrub Hill Station soon after noon and we checked accessible sites.

The following month, on Friday August 10th, I returned to Thurlow country and checked the artificial earth in Ditton Park Wood. I found the skull of a recently killed fox cub in one entrance to the earth.

Saturday September 5th I collected one of the LACS investigations team from Diss station and took him to see the artificial earths in Thorpe Wood, in Suffolk Foxhounds country. We found the usual two and then found that the old third one had been re-furbished. Having three artificial earths in a single wood was some record and marked a major effort by hunt supporters to encourage foxes there.

I joined up again with the LACS team on Wednesday September 12th. We met at Banbury rail station and checked an artificial earth site in Croome country. There had been some tinkering with it since our previous visit. We then stayed at *The White Lion*, Cricklade. We paid in full the night before and told the owner we would leave very early the next morning. When we tried to leave at 5am doors were locked and we had to leave via the fire escape!

We went to the kennels of the Vale of White Horse (VWH) Foxhounds near Cirencester to see if there was any activity. They were only walking their hounds. We went on to check the site of a known artificial earth in a wood by Hinton Parva that is in the adjacent Old Berkshire Foxhounds country. It was a curious site because the central chamber showed three tunnels leading away but we could only find two tunnel exits. The site was less than 100 metres from a pheasant release pen.

I collected my LACS colleague again from Diss station on Friday September 28th and we drove north. We checked the strange artificial earth construction in Cream Gorse Covert in Quorn country and then recorded an artificial earth in neighbouring Fernie Foxhounds country at Gilmorton.

I undertook local investigative work on my own on Wednesday October 24th 2001. Hunt saboteurs had told me about artificial earths in country hunted by the West Norfolk Foxhounds. I searched for one beneath thick undergrowth in a wood near Litcham. I found it by accident when I fell into a pit beside the chamber. I drove on to record another artificial earth in Little Wood near Horningtoft. It also was near a pheasant release pen, just some 50 metres away. It confirmed again what we had been told— that the man who cared for the pheasants (to be shot) usually cared for the foxes (to be hunted).

I had the honour and privilege to work with some of the best investigators. An example was on Saturday November 24th when I drove to Henley-in-Arden station to meet my LACS colleague. We then met IFAW colleagues Kevin Hill and Peter White and together we checked known sites in Croome country. It was my ACIG, LACS and IFAW working together for animals. Both sites checked showed evidence of disturbance since our previous visit.

Wednesday November 28th was significant. I called in at the LACS offices. We had experienced problems with the remote surveillance system camera but after paying nearly £120 to have a lead repaired we could set it up so it worked. Soon it would be put to good use.

We were starting to focus on finding artificial earths in the country of two hunts—the Croome and West Warwickshire and the Heythrop. On Wednesday December 5th, I met my LACS colleague at Banbury station and we searched accessible areas in Croome country. The following day we checked the artificial earth in Heythrop country, in the small copse, Zareba, near Sezincote that I had known about since 1982. Not only was it still there but it had recent modifications and additions. It was clearly a site where hunt supporters were doing their utmost to encourage foxes.

I returned to Thurlow country on Thursday December 13th. When I checked the artificial earth in Ditton Park Wood I found it smelled strongly of fox. The artificial earths were doing their job.

Saturday December 15th 2001 was a notable day for our investigative work. After meeting my LACS colleague at Banbury station we searched for a known old artificial earth in a small copse near Chipping Norton in Heythrop country. The Heythrop Foxhounds always met in Chipping Norton on Boxing Day—so they needed a good supply of foxes for such an important day. [David Cameron rode with the Heythrop Foxhounds and attended their 2004 Boxing Day meet in Chipping Norton.]

We found part of the earth and two freshly dead calves dumped nearby as food for the foxes. They were fresh because the blood was still red on the carcasses. After previously finding chickens, lambs, sheep and even bacon rinds dumped by hunt supporters elsewhere as food for foxes, finding calves was something new.

We then collected two more colleagues from the LACS team and stayed nearby. In the morning, we checked an artificial earth site in Croome country and found more disturbance since our previous visit. When we checked the copse near Chipping Norton with the dumped calves a colleague found the entrances to the artificial earth. As mentioned I maintained surveillance on this site on Boxing Day 2001. On the last day of the year, Monday December 31st, I met LACS colleagues at Banbury Station. We checked several artificial earths in Heythrop and Croome countries. It was bitterly cold with snow on the ground.

*****

Friday January 4th 2002 I met the LACS team in Stratford. The following morning there was a hard frost. We split our forces. Three went searching for artificial earths and found an old one in Heythrop country. The fourth went undercover amongst one of the few hunts to go out.

I returned to the Heythrop country on Sunday January 20th. I checked the artificial earth site where the two calves had been dumped nearby and found that one calf had been moved. Their bodies were starting to rot down. Friday January 25th I met a LACS colleague at Banbury station and we went on to check the artificial earth in a tiny copse near Wootton Wawen in Croome country. One of the entrances had been opened since our previous visit. In the evening, we met another colleague in Stratford and stayed the night there.

The next day we divided our forces again. One went undercover with the Heythrop Foxhounds, posing as a supporter. Two of us searched for artificial earths in the Great Rissington to Stow-on-the-Wold areas. It lashed with rain. We and our cameras were soaked and we gave up when we realized it was impossible to film anything.

Monday January 28th was most interesting. I had a meeting at the LACS offices with Mike Hobday, Andrew Wasley and a camera systems manufacturer regarding surveillance video cameras to help our fieldwork. The next day I bought a fully waterproof camera case to protect my variety of cameras. Whereas my old Nikon F2 was all but indestructible, modern cameras were more susceptible to foul weather and needed protection.

We endeavoured to link hunt meets to known artificial earth sites. When the Heythrop Foxhounds met at Sezincote on Saturday February 16th we observed to see if there was interaction with the known artificial earths in the area. Whilst one from the LACS team went with the hunt posing as a supporter another LACS colleague joined me in monitoring the hunt from distance. It was very foggy and we saw little.

The media showed continued interest in our artificial earth work. With a hunting ban high on the political agenda and hunt supporters claiming that fox hunting was needed to protect farmers from foxes, evidence that hunts were actually building and maintaining homes for foxes and feeding and providing water for them destroyed their arguments. For some time I had been talking to the Anglia Television programme, *Cover Story*, about our success finding artificial earths in Thurlow country. On Wednesday March 6th I met reporters Kate Critchell and Jayne Evans at their Norwich studios. I showed them a compilation video of artificial earth sites. They wanted to interview me at an artificial earth site but had concerns over trespass and disturbing any real site. I was asked to build a mock artificial earth in our small paddock. I did so and thereby gained an idea as to what such creations cost. Two flagstones to make the lid of the chamber cost £19.90. The four nine-inch diameter concrete pipes cost £10.68 each. Some earths we had found used many such pipes.

Hunt supporters would clearly buy in bulk and be given considerable discount but it was still a great investment. Furthermore, the artificial earth sites were often in inaccessible areas where the building materials had to be carried through woodland. The areas in the wood had to be cleared. The tunnels and chamber dug out (unless a badger sett was used). Some earths were so substantial that cement was used for the brickwork of the chamber. Others had steel reinforcements.

Friday April 5th 2002 marked the start of a lengthy expedition. I drove north to meet LACS colleagues at York station in the early afternoon.

We checked the sites of artificial earths in country hunted by the Sinnington Foxhounds. The one in Muscoates Whin where the cubs had been held was destroyed and buried. We found some remains of the second artificial earth in the wood and the body of a dead deer dumped in one corner.

After staying overnight in Thirsk, we spent the next day checking the famous Porter's Parlour in Blencathra hunt country. It was hot and sunny—unusual for the Lake District. We looked for another artificial earth, reportedly in a wood near Torpenhow, but could not find it. It was easy for the entrances to such sites to become overgrown plus some hunt builders were experts at disguising the entrances. In the evening, we checked into a holiday cottage in Portinscale near Keswick we had hired for the week.

We spent Sunday April 7th surveying the Porter's Parlour site. It was every bit as large and complex as the hunt supporters had boasted and clearly had provided generations of foxes for the Blencathra hunt. There were at least ten entrances and over 120m of underground pipework.

(The following year, Barry Todhunter, Huntsman of the Blencathra Foxhounds commented about Porter's Parlour in his local *Cumberland and Westmoreland Herald*, February 15th 2003: "..........*the one they make such a fuss about, which is called Porter's Parlour, was built by an old guy in the 1950s and 1960s as a labour of love.*
That has been to our detriment rather than our benefit, because it is very complicated. We have lost more foxes in that place than I can count and I am happy that it was just about destroyed when they were working on forestry in the area." So, a complex artificial earth like Porter's Parlour is not only a breeding ground for foxes but also provided a safe haven for them—so they can run another day in front of hounds.)

That Sunday evening, I returned home leaving my LACS colleagues to continue their valuable work searching for other artificial earths. On Friday April 12th one phoned to report they had found another artificial earth in country hunted by the Blencathra Foxhounds. It was described as recently built. Saturday April 20th 2002 was memorable. I met my LACS colleagues at 2pm at the picturesque Oxenholme railway station in the Lake District. They guided me to see the new artificial earth they had found at Orthwaite Plantation. The approach was eerie and chilling. We saw a lot of sheep, adults and lambs, lying in the field behind the wood. As we approached they never moved. We realized they were dead.

The artificial earth was in the wood behind the Blencathra meet. The entrances were typical—framed with local stone. However, putting cameras into the entrances we found the pipes were not the usual concrete, or stone or glazed pipe but instead modern new corrugated blue field-drain pipework. It proved that artificial earth to be very new. There was a well-stocked death pit outside the wood. We stayed that night at the wonderful Lancrigg Vegetarian Hotel in Grasmere. In the evening, we met Elaine Milbourn and told her of our find. We spent the next two days doing fieldwork in the locality. There was a lot of countryside to cover and it was easy for hunts to conceal their artificial earths. Monday April 22nd brought more success when we found an area where food was dumped for foxes.

Later investigations revealed that Orthwaite Plantation was owned by Jonathan Hope, a prominent supporter of the Blencathra Foxhounds. Early in 2001, just before the countryside was closed by foot and mouth disease, Jonathan Hope had entertained Prince Charles at a meet of the Blencathra Foxhounds at his Orthwaite Hall Farm.

Douglas Batchelor, Chief Executive of the LACS, was swift to highlight the power of the investigation: *"The findings of this investigation blow apart claims that upland fell hunting is concerned with pest control. The breeding and feeding of foxes for hunting is hypocritical and immoral anywhere, but the fact that we've uncovered that it is taking place in upland areas where hunts have repeatedly claimed to be different exposes a grave deception on the part of the pro-hunt lobby in Cumbria."*

Douglas also attacked the practice of leaving dead animals out on the Fells: *"We believe that animal carcasses are being deliberately dumped as food for foxes in Cumbria by people connected to foxhunting. But we also believe that the careless practices of dozens of farmers are contributing to this situation. The shoddy - and often illegal - discarding of carcasses in open pits, in fields and woodland and on mountain crags is tantamount to laying on a fast food meal for foxes and not conducive to keeping fox numbers low."*

Saturday May 11th was the start of another long-haul investigation. I met one of the LACS team at Banbury station. We checked the site of the artificial earth near Chipping Norton where the dead calves had been dumped nearby. All trace of the calves had been removed but the artificial earth remained. We then collected a colleague from Swindon and recorded the artificial earth in Jugg's Wood, in Tedworth country. We stayed in Marlborough. On the Sunday, we recorded the remains of an old and disused artificial earth in woodland at Ampney St. Peter.

The following week, on Thursday May 16th, I met a film crew from Anglia Television in the car park of Tesco's at Bury St. Edmunds. I guided them to near the artificial earths in Thorpe Wood, in Suffolk Foxhounds country. I was interviewed on a footpath in the wood by a reporter named David. I then took the film crew to my home to show them the mock artificial earth in our paddock. I lifted the chamber lid to demonstrate how the construction was put together.

We constantly received tip-offs from a variety of sources. On Friday May 31st I drove with a LACS colleague to check the site of a known artificial earth in country hunted by the Cottesmore Foxhounds. It was in a wood opposite the kennels near Ashwell prison. It made a welcome change for me to be near a prison and not in it. The artificial earth we were directed to was very derelict. Many bones scattered about the vicinity indicated there had been feeding of the foxes there in the past. Searching elsewhere we found evidence of a second artificial earth that had been removed and destroyed.

We went on to check the covert at Gartree Hill. We found no evidence of any further feeding of the foxes there and the rides through the wood were overgrown.

Channel 4 news broadcast a report about our investigation into artificial earths in Cumbria on Wednesday June 5th. A week later, on June 12th, Anglia TV's *Cover Story* broadcast a report on my artificial earth investigation involving East Anglian hunts. The nation was learning the real nature of fox hunting.

We looked to spread our artificial earth investigations further. On Wednesday June 19th, I drove to Cardiff to meet Mike Hobday, Ralph Cook and one of the LACS investigative team (Ralph was National Secretary of the Hunt Saboteurs Association from 1984 to 1989 and founded the Wales Alliance Against Cruel Sports in 1999). The following day I looked for an old artificial earth in Curre Foxhounds country. It was largely destroyed—I found only the remains of a covered chamber.

Tuesday July 16th, I met a LACS colleague at Banbury station. We checked woods in Grafton Foxhounds country but found nothing of significance. The following day we returned to an old artificial earth in country hunted by the Worcestershire Foxhounds found some years previous by hunt saboteurs. It was still operational.

The following month I embarked upon an artificial earth finding expedition, reacting to information received from hunt monitors and hunt saboteurs. Saturday August 10th marked the start. I drove to Fernie Foxhounds country in Leicestershire and recorded an artificial earth in the quaintly named Dingley Dell. I then drove west and stayed in Wrexham.

The following morning, I photographed an artificial earth in Big Wood, Cefn Parc near Wrexham. That was country hunted previously by the Sir Watkins Williams-Wynn Foxhounds. The next day I searched Flint and Denbigh Foxhounds country. I eventually found a typical artificial earth under a dense mat of brambles in a copse beside a river near St. Asaph. There was a freshly dead adult sheep dumped nearby in the wood.

I returned to stay in Wrexham and the following day found a large artificial earth complex in Nevill's Wood on the Cholmondeley Estate near Wrexham. We were told that Prince Charles always hunted that estate when riding with the Cheshire Foxhounds. The artificial earth was in two parts and in good condition. One chamber had three typical entrances and an additional short entrance. A second artificial earth nearby had a large chamber with two normal entrances and again an extra short entry pipe. There was a badger in residence in the artificial earth as I learned when he looked back at me as I used the 'nightshot' facility to film up the pipe. The finding of artificial earths in Welsh sheep farming areas was significant.

Douglas Batchelor, Chief Executive of the LACS was again incisive, commenting: "*Claims by hunters that hunting should remain in Welsh sheep farming areas because it is essential for pest control are utterly contemptible. Yet again we have undeniable proof that hunters have put an extensive breeding program into place - with the sole aim of subjecting wildlife to an agonising death. The public should not be fooled by claims that hunters have farmers' interests at heart. Barbaric sport is their only concern.*"

During that expedition I learned the value of a hand-held Global Positioning System (GPS) device to give your exact location. It was all very well being given the grid reference of an artificial earth by someone using such a device but in a large wood it was hard to find that grid reference location by map-reading and sight only. Later that month, Tuesday August 20th, I bought a GPS from Maplins.

The Countryside Rallies and Marches were excellent opportunities for field investigators to check sites otherwise hard to access. All the hunt supporters, their friends, aunts and uncles were press-ganged into making up the numbers elsewhere. We, the compassionate side, had our countryside to ourselves. On Sunday September 22nd 2002, whilst Countryside Marchers plodded along the streets of London, I checked the artificial earths in Trundley Wood in Thurlow country. The artificial earth in the corner of the wood had been moved and re-sited. Along the way, I stopped off to photograph a well-attended horse show and gymkhana at Burgate—proof that many equine enthusiasts did not support hunting.

Sunday November 3rd I met my two LACS colleagues at Banbury station soon after noon. We carried out investigative work in Heythrop country. We checked the artificial earth and calf dumping site near Chipping Norton, then the artificial earth near Sezincote. The next morning, we visited the artificial earth near Wootton Wawen in Croome country. There was no noticeable change from our previous visit.

We started to make use of our new concealed video equipment. December 1st marked the start. I collected a couple of LACS colleagues from Diss station and we worked at my home on setting up the newly purchased Remote Surveillance System (RSS) camera. That could be buried in a wood near an artificial earth or fox feeding site and left for weeks. The camera had a sensor triggered by any passing person or creature. The recorder would then come to life and continue to record for a couple of minutes after the last movement was detected. The real bonus was we no longer had to hide in the woods. We could leave these systems dotted about the countryside and all we periodically had to do was change tapes and batteries. The problem was that each unit was expensive.

On Saturday December 14th I met two LACS colleagues at Banbury station. We then installed the new RSS camera by one of the artificial earth entrances in the site near Chipping Norton, in Heythrop country. It took us ages to feel happy that the unit was safely installed. The recording box had to be buried and the lead from it to the camera lens concealed. Then the lens had to be concealed and in that first-generation unit it was quite large. Wherever we put the lens it seemed to us to be easily seen—but it needed to have an open line of sight or would film nothing.

None of us welcomed telling Mike Hobday or Douglas Batchelor that their precious new equipment had been found and smashed by a terrierman. We did the best we could. The next morning when we checked the nearby artificial earth site near Wootton Wawen we found there had been some excavation work at the earth. Then when we checked the artificial earth near Sezincote one of my colleagues saw a fox near the earth.

329

I then dropped my colleagues off for them to change the battery and video tape in the RSS camera at Chipping Norton and collected them afterwards. The nature of our investigative work had changed significantly. From then on we had extra eyes and ears constantly alert in our countryside.

Sunday December 29th 2002 I visited the Chipping Norton artificial earth site and retrieved the RSS camera. On the tape was film of a fox scrabbling at the blocked entrance to the artificial earth. One of my LACS colleagues had on Boxing Day found a strange artificial earth in a small, open, derelict brick building across the minor road. It was described as a 'dropping pot' earth. It was a newly built, small, artificial earth, with two plastic pipe entrances into a chamber made from an old tractor tyre with a lid on. I reckoned any fox would only take up temporary residence there.

My year ended with more fieldwork. I met my LACS colleagues at Banbury station and we carried out investigative work in woods around Stow-on-the-Wold. In one a colleague found a newly built artificial earth in a bank by a stream. There was a pheasant release pen some 100 metres away in the wood.

*****

With the Heythrop Foxhounds meeting in Stow-on-the-Wold on New Year's Day 2003 we left our hotel at 7am and put the RSS camera on the newly found artificial earth. We spent the day searching other coverts for artificial earths, without success. Then, just before darkness fell, we retrieved the RSS camera. There was nothing of significance on the tape.

The next morning, Thursday January 2nd, we installed the RSS camera on the newly found 'dropping pot' site in the brick building near Chipping Norton. Once again in the small area of the building it was difficult to install the lens with any confidence that it would not be seen. Wet weather did not help. I returned to the site to change battery and tape on Sunday January 12th. As I approached I saw a Land Rover with a steel canopy parked near it. A man with short dark hair drove away. I watched him depart then visited the site, uncovered the recording box and made the necessary replacements. When I subsequently reviewed the recorded tape, it showed that man had visited the site, with his terriers, just before I arrived. He was later identified as Gary Whelband, a former terrierman for the Heythrop Foxhounds. Had I arrived about 20 minutes earlier I would have been at the location and caught red-handed which might have been awkward. Except that I had a perfect explanation prepared. You cannot undertake such work without having prepared for every eventuality.

Friday January 17th I met my LACS colleagues at Banbury station again. We first changed the battery and tape in the RSS camera at the 'dropping pot' site. Then we checked the artificial earth near Sezincote. Entrances to the artificial earth there were open. For fieldwork, we developed an effective routine of using mobile phones to maintain discreet surveillance and protect each other.

The next morning, we returned to the Sezincote artificial earth and found both entrances blocked. The Heythrop Foxhounds met nearby. The likelihood was that the entrances had been stopped to prevent any fleeing fox entering. There was also the possibility that there was already a fox in the earth. We checked the 'dropping pot' entrance and found that a cobweb noticed there the previous night was intact. Also, whilst there was a smell of fox within the copse there was no such smell within the earth.

One of our team went undercover amongst hunt supporters. I and another monitored discreetly. We saw the terrierman's quad bike ridden into a nearby wood. Moments later a disorientated fox appeared from out of a ditch. When the hunt moved on we went in on foot and found yet another artificial earth in a wood at Lower Sezincote. There were two quad bikes with six hunt supporters aboard patrolling. We saw one bike ridden around the back of the wood. Moments later another fox appeared.

The next morning, Sunday January 19th, we checked woods in the Over Worton area. We found no artificial earths but when we found a falconer we stopped to chat. Late in the day we returned to the site in the brick building near Chipping Norton and changed battery and tape in the RSS camera. Nothing of significance was recorded.

I spent several days visiting the site of the RSS camera and changing the video tape and battery. The tape would run for an hour. Many 'triggers' were false ones caused by branches blowing across the sensor or by passing wildlife such as birds, rats, rabbits or deer that could access the site.

Friday March 7th I met LACS colleagues in Stratford. The following morning, we removed the RSS camera from the 'dropping pot' site near Chipping Norton and installed it on the artificial earth near Sezincote. When we drove over to check the artificial earth in Croome country near Wootton Wawen we encountered hunters driving away from the cul-de-sac. There was a red coated hunter sat in one of the four-wheel-drive vehicles. The hunt was just finishing. We then found signs of digging at the artificial earth and a fresh dead rabbit dumped nearby. The following morning, we searched for artificial earths near Eyford Hall, where the Heythrop Foxhounds were due to meet the following Wednesday. We found no artificial earth but a large feeding site for foxes. We counted 16 freshly dead chickens dumped and evidence of previous dumping over the years— chicken and what looked to be sheep bones scattered about.

The LACS called a Press Conference in Chipping Norton on Wednesday March 12th 2003 to highlight their findings in Heythrop country. The covert video footage incontrovertibly linked former terrierman, Gary Whelband, to the strange artificial earth near Chipping Norton. Gary was highly regarded within the hunt. An article in the hunts' own magazine, The *Heythrop Hack*, written by a Joint Master, Richard Sumner, praised Gary for his hard work during the late 2000 hunting season: "*I think we owe the Hunt staff a great deal of gratitude for all their hard work, especially Gary Whelband who has done an excellent job of keeping a good fox population.*"

Douglas Batchelor was again forthright: "*Fox hunters invariably deny allegations of fox breeding, blaming gamekeepers, farmers, the Army or just about anybody other than themselves, but our secret footage for the first time provides a direct link between a prominent hunt and artificial earths."* He added: *"These foxes are no longer truly wild. They are being fed, they are being housed, they are being watered, then they are being chased. It is a big embarrassment for hunt supporters as they are trying to say that hunting is necessary for pest control, but it's total rubbish."*

Nicky Driver, a spokeswoman for the Campaign for Hunting responded that there was: *"no deep, dark secret about artificials."* She explained further: *"They are well documented and no one is denying the fact that they are there. There is no story. 'The object of hunting has never been exterminating the fox population. It is concerned with managing the population. You locate them away on the edges of estates and away from game birds, away from livestock, and where they are going to cause least damage."* (*The Birmingham Post* March 13th 2003).

Richard Sumner commented: *"Artificials have been around for years, for centuries. It's nothing new at all."*

We proved that artificial earths are commonly located near pheasant release pens in woods. It is also common to find sheep grazing outside the very woods they are sited in. We also proved that some are relocated and refurbished.

On Friday March 28th I returned to Thurlow country to check some of the sites. I noted the exact locations of some using my new GPS device. I also demonstrated the life-cycle of some of these constructions. The stick-pile in the wood by Shudy Camps, number four on my list, first shown to me by Mike Michalak on April 10th 1994 had all but disintegrated. It was reduced to the corrugated iron tube at the core—placed there to allow easy and safe access for foxes.

I met two from the LACS investigative team at Milton Keynes station on Friday April 4th. We had switched focus to look at shooting as will be detailed later. Two days later, Sunday April 6th, we installed the RSS camera on the artificial earth in Croome country near Wootton Wawen.

I returned to Wales on Saturday May 10th when I met a member of the League team in Brecon. He guided me to see death pits at Crai, Powys. One contained the remains of over 20 dead sheep, was near a fox earth, and on land owned by a hunt-supporting farmer. Such pits clearly worked. When we left, we saw a fox running towards the site. The following day we searched the surrounding area for artificial earths or death pits but found little apart from some old bones—and some very steep hills. Later that month my colleague found the remains of another ten, or more, dead sheep. Some bodies were recently dumped.

As well as routinely changing the battery and tape in the RSS camera other maintenance work was required. On Thursday May 22nd, on a visit to the Croome artificial earth near Wootton Wawen I found that I had to remove growing nettles and other vegetation from the lens's line of sight. That had to be done with great care so as not to draw attention to the location of the lens. Any countryman with experience will note broken vegetation just as a countryman knows there is always a reason for pigeons flying up from a wood.

I returned to Quorn Foxhounds country on Sunday June 8th. I met a League investigator and we checked the artificial earth in the wood near Ulverscroft Priory. I aimed to assess whether the site would be suitable for installing the RSS camera. As we left the copse we encountered the owner accompanied by two dogs, one a Rottweiler. What might have become a difficult situation was quickly defused by my colleague. A school teacher she explained she was looking for sites to take students to. The owner, Michael Bream, was flattered. He explained he had owned the wood for 12 years and was happy to give us permission to visit it. He said he used to have hunt jumps but had removed them as he was too old to fall off.

Sunday June 22nd I met a member of the LACS team at Banbury station at 1pm. We then checked a couple of the artificial earths in Heythrop country before going to Croome country and removing the RSS camera from the artificial earth near Wootton Wawen. I took the camera home for thorough cleaning and checking.

We had an interesting investigation project at the end of August. On Friday August 22nd I collected a LACS colleague and we looked for three artificial earths in a wood near West Tanfield, country hunted by the Bedale Foxhounds. Access was difficult with a gamekeeper prowling about by his pheasant release pens. Trying a different route, we waded across the River Ure. It reminded me of times in Afghanistan when I waded rivers with cameras held above my head. For all our efforts, we found nothing, but when having lunch by the River Ure we saw a kingfisher. We picked up another investigator and we found an artificial earth in Holme Wood near Thirsk. It was the classic design with a large chamber and two entrances, with steel grids for blocking each entrance. We stayed in the area and spent the next two days undertaking investigative work into shooting.

In September we returned to Heythrop Foxhounds country. After I collected a LACS colleague from Banbury station on Tuesday September 9th 2003 we went to the artificial earth site near Stow-on-the-Wold. I used the GPS to get an exact location. When we checked the artificial earth in Zareba near Sezincote we found the water supply to the site had been refurbished. We then checked the 'dropping pot' in the brick building near Chipping Norton and bumped into the landowner and his wife in a Land Rover on the old airfield. Fortunately, with residential areas nearby, they were used to seeing strangers there and there was no problem.

The next morning, we checked the artificial earth in Croome country near to Wootton Wawen. There was proof of recent activity at the site. A brick in one entrance was placed over grass still green plus we found other field signs. When we checked that same site again on Wednesday November 19th it had changed again. Hunt supporters had constricted the entrances, perhaps to keep badgers out. Comparison of images taken on March 8th, September 10th and November 19th that year proved the level of activity at that site.

Next day we found more evidence of recent work by hunt supporters on the artificial earth in the Zareba in Heythrop country. We then checked the other artificial earth near Sezincote and found evidence of animals scrabbling to get in at both entrances. On Friday November 28th, Penny Little telephoned to tell me the Heythrop Foxhounds had a joint meet scheduled with the Belvoir Foxhounds at the Zareba on Monday December 1st. I passed the information to colleagues.

The ACIG and the LACS decided to step up investigative work in Croome country. We were determined to find more of the many artificial earths there. Thursday December 18th 2003 marked the start of an intensive effort. I met LACS colleagues near Pershore. They had found another artificial earth that morning. After our illuminating chat with a former Master of the Worcestershire Foxhounds in a nearby pub we knew there were many artificial earths in the area. We searched a nearby wood without success.

The following morning, I met the LACS team at *The Nightingale*, Sneachill east of Worcester. We then installed the RSS camera on a classic artificial earth in a nearby wood, in country hunted by the Croome. It was the middle of winter and with few leaves on the vegetation it was difficult to conceal the camera lens and microphone. It was in a unit about the size of a green toilet roll tube and had a lead to the recording box. After installation, we feared it could be seen and found but had to take that risk.

I retrieved the camera on the afternoon of Saturday January 3rd 2004. As soon as I arrived I saw there had been recent activity at the artificial earth. The battery in the recording unit had run out but before doing so had recorded revealing footage.

The Croome and West Warwickshire Foxhounds had killed a fox in that artificial earth on Saturday December 20th 2003. The tape and associated timings proved the sequence of events:-

12:59 Hounds run by and over the artificial earth. A horse neighs.

13:00 Hounds are encouraged back to the site.

13:01 Man called out, "*by that lying down log.*" Hounds called back to the artificial earth and marked at an entrance. Hunting horn blown.

13:03 Dismounted hunt servant went to one entrance of the artificial earth.

13:03 A terrierman armed with a spade appeared through the wood and walked to an entrance to the artificial earth.

13:04 The Huntsman, Simon Smith, blew 'to ground' on his horn. The terrierman started digging at the entrance to the artificial earth.

13:06 Second terrierman reached the scene. Both dug at the artificial earth entrance.

13:08 Third terrierman at the scene. The hounds were called away.

13:09 Terrierman opened the chamber of the artificial earth and asked for a torch to look inside.

13:11 Terrierman started digging by the chamber. It was hard work as he took his jacket off.

13:14 Terrierman called out, "*It's in here Terry!*"

13:15 One man asked, "*Have you got a shot at it?*"

13:17 A drain rod was brought up and put to use.

13:18 One terrierman warned about the hounds, "*As soon as they hears a bang they'll be here.*"

13:19 They used the drain rod at one entrance to push the fox towards the chamber. A man exclaimed, "*He's here.*" Another terrierman asked, "*Is it brush or head?*" A terrierman walked to the dug out bit by the chamber. He was clearly holding the gun. Another terrierman noted, "*There's nobody watching.*"

13:19:55 Shot heard.

13:20 Hounds rushed to the scene and tussled over remains.

13:21 Huntsman walked to the scene.

13:23 There were five terriermen at the site.

13:24 Terriermen started putting the artificial earth back together.

13:25 A mobile phone rang.

13:26 Hunt official called out to the terriermen, "*Put it all back together please*," and received the reply, "*Certainly sir!*"

13:28 Terrierman scattered leaves around one entrance to conceal the digging work.

13:30 A terrierman dug at the earth right in front of the concealed camera lens.

13:31 Terriermen left the scene.

No terriers were seen used. The drain rod was deployed to move the fox. Nineteen minutes passed from when hounds marked at the artificial earth to when the fox was shot.

*****

Thursday January 8th 2004, I met my LACS colleagues in the Alcester area and we resumed investigative work in Croome country. We found an old, partially derelict artificial earth near Three Oak Hill Wood. In the evening, we called an informant who had acquired a Croome meet card. It was valuable to correlate hunt meet locations with artificial earth sites.

I met the same LACS lads again on Wednesday January 14th at Broughton Hackett, Worcestershire. They were dedicated and diligent fieldworkers. One took me to see an artificial earth they had found to the west of Lower Cowsden Farm. Whilst we recorded that our colleague found yet another artificial earth to the south of Lower Cowsden Farm. We were just able to record that site before darkness fell.

We spent the Thursday on investigative work at shooting sites. Next morning, following an early start, we mixed shooting and fox hunting work. Another old artificial earth was found by a rearing pen. We then tried to install the RSS camera on the artificial earth to the west of Lower Cowsden Farm. Despite trying several locations, we found nothing suitable and safe. We then went to the artificial earth in the wood south of the farm and installed the RSS camera there. It took 1½ hours to install.

Saturday January 24th two of my LACS colleagues telephoned to report they had found two more artificial earths in Croome country. Sunday February 1st was an example of routine support work. I changed the battery and video tape in the RSS camera. It was a 3 hour drive each way to the site.

My colleagues later moved the RSS camera to above the artificial earth near Wootton Wawen ready for the forthcoming Croome meet there.

Friday February 6th I changed the battery and film tape at the new location near Wootton Wawen, and met my LACS colleagues that evening. On the Saturday, with the Croome meeting in the vicinity, we scouted nearby woods. Another artificial earth was found in a wood near Morton Bagot. There were sheep skeletons about 100m away in the wood. In the evening we removed the RSS camera. Next morning, Sunday, we visited two more artificial earths that colleagues had found. One, in an isolated copse near Peopleton, was judged to be recently built as the tunnels were of blue plastic piping. We installed the RSS camera above that fox home.

Two more LACS investigators were working undercover within the Croome hunt. On Tuesday February 10th when the hunt met nearby they watched them spend a few minutes in the tiny copse where we had installed the camera. The next morning, I visited the site and changed the tape and battery. The camera recorded terriermen at the artificial earth.

My colleagues guided me to another artificial earth they had found in the area; that made six within a circle radius of about a mile. In a wood near a pheasant release pen it had the classic design of two glazed pipes leading to a central chamber.

Wednesday March 3rd was a day that combined educational and investigative work. I gave a talk about my ACIG projects at Writtle College near Chelmsford then drove to Croome country to retrieve the RSS camera. The next morning, I met a LACS colleague at Stratford station and we installed the camera on the artificial earth near Wootton Wawen. It was easier to install because by then we knew where to place it.

Two weeks later, on March 17th I met my LACS colleagues for more fieldwork. During the day, I had searched woodland on the Ragley Estate for artificial earths. I found one in Pearson's Wood, at the end of a main drive from the house. The next day we copied and exchanged video tapes taken in Wales and of the Croome hunt.

When the Croome held their final meet of the 2003/4 season at Aston Hall Farm, home of Joint Master, Rob Adams, on March 13th 2004 the LACS deployed two investigators undercover amongst the hunters. They were equipped with body cameras. Local MP Peter Luff, Chair of the All-Party Middle Way Group on hunting and a good friend of fox hunting addressed the crowd. He praised his own side, "*There are many fine ambassadors for hunting here today, and many people I'm proud to count as friends,*" and mocked us "*the enemy has gone quiet.*" There were at least eight artificial earths near Aston Hall Farm, built and maintained by supporters of the Croome Foxhounds.

The LACS held a Press Conference at the Shakespeare Hotel, Stratford on Tuesday April 6th to reveal our work in Croome Foxhounds country. John Cooper, Chairman of the LACS from 1996, was interviewed on Sky News in the morning. Hunt supporters dismissed the LACS claims as propaganda. Nicky Driver, the community and liaison officer for the Croome and West Warwickshire Foxhounds told *Horse and Hound*: "*The*

Biomedical Primate Research
Centre, Den Haag, Holland,
September 20th 1995.

Biomedical Primate Research Centre, Den Haag, Holland, September 20th 1995.

Top: heavily pregnant hind seeks sanctuary in quarry. Quantock Staghounds, January 20th 1992. Above left: hunters wrestle with stag, Devon and Somerset Staghounds (DSSH), August 25th 1994. Above right: LACS hunt monitors help passing motorist after collision with hound, Tiverton Staghounds, March 25th 1995 (hound was killed). Bottom: Whipper-in with injured hind, DSSH, October 11th 1994.

Above: Kevin Hill plans LACS monitoring of the Devon and Somerset Staghounds, March 27th 1993.

Professor Bateson Inquiry at the Devon and Somerset Staghounds, August 31st 1996. Above: Elizabeth Bradshaw chats with hunter. Left: hunted stag flees through National Trust property at Castle Combe.

Right: LACS staff outside Winchester High Court after victory in Peachey libel trial, June 15th 1992.

Below: LACS Open Days at St. Nicholas Priory, August 2nd 1997.

Right and below: LACS Open Days, August 7th 1999. Right and below right: at Linda Wood children hold flowers sent by Paul McCartney.
Below: Chief Executive Douglas Batchelor addresses supporters.

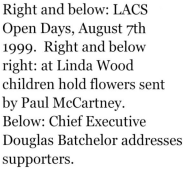

Above: River Barle incident, Devon and Somerset Staghounds, September 29th 1994. Below left: stag engulfed by hounds. Quantock Staghounds (QSH), August 29th 1995. Below right: Huntsman shoots stag. Stag runs away, QSH, April 25th 1996. (Pictures Kevin Hill/LACS).

Above: Blackmore and Sparkford Vale Foxhounds, February 8th 1995. Hounds were made to search for foxes around railway. Right: severed paw. (Pictures Peter White/Joe Hashman/Wildlife Action).

Left: Joe Hashman filmed as Cheshire Foxhound shot, October 30th 1996. Hunt claimed the hound was sick.

Above: Enfield Chace Foxhounds, February 22nd 1992. Right: 'fox in drain incident' New Forest Foxhounds, October 9th 1993 (Pictures from NFAPG video). Below: hounds electrocuted after trespassing on railway line, New Forest Foxhounds, November 27th 1999 (Pictures from video by Peter White/NFAPG).

Above: bear named *Pakise* at Gazimagusa Zoo, Northern Cyprus, June 13th 1997.

Left: Colchester Zoo, March 19th 1991. Elephants perform for onlookers.

Left and below: artificial earth under construction in Vale of Aylesbury Foxhounds country, October 4th 1995.

Artificial earths and log piles in Thurlow Foxhounds' country. Above: a chamber. Left: Lawrie Payne measures a site. Right: Joanna Woolliscroft, Jim Barrington and Lawrie Payne at a site, January 4th 1995.

Some log piles were so large they were visible from aerial surveillance.

Left: Thurlow country flyover, June 21st 1997. Below: log pile, May 8th 1994.

Thurlow Foxhounds. Above: hounds and Huntsman by blocked artificial earth, November 24th 1994. Artificial earth was an active badger sett. With police permission Lawrie Payne (bottom left) unblocked the sett, November 28th 1994. Bottom right: Badger expert, Chris Ferris, seeks evidence at this site, December 1st 1994.

Left and below: Suffolk Foxhounds, Rattlesden airfield, November 20th 1993.

Above: LACS monitors at the meet, East Essex Foxhounds, January 3rd 1994. Right: Thurlow Foxhounds, March 10th 1994

Below: the author (right) monitors a hunt from horseback. New Forest Foxhounds, March 22nd 1994.

Left: Dunston Harriers press hare, September 14th 1996.

Hares netted and driven away to stock fields for coursing at a later date.
Hares were driven over fields into fine purse nets, pulled from the nets
and pushed into boxes. The boxes were loaded into a Land Rover. Six
Mile Bottom, February 10th 1997. Top left: Richard Clarke

Above left: hunters object to being watched, two tyres cut at Essex Foxhounds, March 13th 1995. Above right: Peter White and Kevin Hill monitor the Devon and Somerset Staghounds, August 22nd 1995.

Undercover work with the Ullswater Foxhounds. Above: Elaine Milbourn after fox marked to ground, November 25th 1995. Right: the author wins a prize, November 2nd 1996.

Countryside Rally, Hyde Park, July 10th 1997. Right: steward berates lone young hunt saboteur for making her support for wildlife known.

Sinnington Foxhounds, June 23rd 1998. Two fox cubs confined in artificial earth. Above: cage and water bowl at one entrance. Below: other entrance blocked with dead hen in pipe. Dead lamb dumped nearby.

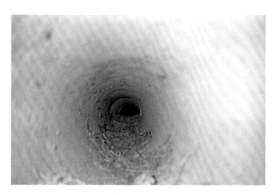

Quorn Foxhounds.
Above and left: artificial earth near Ulverscroft, May 2nd 1998.

Below: dead sheep left for foxes in Thorpe Trussels covert. Eye socket was packed with maggots, May 2nd 1998.

Left: new pipe construction in Cream Gorse covert, June 3rd 1998.
Below: dead sheep and bacon rinds dumped for foxes in Gartree Hill covert, August 18th 1998.

footage shows that the hunt followed the rules to the letter. Yes, a fox was killed, but it was a mangy fox that was shot at point blank range using a licensed firearm. The only issue that arises from the League's footage is that there is an urgent need to communicate to the wider world that there is no deep dark secret about artificial earths. They are not used to breed foxes in captivity. On the contrary, they are a valuable method of providing a habitat for, and sustaining, the fox population." (*Horse and Hound* April 6th 2004)

Doubtless inadvertently, Nicky Driver thereby gifted us one piece of factual information we might have had difficulty proving. By deriding their victim as 'mangy' she confirmed that the foxes hunts breed and feed at their artificial earth sites have a propensity for ill-health.

Hunt supporters have known for over a century that poorly constructed artificial earths create poor foxes. Colonel J.S. Talbot in *Foxes at Home* published in 1906 by *The Field* warned: "*Damp earths, drains etc. which hunted foxes use when they find their regular earths closed in the hunting season, are frequent sources of mange as also are artificial earths, which, unless properly constructed, are worse than all the others put together, and suffice to infect the whole countryside.*

The roof of an artificial earth should be made so low that a fox cannot possibly stand up in it; many of them, however, have chambers two or three feet high, and these soon become very filthy and full of vermin. Mangy foxes use them as they can sit up and scratch inside, which they could not do in a natural earth, and they very soon become infected and remain so." In the appendix to his book Colonel Talbot described how to build an artificial earth but again cautioned: "*Artificial earths, if not properly constructed, may easily become a plague spot in the countryside, as, unless* **perfectly dry**, *they are very apt to give mange to every fox that uses them....."*

I still occasionally checked sites in Thurlow Foxhounds country. On Sunday June 6th 2004 I visited the artificial earth in Balsham Wood and took pictures with a newly purchased digital camera—a Nikon D70 bought with ACIG funds. I marvelled at the benefit of immediately seeing the picture, plus it recorded the time and date of the picture.

Tuesday June 29th marked another significant equipment upgrade. I took delivery of a new RSS camera purchased by the LACS. It had the major advance of recording images in colour plus the camera lens and microphone were concealed in a stick that was much easier to hide at a site.

I was back in Thurlow country on Sunday August 15th. I checked the artificial earth that had become a badger sett in Abbacy Wood where on June 16th 1995 Lawrie Payne and I had problems with the gamekeeper. I found they had made modifications to the earth. Lawrie and I were caught trying to film badgers there. When I re-visited in 2004 I found that hunt supporters had put bars on the entrances to the artificial earth to make it impossible for badgers to use it.

Our investigative work carried on after the Hunting Act was passed on Thursday November 18th 2004. The emphasis just changed slightly.

Tuesday December 21st 2004 I met a LACS colleague at Market Harborough station. We then installed the new stick version of the RSS camera on a nearby shooting site. We also found and recorded a recently built artificial earth in a nearby copse. That was in country hunted by the Fernie Foxhounds. The artificial earth stank of fox and was built of blue plastic drainage pipes.

Aerial surveillance

We also took to the air with our investigative work. The LACS solicitor, Tom Hart, owned a private light aircraft. I had attended many Waterloo Cup hare coursing events over the years. I knew it would be valuable to see the two coursing fields—one at the Withins, the other at Lydiate—from the air. From a few thousand feet, it would be possible to see the relationship between those two fields and the surroundings.

We knew hares were imported into the area in large numbers to sustain the coursing. Was anything visible from the air that might give a clue as to where they were held? I discussed plans with Tom Hart, Jim Barrington and other LACS colleagues. Everyone agreed it was a worthwhile project. Tom Hart kindly offered assistance. We had problems to overcome. We needed good weather for take-off and landing and we needed clear weather over the coursing fields at Altcar near Liverpool.

We made provisional plans for the weekend of July 25th/26th 1992. On Saturday July 25th at 8am I telephoned Tom Hart to ask about the weather forecast. He said it was not good enough that day but should be better the following. I duly called again early the next morning. The forecast was by no means perfect but should be good enough. We arranged to meet at Sywell Airport near Northampton at noon. I drove; he flew. We had sandwiches and drinks for lunch, discussed the Quorn Foxhounds investigations then took off in his Piper Cherokee. It was exhilarating.

When we reached the Altcar area the weather was good. However, I soon found that whereas I can navigate my way around on the ground and am used to reading Ordnance Survey maps, locating where you are from the air is a different matter. Fields, woods and villages look so different from above and pass by so quickly.

I ended up having to find a nearby landmark and then asked Tom to track along the roads from there. There was also the problem that it was not the best aircraft for aerial photography—the low wing obscured some of the view of the ground. However, once we found the fields and Tom banked his aircraft in turning circles I took the photographs we needed. Aerial surveillance was underway. It seemed, and was, a long way from that first Waterloo Cup I had visited in 1976.

At one point Tom declared he was just going to switch fuel tanks. That was apparently a routine procedure. When he started to fiddle with a lever and explained there was some problem I thought he was merely joking—the sort of thing that experienced pilots might do to rookie passengers to put the wind up them. Of course Tom was far too professional for that and was experiencing a real problem. I had visions of us plunging out of the sky to end in a mangled wreck on the Withins but Tom assured me that, if needs be, the plane could glide miles to a safe landing. For all that I was still delighted when he fixed the problem and we could climb and take more pictures from a greater altitude.

Our job done we returned to Sywell soon after 5pm. I thanked Tom for the new insight into hare coursing and the memorable experience.

Aerial surveillance also provided an excellent accompaniment to our investigations into hunts encouraging foxes by building artificial earths and stick and log piles. From altitude, we could see the relationship between woods to each other and to the meets—and prove just how intensively some hunts encouraged foxes. Booking flying time in a light aircraft for aerial photography was difficult. However, booking a short flying lesson, during which photographs could be taken was far easier. I took several such flying lessons during my investigative career.

I first tried flying over the Thurlow Foxhounds country on Saturday June 21st 1997. I drove to Cambridge Aeroclub at Cambridge Airport where I had a 1½ hour flying lesson booked from 11am. We flew around in the Cambridge-Newmarket-Clare-Haverhill areas and I took plenty of photographs. Having spent so much time walking the ground and with the water towers as reference points (particularly that near the Balsham artificial earth) I soon found my way around. A flying lesson included taking the controls—a delightful taste of the freedom of flight.

I also thought aerial surveillance would be excellent for showing the cruelty of cub hunting—where coverts are held up by riders and foot-followers. An aerial view would show a wood ringed by hunt followers, and prove the sordid nature of the trap thereby set for vixen and cubs.

Tuesday September 15th 1998 required another early start. I left home at 4:20am and drove to Henlow Flying Club. We had a tip-off for a cub hunting meet of the Oakley Foxhounds and I planned a search over the countries of the Oakley and Grafton Foxhounds. We took off at 7:50am but had barely been airborne for five minutes before we flew into rain. We flew over and circled around the meet venue but could see nothing through the rain and mist. I returned frustrated.

I tried again four days later—Saturday September 19th. I had another dawn start then drove to the same airfield. There was mist and drizzle along the route but the weather forecast was that the sun would break through and produce clear visibility.

The weather was indeed clearing when I checked in at 7:15am for my flight. I telephoned my eyes on the ground—Penny Little—and she gave me the meets for the Vale of Aylesbury and Bicester with Whaddon Chase Foxhounds. Everything seemed well but then the cloud and drizzle returned with a vengeance and we could not even take off! That was another day lost in frustration, even more so as the hunts would have gone out.

The final act of our investigation into the use of artificial earths by the Croome Foxhounds was a flyover around known sites. After checking flying conditions were suitable, on Tuesday March 30th 2004 I met a LACS colleague at Banbury station. We drove to the Enstone Flying Club at

Church Enstone where I had booked a flying lesson. We met our pilot, Richard, who had 20 years' RAF experience flying a variety of aircraft including Tornadoes. We felt safe as we took off in the early afternoon.

My colleague took the pilot seat next to Richard whilst I sat in the back with cameras. After doing a 'touch-and-go' landing at Wellesbourne airfield we flew to Croome country. We found a landmark and from there it was easy to pick our way around the various sites. The aerial view confirmed the intensive nature of the fox production work in that area. We knew that woodland after woodland contained an artificial earth. I took video film and photographs. After being airborne for over an hour in turbulent air the novice air crew felt slightly queasy on landing.

Lamping with dogs

Hunting foxes, hares and deer at night using powerful lamps and lurchers was an effective means of killing. There was cruelty in the pastime anyway but there was opportunity for extreme abuse. In 1994 the National Anti-Hunt Campaign (NAHC), run by Niel Hansen, carried out an investigation during which they acquired video films of lamping.

A NAHC investigator infiltrated a gang in Yorkshire that used American Pit Bull Terriers (APBT)s crossed with greyhounds to hunt and kill foxes at night. From the films the NAHC produced a campaign video, *Killing For Kicks,* that was launched at a press conference in the House of Commons on October 31st 1994. The 18 minutes of videotape showed cruelty inflicted upon foxes to match the cruelty depicted in the 'Builth Wells' badger abuse video. At night, in the beam of a light, individual foxes are attacked by one, two or three lurchers and greyhounds. The foxes are incapacitated by being stabbed, held by their brush whilst savaged and swung against the ground by the brush. The men delight in their cruelty and at the end pose with their dogs and dead foxes. [Some of the cruelty shown in the video was made illegal by John McFall's Wild Mammals (Protection) Act 1996 that became law on April 30th 1996.]

I ran into problems trying to infiltrate routine lamping. At one hunt where I was deeply undercover a supporter was a keen member of the terrier/lurcher fraternity. He was proud of his lurcher yet had little film of it lamping at night (chasing and catching hares, foxes, rabbits etc. down the beam of a powerful lamp). He asked me to accompany him to film/photograph his dog working. We had little photographic evidence of lamping and the prospect of gaining more was attractive. I said that I would be happy to do so and if he told me when he was next going out I would accompany him. He told me to choose the day and he would fit in with my choice. I could not do it. I could not set the agenda by which wildlife was to die just to gain film. We had to take the role of the 'fly on the wall' recording events that would occur anyway.

Shooting investigations

Whilst searching the countryside for artificial earths we often found sites of cruelty associated with the pastime of shooting wildlife. These ranged from snares and traps to pheasant release pens and gamekeeper's gibbets. Anything illegal we reported to the police.

Just as hunt supporters tipped us off about actions of terriermen associated with their hunt they did not approve of, so did shooters tell us about the behaviour of gamekeepers that offended them.

We also benefitted from informants between the sports. Hunting people often expressed the view that shooting and snaring wildlife involved far more cruelty than hunting. Conversely shooters argued that whereas their pastime centred on killing a creature swiftly the whole aim of hunting was to delay the kill for as long as possible. To put it bluntly hunters and shooters were happy to inform on each other.

Thursday August 10th 1989 produced an example. I met a shooting informant at *The Vine*, Cumnor. He took me to see where illegal pole traps had been set around a nearby pheasant release pen. They were legal Fenn traps set in an illegal manner. Placed on top of a pole they were spring traps designed to catch birds of prey. When we reached the site, the traps were as described but they were not set—they were hanging from the poles.

Later that summer my colleague Mike Michalak telephoned me about illegal (self-locking) snares he had found. Sunday September 3rd, I drove out and duly found fifteen by a pheasant release pen at West Wratting near Newmarket. I closed the snares then telephoned my League colleague John Bryant and arranged to meet him near the site the following Tuesday.

John agreed the snares were illegal so we telephoned the police and guided an officer to the site. Police interviewed Phillip Garrod. He had been the gamekeeper there for eight years. On Wednesday September 6th, I drove to Linton Police Station and gave a statement to PC Morley about finding the illegal snares.

Phillip Garrod admitted setting the snares but claimed not to know the difference between legal and illegal snares (if they had all been banned as we campaigned for it would have been easy). The Crown Prosecution Service (CPS) declined to prosecute recommending instead that he just be cautioned by the police. The LACS then took a private prosecution to bring the matter to court. The resulting case was heard by Cambridge Magistrates on Monday April 2nd 1990. Philip Garrod was convicted under the Wildlife and Countryside Act 1981, fined £100 and ordered to pay £150 costs.

Commenting afterwards Jim Barrington said: "*Snares are vicious instruments which cause any animal caught in them to die in agony. We took a private prosecution because we felt that a mere caution was an insufficient response for such a serious criminal act.*"

I also tried to work undercover within shooting. One good way to gain access was via a recommendation from another branch of 'field sports'. In December 1990, whilst undercover within the Essex Foxhounds I asked supporters about opportunities to see and photograph shooting. Guy Ruggles-Brise invited me to photograph his shoot at Spains Hall, near Finchingfield, Essex on Saturday January 5th 1991.

I drove to the hall for the 9am start and was made very welcome. Guy Ruggles-Brise had three sons, Tim (the eldest), Sam and Jimmy. There were nine guns out that morning. It was a bright and sunny day, perfect for photography. The guns drew lots for peg places then moved two places after each drive. I was introduced to some of the guns—David and Henry. I was told the latter's wife kennelled the De Burgh Bassett hounds. I was guided by the guns where to stand safely to photograph events. Many pheasants were wounded and chased around on the ground by the dogs. It was almost like watching coursing again but with gundogs and crippled birds.

I returned the following week on Saturday January 12th. That morning Jimmy Ruggles-Brise took charge of the shoot. It was another day of fine sunny weather. I was told that Spains Hall prided itself on being a wild pheasant shoot. To preserve the breeding stock the guns were told they could only shoot cock pheasants—there was a nominal fine for each hen pheasant shot. The sexes could be differentiated by the noise cocks made on take off. I chatted with a loader who told me with pride that some of the shotguns they held were very valuable. The guns and beaters were welcoming and accepted my presence as an aspiring 'fieldsports' photographer.

When it came to searching for the hidden side of shooting—snares—Mike Michalak was a diligent fieldworker. Tuesday May 28th 1991 he reported he had found more illegal snares that he had closed. Early the following month, Sunday June 9th, I met Mike and his daughter and they guided me to the site. There were three illegal snares. I alerted the LACS and Cambridgeshire Police.

The next Saturday, June 15th, I met John Bryant at Bottisham Police Station at 11am. We guided PC Macdonald to the site where he removed four illegal snares. We returned to the police station where John and I both made statements. Police arrested two gamekeepers, Roy Brand and William Rolph. The *Newmarket Journal*, October 10th 1991, reported that at Newmarket Magistrates Court both admitted using illegal snares. Each was fined £50 and ordered to pay £25 towards costs.

For wildlife, snares have become the equivalent of landmines in our countryside. They are cheap to buy and freely scattered about. They can kill long after they have been forgotten about. When set in a semi-urban environment they are one of the main causes for cats going missing.

A gamekeeper explained one common trick practised by his colleagues was if they found a cat dead in one of their snares they would remove the body and place it on a nearby road. They would then run the carcase over a few times. Anyone finding a flattened cat would naturally assume the creature was the unfortunate victim of a road accident. Our informant explained that one indicator of the real cause of death was to check the cat's claws. Any cat killed on the road would grip the road in the last instant of life smashing the claws. If the claws on the flattened cat are intact it is likely the cat was already dead when placed on the road.

We found many pheasant release pens some with birds trapped and dead in the mesh of the fencing. Woods containing such pens were often full of corn feeders for the birds. Sometimes we found great heaps of corn dumped on the ground to feed the game birds. Such wanton and lazy behaviour inevitably attracted rats.

Throughout many a drive from my home to Norwich at night I would see rats scurrying along roadside verges. With adjacent fields and woodlands intensively managed by shooting interests the woods were full of pheasant feeders that also provided a near endless supply of food for rats. The rats thrived not only because they had food provided but also the gamekeepers, seeking to protect their gamebirds, strenuously killed their natural predators.

Managing our countryside for sporting interests causes an imbalance in our ecosystems that causes much harm. Ludicrously generous EU farm subsidies that reward landowners for land ownership, not for growing food, have turned our countryside into a playground for hunters and shooters.

Heavily keepered woodlands often stank of death and were silent of life. We regularly found gamekeepers' gibbets with all manner of wildlife strung up on display to rot away. Squirrels, foxes, corvids and just about any creatures not shot for sport were killed as 'pest control'.

I found that monitoring shooting without an invitation could be perilous. Saturday November 16th 1996 became etched in my mind after I ran into real aggression when I stumbled by accident upon a shoot. I had driven out looking for the Isle of Ely or Sportsmans Coursing Clubs reported to be in the Swaffham Bulbeck, Dullingham, Balsham, Fulbourn, Six Mile Bottom areas.

At about 10:30am I found beaters in a field beside the road from Six Mile Bottom to Brinkley. I stopped and saw they were not for coursing but for shooting. I parked off the road on the verge on the left-hand side and took my cameras out. An organiser with the guns on the south side of the road called out that I was in the way and that for safety I should move my car and stand further back towards Six Mile Bottom. He pointed to a gap in the hedge and said I could obtain good photographs from there. I moved back towards Six Mile Bottom to a position of safety where it did not interfere with the shoot. I then took up position on the verge by the gap as directed. The beaters were on the north side of the road driving the birds over the road towards the line of guns standing some distance into the field on the south side.

I took photographs and video of the shooting including several instances of wounded birds being left to flap about on the ground. Standing on the verge by the side of the road I was showered several times by spent shotgun pellets and it struck me that this posed some danger to passing motorists. They could have their cars struck either by the spent pellets or by wounded birds. When the hooter sounded the end of the drive I ran a few metres on to the field to check the condition of a bird that I had observed to fall wounded. It was dead so I took a few seconds of video of it and some photographs. I then returned to the gap in the hedge and was approached by a man who I took to be the head gamekeeper. He was Richard Clarke.

He was burly and looked aggressive so I turned my video camera on to record what was said. I told him I was taking pictures for the League Against Cruel Sports. He was unhappy at my presence, said the shoot was perfectly legitimate, said that I could do what I liked from the roadside but warned me not to step on any private field.

I then drove around to a footpath located to the south, parked and walked along the path. I saw a tractor and covered trailer parked by where the footpath crossed a stream. Dead birds were hung up in the trailer. A young man got out of the driver's cab and walked towards me. I took him to be an underkeeper. I asked him where the footpath went and he pointed to the south up the track. I said that I believed a footpath went straight on also and took out my map to show him. He agreed and asked me what I was doing. I said I was taking photographs. I left him and walked on along the footpath heading north-west.

From a high point on the footpath I saw the shooters congregated by a wood to the north. I waited as they were doing nothing. They looked at me with binoculars. I appreciated that my presence on a footpath with cameras was probably a matter of concern to them. A man driving a covered pick-up drove around to observe what I was doing. He simply sat in his vehicle watching me. I regarded that as bit intimidating so when I had to walk by him I turned my video camera on to record any comments. He said "*Morning*" and I returned the greeting.

I then walked along the footpath looking for the shoot but it appeared to be taking place to the south of me. I returned to my car and drove around to look for them. I parked off the road on the verge near Six Mile Bottom and observed the shooting party stop for lunch at Lark Hall Heath Farm to the south of Six Mile Bottom from about 1pm to 2pm.

When I saw them drive off to the east I drove in the same direction heading for the footpath. I saw people I thought to be beaters but turned out to be a large party of ramblers headed along the footpath towards Crick's Farm. I parked in the same place as before and walked along the footpath as before. A tractor pulling a trailer approached me. Again, I turned my video camera on to record anything shouted at me as it passed.

A beater seated in the back called, "*You're trespassing!*" Another shouted, "*Piss off!!*" I replied to the first claim, "*It's a footpath.*" I heard another beater say, "*That's him aint it?*" There were other comments hard to distinguish. A girl sat on the tailgate of the trailer gestured a V-sign.

The trailer did not stop. Instead it passed me at some speed and disappeared into the distance. I walked further along the footpath to the north-west. About 10 minutes later I was on the footpath when I saw the tractor and trailer return towards me at speed. As the vehicle passed it stopped and Richard Clarke jumped off the back.

Enraged he lunged at me, grabbed my arm, and shouted: "*Turn that fucking camera off!*" I fended him off and turned my camera on to record. It took some seconds to run. He accused me of being abusive to his daughter. Here is the transcript of the exchange:-

Mike Huskisson: "*No, I haven't said a word.*"

Richard Clarke: *"You fucking bastard, if you start being abusive...."*
Mike Huskisson: *"I haven't said a word...."*
Richard Clarke: *"I've got ten fucking witnesses that says you was bloody rude to her."*
Mike Huskisson: *"I never said a word to her."*
Richard Clarke: *"Now, if you don't fuck off, and if you're rude to my daughter again you're in serious trouble."*
Mike Huskisson: *"I never said a word to her."*
Richard Clarke: *"You did. You said "Come on darling let's have your photograph"."*
Mike Huskisson: *"Oh, get out of it...."*
Richard Clarke: *"Yes you fucking did!"*
Mike Huskisson: *"I said "This is a footpath"."*
Richard Clarke: *"So what!? She said "Okay" and you said "Come on darling let's have your photograph"."*
Mike Huskisson: *"No way."*
Richard Clarke: *"There's ten bloody witnesses to it."*
Mike Huskisson: *"Well I never said a thing to her."*
Richard Clarke: *"There's ten witnesses to it!"*
Mike Huskisson: *"I never said a thing to her."*
Richard Clarke: *"There's ten witnesses to it. There's ten witnesses that said you said "Come on darling let's have your photograph"."*
Mike Huskisson: *"I never did."*
Richard Clarke: *"Well, so that's ten against one, eleven against one."*
Mike Huskisson: *"Yea?"*
Richard Clarke: *"Now, why don't you fuck off?"*
Mike Huskisson: *"Because I'm on a footpath and I'm allowed to be here."*
Richard Clarke: *"Yea, but you've been here for three hours. What is the matter with you? Are you fucking mental or something?"*
Mike Huskisson: *"What's wrong?"*
Richard Clarke: *"Nothing's wrong. It's just that you're bugging me because you've been abusive to my daughter."*
Mike Huskisson: *"I haven't said a thing to your daughter."*
Richard Clarke: *".... and I don't like you being abusive to my daughter."*
Mike Huskisson: *"I said "I'm on a footpath" and that's all."*
Richard Clarke: *"Yea and you said "Come on darling let's have your photograph"."*
Mike Huskisson: *"No. No."*
Richard Clarke: *"And you took her photograph. Did you take her photograph?"*
Mike Huskisson: *"No."*
Richard Clarke: *"Eeeer [to tractor driver] Come on. Come on."*
Mike Huskisson: *"No. I never said......"*
Richard Clarke: *"I'm going to phone the fucking police and I'm going to report you as a fucking pervert."*
Mike Huskisson: *"Okay."*
Richard Clarke: *"Taking photographs of young girls."*

Mike Huskisson: "*Okay, you do it.*"

Richard Clarke: "*I bloody will. [To tractor driver] Turn that off! Turn it off! Fucking pervert. He said "Come on darling let's have your photograph", 14-year-old girl.*"

Mike Huskisson: "*Never said a thing to her.*"

Richard Clarke: "*I'm going to fucking phone the police about you.*"

Mike Huskisson: "*Okay.*"

Richard Clarke: "*You're a fucking pervert, looning about here with a camera, there's something wrong with yer.*"

Mike Huskisson: "*Go on then, phone them.*"

Richard Clarke: "*I'm going to do it straight away. You better be in your motor and off. Go on.... we're off to...ridge Hill.*"

Mike Huskisson: "*I'll wait here for the police.*" [Tractor starts]

Richard Clarke: "*Back where we come from Bert. You...any of my staff again...I'll fucking do yer!*"

Mike Huskisson: "*Yea, well I'll be here waiting for the police.*"

Richard Clarke: "*Right. You better be.*"

Mike Huskisson: "*I'm waiting.*"

Richard Clarke: "*That's ten against one.*"

Mike Huskisson: "*That's enough.*"

At that time, I was about ½ mile from my car, on my own, on a footpath. I waited for some minutes to see where the shoot was and then returned to my car to drive around to find them. At about 3:30 pm I observed them on fields to the south of Lark Hall Heath Farm. As there were no footpaths in that area and therefore no point from which I could lawfully film them with any success, and it would soon be dark, I left. I never saw any police officers at the scene.

That encounter had repercussions. On Tuesday November 19th, the BFSS put out a News Release complaining that I had stalked a young girl at the shoot. The 'field sports' media seized upon the tale with glee. *Hounds* magazine, December 1996, ran the following report:-

"*LEAGUE STALKS YOUNG GIRL FOR SNAPS DURING SHOOT*

A photographer claiming to be from the League Against Cruel Sports Ltd was caught stalking a fifteen year old girl during a shoot in Suffolk on Saturday. Not satisfied with taking both still and video shots of beaters from a public footpath, the photographer pushed through a hedge in order to obtain close-up shots of a 15 year old girl who was accompanying the beaters. When challenged as to the purposes of his unsavoury targeting, he beat a hasty retreat!

"*We know that the LACS are against shooting and actively campaign to oppose it, but find it hard to believe that even they would adopt such a course of action to further their ends," said David Bredin, BFSS spokesman in East Anglia, "We have sent details of the individual concerned to the LACS head office asking them to confirm (or otherwise) their orders. We have also asked that such people who are employees of the LACS be issued with an identity card for their use during any lawful 'observations' in which they might he involved.*"

Shooting Times ran the same report on November 28th 1996. Tuesday December 3rd found me at the LACS offices seeking redress. We met the News Editor of *Shooting Times*, showed him my video film of the whole incident and other evidence and invited him to retract his story. He declined. Our opponents were confident that I had no reputation that could be maligned anyway. They were wrong.

Faced with legal action the 'field sports' media settled out of court and printed retractions. *Hounds* magazine Winter 1997 ran the following:-
"LEAGUE AGAINST CRUEL SPORTS
In a recent issue of "HOUNDS" magazine, we suggested that a field sports monitor from the League Against Cruel Sports stalked a young girl for photographs during a November shoot in Suffolk. We now recognise that this report was wholly without foundation and that the monitor's conduct should not have been described in the way it was."

The whole saga proved several things: the aggression and violence of the shooting world; their desire to keep their actions hidden; their willingness to lie and fabricate stories; and the fact that many 'witnesses' count for nothing against one film of what really happened.

The following year, November 7th 1997, I had round two of my encounters with the notoriously volatile Richard Clarke, the Headkeeper at the Six Mile Bottom shoot. Once again I was out looking not for shooting but for hare coursing in the Newmarket area. I bumped into the shoot around midday. Richard Clarke welcomed me in his customary manner. He swore at me, stamped on my foot, barged into me and headbutted my video camera, bending my glasses. Is it any wonder that hunt saboteurs who are there to stop the cruelty, not just film it, are treated so much worse?

Conflict between compassionate people and shooters could also be fatal. On Saturday December 21st 1996 I visited and photographed Byron's Pool near Cambridge. It seemed inconceivable that a gruesome murder could have happened at such an idyllic spot. It was Tuesday January 6th 1976 when William Sweet, a member of the LACS, was shot dead there after an altercation with a man shooting birds. William, aged 50, was taking wildlife photographs between 8am and 9am. The last picture on his camera, found nearby, showed a robin feeding off parasites on a stoat's back.

Peter Littlechild was shooting birds and there was an altercation between the two. William ran off down a wide path but was shot twice in the back and leg. As William lay grievously injured Peter Littlechild calmly reloaded his shotgun and fired a third shot from point-blank range. At Norwich Crown Court in May 1976 prosecuting counsel Mr William Howard did not ask the jury to look at the photographs showing the shotgun wound which killed William Sweet, *"The front left side of the head had been blown completely away." (Cambridge Evening News*, May 3rd 1976). Peter Littlechild was convicted of murder and jailed for life.

We found that many shooting estates celebrated death. Gamekeepers displayed dead animals both to prove their prowess and to deter other wildlife. We became used to the sight and smell of rotting corvids, squirrels and any other creatures that might compete with the game birds, strung up on gibbet lines.

In February 2003 I was told by local hunt saboteurs about a truly shocking stain on nature they had stumbled upon at Road Green, between Hempnall and Woodton, south of Norwich. I visited the tiny copse, behind a small game farm, on Wednesday February 26th. There were eight dead foxes strung up hanging from the trees. Some were freshly killed. It was an appalling sight and an even worse smell.

I assumed that displaying carcasses in such a way was illegal under the 1991 Animal By-Products Order so the next day I telephoned Norfolk Trading Standards to report the site. They said it was nothing to do with them and that I should contact the RSPCA or South Norfolk District Council. I called the latter and they said it was nothing to do with them.

I then tried Norfolk Police. I spoke to a PC White, the Wildlife Liaison Officer at Long Stratton police station. He was both interested and helpful and assured me that he would check out the legal situation. He called back that evening and told me that such fox dumping was not illegal under the 1999 Animal By-Products Order. It seemed the original Order had not been kept in force.

We also looked to expose the intensive rearing of gamebirds for shooting. Later that year, Sunday June 29th 2003, I met my colleagues and we visited a rearing facility at Batsford Park. We saw pheasants at three stages of development including very young chicks.

With the forming of the professional LACS investigations team my ACIG and the League stepped up our work to expose the cruelty behind shooting. January 15th 2004 demonstrated the extent of the war waged against wildlife. Whilst searching in Croome hunt country we found a gamekeeper's gibbet in a wood near Huddington. A team member then found a freshly killed buzzard hidden in a fertiliser bag in the keeper's shed. Another dead buzzard was found in a nearby wood.

As the artificial earth investigation finished we moved the RSS cameras to shooting sites. There was a large rearing facility near Market Harborough that caught our interest. Just before Christmas, Tuesday December 21st 2004, a LACS colleague and I installed the RSS camera overlooking a dump of dead pheasants behind a large rearing shed.

Some of the rearing was so intensive as to be akin to factory farming. Thursday January 13th 2005 marked the start of a three day investigative effort far from home. I met a LACS colleague at Welshpool and we stayed in a bed and breakfast. The next morning, we looked at the nearby Three Valleys Shoot. On Saturday January 15th, we visited Bettws Hall Shooting Hatchery. We simply walked the fields and stumbled upon the site. There were pheasants in raised pens. Others packed into crates for transportation. Some birds never left the site—their remains were trodden into the footwell of a farm tractor. Given that pheasant shooting is often defended as 'natural' it was valuable to have visual proof that it is anything but.

CHAPTER THIRTEEN
Hunt violence

Hunting is a pastime built on violence. Where there is peace and tranquillity in our beautiful countryside, hunters bring violence and death. Hunt supporters are adept at displaying charm and calm to win friends and influence but scratch the surface and violence is there. Hunters can be perfectly friendly—so long as they get everything they want.

Long before there were hunt saboteurs to abuse and batter, hunt supporters could fight amongst themselves over territory to hunt. This report from a hunting magazine details the violent conflict between two hunts near London at the end of the 19th century:-

"The Herts and Essex was run by a Committee with Mr. Frank Judd as field master. An attempt was made to draw a line between the two countries, but the Puckeridge and Mr. Swindell, sheltering under the decision of the MFHA, refused to co-operate. The dispute continued to fester so badly that by the 1892-3 season sabotage and violence were resorted to. The Puckeridge followers formed themselves into a kind of irregular cavalry. At one meet they succeeded in dismounting a couple of members of the Herts and Essex, and on another day hired a trumpeter and galloped pell-mell through coverts which the Herts and Essex were about to draw! On another occasion the Herts and Essex had met in what they considered to be their country but near a covert owned by the Secretary of the Puckeridge. A farmer whose land adjoined the covert told what happened in a letter to the Puckeridge Master, Mr. Swindell: "A party of over twenty members and followers of your hunt have done their best today to spoil the sport of the Herts and Essex Hunt, which I was following, by dressing their horses' legs with oil of aniseed, and with horns and halloaing drew our hounds from the line of their fox at Rolfway, totally spoiling our sport, and at Scales Park the rides and gaps to a considerable distance were stretched across with new telegraph wire, which might, this misty day, have caused some serious accident." It was further alleged that not only was the wire stretched across the rides, but branches and bracken were put in front of it to obscure it and make it more dangerous. Men with sticks lay in ambush ready to pounce on anyone whose horse was brought down! The farmer continued: "I saw your man taking a very active part in the affair. Instead of trying to keep out the Herts and Essex Hunt, he did his utmost to holler them into the covert, and if they had gone there would have been severely beaten." It was complained that serious consequences would have been the result if members of the Herts and Essex, as well as the huntsman and whipper-in, had not refrained from following hounds into what was described as a "death-trap."

The Puckeridge Secretary defended himself: "I have been forced much against my inclinations, to take very strong measures to protect my rights against the constant and intentional trespasses of the Herts and Essex Hounds. The wire used on Saturday was put up to protect my watchers from being ridden down as they were at Pelham." He was referring to an incident where a Puckeridge man was knocked down after he had allegedly attempted to strike a member of the Herts and Essex jumping a fence during a run................By the end of the 1893-4 season Mr. Swindell had resigned, and an arrangement was arrived at whereby the old Puckeridge country should be hunted in its entirety by one pack, and the Herts and Essex be disbanded." (Article, *"The Puckeridge Dispute"*, by John Bridge, *Hounds* magazine. Volume 7, No. 3, January/February 1991.)

The traditional view amongst those who hunt wildlife with hounds has been they can put their hounds wherever they like—until they are told not to. Then when they are warned not to hunt in certain areas they have trouble remembering exactly which land they are banned from, and who told them. The hunting fraternity traditionally greets conflict with violence. Landowners who try to keep hunts off their land may be met with abuse, violence and criminal damage to their property. At least one farmer died trying to keep hunters off his land where they had repeatedly trespassed.

The aggression hunters deploy when dealing with people protecting their own property is multiplied several times when hunters deal with those, usually hunt saboteurs, who are trying to protect our wildlife. Over the years police and courts have, by their ludicrous leniency, given hunters every encouragement to use violence. Some officers have turned a blind eye to hunt violence. It has been an issue of class for UK courts. Whereas dog fighters, badger diggers and those who trespassed to course hares were treated with suitable severity those who hunted with hounds and coursed hares as part of organised clubs, the wealthier classes, the self-styled 'pillars of society' could almost do as they liked.

1976 was a landmark year that set the benchmark for violence by hunters towards those who seek to protect wildlife. The assault by Border Counties Otterhounds supporters on people striving to protect otters was covered at length in *Outfoxed Take Two*. The case of Valerie Waters later that year revealed hunt supporters could not only be aggressive towards wildlife conservationists and cause criminal damage to their property but they could manipulate the system to have their victims imprisoned as well.

The *Sunday Times* August 21st 1977 printed a near full page article under the heading: *"The Hounding of Valerie Waters"* and sub-titled: *"Valerie Waters is a respectable mother, aged 45, married to a tailor. She has not committed a crime or been charged with any offence. But she is in prison—because she helped the police...."*

It was the morning of November 13th 1976 when Valerie Waters drove four young hunt saboteurs to a meet of the Atherstone Foxhounds at Witherley, Leicestershire. I recall Val as a placid but very determined lady. At the meet a rider rapped his crop on the roof of her car and warned her: *"You want to watch out what you are doing today. We're waiting for you."* The threat did not deter Val and her colleagues. As usual they sprayed the area around the meet with Anti-Mate—a proprietary spray designed for use on bitches in heat that overwhelmed the sense of smell in other dogs—perfect for safely masking the scent of foxes. They drove off before hounds left the meet and endeavoured to stay between hounds and their quarry, spraying where required. Though hunt saboteurs always sought to avoid confrontation with hunters, there were inevitably times when the two sides met. Here is the *Sunday Times* description of events:

"*SUBSEQUENT events are in dispute, with each side placing the blame on the other. But what cannot be denied is that Mrs Waters was very severely frightened by an ugly and vicious crowd and her car, a Ford Escort, was vandalised by grown men. It was covered with sump oil, red aerosol paint, de-icing spray and mud, the aerial was broken off, a windscreen wiper was twisted and turf was jammed into the exhaust.*

Mrs Waters's version of events, as described later to her lawyer and the court, was that she was "ambushed" on three separate occasions by hunt supporters working to a deliberate plan. Each time, she says, a car suddenly pulled out across the lane in front of her and another car drew up close behind.

On the first occasion, a man appeared with a bottle of oil which he poured all over the windows of the car. Shortly afterwards, she was stopped again and red aerosol paint and de-icing fluid was sprayed over the roof, bonnet and number plates. The aerial was broken off.

During the last, and most serious, incident, Mrs Waters says her car was surrounded by a crowd of between 50 and 60 men, who were jeering, shouting obscenities and hammering on the roof with their fists. This time she got out of the car because she thought the tyres were being slashed.

Instead she found a man stuffing turf into the exhaust pipe and when she tried to prevent him she was kicked and her hand was cut. The four young men with her, adhering to HSA's "non-violent" policy, stayed in the car although several attempts were made to drag them out. She was hit in the face with a fox's tail before she was able to drive away.

"As I understand it," her lawyer, Ivan Geffen, said last week, "it was the behaviour of a lynch mob. They were shouting 'Kill them, kill them'."

Hunt supporters tell a very different story, while not denying the damage to the car. Their version is that Mrs Waters was never "ambushed" but simply stuck in the heavy traffic that always follows the hunt and that hunt supporters took the opportunity to subject her to a light-hearted "dose of her own medicine."

As George Rowley, a follower of the Atherstone Hunt since he was a child, said last week: "I don't see how she can say she was frightened— she has been making a nuisance of herself at hunts for years."

Mr Rowley, aged 66, a retired garage proprietor, was one of the men later charged with causing criminal damage to Mrs Waters's car. "In fact I didn't actually do any damage, but I took the blame for the rest. All that happened was that I stepped out to stop the traffic as the hounds were crossing the lane. Mrs Waters just happened to be in the first car and I heard one of the long-haired gits with her shout, 'Run the bastard down.'

351

That really made me angry and so when she got out of her car I waved this fox tail I had with me in her face.

"Then she started saying that I had stuffed paper up her exhaust and I hadn't, but she kept on and so I finally stuck some clay up the pipe just to give her something to complain about."

Whatever happened, Tom Waters can certainly testify to his wife's condition when she finally arrived home in Birmingham that evening. "She was as white as a sheet and trembling from head to foot. Her cut hand was bandaged and the car was in a disgusting state."

Ironically, it was Mr Waters who insisted that his wife should press charges—a decision that was eventually to lead to her imprisonment. "If you had told me at the time that Valerie could go to prison without committing any offence and without even being accused of any offence," Mr Waters said last week. "I would have laughed in your face."

Next day, Mr and Mrs Waters drove to Market Bosworth police station where they explained, to a less than sympathetic constable, what had happened. Leicestershire is a hunting county and hunt saboteurs are not generally looked upon with much favour. Only when Mrs Waters said she had a film of the incident, taken from inside her car and on which the assailants might be identified, did the police begin to take a reluctant interest.

Two weeks later, a bizarre little scene was enacted in a darkened upstairs room at Market Bosworth police station. While Mrs Waters's film was shown, a man wearing sunglasses with a coat over his head was ushered into the room to name the people who could be seen vandalising her car. This man has never been identified. His information was to result in four hunt supporters being charged variously with criminal damage, conduct likely to cause a breach of the peace and threatening behaviour. No consideration was apparently given to preferring more serious charges of assault or actual bodily harm."

The four accused were: George Rowley; Kenneth Storer, 47, a night watchman; David Meehan, 40, a miner; and Joseph Loweth, 67, a retired company director. Nearly six months later, on April 19th 1977, all appeared at Market Bosworth Magistrates Court and pleaded guilty. Val Waters was asked to attend court and produce the estimate for repairs to her car.

This seemingly innocuous request may well have been a ruse to get her into the court. All four men were bound over to keep the peace for a year in the sum of £50. George Rowley was additionally fined £10 and ordered to pay £20 compensation on the criminal damage charge. The focus then switched to Val, as the *Sunday Times* reported:

"AFTER the verdict of the magistrates, Mr William Musson, the defending solicitor, got to his feet once more to present a case for Mrs Waters being bound over also. He sought to invoke a fourteenth century Act under which he could ask the magistrates to bind over Mrs Waters to keep the peace, even though she was attending court at the request of the police and only as a witness, not a defendant.

This Act, the Justice of the Peace Act, 1361, empowers a justice "to punish to the intent that people be not by such rioters or rebels troubled, not endangered, not the peace blemished, not other passing by the highways of the realm disturbed, nor put in the peril which may happen of such offenders." [sic]

Mr Musson produced a copy of the Police Review, in which there was an article describing the extra workload put on police officers by the actions of the saboteurs. He pointed out that when hunt supporters retaliated it did not become the protesters to go running crying to the police just because they had been "given a dose of their own medicine."

His argument convinced the magistrate, Mr W. Chappell who ordered Mrs Waters to be bound over for 12 months. Her shock and confusion was adequately recorded by the magistrate's clerk on his notes on her impromptu statement to the court: "I did not know I was on trial today. I have not committed any offence. We are a non-violent association and our sole aim is to save the lives of wild animals. I refuse to be bound over. This is a travesty of justice."

The case, neatly turned against Mrs Waters, was adjourned for two weeks so she could seek legal advice. But for her there was no backing down. "She had made up her mind even before she got home," her husband explained. "She would never agree to be bound over even though she had been told to refuse would mean prison. She is a woman who could never bend on her principles....WHEN Mrs Waters reappeared in court she again refused to be bound over and was sentenced to a month's imprisonment. An immediate appeal was lodged and heard at Leicester Crown Court on July 28 before Judge Guy Dixon.

After hearing evidence of Mrs Waters's saboteur activities from the Atherstone huntsman, Mr Tony Beeney, the Judge said he had no alternative but to send her to prison if she continued with her refusal. It was as if the original trial had been all about Mrs Waters herself."

That night Val was taken to Winson Green prison. She was transferred to Risley prison the next day, classified as a convicted criminal prisoner and refused the visiting rights allowed to a civil prisoner. It took Tom Waters five days and an approach to the Home Office for the prison to be told that his wife should be treated as a civil prisoner.

All appeals for Val to be released were refused. She was released from prison three days early as compensation for the seven she spent treated as a criminal. As for the hunters, here is the last paragraph of the Sunday Times report: "In Leicestershire's hunting country, the four men who, unlike Mrs Waters, were actually charged in court and found guilty of an offence, have not fared too badly. Their legal fees were paid by the British Field Sports Society and the Masters of Foxhounds Association. Their fines were paid by the supporters of Atherstone Hunt. Mr Travers Lisney, a businessman who was joint master of Atherstone Hunt at the time of the incident, says: "I'm very glad she's in prison. She was a bloody nuisance as far as I'm concerned.""

Val carried on with her anti-bloodsports activities and supported a wide range of other activities to help and protect animals. Tragically she was diagnosed with cancer at the end of 1997. She continued to campaign for as long as she could, but her illness worsened and on February 24th 1998, aged 65, she took her own life to avoid the suffering and indignity of the final stages. After the Labour win in 1997 she knew hunting would be banned—albeit that she did not live to see it.

The lesson from Market Bosworth Magistrates was not lost on the hunting fraternity. Whatever happened in the hunting fields, hunters would always be perceived by the legal authorities to be the victims. To add to the mix hunting enthusiasts have deployed a very effective dirty tricks department. They have sought to have animal rights campaigners wrongly blamed for all manner of offences ranging from theft of hounds to the planting of 'bombs'.

The deviousness of the hunting fraternity is best exemplified by the 1990 case of leading hunting enthusiast Alan Newberry-Street, Director of the British Hunting Exhibition – a mobile bloodsports display supported by the BFSS and the MFHA. He placed a nail bomb beneath his own Land Rover in his home village of Seavington St. Mary, Somerset. He then telephoned the police, claimed to be a spokesman for the 'British Animal Rights Society' and told them where to find the bomb. Police sealed off the village, began evacuating it, including an old people's home. The Bomb Squad were called down from Herefordshire along with more than 80 police officers. However, officers were puzzled when they asked Newberry-Street to look under his Land Rover but saw him locate the device by feel alone. They stopped being puzzled when they found a nail, identical to those used in the bomb, under a cushion on the driver's seat. When questioned about this coincidence, Newberry-Street confessed that he had put the bomb there himself. At Taunton Crown Court in October 1990 the prosecution reported him as saying: "*I did it to discredit the Animal Rights and Hunt Saboteurs Associations.*" He asked for two similar offences (hoax calls about bombs in London) to be taken into consideration. Alan Newberry-Street was jailed for 9 months.

In any conflict between hunter and hunt saboteur it is obvious where the violence comes from. Hunters delight in violence. Conversely, hunt saboteurs are peaceful, usually either vegetarian or more likely vegan.

Some unsavoury individuals were associated with bloodsports. Hare coursing enthusiast Clement Freud exuded a veneer of charm and respectability but was a predatory paedophile who sexually abused and raped young girls. He wrecked lives in pursuit of his fun. Another hare coursing fan, Clarissa Dickson Wright, had inherited £2.8m from her mother in 1975 but spent it in 12 years of heavy drinking. She was made bankrupt three times. She happily wrecked other businesses in pursuit of the wealth to fund her pleasures. Both were participants in and passionate defenders of bloodsports. Both were media darlings.

There were too many incidents of hunt violence to mention them all. The case of Eddie Coulston who was nearly killed by a hare courser at the

1984 Waterloo Cup was mentioned in Chapter 1. It was said at the time that if hunt violence continued unrestrained it would lead to a death. Seven years later the first hunt saboteur was killed at a hunt. Michael Hill was killed aged just 18 whilst protesting following the meet of the Cheshire Beagles on Saturday February 9th 1991. The hunt met at *The Red Lion*, Little Budworth, (near Oulton Park Motorcycle Racecourse). All afternoon there had been repeated scuffles. Hunters had thrown punches at saboteurs and used a wheel brace against one saboteur. Towards the end of the day, still with no kill recorded, the huntsmen boxed up their hounds in the small blue trailer which was being towed by an open-top pick-up truck.

Kennel Huntsman, Alan Summersgill, together with another hunter, jumped into the pick-up. Three saboteurs nearby, on impulse, leapt onto the back of the pick-up hoping to stop the man driving the pack off to another location to continue hunting away from the hunt saboteurs.

However, Alan Summersgill immediately drove off at high speed, with the three saboteurs clinging on. He drove erratically and at speed for five miles, around country lanes, in icy conditions, towing a pack of hounds and with three saboteurs perched on top.

The three were terrified. They tried to keep a grip and feared what might happen at their destination. They decided that if the vehicle stopped for a junction, or slowed enough, they would jump off and run away. Tragically it seemed that Mike panicked and, in fear of his life, jumped from the pick-up as it rounded a bend and slowed. He failed to clear the truck properly and was caught between the truck and trailer which crushed him.

Alan Summersgill would not stop. He drove on for a further mile and only halted when a hunt saboteur smashed the back window into the cab. That saboteur was attacked with a whip as he tried to stop the vehicle. When it did stop, the saboteur ran back the mile to where Mike's prone body lay in the road. Another hunt saboteur ran to a nearby house to call the ambulance (this was before mobile phones were commonplace).

Alan Summersgill simply drove off, flagged down a police car shortly afterwards and later in the afternoon handed himself into a police station. Police treated the case as a tragic road traffic accident. One suspects they would have reacted differently had the roles been reversed. [In March 2009 when Trevor Morse, a hunt supporter, tried to stop a hunt monitor in a microlight from taking off and was tragically killed by the spinning propeller the microlight pilot was initially charged with murder but subsequently acquitted by the jury of manslaughter charges].

Two years later a second young hunt saboteur was killed. On Saturday April 3rd 1993 15-year-old Thomas Worby, from Milton Keynes, was with a group of hunt saboteurs at the Cambridgeshire Foxhounds on his first hunt sabotage. The day had been a successful one for the saboteurs, a fox having escaped unharmed when hounds on his trail were called out of a covert near Low Farm, Waresley, Cambridgeshire.

The hunt eventually boxed up their pack. No-one told the hunt saboteurs the hunt had finished early for the day—it was the day of the Grand National (the race that never was as it was declared void after a series of mishaps at the start). Huntsman, Tony Ball, an irascible character, who appeared to delight in using his horse as a weapon, drove his hound van down a narrow lane away from the meet, as about 30 hunt saboteurs strolled along in front. When Tony Ball began revving the engine and nudging his vehicle forwards the hunt saboteurs quickly scrambled to the side and out of the way. Tragically Tom Worby's jacket apparently snagged on the left wing mirror and he was dragged along and fell under the rear wheels of the heavy lorry. He died shortly afterwards. 53-year-old Tony Ball was questioned by Cambridgeshire police. The CPS decided to take no action.

In the aftermath, out of concern for the feelings of his family, the hunt saboteurs who were present and witnessed the horrific manner of his death were restrained in their comments. They said little beyond expressing sincere regrets. In contrast the hunting side had no such qualms and attributed blame to everyone but themselves. The media joined in with condemnation of the saboteurs and allegations about the extreme right-wing views of the group that recruited Tom. One beacon of light and truth out of all the press comment was Edward Pearce's commentary in the *Guardian* on April 10th 1993. Here is an extract:

"Young saboteurs present in Cambridgeshire, had as their first experience after seeing the tragedy, the refusal of three huntsmen on horseback to go to a house to phone an ambulance! A desperate, distressed request from youngsters who had seen Tom Worby with blood coming out of his ears, received the answer: "Oh we're not going that way." Their second experience after police had summoned an ambulance, was to walk through jeering hunt supporters and hear taunts, laughter and cries of "He deserved it.""

On the Saturday following Tom's death the Cambridge HSA called a peaceful public meeting in Parker's Piece, Cambridge. The theme was 'Hunt Violence Kills'. It was well attended and a host of speakers called for more protection for those who seek to protect our wildlife. My colleague, Rorke Garfield, a veteran hunt saboteur, gave a particularly moving speech urging young hunt saboteurs to continue their peaceful but forceful actions to safeguard wildlife. There were no calls for revenge.

An inquest was held in Huntingdon on September 7th 1993. No jury was summoned. The Coroner returned a verdict of 'accidental death'. Here is the statement released by Cambridge HSA in response:-

"Report on the inquest held in Huntingdon on the 7th of September 1993 into the circumstances of the death of hunt saboteur Tom Worby on the 3rd of April 1993 under the wheels of the hounds van of the Cambridgeshire Foxhounds driven by huntsman Anthony Ball

Tom Worby's parents, the hunt saboteurs witnesses and the hunting fraternity were each represented by their own solicitor. The inquest started with an application brought forward by Tom Worby's parents that the inquest should be heard in front of a Jury. Their solicitor argued that the law requires a Jury if the circumstances under which the death took place are likely to reoccur. Given the fact that another hunt saboteur, Mike Hill, had died under similar circumstances in February 1991 on a protest at the Cheshire Beagles, and given the increased amount of violence on hunt protests in the last season, the Coroner "has no option than to allow for a Jury". Nevertheless the Coroner declined.

Then the hunt witnesses were questioned. Some of them, who spoke of about up to 13 saboteurs hanging on to the hounds van just before the incident occurred, were quickly exposed as having a too vivid imagination. It turned out that there was not one single witness on the hunt's side, who had actually seen what had happened. In the van at the time of the incident were three people. First Christopher Ball, the Huntsman's son and a paid Terrier-man was asked what he saw. He said basically that he was too frightened to have seen anything. He saw Tom Worby level with the window on his side of the van, but he didn't care about what happened to him or why he disappeared. Next Anthony Ball, the huntsman and driver of the van was asked. He said that he just caught a very brief glimpse of Tom Worby at the window, but he drove on when the road was clear. He said he had no idea that any accident might have happened.

The next witness was Amanda Sutton, the kennel groom, and the third passenger in the van at the time of the incident. To the amazement of the audience she said under oath that Christopher Ball told his father that he had 'just driven over an Anti'. She also witnessed that Anthony Ball tried to inform a police officer soon after the incident that something had happened by waving and calling out of the window, before driving home without any further delay. Her statement clearly contradicted those of the other two witnesses in the van, but the Coroner was not impressed, indeed in his summary he didn't even mention this fact.

Next only six out of more than 20 hunt saboteur witnesses were questioned. They unequivocally claimed that Anthony Ball drove too fast, dangerously nudging them from behind with the van when they were on their way back to the road. Some were pushed by the van into the ditch on the side of the track, some narrowly escaped the van when it was gaining speed. Overall the picture emerged that the van was driving reasonably slow up to a point, when it suddenly roared the engine and gained speed. Since the track is just about wider than the van, where it happened and since the track has a hedge on one side and a ditch on the other, it appeared to have been very difficult to escape the van. Some witnesses saw Tom Worby being caught by the van. They say they saw him hanging on the wing mirror and banging on the window to get the driver to stop the van. Some witnessed Tom Worby losing his grip, falling and rebouncing back from the hedge underneath the back wheels of the van.

The hunt saboteurs witnesses were very rudely questioned by the hunt solicitor and eventually told they were lying. In complete contrast to his understanding and supportive behaviour towards the hunt witnesses, the Coroner questioned the credibility and consistency of the hunt saboteurs witnesses's statements. One of them he rejected altogether.

In his summary he basically exactly repeated Anthony Ball's witness account. He called the hunt saboteurs a "mob" and doubted their compassionate feelings towards animals since they supposedly had no such feelings for the animals inside the van. He also claimed that the Cambridgeshire Foxhounds, and especially their huntsman Anthony Ball, had generally an amicable relationship with the usual hunt protesters, which is why it was unlikely for him that Anthony Ball would have acted out of anger, when he drove over and killed Tom Worby. Having been a hunt protester at the Cambridgeshire Foxhounds for the last three seasons, I can safely say that it was the complete opposite: this huntsman always and very easily lost his temper. WE were non-violent and friendly towards him, yes, but not the other way round. We of the Cambridge Hunt Saboteurs have about 20 documented incidents when Anthony Ball attacked members of our group or our cars. He also threatened and actually tried to ram us with his van, the very same van under which wheels Tom Worby died.

In summary, the Coroner gave the verdict of "accidental death". The hunt saboteurs have since then announced their intention to appeal against this verdict to bring the case to the High Courts, where it should be heard in front of a Jury."

The hunt saboteurs attempted to appeal against that verdict asking for a new inquest to be held in the presence of a jury. They were refused legal aid so could take it no further.

Tom Worby's family were initially coaxed by the media into condemning the hunt saboteurs who recruited him. However, after meeting those campaigners and after hearing the evidence given by the hunt witnesses in court they too felt it was not the one-sided picture painted by our press—and that another inquest before a jury was needed.

With the benefit of hindsight Tom was too young to be taken out to sabotage a hunt. However, he was a few weeks short of his 16th birthday and it can be hard to gauge age. Most hunt saboteurs regard it as wise for anyone on their first hunt sabotage, whatever their age, to have some expert to chaperone and guide them. Newcomers to wildlife protection cannot believe just how violent and callous hunters can become in the heat of the moment. There was fault on the compassionate side but there can be no doubt where the real blame lay. Tony Ball only had to stop, to allow Tom to free himself, and then drive on. Those riders who refused to call an ambulance are in stark contrast with the many hunt saboteurs and monitors who time and again have put their differences with hunters aside to help injured or stranded hunters or help hounds or horses.

Violent attacks by hunt supporters on hunt saboteurs continued unabated. There was nearly another fatality at a cub hunting meet of the Old Surrey, Burstow and West Kent Foxhounds on the morning of September 1st 2000. Steve Christmas, a hunt saboteur from Croydon, was peacefully protesting with colleagues when gamekeeper and hunt supporter, Martin Maynard, drove at the group. Steve Christmas was hit as he fled then deliberately driven over.

Steve nearly died. He was airlifted to hospital and spent four weeks in intensive care with a crushed pelvis, broken ribs and abdominal injuries. The CPS initially prosecuted Martin Maynard for Grievous Bodily Harm with Intent but dropped the case the following year giving as a reason the fact that one witness was imprisoned for an unrelated offence. The four-wheel-drive vehicle driven by Martin Maynard was untaxed and uninsured—he was fined £75 for those offences. Four years after he was nearly killed Steve Christmas was awarded £18,500 compensation by the Criminal Injuries Compensation Authority. His injuries proved life-changing. When hunt saboteurs protested outside the hunt kennels the day after that near-fatal assault they were greeted by hunt supporters armed with pickaxe handles who taunted them. Some windows at the kennels were broken. Watching police arrested no-one on the day but some weeks later 26 people identified by CCTV had their homes raided. They were arrested for 'violent disorder' and later 18 were charged with Conspiracy to Commit Violent Disorder. There were three trials. Those found guilty received lengthy Community Service Orders.

Hunt stewards and blocking footpaths

Over the years hunts tried various tactics to deal with hunt saboteurs, everything from outright violence to hiding from saboteurs. In the early 1990s they developed a plan of action that revolved around the use of hunt stewards or hunt marshals to deal with anyone who interfered with the hunt. When a hunt operated on private land with the permission of the landowner that same landowner had property rights and could deal with trespassers. When people are identified as trespassers they can be told to leave and should do so by the shortest route to the nearest public highway.

If the trespassers refused to leave or ignored demands to leave then the landowner is entitled to use 'reasonable force' to eject the trespasser. That does not mean that they have a free hand to assault trespassers, run them over or batter them. The idea of hunt stewarding was that the landowner gave authority to a group of hunt supporters—fit young lads—to act on his behalf and eject people interfering with the hunt. If the hunt did not have enough volunteers they might hire professional security staff–or pay men from their local rugby club.

For hunt supporters, such stewarding did not solve the problem of hunt saboteurs altogether. Stewards could stop hunt saboteurs interfering at dig-outs to save the lives of trapped and exhausted foxes but our countryside, thankfully, is criss-crossed by public footpaths and bridleways and there were many legal ways for hunt saboteurs to get close to hunters.

Hunt followers were irritated that the general public could share the countryside with them. They explored ways to limit the use of footpaths. They found an ancient court judgement that declared that a footpath could only be legally used for transit from A to B. You were not allowed to stand still on any footpath. Some hunters instructed their stewards to ensure no one trying to protect wildlife loitered along a footpath. If you, as a hunt monitor, stood still on a footpath to film the hunt on the other side of the adjacent field it was not long before a hunt steward barged you in the back and told you to 'move on'.

Essex Foxhounds followers pushed this further. In the early 1990s they conceived the idea that the landowner over whose land the footpath ran could close that footpath to people he suspected would use it improperly (did not like the look of). The theory was floated with Essex Police as a general thing but of course Essex hunt stewards were only interested in barring opponents of hunting from the footpath.

We reached the stage whereby in Essex in 1993, on hunting days, footpaths near where the hunt met would be closed to those who sought to protect wildlife. Hunt stewards would block entrances to a footpath and only let by people who they deemed to be acceptable. It was a young Nick Herbert, a keen supporter of hunting and the Essex Foxhounds who, I was told, was a proponent of this concept. He went on to become an MP—and in 2010 David Cameron made him Policing Minister, charged with the responsibility of enforcing the Hunting Act 2004.

January 9th 1993 was a significant day. I followed the Essex Foxhounds as an observer with Lawrie Payne the LACS regional representative. The hunt met at Felsted. Hunt stewards were out in force as were local hunt saboteurs. When Lawrie and I tried to use a footpath to watch hounds going into covert our way was blocked by the stewards and we were forcibly ejected from the public right of way.

Essex police officers watched this happen. When I complained to one officer that my right to use a public right of way was being denied he replied that the hunt had told Essex Police that they had legal authority to do precisely that. I complained that they had no right in law to block a highway in that manner, all the more so as I was only seeking to observe the hunt, not interfere with the hunt.

The officer was adamant. The hunt claimed they had the right to close the footpath and Essex police accepted that. If I or anyone else did not like it, we should take the matter to court. I did not view that as greatly helpful. I could see such actions would lead to conflict.

We encountered similar behaviour from hunt stewards on Saturday January 23rd when the Essex Foxhounds met at *The Butcher's Arms*, North End. That day there were some 200 hunt saboteurs out as well and as expected intense conflict developed with the hunt stewards. It led to what became known as the Battle of Stagden Cross.

The Metropolitan police were summoned to help their Essex colleagues and turned out in force—some 30 police vehicles and the police helicopter. I ran up one footpath to film the most vicious fighting where the hunt stewards were attacking the hunt saboteurs. The police helicopter landed nearby and two officers emerged to try to contain the violence.

When he saw the police one big burly hunt steward threw himself to the ground and rolled around like a football striker seeking a penalty. He was frantically rubbing his eyes and complaining that chemicals had been thrown in his face and blinded him. Some hunt saboteurs carried bottles of 'sab special' a harmless concoction of strong smelling liquids used to mask the scent of hunted animals. Doubtless in the mêlée some of that was splashed around; none was sprayed deliberately into anyone's face.

From about 11:45am the hunt ended up bottled up in a farm at Stagden Cross and did no further hunting that day. There was a thin blue line of police officers between the two sides trying to calm the situation. I ventured into the perilous ground that is the middle to help. Hunt saboteurs complained they had been punched and kicked and blood streaming from wounds proved it. They wanted the police to arrest their assailants but the police were happy to just end the violence. I calmly pointed out to saboteurs that with the hunters contained in the farm yard there would be no hunting so their job was done.

The LACS were determined to resolve this situation peacefully. Tuesday February 16th, I left home at 7:15a.m. to meet Jim Barrington, Angela Smith, and Lawrie Payne. We had an arranged appointment with Assistant Chief Constable Geoffrey Markham at Essex Police HQ in Chelmsford. We sought to clarify our use of footpaths on hunting days to monitor hunts. We achieved nothing. We were told police had received legal advice that it was lawful for hunt stewards to remove people from a footpath if they judged those people were not using the footpath properly. We learned the hunt had received legal advice that they could go further—their stewards could even deny access to the footpath to people they suspected did not intend to use it properly. Essex police accepted that advice and advised that if we did not like it the LACS would have to take the matter to court. We discussed the bizarre situation and agreed that the LACS would have to lead the line in upholding citizen's rights in our countryside. If landowners could legally decide who used footpaths over their land where might it end? We resolved to liaise with the media and chose the BBC programme *Countryfile* who at that time were still interested in upholding the rights of all in our countryside.

Jim Barrington planned to force the situation to a conclusion. It was March 6th when Lawrie Payne and I met Jim in the Essex countryside. Once again we tried to observe the activities of the Essex Foxhounds. They met at Pleshey. From the road, we saw the hunt in distant fields. A footpath headed towards the scene so we set off down it. I kept my video camera running. A group of hunt stewards duly blocked our way. We asked to use the footpath only to see, photograph and film the hunt but our way was blocked. Everyone was calm and reasonable. We were not just blocked—we were forcibly ejected. That occasion there were no hunt saboteurs out, but there was a film crew from *Countryfile*. Incidents they filmed were included in the *Countryfile* programme broadcast on March 14th 1993. Even neutral observers considered hunters to be behaving in a high-handed fashion. Rural folk value their footpaths.

What caused exceptional outrage was the knowledge by many rural dwellers of the ways hunters themselves misused footpaths. For example, hunt riders commonly rode along footpaths. When they did so after wet weather with the ground soft their hooves would sink in to a considerable depth and caused a lot of damage. People could stumble in the deep holes

361

and twist or break ankles. If the public subsequently complained to the Council about the state of the footpaths the Council had to reinstate those paths at public expense. Such damage happened in some parts with depressing regularity.

Essex police advised the LACS to take the matter to court and the LACS did. They took legal action on behalf of their Executive Director, Jim Barrington, and Essex regional representative, Lawrie Payne. That ended in an out of court settlement whereby the Essex Foxhounds paid a substantial sum to the two men in compensation. Lawrie Payne gained a new video camera with which to expose hunting, courtesy of the Essex Foxhounds. LACS hunt monitors were then allowed to make unhindered use of all footpaths and other public rights of way in Essex. The LACS also acquired a copy of the BFSS manual for Masters of Foxhounds entitled *"Hunt Stewarding"*. Marked *"strictly confidential"* it made interesting reading and included the following:

"If sensible but tough, fit young men are not available to the hunt as volunteers, then you will have to consider hiring men. You will probably have to pay £20 for a local man, more if he has to travel. Ex-soldiers are likely to cost more, in the region of 40. Highly qualified professional security men cost about £100 a day. It is essential that your men are fit and robust. It helps if they are solidly built. But they must not be thugs. It goes without saying that you should not use anyone who has a criminal record."

At the back, appendix F, entitled *"Advice On Media Relations"* included this that hinted at the true financial burden of hunt stewarding:
"You should not, under any circumstances, reveal how much the use of stewards is costing your hunt, nor should you allow yourself to be drawn into commenting on the effect it may be having on hunt finances."

Countryfile, that had been excellent at reporting country issues in an unbiased manner, rapidly descended to become little more that the propaganda mouthpiece for the BFSS and and its successor, the Countryside Alliance (CA). One of their journalists was embarrassed by that turn of events, but explained that it was made clear that if they wanted access to the UK countryside, they should abide by the pro-hunting and pro-shooting sympathies of those who own most of that countryside.

As attempts to ban hunting moved up the political agenda the hunters became more threatening. The following was penned under the name 'Nimrod' in *Countryman's Weekly* July 7th 1995:
"Nobody has yet thought through, or dared to suggest, what would happen if hunting were to be banned. Would we all sit down meek and mild, as 20,000 hounds are shot, hundreds of horses put down and lurchers, whippets, terriers and greyhounds made redundant and potential instruments of a criminal act? If you think there has been social unrest over the export of a few calves, be prepared for the countryside to rise up in bitter anger at any attempt to end its sports."

That was a violent road that culminated in hunt supporters viciously attacking police officers in Parliament Square.

CHAPTER FOURTEEN
The ACIG works with colleagues in Ireland

After some work in Ireland previously described I was delighted to work with colleagues across the Irish Sea throughout the 1990s. In the autumn of 1993 I accompanied Jim Barrington on a week-long expedition to Ireland at the invitation of the Irish Council Against Bloodsports (ICABS). November 6th to the 13th was a week that proved informative, enjoyable and at times alarming.

ICABS had led a brilliant campaign against hare coursing in Ireland and sought similar success against fox hunting and stag hunting. At that time, English foxhunters boasted that were hunting to be banned in the UK they would simply cross the Irish Sea for their fun. Many already took hunting holidays in Ireland. That being so we felt it only right that we also should cross the Irish Sea to give our support to ICABS campaigners. If England could export cruelty it could also export compassion.

Our mission that November was to spread the word, encourage and inform supporters of ICABS and the public through a series of well-advertised public meetings. Colleagues from ICABS booked all the venues and made the necessary arrangements.

As a preliminary I crossed to Dublin on Saturday November 6th and spoke at the annual ICABS conference on the purpose and value of hunt monitoring. The following day I accompanied their wildlife research officer, John Tierney, on an undercover trip to video and photograph Trim Coursing Club. We used a hidden video camera to film—with the lens hidden in a jacket and the recorder in the pocket.

It was park coursing that, as previously described, differed from our open hare coursing in that hares were held captive in an enclosure at one end of the field. I had seen such coursing at Clonmel, their big annual event that is the equivalent of our Waterloo Cup, but this coursing at Trim was almost farcical.

Under pressure from ICABS the coursers appeared to have been instructed by their own hierarchy to tone their pastime down and do their best to avoid kills. The result, as we observed, was the hare was often halfway up the field before the dogs were even slipped and in many cases she disappeared into the escape hole before the dogs had reached the scene! Many courses were just a straight race between two dogs to see which reached the other end of the field first. The hare was superfluous. They could have done just as well with a child's toy rabbit winched in on a piece of rope. Only on two occasions in the first session did we see a hare even forced to turn and both times she escaped.

At the time, from the semi-final stages of Irish Park coursing, the dogs had to be muzzled. On the face of it that appeared to be humane, to have solved the problem of cruelty in coursing. However sadly it was soon clear that it was not the case. Incidents were reported where hares were killed by muzzled dogs. They can only have been bludgeoned to death.

From January 1994, it was reported that all Irish Park coursing would be done with muzzled dogs.

Merely muzzling the dogs left many cruelty issues unresolved. For so long as live hares are used there is obvious cruelty in the catching, holding, transporting and release of those hares. Hares are timid wild creatures that do not appreciate being handled by man.

During our Trim observations the most fearful screaming that we heard from a hare came from the release area. We did not know what happened but when we filmed at the release zone we saw hares being cajoled along a compartmented channel by a courser with a stick. Perhaps a terrified hare was cajoled too hard or perhaps she was trapped beneath one sliding door? That afternoon we returned to Dublin and met Jim Barrington and Aideen Yourell from ICABS. In the evening we drove to stay in Waterford.

The next morning, Monday November 8th 1993, we searched for the Kilkenny Foxhounds meeting at Ballyduff, near Thomastown but found them very elusive. That evening Jim and I gave an illustrated talk at the Tower Hotel, Waterford. It was well attended and, as expected, some of the local hunting fraternity turned up. They left dumbfounded and disheartened at seeing the visual proof of the measure of cruelty perpetrated by their English counterparts.

The next night we were at Cork for what proved to be an extremely lively meeting. We arrived to find a substantial contingent of grim faced hunters in attendance together with many ICABS supporters. Sadly, there appeared to be precious few members of the general public in the room.

The hunters listened to our presentation in stony silence with only a few heckles. It was during questions at the end that mayhem started. One burly hunter suddenly stood up and lashed a chair over the head of an ICABS supporter in front of him. The hunter then sat down again behind him as if nothing had happened! He looked the sort of guy that had not slugged anyone with a chair since—oh, as long ago as the night before.

With blood streaming from his head the ICABS man was taken to hospital where he had eleven stitches inserted into his wound. The Gardai (police) were summoned but before they arrived the hunter had left the room with some of his friends thwarting all attempts to stop him. That incident was widely reported in the Irish media. Hunters that remained to argue their viewpoint in a more intelligent manner denied all knowledge of the man.

Our meeting on Wednesday was at Limerick, known as knife city to the locals. We were warned beforehand that hunters were preparing a show of strength. The meeting was duly packed, with standing room only at the back, but there was no violence within. That occurred at the front door where a sizeable number of hunters were irate at being shut out. Apparently, they had driven miles to attend the meeting and were enraged to find the room full—so enraged that when the doorman tried to close the doors they assaulted him.

The Gardai were called again. As I stood up to speak I was passed a note saying the Gardai were advising ICABS to curtail the meeting as they would not be able to contain any further outbreaks of trouble. Not the most reassuring of circumstances in which to talk.

Our last meeting was on Thursday November 11th in Galway. We took care to drive through The Burren along the way. It was therapeutic to be immersed in such beauty. Our meeting was at the Ardilaun House Hotel. Again, we had to prepare for trouble but thankfully none was forthcoming. Some hunters attended but were well mannered. They listened, asked questions, argued their viewpoint in the bar afterwards, then left. Would that all our opponents were that civilised. Next morning we saw more of the wonders of Ireland when we took a diversion to Connemara and stopped off for photographs at the quaint 'Quiet Man' bridge (named after the John Wayne film) near Oughterard.

In July the following year I returned to Ireland to help ICABS again. Friday July 8th 1994 was most enjoyable. Trevor Sargent TD (equivalent of our MP) met me at Dublin airport and took me to join in the Green Party celebrations in the city. I returned to Mullingar with Aideen and Joan Yourell and the next day photographed the formal opening of the new ICABS office in Mullingar. Tony Gregory TD (1947-2009), Trevor Sargent TD and the ICABS President, Hugh Leonard (1926-2009) were present. Hugh Leonard was a forceful advocate against cruelty. One of his quotes was: "*Hare coursing isn't a sport. It is barbarism, promoted by those who have ascended the wrong limb of the evolutionary tree.*"

We worked hard to raise funds. After running the London Marathon in 1994 I ran the Dublin Marathon on October 30th 1995 to raise funds for my ACIG. My ICABS colleague, John Tierney, ran as well. From the start, we did street theatre for the media to highlight our cause. I dressed in black hunting gear and carried a cardboard cut-out of a horse's head. John Tierney dressed in fox costume. RTE (Irish television) interviewed me before the start. We set off with me blowing the hunting horn as the English Huntsman chased the Irish fox. I carried a map so as not to get lost in the back streets of Dublin and finished in 5 hours 50 minutes. John achieved a commendable 4 hours 15 minutes.

On February 23rd 1996 I joined ICABS colleagues Aideen Yourell and Catriona Smyth for undercover observation of the Irish Cup coursing event at Clounanna, Adair near Limerick. After an uneventful morning in the afternoon we saw hares buffeted by the muzzled dogs. One dog collapsed when led away from the escape zone after a course. That dog, *Nought to Sixty*, was carried off and died soon afterwards. Later we saw a hare caught by the dogs and bludgeoned on the ground by them. The hare appeared to be killed. I filmed some courses by shielding my camera and having Aideen and Catriona either side of me to shield my actions.

The following day, with ICABS colleagues Aideen Yourell, Mona Ward and Mary Chundee, I attended the meet of the Westmeath Foxhounds at Jamestown Court. Mona and I posed as hunt supporters and walked in to photograph the meet. Hounds were taken first to draw adjacent woodland. A couple of lads swinging spades walked out from the wood and a fox was immediately found. Whilst Aideen and Mary followed the hunt, Mona and I scouted the wood for artificial earths, but found nothing.

The next day Aideen and I returned for the last day of the Irish Cup Coursing event at Clounanna. It was bitterly cold. There was snow on the fields but the roads were clear. I filmed the finals from a concealed position in the car park. We lingered to photograph the presentation of the trophies.

In December 1996 I was back in Ireland working undercover with ICABS colleagues to expose bloodsports. On December 14th, along with Philip Kiernan, I attended the meet of the Westmeath Foxhounds at Bunbrosna. We took the undercover role. I chatted merrily with the riders until I met a lady who said she lived in Woodbridge, Suffolk. Too near me for comfort. When I saw her ride off to talk to the Master I kept my distance thereafter. We saw a fox escape towards Lough Iron.

The next day along with a larger team of ICABS colleagues we monitored the Park Coursing event held at Castletown Geoghegan near Mullingar, County Westmeath. A public road ran the width of one small field away from the coursing venue. The ICABS team staged a banner demonstration on the roadside verge against the cruelty of the coursing whilst a colleague and I endeavoured to film the coursing from amongst the banners. We were soon spotted. Within minutes some of the coursing lads came out towards us and one advised me to be very careful with my camera.

The ICABS protestors were told they were not allowed to demonstrate. At this their organiser, Aideen Yourell, used her mobile phone to summon the Gardai. The arrival of the local beat officer took the heat out of the situation and we could carry on with our protest and filming.

The coursers clearly loathed being filmed but there was little they could do. The slips given to the hares seemed unusually long and as a result several hares had reached the sanctuary of the escape zone before the dogs were even up with them. On some occasions the slips were so long that one or both dogs ran 'unsighted'. That was when the dog lost sight of its quarry and just bounded gaily but aimlessly up the field. Even though that course might be re-run it amounted to poor coursing and could have been avoided by using an artificial lure and a regulation length slip.

Our first indicator that a hare was in the field and the course was on was when the lady judge spurred her horse up the field towards our left. The tiny fleeing hare would come into view with the dogs pounding after her to the cheers of the crowd. Most hares escaped. On one occasion the hare was flicked forwards by a dog in a cartwheeling manner. When she tumbled over and over we feared for her. Thankfully she had not been injured and was soon on her feet again. She darted off to safety leaving the dogs frustrated.

We witnessed another similar mauling from which the hare survived. It is fair to say that on both occasions if the dogs had been un-muzzled the hares would have died. Muzzling the dogs increased the chances of hares escaping but hares could still be injured and killed by muzzled dogs. We saw two maulings where the hare was hit by the dogs but managed to escape. We also saw two occasions where the unfortunate creature was pinned to the ground by one or both dogs and given a real battering. Each time a supporter, who in British coursing would be known as the picker-up, dashed on to the field to 'rescue' the hare.

He clutched the battered little body to protect her from the dogs. Was she dead? Was she alive? With the dogs held by their handlers he could have proved that she was alive, if she was, by replacing her on the ground allowing her to make her own way to the escape zone. He declined and instead carried her body to the escape area. I saw no signs of movement on either occasion from the hare.

When hares were mauled or pinned to the ground there was silence from the crowd. That was in stark contrast to the raucous cheers and jeers heard from coursing supporters on this side of the Irish Sea when hares were caught and ripped by the dogs. It could be that the Irish were more civilised than our yobbish louts or perhaps they feared a more imminent ban on their activities and consequently were on their 'best behaviour.'

The coursing continued to its natural conclusion sometime in the afternoon after which the few supporters who watched, and in some cases bet on the results, drifted home. We stayed to see what happened to the hares—those not coursed and those coursed and caught again.

Hares were caught before the meeting and held in an enclosure to be released at the appointed time. Afterwards those in a fit condition are supposed to be released. However, hares are not easy to catch in the first place and ICABS supporters have often wondered as to the true nature of the 'hare release' that takes place afterwards.

It appeared an ideal time to follow those coursers with the hares to see what happened. It was soon clear that despite being told by supporters that we could watch the hare release we were in fact to be involved in a 'game of cat and mouse'. After a lengthy delay to catch, count and check the hares (we were told that two had slight marks on them and two were 'missing') the van carrying the hares set off down the narrow lanes followed by a car driven by a coursing supporter.

Memories of following the secretive otter hunters back in the early 1970's in the UK led me to suspect that the back car would simply block the lane allowing the front vehicle to proceed unobserved. The Irish coursers had thought of an added refinement to this technique. Our convoy proceeded down through a farmyard whereupon their rear vehicle stopped and blocked us. The lead vehicle, carrying the hares, disappeared from sight. There was an ICABS car behind the road blockage and then mine. I was about to get out and film the blocked road when the ICABS car suddenly reversed. I looked right and coming down the farm drive towards us was a burly gypsy type 'gentleman' backed up by several young lads, at least three of whom were brandishing shotguns!

I believe discretion to be the better part of valour so I hastily nipped back into my car and beat a hasty retreat. We called the Gardai again but as the light faded so did our hopes of seeing those hares released. We have only the word of the coursing fraternity that they were.

The following year I returned to Ireland to help ICABS colleagues. On Tuesday February 4th 1997 I caught the Ryanair flight from Stansted to Dublin, picked up a hire car and drove out to Mullingar where I met Aideen Yourell. The next day I drove Aideen and Joan Yourell to Dublin for the ICABS Press Conference at the Powers Hotel. Three TDs attended and I met John Fitzgerald, a most determined campaigner.

The next morning, Thursday February 6th, I drove Aideen to look at the deer in the park at the Ward Union kennels at Green Park near Dunshaughlin. We saw a chap herding the deer like cattle—with a stick.

The next day Aideen Yourell and I went to the meet of the Ward Union Staghounds. On the way, we took another look at the deer in the park at the kennels. The meet was at Stamullin at 1pm. As Aideen was then well-known to Irish hunters it was more a matter of monitoring the hunt rather than any attempt at undercover work. At the meet we went into the pub for coffee. Aideen was soon recognised and we heard mutterings of discontent from the assembled hunters. We saw the deer released from the cart at 1:30pm. He was caught again about an hour later some miles to the north. I caught the 6:55pm flight home that evening.

In 1997 ICABS acquired a shocking video that proved the cruelty inherent in fox hunting. They released the video to the media at a press conference in Dublin on Wednesday March 5th 1997. Taken in 1986, with the agreement of the South Union Foxhounds based in County Cork, the film shows a day's hunting. A fox was hunted to ground, dug out by at least four terriermen, attacked by a terrier, placed in a sack and then thrown in front of the hunt for hounds to chase and kill. The Huntsman whooped with glee as he baited his hounds with the dead fox. As graphic proof of the cruelty at the heart of hunting the film is without equal.

The video was made to promote the hunt. As well as the day's hunting (where doubtless the hunters were on their best behaviour) there were scenes of a hunt social at which hunt officials were interviewed about fox hunting and there was a visit to a supporter who cared for a tame fox.

In early summer the following year I returned to Ireland to help ICABS colleagues on one new area of animal abuse and another sadly all too common. It was Sunday May 17th 1998 when we observed the ostrich egg and spoon race at Punchestown Country Fair at the racecourse near Naas. The concept of wee jockeys riding Ostriches seemed to enthral the media—but opportunities for abuse were obvious.

Organisers had planned to run the Amberleigh House Ostrich Derby with a prize fund of IR£5000. Professional jockeys were booked to ride the 11 ostriches. However, pressure from animal welfare groups, including ICABS, caused the event to be called off. The Irish Department of Agriculture asked for the race to be cancelled on cruelty grounds and the Minister for Agriculture, Joe Walsh, said he would ban the race if it was not called off. Organisers then announced the ostriches would merely be on show at the event. When Aideen Yourell and I visited the Fair, we found it went a bit further. The replacement event was an 'egg and spoon' race with the jockeys running over an obstacle course. To add to the 'fun' (danger?)

368

the ostriches were released into the running area and some chap blew a hunting horn to much cheering from the crowd.

The birds appeared stressed and it seemed fortunate that no-one sharing their enclosure was kicked. Abuse of ostriches for entertainment has a long history. During the imperial period of Rome, they were paraded at festivals. Julius Capitolinus writing around the 3rd century AD tells of 300 ostriches, painted red, being released for the amusement of the Emperor Gordian III and his court. At a similar period, the Egyptian tyrant, Firmus, ordered ostriches to be harnessed to his chariots. It was also said that he could eat a whole ostrich in a single day. Egyptian and Roman ladies of noble birth rode ostriches on ceremonial occasions.

I then spent the following three days in Ireland looking for evidence of badger snaring. I walked many a mile with Aideen Yourell and Philip Kiernan. We found no snares but I did find a mucky Irish bog-hole—that I fell into.

In January 1999 I made another trip to Ireland to help ICABS colleagues. During it I secured the most powerful film I ever gathered demonstrating the cruelty and violence at the heart of carted stag hunting. The expedition started innocuously enough when on Saturday January 16th I caught a morning Ryanair flight from Stansted to Dublin and was met at the airport by Aideen Yourell. Aideen drove me to Mullingar where I checked into the Austin Friars hotel. Whereas it had been sunny in both Stansted and Dublin I walked to the shops in Mullingar in a blizzard.

The next day I spoke at the ICABS investigations and tactics meeting in Portlaoise. Many enthusiastic campaigners attended including Aideen Yourell, Philip Kiernan, Dick Power (1927-2011) and John Tierney. That evening we enjoyed an Indian meal in Portlaoise. Overnight the meal struck back with a vengeance as I became closely acquainted with my hotel toilet.

Others at the meal were similarly afflicted. Next day I was so ill I had to see a doctor. Even that afternoon I was unable to hold anything down. We planned to attend the meet of the Ward Union Staghounds the following day, Tuesday January 19th. Would I recover in time?

Thankfully on waking on Tuesday morning I felt well enough to go. I phoned the hunt kennels and they told me the meet details. Aideen was still stricken but Philip was well enough to accompany me. He picked me up from my hotel and drove us to the meet at *The Hatchet*, just south of Culmullin cross roads, north-west of Dublin, at 1pm.

At the meet, we took photographs and film of the deer in their cart and hounds being unboxed. I then set off to follow the deer cart to the point of release. On the way, a rider leant out of her saddle and said to me in friendly fashion, "*You're Mike, aren't you?*"

I could only smile in agreement. I was truly astonished that she had recognised me when so many English hunters failed to. I knew that some hunts in East Anglia warned their followers about me but surely not in the wilds of the Irish Republic? The explanation came moments later when she introduced me to a colleague: "*Here is Mike, he's a photographer from London, from the* Sunday Times."

I was being confused with a true professional and felt flattered. It all became clear when Philip caught up. He told me that world-renowned boxer Steve Collins was riding with the hunt that day and there was a professional photographer named Mike King, not from the *Sunday Times* but from the *Sunday Telegraph,* out to do a story on him.

We formulated a plan. The *Sunday Telegraph*, a very pro-hunt paper would do a typical shallow puff for hunting. If we monitored and paid close attention to what happened, particularly on the fringes, we might show what happened behind the glamorous façade that was the limit of their interest.

To achieve that we needed luck and we got it. Early in the afternoon we were at the tail of a line of cars following riders that we had seen moving across the fields. The cars stopped and I saw their occupants jump out with real urgency and look to their left. I did likewise. As soon as I was out of the car I heard that dread sound of staghounds baying their quarry. I had first heard this as a young hunt saboteur back in the mid-seventies, some 24 years before. A small field away I saw hounds milling around the back of a barn. I guessed the deer to be in or near it so ran back up the road, seeking access to the land, following a stag hunt supporter. When he nipped down the side of a bungalow, through an open gate and climbed over a closed gate I did likewise.

The baying sound was incessant. I knew hounds were up close and personal with the deer. I checked my cameras. On clearing the gate and running into the field I saw the stag break away from the building on my right and run to my left with the baying hounds keeping close company.

I turned on my video camera. The field was a boggy quagmire. The deer reached some bales then turned to face the hounds. I heard a shouted warning from other supporters flooding into the field behind me to watch out for the photographer (me?!) but ignored it. The image of the deer standing all alone was stark through my black & white viewfinder. A deluge of rain then struck and the deer broke away. I turned my video camera off and put it under my jacket to shield it both from the supporters around me and from the inclement weather.

The stag ran to my left, towards a railed farm gate it could never clear. I turned my camera on again. The deer banged into the gate, bounced back, and a hound snapped at his ankles. The stag ran on ahead of me seeking the protection of the hedgerow at the field's edge. Hunt supporters rushed by me. One leapt at the head of the deer and wrestled him. I thought no wonder they cut the antlers off. A good spread of antlers might be easy to grab but can also do a lot of damage.

The hounds piled into the fray with the most appalling baying sound. Two black jacketed hunt riders joined the mêlée and tried to beat hounds back. The struggling deer was forced to his knees in the mud by followers. He was a pitiful sight. The best I could do to help him was to stay at distance and record his torment. The air was assailed with colourful expletives as hunters cussed each other.

When eventually the deer was subdued and hounds cleared away supporters started to drift back towards me. That was my cue to leave. I concealed my camera, turned and strolled away. The stag was caught around 2:45pm. Philip Kiernan took my place in the front line and photographed the bewildered animal manhandled back into his cart.

I left my film with ICABS who expertly handled the subsequent dealings with the Irish media. A photograph and excellent write-up was published in the *Irish Sun*, Thursday January 21st 1999 with more national coverage on the Sunday. ICABS spokeswoman Aideen Yourell was quoted in the *Irish Sun* as follows: "*The Ward Union have always denied inflicting cruelty on deer by virtue of the fact that it is not killed. Yet they see nothing wrong in submitting it to needless terror, exhaustion and injury.*" My film was also shown on RTÉ (Ireland's National Television and Radio Broadcaster). Reflecting afterwards I was truly puzzled to see a boxer of great repute involved. Boxers fight each other on strictly equal terms with weigh-ins etc. to ensure fairness. How could any boxer regard it as sporting to participate in such gruesome bullying? The deer ran, stood and suffered alone, one against many.

Obviously, our main concern was for the suffering endured by the hunted deer, but what of the torment endured by the 'spare' deer? His fate was to be bumped about the narrow lanes for hours following the hunt, ready to be used if needed. Philip dropped me back at Maynooth to catch the Dublin bus and from there I caught my flight home.

On Tuesday February 23rd, I received a fax from ICABS telling me the Gardai were interested in the Ward Union incident I filmed. The following month debate arose as to whether the deer hunted by the Ward Union were domesticated or wild. As the deer had their antlers cut off, were kept in fenced fields by the hunt kennels and were fed and watered by hunt staff they looked to me to be as domesticated as any farm cattle or sheep.

Following up the Gardai interest I was asked to telephone Rotherhithe police station on Monday May 17th. I called again the following day and arranged to give my statement to PC Dave Flint on Wednesday June 2nd. That day was frantic. As soon as I gave my statement I was driven at speed by a Festival official in a new Range Rover to debate against Professor Roger Scruton at the Hay Festival. I lost by a large margin. Nothing came of the Gardai interest in the Ward Union.

The only work I undertook in the north of Ireland was in 1999. On Monday April 26th, I caught a flight from Luton to Belfast and was met at the airport by Lorraine Busby. I went to the Save our Stags meeting in Belfast that evening. Save our Stags campaigned against carted stag hunting by the County Down Staghounds.

The next day I helped this wonderful group with their presentation in the Private Members Dining Room at Stormont. I showed my video taken earlier that year at the Ward Union Staghounds; it caused a stir. Twelve Northern Ireland Assembly Members from across the political spectrum attended—but there was a reminder of the political divide when two politicians declined to be photographed sharing the same platform.

Save our Stags organisers displayed a huge banner on the steps of Stormont and handed in a petition signed by 102,033 calling for the banning of carted stag hunting in the north of Ireland. Lorraine very kindly then took me on a guided tour of Belfast and I saw places that I had only previously seen on news reports of atrocities there. I caught the evening flight home to Luton.

In the summer of 1999 I returned to Ireland to help ICABS in a court case. Tuesday June 29th, I caught the noon flight from Stansted to Dublin. From the airport, I caught the bus to Dublin and then picked up the Galway bus intending to be dropped off near the ICABS office in Mullingar. I foolishly alighted early and ended up having to walk the last 3½ miles. In my youth I would have run it!

I was back in Ireland in November that year. On Friday November 12th, I flew to Dublin then caught the bus to Kinnegad where Aideen Yourell met me. I then checked into a Mullingar hotel. The next morning, we drove to the meet of the Galway Blazers Foxhounds at *The Green Briar*, Moyveela Cross Roads. We met a local ICABS supporter who followed the hunt by bicycle. Surprisingly Aideen and I were accepted as genuine hunt followers but not much happened.

We had more success the next day. On Sunday November 14th Aideen and I drove to the Co. Cavan and District Coursing Club Park meeting at Augherera, Crosserlough near Kilnaleck at noon. We estimated about 200 coursers present. The first hare coursed was knocked about by the muzzled dogs. In the crowd, it was very difficult to take photographs or film. Hidden cameras were difficult to use at hare coursing. They usually had a fixed wide-angle lens, good for filming close to such as at a livestock market, or a fox dig-out but all but useless at a hare coursing event where most action took place further away.

Eventually, after lunch I went ostensibly for a 'comfort break' in the bushes, but in fact I crept around the back of a hare pen and found a dead hare lying in the pen. I filmed and photographed her. She could have died from a variety of causes. The most likely being injuries sustained on the coursing field; the least likely being old age.

I stayed in Ireland and on Tuesday November 16th Aideen and I paid another visit to the Galway Blazers Foxhounds meeting at the Laragh Ryan Lounge, Crumlin, north of Athenry. Pupils from a nearby school turned out to see the hounds meet. Again, Aideen and I were accepted as genuine hunt supporters. At one point I took film and photographs of the hounds and riders on an old railway line.

It was a while before I worked in Ireland again. I had planned a visit in the autumn of 2003 to see the Ward Union Staghounds and hare coursing but with my father desperately ill I cancelled my trip and a colleague took my place. After that I became embroiled in gathering the evidence for the final push in support of the Hunting ban in England and Wales. After the Hunting Act took effect in February 2005 I returned to carry out more investigative work in Ireland but that is a subject for my final book.......

CHAPTER FIFTEEN
Spreading the facts. Talks, debates and letter writing.

Talks

Essential elements in my campaigning work were encouraging others to help; informing people about our work in the hope they would financially support it; and spreading the facts about cruelty to animals, particularly into schools and colleges. This was done by talks, usually illustrated with a slide-show followed by questions and answers.

When I spoke to animal rights groups, hunt saboteur groups and LACS support groups I tried to encourage the audience to join my style of lawful campaigning and investigative work. I also sought new recruits firstly for my ACIG and then later for the AWIS.

Talks in schools, colleges and universities were targeted more at educating and informing. I preferred to show slides rather than videos because a slideshow could be tailored to the audience. Nothing today matches the visual impact of a 35mm colour slide projected onto a large screen in a darkened room. Obviously with younger pupils the more gruesome and shocking images were withheld.

I took care at every student venue to request that the teachers also invited our opponents in for their view. I had nothing to fear from those who defended bloodsports. I was happy to talk before them, alongside them or after them. My sole concern was that pupils should hear both sides of the argument to enable them to take a view based on facts.

Teachers told me how they appreciated such talks as even their most quiet pupil could usually be relied upon to express an opinion about cruelty to animals. I loved the interaction with students—most memorable were the sometimes fiery debates with those vehemently pro-hunt.

Today students are often left to do all their research on the Internet. Yes, that gives access to a mine of information but no intelligent interactive debate. I venture that nothing helps young inquisitive minds more than open and frank exchanges with people who have seen it and done it.

I gave countless talks to animal rights groups, educational establishments and to audiences ranging from Young Conservatives to prison inmates! Far too many to mention more than the highlights here.

Not all my talks were well-attended. On Thursday February 21st 1991 I was away from home from 8am to 9pm as I drove to give a talk about my work to students at the North Staffordshire Polytechnic. Four turned up, one of whom was a hunter.

September 22nd 1992 brought another return to familiar ground when I gave an illustrated talk to Cambridge Animal Rights. The Cambridge HSA were organised by a great guy—Dave Fox—who had helped me with investigative work. At my talk a chap took a seat in the audience and introduced himself as a Joint Master of the Cambridgeshire Foxhounds. His name—Geoffrey Fox! It seemed a bit surreal to have two Foxes listening to one anti-hunt talk.

The following month, on the evening of Thursday October 15th I gave a talk in Watford to Dacorum Animal Rights Group. It was notable for me because someone in the audience was so captivated by my eloquence, wit and wisdom that they fell asleep. I recalled that years before I had accompanied Richard Course whilst he gave a talk to a group of pensioners in London. The room was hot and many fell asleep but Richard took it with humour and grace. Public speakers need a lesson in humility occasionally.

Our opponents would sometimes pack out my audiences. I was always flattered when they did and seized the opportunity to explain some seldom seen facts in their chosen pastimes. Personally, I regarded it as a foolish tactic on their part as the speaker exerts full control over a meeting. The speaker orchestrates the format and can take or decline questions at will. The ace the hunters could and did play was to listen to it all and then call for a show of hands to see how many in the audience agreed with me— lo and behold, when they had packed the audience, few did. My ace, never played, was to close the meeting and walk off.

*****

An example of audience packing occurred on Tuesday March 2nd 1993. Marian Lanham had invited me to talk to her LACS Support Group at the Hawth Theatre, Crawley. The event was advertised in *Shooting News*, a magazine for shooting and hunting enthusiasts. It was no surprise that my opponents turned up in considerable numbers but they were well behaved and there was no trouble.

There were more problems the following day. I had been asked to talk to Birmingham Animal Rights along with Robin Webb from the Animal Liberation Front (ALF). Someone phoned in a bomb scare and the event was cancelled. The evening was not completely wasted for me though as I met Ronnie Lee, a comrade from the past I had not seen for years. Ronnie, founder of the ALF, had served many years in prison for taking direct action to save animals. We had worked together as hunt saboteurs to protect wildlife from hunts in the early 1970s.

There was something about that month. On March 24th I gave a talk to Bedford Animal Concern. The meeting was packed with enthusiastic supporters and my lecture well-received. Problems were revealed afterwards. In the venue car park cars that displayed anti-hunt stickers were in some way damaged, mostly by having paint and bodywork gouged. Steve Watson, organiser of the event and a renowned field investigator found the locks on his car jammed with superglue. A clue as to the culprits was that my car which of course wore pro-hunt camouflage, BFSS and NFU stickers and the like, was undamaged.

June 22nd 1993 found me back behind high walls when I spoke to prisoners in the Lifers' Wing of Maidstone Prison. It made a refreshing change for me to be in a prison without being the wrong side of the cell door. I could but guess at the hideous crimes my audience had committed but they would be released sometime and I sought to generate some measure of empathy towards those over whom they would hold power.

On Monday September 20th that year I gave another talk to a meeting packed by hunt supporters. It was at Loughborough Library and I estimated my audience were 90% pro-hunt. Probably many were followers or supporters of the nearby Quorn Foxhounds.

The following month, Tuesday October 26th, I gave a talk to the Birmingham HSA Group at The Custard Factory, Birmingham. My diary notes that I was heckled throughout by a very drunk Asian gentleman. It was unclear if he was for or against bloodsports, but he was very vocal.

Winter weather was a bane for the planning of talks. For long trips, I would usually give myself an hour to spare to allow for traffic hold-ups. That often meant I arrived early, but not always. Tuesday November 23rd 1993 exemplified the problems. I set out to talk to Devon Animal Rights at Totnes. Everything was well until I reached near Swindon when a blanket of fog descended. There was first a lane squeeze on the M4 then police closed the motorway.

Having to use the minor back roads put me at the venue one hour late. Such a delay for a school talk would have been fatal, as the lesson slot would have passed, but at that group talk I arrived to find an amicable, if passionate, debate taking place between our side and the numerous hunt supporters who turned up.

*****

Wednesday July 27th 1994 was strange. I gave a routine talk in the evening to Wolverhampton LACS Support Group. Nothing unusual except I was surprised to see Jim Barrington with Joanna Woolliscroft seated amongst my audience. Neither had anything to learn from anything I said.

I encouraged as many as possible to take part in hunt monitoring work. With many people watching and taking video film of hunts we would gather proof of both the cruelty imposed on our wildlife and the mayhem and havoc that hunts caused. I also knew that video cameras, certainly when used by several individuals covering each other, could deter hunt supporters from some of their wilder excesses.

Hunt supporters knew if they smashed one camera they would have to smash them all and furthermore merely smashing the camera was not enough. Photographic film and cine film once exposed to light was ruined but video tape could be retrieved. Violent hunters would have to steal the video cameras. The LACS worked hard to encourage supporters to take direct action in the hunting fields. They held a Hunt Monitors Conference at Goldsmiths College, London over the weekend of September 3rd and 4th 1994. The event was packed with 140 supporters from all over the UK and Ireland. It was a marvellous opportunity to exchange ideas and learn from each other's experiences. I spoke on the Sunday.

ICABS organisers had kindly attended our conference and I returned the compliment by attending theirs a few weeks later. It was Friday September 30th when I caught the Ryanair flight from Stansted to Dublin. I then travelled by bus and train to Mullingar where the ICABS office was. Next morning, I accompanied Aideen Yourell and colleagues to the ICABS AGM and Conference in Dublin. My colleagues Graham Hall and

Donal MacIntyre shared the Edward White Memorial Award for their magnificent undercover work to expose the cruelty in bloodsports (Donal MacIntyre had filmed for a BBC documentary greyhounds in Ireland being blooded with live rabbits). I spoke about hunt monitoring and showed videos of my work in England.

On the afternoon of Saturday October 8th, I met Marian Lanham and spoke about LACS campaigns at *The Queens Head*, Brighton. Just four people were in the audience, including Marian!

School talks gave a guaranteed audience but could be at awkward times—and it was imperative never to be late. An example was Wednesday November 2nd when my alarm sounded at 4:30am for me to drive to give early morning talks at Canterbury College. I gave two illustrated talks, each for 1½hours. Thoughtful interactions with the students soon made me forget the slog of getting there, and home again.

Talks were excellent opportunities to meet like-minded colleagues. Sunday November 20th 1994 I spoke at the Southend Earth First Exhibition. I arrived in time to hear Teddy Taylor MP speak. Iain Blake-Lawson from the LACS spoke then I had a short ½ hour slot. I had a good chat with Niel Hansen from the National Anti-Hunt Campaign (NAHC). Niel did an excellent job taking our campaigns to the streets. He told me that in Southend the previous day he had collected 1200 signatures for his anti-hunting petition and raised hundreds of pounds in donations.

Tuesday November 29th found me at a noted seat of learning. I had the pleasure of talking about the work of the ACIG to students at the University of East Anglia, Norwich. It was at the invitation of Mike Radford from the School of Law. I showed slides and answered many questions.

*****

I covered some distances giving talks. On Wednesday August 30th 1995 I was in Wolverhampton in the evening talking about my work. Steve Wilde had invited me to speak to his LACS Support Group. The following evening, I spoke to another LACS Support Group, in Newport, Isle of Wight. Whenever possible some or all my family accompanied me.

*****

I aimed to present the results of the latest investigations at talks; for instance Monday March 11th 1996 when I spoke at a public meeting in Saffron Walden about live exports. Joan Court from Cambridge chaired the packed meeting that included many taking an interest in animal welfare issues for the first time. I shared the platform with Terry Woods. I showed our AWIS campaigning video, *UK Calves*, that detailed my investigative work with Lawrie Payne and Janet Taylor the previous summer.

I gave talks in a very pleasant location in September that year. On Monday September 23rd, I caught the noon flight from Stansted to Jersey and met long-standing ACIG supporters Jennie and Mike. They kindly gave me a guided tour of their beautiful island. That evening I spoke about my ACIG work to an animal welfare group at the Jersey Arts Centre. The following morning, I talked to D'Hautree School about investigative work to help animals. Then in the afternoon I was interviewed by BBC Radio

Jersey and in the evening met dedicated supporter Joya Ghose. On my final day, Wednesday September 25th, I spoke to students at Highlands College in the morning before catching the afternoon flight home.

*****

As well as talks I assisted on LACS stands and Press Conferences. The following year on Saturday February 22nd 1997 I helped at the LACS display in Eastbank Square, Southport protesting against the cruelty of the Waterloo Cup. Tony Moore (1934-2013) from Fight Against Animal Cruelty in Europe (FAACE) and Ralph James were there as well. We erected a giant inflatable hare that we named 'Harriet'. Hundreds signed our petition against hare coursing and people were generous with their donations. Problems only arose when 'Harriet' proved an irresistible target for young lads to lark about with and we had to deflate her.

Two days later, Monday February 24th, I assisted the LACS Press Conference against hare coursing. It was at the Alicia Hotel, Sefton Park, Liverpool. Before the event I helped John Bryant and colleagues erect 'Harriet' again. Tony and Vicki Moore attended. Vicki was still recovering from horrific injuries she suffered when gored by a bull in June 1995 whilst investigating and exposing Spanish Blood Fiestas. Vicki had been tossed in the air ten times and suffered multiple injuries. A seven-hour operation saved her life but she remained on the critical list for nearly four weeks.

Although far from fit, Vicki returned to Spain the following year to continue her work. For me it was an absolute pleasure to meet her. Over many years campaigning I have met many courageous activists. Vicki Moore ranks up there with the best of the best. She told me that many Spaniards regarded her as a walking miracle. She survived injuries that were not survivable; in consequence, they listened to her almost with reverence. Vicki sadly died on February 6th 2000.

The Press Conference was a great success. The presence of celebrities and local politicians attracted great media interest.

I occasionally participated in television programmes. One was on Tuesday June 24th 1997 when I went to Anglia Television studios, Norwich for 'The Time, The Place' debate about hunting. I sat next to my erstwhile friend Jim Barrington. His new colleague Janet George was there. Australian Janet George was an acerbic character and an effective Press Officer for the BFSS/CA. The *Times* Diary, April 17th 1998, delighted in recounting a tale of how she took legal action against her local hunt, the Wheatland Foxhounds, after they trespassed on her farm, an incursion that forced her to put down two pedigree ewes. She complained, "*They said they didn't know my farm was there, but they bloody well should have done,*" threatened to "*bite the balls off*" the Master but settled for £2,000 compensation from the hunt. Janet told the *Times*: "*There are some dim people in the Wheatland. Their attitude is that the hunt is everything. There is no place place for those prehistoric diehards. One out of every five hunts makes this sort of mistake.*"

In the debate our side was well represented by Kevin Saunders, the LACS Press Officer, Penny Little and Janet Smart. The programme conducted a poll that received 30,000 votes. Our side won by 81% to 19%, which reflected the general view throughout the country over the issue. Jim Barrington seemed awkward and ill at ease. There was none of the fluency and wit with which he had previously advanced the anti-hunting cause. After the programme, we went for a meal together and it was clear he was a troubled man.

*****

Whilst I mostly spoke against the cruelty inherent in bloodsports I did occasionally talk against vivisection. An example was Tuesday March 17th 1998 when I gave a talk for Animal Aid to students at Tuxford School, north of Newark-on-Trent about the cruelty and failures of vivisection. Tuxford was a welcoming school with thoughtful pupils and cheery staff and my talk there was for some years an annual event.

Monday November 23rd 1998 I promoted the work of my ACIG to Animal Care students at Writtle College near Chelmsford. That was an excellent opportunity to talk to students who would soon be at the front line themselves about the reality of animal cruelty.

*****

I travelled the country giving talks. We needed more recruits in the front line to help with the work and my ACIG needed more funds. The following year on Tuesday February 16th 1999 I gave an illustrated lecture about my ACIG to Shoreham Protestors group at St. George's Hall, Hove. The venue was packed with more than 70 people. On Wednesday February 24th, I spoke at Reading College then on Monday March 1st the venue was the LACS Support Group meeting in Essex.

On April 20th 1999 I spoke to Gamlingay Young Farmers Club at Gamlingay Village College. It was interesting for me as I had spent some of my teenage years living at nearby Abbotsley and when the local hunt, the Cambridgeshire Foxhounds, showed me the cruelty inherent in hunting it set me on the course of opposition to the pastime. It was also close to the place where young hunt saboteur Tom Worby was run over and killed in April 1993.

Tuesday May 5th was a memorable day for talks. First I drove north to give another talk at Tuxford School for Animal Aid about vivisection. Afterwards, instead of heading home I drove further north to Doncaster. There I gave two talks about the work of my ACIG. The first was to Kirk Sandall Youth Club, the second at Armthorpe Youth Centre.

Both talks were hard work but gave real joy. They were hard because the youngsters were only there by choice, they could walk out at any time. Secondly there was the inevitable propensity for teenage lads to impress the girls present with macho callous attitudes. I won them round to my view that it was manly to be compassionate and only the cowards who were cruel. Real men are kind to animals.

That was a front line for animal welfare every bit as much as working undercover within hunting or vivisection, or hiding up somewhere to maintain observation. Setting youngsters on the path to compassion avoids a lot of cruelty down the road. From Doncaster youth clubs in May I switched to the House of Commons in July when I spoke about hunting to MPs on the afternoon of Wednesday July 14th. My talk followed that by a man from MORI. I was somewhat intimidated by the presence of so many MPs in the audience including that formidable speaker and passionate advocate for animal welfare, Tony Banks MP.

In September 1999 I did more talks at long range. I spoke to the Animal Rights Group in pretty Perth on the evening of Monday September 13th then stayed with supporters nearby. The next morning, I accompanied Steve and Catriona to see the glorious beach at Montrose. In the afternoon, I spoke to pupils at Webster's High School, Kirriemuir and in the evening to students at the University of Dundee. The following day, Wednesday September 15th I gave three talks to a succession of three classes at Webster's High School in the morning then in the evening spoke at a public meeting at the Montrose Basin Wildlife Centre.

The next day I met Jill Russell and other ACIG supporters, Myrna and Fay, even further north in Aberdeen. Jill had laboured hard to edit and compile Melody MacDonald's book *Caught in the Act* about the Feldberg investigation. It was a pleasure to meet and chat at length about past, present and future ACIG projects.

*****

In the New Year, I was pleased to return to Cambridge on Monday January 17th 2000 to meet Joan Court (1919-2016) again and talk to her excellent group, Animals, People and the Environment. I was delighted to emphasise that ours was not simply an animal issue. Caring for the well-being of our fellow creatures was about caring for all around us.

Wednesday May 17th 2000 was notable. I made a significant achievement for a man imprisoned twice for animal rights activity—I spoke to an audience of police officers about my lawful work for animals. For an hour and a half, I spoke and answered questions at the Ministry of Defence Police Wildlife Liaison Officers Foundation Course at the Police Training Centre, Wethersfield, Essex. I showed my slides and also video film taken by Kevin Hill undercover amongst hare coursers on the bank side at the Waterloo Cup. The interaction with officers was excellent.

I returned to talk at Writtle College on Tuesday November 7th. I showed slides and video to 36 students studying for a 'Country Sports' module. The questions and answers element was lively and valuable.

Some 'talks' were more a matter of keeping the media informed. On Thursday December 7th CBS News hired me to visit their office in Knightsbridge, London. I discussed the anti-hunting campaigns with a journalist. Later in the month CBS collected a video tape showing some of my work exposing the many artificial earths in Thurlow Foxhounds country. I later met Stephen Milne from CBS at the Boxing Day demonstration against the hunt in Maldon.

*****

The following year, on September 26th 2001, I lectured again to Police Wildlife Liaison Officers at the Police Training Centre, Wethersfield. I was accompanied by LACS Committee Member, hunt monitoring colleague and ACIG supporter, Donna King. My diary records there were high level security checks including having my car searched. It was no surprise after the terrorist outrages in the US on September 11th.

I returned to talk to more Wildlife Liaison Officers at the same venue the following month, on the afternoon of Tuesday October 2nd. I welcomed the opportunity to explain fully to fellow professional wildlife crime investigators the actions of bloodsports enthusiasts in our countryside.

Occasionally with school talks I would be told that the class before me were uncommunicative and unlikely to ask many questions. I enthused over the challenge to incite responses. One such example was Tuesday November 20th when I gave a talk about my work, illustrated with slides, to a 6th form group at St. Albans School. I was assured the students would not ask many questions but they certainly did.

*****

From 2002 requests for talks tailed off as gathering information from the Internet took over. The AWIS funded my talks so I never charged but donations towards expenses were always welcomed. Perhaps it just became easier to ask pupils and students to look up the information from both sides online.

Between December 31st 1997 and December 31st 2002 the individuals that make up our society seemed to lose some of their ability to talk to each other in person. My eldest son created a web site for my ACIG in 2000. Digital cameras took the place of film cameras. Slides shows were replaced by PowerPoint presentations. Personally, I missed the opportunity to exchange thought and ideas with colleagues at group meetings and with students. Talks became occasional. On Thursday April 25th 2002 I spoke in Croydon at the meeting of the group Surrey Fighting For Animals. Later that year, Wednesday November 6th, I gave an illustrated talk to the local HSA group in Canterbury. It was a joy to be back in the old city and the audience were very generous in their support for my ACIG/AWIS.

*****

Talks were few and far between in 2003. Monday March 31st I spoke about the work of my ACIG to the Animal Rights Group at Sheffield University. I was always keen to show that the work that I undertook could easily be done by others. I returned home at 2:30am.

Sunday November 16th found me back in Cambridge when I gave a short talk at a regional Animal Rights meeting. It was a truly positive encounter and I sold eleven copies of *Caught in the Act*.

*****

The following year, Friday March 26th 2004, I gave another talk about my anti-vivisection work to the Upper Sixth Form at Tuxford School. It was distinctly satisfying because the students had heard a speaker from our opposition before me.

In April, on Tuesday 20th, I gave my usual talk at St. Albans School, against hunting. I showed two videos, both taken by colleagues working undercover. The first was of the 2000 Waterloo Cup, the second of a fox killed by the Plas Machynlleth Foxhounds. Students were shocked.

On the evening of Saturday September 4th, I spoke about the investigation work of my ACIG at the International Animal Rights Gathering held near Tonbridge. It was a marvellous opportunity to meet like-minded campaigners from around the world.

With the hunting side demonstrating their propensity for violence by fighting with police officers outside the House of Commons my talk to an Animal Rights Group in Cambridge on Sunday October 10th was all about self-defence. I described how to avoid confrontation and how to protect yourself and your friends if violence was forced upon you.

With the passage of the Hunting Bill dominating the media I expected a good audience when I turned up at the University of East Anglia on Thursday November 4th 2004. I was billed to talk to the Politics Society about campaigns to abolish hunting. My audience consisted of four.

Debates

When it came to formal debates I had a near unerring ability to lose. Whereas my colleagues Richard Course, Jim Barrington and later Douglas Batchelor usually won I could be relied upon to lose. Debates are won or lost on wit and humour rather than passion. Perhaps I was a bit too close to the events to be anything other than passionate. My inadequacy in that area made it even more surprising that on the most illustrious debating forum to which I was ever invited, my opponents ran away.

Wednesday February 7th 1996 brought a frantic call from Jonathon Wolf of the Oxford Union Debating Society asking me to speak in the Oxford Union debate the following evening on the issue *"This House believes that a civilised society cannot permit hunting and shooting."* He told me that Jim Barrington who had left the LACS but still claimed to oppose hunting had been booked to speak but had pulled out just that very day. Two Labour MPs also booked to speak in favour of the motion also had to withdraw at the last minute due to a three-line whip in the House of Commons. The LACS had been asked but were unable to field a speaker.

I had never previously participated in such a formal debate and the prospect of starting in at the deep end at the Oxford Union terrified me but in the absence of anyone else from our side I accepted the invitation and booked a room in an Oxford hotel. The next morning, I made preparations and at 2pm was about to leave when another urgent call came from Oxford. My three opponents for the debate, including Janet George, Chief Press Officer of the BFSS and Jonathon Young, Editor of *The Field* had proclaimed that if I turned up to speak they would walk out.

They advised the Oxford Union Debating Society it would taint their organisations for them to share a public platform with a man who had my criminal record for animal rights activity. The Debating Society was clearly embarrassed but in the face of that threat the Oxford Union reluctantly withdrew their invitation to me. They apologised profusely.

My colleagues, Penny Little and Miles Cooper, attended the debate and told me the outcome. The motion was proposed very ably by three undergraduates. For all their eloquence, the proposition was rejected by 157 to 67. One galling feature of the aftermath was the bloodsports brigade mocking what they described as the inability of our side to field a speaker! Janet George boasted in *Countryman's Weekly* (February 23rd 1996), *"The result proved conclusively that when fieldsports are subjected to intelligent and intense examination, they totally justify their continuation."*

Only a few from the hunting and shooting side declined to debate with me. Tuesday October 28th 1997 I debated against Marigold Thompson, Master of the West Norfolk Foxhounds, at Norwich Trades Council. Mrs Thompson was accompanied by her Field Master and Huntsman—Ian Higgs. The latter seemed a particularly affable chap.

I met Marigold Thompson again at another debate the following year at Fakenham College on Wednesday February 4th 1998. The motion was *"This House would ban Fox hunting"*. It was marvellous to see the passionate involvement of so many students in the verbal jousting.

Friday November 20th was significant because I had the honour to debate the hunting issue against Professor Roger Scruton at the University of London, Institute of Education. My colleagues Ben Stewart from the LACS and Dave Wetton came along to listen. I faced a truly formidable intellectual opponent. I was rattled when I ran my usual line that we needed to be compassionate and protective towards those we hold power over and someone from the audience asked why? I took it as a given that we should be but I guess it is often not in our best interests to be caring. I said that it is fine for a man to stand alone when fit, young and strong but he would marry and have children and would surely expect others to be considerate towards his wife and children. Furthermore, even the toughest grow old and weak and then they would expect others to be considerate towards them. So, give to others as you expect to receive.

1999 brought more debates. On Wednesday February 10th, I left home in the snow heading for the exclusive girls school, Benenden School, near Cranbrook, Kent. I had hoped to call in to see Alan Clark MP (1928-1999), who lived not far away, but as he pointed out it being a Wednesday he was in the House of Commons for Prime Minister's Questions.

Tragically Alan died later that year on September 5th so I was never able to thank in person the man who gave me so much support whilst I was in prison, and my ACIG so much support subsequently. That was a real shame as he was a passionate supporter of animal welfare causes—and as readers of his autobiography will know he knew a thing or two about how to deal with the judiciary. [Jane Clark subsequently kindly invited me to the memorial service for Alan held at Westminster Abbey on Tuesday February 1st 2000. I was delighted to attend along with Jane Fegan who for years had been a cheerful and knowledgeable voice in the LACS office.]

As for the debate, I was up against William Meakin, the Honorary Secretary of the West Kent Foxhounds. I lost the vote 26-16.

I sustained another defeat on Wednesday June 2nd in the previously mentioned debate at the Hay Festival, Hay-on-Wye. I lost badly and returned home at 2:45am. Thursday July 8th 1999 provided a rare event when I won a debate. I was pitched against Alison Hawes from the Countryside Alliance at an Oxford School. Win or lose I was delighted that the Countryside Alliance were then willing to share a public platform with me. It seemed grossly unfair to deny students the opportunity to hear both sides of this issue forcibly debated.

During the evening of Thursday October 21st, I participated in a debate organised by LM (Living Marxism) magazine at the Friends Meeting House in London. It was Dr Richard Ryder and me up against Professor Roger Scruton and Mick Hume, Editor of the magazine. There was no vote but looking at the audience we judged that had there been we would have lost by around 60-40. On the way in I was accosted by a bullish hunt supporter who took me to task over the *Games for the Gutless* leaflet produced by my ACIG. He assured me he was not gutless and if he ever met me in the hunting field he would punch me harder than I had ever been punched in my life. By then I had done enough martial arts training to have experienced being hit hard—by lads who genuinely could hit—but I thanked him for his warning and said I would look out for him.

The next evening, I had a mini-debate at the behest of Anglia TV outside the kennels of the West Norfolk Foxhounds. I was up against the formidable George Bowyer, a Joint Master of the Fitzwilliam (Milton) Foxhounds. George, the son of Lord Denham, was a true hero of the Countryside Alliance. His protest song, *Guardians of the Land (The Marching Song)*, was released on August 10th 1998. Heavily promoted by his hunting friends it reached number 33 in the UK Singles Chart.

The media were voracious for interviews about the hunting issue. The following Sunday, October 24th, I went to the Royal Norfolk Showground for an interview for the BBC 2 programme *The East at Westminster*. I was up against Miles Gadsby from the Union of Country Sports Workers (UCSW).

In March 2000 I participated in another debate way up north. It was Tuesday March 14th when I drove to stay with my good friend Elaine Milbourn in Cumbria. The next afternoon I debated the hunting issue at Beacon Hill School, Aspatria. I was against Tom Fell, a local and eloquent spokesman for the CA. I lost the vote 32-24 with 4 abstentions. That evening I spoke about my ACIG at a meeting of the Cumbrian Humanist Society.

I met Alison Hawes from the CA again for a debate at Bristol Cathedral School on Friday April 30th. She was accompanied by the Master of the Mendip Foxhounds and two hounds. They brought hounds to claim that, were hunting to be banned, thousands like those would be killed. Their plan backfired badly. I explained to the pupils that hounds like that would never die of old age, nor even grow old. In the routine course of hunting thousands were killed long before the natural end of their lives. Furthermore, those two were lucky. Many were bred that did not even make it into the pack—being killed as puppies for a variety of reasons.

I then urged the pupils to look the hounds in the eyes. Those dogs were trusting. They would hunt any scent they were taught to hunt. I asked the students would they really teach and encourage those dogs to hunt the scent of a wild animal that could lead them over railways lines and main roads where many hounds are injured and killed each season when the alternative is to hunt humanely over safe routes? Part of the deal of dog ownership is to be fair to your hound—and putting them into mortal danger for your fun is far from fair.

Perhaps the most prestigious debate I participated in was at the Durham University Union Society after the Hunting Act was passed. It was a very formal 'black-tie' affair. I made use of my late father's dinner jacket. I partnered hunt monitor and LACS Support Group Coordinator Lynne Edwards and Durham student, Erin O'Brien, proposing the motion: 'This House would ban hunting with dogs.' We were against Kate Hoey MP, George Bowyer MFH and Lucy Higginson, Editor of *Horse and Hound*. We lost by a margin of around 70% to 30%. I reached home at 4:30am.

Letter Writing

Writing letters for publication in local and national newspapers was a vitally important way of getting the facts about the cruelty inflicted upon animals into the public domain. When I started as Press Officer at the LACS in April 1981 the Executive Director, Richard Course, impressed upon me the value of such letters. He judged the letters page to be one of the most widely read pages in any paper. I sent many letters including some abroad. Here is an example in response to a storm of outrage by the Irish hunting fraternity after a somewhat lively protest against a hunt in Co. Waterford. My letter was published by *The Irish Times*, January 22nd 1996:-

"HATLESS HUNTSMAN

Sir-- It is distressing to learn about the huntsman having his hat knocked off at a protest in Co. Waterford. I totally condemn violence and urge protestors to keep their cool whatever the provocation from those who derive fun from persecuting wildlife. However it ill-becomes the hunters to seek public sympathy for this incident. For a start, the violence that they inflict on wildlife is infinitely worse. Secondly, hunters themselves know a thing or two about dishing out violence to opponents.

I spoke against hunting at a public meeting in Cork on November 9th 1993. Whilst I was answering questions from the audience a hunt supporter smashed a chair over the head of an anti-hunt person sitting in front of him, splitting open his scalp. The hunting brigade, who knew the assailant, then closed ranks to conceal his identity.

Finally, it should be noted that any riding hat which can be that easily knocked off is probably unsafe anyway. The chin-strap is the recommended safety aid, but for the chinless wonders who ride to hounds it is probably of little use.

Yours etc., M.J. Huskisson. ACIG"

As the Hunting Ban moved up the political agenda I stepped up my writing campaigns. The climax was in the autumn of 2004 when in a period of about six weeks, with the help of my whole family, we mailed out nearly 3000 letters, many accompanied by photographs, for publication. Some examples of my letters are included in the Appendix.

384

CHAPTER SIXTEEN
Political campaigning. A Labour Government from 1997 put abolition back on the agenda. The Lord Burns Hunting Inquiry.

It was the task of investigators to uncover the truth about the abuse of animals in the hunting fields, vivisection laboratories and factory farms. It fell to political campaigners to translate the resulting public anger into Parliamentary action to render the cruelty illegal. The baton of compassion then passed to the police and judiciary to enforce the new legislation.

The LACS was particularly well served with political campaigners. Richard Course was one smart tactician. His actions in the late 1970s and early 1980s whilst at the helm of the League (described in *Outfoxed Take Two*) made him lead architect of the hunting ban. At the League, he recruited Angela Smith in 1982 as Political Officer. Angela, even more astute, achieved success after success until leaving in 1995.

Chris Williamson, a clever and determined political campaigner served on the LACS Executive Committee for years (Chris was Labour MP for Derby North from 2010 to 2015). The redoubtable Lord Soper was LACS President from 1967-1997. David Coulthread took the role of Head of Political Affairs at LACS in September 1995 and held it until 2001 when Mike Hobday took over. Samantha Arditti joined the League political department as Political Officer in 1996. The League had assembled a formidable team for the struggles to come.

David Coulthread maintained and extended the effectiveness of League campaigns. The Wild Mammals (Protection) Bill that was originally drafted by the League was presented to Parliament by Labour MP Alan Meale and with all-party support became effective on April 30th 1996. That Act was the first British legislation to protect all wild mammals from acts of brutality. That same year three big UK groups, IFAW, LACS and the RSPCA, combined to launch the Campaign for the Protection of Hunted Animals (CPHA) at a House of Commons press conference on Wednesday July 24th.

In a statement the CPHA said that using dogs to hunt or kill wild animals was, "*fundamentally cruel*", and added: "*When decisions are taken to kill wild animals, then, without endorsing such decisions, the most humane and target-specific method possible should be employed. Using dogs to hunt, pursue and/or kill foxes, deer, mink and hares does not meet these criteria and should therefore be abolished.*"

LACS Chairman, John Cooper, observed: "*Hunting with hounds is a sport which causes a great deal of suffering to British wildlife. There is simply no place for such a sport in a modern civilised society. Hunters can keep all the traditional, social and equestrian aspects by switching to draghunting—the humane alternative.*"

BFSS members who attended the press conference were invited to ask questions but declined. However, in an interview for *The Scotsman* a BFSS spokesman lamented: "*We are worried about this development—it combines the money of IFAW, the respectability of the RSPCA and the dirty tricks we know the League Against Cruel Sports has up its sleeve.*"

In the political arena Richard Course had ensured a League presence at the party political conferences—where they were always well received. In 1996 David Coulthread ditched what had become the traditional LACS stands for conference use and took a new 'Fountains of Blood' stand to the party conferences, working with IFAW. The stand was impressive, thought-provoking and won widespread plaudits, and plaudits mean prizes. The stand won first prize at the TUC, Liberal Democrat and Labour conferences. Hopes for a clean sweep by also winning at the Conservative conference were dashed when LACS and IFAW were refused a stand. The League participated in a successful fringe meeting held by the Conservative Anti-Hunt Council.

For some years, there had been increasing pressure from the Devon and Somerset Residents' Association for Deer Protection formed by Diana Wilson, Doreen Cronin and Richard and Daisy Hall. Deer protection experts such as Ian Pedler (author of *Save our Stags* (2008)) added their voice and with many films appearing proving the cruelty in stag hunting the National Trust came under severe pressure to ban hunting on the land they owned in the West Country.

On September 27th 1994 Kevin Hill filmed a stag killed on National Trust land at Horner. A rider was recorded whipping the exhausted stag to run further. In response, the National Trust commissioned an inquiry into stress suffered by hunted deer. This was led by Professor Patrick Bateson, Professor of Ethology at Cambridge University. Over two years, with the cooperation of stag hunters, Professor Bateson and research assistant, Elizabeth Bradshaw, took and examined blood samples from deer that had been hunted and killed.

Many wondered whether you needed a scientific inquiry to tell that deer hunted all day to the point of exhaustion suffered. Conversely hunt supporters must have been confident that the results would show nothing out of the normal for a prey species. Physical changes to a body caused by over-exertion have long been known about—it is the whole question of myopathy. Tragically, young, fit soldiers on exercise, on occasion, die of 'exhaustion'. Could the anecdotal be turned into measurable, quantifiable science? That was the task for Professor Bateson. [Dr Henshaw had previously described myopathy in deer, see 1989 article "*Frightened to Death*" in appendix].

When their report was released at the headquarters of the National Trust on April 9th 1997 the effect was devastating. It revealed the full measure of suffering inflicted upon red deer purely for entertainment. The National Trust Council acted swiftly, deciding unanimously to ban the hunting of deer on its land.

The National Trust explanatory document "*Statement on decision not to issue licences to hunt deer with hounds on Trust land in the West Country*" was clear: "*The Report's conclusions were clear and unequivocal. They state that hunting with hounds causes suffering to red deer which is far outside their natural expectations, far greater overall than that caused* by shooting by rifle and broadly similar to that experienced by deer that have been severely injured, for example by road accidents."

Here is an extract from Professor Bateson's report:

"*19. The study produced clear-cut scientific results. These show that lengthy hunts with hounds impose extreme stress on red deer and are likely to cause them great suffering. The hunts force them to experience conditions far outside the normal limits for their species. These stresses are at least at the same level as for severely injured deer and usually last for hours in the case of deer which are killed and much longer in those that escape. We could not judge, for the latter group, the likely extent of recovery but this does not efface the reality of the suffering caused. Moreover, the potential for such suffering occurs with every hunt.*

20. The alternative of shooting red deer, already accounting for most of the culling on Exmoor and the Quantocks, produces on average much lower levels of individual suffering. Thus, I estimate that 130 hunted deer that are killed each year by the Hunts and roughly a further 100 that escape will experience unacceptable levels of suffering whereas only seven or so of the 130 at present killed by hunting would have such problems if they were shot.

21. I conclude that the level of total suffering would be markedly reduced if hunting with hounds were ended. Hunting with hounds can no longer be justified on welfare grounds, taking into account the standards applied in other fields of animal welfare...."(The Behavioural and Physiological Effects of Culling Red Deer. Report to the Council of the National Trust. Professor Patrick Bateson, FRS. 1997.)

After the National Trust banned stag hunting on their land on grounds of cruelty political pressure increased on the Government to ban all hunting throughout the UK, for the same reasons.

Hunt supporters were duly outraged. Janet George wrote in e-mail correspondence on April 16th: "*The science is crap - the way in which blood samples were taken alone should make the report worthless - never mind the crazy assumptions, but it's manna from heaven for the anti brigade.*"

Two days later, in another e-mail, Janet George elaborated on the greater threat: "*This Report will finish staghunting in the UK if we can't prove it is rubbish - and that brings the axe ever closer to fox hunting. The RSPCA and others are proposing a similar study on foxes (which may buy us time) but we won't touch it until we work out what went wrong with the methodology with this one.*" The BFSS scoured the world for 'experts' to criticize Professor Bateson's findings.

After the report was released Professor Bateson and Charles Nunneley, Chairman of the National Trust, hoped that once stag hunters read it and learned just how cruel deer hunting was, most would not wish to carry on hunting. They did not understand the stag hunter's mind—it is exactly the cruelty in the long punishing hunts that attracts them.

A similar mistake is made by observers considering other bloodsports. People think along the lines: if only fox hunters could see the pain inflicted when a fox is dug out they would give up; surely no-one who heard the cries of pain and terror when she is caught could continue hare coursing? This is a mistake. Whilst it can happen, by and large the hunting fraternity know full well the cruelties that underpin their pastimes, view them as essential for their games to work, so accept them. For a few it is the very cruelty that attracts them. Stag hunters rejected the Bateson Report and proclaimed their determination to carry on.

When the deleterious effects of prolonged hunting were highlighted all hunting had a problem. Hunting with hounds, whether of fox, deer, or hare, had at its heart the notion that the hunt should be prolonged for as long as possible to give followers the lengthy chases they sought, desired and paid for. An exhausted fox would be given a start after bolting. A hare to be coursed would be given a start before the dogs were unleashed. In stag hunting every opportunity was taken to prolong the hunt—to the point even of holding the hounds back and whipping on deer reluctant to run.

The day after the National Trust announced their ban the Devon and Somerset Staghounds hunted a stag to exhaustion in temperatures well above 70°F (21°C). After shooting the stag supporters celebrated their kill with ice-creams from a following van.

During the Bateson inquiry, hunters had full control over how samples were taken and from which deer. Colleagues and I observed many hunts during the study period. Some deer subjected to the most stressful hunts were never sampled—for the simple reason that they were never caught. Stag hunters may not have been able to guarantee any specific deer would be caught, but they could certainly ensure that a deer would not be caught. It was in their control to call their hounds off.

In response to the report John Bryant, the Chief Officer of LACS observed: "*The League has been saying since the day it was formed in 1924, that selecting a strong, fit deer and chasing it for hours to exhaustion with a pack of dogs, is outrageously cruel, and cannot be compared to natural predation by wolves which select weak and injured prey which they can bring down in an ambush or after a short chase. Commonsense dictates that fox hunting, which is equally unnatural, must also be cruel. The hunters have chosen to reject the scientific truth and therefore we will have to rely on Parliament to put an end to such bloodsports.*"

The first scientist brought out by the BFSS to denigrate the Bateson report was none other than Professor John E. Cooper—my old foe previously employed as Veterinary Conservator at the Royal College of Surgeons. His reputation was hardly enhanced by the RCS saga—albeit that the college was eventually acquitted on appeal on a legal technicality. Later, during a libel trial over an episode of *The Cook Report* it was revealed that John E. Cooper had admitted that some dogs used by the RCS for transplant research were former domestic pets.

Despite not having seen the data collected from the survey; nor being involved in the study at any stage, nor even speaking to Professor Bateson, Professor John E. Cooper, through the BFSS questioned the methodology: "*differences in methods of sampling, storing and transporting blood could lead to misleading results.*"

With the 1997 election looming, there were increasing signs of militancy from the hunting fraternity. On Boxing Day 1996 the *Daily Express* reported comments by Janet George, Chief Press Officer of the BFSS, regarding Labour's plans to allow a free vote on the hunting issue. Janet threatened: "*This measure will be the equivalent of the poll tax for Maggie Thatcher. If any Bill goes further through Parliament we could cause chaos on the motorways. Imagine what 5,000 horse boxes could do on the M25, M5 and M6.*"

The next day another BFSS spokesman threatened to bring central London to a standstill with horseboxes and tractors. The Cardiff *Western Mail* reported that Welsh hunters threatened to send queues of horseboxes miles in length along the M4 and set up roadblocks to cut off traffic into London, where they would stage demonstrations "*larger than those against the poll tax.*" The *Folkestone Herald* reported that the BFSS intended to "*create motorway chaos with blockades*" and quoted Janet George: "*It will be a demonstration the like of which they have never seen. If Labour wants a fight, it will get a fight.*"

In a clear threat to defy any hunting ban the BFSS also distributed thousands of pre-printed postcards for its supporters to send to Labour leader Tony Blair pleading: "*Please don't make us criminals.*"

The topic was discussed in a BBC Radio 5 debate on December 27th 1996 between LACS Chief Officer, John Bryant and Janet George. Presenter, Diana Madill, asked Janet George whether hunters would disobey a law banning hunting. Janet replied: "*I think that that's a very real possibility because I think that we do not accept that there is any case for banning hunting.*"

John Bryant responded by accusing Janet George of hypocrisy: "*These are the people that have attacked hunt saboteurs for defying the aggravated trespass provisions of the Criminal Justice Act. How often have we heard hunters piously stating that they respect the right of people to oppose hunting as long as they stay within the law? Now, because they don't agree with a law to protect wild animals from being hounded to death, they are threatening to defy the will of Parliament. Such hypocrisy is sickening.*"

David Coulthread and John Bryant (John shared the CEO role at LACS with Graham Sirl after the departure of Jim Barrington) made a formidable campaigning team. Together they produced the 'Pack of Lies' campaigning diary for 1997 sent to every anti-hunt candidate with a reasonable chance of election in 1997—that was over 1,500. The diary outlined 52 outstanding lies from hunt supporters—and the answers to them. The diary demonstrated that anti-hunters had won all the technical arguments but that was a far cry from securing a ban on hunting.

In the run up to the 1997 election the LACS made clear the position of the three major parties regarding hunting. Labour pledged a free vote on hunting. If that vote was successful they promised Government support for the abolition of hunting. Labour also promised to suspend hunting on all publicly owned land if elected. The Liberal Democrats confirmed their commitment to the abolition of hunting and their support for a free vote on the issue. The Conservatives maintained the issue was a matter of individual conscience.

Sections of the media saw the many flaws in the arguments spouted by hunt supporters. This is an extract from an editorial published by the *Northern Echo*, April 22nd 1997: "*Labour peer Lady Mallalieu has come up with an interesting argument against banning hunting with hounds:* "To introduce legislation that does not have the support of those affected is a recipe for civil disorder," *she says. I am sure many people can see her point - among them burglars, muggers, murderers and arsonists, whose crimes would never have been outlawed if only they had had a say.*"

In anticipation of an incoming Labour Government the hunting fraternity set up the Union of Country Sports Workers (UCSW) in April 1997. Chairman was computer consultant John Fretwell, Kennel Huntsman of the Stowe Beagles. The new Union claimed 125,000 jobs would be under threat if Labour won.

Barry Leathwood, national secretary for the rural workers section of the Transport and General Workers Union, commented about the newcomers: "*As the only trade union representing rural workers, we are extremely concerned about protecting jobs and creating new employment in the countryside, by expanding drag-hunting for example. The scare-monger tactics of this new group do nothing towards an informed and accurate debate on field sports and the future of the countryside.*"

Close to the election hunt supporters launched vicious attacks on LACS property. On the evening of April 29th industrial style Chinese firework rockets, designed for use in public displays, were fired at the League's West Country Office at St. Nicholas Priory, near Dulverton.

The outcome of the May 1st 1997 election did not improve hunter's humour. On May 15th/16th the League's exhibition van parked at the Devon County Showground was wrecked overnight. Headlights and windows were smashed; paint-work gouged; tyres and awning slashed and sales goods and leaflets scattered around the show ground. Hunters were determined to snuff out the LACS message. £4,000 worth of damage was caused.

Police arrested prize-wining farmer and hunt supporter Robert Venner whose family helped establish the Tiverton Staghounds. He admitted his drunken wrecking spree and said he took exception to the LACS being allowed a stand at the Devon County Show. Robert Venner was charged with Criminal Damage and was due to appear before Exeter Magistrates. However, police settled the matter when he paid £4,100 in compensation and accepted a police caution. Outside the court wealthy Robert Venner, who was egged on by others, commented: "*The incident was a practical joke that went wrong. I tried to climb their flagpole and pinch their flag. I should not have done what I did and I have paid for the repairs.*" (*Western Morning News*, July 24th 1997)

The League Chief Officer, Graham Sirl, complained the League was not consulted over how the case was resolved and expressed outrage over the leniency: "*I'm happy we've got the money but the police have been quite pathetic in just giving him a caution. We're always branded as extremists, those who resort to violence to get across our point of view. But when it comes to the opposition being violent to property and frightening people, they fail to come down heavy. This is just a slap across the wrist. There are people who do far less and get suspended sentences"* (*North Devon Journal*, July 31st 1997).

In Waveney, I had campaigned for local Labour candidate, Bob Blizzard. Then I spent election day campaigning with Lawrie Payne for our good friend Angela Smith, Labour candidate in Basildon. I had known Angela since Richard Course first employed her as a Political Officer at the LACS in the early 1980s. Angela proved to be an intelligent and determined campaigner for animal welfare. Along with colleagues such as Richard Course initially and later Jane Springford and Kevin Flack she took the League striding forwards politically.

Angela Smith won in Basildon as Labour won in the country with a huge 179 seat majority. The BFSS Chairman Charles Goodson-Wickes lost his Wimbledon seat to Labour with an 18% swing. The Labour victor, Roger Casale, made animal welfare and the abolition of hunting one of the main issues of his campaign. Former BFSS Chairman Nicholas Bonsor also lost his seat as did another BFSS hunting fanatic, Nicholas Budgen. Bob Blizzard won in Waveney and proved to be a dedicated, principled and compassionate MP.

We had the first Labour Government since 1979 and hopes were high for a new more compassionate and caring world. The Labour Party had given a wide range of animal welfare commitments during the election campaign. Many people, particularly youngsters, gave their support to Labour as a result. The Labour manifesto promised a free vote on whether hunting wildlife with dogs should be banned. It was certain that such hunting would be banned; the only question was when.

Whilst the hunting fraternity rank-and-file were distraught that their Conservative allies had lost the election so badly many leaders did not appear too dismayed. Some privately boasted they had good friends high amongst the Labour Government and they expected any ban to be delayed and weakened. Their allies included senior MPs like Jack Straw, who worked behind the scenes, as well as the openly pro-hunt Kate Hoey (previously a member of the LACS, Kate Hoey switched sides to become a stalwart supporter of hunting and was Chairman of the Countryside Alliance from 2005-2014).

Michael Foster, Labour MP for Worcester, drew first place in the first ballot for Private Members Bills after the election. On Monday June 16th, he announced he would introduce a bill to abolish the hunting of wildlife with dogs. In July 1997 at a press conference to set out the principles of his proposed bill he said: "*There is no place in modern Britain for 'sports' which cause unnecessary suffering to over 100,000 animals every year.*"

Thursday July 10th 1997 was a momentous day for the hunting fraternity. The Countryside Alliance (CA) was born out of the merger between the British Field Sports Society, the Countryside Business Group and the Countryside Movement. The latter outfit, run by Sir David Steel on a remuneration of £94,000, had collapsed owing over £1 million. The Countryside Business Group was set up with the declared ambition to raise between £3 and £5 million each year to preserve hunting and shooting. Chairman was Hugh Van Cutsem. In the first year, the group raised an estimated £700,000, most of which came from the gun lobby.

Many perceived the name 'Countryside Alliance' to be more anodyne that the disreputable and discredited BFSS. The new group launched by holding a 'Countryside Rally' in Hyde Park, London from 11am to 2:30pm on Thursday July 10th 1997. It was attended by some 80,000 (Royal Parks official figure). Many City businesses gave employees time off to attend. Many parents encouraged their children to play truant from school to swell the numbers.

The rally was called to raise concerns over a variety of issues from hunting to loss of jobs in the countryside and the closure of rural post offices, schools and hospitals. It was a thin veneer of respectability. Speaker after speaker did not address a single issue other than the fear of hunting with dogs being abolished. I attended as an observer and photographed and took video film of the event. Few that I spoke to, or overheard chatting, seemed to know much about the reality of hunting. One who knew was Lynn Sawyer, the former Essex Foxhounds follower who changed sides. She courageously climbed a tree behind the main stage and displayed an anti-hunt banner.

Another who knew the truth was Ruth, a young hunt saboteur from Brighton, who took prime position at the front and middle of the crowd—and called out questions the speakers did not want to hear. Some of the less savoury heroes amongst the crowd gravitated towards her and threatened her with all manner of mischief if she did not shut up. She courageously ignored their threats, made her points and was protected by the professional security men at the event.

Threats were in the air. There was a great deal of militant talk from the platform. David Jones, Huntsman of the David Davies Foxhounds declared: "*This is the last peaceful march, and this is the last peaceful rally.*" John Fretwell from the UCSW said: "*Starting today, you're the soldiers.... We must all go back home and be prepared to fight our cause.*" Eric Bettelheim the American financier who set up the Countryside Business Group, compared, without a hint of embarrassment, the rally to the beginning of the American Revolution. *Daily Telegraph* columnist Auberon Waugh even suggested the idea of poisoning the water supply should hunting be banned.

In the summer the LACS magazine, *Wildlife Guardian*, won the *BBC Wildlife Magazine*'s competition to find the 'Best Environmental Newspaper'. John Bryant, Chief Officer of the LACS and Editor of *Wildlife Guardian* received the award in a ceremony at BBC Television Centre, London on August 20th 1997.

On September 8th Michael Foster launched a 'campaign bus' tour from Reading in support of his bill. In a sign of things to come hunt supporters turned up to harangue Michael Foster, his fellow MP Martin Salter and members and supporters of IFAW, LACS and the RSPCA. Michael Foster also reported receiving hate mail including death threats. Undeterred he published his Wild Mammals (Hunting with Dogs) Bill on November 5th 1997. The Bill was presented as being a "Bill to make provision for the protection of wild mammals from being, pursued, killed or injured by the use of dogs." The Bill's sponsors were: Jackie Ballard (Lib Dem), Ivor Caplin (Lab), Ian Cawsey (Lab), Margaret Ewing (SNP), Roger Gale (Con), Simon Hughes (Lib Dem), Nigel Jones (Lib Dem), Jackie Lawrence (Lab), Kevin McNamara (Lab), Angela Smith (Lab), and Sir Teddy Taylor (Con).

The Campaign for the Protection of Hunted Animals (CPHA) urged supporters to lobby their MPs to support the bill. Caring people responded magnificently. Several MPs reported receiving letters from anti-hunt constituents that outnumbered those from pro-hunt by a ratio of 100 to 1. John Bryant left his position at the League and moved to work as an adviser to the CPHA. His role as Editor of *Wildlife Guardian* was taken over by Kevin Saunders, the LACS Press Officer.

In March 1987, as a young hunt saboteur, Kevin Saunders had been seriously injured whilst trying to protect wildlife from the Essex Foxhounds. He had been calling hounds out of covert when Whipper-in, Martyn Blackmore, rode up and demanded to know how long he wanted to live. Kevin's wife, Carol, pointed her camera at Blackmore to discourage him. When Kevin turned his back and walked to his car, Martyn Blackmore smashed the bone spike of his whip handle onto Kevin's head. As he collapsed to his knees Kevin was struck again. Kevin later said: "*On the way to hospital I realised my ear was hanging off and my whole head was covered in blood. I received seventeen stitches to my ear and one to the top of my head.*" Martyn Blackmore was cleared of assault at Chelmsford Crown Court when he claimed he only struck out because he feared being unsaddled (*HOWL* 37, Autumn 1987).

Kevin was to suffer even more severely for his willingness to stand against cruelty and violence. It was Thursday November 9th 1995, almost a month after he was sacked from the League by Jim Barrington, when he was on the London underground and saw a man being violently assaulted. Kevin immediately went to the aid of this stranger, saved him from a violent beating but, for his trouble, was knifed in the back by the assailant. Kevin nearly died—only the close proximity of a major hospital saved his life. He suffered a collapsed lung, a pierced diaphragm and lost his spleen. After Jim Barrington left the LACS, Kevin was reinstated, but the injuries he suffered that November day proved to be life-changing. He was plagued by ill-health afterwards and tragically died in 2012.

The Second Reading of the Foster Bill was on Friday November 28th 1997. The Commons was packed when soon after 9:30am Michael Foster stood to move his bill. He spoke for nearly an hour before concluding:

"When we were elected to the House, we all wanted to change the world, or at least a small part of it. Today we have an opportunity to make a modern Britain. The House will be judged by future generations on our actions today, just as we judged the actions of our 19th-century predecessors (who banned dog-fighting, cock-fighting and bear baiting). *I urge every Hon. Member to stand proud, to make a mark and to vote to end the unnecessary, cruel and outdated practice of hunting with dogs."*

Amongst those speaking against the bill was former Conservative Environment Minister John Gummer who said: *"....there is no question of extinction, and therefore no need to protect foxes....This is not an issue of cruelty; it is an issue of sentimentality."*

One of the most eloquent speeches in favour of the bill came from Labour MP Paul Flynn: *"The debate is about how we treat other species and our relationship with them. The compassion and consideration that we show those species is a mark of our civilization. We cannot treat them as quarries for our entertainment or pleasure. They are creatures like us, with nervous systems. They feel pain, suffering and fear, just as we do. We cannot treat them as targets or a collection of inert, non-suffering chemicals. That demeans us as human beings."*

Speech of the day came from Conservative Ann Widdecombe. Her words included: *"It is important to ask ourselves a simple question. Is hunting so wrong that we wish to abolish it? If it is, all else flows from that. We do not need to be concerned about jobs or liberties to do wrong; we need only ask whether it is so wrong that it should be abolished."*

In the early afternoon George Howarth, the Parliamentary Under-Secretary of state for the Home Department rose to speak for the Government. He was incisive: *"In the late 20th century, as we move to a new millennium, the spectacle of hunting is unacceptable. The idea of people riding horses and chasing a pack of hounds to hunt down, sometimes in the most cruel way, a quarry that is sometimes killed in the most appalling way is beyond the scope of most people to understand. They wonder how it can possibly be considered a sport."* Pressed by MPs as to whether the Government would give the bill time George Howarth was evasive but said there was no reason why the bill should not progress successfully through Report stage and Third Reading to the House of Lords. He ended with a warning to the unelected Lords: *"If the Lords want to take on the House of Commons, then let them do so. They will find that the public believe as we believe—that hereditary peers should not have that right."*

When it came to the vote the result was decisive. 411 MPs from all three major parties voted in favour, and just 151 against. It was a record-breaking vote—the largest number of MPs voting for a Private Member's Bill and the largest ever majority (260) in favour of such a bill. Turnout by MPs was all the more remarkable given that it was a Friday, the day when they usually leave the Commons to work in their constituencies. The bill then moved to the Committee stage. That stage was completed on February

25th 1998, despite a last-ditch attempt by the Committee's pro-hunt members to talk the Bill out.

To demonstrate their opposition to the Foster Bill the CA organized a large protest march on Sunday March 1st 1998. The BBC estimated some 250,000 joined this protest against the bill and against other perceived threats to rural life including plans to build on greenfield sites, falling farm incomes, plans for 'right to roam' legislation and the banning of 'beef on the bone'. Many rural employees, particularly those living in tied accommodation, were given little option but to march.

Dave and Cee Wetton were voices for compassion as the marchers plodded by. Armed with their "Ban Bloodsports" banner they took a position on the corner of the Embankment and Northumberland Avenue some 100m ahead of the start point for the march, where marchers would see them. It was no surprise that Dave and Cee were subjected to a loud chorus of boos, hollers, catcalls, 'wanker' and middle-finger gestures. They responded with various taunts including, "*Flat hats for flat heads!*"; "*Forelock doffers*"; and "*Welcome to civilization!*" Some drunk terriermen made lunges for their banner; one did later snatch it but was arrested.

The LACS at that time was blessed by having in their employment Ben Stewart. I recall the young man in his early days at the League being as quiet as a mouse. He soon evolved into one of the most fastidious, determined and dedicated researchers I have ever met. He left the LACS and went to prove his activist credentials at Greenpeace.

Later in 1998 a LACS investigation revealed the CA had sold the names and addresses of 30,000 of its members to the Conservative party. Those on the list promptly received a letter from William Hague requesting a donation to the Conservative Party. In response Conservative Central Office received tens of thousands of pounds. The League sent a copy of William Hague's letter to the *Times* who ran a story under the caption: "*Tories cash in on the countryside marchers*." CA Chairman Charles Goodson-Wickes called the affair a 'major embarrassment' and promised that members' names would never again be sold.

Such harvesting of names and addresses had been done before. When the Countryside Movement was set up, a spokesperson claimed that the organization was not a pro-bloodsports movement. Chairman, David Steel, had said: "*I do not approve of hunting.*" But at the time of its inception the Countryside Movement had registered the BFSS as a recipient of the details of its database. A list of 105,000 country folk gathered by the Countryside Movement was passed to the BFSS. The database included the names of National Farmers Union members whose details had been given to the Countryside Movement, and thus to the BFSS, without the knowledge of those individuals. Some farmers reported receiving letters stating that unless they wrote refusing membership their names would be included on the Countryside Movement's list of supporters.

Hunting folk always had a problem with numbers. My best estimate is that there were only some 40,000 actively involved with hunting wildlife with dogs. To garner support from shooters and fishermen they recited the

395

mantra that 'if hunting is banned first, you will be next.' The problem for hunters was that too many in their ranks were inherently aloof, arrogant and ignorant. They seldom thought twice about disrupting shooting activities with their hounds and hunt apologists seemed incapable of promoting hunting without denigrating shooting. Their argument ran along the lines: 'Hunting is one means of killing the fox instantly and as such is infinitely better than shooting which results in wounded foxes crawling away to die in agony from gangrene.'

To many shooters and fishermen, it was as if the three sports were drowning in a small pool and the huntsman was keen to sit on the shoulders of either of the others to keep his head above water. It is likely that fishermen and shooters who marched did so not out of any real love for hunters but rather out of recognition that were hunting to be banned those interested in protecting animals from unnecessary cruelty would indeed switch their full focus to their pastimes.

The hunt tactic their strategists deployed to perfection then and maintain to this day, was to build a smokescreen of rural concerns around hunting. People rightly concerned about the closure of rural schools and rural post offices, even pubs, were encouraged to march against the Government—and support the CA.

From talking to a politician close to Tony Blair at the time it is clear Tony was severely rattled by the numbers on the March—more so as it was so early in his reign as Prime Minister and he had yet to gain the bullish swagger that marked his later years.

The CPHA responded to the March by proving their electoral power. It was March 5th 1998, the day before the Foster Bill started its Report stage, when three senior officers from IFAW, LACS and the RSPCA handed a one million signature petition to 10 Downing Street. Collected by the CPHA in just two months it said: "*Noting that the Wild Mammals (Hunting with Dogs) Bill received a Second Reading on 28th November, we, the undersigned, call for legislation to be enacted to end hunting with dogs as soon as possible in the lifetime of this Parliament.*"

That same day, a rival petition raised by the CA and the British Association for Shooting and Conservation (BASC) was handed in. Theirs amounted to half a million signatures, took around nine months to collect and was a broad plea to protect all 'country sports and the countryside'.

However, the Bill stalled when it ran out of time during the Report stage after pro-hunt MPs tabled hundreds of amendments. On the first day, March 6th, former Conservative Minister, Douglas Hogg, tabled no fewer than 102 amendments (Douglas Hogg was the Minister many blamed for the mishandling of the BSE crisis. More recently he was exposed by the *Daily Telegraph* in 2009 for claiming upwards of £2,000 of taxpayer's money for the cleaning of the moat at his Lincolnshire country pile—Kettlethorpe Hall).

More amendments were tabled by pro-hunt MPs the following week. Two days of outrageous filibustering ended on Friday March 13th 1998. A small group of mainly Conservative MPs but including Kate Hoey for Labour, had wasted two five hour sessions preventing the Bill reaching its Third Reading. Hunt supporters proclaimed the Foster Bill dead—but conservationists hoped the Government would make more time available to meet overwhelming public demands to see wildlife properly protected.

Speaking for the CPHA after Michael Foster's Bill was adjourned on March 13th, Kate Parminter from the RSPCA said: "*A ban on hunting with dogs is what the people want, what Parliament wants, and seems to be what the Prime Minister wants. This issue will not go away and the Government will have to respond.*"

In June 1998 the CA was torn apart by internal wrangling. The row was essentially between Edward Duke, the newly-appointed Chief Executive, and Janet George. A letter expressing no confidence in Edward Duke signed by Janet George, Roger Loodmer the Finance Director, and John Gardiner the Director of Public Affairs was sent to the Chairman of the board, Charles Goodson-Wickes on June 12th. The CA board met and decided to put Edward Duke on 'probation' and pay off Janet George. She immediately declared that she would sue the CA for sexual discrimination and unfair dismissal and stated she was, "*angry as hell.*" She lost no time in confirming their whole strategic plan to hide hunting behind a large raft of rural concerns saying: "*We must wrap up hunting in the rural fabric, because everyone hates hunting and loves the countryside*" (*Wildlife Guardian*, Issue 40 Spring 1999).

The hunting press rallied to support Janet George. Arnold Garvey, Editor of *Horse and Hound* observed that the CA had: "*snatched defeat from the jaws of victory.*" Days later Dr Charles Goodson-Wickes resigned.

In July 1998 Michael Foster withdrew his bill because of what he described as the cynical tactics of his opponents. A CPHA spokesman explained: "*Our campaign goes on regardless. Michael knew plans were being made to scupper his bill and he did not want to hold up any other worthy bills on the list by keeping his on it.*" On July 29th Tony Blair stated: "*The Home Secretary has discussed with* (Michael Foster) *and others ways in which we can make progress on this issue.*" Hunting and hare coursing continued through the 1998/99 season.

Tony Blair confirmed that any Bill to ban hunting wildlife with dogs would not proceed until the House of Lords had been reformed. A new campaigning group appeared with the launch in London on Monday November 30th 1998 of Deadline 2000. At a packed meeting in Westminster, John Rolls, the RSPCA Director of Communication, declared that IFAW, LACS and the RSPCA were committed to work together to ensure that hunting would not survive into the next millennium.

The *Mail on Sunday*, December 6th 1998, reported the Government favoured legislation by which hunting would be banned across the UK, whilst hunts would be permitted to apply for an exemption if the population of a county voted to retain hunting in a referendum.

In April 1999 Douglas Batchelor was appointed Chief Executive of the LACS. It proved an inspired appointment. Initially Douglas appeared to be your friendly bank manager type figure but he proved adept at welding an effective team together. He extracted the very best from every member of his team and identified and exploited the many weaknesses amongst those who supported bloodsports. In my area of concern Douglas gave full support and a free rein to the investigative side of the League's work. He was at the helm to see hunting banned.

On Sunday May 23rd 1999 the LACS Chairman, John Cooper, launched a new League campaign with a caricature of a Huntsman in a bath of blood and an uncompromising message for Tony Blair: "*It's time you ended this bloodbath. Ban hunting now, Tony.*" IFAW, LACS and the Countryside Protection Group also produced a campaigning video entitled 'Out of Control in the Countryside' that detailed the mayhem and havoc caused by hunts the previous season.

There was a by-election in Eddisbury on June 22nd. When Tony Blair joined a rally in Winsford in support of the Labour candidate, Margaret Hanson, he was effectively ambushed by hunt supporters encouraged to attend to 'tread on Blair's toes.' Tomatoes were thrown, supportive balloons popped and a children's brass band was drowned out by jeering. LACS investigators identified four Hunt Masters present for this unruly protest and the terrierman of the local Cheshire hunt.

July 8th 1999 proved significant. Prime Minister Tony Blair was tackled about the hunting issue on the BBC programme Question Time. He said: "*It will be banned. We will get the vote to ban as soon as we possibly can. We are looking at ways of bringing it forward in future sessions. We will try if we possibly can to give it space in the upcoming session or the one after that.*" Tony Blair wrote of that incident in his autobiography *A Journey* (page 305): "*On a TV programme I stupidly gave the impression it would indeed be banned. Of course I had voting form, having voted to ban it or said I wanted to or signed some petition or something. Anyway, I repeated my 'position' rather than reconsidering it. The moment I did so, I was defined. And so trapped. By the end of it, I felt like the damn fox.*"

Two days after his announcement on Question Time Tony Blair was in Scarborough, Yorkshire for a Labour Party conference. As his car rounded a corner some 250 pro-hunt protesters rushed through a police cordon. Objects were thrown at the Prime Minister's car. Violent clashes between police officers and hunt enthusiasts ended in three arrests for what officers described as 'public order offences'.

Monday July 12th 1999, in the House of Commons the Home Office Minister, George Howarth, answering oral questions from three Labour MPs confirmed the Government intended to legislate on hunting with dogs. He said they were considering three options: the introduction of specific Government anti-hunting legislation; the amendment of a planned Government bill to include provisions that would end hunting; Government support for a Private Member's Bill.

George Howarth had said that proposals would be published before the summer recess of Parliament but that did not happen. At the time animal welfarists expected plans to ban the hunting of wild mammals with dogs to be included in the Queen's Speech in November 1999.

Later that month the Labour MSP Mike Watson announced plans to put forward a private member's bill in the Scottish Parliament to ban hunting with dogs in Scotland. In Scotland Advocates for Animals, IFAW and the LACS supported this under the umbrella organization Scottish Campaign Against Hunting with Dogs (SCAHD).

A couple of months after Question Time Tony Blair repeated his commitment to banning hunting. On September 30th 1999 on BBC Radio 4 he said: "*I am opposed to hunting.....Parliament will have a chance to see this through.*"

Many tactics were deployed to delay the bill to ban hunting wildlife with dogs. It was suggested it would have to wait until the House of Lords— that was packed with pro-hunt peers—was reformed. On November 11th 1999 the Home Secretary, Jack Straw, declared a bill would be given Government time, but only after the completion of an inquiry into the hunting issue: "*The Government's manifesto commitment was for a free vote on whether hunting with hounds should be banned. Such a free vote took place during proceedings in the 1997/98 Session on the bill to outlaw hunting with dogs sponsored by my hon. Friend, the hon. Member for Worcester (Mr. Foster). His bill received a Second Reading by 411 votes to 151. I well understand the frustration of many hon. Members that no legislative conclusion followed. I am, therefore, pleased to announce that the Government will offer reasonable time, if necessary, and drafting assistance for this issue to be considered by the House of Commons through a Private Member's Bill on a free vote. We shall consult the House authorities, as appropriate, on how this can best be taken forward. The Government have decided that there should first be an inquiry. This will be a committee of inquiry not into whether hunting is right or wrong, which is a matter for Parliament to decide. Instead, the inquiry will be put in place better to inform the debate. The inquiry will look at the practical issues involved in hunting with dogs, how a ban could be implemented and what the consequences of a ban would be. It will provide an opportunity for the facts about hunting to be considered. Also, it will enable an examination of the effect on the rural economy, agriculture and pest control, the social and cultural life of particular areas of countryside, the management and conservation of wildlife and animal welfare of hunting and if hunting were to be banned. The inquiry will take evidence from all interested parties. The inquiry will be chaired by the noble Lord, Lord Burns. It will be asked to report by late spring next year. The names of the other members of the inquiry will be announced as soon as possible. The report will be put before Parliament. Once the inquiry has reported, the Government's offer of time and drafting assistance will take effect.*"

Jack Straw MP appointed the Committee of Inquiry in December 1999 to look into hunting with dogs with the following terms of reference:- Page 1: "*To inquire into: the practical aspects of different types of hunting with dogs and its impact on the rural economy, agriculture and pest control, the social and cultural life of the countryside, the management and conservation of wildlife, and animal welfare in particular areas of*

England and Wales; the consequences for these issues of any ban on hunting with dogs; and how any ban might be implemented."

Members of the Inquiry team were Lord Burns, Lord Soulsby of Swaffham Prior, Professor Sir John Marsh, Professor Michael Winter and Dr Victoria Edwards. Civil servants in charge of organizing events were Brian Caffarey, Secretary to the Committee of Inquiry, and Mark Sanderson. Lord Soulsby was President of the Royal College of Veterinary Surgeons and Professor of Animal Pathology at Cambridge University.

Before the selection of the Inquiry team animal welfare groups had been invited to submit names of academics who might sit on the panel. None they suggested was selected. Instead Jack Straw appointed an Inquiry team calculated to be at the very least sympathetic to hunting. *The Observer*, February 6th 2000, reported salient facts under the heading *"Blood sport inquiry's hunt links revealed."* Lord Soulsby had offered his services 'free' to the BFSS to counter the report by Professor Bateson that showed the cruelty suffered by hunted deer. Professor Winter had been on hunts as a child and an adult. Sir John Marsh was a governor of the Royal Agricultural College, which owned a pack of beagles. Dr Victoria Edwards was a member of the Advisory Council of the Royal Agricultural College.

John Cooper, Chairman of the LACS said: *"How can our members have any confidence in this process? The more we learn about the inquiry members, the more obvious it appears that we have been stitched up."* Ian Gibson, Labour MP for Norwich North, said: *"I am astonished that three years into a Labour Government pledged to ban hunting we are having a debate about the make-up of a so-called independent committee. It is simply unbelievable that its members seem to be biased one way."*

It is important to understand exactly what the Inquiry was asked to do. On page 1 of their report the Committee note: *"We were helped by the terms of reference, which asked us to concentrate on the factual and analytical background to hunting. We have addressed those issues and we have not attempted to answer the question of whether or not hunting should be banned. In particular, we have not sought to find a compromise solution, which we regarded as outside our terms of reference."* On page 7 the Committee clarify their role: *"We were asked to focus on the hunting with dogs of foxes, deer, hares and mink. The use of dogs solely to locate or retrieve quarry was excluded from our terms of reference. We were not asked to recommend whether hunting should be banned. Nor were we asked to consider moral or ethical issues."*

The Committee was not asked to decide whether hunting wildlife with dogs was cruel. They were not asked to decide whether hunting should be banned—that was left to MPs to decide. The Committee was not asked to look at hunting in Scotland or Northern Ireland.

An integral part of the Inquiry was a succession of visits by members of the Inquiry team to see hunting and coursing. For each visit, it was decided there would be observers from both sides—Deadline 2000, the focus group of the CPHA, and the CA would both provide observers. The CPHA appointed Graham Sirl and me to share being their observers.

My task, as I saw it, was to ensure that these outsiders who may have seen little or nothing of the pastimes before saw something of hunting and coursing as I knew them to be. You can only ever see the full reality of hunting if your fellow hunters perceive you to be 'one of them' but I wanted these Parliamentary observers to see more of the activities than the meaningless glamorous façade shown to our media.

*****

The first visit scheduled was to the Bicester with Whaddon Chase Foxhounds at Priors Hardwick, south west of Daventry, on Thursday January 27th 2000. I was to rendezvous with the Inquiry team at Banbury station at 9:30am. I stayed in Banbury the night before and was at the station on time. I waited and waited but no-one arrived. In time, I phoned the LACS office and learned the visit was cancelled due to frost.

Whilst it was bright and cold I expected that hunt to meet as they had a reputation for hunting whatever the weather, and until the last rays of light faded. I went to the meet and true enough found hunting had simply been delayed an hour. Hunt monitors were out. They told me the whole day was strange. It was on a Thursday but was not in their usual Thursday hunt country. The area selected for this meet was regarded as being much 'safer' for the hunt.

I filmed the meet and some hunting over nearby countryside. I saw a bobtailed fox fleeing the hounds. In the absence of the Inquiry team I was unwelcome on the land. With it hard to monitor the hunt in that area I left after a short time. It was a lovely sunny afternoon.

*****

My first real visit with the Inquiry team was to the meet of the East of England Coursing Club at Twenty, west of Spalding, on Friday February 4th. That was a coursing club and area I knew well from previous undercover work. The Inquiry team were Lord Burns, Lord Soulsby, Dr Edwards and Mark Sanderson organising the visit. It was the first day of the Barbican Cup, a two-day meeting. The Inquiry team was given the rendezvous of Ely railway station, some 50 miles away, at 9:00am. As always for English coursing the first brace of dogs was due in the slips at that time. Clearly visits were to be a relaxed affair.

I arrived at Ely on time and met Mark Sanderson in the company of well-known hare courser Michael Darnell. Lord Burns, Lord Soulsby and Dr Edwards arrived by train and I was introduced. We split our party for the hour drive to the meet. Michael Darnell had a four-wheel-drive vehicle driven by his son. He took Lord Burns and Lord Soulsby whilst Dr Edwards and Mark Sanderson travelled with me.

On arrival, we drove up a track and met the person selling the entry cards. I was intrigued as to whether we would be expected to pay. Michael Darnell stepped out and spoke to the lady. We were all given free £5 entry cards. We were directed further up the track and parked at the end of a line of vehicles. We were introduced to Simon Hart, the Head of Public Relations for the Campaign for Hunting, there to observe for the CA.

401

Hare coursing was under way in a nearby field and we were guided to a suitable observation point. I needed more evidence than merely my recollections so I took out my still and video cameras. Lord Burns and Dr Edwards also used cameras. We were introduced to Charles Blanning, the keeper of the Greyhound Stud Book. He ran the National Coursing Club offices in Newmarket. At a suitable opportunity, the mounted judge, Bob Burdon, was introduced to us. I knew both well from previous visits. From his lofty mounted position Bob discussed coursing matters with the team. I noticed Simon Hart whispering to Charles Blanning.

We saw two hares killed, both a considerable distance from us. None of us could see whether the hares were killed by the dogs or by the Pickers-up. On both occasions the Pickers-up were seen to break the hare's neck. When the first hare was caught around 35 seconds elapsed before the Picker-up retrieved the hare from the dog. When released from the dogs the hare appeared to make a dash to escape and the Picker-up caught and killed her. He turned, shielding this from our view.

When the second hare was caught, I heard her crying. There was a strong wind that obscured sounds but I had heard those pitiful cries too many times before and discerned them. I asked Dr Edwards but she said she heard no crying. Simon Hart, who admitted he had seen very little of coursing before that day, heard nothing. Some of the cruelties of coursing could easily pass unnoticed.

I asked that the Inquiry team be shown the body of the first hare killed. The coursers said that would be no problem and it should have been easy as the body was nearby but the team never saw that body. I asked several more times but it was never produced.

We did see the body of the second hare killed, a male. The only visible injury was a cut producing blood from just in front of a back leg. This body was shown to Lord Burns, Dr Edwards and me. Lord Soulsby was nowhere in sight. Knowing that Lord Soulsby was a senior vet I thought he should see the body too. We eventually found him back with the supporters' vehicles. We walked up the track to a suitable place and the dead hare was tipped out of the bin-liner on to the ground. Lord Soulsby crouched down and felt his neck.

Lord Soulsby: *"Did it have its neck broken...er..by the hunt?"*
Mike Huskisson: *"The Picker-up....."*
Hare Courser: *"No, the dog.....the dog went for it"*
Hare Courser: *"First grab...."*
Mike Huskisson: *"Sorry?"*
Hare Courser: *"First grab was the back of the neck..."*
Hare Courser: *"And when it come forward the other one got hold of the other end."*
Mike Huskisson: *"Right."*
Hare Courser: *"And actually it was dead before the other one collared it..."*

There was a pause while Lord Soulsby examined the hare. A vehicle horn sounded indicating we were blocking the way. A hare courser apologised to Lord Soulsby and indicated that there was room to continue his examination to the side.

Lord Soulsby: *"No, that's fine. The....er...It seems to have been got by the by the neck....."*

The hare was indeed "got by the neck". We had seen the Picker-up break his neck. What was disputed was who broke the neck—Picker-up or dog? Pickers-up had no need to break the necks of dead hares.

I suggested the Inquiry team see the Slippers' view of coursing, a view that I, when posing as a coursing supporter, never had. I felt sure the coursers would feel obliged to help and they did. Lord Burns joined the Slipper in his shy to see the dogs released. He had been in the shy when the dogs were released that resulted in one of the kills. I hoped that all Inquiry members would have a turn in the shy but only Lord Burns did.

For the last coursing beat that we saw I waited with Dr Edwards next to the area where the dogs were gathered before being put in the slips. We waited for Lord Burns, Lord Soulsby and Mark Sanderson. We saw the beat line coming in and I was torn between waiting with Dr Edwards for the others and making my own way down the flank line to film, and thus record for the Inquiry team, whatever occurred. However, I had been instructed not to leave the Inquiry team so I waited with Dr Edwards.

Realising the need for urgency she said that we should go on and leave the others to catch up. We did. Lord Burns and Mark Sanderson quickly joined us but of Lord Soulsby there was no sign. He stayed far back from where the hare was likely to be caught, near the slip Steward. Aged Lord Soulsby had mobility problems that I feared would cause problems at other very rural events.

We saw one dog suffer a severe impact when misjudging a jump over a ditch whilst in close pursuit of a hare. In obvious pain the dog howled and cried. Dr Edwards heard this too and accompanied me to the scene. Luckily the dog, we were told, did not have a broken leg. After a period to recuperate he was carried away. Lord Soulsby, the veterinary expert, was too far away to know any of this. I saw the injured dog carried past him. Later I sought his opinion of the injury but he told me he had not checked the dog himself and repeated the courser's diagnosis.

By 3pm the Inquiry team had seen enough and left. The coursing that started without us ended without us. The Darnells drove Lord Soulsby back to his home. Simon Hart and I ferried the remainder of the team to Peterborough railway station (much nearer than Ely). I had the pleasure of Lord Burns' company whilst Dr Edwards and Mark Sanderson travelled with Simon Hart.

Aside from the kills, the most memorable feature of the day was the shortage of hares. We arrived an hour after the start and yet they had run just three courses in our absence. Lines of beaters walked in again and again with few hares to show for their efforts. The coursers told the Inquiry team that this was due to the efforts of poachers, often working at night. These coursers were keen to stress to the Inquiry team the great cruelty caused by those who poach hares using coursing dogs.

As the hares were clearly present on the farmland in very low numbers they could not be described as pests. It was usually claimed that where there was coursing there would be hares. It was not the case here. Furthermore, for all their complaining about the shortage of hares what was certain was that at day's end there were at least two hares fewer. Again many beaters employed for the day were students playing truant from local schools.

*****

My next visit was the following week when I joined the team for the meet of the Border Foxhounds far to the north at Heatherhope in Scotland to the south-west of Jedburgh on Wednesday February 2nd 2000. I drove north the evening before. I was booked in at the prestigious Percy Arms Hotel, a well-known hunting establishment, the rendezvous for the Inquiry team in the morning. The last half hour of my drive over the open moorland was through a blizzard.

When I checked in I was told: *"Oh! The rest of the Inquiry Committee have phoned to say they will be a bit late."* At 9:30pm Lord Burns, Professor Winter and Brian Caffarey arrived. Lord Burns and Brian Caffarey had travelled up by train whilst Professor Winter took the aerial route from Bristol. We all enjoyed dinner together.

Michael Hedley, Joint Master and Huntsman of the Border hunt and Simon Hart, joined us. During the conversation at the dining table Michael Hedley told us his hunt operated over some 200,000 acres. He explained that a lot of the country they hunted was Ministry of Defence or Forestry Commission land. He claimed all landowners in their hunting country made them welcome. He said that they killed about 200 foxes a year and that they dug out a lot, about a third. Simon Hart stayed with Michael Hedley at the hunt kennels nearby. We learned the hunt had arranged for two expert guides, Barry Richardson and Gordon Wright, to collect us in a Land Rover 110 from our hotel the following morning.

The day dawned bright and dry. There had been little further snow. We were collected at 9:15am and told there would be a drive of about an hour to the remote meet. I boarded the Land Rover with the rest of the Inquiry team. Simon Hart chose to follow in his car.

The meet was high up in the Cheviot Hills on the Scottish side of the border. The previous Friday Simon Hart had opined that for a Wednesday meet in Border Hunt country there would be few riders and followers. There were more than a few. A couple of supporters introduced themselves to Lord Burns as being followers of the Bicester with Whaddon Chase hunt. They declared they were sad he had not been able to see their hunt so they had come to see him.

At the meet at the end of a track in the hills, one of the wildest and remotest places imaginable, a couple of television crews strolled up! The local Border TV crew were doing a 'fly on the wall' type documentary, "A day in the life of a hunt". The presence of a Sky TV crew caused considerable consternation to the Inquiry team. They asked the Sky TV reporter how they

404

knew about the event; he merely said that his colleague in London had been told.

Sky television interviewed Lord Burns and Michael Hedley. I was as usual laden with cameras. At the 10:30am meet Lord Burns took photographs. Professor Winter did not appear to have his camera with him. The high number of supporters at the meet riding quad bikes was noticeable. A liberal amount of drink was passed around. Eventually Michael Hedley set off on foot with the hounds at about 11am. We watched from the vehicles then drove in pursuit as the hunt appeared to drift to the north-west towards Hownam.

We found the Sky TV crew parked by the road. They had their camera mounted on a tripod trained on the distant hillside. It was about twenty minutes to noon. Lord Burns was the first of our team to see the fleeing fox that had caught the cameraman's attention. We stopped, jumped out and observed a big fox making his way with no great rush from left to right on the hillside across from us. He disappeared near some buildings to our right. The hunt was some way behind with their hounds running widely scattered. In due course the lead hounds came by giving cry. Simon Hart timed them as being four and a half minutes behind. They appeared to be running right on the line of the fleeing fox.

One of our hunt guides advised us to turn around and drive in pursuit which we did. We noticed a cluster of quad bikes parked to our left. We stopped but the riders indicated that the hounds had gone on. We drove on and next saw hounds milling about in a field of grass to our left. I feared they had already killed the fox. We parked and made our way to the scene. Simon Hart was there first, chatting to hunt supporters standing around. A hunt follower coming away told me hounds had marked the fox to ground. I wondered what the hunt would do next.

The hounds were digging and baying at the edge of an old stone wall. We rushed to the site as did the Sky TV crew. They trained their professional camera on the hounds. I did likewise with my small digital video camera. The whole Inquiry team were swiftly at the scene. Riders on quad bikes and horses were there as were many other hunt supporters but not Michael Hedley. I noticed a hunt terrier given a ride on a quad bike. I heard hunters use their radios to discuss the situation with Michael. It was decided to 'give the fox best'. That fox was lucky to have gone to ground with the eyes of observers for the nation upon his sanctuary.

To my knowledge the landowner was not present. If he was he did not introduce himself in my hearing. The Inquiry team was not told whether the landowner wanted the fox killed or left. They were told the fox was left out of fear that the wall could collapse if hunters dug under it. I saw no effort made to ascertain the nature of the underground tunnels near the wall. Sky TV interviewed Lord Burns and Professor Winter by the wall overlooking the scene.

After that incident the hunt was mostly confined to distant high hillsides apart from one occasion when they came near us, close to a small reservoir by Heatherhope. I had previously ascertained from the Hon. Sec.

of the hunt, Lt. Col. Cross, that the hunt did have one artificial earth that he knew of, albeit an old one. I discussed this in the presence and hearing of Lord Burns, Professor Winter and Brian Caffarey. Lt. Col. Cross said he did not know why the artificial earth had been built.

When we approached the reservoir our guide cheerfully informed us the previous shepherd to the current one by the reservoir had so disliked the hunt that he used to wire up the gates whenever the hunt visited and his actions made it very difficult for the hunt. Given the claim from Michael Hedley the previous night that every landowner welcomed them there was evidently a difference in attitude to the hunt between those who owned the land and those who worked it.

With the hunt roaming the distant hillsides and ourselves confined to the hunt Land Rover there was little of interest to see. At one point, I noticed Lord Burns asleep in the front passenger seat. He slumbered and we sat in the vehicle whilst the hunt hunted. He stirred and I waited until he was fully awake. Knowing his role as a Director of Queens Park Rangers football club I commented, *"This is about as exciting as watching a football match from outside the stadium!"* He laughed and added that in his opinion it was worse because at least outside a football stadium you could hear the sounds of the crowd.

Professor Winter had a flight booked at 6pm so we left the hunt at 3:15pm, before they had finished. In consequence, we missed the main action because when I phoned Michael Hedley the next day he told me they killed two foxes that day. When we left, we were unaware of any kill.

*****

Our next visit, two days later, was to the meeting of the Kimberley & Wymondham Coursing Club at Kimberley on Friday February 11th. This was a venue I had previously attended undercover. The rendezvous was Norwich railway station at 8:20am. I caught the train from Diss and, by pure coincidence, found myself seated behind Brian Caffarey who I observed ploughing through a lengthy tract from the National Coursing Club.

Amongst the influx of commuters heading for work Professor Marsh met us at Norwich station and drove us in his aged but sturdy Volvo to the venue for the day's coursing at the small village of Kimberley, to the south-west of Norwich. It was a lovely sunny morning.

Brian Caffarey had been advised by the Coursing Club to look out for their direction signs to the coursing meet. Such signs were never big advertising boards saying 'Live hare coursing this way'. The clubs preferred small, and more anonymous (several inches high) coloured direction arrows or similar sized arrows bearing only the club initials.

Finding the exact venue was not easy and necessitated several turn arounds. We ended up just following cars that looked to contain coursing supporters. The name Hall Farm had been mentioned. I recalled the location as having been the site of a hare hunt by the Dunston Harriers that I had attended the previous autumn. It was still hard to find the coursing. We ended up amid several cars of bemused and lost coursing supporters.

Eventually the correct site was found. We met Simon Hart at the meet. The entry card, again given to us free of charge, declared a start at 9am sharp and we appeared to be about half an hour late. However, we missed nothing, the start was delayed an hour due to frost.

Coursing dogs had enough problems to contend with in the form of adverse ground conditions such as sharp flints and in the autumn short sharp stubble. Both lacerated their paws. Frozen ground was an additional hazard easily avoided by waiting for the sun to rise. Given a meet card I showed the Inquiry team the warning typed in bold on the back:-
"PHOTOGRAPHY, BOXES, STOOLS ETC. STRICTLY PROHIBITED"

There was another warning, in bold on the front:-
 "Anyone found returning to the running grounds and poaching will be reported to the NCC and will lose their membership of K&WCC".

The initials represented the National Coursing Club and the Kimberley & Wymondham Coursing Club. The need for such a caution was recent. From my undercover days, I had two other meet cards for the Kimberley & Wymondham Coursing Club, both for coursing at Kimberley. One dated Monday 4th March 1985; the second Monday 15th January 1990. Neither contained any reference to the caution against club members returning to the running grounds and poaching. Clearly this 'difficulty' for the organisers of coursing was a new phenomenon.

When coursing started, it was soon apparent there was almost a queue of hares waiting to be driven on to the coursing field. The slip length given appeared to be the normal. The conditions of the ground and the field topography must have favoured the hares as none was killed. One however was caught by the dogs right in front of us and flicked up in the air. Thankfully she landed intact and was able to escape.

Soon afterwards we noticed the highly experienced Slipper, Bob Blatch, struggling in the slips. His two canine charges, waiting in their paired collars, were having a fight. In many years observing coursing I had seen such fights occur before but they are a rarity. That they do occur is evidence of the measure of excitement and expectation engendered in the dogs. The coursers explained to the Inquiry team that the fight was due to the dogs involved being puppies.

We had seen many of the coursing supporters on our visit to the East of England Coursing Club at Twenty, the previous Friday. Many had also travelled large distances. One I spoke to had driven up from Kent to attend both venues.

Thankfully there was only one hare killed. It was a curious kill because the hare was caught by a single dog running on its own. I had seen that happen before but it was a rare event. The course lasted more than 50 seconds before the hare was caught. The Picker-up, or trainer, moved in quickly and obscured the condition of the hare from our view.

I suggested to Professor Marsh and Brian Caffarey they look at the body. The coursers appeared willing to oblige but I recalled that with the first hare killed at the East of England the coursers had appeared likewise willing to help but had never actually produced the dead hare. This time their willingness was never tested as Professor Marsh declined my suggestion saying he did not think they would gain anything from examining the dead body.

The coursing ended at about 3:15pm. The final course scheduled was not run due to one of the dogs involved being withdrawn. The whole Inquiry team stayed until the end. Brian Caffarey told me he had counted 32 courses run. Whilst welcome, the low kill ration of 1 out of 32 was wholly unusual and in no way representative of the usual threat to the hare posed by coursing (I have seen reports of kill ratios as high as 82% over a full day's hare coursing). However, I could not identify any unusual difference to the organisation of the coursing that day.

I was pleased Professor Marsh took a turn in the shy observing the Slipper working at close hand. During the day, I discussed with Professor Marsh the level of economic input provided by such a coursing club. Whilst the meet was at Kimberley Green there was no equivalent to the hunting 'stirrup cup' at the local pub. The meet was merely a rendezvous point from which to follow direction signs to the coursing field. There was some input of money to the locality by the payment of beaters. Refreshments were provided by a mobile catering vehicle which appeared to be the same one as seen previously at the East of England coursing fixture. With a two-day meeting, as this was, trade might have been provided for local hotels, Bed and Breakfasts and the like but given the need to accommodate the coursing greyhounds this cannot have been taken up by all. Most importantly the club only advertised 10 days' coursing in their entire 1999/2000 season and given that they had several venues at which to course their presence could not be portrayed as a significant input into local economies.

*****

There were then three visits by the Inquiry team of which, as I did not attend, I will only report the salient facts reported to me. Graham Sirl was the CPHA observer at all three. On February 15th 2000 they saw the Alresford Coursing Club meeting at St. Mary Bourne. Initially they were placed in a position where they were unlikely to see any kill. Realising this Graham asked they be moved and within five minutes a hare was killed just metres from them. The hare was heard screaming and it took all of 22 seconds for the Picker-up to reach the scene and retrieve the live hare. The Picker-up claimed the hare was dead when he reached her. When another hare was caught alive, and heard screaming, Professor Winter accompanied the Picker-up to the scene. One hare was coursed by three dogs when a dog waiting to go into slips broke free. The final course failed owing to shortage of hares. Over the two-day event four hares were killed. The coursing steward told the Inquiry team that dogs were injured the previous day by flints on the adjacent fields. On the day of the visit one dog was injured following a collision.

*****

Two days later, on February 17th, the Inquiry team attended the meet of the Devon and Somerset Staghounds at Wheddon Cross. This was

408

the hind hunting season. Hind hunting started on November 1st and ran through to the end of February. The hinds were pregnant throughout; by mid-February they would have been heavily pregnant. The first hind hunted was lost in thick gorse. They returned to the starting area to draw for a second. That hind ran precisely the same line as the first and ended up on Dunkery Beacon before running onto National Trust land at about 3pm. The hunt then ended for the day. The Inquiry team were with the hunt for the full duration.

Tom Yandle, guide for the day of the visit, High Sheriff of Somerset and Chairman of the hunt, had told the Inquiry team that the Snowdrop Valley they went into was usually closed at that time of year but had been opened especially for the team. Graham Sirl checked this claim with the Exmoor National Park Authority and was told the road into Snowdrop Valley had been opened to avoid any congestion with the scheduled coaches which are run at that time of year for visitors to see the Snowdrops. The hunt had in fact refused to change their meet. Exmoor National Park also confirmed they had received complaints the next day about hunt vehicles being driven over the verges and destroying the snowdrops.

As well as being pregnant, hinds were further handicapped by the fact that they tended to run with the previous year's calf by their side. This has long been acknowledged in hunting literature as this quote shows: "*At first the hinds will perhaps run round and round in a most exasperating way, and many days are marred by the hounds changing on to fresh deer when their hunted one is more than half beaten; nevertheless the sport is often first-rate. Especially is this the case after Christmas, as by that time the calves are able to take care of themselves, and a mother when pressed by the hounds will leave her offspring and go straight away, instead of ringing round to the place where she hid the little one under a bush in the morning.*" (*Fur, Feather, & Fin Series* Edited by Alfred E.T. Watson. Red Deer. Longmans, Green, and Co., 1912. Page 238-9. Stag-Hunting section by Viscount Ebrington, Master Devon & Somerset Staghounds 1881-87).

*****

Then on Saturday February 19th the Inquiry team visited the Old Berkeley Beagles meeting at Grendon Underwood between Aylesbury and Bicester. The hunt moved off at around 1pm. The Inquiry team left at 4pm with the hounds still hunting but with darkness approaching little was missed. There was an abundance of hares in the area hunted. Joint Master, Robert Knight, told Professor Winter that the beagles were not bred for speed. He added that he could make them faster by cross-breeding.

Professor Winter ran with the hunt staff following the hounds. He saw them running backwards and forwards for three quarters of an hour in a wood that turned out to be owned by the Woodland Trust. Graham Sirl filmed the hunt staff crossing a railway line near Quainton to the north west of Aylesbury. The line was used twice daily by trains from London. He pointed this trespass out to Lord Burns.

Hunt President, John Robinson, told Lord Burns that beagling did not control the numbers of hares. He said hare numbers were controlled by foxes killing leverets (which were around at that time of year). He also told Lord Burns it was not necessary to have any other form of hare control on Knapps Wood Farm, which was where they hunted that day.

*****

I then returned to the field for a visit to fox hunting proposed by the CA. This was the Thurlow Foxhounds meet at Great Bradley Hall on Monday February 21st. The Inquiry team were Lord Soulsby, Dr Edwards and Mark Sanderson. Simon Hart and I were the observers. The CA arranged transportation for the Inquiry team and our movements during the visit were determined by the Joint Hon. Sec. of the hunt, Paddy Bell.

The Thurlow is an old hunt. The first Master of whom much was known was James Paton, Master from 1770-1800. The present hunting country is small, covering some 18 miles by 11 miles. It was formed as the Newmarket and Thurlow hunt in 1884. In 1970 that hunt amalgamated with the Puckeridge to form the Puckeridge & Thurlow hunt but in 1992 the hunts divorced and the hunt reverted to its original name.

There has been a long tradition of preserving foxes in Thurlow hunt country. Michael Brander in *Portrait of a Hunt The history of the Puckeridge and Newmarket and Thurlow combined hunts* (Hutchinson Benham Limited, London 1976) writes on page 93 of the Newmarket and Thurlow in the 1920s:- "*At this time the country was being hunted five days a fortnight and the old strife between hunting and shooting interests had entirely ceased. Everyone was dedicated to foxhunting and no one shot on hunting days any longer and keepers did not kill foxes. Poisoning and trapping were no longer hazards to be suffered in silence. Mr C.F. Ryder of Thurlow Hall was a keen fox preserver and General Sir Charles Briggs, ex-cavalry commander and successor to Mr R.W. King as chairman of the hunt committee, rented the shooting of several of the best coverts on the Wickhambrook side of the country as well as maintaining supplies of foxes in his own.*" And adds on page 97:- "*Just how considerable a fox preserver Mr C.F. Ryder had become may be a little hard to appreciate without outside evidence. In his first season Mr Deacon personally counted twenty-two litters of cubs within a two mile radius of his house.*"

We met at Whittlesford station at 9:05am and drove in convoy to the hunt kennels at Wadgells Farm, Great Thurlow. We were given a guided tour of the premises by an elite team: Joint Master and Huntsman, Edmund Vestey; Joint Hon. Sec. Paddy Bell, and Kennel Huntsman and 1st whipper-in, Chris Amatt. Edmund gave us a little green booklet "*A List of the Thurlow Foxhounds*". The Inquiry team were introduced to a hound entered to the pack way back in 1991. I was surprised they retained a hound that old in the kennels but on checking the booklet it was clear that at the time they had three hounds in kennels entered in that year.

The Inquiry team were impressed by the care lavished on the hounds. It was not always the case at that hunt. I recalled the incident I had witnessed when monitoring back in March 1994 and I saw a Thurlow hound nearly killed on the A604—and the Whipper-in to whom I complained was anything but concerned.

We learned the Thurlow made no charge for their collection of fallen stock. In the yard, I asked Edmund Vestey about artificial earths. We knew the Thurlow Foxhounds had at least 31 and at least 16 stick piles. I asked if he could arrange for the Inquiry team to see an example. He said they had nothing to hide and would be happy to do so. We were assured the foxes they caught were old, infirm, sick or injured.

In time our party was driven to the meet. It was clear from greetings exchanged there that Lord Soulsby was in the company of plenty of friends, but that was not surprising as he lived nearby. There were many riders and followers gathered. Hunters explained that as being due to the fact of its being half-term rather than any attempt to bus in supporters.

Hounds were taken into Hart Wood for the first draw and we followed. I know of no artificial earth in Hart Wood. I asked Paddy Bell, our guide and driver, if there was an artificial earth there he could show to the Inquiry team. He replied that he did not know and that I knew more than him about artificial earths in Thurlow Hunt country. Given his prominent position within the hunt and as Land Agent for the Thurlow Estates I was surprised.

We parked by a pheasant release pen in Hart Wood and got out to listen and watch. A deer ran by through the wood but the hounds made no attempt to pursue him. Paddy assured our team that if they did not find a fox in that wood they certainly would in the adjacent one. He was right. The fox, pursued by the hounds, left the wood then returned, ran around and around then went to ground. Dr Edwards, Mark Sanderson, Paddy Bell, Simon Hart and I trekked over wet farmland to the scene. Lord Soulsby declared the walk beyond him and returned to the Land Rover. That deprived us of his veterinary expertise at any dig-out. However, before we reached the adjacent covert a rider told us they had decided to leave the fox.

Delighted though I was for the fox I asked—why? Was he in a natural earth? He told us that as far as he knew it was in a natural earth but he had not seen the site himself. He did not know why they decided to leave the fox. It seemed unusual and I pressed for an answer but answer came there none. Someone knew why but failure to explain the reasons to the Inquiry team prompted all manner of speculation. Was the fox in a badger sett? Was he in an artificial earth? Did they fear the fox to be a pregnant or nursing vixen?

We turned about and returned to join Lord Soulsby. I suspected the hunt would only display to the Inquiry team exactly what they wanted them to see. Paddy Bell said the hunt would head for Carlton and we should also. With an artificial earth in Carlton Wood and a stick pile in an adjacent copse they would be likely to find a fox. As we were about to leave we heard hounds returning and we queried with Paddy Bell that we might be better to stay. He was adamant that we should drive around so we did. He was taking us on a guided tour of his hunt as tourists might be taken on an escorted tour of the Pyramids. He was amenable to making subtle changes such as lingering a little longer if members of the Inquiry team wished but he never viewed his role as being merely that of a chauffeur, going where

411

and when the Inquiry team wanted, at their bidding. The Inquiry team would have gathered more useful evidence had they been given freedom to travel wherever they wished and in their own transport.

We were driven to a position between Park Grove (where there is an artificial earth) and Lophams Wood (where there is another artificial earth). We looked back across the fields and saw hounds in Hart Wood, exactly where we had just left and from where Paddy Bell had insisted we should leave. Hounds streamed out towards Carlton, then returned. As we looked towards Park Grove a fox crossed the open field from left to right. There was a deer settled down in the open in the same field. Hounds appeared and although they were slow to follow the scent of the fox they were, admirably, totally disinterested in the deer. I noticed the hunt placed a rider in a strategic position to ward off any riot after the deer.

We followed the hunt down towards Temple End. The fox was not to ground but hunt opinion was that he was close at hand. Whilst they tried to stop the hounds casting off for a fresh fox exactly that occurred. A fox jumped up from long grass at the back of the farm giving the Inquiry team a grandstand view of the hounds coursing this fox at close quarters. The fox, little bigger than a cat, dashed past the bulk of the mounted field waiting in the farm yard. The contrast in size was memorable.

That fox was pursued out towards the old Bomber Command airfield at West Wratting, then hunted back towards Temple End, then lost. Following in the wake we saw some further hunting and then saw hounds marking at what appeared to be a drain in the distance. Paddy Bell drove us to the scene. Simon Hart was quickly out of our vehicle and strode forward to chat with Edmund Vestey, out of our hearing. The terriermen drove up in their Land Rover.

Simon returned and told the Inquiry team the hunters were happy for them to see how they would usually deal with the fox. For safety, they would have to stand back when the fox was shot. I knew then that the hunt was determined the Inquiry team should see a fox killed that day. The Inquiry team considered the offer and agreed, as they felt it necessary to see the kill. To my knowledge the opinions of the landowner were never canvassed—if the land was owned by Edmund Vestey they could easily have declared that fact. Nor was there any mention of the fox being 'old, sick or infirm', nor any claims of it being a 'pest'.

I suspected a very clinical exercise was to be played out. There was just one problem: the fox it seemed, was not willing to play his role. The terrierman, Dean Smith, had explained his plan of action to the Inquiry. They would net one end of the pipe then put a terrier into the other end to drive the fox into the net. Then they would shoot the netted fox. First they had to check there was a fox in the pipe. Dean crouched down and peered into the dark tube. He announced, with some regret, that it must have been a false mark. There was no fox in the pipe.

The Inquiry team, particularly Dr Edwards, appeared relieved that they were not going to see the fox trapped and shot. They also appeared a bit sceptical of the explanation given. If the fox was not in the pipe where had he gone? He cannot just have vanished. If he had run off why had hounds not picked up his scent and pursued him? What was going on?

This was part of the learning curve for those inexperienced in the ways of hunting wildlife with dogs. Such hunting is not an exact science. Hounds are canines that can be confused and fooled. Whereas they hunt the fox for fun, he flees from them for his life. The motivation is different.

There were various plausible scenarios. The fox could have run through the pipe and away and hounds failed to detect his departure. The fox could have run to the pipe but declined to enter and backtracked or run off at a tangent, with the hounds not picking up this ploy. What is certain is that in a hunting country where there are a lot of such pipes—field drains and artificial earths—hounds will be used to marking at pipe entrances. Perhaps at the first sign of difficulty with owning the line of a fleeing fox they mark at the nearest pipe entrance.

The Inquiry team made their scepticism obvious. I was offered to look up the pipe in case I did not believe the hunt. I did not bother. I suspected from their whole demeanour they wanted a fox to be in there so they could demonstrate a reasonably quick and clean kill to the Inquiry. We climbed back into our hunting transport and Paddy Bell drove us back to the old airfield. Soon afterwards there was another mark by hounds at another drainage pipe. We drove as near as we could, then we disembarked and walked towards the sounds of the hounds baying. Simon Hart again went ahead to have a word with the hunters at the scene. However, before either the team and I or the terriermen reached the site Simon returned with the news that the fox had bolted of his own accord from the pipe. The Inquiry team exchanged slightly baffled looks.

Hounds were then taken to draw Lophams Wood. It was explained to us that this well-known covert was deliberately planted to be 'warm' and thereby attractive to foxes and a range of other wildlife besides. I also knew it held an artificial earth and wondered if Paddy Bell would show it to us, and indeed if he would show us the same artificial earth that I knew of.

As we walked into the covert Dr Edwards, Mark Sanderson and Simon Hart strode ahead with Paddy Bell. I strolled behind keeping Lord Soulsby company. We chatted about the pleasures of drag hunting in various parts of the world. As the hounds circled Lord Soulsby returned to the Land Rover. I joined the others at one of the junctions of the rides in the wood. The hounds were in full cry in the undergrowth. I saw the hunted fox crossing a ride some distance beyond them. I stifled my exclamation out of fear that Paddy Bell would holloa to put the hounds right. Simon Hart saw what had happened and, surprisingly, shared the difficulty of my position. I wanted to tell Dr Edwards and Mark Sanderson what had happened, to keep them fully informed as to the course of the hunt, but my top priority was not to imperil the safety of the fox.

Simon Hart did not holloa either; nor did he when a short while later he saw the fox cross the ride nearby with the hounds floundering to pick up his scent. He explained that in his view his role was not to interfere in the normal course of the hunt.

With it apparent there would be a quiet spell, Paddy Bell offered to take the Inquiry team to see an artificial earth in the wood and duly took us to the site of the one I knew of. We are told by some hunters that such earths are not built for foxes to breed in but instead to locate foxes where they do no harm. Of the 31 artificial earths I know of in Thurlow country, some are placed precisely where foxes might be accused of being a threat. No fewer than 8 are located in woods that also contain a pheasant release pen (and one of the commonest reasons offered for reducing fox numbers is the threat they allegedly pose to such shooting interests). One of these artificial earths is barely 40 metres from a release pen.

The Inquiry team examined this artificial earth. They were told the Thurlow hunt had put in no new artificial earths recently. Whilst admitting they had fed the foxes in their hunt country they said that such practices had stopped once they realised that doing so was illegal.

Paddy Bell then drove us back to follow the hunt who were in the vicinity of the old airfield again. There were plenty of foxes about. The hunting from our perspective was a matter of drive, stop, look, drive on, stop look and so on in increasingly frantic fashion. Eventually a fox was marked to ground in the corner of Lophams Wood. We drove across a field to the scene and again Simon Hart jumped out and went ahead to have a word with the terriermen. Simon returned and I feared for the safety of the fox. It was 3:05pm; the fox had been marked to ground some time earlier.

The fox was in a shallow rabbit warren. Simon Hart told the Inquiry team the hunt invited them to see how they would usually deal with a fox in such a situation. There was general agreement to watch and whilst it appeared that Lord Soulsby would have difficulty reaching the site in the wood, to his credit he did eventually do so.

No-one identified himself as the landowner and said that he or she wanted the fox killed. If the fox was to ground on Thurlow Estates land and Paddy Bell, as Land Agent was responsible, he did not say so. I had earlier asked Paddy if they would be hunting on Thurlow Estates land that day and he told me, no. No-one offered any reasons why the fox should be killed. There was no claim of local damage caused by foxes, no claim that the fleeing animal had been seen to be old, injured or infirm. It appeared to me that this hunt was keen to seize their opportunity to demonstrate to the Inquiry team that a fox could be dug to and killed with little difficulty. From a shallow rabbit warren that was hardly surprising. In drier weather conditions the hounds might easily have extracted the fox themselves.

We dutifully walked forward to see the final act. The terrierman, Dean Smith, and his assistant were at the warren. I saw the entrances had been blocked. We were told that, in the interests of our safety, when it came to the moment to shoot the fox, we would have to stand well back (they were using a free bullet pistol, not a captive-bolt and feared the effects on the Inquiry team of an unforeseen ricochet).

The blocking material used in the entrances was packed earth or, more simply, a spade thrust in. A small white terrier named Susie was put in. We heard barks and yelps as she bayed the fox a short distance below ground. Susie was brought out, checked, and put back into the fray on several occasions. Whenever she was visible she appeared uninjured, however injuries can lurk below the fur, invisible to the eye. No-one from the Inquiry team asked to check the condition of the terrier.

The hounds were held in check in the grass field adjacent to the wood. The riders milled about. They became impatient for something to happen. On several occasions one rode up and called out, asking how much longer it would take. The reply was always "*Not long!*" I asked why the hounds were being held waiting.

The Inquiry team were told that MFHA rules prevented a fox being bolted from such a situation, so that was out of the question, and the hounds were only held so they could eat the dead fox. That was not unusual hunting practice. It was reckoned that if hounds got a taste of their fox in such circumstances it would keep them sharp, focused and hunting the right quarry.

However, at about 3:25pm, they must have found the waiting simply too boring because hounds and hunters outside the wood left. I assumed they drew for another fox elsewhere. With the fox's room for manoeuvre considerably restricted the terrier was extracted and Simon Hart volunteered to return her to the terrierman's Land Rover.

Near the end of the dig Lord Soulsby enquired how many people out hunting would normally see such a dig-out and kill. Paddy Bell said very few. It was stressed that such a dig-out was not part of the entertainment and indeed MFHA rules barred too many people being present at such times. That rule also prevented undercover cameramen from recording exactly what happened on such occasions, when Government Inquiries were not present.

Eventually, by digging the roof off the shallow tunnels the fox was cornered in a small area below ground. Dean's assistant commented that he could see the brush of the trapped and helpless fox. He forced his spade into the entrance of the tunnel to thwart any attempt to escape.

Dean advised he was ready to shoot and, as requested, we moved back. He loaded his pistol, reached into the hole and fired. I noted the time as 3:35pm. He pulled the body of the fox out and displayed it on the ground. Dean examined the teeth and estimated the age as 2-years old. He had been shot through the top of his head. Until that finality he had been a young, healthy dog fox. His body bore no signs of old injuries.

I had taken video film and photographs throughout. Dean commented: "*I hope we're not going to be on News at Ten or anything now.*" I was not surprised that such hunt enthusiasts should be keen for their actions to be kept out of public view. Paddy chipped in something to the effect that it was part of the agreement that pictures taken would be private to the Inquiry. That was news to me.

The hunt had continued elsewhere but the Inquiry team decided not to follow any further. We boarded our Land Rover and Paddy Bell drove us back to the kennels. Lord Soulsby sat in the front passenger seat next to Paddy Bell and casually asked what would happen to the body of the young fox. Paddy replied that it would be taken away by the terriermen and dumped in the incinerator at the kennels. We returned to the kennels and parted company, leaving the hunt to carry on in our absence.

On March 26th 2000 I returned to Lophams Wood and paced out the distance between where the fox was killed and the artificial earth where he may well have been born. The distance was no more than 370 metres.

The Inquiry team had spent their day in prime Thurlow Foxhounds country, an area of countryside that had for years been dedicated to the pursuit of foxes for sport. As long ago as 1827 the Thurlow Hunt Club was set up with one of its aims being to preserve foxes which were apparently in short supply at the time. Later in the same century the Thurlow Hunt Club was restarted and at a meeting in Newmarket on May 31st 1859 some resolutions were agreed to, of which the following are of notable interest:-

"*1st - That the Club called the Thurlow Hunt Club be revived and re-established.*

2nd - That the object of the club shall be the preservation of foxes in the district known as the 'Thurlow Country'..............

5th - That the following Gentlemen, having consented to attend to the preservation of Foxes in the covers attached to their respective names, form a Committee of management, viz:"

There then followed a list of people and covers of which only the following are relevant to this Inquiry visit:-

"*THOMAS NASH, Carlton wood*

W. TRAYLER, Hart, Temple, Lophams, Thurlow Groves"

The resolutions continued:-

"*6th - That subscriptions be received from Gentlemen residing in the Thurlow Country, and others disposed to contribute; (no one subscription to exceed the sum of £5) and such subscriptions to form a fund for carrying out the objects of the club.*

7th - That Cubs shall be purchased, and turned down at such parts of the Thurlow Country and in such covers as the Committee may determine.

8th - That one sovereign shall be given to any keeper, woodman, or servant, who shall take care of and rear any of the purchased Cubs.

9th - That the sum of £2 shall be given to any keeper, or woodman, in whose woods or covers a litter of foxes shall be bred and reared.

10th - That a donation of a sovereign shall be given to every keeper or woodman, in whose woods or covers there shall be 'a find' and more than one 'find' on the same day shall not entitle the same keeper or woodman to more than one donation.

12th - That at such annual meeting the conduct of any keeper or woodman, who may not have had during the preceding year any claim for a 'find' may be considered, and the meeting shall have full power, if the members present think proper, to award any compensation to such keeper or woodman, for care or trouble they may have had in the preservation of Foxes.

12th[sic] *- That if any complaint of the loss of fowls &c, by any person not* *being a member of the club, be laid before such meeting, such complaint be considered by the members present, who shall have the power, if they think proper, to award compensation out of the funds of the club."*

Michael Brander noted the significance of this latter resolution on page 46 in his *Portrait of a Hunt*:-

"In the 1850s the idea of making good losses of poultry was comparatively advanced. It was unusual, to say the least, before this for the hunt to consider claims for damages of this nature. When, however, it was decided to set about breeding foxes deliberately, it must have been felt that some form of compensation must be made to those who had suffered by it."

This attitude towards foxes continued to more recent times as evidenced by the following reference again from Michael Brander on page 98 of his book, concerning a Newmarket and Thurlow hunt press announcement made in September 1939:-

"Mr. E.H. Deacon, Master of the Newmarket and Thurlow, has left to join his Regiment, and his wife has been elected joint-Master, and will carry on in his absence, with G. Samways as huntsman. Fifteen couple of hounds have been put down. As from Saturday, September 30th, no claims will be recognised or paid for damage done to poultry by foxes for the duration of the war."

*****

I left the Thurlow country and drove far north to stay at a hotel in Crosby, near Liverpool. The next morning, Tuesday February 22nd, I joined the Inquiry team for the first day of the Waterloo Cup meeting at the Withins, Altcar. The visiting party were Lord Burns, Lord Soulsby and Brian Caffarey with Simon Hart and me as observers. I was keen for people with influence to see that annual festival of cruelty that I first attended as a young hunt saboteur back in 1976.

Almost 50 years before a previous Government Inquiry, the one whose Chairman was John Scott Henderson K.C., declared coursing such as carried out at the Waterloo Cup to be cruel. And that was a Committee that viewed gassing with cyanide as a humane method for destroying animals which live underground! Their finding that the Waterloo Cup was cruel appears in paragraph 280 of the Scott Henderson report:-

"Having regard to the meaning which we have given to the word "cruelty" in reference to wild animals, as set out in paragraph 11, we should not regard the degree of suffering which is involved in coursing as constituting cruelty in so far as it is used as a method of control. But coursing is also practised as a sport and, as pointed out in paragraph 274, the National Coursing Club do not claim that the control of hares is an object of coursing as carried out under their rules. No doubt, however, hares are kept down in number in some localities as an incidental result of the coursing meetings held there and, although the primary object of the meetings is sport, more shooting of hares would be necessary if coursing did not take place. In so far as that is true, on the principles we have adopted for our enquiry, the suffering caused to hares coursed at such meetings would not constitute cruelty. But that obviously does not apply

417

to the coursing that takes place at, for example, Altcar, where hares are far more numerous than they would be if their numbers were controlled by ordinary methods, and the same is probably true in varying degrees in other places. Consequently, the suffering which is caused to hares coursed at such meetings comes within the definition of cruelty which we have adopted."

The arrangement was for the Inquiry team to rendezvous at the Countryside Alliance tent at The Withins at 10am, half an hour after the coursing started. I arrived at the tent on time and met Simon Hart. No-one from the Inquiry was present. Lord Burns, Lord Soulsby and Brian Caffarey arrived at about 10:30am. They were introduced to prominent officials from the CA. I saw Sir Clement Freud (1924-2009), a notorious supporter of hare coursing, lurking in the tent.

[Clement Freud was Liberal MP for the Isle of Ely from 1973-87. He resolutely defended hare coursing both in the House of Commons and in the media and was regarded as one of the best advocates for 'fieldsports'. On June 14th 2016, nearly seven years after his death, he was exposed as a predatory paedophile. He sexually abused a ten-year-old girl and continued to abuse her when he brought her up as a daughter until she moved away aged 19. He abused another girl in the 1970s when she was aged 11 and raped her when she was 18 by which time he was a Liberal MP. The rape was so brutal that his victim bled for a week. Invited to comment Lady June Freud said: *"This is a very sad day for me. I was married to Clement for 58 years and loved him dearly. I am shocked, deeply saddened and profoundly sorry for what has happened to these women. I sincerely hope they will now have some peace."* (*The Telegraph* June 15th 2016) Another woman said that as a 19-year old student at Dundee University in 1975 she was attacked by Clement Freud when he was rector of the University. His victim said: *"He was a national wit and author, but he was abusing his power to prey on young girls."* (*The Guardian* June 21st 2016)]

The Hon. Secretary of the Waterloo Cup Coursing Club, Ronnie Mills, was introduced as our guide for the day. Soon afterwards Ken Livingstone MP arrived with a considerable media entourage. Robin Page, who had been selling copies of his new book *The Hunting Gene* from a car boot type pitch near the CA tent was one of the first to berate him. Vinnie Faal a notorious lurcher enthusiast from Manchester was also quick to harangue the MP.

Ken went to watch the coursing, with his attendant media circus, whilst we were left being introduced to a variety of coursing stalwarts. Eventually Lord Soulsby disappeared to see the coursing with one supporter and Lord Burns, Brian Caffarey, Ronnie Mills, Simon Hart and I went to watch it from the entry point where the dogs were first taken on to the field. Lord Burns asked to be taken into the shy to see the dogs being slipped. Ronnie Mills replied that he was happy to do so but only one of us at a time would be allowed into the shy. He took Lord Burns and I stayed with Brian Caffarey whilst Simon Hart went off elsewhere.

We were given coursing cards. Typed on the back, in bold text, was the following warning:-

PHOTOGRAPHY NOT ALLOWED WITHOUT PERMISSION

When a hare was driven into the coursing arena and the dogs were released I started to take film and photographs. The lady taking the details of the dogs, who I assumed was the Slip Steward, asked if I had the authorisation to take photographs. I said that I was doing it as part of the Hunting Inquiry and advised her to check the matter with Simon Hart if she had any problems. He of course was not about and nothing further was said. Quickly we saw a hare caught. The Picker-ups were not able to reach her and do their job as the dog with the hare returned to its handler. He was seen to dislocate her neck. Lord Burns returned from the shy. Once again the hare had been caught when he had taken up that position.

I suggested to Lord Burns and Brian Caffarey that we walk up the path towards the incoming beaters to see the hares gathered in the beat funnel just off the coursing field. Ronnie Mills was happy to take us.

On the way, I had an encounter of note with a chap from the coursing fraternity whom I had befriended way back in the early nineties. He of course did not know who I was, either then or now, and he was genuinely friendly. I responded in kind but I was unwilling to linger long. I quickly walked off with Lord Burns and explained that such an experience was an unsavoury aspect of undercover work. By adopting such a role one inevitably befriends people who would greatly dislike you if they knew your real identity. When they are cruel ignorant thugs, such deceit causes no qualms. When they are not, as with this chap, it causes unease.

We walked forward as far as we could to the point where I had expected to see many hares milling about in the beat funnel but there were surprisingly few. We chatted to a beater standing at that point who, by his appearance and demeanour, had considerable experience of such a role. Lord Burns asked how they stopped too many hares being driven on to the coursing field at once. The beater pointed to a small stack of straw bales right in the middle of the funnel, in line with the Slipper's shy and told us there was someone hiding there whose job was to jump up whenever one hare went by and stop others following. Waterloo Cup coursing was clearly an efficient operation. It had to be with the entry card for spectators costing £10 and the prize for the winner being £4,000 plus a trophy.

On closer inspection of the beat funnel Lord Burns saw many hares moving about, unwittingly waiting their turn to enter the arena. We then returned to the main coursing crowd as Lord Burns was anxious to be present when the expected pro-hare demonstration arrived. We called in at the CA tent and it was at about that time that I was tackled by Lord Soulsby who felt I had misled him regarding the movement of hares to the Waterloo Cup.

The previous day, when driving Lord Soulsby to the Thurlow Foxhounds visit, I told him they regularly shipped hares to the Waterloo Cup. I said they needed many hares for the Waterloo Cup (it is a 64-dog stake and there are two subsidiary competitions, the Waterloo Plate and the

Waterloo Purse) and it could only happen because they had in the past netted hares in other parts of the country and moved them up. I was at pains to stress they were not moving them up and releasing them from boxes on the day. I said that we had no proof as to exactly when they moved them up but there had been something in their rules to the effect that it should be no less than six months beforehand.

Lord Soulsby was under the impression that I had told him that hares were shipped up for that Waterloo Cup just beforehand. Conversely he had spoken to one of our opponents who had denied that hares had been shipped up in her memory. There followed a brief dispute between myself and a CA representative as to what the National Coursing Club rules on the topic were. I mentioned the 'six months' rule but this was laughed at. When I invited her explanation as to what the current rules were regarding the movement of hares for coursing nothing was forthcoming.

That was farcical. They must surely have known what their own rules were on a such a sensitive topic as the movement of live hares about the country by coursing enthusiasts. In desperation, I looked around and saw Sir Mark Prescott, to whom we had been introduced earlier, standing nearby. Now we may stand on opposite corners of the ring when it comes to coursing but I knew him to be better informed than almost anyone on the running of the Waterloo Cup. He was also at times surprisingly candid.

I invited Sir Mark Prescott to explain to Lord Soulsby the situation regarding the movement of hares to the Waterloo Cup. He was pleased to oblige. He explained that coursing had all but ended in the late seventies due to shortage of hares. In the early eighties, they had shipped a lot into the area. I asked when was the most recent time that they had imported hares and he said that it was when the Waterloo Cup had been cancelled due to frost and snow in the early nineties. I asked exactly how long ago that was and he said *"Three to five years"*. Most significantly the National Coursing Club Rules on the relocation of hares by coursing enthusiasts for coursing purposes appear to have changed over recent years.

For an area of land, such as where the Waterloo Cup was staged, there was a natural carrying capacity for hares. That was dependent on the habitat, food supply, local topography, and not surprisingly the influences of man such as roads and the proximity to towns from whence people with lurchers might come to course them. The hare population could not be raised and sustained above natural levels without regular importations. Overpopulated hares soon disperse.

For the Waterloo Cup, many hares were needed. If the natural population found on local fields could not provide enough for coursing at the end of February, would introducing some in March, for coursing 11 months later solve the problem? Clearly not, as hares would not stay there over and above the natural carrying capacity.

So how long before might they have been moved there for them to still be there when required for coursing? 6 months? 3 months? Or the week before? For years, there was a battle of wits fought between animal welfare investigators trying to prove just how short a time before the Waterloo Cup the hares were moved and coursing authorities trying to ensure that we knew as little as possible about their movement of hares. It would be fair to admit that with a few exceptions the coursers won. For a pastime that claimed to fear nothing from close public inspection they were at times remarkably secretive.

However, their evidence submitted to the Hunting Inquiry resolved the situation. The changes in time allowed held the key.

Rules of the National Coursing Club, as revised April 1972, included the following regarding the movement of hares:-

"(S) Illegal Practices

(1) The Club will not under any circumstances countenance any of the following practices, namely :-

(a) The use of ground for coursing into which hares have been artificially moved or transported during the previous six months :

(b) The use of ground for coursing where the hares have not been at liberty during the previous six months :

(c) The use of ground for coursing which in the opinion of the Standing Committee is designed to restrict artificially the complete freedom and liberty of the hares.

(2) The Standing Committee may, if upon due enquiry it finds that any affiliated club has been guilty of any of the foregoing practices, order that such Club be expelled from affiliation and disqualified from becoming affiliated for five years."

This appears to have been changed at least once since 1972 because a more recent rule book of the Coursing Section of the Saluki or Gazelle Hound Club, that is based on National Coursing Club Rules, includes:-

"21. Illegal Practices

The Section will not under any circumstances countenance any of the following practices:

The use of running ground for coursing into which hares have been artificially moved or transported during the preceding three months.

The use of running ground for coursing where the hares have not been at liberty for the preceding three months and the use of ground which, in the opinion of the Committee, is designed to restrict, artificially the complete freedom and liberty of the hares."

Note how the six months rule was reduced to three months. It was reduced further. The National Coursing Club submission to the Hunting Inquiry, posted on the Internet, included the following reference to this aspect of their rules:-

"(S) Illegal Practices

(1) The Club will not under any circumstances countenance any of the following practices. namely:-

(a) The use of ground for coursing which is designed to restrict artificially the freedom and liberty of the hares.

(b) The use of ground for coursing where the state of the going or the arrangements on the field hinder the escape of the hare.

(c) The use of ground for coursing of which the hares coursed have insufficient knowledge.

(2) The Standing Committee may, if upon due enquiry it finds that any affiliated club has been guilty of any of the foregoing practices, order that such Club be fined a maximum of (see appendix) and/or expelled from affiliation and disqualified from becoming affiliated for five years."

From six months to three months, then to *"insufficient knowledge"*. Who was to judge when a hare netted in one area, boxed up and transported to another for coursing had sufficient knowledge of her new locality? How could you tell? Was it a matter of allowing the hare one year, one month, one week or one day? Clearly the period was short enough to trouble some coursing enthusiasts who declined to attend the Waterloo Cup.

In early February 1997, an anonymous phone call to the LACS alleged that hares were to be captured in nets, for transportation to Altcar for the Waterloo Cup, on Monday 10th at the Six Mile Bottom estate near Newmarket, Suffolk. LACS Executive Committee member Lawrie Payne and I went to the venue and encountered the headkeeper, Richard Clarke, and colleagues. In the face of considerable intimidation and threat, including being barred from access to a public road, we filmed hares being captured in nets, transferred to cramped boxes and loaded into a Land Rover. Supervisor of the whole operation was David R. Midwood, Chairman of the Waterloo Cup Committee. His role as Chairman of the Waterloo Cup Committee was confirmed by the meet card given to members of the Inquiry team on their visit.

David Midwood, and later the BFSS, denied the hares were going to Altcar and between them at various times gave the destinations for the hares as Dartmoor, North Wales, Shropshire, Lincolnshire, Leicestershire and Surrey. They claimed the operation was conducted by *The Hare Conservation Society*—a little known organisation run by a Mr W.B.K. Steadman who was also a member of David Midwood's Waterloo Cup Committee as well as the BFSS's Coursing Committee.

Our video of the hare netting was handed to Professor Stephen Harris for comment (Professor Harris conducted the national hare survey for the Government's Joint Nature Conservation Committee). In his report to the LACS Professor Harris found: *"The operations portrayed in the video were grim; they were likely to cause considerable stress to the animals and maximise the chance of injuries."*

He added the hares should have been covered and noise should have been kept to an absolute minimum. He was particularly critical of the handling of a hare while it was extracted from a net. The animal was held off the ground and the Professor said that if it had kicked it could have fractured or injured its spinal column due to the power with which hares can flex their backs using their hind legs. He also said the boxes used were only suitable for holding hares for brief periods because there was no way the hares could be fed or watered.

He saw it was raining during the operation and he warned that putting wet hares into boxes in which they could not dry off posed risk of fatalities. He complained that the handling of the hares was *"haphazard and showed no care for the animals"*, and that stacking the boxes on top of each other, (one on its side) was *"disgraceful"*. Finally, Professor Harris pointed out the time of the hare capture (February 10th) coincided with the period when female hares were either heavily pregnant or already had dependent offspring. In his view: *"Removing hares at this time of the year will lead to young dying of starvation and a great deal of trauma to pregnant does"*.

Coursing enthusiasts who knew about the regular movement of hares to Altcar, and were prepared to talk, reported that at the Waterloo Cup hares driven on to the coursing field that turned around and ran back into the beat funnel, or ran into the crowd, had been shipped in recently.

Whatever the Rules of the National Coursing Club in 1997, and wherever those hares went, if a similar operation had been mounted in 2000 with hares netted in early February for transportation to Altcar for release into the area ready for the Waterloo Cup starting on February 22nd there would have been no breach of the National Coursing Club Rules. Twelve days or more, could clearly be argued, gave hares the 'sufficient knowledge' required.

The Waterloo Cup had been dependent for some time for its running on the regular importation of hares. The *Waterloo Cup **Report and Annual Accounts 1981*** includes the following reference to the movement of hares under the section *Report of the Committee to the Waterloo Cup Nominators* :-

"The Committee annex an Income and Expenditure Account for organising the 1981 event which reveals a serious deficit of nearly £2000. The Committee consider that there is limited scope for reducing expenditure and therefore they must concentrate effort on finding a way to increase income. It will be noted that no expenditure is included in this account for hare restocking for breeding purposes which the Committee are satisfied must in future be an annual necessity."

The accounts for the following year revealed a figure under *"Sundry Expenses"* of £363 paid for *"Hare re-stocking"*. One might ask the pertinent point if the hares need to be shipped up so regularly to Altcar what is the fate that awaits them? There was no indication that hares that survived the Waterloo Cup were netted again and shipped back to whence they came. Many were doubtless killed by lads with lurchers, or on the roads.

The movement of hares for coursing had been considered by the Scott Henderson Committee. They give the following finding in paragraph 275 of their 1951 report:-

"The allegation that hares are specially imported for coursing gives rise to the further suggestion that they may not be familiar with the ground over which they are coursed and may consequently be at a disadvantage. This objection is said to apply more to the large, organised meetings than to the

smaller, local meetings, but as the movement of hares within six months of coursing is forbidden we think that hares are in fact sufficiently familiar with the ground over which they are coursed."

At that time the National Coursing Club had their 'six month' rule in force. What would the Scott Henderson Committee have made of it being reduced to 'three months' and then to the near meaningless term 'insufficient knowledge'? This point concerned Lord Burns as the following exchange during the Oral evidence session on Monday April 10th 2000 showed:-

"THE CHAIRMAN [Lord Burns]*: "How do you know when a hare shows knowledge of its area and secondly typically how long do you think that gap is? There may not be a rule about the gap there should be, but do you have any indication that you can give as to what it typically would be?"*

MR BLANNING: *"We have no indication no, because when hares are moved they are given a considerable amount of time to get used to their new surroundings. The calendar, if you like, dictates this because hares are mainly moved in the late winter or early spring. That is when the hare shoots are usually going to take place and the hares are moved from estates where otherwise they would have been shot for control purposes. So what is happening is that the hares are being put down, often in late February, early March and then, of course, they are outside the coursing season. The coursing season does not start again until the following September."*

THE CHAIRMAN: *"So that would be six months, effectively?"*

MR BLANNING: *"Yes"*

When a wild animal, such as a hare, is moved it needs to gather 'sufficient knowledge' quickly or it is dead.

At some point in the morning Lord Soulsby went to view the coursing from the Slipper's shy. Lord Burns was keen to see the arrival of the march of people protesting against the cruelty of coursing. We moved to watch. He asked me to introduce him to a marcher so he could have a discussion with them. He had previously cleared this proposal with a senior police officer. I obliged but to be honest, with all the cacophony of noise, I am not sure either heard much.

Lord Burns then expressed keenness to see coursing from the crowd standing on the bank side. Ronnie Mills was happy to facilitate this so led Lord Burns, Brian Caffarey, Simon Hart and myself round to the bank side. Lord Soulsby did not join us. Instead he wandered off in the direction of the CA hospitality tent. He had earlier remarked to me how good their Game Soup was. We reached the bank, stood amongst the crowd and watched some coursing. There was no kill. We left at about 12:45pm and returned to the Nominators' enclosure. That was the last coursing we saw at that Waterloo Cup.

Outside the CA tent I encountered Clarissa Dickson Wright sounding off to a television camera crew about her knowledge of and love for coursing the hare. In her book, *Spilling the Beans,* she described how she first discovered coursing in the autumn of 1997. For our media that made her an expert. Amongst other quotes she offered the following:-

"If I were a hare I would rather die on a day like this, if I were to die, and as I said it was only 1% last year, you know with the crowds cheering and doing something I knew how to do than be run over by a car. Are we going to stop driving?"

Soon afterwards, at about 1:30pm Lord Burns and Lord Soulsby declared they had seen enough and as they had a flight to catch they decided to call an end to this visit. They left and I was obliged to leave also. There was a break in the coursing for lunch but it then continued until 4.15p.m. The Inquiry team had left the coursing like leaving a football match at half-time. They had seen very little coursing that day.

As well as me with the Inquiry team the CPHA had undercover monitors filming from amongst the coursing crowd. Their evidence confirmed the difference between the coursing on show for the Inquiry team and that which occurred after the latter left. This was frustrating for those keen to see the full horror of coursing exposed but it was by no means unusual. The first part of the first day was when television cameras and press photographers were in attendance. Once they had their required images and left the coursers resumed the real business.

My colleague Kevin Hill, filming with an IFAW team for the CPHA, secured highly revealing sequences. Kevin filmed that first day from the bank side. His video proved some of the attitudes from the crowd of coursers that should have been seen and heard by the Inquiry team.

At 11:50am a hare was caught and became the victim of a tug of war. The Picker-up released the hare and struggled to kill her. From a courser near the camera there was the loud demand: *"Kill the cunt!"*

About fifteen minutes later another hare was caught. Once again the Picker-up was required to dispatch the hare. This time there was this clear shout of encouragement from coursing supporters: *"Go on.........wring its neck!"*

Another quarter of an hour or so elapsed and another hare was twisting and turning as she fled for her life. As she ran, her canine tormentors were encouraged thus: *"Fucking have it!"* Eventually this hare escaped by heading back past the Slipper's shy towards the beat funnel.

The behaviour of some country sports enthusiasts matched their language. A pair of drunks wallowed about in one of the ditches trying to fight each other, before shaking hands. Later a lad climbed on to the field before the coursing field and pulled his pants down to moon to the crowd.

A strange event occurred at about 12:50am, just after the Inquiry team had vacated the bank side, and headed back towards the Nominators' enclosure. A hare was driven on to the coursing field. She was clearly weak as the dogs were not slipped. She was so weak she simply flopped over in a pathetic heap. She was then killed by a Picker-up. What was the back story for that hare? Was she injured or diseased? Was she pregnant and exhausted through being driven backwards and forwards by the beaters?

If the Inquiry team were to fulfil the role asked of them all the hares caught at that Waterloo Cup would have been given post mortem examination. Out of all the hares that died the one that just collapsed may well have been the most important to examine. On the day, the Inquiry team knew nothing of that incident even occurring.

A significant incident occurred at 4:05pm on that first day. It involved a pair of dogs running in the second round that included *Duxbury*. The nominator and owner of the dog was Len Elman who had earlier been introduced to the Inquiry team. The sequence of events for the death of the hare was:-

Gary Kelly slips the dogs.
19 seconds later the hare was caught by one dog.
2 seconds later the hare escaped.
1 second later the hare was caught again. Both dogs tussled over her.
8 seconds later one dog won the tussle and ran off with the hare.
8 seconds later the hare escaped again and ran off.
1 second later the dog caught the hare again.
2 seconds later the hare escaped again.
1 second later the dog caught the hare again.
3 seconds later the hare was dropped and ran off again.
7 seconds later the dog caught the hare again.
9 seconds later the hare was dropped and ran off again, this time in a clearly injured state. A watching courser shouted, "*Get the fucking hare!*"
7 seconds later, with the dog clearly exhausted, the Picker-up dived on the hare and she was killed soon after.

At least 49 seconds elapsed from the moment the hare was first caught to when she was killed. The hare escaped from the jaws of the dog(s) no fewer than five times. There were at least five men wearing the yellow arm-bands of a hare Picker-up in close proximity whilst this coursing of a crippled hare took place. This greatly entertained the crowd. They cheered when the hare was first caught and they both cheered and laughed when a Picker-up eventually dived on the hare.

There were other investigators watching. The last course ended in a kill at 4:15pm when the light-coloured dog wearing the red collar caught the hare. There were cheers and applause from the watching crowd. The black dog in the white collar grabbed the other end of the hare and both dogs tussled over her. A Picker-up dived in and grabbed the white collared dog. The canine wearing red ran off with the hare. This was accompanied with the following commentary over the public-address system:-

"*Just to remind you Ladies and Gentlemen, after a really cracking day's coursing - I'm sure you'll agree that the sixty four courses we've seen today have been as good as you'll get, and er... everyone's put a lot of effort and hard work into ..er..producing this coursing today - tomorrow of course we're at the Lydiate.*"

The dog ran off with the hare past the flank line who made seemingly half-hearted attempts to stop her. The crowd left happy.

It was clear when reviewing undercover film taken by Kevin Hill and other IFAW/CPHA monitors on all three days at the Waterloo Cup 2000 that time and time again hares ran back towards the Slipper's shy and the beat funnel to escape. Hare coursers assured us, and the Inquiry team, that certainly on the first and third days when the coursing was staged at The Withins if the hares had sufficient knowledge of their immediate environment they would run towards the rhododendron end purposely created for their escape. That so many hares did not do so suggested they lacked 'sufficient knowledge'.

The last rule in the little green book supplied by the National Coursing Club used to be as follows:-

"47. Interference with a Course
No person shall interfere, by shouting, waving or in any other way with the running of the hare or the dogs, or by seeking to influence or divert the hare in any way, or by holloaing a dog on."

That rule was ignored time and time again by the Waterloo Cup crowd. I left the Withins and drove home to recharge my camera batteries for the next day.

*****

The following morning, Wednesday February 23rd, I joined the Inquiry team to see the Waveney Harriers from their meet at Wingfield in Suffolk, east of Diss. The team were Lord Burns, Professor Winter and Brian Caffarey. Observers were Simon Hart and me.

The Waveney Harriers began as a pack of foxhounds about 200 years ago. In 2000 they hunted primarily hare and the occasional fox because there were many hares and few foxes in their part of East Anglia.

Our rendezvous was the busy commuter hub, Diss railway station, at 10am. I arrived on time to find Professor Winter waiting. He had travelled to Diss the previous night and stayed nearby. I took the opportunity to chat about occurrences to date, including events Graham Sirl told me about. Professor Winter confirmed that during their visit to the Old Berkeley Beagles on February 15th the hounds ran into woodland owned by the Woodland Trust (he had seen the sign). I asked him about their visit to the Alresford Coursing Club on February 19th. I was keen to hear what he saw with the Picker-up when the second hare was caught. He said that when they reached the hare she was alive and screaming.

At about 10:15am Waveney Harriers' Joint Master, John Ibbott, drove up. We had a short conversation before the London train pulled in and Lord Burns and Brian Caffarey alighted. The latter travelled with me; Lord Burns and Professor Winter were driven by John Ibbott to the 11:30am meet where Simon Hart was waiting.

The hunt had just 11½ couple of hounds out. Later I queried that small number with Simon Hart. He told me they took few hounds out if there were a lot of hares about to avoid the pack splitting. He said he had once hunted with only 9 couple. I assumed that was in his time as Master and Huntsman of the Royal Agricultural College Beagles in 1983-1985.

We left the meet with all of us seated in a four-wheel-drive driven by John Ibbott. We saw hounds drawing across a field. The first field we were taken into was full of hares. Lord Burns was again the first of our team to see the fleeing quarry. Quickly we piled out of our vehicle and into the field. The hounds came by in full cry, dashed across the field, swinging to the left and right. In no time at all we saw them clustered around what I took to be the kill. This seemed strange as it occurred so quickly.

The strangeness was emphasised by the absence of the usual horn blowing from the Huntsman to celebrate the kill. Furthermore, he urged his hounds on. I suspected hounds had killed not a hare but a rabbit suffering from myxomatosis. In the later stages of that disease, a shameful gift from scientists and farmers to wildlife, such poor creatures hobbling about blind in the fields are temptations few hounds can ignore. On several occasions when monitoring the nearby Dunston Harriers that season I saw them kill such rabbits. At first Simon Hart thought they were scavenging long dead material but later agreed it was probably *"a bunny"*.

The Inquiry team spent time observing the hunt operating in and around this field. Hares and hounds ran in all directions. It was clear that, mercifully, scenting conditions were poor. Once, when I was with Professor Winter and Brian Caffarey, we watched Lord Burns and Simon Hart walk ahead into the middle of a field. Simon then beckoned us over silently. On approaching we saw a hare squatting down on her form just in front of them. I filmed as we approached. When we were near Simon strode forward to put her up and she ran off in safety. Lord Burns marvelled at how she held her nerve and sat so tight.

I was pleased Lord Burns empathised with the hare. Twice I heard him expressing regret that he must be some bad omen for the species as on both occasions when he joined the Slipper in the shy at coursing meetings the hare was killed. He said that if, as coursers claimed, the average was for one hare to be killed out of every ten coursed then for him to see two out of two killed when he was in the shy was singularly unlucky.

The great expert on the pastime of hunting hares, Captain J. Otho Paget, would have warned him of the threat posed to his enjoyment of hare hunting by sympathising with the hare. In his book, he cautioned:-
"In hunting, whether it be of fox or hare, every follower should identify himself with hounds' aims and give his entire sympathy to them. If he allows himself to sympathise with the hare, his pleasure in the chase will be neutralised and he might as well go home at once." (**The Art Of Beagling.** Captain J. Otho Paget. H.F. & G. Witherby. 1931. Page 217)

On another occasion, I was with Professor Winter. We stood behind Lord Burns who was with hunt supporters, including two young children, all watching the hunt in the distance. On hearing and seeing the dogs running one very young girl started chanting, *"Chase the hare! Chase the hare!"* Professor Winter had two young children and I had three. We looked at each other and he said: *"Well, at least it wasn't Kill the hare! Kill the hare!"* Moments later the girl in question expressed the hope that they wouldkill the hare. Professor Winter and I again exchanged looks, this time of real sadness.

We were driven on and followed the hunt. At one point a chap came out and ordered us off his land. This caused consternation to the Inquiry team until John Ibbott explained we were hunting with permission. This clearly satisfied the man as he allowed us on.

From the garden of one cottage we heard hounds in full cry followed by irate shouting. I opined that some person or hound was misbehaving. That the culprit had four legs rather than two became clear when a couple of deer fled the wood near the sounds of hounds. The deer quickly disappeared behind some scrub. My opinion that the hounds were rioting was mocked and dismissed by nearby hunters. My analysis was confirmed when the quarry came back into view—a fine pair of deer with many hounds in full cry after them. The whole Inquiry team present that day saw this spectacle.

The Huntsman was far from delighted to look across the fields and see us watching as he struggled to retain control of his charges. Oblivious to his guttural shouts his hounds chased the deer around the corner to our right, then appeared to scatter in all directions. Some possibly continued to chase these deer. Others appeared to run in every direction after the numerous hares that were fleeing. I was with Lord Burns and John Ibbott. We counted 5½ couple (one hound less than half the pack) chasing a hare but they lost her.

Simon Hart, who had been some way away from us, told us he had seen Fallow deer. John Ibbott identified the deer his hounds rioted after as Red Deer. Whatever, there certainly were deer about and these hounds were nowhere near as steady in their presence as their counterparts at the Thurlow Foxhounds had been two days previously.

The Inquiry team needed to catch the 3:17pm train from Diss for Lord Burns to speak at a meeting attended by Ken Clarke MP (with whom he told us he had been around the world twice). At about 2:20pm we left the hunt and returned to the meet. The hunt continued in our absence.

Lord Burns and Brian Caffarey were dismayed to discover the car in which John Ibbott had collected them from the station was not parked where left at the meet but instead was being driven by Mrs Ibbott, who was following the hunt. Lord Burns and Brian Caffarey had left a lot of their possessions, including papers, in this car.

To locate his partner John Ibbott made frantic calls on a mobile phone borrowed from one of the Inquiry team. He then drove off at high speed to retrieve his car. All the boundless efforts made by the hunting fraternity the length and breadth of Britain to ingratiate themselves with this Inquiry team looked at risk. I waited as the Inquiry team kicked their heels in frustration in the farm courtyard, anxiously checking their watches. It was clear they viewed that incident as but another example of the chaos they had seen that day.

The missing car was found and we split up. Professor Winter accompanied me whilst Lord Burns and Brian Caffarey went with John

Ibbott. We returned the team to Diss just in time for their train. As we left the hunt we had to pull to one side of the road to allow Huntsman and hunters to pass. I called out to the Huntsman to query the nature of the first kill. He confirmed it had indeed been a rabbit with myxomatosis. Whilst with the hunt they did not kill a hare to our knowledge.

During the day, I enquired what harm was caused locally by hares. John Ibbott said that people nearby trying to grow oak trees did not like hares at all. I heard nothing else about hares being harmful. We have planted many fruit trees on our land and are well practised at providing young trees with wire shields that provide humane protection not just from hares but from rabbits as well. As we saw that day hunting with hounds was anything but humane and anything but effective.

The Waveney Harriers were trained to hunt the scent of hares and foxes. This confirmed the adaptable nature of such hunting dogs and supported the opinion there would be no insurmountable problems associated with converting such hounds from hunting live quarry to the humane alternative.

*****

Graham Sirl was back on duty for the Inquiry visit to the Brecon and Talybont Foxhounds at Felindre on Saturday February 26th at 11am. This was a visit to his local hunt requested by Lord Burns. Graham counted 12 riders following and about 15 cars. Hunt and supporters communicated using CB radios.

A fox was found and hunted and Simon Hart confirmed the pack split. One portion marked their fox to ground on the side of a high escarpment. Brian Caffarey and Simon Hart went to watch the dig. Lord Burns stayed with Graham Sirl. Some 45 minutes after the fox was marked to ground he was shot and his body shown to Brian Caffarey and Simon Hart. Brian later told Lord Burns the fox was in very poor condition with signs of mange. Terriermen buried the carcase in the earth.

The fox had sought sanctuary in an earth in some very rocky hard ground. The terriermen had considerable difficulty digging around some of the boulders. The landowner for the area in which the fox was marked to ground was not identified nor were his views canvassed as to whether the fox should be killed. It may be the hunt already knew his or her views but if so they never made the fact known to the Inquiry team.

No reason was put forward as to why this fox needed to be killed. No accusations of local fox damage attributable to him were made, nor was it claimed they knew him to be injured, in poor condition or mangy before he was killed. The reason given to Brian Caffarey for burying the fox, rather than showing him to Lord Burns (the body was not heavy and distance not far), was the fox was in such a poor state.

The burial of the body was convenient for the hunt. It denied anyone the opportunity to examine the fox closely to see if he bore any injuries resulting from the lengthy fighting below ground with the terriers. So far as Graham was aware the fox was not sexed nor was any estimate made as to his age. As Graham Sirl stood with Lord Burns, waiting for the duration of the dig-out, he noticed the body of a dead sheep nearby—there was an abundance of food for local foxes. Another hunt was witnessed by the Inquiry team but that fox was lost. At about 3:30pm Lords Burns said he had seen enough so the Inquiry team packed up. The hunt continued.

*****

The next Monday the entourage moved to north Wales for the meet of the Plas Machynlleth Foxhounds near Machynlleth on February 28th. There were Professor Winter, Dr Edwards and Mark Sanderson from the Inquiry team and Simon Hart and me as observers.

I left home at midday on the Sunday and drove to the luxurious and expensive Ynyshir Hall near Machynlleth. I would never usually stay at such a prestigious establishment but the LACS rightly felt I should stay in the same hotel as the Inquiry team (believing, correctly, that the CA would). I arrived in heavy rain to find Adrian Simpson from the CA there. Adrian for many years wrote a column in *Shooting News* about and in praise of terrierwork under the pseudonym 'Daergi'. He had a brooding malevolence that inspired unease.

The Plas Machynlleth was originally a pack of Foxhounds officially recognised by the Masters of Foxhounds Association. It was last listed in Baily's Hunting Directory 1971-72. At that time the hunt had 12 couple of hounds and was described: "*This pack is owned by the farmers and run by them to keep down the foxes. Hunting is practically confined to foot.*" Rendezvous for the Inquiry team was the cross in Machynnlleth at 9am. From there we drove in convoy to a point to the east, near the meet, where we left our cars. We were then divided up into hunt transport provided. Unlike previous visits elsewhere there was no single large vehicle to accommodate all the Inquiry team. I ended up in a car with Mark Sanderson, Simon Hart and his colleague Adrian Simpson. Professor Winter was in another hunt vehicle and Dr Edwards in another. Consequently, I heard nothing of what was said to Professor Winter or Dr Edwards when they were driven by hunt followers. It was a small but irritating flaw in the set-up of the observation system for that visit.

When I broached the matter later with Mark Sanderson he explained that, as always, they requested a large vehicle be provided to accommodate all the team. Suitable four-wheel-drive vehicles were common at hunts. It was regrettable that lack of one compromised the effectiveness of the planned team observation effort.

We reached the meet which was at 10am up some isolated track in nearby forestry. Numerous men toting shotguns were gathered. In due course hounds were driven up in a van. The Huntsman, Ken Markham, employed full time by the hunt, told us he had 17 hounds out. I was pointed out to the assembled guns and they were told that I was the man from the LACS and they should take great care not to inadvertently shoot me in the forest. Everyone laughed.

The Inquiry team were assured that every farmer within the operating area of the hunt supported the hunt. The hunt meets on Tuesday, Thursday and Saturday. But this was a Monday! When I queried this I was

431

told that this day had been especially arranged for the Inquiry team visit. Whether a planned meet was brought forward or a new meet arranged was never revealed.

It was soon clear that not all who hunted that day attended the meet. We learned some had already gone ahead to high points, presumably to the strategic places. I asked them how many guns were out and the number 20 was offered. The hunters stressed that all involved that day were full time farmers. These people knew a lot about their local fox population. They knew where their earths were and the runs foxes would take. The hunters discussed where to place their guns and said of the foxes: "*It's surprising how they will stick to paths.........they tend to run the same ways every time......so these boys know more or less where to go you know and they will stick there....*" This was emphasised again later: "*Foxes will mainly run the same paths, like we use the road they use certain paths.*"

The hounds were cast into the forestry to seek out and hunt their quarry in the usual way. I asked if hounds ever killed the foxes themselves. We were assured they could, and did. A pair of terriers linked by a couple collar accompanied the hunt. These were to be used if the fox went to ground. I asked if the terriers would kill the fox below ground but was told that was not the idea. Rather, the aim was to bolt foxes to the guns or dig to them and kill them.

It was a sunny morning, surprisingly warm in the sheltered hollows for late February. However, there was snow on higher ground and a biting wind was blasting over exposed areas. I expected to see foxes slaughtered. With little of the usual meet ceremony the Huntsman set off on foot with his hounds and we drove in a convoy of hunt vehicles, mainly of four-wheel-drives, most of recent vintage. We had a good view of the tracts of forestry interspersed with tracks with hunt vehicles dotted at strategic sites. Figures dotted the high snow-covered skyline in a scene reminiscent of the film *Zulu*. That this was a more modern conflict was proved by the crackle of radios as hunters exchanged information.

One of the Inquiry team asked about the gun cartridges used that day. A hunt official, I believe Emyr Lewis, cut open a BB cartridge to show us the large size of pellets being used. A cartridge used for pheasant shooting was produced and cut open for comparison.

There was little sound of any activity on the first draw. We were then driven to an elevated position, amid snow, with a bitter freezing wind whipping over us. In the distance, we could see one of the guns taking up a position of concealment in the snow. Other guns had equally cold positions dotted along the tracks in the forestry.

We lingered a while and then were driven up and down a snow-covered track with men brandishing shotguns dotted along its length. One of our hunt guides periodically stopped and asked these individuals for information. His questions and their answers were often conducted in Welsh so I at least had no idea what was said. I failed to see that speaking in a foreign language helped inform the Hunting Inquiry.

Thurlow Foxhounds' fox feeding site near artificial earth. Above: dead chickens dumped, January 4th 1995. Right: same site, January 12th 1995 (Lawrie Payne takes video film).

Below: hunt saboteur, Tim Nickerson, saves hare by stopping hounds after hare has run behind him. Dunston Harriers, October 19th 1999.

Ward Union Staghounds, January 19th, 1999. Right: stag dragged back to cart (picture Philip Kiernan/ICABS).

Work with ICABS.

Left: hare released for coursing, Trim Coursing Club, November 7th 1993.

Below: protesting against and filming at Castletown Geoghegan Coursing Club, December 15th 1996.

Above left, above and left: hares in pen and hare dead in pen, Co. Cavan Coursing Club, November 14th 1999.

Maldon, December 26th 1996. Above: LACS officials with poster using my photograph taken at the Dulverton West Foxhounds, October 8th 1982. Left: local people protest against the Essex Farmers' and Union Foxhounds, December 26th 1996.

Ulster people and politicians unite against carted stag hunting, Stormont, April 27th 1999.

Visits with the Lord Burns Hunting Inquiry. Above: Border Foxhounds, February 9th 2000. Below: Thurlow Foxhounds, February 21st 2000. Bottom: Waterloo Cup, February 22nd 2000.

Left: Paddy Bell, Joint Hon. Sec. Thurlow Foxhounds, shows the Inquiry team an artificial earth, February 21st 2000.

Above: Plas Machynlleth Foxhounds, February 28th 2000.
Top left: different size of pellets demonstrated. Below: Staff College and
Royal Military Academy Sandhurst Draghounds, March 19th 2000.

Above and left: the
'kill' was a rag and
a bucket of
biscuits.

Above right: Lawrie Payne and Lord Burns, Essex Farmers' and Union Foxhounds, March 22nd 2000. Top left: Hunting Inquiry, April 6th 2000. Left: Hunting Inquiry, April 10th 2000.

Wickwar Park Coursing Club (drag coursing), April 30th 2000.
Above: greyhounds close on lure.

Ytene Minkhounds, May 20th 2000.
Right: a ride in the hound van at the end of the day.

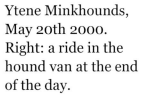

Above: Thurlow Foxhounds' artificial earth in Trundley Wood, May 5th 1997. Right: the same site, June 5th 1999, after renovation. Right: two cubs playing in summer sunshine on nearby ride, June 5th 1999.

Below: protests against Greyhound 2000 hare coursing event. Bottom left: street protest in Newmarket, December 10th 2000. Bottom right: making the point at the hare coursing event, Six Mile Bottom, December 11th 2000.

Heythrop Foxhounds' artificial earths.
Top left: concealed entrance to pipe, Zareba, January 15th 1984.
Left: same entrance, January 18th 2003.
Below: team install hidden camera, March 8th 2003.
Middle: outside Zareba.

Above: 'dropping pot' near Chipping Norton, December 29th 2002.
Right: hidden camera records hunt terrierman at site, January 12th 2003.

Heythrop Foxhounds. Above and right: dead calves dumped to attract foxes for Boxing Day meet, December 15th 2001. Below: blocked artificial earth. Below right: hound by calf, dumped nearby, Boxing Day 2001.

Below: fox scrabbles at blocked artificial earth entrance, December 2002.

Above: calf rots, January 20th 2002. Left: investigator films chickens dumped as food for foxes, March 9th 2003.

Top left: Vale of Aylesbury Foxhounds' artificial earth, September 18th 1997. Above left: Duke of Beaufort's Foxhounds artificial earth, August 13th 1999. Above right: badger resides in Cheshire Foxhounds' artificial earth, August 12th 2002.

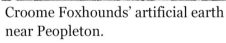

Croome Foxhounds' artificial earth near Peopleton.

Above right: surveillance camera system before being buried, February 8th 2004.

Right: concealed camera records hunt terriermen at site, February 10th 2004.

Artificial earths in Croome Foxhounds' country. Above: near Wootton Wawen, January 25th 2002. Note sheep in adjacent field. Right: terriermen at earth.

Left: Investigators install hidden camera at artificial earth near Sneachill, December 19th 2003.
Below: camera films as fox is evicted with drain rod and killed, December 20th 2003.

Artificial earths in Blencathra Foxhounds' country.

Top five pictures: Porter's Parlour, November 2nd 1996 and April 6th 2002.

Left and below: Orthwaite plantation, April 20th 2002. Bottom centre: investigator films death pit.

Above: aerial surveillance of Croome Foxhounds' country, March 30th 2004. Left: artificial earth site near Wootton Wawen arrowed.
Right: investigator at the controls. Below: illegal hare coursers near Burwell, February 10th 2002. Courser slips dog against hare (arrowed).

Below: mink hunters near Withersdale Street. A few were keen to block my camera, May 15th 2004.

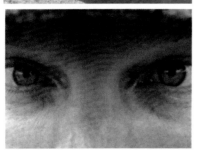

Hidden side of shooting.
Above: corn dump for pheasants.
Above right: discarded cartridge
cases, January 1st 2002.
Right: dead foxes displayed near
game bird rearing site, February
26th 2003.

Left: Dick
Course with
Neil Kinnock
MP, May 29th
1984.

Below left: LACS Chairman, Mark
Davies presents award to John
McFall MP, June 20th 1995.
Below: Tony Banks MP at CPHA
reception, November 23rd 2004.

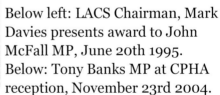

Game birds. Right: Lawrie Payne with shot birds dumped in death pit (above), Cambridgeshire, January 30th 1995. Below: Bettws Hall Shooting Hatchery, January 15th 2005.

We heard hounds in cry but they appeared to have split. The Huntsman seldom blew his horn. Supporters, in touch by radio, appeared to know what was going on but as no-one in our car had a radio with which to link in it was all a mystery to us. In time at one of the pauses we learned from Emyr Lewis they had two foxes running. We heard a couple of shots close together followed by a third shot sometime later. We were driven down the track towards this action. A pool of blood stained the snow. A dead fox lay nearby. None of the Inquiry team saw the fox shot.

Dr Edwards enquired who shot the fox. She then asked the chap who claimed responsibility to explain events. He said when he shot the fox it had gone down and he had given it a second shot to finish it off. We were guided to see the fox. 'It' was identified as a vixen; about two years old. It appeared that prior to death she was healthy and was carrying no old injuries. This had all happened at the opposite end of the forestry to where the chap was entrenched in his snow hole waiting to take a shot.

We were then taken away up a nearby track to look for the hunt. I lingered to change some tapes and noticed in a field of sheep to my left the remains of some long dead sheep, more food for foxes. It was often claimed that such casualties were left where they died because of problems removing them from the high fells. But these carcases were just a short throw from the farm track.

Earlier one hunter informed us that within the local area in the previous ten years the sheep population had doubled. Certainly, on the drive to and from the venue, the countryside had appeared full of sheep. Inevitably there will be casualties, for a variety of reasons. When simply left to rot in the fields where they lay it was no surprise foxes abounded.

At the beginning Dr Edwards had hoped we could be away at about 3pm. Emyr Lewis responded that the hunt usually finished any time between 3pm and 7pm. Perhaps mindful of a request to leave early, at about 2:15pm we were led back to where supporters had gathered by their vehicles, by where we were shown the first fox body. There was a second dead fox displayed on the ground. A young dog fox he was the subject of considerable comment as he had a gloriously resplendent brush.

We left at about 2:30pm and were driven to collect our cars. The hunt continued. We then drove in convoy to the home of Emyr Lewis. He and his family made us very welcome and served a splendid tea in their splendid home in a splendid location. The walls were adorned with photographs including some of Emyr Lewis in the company of Prince Charles. This was the social side of hunting very much to the fore. As we enjoyed the lavish fare I wondered how the chap was getting on in his snow hole. Before we left Emyr Lewis gave us a package of information concerning his hunt. This made interesting reading. There was a list of hunt meets for the 1999/2000 season together with their tally of foxes. In the 66 meets up to but not including that date they had killed 131 foxes. The most they had killed after any meet was 10. Conversely, after 11 meets they had killed no foxes at all. I thought again of that fella sitting in his snow hole for hours without having a shot. I guessed he was used to it.

At our Monday meet we were told there were 20 guns out and we were assured that on Saturdays there would be many more. I made calculations. Even just 20 men with guns averaged over 66 meets would amount to 1,320 man days. A tally of 131 foxes meant that on average it took just more than 10 man days to kill each fox. That is ten full farming day's work for each fox killed and that only accounted for the guns. It included no figure for the operation of the hunt itself, the hounds etc. Nor was there any cost allowance for the attendance of other helpers and followers. It would be not unreasonable to estimate the total cost to kill each fox at about £1,000.

Such economic factors were relevant when considering gun packs that were portrayed as necessity rather than 'sport'. The costs had to be set against the alternatives. Most lambs lost died from hypothermia or poor nutrition. Their bodies were then scavenged by foxes. The £1000 freely spent year after year killing each fox might be better employed on providing remedies for hypothermia or poor nutrition. Money spent on alleviating hypothermia, if invested in hardware, would be largely reusable from year to year. The ten full farming days devoted to killing each fox could, if directed elsewhere, go far to reduce the real threat to lambs. Clearly 'sport' was more important than was admitted.

Before thought is given to alternative means of killing foxes in the absence of hounds, consideration needs to be given to a cost-benefit analysis over the presence of foxes. Foxes cause no harm to forestry and are a real benefit to farming through predation on rabbits and the removal of carrion. Many farmers regard foxes as beneficial rather than harmful.

I sensed that whatever such gun packs may claim about their hunt being a necessity rather than 'sport' they were glad that foxes were there. Followers enjoyed their day, never spoke of wiping out foxes and I felt that if there were no foxes in that part of Wales they would introduce them.

Within the information package provided by this hunt for the Inquiry team was a cutting from *The Western Mail* November 25th 1997. A piece largely supportive of the Plas Machynlleth included this:-
"It makes more sense for farmers to kill vixens when they are still carrying their young but, surprisingly, they leave them to give birth and allow the cubs to grow to an age where they start to become a nuisance to farmers like Will Lloyd."
[Will Lloyd was a local farmer who it is said had no fewer than 12 ducks stolen by a fox cub [sic]. The Plas Machynnlleth foxhounds were called in together with about 15 guns but after a half hour search of the woodland where they judged the culprit to be found nothing and gave up. True, they went on to kill two foxes elsewhere that day but there was no claim that either was responsible for the duck killing outrage.]

The above comment from the reporter, Duncan Higgitt, was pertinent. By their actions whatever else hunters may have in their minds regarding the control of foxes it was clear that first and foremost was the need for the fun gained from that means of control.

434

Finally, the statement from Emyr Lewis, copies of which were passed to the Inquiry team included the following under the section *"Social and Cultural life of the countryside"*:-

"Farmers on hill farms spend a tremendous proportion of their lives working in solitude. The state of agriculture during the last few years has added a considerable strain on every farmer. Mid Wales has, in recent years, caused alarm among experts who have discovered its high farming suicide rate and attributed it, among other reasons, to a lack of opportunity to meet with other people.
A day out hunting gives a farmer a break from the day to day solitude and the enjoyment of meeting and talking to other farmers is an absolute lifeline for many a depressed farmer."

Is killing honestly a cure for depression? Even if it is, does sitting alone in a freezing snow hole all day without having sight of a fox make you more, or less, depressed?

The whole question of sheep farming in upland areas caused considerable debate. Graham Harvey in his insightful book *The Killing of the Countryside* (1997) exposed the real harm caused by poorly directed farm subsidies. In 2001 foot and mouth was unleashed upon our countryside and spread by the greed, ignorance and callousness of a few livestock farmers. With the public moved by images of farmers in tears over their lambs being sent early for slaughter the naïve Labour Government was fooled by the unholy trinity of farmers, livestock auctioneers and vets into paying excessive compensation. Many farmers accrued even more wealth.

[The National Audit Office report to Parliament in June 2002 revealed that the outbreak cost some £8 billion. *New Scientist*, July 30th 2001, reported UK farmers may have deliberately infected their livestock with foot and mouth disease to benefit from substantial compensation packages: *"Nuala Preston, a farmer in Newport, Pembrokeshire, revealed on 29 July that a man had telephoned her to offer her an infected sheep for £2000. "I was so horrified I slammed the phone down," she said. "I was absolutely appalled that anyone should dream of doing that. But I think some farmers on the brink of desperation and bankruptcy might be tempted to go for it because at least they would get compensation for their animals." Farmers can receive £90 compensation for a sheep slaughtered from an infected herd – at least double the market value. Sam Harrison, a spokesman for DEFRA, says the department has been in contact with Preston to investigate her claims. He said they are also investigating "an individual suspected of spreading foot and mouth by deliberate infection"."*]

After an enjoyable tea courtesy of Emyr Lewis we left and I was home just before midnight.

*****

A week later, on Monday March 6th, Graham Sirl was back as an observer when the Inquiry team visited the meet of the Irfon and Towy Foxhounds. The team were Lord Burns, Lord Soulsby, Professor Marsh and Brian Caffarey. Simon Hart observed for the CA. After meeting at Port

Talbot station the team were driven in hunt transport to the meet between Myffai and Twynllanan. The hunt moved off in thick fog around 11:30am. There were some 30 guns out. It seemed the first woodland drawn was blank. After lunch hounds were heard running followed by shots—but they may have come from a nearby army firing range.

After hounds were put into a third conifer woodland the team heard at least two shots. The team were escorted around the track and shown their first dead fox of the day. A dog fox, about three years old, he was shot cleanly through the chest at reasonably close range. After further holloas from hunt supporters and shots the team were shown a second dead fox. This was a very young vixen, neither pregnant nor lactating. She too had been killed cleanly. The team were told the tally after 2½ hours' hunting was four foxes shot plus one killed by hounds. After examining the second dead fox shown to them the team left at 2:30pm. They were told the hunt used terriers to deal with any foxes that went to ground and any foxes left injured by the guns were followed up by the hounds. That was the third visit by the hunt to those woods that season. To that date in the 1999/2000 season the hunt had killed 146 foxes with the most killed on one day being 14.

*****

The following week the Inquiry team visited a Fell pack. Graham Sirl and Simon Hart were the observers when the team attended the meet of the Coniston Foxhounds at High Yewdale Farm, Holm Fell on Tuesday March 14th. The team were Lord Burns, Professor Winter, Dr Edwards and Brian Caffarey. Everyone stayed at a nearby hotel the night before. After dinner, there were discussions with hunt officials. Roger Westmorland, a Master, explained how their hounds were returned during the summer to their puppy walkers and that after six or seven seasons' hunting most hounds were retired to the same puppy walkers to live out their lives as normal pets. The closeness of hunter to hound at that pack dated back to its formation. According to *Baily's Hunting Directory* the pack was established in 1825, "*as a trencher fed pack to run fox, marten and hare.*" The team were told it cost £25,000 a year to run the hunt of which £3,000 was raised by subscription. Up until then they had killed 70 foxes that season with a quarter of the kills resulting from dig-outs. Numbers of kills had risen with other Fell packs experiencing a similar rise.

At the meet, a coffee morning event, the Inquiry team were greeted by senior members of the hunt—and by a television crew from the BBC programme *Countryfile*. The hunt set off around 10am. Professor Winter walked with the Coniston Huntsman and was never seen again by Graham Sirl that day. Professor Winter used his mobile phone to call Lord Burns at around 12:30pm saying he was on top of a hill near the meet. Graham stayed with the rest of the team who saw hounds drawing. Graham was introduced to Barrie Wade from the National Working Terrier Federation.

Hounds were seen drawing, were heard in cry and the Inquiry team followed, on National Trust land. In time, they ended up in a disused quarry from whence they could see hounds running on a scent in the distance. The pack had split and groups of hounds hunted independently across the valley bottom. The television circus then took over. There were several interviews and *Countryfile* tried to follow Lord Burns and hounds. In time the Huntsman appeared with the full pack and Lord Burns was invited to stop him for a further television interview. Hounds were then drawn along the side of the Fell in full view of the television camera. When hounds disappeared from sight the Inquiry team decided to call it a day. It was just 1pm. The hunt continued. Apart from Professor Winter, whose whereabouts were unknown, the Inquiry team saw nothing further of the Coniston that day. Graham was not told of anything being killed—the reason given for that was bad scenting conditions.

*****

Graham Sirl was again the CPHA observer when the Inquiry team visited the meet of the elite Duke of Beaufort's Foxhounds at Hawkesbury on Saturday March 18th. The team were Lord Burns, Professor Marsh, Professor Winter, Dr Edwards and Brian Caffarey with Simon Hart the CA observer. The CPHA had suggested the team visit an elite hunt, such as the Duke of Beaufort's or the Quorn. The choice of hunt, date and venue was made by the Inquiry team and the CA.

The rendezvous was the hunt kennels in the grounds of Badminton at 10am. Graham Sirl arrived to find the television crew from *Countryfile* already there. A *Times* reporter also planned to attend but never appeared. This elite hunt put out their elite team to greet the Inquiry—Chairman Antony Brassey, Joint Master and Huntsman Captain Ian Farquhar and Lord Mancroft. The team were told the hunt had killed 80 brace to date (160 foxes); of which 15% were dug out. The hunters thought their fox population was rising and that mange was more noticeable that season. Asked about artificial earths Lord Mancroft claimed they had 'hundreds', most built by the late Duke of Beaufort. He expressed sadness that some of their earths had been vandalised and the foxes in them killed by gangs coming out of Swindon and Bristol (these could only have been country sports enthusiasts equipped with terriers and perhaps lurchers as well).

[Lord Mancroft was an interesting character. On November 8th 1987 the *Daily Telegraph Magazine* welcomed his appointment as Joint Master to the VWH Foxhounds: "*Now Lord Mancroft is off heroin, he has joined the hunt.*" (*HOWL* 38, Winter 1988). Eton educated Lord Mancroft retained that post from 1987-89. Prior to that, during his seven-year spell as a junkie, he even stole from his sister to fund his drugs. In 1997 he participated in negotiations with defectors from the LACS—Jim Barrington, Mark Davies, Howard Hodges and Steve Watson. In a full-page article in the *Weekend Telegraph*, Saturday February 8th 1997 Lord Mancroft gave the memorable quote: "*Terrier work is not part of the fun of the hunt, it's the price we pay for hunting.*" For a man whose health issues were largely self-inflicted Lord Mancroft had surprising contempt for professionals who helped him. In 2008 after being treated in a hospital for septicaemia (complicated by his having Hepatitis C) he complained of the NHS nurses: "*The nurses who looked after me were mostly grubby - we are talking about dirty fingernails and hair - and were slipshod and lazy. Worst of all,*

437

they were drunken and promiscuous." Daily Telegraph February 29th 2008. Lord Mancroft, a supporter of the Middle Way Group, was Deputy Chairman of the CA, the pride of hunting and a member of the exclusive Pratt's Club.]

Captain Farquhar took the Inquiry team on a guided tour of his hunt kennels and stables. With an annual operating budget of £400,000 these were impressive. They were then all driven to the meet by hunt supporters in two vehicles. At the meet, they met well-known hunting author and intellectual, Professor Roger Scruton.

The hunt moved off at around 12:30pm with other CPHA monitors watching. Soon afterwards, when the first woodland drawn was found to be blank, Lord Burns left. Whilst hunting near Hawkesbury Monument the team met the Beaufort Hunt Stewards. Unusually these were keeping well away from the CPHA monitors. At one point Graham saw a fox flee a covert but as the others from the Inquiry team had left their vehicle they missed this. More hunting followed and then Captain Farquhar returned with his hounds. He stopped to inform the team that they had just killed a mangy fox—and that they had killed another mangy fox earlier. Graham asked their driver and guide what happened to the carcasses and was told they would have been buried. Soon afterwards the remainder of the Inquiry team left; it was around 3:30pm. The whole flavour of the hunt then changed.

CPHA monitors continued to follow and reported that with the Inquiry team present the hunt was little more than a hack about the countryside. With them out of the way the hunt crossed the A46 to their preferred hunting country, visited Park Wood where there is an artificial earth and hunt stewards reverted to their usual intimidating and aggressive selves. The hunt continued till around 6pm. Within four miles of the meet CPHA monitors knew of five artificial earths. In Duke of Beaufort's hunt country CPHA monitors knew of 12 artificial earths. At two food was found dumped by hunt supporters near the artificial earth. At a third food was found dumped elsewhere in the wood.

*****

My next visit was the following month when I joined the Inquiry team on their mission to see a drag hunt. That was the meet of the Staff College and Royal Military Academy Sandhurst Draghounds at Puttenham between Guildford and Farnham on Sunday March 19th 2000. It was a lovely sunny day. The Inquiry team were out in force with Lord Burns, Lord Soulsby, Professor Marsh, Dr Edwards, and Brian Caffarey present. The observers were Simon Hart and me.

I left home early for our rendezvous, Guildford railway station, at 11:45am. I arrived in good time and saw Lord Soulsby waiting there having caught an earlier than expected train from Waterloo. I beckoned him over and invited him to sit in the quiet of my car. It was an excellent opportunity to discuss his impressions to date. I then noticed Dr Edwards drive up. When I walked to greet her, I saw the rest of the Inquiry team assembled in the car park. Lord Burns and Professor Marsh had driven. Brian Caffarey and Simon Hart had let the train take the strain.

We met some people from the hunt and decided to drive in convoy to the nearby meet at Suffield Farm, Puttenham, at 12:30pm. Lord Soulsby stayed with me and we continued our discussions. At the meet, we were still somewhat early. The hunt Kennelman, Bryan Robinson, was introduced. Helpful and forthcoming, he showed the drag and the scent they intended using. Bryan was quizzed by the Inquiry team about how the hunt operated and if they could create variety. He responded: "*Now and again for a bit of a change we'll do one of the lines backwards.*"

Asked about the riders he revealed: "*Some of them go foxhunting. Some of them don't.*"

And about the hounds: "*We use foxhounds.........we get given them by packs of hounds who um find that they either don't hunt foxes, or they are not quick enough, or they are too quick, or they misbehave in any way.*" He told us that he expected 30 or 40 riders out on the day.

Dr Edwards asked Bryan: "*It's sometimes said that it is too fast in terms of offering an alternative. Is there any way you can slow it down?*" Bryan replied: "*There are ways you could slow it down by the means that you said by putting checks in the line*" (creating artificial checks in the lines laid such as by lifting them had been discussed).

Asked about the suitability of drag hunting for children he said: "*We have children's versions but it's done at the same speed. All we have is smaller jumps.*"

Lord Soulsby asked: "*What would the proportion be of er fox hunters to drag hunters today?*" and elicited this reply: "*Of everybody here today I would say that a good 95% have fox hunted at some point.*" Lord Soulsby enquired further: "*During the year or at any time in their life?*" Bryan replied: "*In the last two or three years?*"

Professor Marsh confirmed the close link between fox hunting and drag hunting locally when he asked: "*Is foxhunting available in this area readily?*" Bryan Robinson confirmed the intimate link: "*Yea. The Surrey Union were over the jumps that we're going to jump today, yesterday.*"

Bryan then departed to take the runner, a young lad, to lay the drag. A senior lady from the hunt, introduced as Pat, took up the description of how it worked. She cleared up a lot of the uncertainties concerning the sport: "*Do remember you can't go any quicker than hounds can hunt................I've actually hunted drag hounds for twenty years. In all those years I've had foxes cross over the track.....um.....between the runner running and then hounds....I mean literally you know not far ahead of them and really hounds have been far less likely to follow a fox than they have a deer.............I've had foxes cross galloping in front of me and hounds have been...they've just carried straight on.*"

Asked what type of hound could be used for drag hunting she replied: "*Any scenting hound theoretically could be used to go drag hunting.*" As their name suggested there were close links between this hunt and the army. Pat told us:

"*An awful lot, funnily enough, of past Foxhound Masters have come through the drag hunt in their time in the army...........B. Fanshawe for* one.......*Simon Clarke for another.*" This was a reference to the Brian Fanshawe who had set up these visits for the Inquiry team. [Not all hunts have the followers their name suggests—few if any miners follow the Banwen Miners Foxhounds.]

I sensed that Simon Hart at that visit was somewhat withdrawn. He usually took a leading role, ensuring the Inquiry team were well briefed as to what the hunt intended. On that occasion, he stayed more in the background. The meet was in the grounds of the farm. There were seven couple of hounds out. They were foxhounds taken in as drafts from nearby fox hunts. After a few words from the Master to the assembled supporters we set off. Again, there was no suitable four-wheel-drive to take us all so we divided. I joined Professor Marsh in a four-wheel-drive driven by Karen Robinson with their two boys as company in the back. I was fascinated to learn that her husband, Bryan, had been the terrierman at the Sinnington Foxhounds when Adrian Dangar was there.

We learned that three lines were to be laid and that that would be their last hunt for the season. We were driven to a point in a nearby field from where we could see the hounds and mounted field arrive. The hunt then set off around the three sides of a square around us. I enjoyed seeing lots of people having fun and knowing no animals were being tormented.

The hounds ran well but evidenced the heat of the day as they laboured somewhat as they slogged up the grass slope near us. There was plenty of interest from the assembled supporters as they watched the riders negotiating an awkward-looking jump to exit the field. We were then driven to another point at a fine house. It was noticed that the front offside tyre on Pat's car was almost flat. She, and the members of the Inquiry team with her, transferred to another vehicle and her car was left to be repaired later. It crossed my mind that if it had been the more common animal hunt, with opponents to such cruelty out, the latter would have been wrongly blamed for that 'sabotage'. Taken to the end of the second line we saw the mounted field galloping up over a long expanse of grass and taking jumps. The jumps were not compulsory; most could simply be ridden around if preferred. Neither drag line was long. I found this hard to reconcile with the often-made claim, from those seeking to retain fox hunting, that drag hunting requires much more space.

Once we ended up on a narrow track through a wood where hounds were being held at a check. This was the opportunity for everyone to get their breath and for the new drag line to be laid. Lord Burns strode up and took photographs. I did likewise but encountered the very rare occurrence of a jam in my normally ultra-reliable Nikon F3. Whilst I endeavoured to resolve this the hunt passed me by and I was left behind the long trail of riders. My transport kindly waited but regretfully I delayed them.

We were then driven to the end of the last line. We arrived in time to observe the young runner appear out of the wood, trailing his drag. He ran up the field towards us, circled and ended up where Pat was waiting with a large bucket of biscuits. She called out that this was the 'kill' for their hounds. I was intrigued to see if hounds followed the exact line. They came out of the wood in cry and duly did. To add to the interest, we could have suggested to the runner that he take a certain route. He might have done so. Had it been an animal hunt the quarry would probably have taken one look at us all standing in the open field and stayed in the wood.

Wagging sterns proved the hounds' pleasure at gaining their reward. The mounted field appeared and it was clear they had enjoyed a good ride. Bryan Robinson approached me to chat. I took the opportunity to discuss his days at the Sinnington Foxhounds. Apparently, he worked for 18 months at that hunt as terrierman. Having seen a pair of cubs incarcerated in an artificial earth, with a tiny cage on one end, in a wood owned by the Sinnington Foxhounds I asked him about the treatment of foxes and in particular the movement of cubs about their country. I surreptitiously recorded our conversation:

Bryan Robinson: *There was a policy in Yorkshire with the keepers, rather than shoot all the foxes, because they've obviously got to look after their pheasants,*

Mike Huskisson: *Right.*

Bryan Robinson: *What they do is they'll find a litter of cubs; they'll know for example in that wood there is a litter of cubs*

Mike Huskisson: *Right.*

Bryan Robinson: *So they'll go out and shoot the vixen,....Oh! that's bloody horrible,.....they've shot the....how'll the poor cubs...*

Mike Huskisson: *Right.*

Bryan Robinson: *Then they'll go there every day and feed the cubs, they leave chickens and stuff out for them...*

Mike Huskisson: *Oh, right.*

Bryan Robinson: *Cos they then...they can control then whereabouts on their patch the foxes are...*

Mike Huskisson: *Right.*

Bryan Robinson: *Yea?*

Mike Huskisson: *Right.*

Bryan Robinson: *So, it's a way of ensuring that there's foxes there for the people to hunt when they go hunting but also a way for the keeper being able to dictate where on his patch the foxes are.*

Mike Huskisson: *Right.*

Bryan Robinson: *Yea. Do you follow what I'm saying?*

Mike Huskisson: *Yea.*

Bryan Robinson: *So, it's common practice. They'll shoot them, shoot the mother once the cubs are big enough to be sort of on on solid flesh...*

Mike Huskisson: *Right.*

Bryan Robinson: *Shoot the mother and they will then to all intents and purposes rear the cubs.*

Mike Huskisson: *Right.*

Bryan Robinson: *But all they actually do is go and feed them.*

Mike Huskisson: *Right.*

Bryan Robinson: *And they are then able to keep track of where the foxes are on their patch which at the end of the day every good keeper wants to know where his foxes are, doesn't he?*

Bryan Robinson was an experienced gamekeeper, terrierman and Huntsman. His description, for the Inquiry team, portrayed the reality of how foxes were treated for sporting purposes. It made a mockery of claims that foxes were hunted in their wild and natural state. The relationship between a vixen and her cubs is intimate and vital. The vixen teaches her offspring how to hunt and how to survive in the wild. If, in the interest of the sport of men and women, she is killed and her cubs fed from the moment they are weaned by man (and on chickens!) what is the exact measure of harm caused to those cubs? They find it hard to fend for themselves in the wild and until they fell victim to the 'sport' for which they were spared, doubtless fulfilled the jaundiced view of some by being the very threat to farming interests for which their species was damned.

It was timely that in the **Gamekeeper & Sporting Dog** section of *Countryman's Weekly* May 5th 2000 under the *Looking Back section taken from The Gamekeeper, 1913* there was the following:

"*Mistake of hand rearing a litter of fox cubs*

Every gamekeeper who has foxes to contend with naturally does his best to prevent damage to his game, some following one system and others another, but it has always been my practice to interfere with the litters as little as possible.

However, I have recently determined to be still more careful in that particular owing to what has lately occurred. I found that the vixen belonging to a litter of cubs on my ground had somehow been destroyed, and I had to feed the youngsters regularly at their earth, or they must have died.

My lad used to take them dead rabbits, rooks, and anything we could procure every evening, and so carefully did we see to their wants that all survived and a healthier lot of cubs could not be found.

Nevertheless, they repaid us badly, for I never met such bold foxes as these finally became. They stole fowls and pheasants under our very noses, and all the devices which generally are so successful as scares were in their case of not the slightest use.

They simply ignored them, and the appearance of a scare only served to inform the cubs that something was to be had near it.

This boldness I attributed to feeding them continually on food which had been handled, and they thus got accustomed to the scent of man and associated it with food. In fact, they welcomed it, and were constantly to be seen about our haunts and where an ordinary fox would not have dared to venture.

As long as one remained unkilled by hounds we were made conscious of its presence by irritating losses, and were rather pleased than otherwise to find out that they were the first to succumb to the pack.

Plainly, hand-reared cubs are worthless both from a hunting and shooting point of view, and I would sooner have three wild-bred litters than one hand-fed. LEICESTERSHIRE"

Risks associated with treating foxes in this wholly unnatural manner were clearly known for years. After my illuminating chat with Bryan we were driven in convoy back to the meet and invited in for very pleasant drinks and nibbles. This was one of the few occasions where the Inquiry team stayed out for as long as the hounds. I volunteered to drive Lord Soulsby, Brian Caffarey, and Simon Hart back to Guildford station for their train. We left at 3pm. Whilst it was fortuitous that drag hunting offered a ready-made and easy alternative to live quarry hunting the campaign to end the cruelty of the latter was not dependent on the existence of an alternative. If Parliament decided in its wisdom that a cruel pastime should be abolished there was no onus on anyone to offer an alternative outlet to those who formally delighted in that cruelty. A conversion to drag hunting was promoted as an alternative to the threatened slaughter of hounds and horses when animal hunting was banned.

Drag hunting took many forms. E.W. Martin in his 1959 book *The Case Against Hunting* quoted a *"great authority on hunting, Lady Florence Dixie"* as follows: *"Drags can be run fast or slow, according to the way they are laid. My husband owned a pack of harriers and a pack of beagles, and I was able to get him often to hunt them on drags, and have often ridden with the harriers and run with the beagles. When a very fast, non-hunting run was wanted with the harriers, the drag was laid straight and continuously, and hounds ran fast, and riding was like a steeplechase, without a pause, except when any of us came a cropper! When a hunting run was required, we laid a catchy drag, twisting here and there, lifting the scent copying as near as possible the wily ways of Reynard. With the beagles we imitated a hare, who is a ringing, not straight-running, animal, lifting the scent, doubling back, and so on, and, in fact, we brought thus two competitors into the sport, i.e. the drag layer versus the huntsman, and pitted their wiles and their cunning against each other. I may be accepted as an authority, as few have perhaps ridden in harder-fought hunting runs than I - fox, stag, harrier, guanaco, ostrich, and suchlike - and I have had considerable experience with beagles as well, on foot."*

*****

The following week we were back out fox hunting for the Essex Farmers' and Union Foxhounds meet at Woodham Ferrers on Wednesday March 22nd 2000. The Inquiry team were Lord Burns, Professor Marsh and Mark Sanderson, with observers Simon Hart and me.

This visit was proposed by the CPHA who wanted the Inquiry team to meet local people who experienced problems from hunting. The rendezvous was Ingatestone station at 10am. I arrived on time to find the car park full with vehicles left by commuters making their daily trek to London. I found Professor Marsh already there waiting in his trusty Volvo. It was another lovely sunny morning.

We waited and waited. Trains came and went but there was no sign of our colleagues expected from London. Professor Marsh turned on his mobile phone to find a message from Mark Sanderson. The rest of our team had missed their scheduled train, were on a later one to Shenfield, and would be driven to meet us. In due course, they turned up in a Range Rover driven by a hunt supporter.

Simon Hart had inadvertently caused the delay. Thinking he could buy a ticket on the train, as is common in rural areas, he had tried to board it without a ticket, found the barrier system at Liverpool Street prevented him and whilst he purchased his ticket they all missed the train.

There was no harm done. We arrived at the meet at 10:50am and parked in the crowded pub car park. Clearly many hunt followers did not have to join the commuting rush to work. Lord Burns and his team were introduced to the usual succession of hunt supporters. The team were then squeezed into the packed pub and offered all manner of alcoholic beverage. They imbibed only coffee. When we first arrived, I noticed my LACS colleague Lawrie Payne, taking time off from his Fire Service profession. Lawrie waited with people I took to be those troubled by the hunt and keen to talk to Lord Burns and his colleagues. In the pub, I informed Mark Sanderson that there were some individuals outside to whom the Inquiry team should speak. With some difficulty, we disengaged Lord Burns from all the hunt followers keen to catch his ear and took him and Professor Marsh out to meet the opposing view.

I left them to converse in comparative peace and chose instead to chat with Simon Hart about the shortly expected arrival of his first child. I wished he and his partner well. I raised with Simon information that was being swapped around on the Internet containing allegations as to what I had said, or not said, to Lord Soulsby concerning the movement of hares for the Waterloo Cup. This Internet gossip appeared to source the information to a CA newsletter, and beyond that to Simon as the original information source. As we had all agreed that we would publicise nothing about what we had seen, heard, or done at these visits, until they were over, this caused him some embarrassment. He denied ever telling anyone about what I said to Lord Soulsby and he was right as he had not been party to our conversation.

Simon called his colleagues at CA Headquarters, then told me that in his opinion the source of their leak was a Press Officer who had left their organisation. I was sure he was right but the incident and the hyperbole surrounding it highlighted the difficulty we had ensuring it was only the facts about hunting with dogs that were passed to the Inquiry team.

The hunt had their meet with the hounds by the pub and departed whilst Lord Burns and Professor Marsh were still engaged in discussions with locals angry over the behaviour of the hunters. Some were from the local Badger Group there to report the difficulties they experienced with sett blocking by hunt supporters. They had setts blocked with the wrong material and seldom were setts unblocked after the hunt. Another petitioner was from a local village keen to explain efforts made to keep the hunt out of her village. I later enquired from the local Badger Group, the North-East Essex Badger Group, about the events on the actual day of the Inquiry team's visit and was sent the following:-

"22-3-2000 the day of the Burns Inquiry visit. Setts at Radar Hill A found stopped but to our surprise some of the holes had been re-opened by badgers. Radar Hill B also found hard stopped. Police and RSPCA informed."

Undoubtedly the Inquiry team heard about this but equally they saw little hard evidence. Lord Burns was in a rush to leave to return to London and did so shortly after the hounds set off. After his departure, we were at the whim of whatever Professor Marsh decided to do. At first it seemed he was going to leave straight away also. Later that he would follow the hunt for a short while before leaving. The hunters were keen for him to do so and had transport waiting. In the end one lady Joint Master offered to buy us all a coffee in the pleasantly laid out pub garden. Professor Marsh chose that option and we joined him. We had an amicable discussion, saw nothing of the hunt in action and left at about 12:15pm. Professor Marsh gave Mark Sanderson and Simon Hart a lift to the station. It was eminently civilised but hardly what we were there to do.

*****

Two days later the Inquiry team returned to the Lake District for the meet of the Blencathra Foxhounds at *The Swinside Inn* on Friday March 24th. Professor Marsh and Mark Sanderson attended for the Inquiry; Graham Sirl and Simon Hart were observers. At a meeting the night before the Inquiry team were introduced to three Blencathra Joint Masters and their wives. The hunters declared they had 1000 subscribers and operated on an annual budget of £30,000. They claimed to kill on average 70 foxes a season. There was no mention of mange in foxes but hunters spoke of their foxes appearing tamer—they put that down to the increase in visitors to the Fells making foxes more used to seeing people. Unlike the Coniston they did not report an increase in fox numbers.

In the morning, they were introduced to Jim Bennett, a Joint Master, and given a half hour tour of his kennels by Barry Todhunter, the Huntsman. Then it was on to the meet at *The Swinside Inn*, Newlands Valley, where they enjoyed coffee and biscuits with a crowd of about 60, including staff and Masters from neighbouring packs.

A farmer appeared at the meet carrying a plastic sack from which he pulled a decapitated lamb, a sight calculated to shock. He told Professor Marsh the lamb had been killed by a fox the previous night. Graham Sirl intervened to ask the key question: had the lamb been dead or alive when attacked by the fox. Too often dead lambs are found scattered about Lakeland fields. Foxes are highly efficient (and should be valued as) scavengers of carrion, including dead lambs. The only relevant question was what killed the lamb? Fox, misfortune, or poor husbandry? [In October 2016 the National Animal Disease Information Service web site stated: *"Lamb deaths from birth to three day-old in the majority of UK flocks ranges from 10 to 25 per cent which represents 2 to 6 million dead lambs annually....*" Animal Aid point out that this high mortality is not due to foxes or other predators but rather to exploitation and neglect by farmers themselves. Foxes are convenient scapegoats.]

Some pro-hunting farmers appeared on debates and claimed to have sat and watched as foxes killed their lambs, with foxes even waiting in packs for ewes to give birth. Such nonsense invited the retort that to have sat and watched that happen proved what poor shepherds they were. Invited to explain how he knew the lamb was killed by a fox this farmer stuttered and stammered but gave no definite answer. The exchange proved the value of having knowledgeable observers with the Inquiry.

The hunt moved off between 10:30 and 11am to draw woodland behind the hotel. Their aim seemed to be to return to draw in front of the hotel where supporters were. Many followers set off with Barry Todhunter. Time passed; then a supporter returned with news that caused concern to the assembled Masters. The fox and hounds had just gone through the village. The sounds of horn and hounds were then heard in the valley behind the hotel. Graham Sirl returned to the Hotel car park. The hounds, in the distance at first, came nearer and nearer. Soon there was an influx of supporters who were greatly excited after seeing the fleeing fox. This fox was turned at the road and headed across the fields in front of the car park from left to right. It was obvious the fox was totally exhausted. Hounds were well on the line of their victim and it seemed the lead hounds were coursing him rather than hunting by scent.

The fox tried to head for the sanctuary of the woodland where he had originally been found but was headed by hunt supporters standing on the road. He performed a complete U-turn, back towards the hounds, and ran into the tail end of the pack. He was caught and killed by hounds to the great excitement of the watching supporters. Even clapping was heard. Commenting on this later Professor Marsh compared their reaction to that of the crowd when a goal is scored in a football match.

Simon Hart commented: "*Text book hunt I would say,*" and added about the obviously exhausted condition of the quarry: "*There must have been something wrong with the fox.*" The Inquiry team then retired to the hotel for coffee as Professor Marsh was cold. Professor Marsh commented on the speed of the kill at the end. After about twenty minutes the hunt returned to the area of the hotel and then moved off to draw near the fell.

The Inquiry team left the hunt at about noon and were driven back to Penrith by Simon Hart. The hunt continued in their absence. On the train journey to Preston Graham Sirl discussed the day with Professor Marsh. The latter revealed that Blencathra Huntsman, Barry Todhunter, had claimed the fox they had seen killed had been the very same rogue fox that had attacked sheep the previous night. Professor Marsh appeared none too convinced over that claim.

*****

The following Tuesday, March 28th, the Inquiry team were back in the Fells when Lord Soulsby attended the Blencathra Foxhounds meet at the Mary Mount Hotel, Borrowdale. It was agreed that as it was essentially a repeat of the visit made the previous Friday, neither the CPHA nor the CA would send observers. The hunting fraternity of course had plenty of people present to make their views known (unopposed) to Lord Soulsby.

As to what Lord Soulsby saw *Hounds* magazine (April 2000) reported under the Fell Hunting News section: "*On the following Tuesday, Lord Soulsby visited a meet at the Mary Mount Hotel, Borrowdale and was able to see 'terrier work' and a fox bolted from a rocky boran before eventually being overtaken by hounds.*"

*****

At the end of that week it was back to stag hunting when the Inquiry team attended the Devon and Somerset Staghounds meet at Molland Moor Gate on Saturday April 1st. The Inquiry team were Lord Burns and Dr Edwards along with Brian Caffarey and Mark Sanderson. Grahame Sirl observed for the CPHA with Simon Hart for the CA for the first part of the day and then Richard Walton.

The day started at 6am with a drive to see deer being harboured. In attendance were Lord Burns, Dr Edwards, Brian Caffarey, Mark Sanderson, Graham Sirl, Simon Hart, Tom Yandle and the harbourer for the Devon and Somerset Staghounds—Martin Lock. Tom Yandle explained the latter was one of three, all paid by the hunt. Tom Yandle drove the team in one vehicle to Anstey Common to await the dawn. It was extremely foggy and it was difficult to see across the valley. In the growing light about a dozen deer were picked out some 5 miles away across the valley but it was impossible to tell their age or even their sex. Another group of deer were spotted near Anstey Gate amongst which was what appeared to be the quarry, a spring stag. It was explained that the hunt was looking for a stag about 3, 4, or even 5 years old with antlers, Brow, Bay, Two a-top. Martin Lock explained they could get closer because the deer would be used to vehicles driving to the nearby farm. When close enough for a clear view Martin Lock declared there was no suitable deer to hunt in the group. He explained he was looking for a poor stag unsuitable for breeding and that he looked for antler formation and body condition.

The Inquiry team were then taken to West Molland Barton Farm to see the farmer about a group of stags recently seen on his farm. They were driven into a coniferous plantation owned by the Molland Estate and shot over by the Holland & Holland shoot. There were feed bins and 6ft high pheasant enclosures everywhere prompting the aside from Tom Yandle that he did not know how they justified that shooting business that released over 60,000 birds. A small group of hinds was seen but no stags. The Inquiry team then returned and met a farmer coming out from the field above the woodland. He informed Martin Lock there had been a big group of deer there earlier that morning but he had frightened them away when feeding.

The Inquiry team went back into the woods and took a higher track. They soon came upon the stags that were nearly all 'warrantable' (suitable to hunt). The deer moved off and the Inquiry team moved back along the road. After a short journey, they stopped and looked out across the fields to see 27 stags coming along the field about half a mile away. Amongst these stags was one with a broken antler. Martin Lock told the Inquiry team however that it was very unlikely that they would hunt one of these deer that day as there was a meet scheduled for the farm the following Tuesday. Tom Yandle said it was always left to the harbourer to decide which deer to hunt. The Inquiry team left and returned to Dulverton at 9am. It was unclear at the time whether any of the deer they had seen would be chosen for hunting. It turned out the hunted deer was eventually selected from the herd seen at West Molland Barton.

They reassembled at Dulverton at 10:30am. Professor Marsh had made the trip down and been expected to take part but sadly owing to illness he remained in the hotel. The Inquiry team were taken to the meet. They were greeted by the spectacle of hunters assembled on one side of the road with the local LACS Support Group on the other making clear their support for the deer. Again, a television crew from *Countryfile* were present. Adding to the media circus were reporters from the *Western Morning News*. The hunting fraternity had also arranged for reporters for *Horse and Hound* and *Shooting Times* to be present.

Lord Burns and his Inquiry team spoke to representatives from both sides. Hounds were gathered at the back of the horse boxes. Lord Burns spoke to Joint Master, Diana Scott. Graham Sirl noticed the harbourer, Martin Lock, talking to the Huntsman, Donald Summersgill. Without any introductions or speeches hounds were taken off, followed by the hound van. Graham Sirl quickly saw they were moving some distance away to draw for the stag. The Inquiry team trailed behind in the hunt Land Rover and were driven into a field to overlook West Molland Barton.

Graham deduced the quarry for the day would be the stag with the broken antler seen earlier. For about half an hour the Inquiry team observed as hounds pushed a bunch of stags around the three fields in their view. In time the hounds took off, moving towards East Anstey. The Inquiry team followed.

The following hunt report for that day in the local *West Somerset Free Press* detailed what occurred: "*Fog cleared on cue, and tufters were taken to West Molland Laurels, where a one horned stag, with a fine herd of other stags, was harboured. After a circuit of Park Hill the right stag, with one other, came away over Higher Hill to Veyseys, and crossed into King's Wood. Re-crossing the road to Veyseys on the right stag now, they ran back to West Molland Laurels, and across to Natty Cleave. Having worked up to their stag at the top end of Redlands, it was down to Natty Cleave once more, across to West Molland Wood, and, after a brief check with fresh stags, in through The Rookery and up Gatcombe. The hunted stag climbed up over the event course to lie up beside the Cuzzicombe fence, and, having been stopped off more fresh stags, hounds were taken there and fresh found. Now it was back down Gatcombe to Redlands, down as far as Natty Cleave, and up Redlands again, to just touch Barton, before sinking to the water below Barton Bridge, to take their stag under The Rookery at around 3.30p.m.*"

That was the view for an informed and experienced hunting

448

correspondent. For the Inquiry team, it was somewhat different. They caught up with the hunt when the hounds were stopped and taken back to the area of the meet to draw again. They were not informed as to why. After about half an hour they were driven back to their previous observation point and parked. Perhaps in consequence of the early start coupled with the warm vehicle Lord Burns promptly fell asleep. At around 2:15pm the Inquiry team observed the hunted stag, mixed up in a much larger bunch of deer, crossing below them heading towards Twitchen. The team were driven in pursuit but their progress was hindered by the volume of traffic and riders. Graham Sirl estimated there were at least 100 riders out plus about 80/90 vehicles of followers. The Inquiry team broke away from following the hunt to head for the local offices of the LACS at St Nicholas Priory and a pre-arranged meeting with CPHA representatives. In consequence, no-one from the Inquiry team saw the deer killed.

*****

The Hunting Inquiry then held Oral Examinations of witnesses at the Posthouse Hotel, Coram Street, London. On Thursday April 6th 2000 the morning session heard about hunting; the afternoon about economics. I gave evidence in the morning session. I attended another session the following Monday, April 10th, from 10am to 5pm. I then caught the train to Coventry to be an observer at the meeting between the Inquiry team and CA supporters. The meeting was at the Hylands Hotel from 7:30pm to 9pm.

During the meeting Robin Page made the following plea:- "*As a farmer and countryman then my visits to hunting areas have left me totally depressed because I find the farming situation is absolutely desperate. I have seen people in the Lake District burning wool. I have seen piles of day old calves in the kennels of Edmund Porter in the Lakes because the farmers cannot afford to keep them.*
Eight miles away from me a farmer's wife has blown her brains out in the kitchen because farming is desperate and farming people and country people are desperate at the moment.
And what hunting is actually doing is it's holding people together. It is binding communities together and it is actually giving traditional country people something to live for.
And I do not hunt. And I do not shoot. And I do not fish but I regard them as my people and I worry about them and I hope that for God's sake that our politicians will soon wake up to the fact that there is a crisis in the countryside and many country people regard an attack on hunting as the final straw. It is a final straw driving people to desperation. They are despairing. They are bewildered. They feel victimised and they are angry. And they are very angry, some people.
I was at the Ludlow Point-to-Point yesterday and because of my column in the Daily Telegraph *I was approached by one person after another saying: "We are desperate. Thank you for writing about us."*
One man said: "I leave my farm next week. I am bankrupt. The only thing which stops me killing myself is my hunt work." His wife stood by him and his child was by his wife and the child was in tears. That is the

real state of the countryside which our people cocooned in London do not see and do not want to see."

The Committee of Inquiry appeared greatly moved by this plea. Robin Page was a highly intelligent man with a wealth of contacts amongst the hunting fraternity. He was invited to speak to the Committee of Inquiry (I had on an early hunting visit heard members of the Inquiry team say that Robin Page and Roger Scruton were two they should certainly interview). Robin Page knew that with a stenographer present taking notes, his words were 'on the record'. Can there ever have been a more succinct expression of the inherent selfishness in the hunting fraternity? What lasting harm might have been done to that child by hearing their father threaten to kill himself? To make his wife a widow and his child an orphan if he ever had to end his 'hunt work'? As a husband and father, I found that attitude impossible to comprehend.

*****

The next field visit for the Inquiry team was later in the month in Germany. On Tuesday April 25th Lord Burns, Dr Edwards and Brian Caffarey attended the meet of a drag hunt near Dusseldorf. Observers were Simon Hart and a RSPCA official for the CPHA.

*****

My next visit was at the end of that month when I joined the Inquiry team for their trip to see the humane version of hare coursing. This was at the Wickwar Park Coursing Club (under National Drag Coursing Club rules) at Wickwar, north-east of Bristol, on Sunday April 30th. I say 'team' but it was only Dr Edwards and Brian Caffarey. I was observing for the CPHA and I expected Simon Hart to be there for the CA.

The rendezvous for the Inquiry team was at the venue at 10am. I arrived on time. There had been heavy rain the previous few days, making the ground very wet, but that day dawned lovely and bright and was forecast to be very warm. When I spoke to Mark Sanderson to learn the arrangements he advised that I leave my car outside the venue as the ground was very wet. That was wise. The organisers had a tractor on hand that was put to frequent use to rescue vehicles bogged in the mud.

First brace was due in slips at 10:30am, rather more leisurely than live hare coursing in England. There was no sign of Simon Hart but I noticed another chap wandering about wearing a CA badge. I wondered whether Simon had been substituted. He told us their first child had just been born and I knew well myself the toll from sleepless nights with young babies. An aristocratic looking chap drove up in a K-registered white Range Rover and when the CA badged man seemed to know him I assumed one or other was the observer from our opposition.

I introduced myself to event organiser Bob Tovey. He said to buy an entry card and I found the chap selling them. For that type of coursing I was happy to pay the fee of £3. At about 10:15am Dr Edwards drove in with Brian Caffarey and a man who turned out to be her husband, Rick. He was sporting a sophisticated looking Sony video camera. I took them to find Bob Tovey. This involved some searching and waiting as he was fully occupied with the organisation of proceedings. We gathered and were introduced. The chap I first noticed wearing the CA badge turned out to be Mal Treharne, their local spokesman. His colleague in the white Range Rover was Keith Gardner, Chairman of a local coursing club called the South Marsh. I told him I had not seen his club listed on National Coursing Club events. He explained the South Marsh was a club for any breed of sight hound, not just greyhound. They apparently operated on the Somerset levels. It was quickly clear that Bob Tovey held no great affection for him.

Bob Tovey, a short, weather-beaten and clearly knowledgeable character, explained what his Drag Coursing Club was about and how they operated. He said he had been organising such drag coursing since 1992. It had nothing to do with lure coursing. There were no seasons for drag coursing; it was only stopped by bad weather. He gave Dr Edwards and Brian Caffarey each a set of the National Drag Coursing Club rules.

Dr Edwards asked if Rick could video the event. She explained she was the only member of the Committee of Inquiry able to attend that day and would like film to show to her colleagues so they could see what took place. Bob Tovey said we could take as much film and photographs as we liked. He told us he also ran a live hare coursing club (he was Secretary of the Yeovil & Sherborne Coursing Club, as listed on the National Coursing Club fixtures list 1999/2000). He was unable to talk for long as he soon left to carry on with making the arrangements for the day. I was delighted to see my friends and colleagues Kevin Hill and Peter White from IFAW.

The venue was a large grass rectangular field with a steep slope at one end. On the long side of the field, away from the entrance gate, was the coursing area. At the low end, near one corner, was the Slipper's shy. It was like the shy used at live hare coursing—a camouflaged screen. In addition, in a style reminiscent of the Park Hare Coursing I witnessed in the Republic of Ireland, there was a post at each side of the shy with a red disc on one side and white disc on the other. This indicated the corresponding colour of collar of the dog in the slips.

The running ground was a straight line up the hill. On the brow of the hill were two posts marking the finishing line; beyond them some bales of straw and the catch-up area for the drag. There was a car parked on the brow of the hill at right-angles to the running ground. It had its front elevated on a jack and the front offside wheel had been removed and replaced with a drum. That created a very effective improvised winch.

The object to be dragged was cleverly designed for maximum enticement of the dogs. It appeared to be a commercial fishing float with a ball of material that looked like hessian or rag. Most ingenious was the incorporation of a squeaker that squealed as the object was dragged. I commented to the Inquiry team that it mimicked the sounds emitted by a hare when caught. Slipper, Brian Pether, introduced himself to the Inquiry team. I asked if he had slipped at live hare coursing events and he replied he had, since 1967.

There were six eight-dog stakes listed on the card. With each stake involving seven courses to run off there were 42 courses scheduled. There were also plans to run whippet coursing and some trials. It was to be a busy day. Proceedings started on time at 10.30a.m. Initially we gathered near the finishing post. A pair of greyhounds were called forward and put in the slips in the usual manner. Bob Tovey rode a motor bike to carry the drag down to a point behind the Slipper's shy. A chap sited it correctly and then waved a green flag to indicate to the car driver that all was ready. The latter engaged gear and let the clutch out to start his winch spinning. The drag whizzed past the Slipper's shy causing his two charges to strain at the slips. He gave the drag a start of some 50 metres then slipped the dogs. They bounded up the field towards us. As the slope took effect the dogs strained for the lead. I filmed the contest. When the drag reached a cover, sited in front of the straw bales, the dogs pounced on their squealing quarry, but there was no pain. A red or white flag was raised to indicate which dog, which colour collar, crossed the finish first. Watching supporters marked their cards just as they do at live hare coursing. Bob Tovey rode up to retrieve the drag and took it back to the start. The pulling line was paid out and the dogs for the next course were called forward by the Slipper. That was the rhythm for the day. Some dogs were muzzled; some not.

After observing from the finishing area, we moved down to see the view from the Slipper's shy. Brian Pether told us the only improvement he sought in the organisation of the event was to have stricter authority over the bringing forward of dogs to the slip steward. This should happen crisply and quickly instead of there being any delay. Owners and trainers being somewhat lethargic at bringing their dogs forward was clearly a problem common to all coursing.

Bob Tovey was keen to tell the Inquiry team about his experiences netting and moving hares but there needed to be a pause in proceedings for him to do so. We then moved back up the slope towards the bulk of the crowd. I counted 35 parked vehicles. The Inquiry team, with Rick as cameraman, moved off and conducted improvised interviews with Dr Edwards admirably fulfilling the role of interviewer. She asked one watcher whether he thought the proceedings as enjoyable as hare coursing. He answered, *"Yes"*. Dr Edwards questioned the farmer who owned the field. He said the club met there about three times a year and his field was used for other purposes, including microlights. He also said there was no live hare coursing on it.

Lunch was scheduled for 1pm when there was planned to be a natural break in the running of the event. For some reason that was delayed. At about 1:55pm the winch line broke. As the drag was metres short of the finishing post this caused consternation. Would the dogs be put back in the slips for the course to run again? That would impose the penalty on the winning dog of in effect having to run almost an extra course compared to the dog it would encounter in the next round. The problem was solved by the diplomatic withdrawal of one dog. For one course a dog was noticed running 'unsighted'. He had lost sight of the drag, possibly after being distracted by something to the side of the running field. It was not uncommon in live hare coursing for one or both dogs to run 'unsighted'.

There was betting taking place. As we stood watching from the high point of the field we could hear the odds being called out. Soon after 2pm we had an opportunity to talk to Bob Tovey at more length about his great knowledge of the movement of hares. Bob, a man with 50 years' experience of coursing, was asked before the Inquiry team about the netting and movement of hares, in particular for the Waterloo Cup:-

Kevin Hill: "*What about like the Waterloo Cup. Have you put them down there?*"

Bob Tovey: "*I have put them down, yea.*"

Kevin Hill: "*What, what sort of space of time before?*"

Bob Tovey: "*I put them down a few days before, a week before.*"

Brian Caffarey: "*That was quite a time ago though, wasn't it?*"

Bob Tovey: "*I haven't done any netting since nineteen ninety...not for the Waterloo Cup I'd never do any again...since nineteen ninety three. But it still goes on. It still...every year.*"

Bob Tovey told of hares that suffered from syphilis being moved by others for coursing. He said he had moved hares for coursing, for beagling and for conservation. He then only moved hares for conservation purposes. He described petty squabbles between coursing clubs: "*One coursing club will even shoot another coursing club's hares so that they don't have a successful meeting, they are that stupid.*" He complained that people doing drag coursing had been intimidated and threatened by supporters of live hare coursing. He stressed he was not opposed to live hare coursing. He merely wanted to see drag coursing flourish irrespective of what happened to live hare coursing. After that the Inquiry team and Mal Treharne left. At about 2:30pm there was a thirty minutes' break for lunch. Usually when the Inquiry team left I had to leave, but that day was different. It was cruelty free and I had paid for my entry card so I was happy to stay to see the finals and the presentation of the cups. I watched the finals followed by whippet coursing and some trials. I then took film and photographs as the trophies were presented before departing at about 4:30pm.

I was delighted the Inquiry team saw the advantages for all in that type of coursing. For hares, there were no kills, no being driven over the fields by beaters, no terrors of the course for those that survive and no being netted and shipped about the country in small boxes to sustain coursing. For the dogs, there was no running over grounds that caused injury—such as short stubble or where sharp flints abounded. There was no running over fields where there were ditches or through hedgelines off the coursing field where barbed wire might lurk. Because the coursing was limited to the running field there was no risk of over-exertion in dogs chasing hares that have fled the coursing fields and disappeared far away. There were also no lengthy waits in slips on freezing cold mornings for hares to appear.

The supporters enjoyed advantages as well. There was the certainty that no animal suffered to entertain them. There was also the knowledge that if they entered their dogs into the competition they would get a run that day, weather providing. There is no question of hare shortage causing parts of the day to be abandoned.

Live hare coursing enthusiasts claimed one big disadvantage with such humane coursing was there was no twisting and turning. This was a straight line course up the running field. Whilst manifestly true what was the effect? In live hare coursing the dog first up to turn the hare usually won. It was rare indeed for the dog that was second to the hare to win. The points advantage gained by the first dog was hard for the other dog to overcome. Therefore, drag coursing, in which victory went to the first dog to the winning post was an almost perfect simulation.

In some ways drag coursing was in reality a better test of the merits of the dogs. In live hare coursing, typically when the dogs were slipped on a weak hare, one dog could bound up, catch the hare, and the course was over. This could not happen in drag coursing and indeed the lead could change over the running field particularly one where a slope took effect. Then there was the effect created by the presence of the crowd to consider. A wild hare fleeing usually veered away from any crowd. That favoured the dog on the side she veered to. In drag coursing the drag was obviously unaffected by crowd sounds and was pulled so as not to favour either dog.

*****

Early in May I was an observer at another meeting between the Inquiry team and CA supporters. That was on Friday May 5th at Armley Mills Museum, Leeds from 7:30pm to 9pm. The venue was packed. Present from the Inquiry Committee were Lord Burns and Professor Marsh. One speaker was Peter Hole, a former Master (for 19 years) of the Colne Valley Beagles. He told the Inquiry: "*I love the hunting of the hare.*" He described how he had attended the Waterloo Cup that year and was keen to emphasise the strength of his support for hunting: "*I certainly, a former bank manager, would be willing to submit to imprisonment to defend my sport.*"

*****

My final visit with the Inquiry team was to the Ytene Minkhounds meet at Langton Long, south east of Blandford Forum on Saturday May 20th 2000. Team members present were Professor Marsh, Professor Winter, Dr Edwards and Brian Caffarey. Simon Hart and I were observers. The Inquiry team were originally scheduled to attend two meets of the Ytene Minkhounds—on April 8th and April 22nd. Neither visit took place. They were cancelled, we were told, because the waters were too cold. Then in May we learned a visit had been set up for May 13th or May 20th. The latter date was selected. Our rendezvous was Manor Farm, Langton Long at 11am. I drove down the night before and stayed in Fiddleford. In the morning, I reached the meet about ten minutes early to find Professor Winter waiting, parked outside. As I drew up Professor Marsh and Brian Caffarey pulled up, coming from the opposite direction.

There had been discussion between my colleagues at the LACS and Brian Caffarey concerning the content of the submission regarding these visits I had sent to the Inquiry Committee on May 11th. My submission had not been put up on their web site as the Inquiry was unhappy about some of its contents. My report revealed I was using recording devices to prove

454

who said what to whom. I do not take shorthand and have learned that on occasion you must be able to prove what was said.

Accordingly, I was somewhat apprehensive as to the welcome I would receive. I was prepared to be barred from the event, by the hunt if no-one else. It turned out there was no problem at all in that regard. There was a real problem though in finding the hunt. We waited in early summer sunshine with no sign of any mink hunters. After a while Dr Edwards drove up. I asked whether Lord Burns and Lord Soulsby would be attending. I was told that Lord Burns had hoped to but could not. Lord Soulsby had intended to but, as he had to be back at his home near Cambridge by 4pm, and did not drive, it was simply impractical.

We waited. A farm tractor came and went. Some cars carrying people who looked to be mink hunters drove by. When a Land Rover with terriers in a box went by Brian Caffarey suggested one of us drove around to see if we could find the hunt. I volunteered but found no sign of hunters in adjacent fields, nor on our side of Langton Long. I returned to the waiting members of the Committee. Dr Edwards asked at the farm and a vehicle drove by that we stopped. Between the two sources we ascertained that if we drove back to Langton Long and turned down the track on the left, past the church, we would find the hunt. We did so and saw Simon Hart waiting on the road by the track.

We drove in and parked on the grass amongst numerous supporters' vehicles. I prepared my cameras and walked to join the introductions. The meet was at 11:30am. It was a few minutes before and hounds were still held in their vehicle. Simon Hart introduced the Inquiry team to key figures in the hunt—Rose Whitcomb and Bob Tucker who were Joint Masters and Tony Smart who was Huntsman as well as Joint Master. We were also introduced to the landowner for the meet. After some brief chats and a short speech from Bob Tucker we set off on foot along the northern bank of the River Stour. We had been warned to expect to do a bit of wading if we wished to keep up with the hounds. There were 10½ couple of hounds out. These were a mixture of pure otterhounds, cross-bred otterhounds and re-trained foxhounds. Plus, there were numerous terriers in attendance. Most of these were held on couples or leads but some ran free. I estimated about 50 foot followers trailed along behind the hounds. I recognised Desmond Hobson, who had given oral evidence to the Inquiry Committee at one of the hearings, proudly wearing his Ytene Mink Hunt sweatshirt.

We had not gone far before there was a need to wade. It was a short stretch of knee deep water. The greatest difficulty appeared to be caused at the entry point into the water. Professor Winter, Professor Marsh, Dr Edwards, and Brian Caffarey gamely took it on. Of the quartet Professor Marsh paid the greatest price as the sole of his boot came adrift and had to be pulled off. The Inquiry team had been baptised into the pastime of mink hunting. Simon Hart and I also waded across as did the bulk of the mink hunters. This all generated a great deal of amusement amongst the assembled throng. The hounds waited, appearing somewhat baffled as to the delay. As for the mink, there was no sign.

Some supporters were on the southern bank of the river. The hounds crossed to and fro showing little interest. On the far side of the river I saw the village of Charlton Marshall and the houses lining the busy A350. I wondered if any residents had noticed our progress. We seemed to be in a strange time-warp as there was little sign of other people. One could almost transfer back rather more than a quarter of a century ago to the time when that river was hunted for otters by the Bucks and Courtenay Tracy Otterhounds. I asked our guide for the day, Bob Tucker, about those days and it was clear they held fond memories for him. The otter hunting I saw as a young hunt saboteur held no happy memories for me.

There is a U-bend in the River Stour across from Charlton Marshall. We by-passed that as the hounds were taken out of the water and we marched in procession across the fields. The hounds were put in again just across from Manor Dairy Farm. There is an island in the river there. We had another longer and deeper wade. Perhaps wisely in view of the state of his footwear Professor Marsh declined that opportunity for a dip. On the island hounds spoke for the first time. No-one saw a mink but hounds spoke and supporters reckoned they had detected the drag of a mink. Nothing came of it though. I later heard Tony Smart say that was the first time he had seen a deer in that area. We carried on.

Supporters enthused over how nice it was to walk such beautiful countryside. They pointed out that with no footpaths along the riverbank there they would not normally be allowed such access. Heading south along the river bank we reached an area where it divided. We waded again. Suddenly hounds spoke with an urgency and enthusiasm that suggested there might be a mink nearby. I think it was an old mill race. When hounds piled into some dense undergrowth reaching down to the river I kept a close watch on the water surface, fully expecting to see a fleeing mink. Instead there was a sharp squawk of indignation and a moorhen dashed out and took flight. Hounds remained excited and Tony Smart cast them up and down on both sides of the river. Supporters stood in midstream as did Professor Winter and Dr Edwards. I noticed hunters scouring the heights of trees lining the river looking for any mink taking refuge. I heard one supporter telling another about a previous day when they fortunately had a follower able to run up trees "*like a monkey*" to dislodge any mink seeking sanctuary at altitude. It was portrayed as wonderful entertainment.

I have seen many mink hunts in many different locations and in my opinion this hunt on this day appeared distinctly reticent in their pursuit. True enough the hounds were cast hither and thither and the supporters stomped about on the vegetation with enthusiasm but it seemed that no-one definitely saw a mink.

There was one shout of, "*There he is!*" which brought an enthusiastic response. The eyewitness described seeing a mink leave the water by a tree on the riverbank but when the hounds were taken to the exact spot mere moments later they showed no interest. The supporter, somewhat shamefacedly, then conceded it might have been another moorhen he saw. If there had have been a mink in that area that distraction probably saved his life. There was more casting about, more speaking from some hounds, some unwarranted suspicion the quarry was up a certain tree and then it was decided to move on. I asked Tony Smart what he thought had happened. It appeared the 'mink' had gone up a small brook towards the houses and the busy main road and they had decided not to press after it.

Hounds were then taken on a short excursion up the River Tarant but as soon as we reached the road we headed back towards the River Stour. At this point we parted company with Professor Marsh and Brian Caffarey as the former needed to be away. We carried on and hunted another mile of riverbank. Again, there were supporters on both sides and the hounds were encouraged to cross and hunt both sides.

After another mile of footslogging we reached Crawford Bridge at about 4pm. Hounds had shown no further interest and it was decided to call it a day. Professor Winter and Dr Edwards had accompanied the hunt from start to finish; no-one could have asked more of them. We were told the hunt had kindly arranged for transport to return us to our vehicles at the meet. It turned out to be a small van used to transport hounds. Rose Whitcomb helpfully told us it had bedding down and that as far as she knew the dogs had not wet it. Professor Winter and Dr Edwards clambered in. Simon Hart and I followed and two hunt supporters squeezed in afterwards. We sat or squatted on the floor. I went to kneel but rapidly changed my mind when I found it to be very wet with hound knows what!

We bumped our way back to the meet. When I thanked Rose Whitcomb for the lift she replied: "*Don't thank me, I would have left you to walk!!*" Her venom towards me surprised team members who heard it. I thanked the members of the Inquiry and we went our separate ways.

Mink hunting posed a very real threat to otters. The entry for the Ytene Minkhounds in *Baily's Hunting Directory* (1999-2000) said the hunt "*was formed in 1978 to hunt mink in the country of the former Courtenay Tracy Otter Hounds.*" The habitat the Ytene Minkhounds operated in was good otter country. Of the threat to the otter posed on that actual day Peter Irvine, the North Dorset Area Co-ordinator of the Dorset Otter Group, wrote to me:-

"*The Stour and its tributaries have traditionally been a stronghold for the otter and they are now playing a particularly important part in the gradual but still only partial recovery of the otter population.*

The mink hunt which took place on Saturday 20th May from Langton Long Blandford to Crawford Bridge covered a stretch of the Stour which provides a particularly rich habitat for the otter. Positive habitat factors include the following:

A good fish supply

A rural environment which is normally not disturbed by dogs or humans and certainly not in large numbers.

Areas of dense bankside vegetation which provide plenty of cover and opportunities for 'lying up' during the day. The stretch of the river near

Keynston Mill is a particularly good example with very good cover and the added benefit of the mill pond and other water features which attract otters...............

An adult otter accompanied by a young otter was recently sighted on the Stour near Charlton Marshall. Female otters can have a territory covering several miles and overlapping territories can mean that an otter with her young could be found at a wide number of different locations."

Many worked hard for the successful re-introduction of the otter to its former haunts. An indication of the attitude of some hunters comes from the following extract from the entry for the Courtenay Tracy Otter Hounds Club in *Baily's Hunting Directory* (1980-81):

"The club was formed in March 1978 following the cessation of the Courtenay Tracy Otter Hounds as an active pack. Its aims are (a) to retain control over the waters of the former Courtenay Tracy Otter Hounds, pending a possible resumption of otter hunting;....."

The Hon. Sec. of the Courtenay Tracy Otter Hounds Club at the time was a Mr R.O. Tucker—the same Mr R.O. Tucker who was then, and was in 2000, a Joint Master of the Ytene Mink Hunt.

*****

The last visit by the Inquiry was on Wednesday June 7th 2000 when they saw lamping at Vernham Dean north of Andover. It was a planned visit to watch the professional culling of foxes that had been repeatedly cancelled. The Inquiry team were Lord Burns, Lord Soulsby, Professor March and Mark Sanderson. Observers were Graham Sirl and Simon Hart.

Graham arrived at the rendezvous—Conholt Park near Vernham Dean—at 9:30pm and met Professor Marsh, the well-known fox expert David Macdonald, the gamekeeper and two assistants. Simon Hart arrived soon afterwards. They went on to meet the rest of the team at the gamekeeper's cottage at 10:30pm. They were introduced to the estate landowner, Dutch billionaire Paul Van Vlissingen (1941-2006). Paul bought Conholt Park in 1994. He and his long-term partner, the writer and art historian Caroline Tisdall, made it their permanent home. [Caroline Tisdall is now Professor of the Department of Rural Future at Oxford Brookes University. She likes angling, shoots, stalks and hawks and has boasted she *"would die in a ditch to defend hunting"*. She is a board member of the Countryside Alliance Foundation.]

Paul explained that Conholt Park amounted to 2,500 acres of woodland and grassland that he used as a private shoot. He explained that they put down (released) 20,000 birds each year, pheasant and partridges. They discussed predator control. Gamekeeper, Chris, demonstrated how he set a snare and measures he took to avoid deer being caught in snares. He told the team he set about 80 snares on the estate and checked each twice daily. He estimated he killed 20-30 foxes a year by snaring and that in total they killed about 200 foxes a year with the others being killed by lamping or fox drives. The local hunt, the Tedworth Foxhounds, visited the estate twice a year and killed around a couple of brace (four foxes).

Chris killed a wide variety of wildlife that threatened 'his' pheasants and partridges. He gave the following annual tally of native predators killed by his tunnel traps (Fenn traps set in a tunnel): 68 stoats; 32 weasels and 6 polecats. He stated he did not aim to control rabbits or hares—and that he left the rabbits in the hope and expectation that foxes would take them in preference to his reared birds.

Between 11 and 11:30pm they set off in two vehicles. Graham Sirl was allocated to one in company with Mark Sanderson, Simon Hart and David Macdonald. Graham noted that most of the fences and gates on the estate had been taken down, presumably to allow easy access. They drove for about 20 minutes. Graham observed an occupant of the vehicle in front using a light with a red filter on to sweep across the land. When the eyes of a fox were picked out in this eerie light the vehicles stopped. A person in the lamping vehicle called the fox by making squeaking sounds. Such plaintive squeaks are made by special devices, or something as simple as blowing a blade of grass, to mimic the sounds of a rabbit or hare in distress—the idea being to lure the fox closer by the prospect of an easy meal.

The unwitting fox approached the vehicle and a loud, unsilenced shot rang out. The gun was described as a .2250 rifle. The Inquiry team were driven to see the body of the fox. Shot cleanly and killed instantly he was described as a 4-5 months old cub. Chris told Graham they had killed the vixen earlier and knew her cubs were still in the area. There was one cub less. The cub had been shot at a range of about 100 metres. The marksman was asked how often the quarry ended up injured when he fired. He claimed that in his experience the fox was killed cleanly on 99.9% of occasions. He was asked at what maximum range he could shoot a fox. Shining his light in the direction of some trees to indicate distance he estimated he could shoot a fox at up to 200 metres.

After the cub was shot and examined the Inquiry team were asked if they wished to carry on and see more. Lord Soulsby said they had witnessed what they wanted to see and could leave. So they did. They drove back to the gamekeeper's cottages at about midnight and went their separate ways.

*****

Questions were asked about how the visits were conducted and the value of them. Did the Inquiry team see much 'real' hunting and coursing? In 2000 most of the hunting and hare coursing the Committee of Inquiry set out to observe was open to public view. Meets of many Foxhound packs and of nearly all Staghound packs were advertised in *Horse and Hound* and local papers. Some meets of Harriers and Beagles were likewise publicised. The phone numbers of all hunts were listed in *Baily's Hunting Directory* and their meets could, with a little encouragement, be gained over the phone. The National Coursing Club published an annual fixtures list. Venues were not given but contact details for the Club Secretaries were and in practice it was not hard to elicit the required information. With the Welsh gun packs, it was harder, but still not impossible to find out meets. Lamping was different. Finding out where that took place was usually a matter of knowing the individual(s) involved. Given that the hunting and coursing were all comparatively easy to access there were options open to those planning these Inquiry visits. There could have been open visits, secret visits or a mixture. Some visits could have been made with the agreement of the hunt concerned with only a CA observer present and no-one from our side if in return a similar number of visits were made to hunts at our instigation with only ourselves having foreknowledge and attending, and not the CA.

From the point of view of gathering information regarding the true nature of hunting and coursing with dogs it is unfortunate that a poor option for visiting was selected. Further, perhaps for reasons of economy, within this poor option the way the visits were conducted was hardly conducive to acquiring the most accurate information.

It appeared that apart from the initial request as to what they would like to see the agenda throughout was mainly set by the CA. Of the 22 visits, no fewer than 17 were at the behest of the CA. Three were at the request of the CPHA. These were the Essex Farmers and Union Foxhounds, the German drag hunt, and the drag coursing club at Wickwar. At the Essex Farmers and Union Foxhounds no hunting was witnessed. The visit to the Brecon and Talybont Foxhounds, was at the request of Lord Burns and the second visit to the Blencathra Foxhounds, by Lord Soulsby alone, was because the latter missed the earlier visit.

Perhaps the aspect that caused most concern was that at all the hunting visits, but not the coursing where it did not apply, the transportation and guides were provided by the hunting fraternity (a possible exception to this was at the German drag hunt where I do not know what transport arrangements were made). In effect the Committee of Inquiry embarked on an escorted tour of the hunting field.

The Inquiry team chose the start and finish times but apart from that they largely went where the hunting fraternity wanted them to go and saw what the hunting fraternity wanted them to see. It was hardly surprising that little untoward came into view. There was evidence that the worse cruelty that occurred on the days of the visits took place when the Inquiry team were safely out of sight. For all their good intentions it is clear, with hindsight, that this Hunting Inquiry had about as much hope of successfully witnessing the cruelty that evidently concerned the public as would sending a Home Office Inquiry team on an arranged visit to check for cruelty in boarding schools or children's homes.

Early on I heard Lord Burns explain their visits were important for the Inquiry to get a 'flavour' of the hunting field. To gain an impression of who took part. It was said that members of the Committee had already seen plenty of videos of fox hunting, stag hunting etc. but these were somewhat dismissed with the view that such videos could be edited and used to portray any viewpoint. The Hunting Inquiry wanted to see the 'real thing' but for all their honest endeavours and for all the miles they travelled I feared they saw but a fraction.

CHAPTER SEVENTEEN
**2000, political work, Burns Inquiry report published. The road
to the Hunting Act (2004).**

The decision to have the Lord Burns Hunting Inquiry secured the safety of the 1999/2000 hunting and coursing season. The LACS expected hunting might be banned as early as before the start of the 2000/2001 season. It could have been but more years were to pass. On March 1st 2000 Mike Watson MSP introduced his Protection of Wild Mammals (Scotland) Bill to the Scottish Parliament. The following month Jack Straw suggested a solution to the hunting problem by offering MPs a choice of three options: outright ban; stricter regulation of hunting; or no change.

It was June 9th 2000 that the Report of the Committee of Inquiry into Hunting with Dogs in England and Wales was published. If the hunters had expected that their friend, Jack Straw, would ensure it was supportive of hunting they were sorely disappointed. Here are key extracts from the summary of their findings:

1) Foxhunting
The evidence which we have seen suggests that, in the case of the killing of a fox by hounds above ground, death is not always effected by a single bite to the neck or shoulders by the leading hound resulting in the dislocation of the cervical vertebrae. In a proportion of cases it results from massive injuries to the chest and vital organs, although insensibility and death will normally follow within a matter of seconds once the fox is caught. There is a lack of firm scientific evidence about the effect on the welfare of a fox of being closely pursued, caught and killed above ground by hounds. We are satisfied, nevertheless, that this experience seriously compromises the welfare of the fox. (Paragraph 6.49)
Although there is no firm scientific evidence, we are satisfied that the activity of digging out and shooting a fox involves a serious compromise of its welfare, bearing in mind the often protracted nature of the process and the fact that the fox is prevented from escaping. (Paragraph 6.52)
It is likely that, in the event of a ban on hunting, many farmers and landowners would resort to a greater degree than at present to other methods to control the numbers of foxes. We cannot say if this would lead to more, or fewer, foxes being killed than at present. (Paragraph 6.58)
 None of the legal methods of fox control is without difficulty from an animal welfare perspective. Both snaring and shooting can have serious adverse welfare implications. (Paragraph 6.59)
Our tentative conclusion is that lamping using rifles, if carried out properly and in appropriate circumstances, has fewer adverse welfare implications than hunting, including digging-out. However, in areas where lamping is not feasible or safe, there would be a greater use of other methods. We are less confident that the use of shotguns, particularly in daylight, is preferable to hunting from a welfare perspective. We consider that the use of snaring is a particular cause for concern. (Paragraph 6.60)

In practice, it is likely that some mixture of all of these methods would be used. In the event of a ban on hunting, it is possible that the welfare of foxes in upland areas could be affected adversely, unless dogs could be used, at least to flush foxes from cover. (Paragraph 6.61)

2) Deerhunting

Although there are still substantial areas of disagreement, there is now a better understanding of the physiological changes which occur when a deer is hunted. Most scientists agree that deer are likely to suffer in the final stages of hunting. The available evidence does not enable us to resolve the disagreement about the point at which, during the hunt, the welfare of the deer becomes seriously compromised. There is also a lack of firm information about what happens to deer which escape, although the available research suggests that they are likely to recover. (Paragraph 6.33)

Stalking, if carried out to a high standard and with the availability of a dog or dogs to help find any wounded deer that escape, is in principle the better method of culling deer from an animal welfare perspective. In particular, it obviates the need to chase the deer in the way which occurs in hunting. (Paragraph 6.39)

3) Harehunting

There are two areas of welfare concern in respect of hare hunting and coursing: the chase and the "kill". Although no scientific studies have been carried out, there is evidence that, in the case of coursing, there can be a significant delay before a hare which has been caught by the dogs is dispatched.

There is a lack of firm scientific evidence about the effect on the welfare of a hare of being closely pursued, caught and killed by hounds during hunting. We are satisfied, nevertheless, that although death and insensibility will normally follow within a matter of seconds, this experience seriously compromises the welfare of the hare. (Paragraph 6.67)

We are similarly satisfied that being pursued, caught and killed by dogs during coursing seriously compromises the welfare of the hare. It is clear, moreover, that, if the dog or dogs catch the hare, they do not always kill it quickly. There can also sometimes be a significant delay, in "driven" coursing, before the "picker up" reaches the hare and dispatches it (if it is not already dead). In the case of "walked up" coursing, the delay is likely to be even longer. (Paragraph 6.68)

In the event of a ban on hunting and coursing hares, it seems likely that a few more would be shot than at present. There are concerns about the welfare implications of shooting hares because of wounding rates. (Paragraph 6.69)

4) Minkhunting

There is a lack of firm scientific evidence about the welfare implications of hunting mink. There seems reason to suppose, however, that being closely pursued, caught and killed by hounds, or being dug out or bolted, seriously compromises the welfare of the mink. The kill, by the hounds or by shooting, is normally quick once the mink is caught. In the absence of hunting, more mink would probably be killed by shooting and, mainly, trapping. These methods involve welfare implications but we do not have sufficient evidence to conclude how they compare with those raised by hunting. (Paragraph 6.71)

The Inquiry team made other pertinent observations. About the effects of hunting on other wildlife they noted (6.75): "*There is some evidence that hunting incidentally affects the welfare of wildlife. In particular, we have been informed about the stopping-up of badger setts and a few isolated cases of disturbance to otter - both of which are protected species - and wildfowl during mink hunting. The frequency of such incidents is disputed.*"

They noted the harm caused by rioting hounds (6.76): "*The welfare of pets which are attacked by hounds is clearly compromised, and their owners suffer great distress.*"

They considered the question of injuries caused to terriers when foxes are dug out (6.82): "*We discussed in paragraph 6.51 the question whether fights occur between terriers and foxes underground in the course of digging-out/terrierwork or bolting (eg from rockholes). As we indicated, there is no firm information on this, although we are satisfied that fights do occur from time to time and that these would involve some compromise of the welfare of the terrier.*"

About the role of hunting in habitat conservation they observed (7.42): "*Hunting has clearly played a very significant role in the past in the formation of the rural landscape and in the creation and management of areas of nature conservation. Nowadays, however, hunting with dogs is likely to form only a relatively minor factor in determining farmers' and landowners' land management practices. It still plays a role, though, in certain localities in respect of woodland planting and management.*

Hunting exerts much less influence than agricultural market and policy trends, the management of game for shooting or incentives under agri-environment schemes. With the possible exception of hare conservation, a ban on hunting with dogs would be unlikely to have a major impact from a conservation perspective. In the case of the hare, on those estates which favour hare coursing or hunting, rather than shooting, a ban might lead farmers and landowners to pay less attention to encouraging hare numbers. The loss of habitat suitable for hares could have serious consequences for a number of birds and other animals."

On drag and bloodhound hunting they found this (8.44): "*Drag and bloodhound hunting are different from live quarry hunting. In particular, they involve the laying of a man-made trail. They lack the unpredictability and, consequently, some of the interest associated with a live quarry. The hound work, especially in the case of the draghounds, is less subtle and complex.*

(8.45): There would be greater incentive, in the event of a ban, to expand the number of drag and bloodhound packs and the level of participation in both sports. Because bloodhounds are in short supply, and are not easy

to breed, any growth in the short term would mainly come from using foxhounds for draghunting. The scope for expansion is impossible to predict with any accuracy at present because the existence of hunting as a complementary activity means that there has been little motivation in practice to develop the sports. The popularity of horse riding, however, suggests that greater efforts would be made to develop substitute activities in the event of a ban on hunting. The kinds of opportunities that drag and bloodhound hunting already offer in some areas might be expanded. There is some scope for adjusting the level of skill required in drag and bloodhound hunting to riders of different ability levels. There is also possible scope for developing other forms of cross country riding, possibly on a fee-paying basis."

And this about drag coursing and the role for these humane activities in providing attractions for rural communities (8.52): "In the event of a ban on live hare coursing, drag coursing might have some appeal, especially to those owners of greyhounds who are essentially interested in racing their dogs. It would have less appeal for those people who particularly enjoy the contest between the hare and the dog.

It is unlikely that either drag and bloodhound hunting or drag coursing would of themselves mitigate to any substantial extent any adverse effects on the rural economy or the social life of the countryside arising from a ban on hunting."

They commented on the trespass, disruption and disturbance caused by hunts (9.8): "There are too many cases of trespass, disruption and disturbance. These are most common where hunts operate too close to residential areas and interfere with the movement of traffic on roads. We do not want to exaggerate these problems but they can cause distress to the individuals and families involved. To some extent hunts could avoid these problems themselves, by being more selective about the areas in which they hunt. This would be likely to lead to fewer hunts. Steps that might be taken, in the absence of a ban, include: restricting hunting in certain parts of hunts' countries; reducing or amalgamating the number of hunts; requiring permission to be obtained in writing on a regular basis from farmers and landowners; penalising trespass, or repeated trespass, over land where permission has not been given; and improving means of seeking and obtaining redress."

They recommended that in the absence of a ban hunting should be more open to scrutiny (9.10): "In the absence of a ban, organised hunting should be conducted on a more open basis than at present in order to provide greater reassurance that approved procedures are being followed. One possible option would be the appointment of individuals as independent monitors who would have the freedom to take photographs and video evidence. Their task would be to observe organised hunting and to take up with the hunt, and others as necessary, any concerns that they might have about the way in which it is being conducted. They might also serve as a channel for complaints by others. It would no doubt be helpful if monitors were appointed by a reputable, independent body."

When it came to considering cub hunting it is clear the Inquiry were sceptical over claims from the hunters. Here is what they found: "*9.11 We described in paragraph 2.29 the practice of autumn/cub hunting of foxes. The MFHA and the Countryside Alliance, in their evidence to us, argued that autumn/cub hunting serves a number of useful purposes. They pointed out that a survey of hunts carried out in January 2000 showed that some 40% of the foxes killed by the registered packs were killed during autumn/cub hunting and that it takes place at a time when the fox population is at its highest and most concentrated. [529]*

(9.12): It is also argued by the hunts concerned that autumn/cub hunting is useful in dispersing the fox population, thus reducing their concentration in any one area. [530]

(9.13): The third purpose served by autumn/cub hunting, in the view of the MFHA and the Countryside Alliance, is that it serves as a very useful means of introducing young hounds to hunting. Autumn/cub hunting takes place in a comparatively confined area and with fewer riders and other followers around to distract them. [531]

(9.14): It does not seem to us, from the evidence we received, that these arguments are wholly persuasive. As we noted in paragraph 5.36, there is little evidence that, in spite of the numbers killed, this activity is particularly effective in reducing fox populations or that dispersal has the benefits which the MFHA claim. It is clear too that it is not necessary to practise autumn/cub hunting in order to train young hounds. A number of packs, including the Fell Packs and the Welsh gun packs, use other methods.

(9.15): Those who object to autumn/cub hunting also point to the practice of "holding-up" i.e. the steps taken to prevent the escape of foxes from the wood or coppice. We are aware of the concern which some people feel about this practice and, more generally, about the principle of using young foxes (whether fully grown or not) to train young, inexperienced hounds.

(9.16) In the absence of a ban, consideration could be given to a number of options for responding to the concerns about autumn/cub hunting. These options include: prohibiting the practice entirely; introducing a closed season for hunting foxes, so that hunting would start at a later date than it does at present; permitting it only in those areas where it was clearly necessary as a means of controlling fox numbers; and prohibiting the practice of "holding up"."

The Inquiry commented on the vexatious issue of digging out (9.17): "*Digging out and bolting foxes with the use of terriers was a topic which also aroused strong feelings on both sides of the debate. On the one hand, it was argued, especially by hunts, farmers in upland sheep-rearing areas and gamekeepers, that digging-out or bolting (see paragraphs 2.23 to 2.25) was very important in controlling the number of foxes. [532] It was pointed out that, in some areas, well over half of the foxes killed by hunts resulted from digging-out and that it was the only legal means of killing foxes underground. [533] Moreover, as we noted in paragraph 5.27, it* seems likely that an even larger number are killed as the result of terrierwork by other groups and individuals. There is also the issue that terriers may be used to dispatch orphaned cubs.

On the other hand, many opponents of hunting clearly felt that it was wholly unacceptable that a fox, having gone to ground, whether in a natural or artificial earth, should be dug-out or bolted. Their concerns were exacerbated by reports of injuries received by foxes and terriers fighting underground.

Another point which needs to be borne in mind is that the fact that digging out foxes is a legal activity makes it more difficult to take action to combat badger-baiting since those who appear to be intent on the latter can argue that they are planning to dig out foxes.

Digging-out and bolting foxes is a complex issue because of the perceived needs in different parts of England and Wales. In the absence of a ban, serious consideration could be given as to whether this practice should be allowed to continue and, if so, under what conditions. Possible options would be to ban it altogether; confine it to those areas where it is considered necessary as a means of controlling fox numbers or in the interests of animal welfare; make the practice subject to the general legislation on cruelty by removing the present exemptions for hunting; or improve monitoring by the hunts and by any independent monitors."

And they said this about stopping up (9.21): "*Another practice which gives rise to particular concern is that of stopping up foxes' earths, badger setts and other possible refuges before a foxhunt begins (see paragraph 2.20). As we noted in Chapter 7, we received a good deal of evidence about this activity, especially from badger watch groups. [534] They argue that there are still far too many instances in which hunts and others are illegally stopping-up badger setts by using hard material or soil cut back from the sett itself.*

The Countryside Alliance argued that there was no evidence of any malpractice. [535] Whilst we accept that there is a lack of firm evidence linking malpractice to the hunts, we do not think we can disregard entirely the written and oral evidence we received from badger protection groups and their supporters on this issue.

We recognise that badgers are now more numerous than at the time when they were first given legal protection. We also recognise that, if hunts were not permitted to stop up badger setts, foxes would be more likely to go to ground there and would have to be left. Similarly, we recognise that if the same prohibition applied to foxes' earths many more foxes would escape unscathed. However, consideration could be given to both of these issues in the absence of a ban.

There have been many suggestions put to us that, at times, hunts and others contravene the law relating to the stopping-up of badger setts. One option, in the absence of a ban on hunting, would be to remove the present exemption for hunts. In the case of stopping-up of foxes' earths, there are a number of possible options which could be considered in the absence of a ban. These include: prohibiting the practice entirely; confining it to those areas where it is considered necessary in the interests of controlling fox numbers; or otherwise limiting the circumstances in which it may be done or the way in which it can be carried out."

The Inquiry was scathing about the use of artificial earths by fox hunts (9.25): "*It is clear that it used to be common practice, especially in the case of hunts in lowland England, to provide artificial earths for foxes, particularly when planting new coppices or coverts. We received no firm evidence that this is still being done but we were told that some existing earths were still being "re-furbished" and even that foxes were being encouraged to use them by, for example, providing food. [536]*

The Countryside Alliance told us that, given that the purpose of hunting in many areas was to preserve a sustainable and healthy fox population, they did not consider that the practice of providing artificial earths was objectionable if the particular locality did not already offer suitable habitat. They argued that this balance between preservation and control was seen in other contexts such as game shooting and fishing. [537] It was also put to us that artificial earths could be useful in helping to ensure that foxes' earths were in suitable places: for example, away from chicken runs. We consider, however, that it is hard to reconcile any use of artificial earths by the hunts with the argument that foxes are a pest and that their numbers need to be controlled through hunting.

The active use of artificial earths, with a view to hunting, is inconsistent with the stated objective of controlling fox numbers through hunting. In the absence of a ban, hunts could be required, or encouraged, to end this practice."

The Inquiry team commented upon interfering with the quarry's flight (9.28):

"*Deliberately interfering with the flight of the quarry takes place in a number of situations, for example:*
- *preventing the flight of young and adult foxes during autumn/cub hunting (see paragraph 9.15 above)*
- *attempting to prevent the quarry from going onto land where the hunt does not have permission to go*
- *trying to keep the quarry - and therefore the hounds - away from areas such as roads and railway lines*
- *attempting (on the part of hunt saboteurs) to rescue the quarry or to help it make its escape.*

The research which we commissioned on the welfare of hunted deer indicated that close contact with human beings, including attempts at interfering with its flight, had a noticeable effect on the deer. [538] Such interference, whether in relation to deer or other animals, also seems to sit uncomfortably with the notion that hunts usually embrace of hunting an animal in its "wild and natural state".

There is concern about deliberate direct interference by people with the quarry's flight. In the absence of a ban, action could be taken to amend, where necessary, the rules of the relevant associations and to ensure that such interference does not take place unless it is in the interests of the

467

safety of the people or animals involved. In particular, provision could be made to ensure that there was no interference with the flight in order to prolong the chase, prevent the quarry escaping or to prevent it entering land where the hunt did not have permission to go."

The Inquiry was positive about recommending a closed season for hares (9.31): *"We noted in paragraphs 2.48 and 2.54 that there is no legally-prescribed closed season for hunting and coursing hares but that the rules of the relevant associations forbid hunting after the end of March and coursing after 10 March.*

We also noted in paragraph 5.78 that hares breed from February onwards - and, indeed, we understand that hares sometimes produce leverets in January. [539] In our view there is a case for having a legally-prescribed closed season for killing hares. This ought, logically, to apply to all forms of killing, including shooting.

There is understandable concern that the seasons for hare coursing and hunting are too long in relation to the hare's breeding season. In the absence of a ban on hunting, an option would be to introduce a closed season. Consideration would also need to be given to whether a closed season should apply to shooting."

They also expressed concern about the practice of stag hunts hunting hinds with calves (9.34): *"Concern was expressed to us about the practice of hunting hinds with calves. It was argued that, at the start of the season, hinds may have a totally dependent calf at foot; that calves have great difficulty in keeping up with a chase; and that eventually the hind is forced to abandon it. [540] The MDHA argued, on the other hand, that by November last year's calves are able to thrive without their mother and said that any hind with a late-born calf would not be hunted. [541] We simply record that, whatever the precise degree of dependence, a number of people clearly find it distressing to see a hind and calf being chased and to observe the apparent dilemma of the hind about whether to stay with the calf or to pick up speed and leave it behind.*

Hunting hinds with a calf gives rise to understandable concern. It puts the hind in a position of having to choose between saving itself and staying with the calf. We are not able to say how often this situation occurs but action could be taken to end this practice in the absence of a ban."

Paragraph 9.36 was prophetic: *"All these concerns about these practical aspects of hunting would be resolved, in principle, by a ban on hunting, subject to any exemptions or exceptions which were considered necessary."*

They were surprised over the lack of formal control of hunting (9.48): *"We think it is perhaps surprising that, without a greater measure of regulation, hunts should be able to go into the countryside with the responsibility for a pack of hounds that are often not under close control, and which can have a marked effect on the lives of other people."*

The Inquiry foresaw problems in implementing a ban when they said this about how any ban might be enforced (10.37): *"In principle, the enforcement of legislation can be carried out by a number of different*

468

agencies, including the police, local councils or bodies, such as inspectorates, established specifically for the purpose.

The last two approaches seem to us to be more appropriate in the case of regulating or licensing an activity, rather than simply enforcing a prohibition. Accordingly, we think that, in the case of a ban on hunting, the obvious course would be to look to the police to enforce the legislation in the normal way.

It was put to us by the Countryside Alliance and others that the police might face certain difficulties in enforcing a ban. The main arguments advanced were that:

- the law would be strongly resented by many people, some of whom would not comply with it
- because the police are reluctant to enforce legislation where there is a lack of public support, they would not seek to give it a high priority
- police resources were, in any case, already heavily stretched, which would also encourage them to give enforcement a low priority
- the police would find it difficult to enforce a ban because many of the activities take place in fairly remote areas and, with the exception of hunting by the registered packs, many of the activities would not be very visible. [549]

We recognise that enforcing legislation of this kind would pose difficulties for the police and the prosecuting authorities. We also recognise, however, that similar difficulties are experienced in other areas of the law. It would be for Parliament to weigh up these arguments, amongst others, in considering whether a ban should be introduced and the form it should take.

Legislation implementing a ban might well pose some enforcement difficulties for the police. These matters should be considered by Parliament when examining a Bill."

The Inquiry also commissioned post mortems to be done on animals killed by hunts and coursing. What did the post mortems, carried out for the Inquiry by the University of Bristol, reveal about the death of foxes caught above ground by hounds? Was the 'quick nip to the back of the neck' fact or fiction? Here are extracts from the Report's findings:-

"Fox 3 (Royal Artillery Foxhounds, Salisbury Plain, 3rd April 2000)
This animal was hunted with hounds for approximately 15 minutes. The fox was killed on the surface by the hounds.
Cause of death
Profound trauma by repeated dog bite. Post mortem examination revealed little tissue damage in the head, neck and shoulder region, pronounced damage to the ribcage and thoracic organs, and profound damage to the abdomen. It is probable that trauma to the abdomen, hindquarters or chest were the cause of death in this animal.
Fox 4 (Royal Artillery Foxhounds, Salisbury Plain, 8th April 2000)

This animal was hunted with hounds for less than 2 minutes. The fox was killed on the surface by the hounds.

Cause of death

Profound trauma by repeated dog bite. Post mortem examination revealed little tissue damage in the head, neck and shoulder region, pronounced damage to the ribcage and the thoracic organs, and profound damage to the abdomen. It is probable that trauma to the abdomen, hindquarters or chest were the cause of death in this animal. It is not possible to determine the time period from first bite to death from this post mortem material"

Neither fox was stated to have been killed by the 'quick nip to the back of the neck'. The post mortems revealed notable cruelty during digging out:

"Post Mortem findings.

Fox 1. (Cotswold Foxhounds, Miserden Park, Nr. Cirencester 1st April 2000)

This animal was hunted by the hounds for approximately 31 minutes. The fox went to ground and a terrier was sent down. After 9 minutes, the fox left the earth and was shot as it left the hole.

Apparent Pre-death trauma

Haemorrhage in the soft tissues of the lateral aspect of the proximal right antebrachium (the upper outside region of the forearm) provide evidence of some trauma before death.

Cause of death

Death was caused by a free bullet shot to the head with a .22 calibre single shot pistol"

It is clear that fox 1 was bitten before death, not an 'instant kill'.

"Fox 2 (Royal Artillery Foxhounds, Salisbury Plain 3rd April 2000)

This animal was hunted with hounds for approximately 7 minutes. The fox then went to ground and a terrier equipped with a radio collar was sent down. After approximately 25 minutes of digging, the fox was revealed, the terrier removed, and the fox shot in the hole with a .22 calibre single shot pistol. Two shots were required.

Apparent Pre-death trauma.

1) Pre hunt

a) Presence of shotgun pellets in the left side of the head, the left forelimb, the abdomen and the left hindlimb. These pellets are from a past shooting, from the left side of the animal. Dissection of individual pellets showed them to be walled off in fibrous tissue indicating healing of the pellet wounds.

2) Post commencement of hunt

b) Multiple bite wounds on the face and the top of the head.

c) Damage to the right eye.

d) Bite wounds, haemorrhage and oedema in the region of the larynx and lower neck.

e) A .22 calibre bullet in the muscle tissue of the left shoulder region and some radiographic evidence of damage to the vertebra of the neck in the

region of the 3rd and 4th cervical vertebrae. The shooting of this fox was observed, and it was apparent that this first bullet did not kill the animal. Cause of death
A second shot with a .22 calibre bullet caused death."

Having survived an earlier shooting fox 2 was hunted by hounds then savaged below ground by a terrier. He was then wounded by a shot in the shoulder/neck region. The pistol was reloaded and the fox eventually killed. Post mortem reports on the bodies of coursed hares were notably shocking (6.64):

"We arranged post mortems on the carcasses of twelve hares which had been killed during organised coursing events. These were carried out by the Department of Clinical Veterinary Medicine at the University of Cambridge. There were difficulties, however, in determining the cause of death in some cases because the neck of the hare is almost invariably broken by the "picker-up" as soon as the hare is retrieved from the dogs. The findings were that the cause of death in one case was probably fatal injuries caused by the dogs. In six other cases it was not clear whether the actions of the dogs, or the picker-up, had led to the hare's death. In the remaining five cases the picker-up was judged to have been the cause of death."

Hare coursers claimed their dogs always killed the hare instantly. These post mortems revealed the truth. The italics below are extracts from the Inquiry Report. Of twelve hares examined eight were female, four were male. Of the eight females five were pregnant and of these three were lactating. Two of the pregnant hares were assessed as being in 'early' pregnancy, two in 'mid term' pregnancy and one was described as 'full term' pregnant. Three were found to contain two foetuses each and two contained three foetuses.

Hare reference number 5 was assessed as 'full term' pregnant. Her reproductive status was described: "Mature Female. Advanced late pregnancy (two large fully-haired foetuses, weighing 176 and 162g resp. located one in each uterine horn). Milk in mammary glands." Her state was summarised: "This heavily pregnant female hare was in good condition. The large size of the foetuses and presence of milk in the mammary glands suggests she was close to giving birth. Recent severe traumatic damage with local haemorrhage was present, involving mainly the right side of the thorax. Some of the injury to the left hindleg was not associated with haemorrhage and may have occurred after death."

For that hare it was not possible to assess whether she was killed by the dogs or the Picker-up. One of the females killed, that was not pregnant, was judged to be recovering from a previous non-lethal, shooting episode as she had shotgun pellets beneath her skin.

What of the condition of the males post mortemed? Hare number 2 had "Nostril and genital lesions suggestive of hare syphilis". Hare number 6 had "Genital lesions suggestive of hare syphilis". Hare number 8 had "Area of corneal opacity in the right eye". Finally, hare number 10 had "Nostril lesions suggestive of hare syphilis".

471

Of these four hares, one had been killed by the Picker-up and for the remainder it was unclear whether they were killed by the Picker-up or by the dogs. Of the twelve hares post mortemed ten were either pregnant, injured by shot, suffering from syphilis or had impaired vision.

*****

The Lord Burns Inquiry was estimated to have cost over £500,000. Publication of their Report increased public pressure to ban hunting. In response hunters stepped up their militant protests. In July 2000, pro-hunt protesters organized under the title of the Rural Action Group (RAG) blocked the Severn Bridge to coincide with the Parliamentary debate on the Lord Burns Inquiry report. South Wales police labelled the action 'irresponsible and dangerous'. One West Country newspaper described RAG as 'anarchists with manners'. In response RAG threatened that they would 'shut down every motorway in Britain if we have to.'

Arnold Garvey, Editor of *Horse and Hound*, supported the actions of RAG saying: "*I commend our Welsh friends for their initiative.*" One prominent protester was Brian Hughes who held various positions within the Llangeinor Hunt and was Chairman in 1998. The 'Peoples Fuel Lobby' who specialized in picketing fuel depots causing fuel shortages and great public inconvenience was headed by David Handley, Master of the Monmouthshire Foxhounds from 1985 to 1987.

Arnold Garvey had demonstrated his own regard for rules and regulations when in May 2000 he took his seven-week-old Jack Russell puppy hidden in his hand luggage on a Go flight from London Stansted to Rome. British Airways Go-Fly (1998-2005) services banned all animals on their flights. Arnold admitted not telling the airline he intended to travel with a pet. He explained the dog was a present for his sister in Rome and therefore did not require a pet passport and that he had all the necessary paperwork. It was only when the puppy escaped and urinated on another passenger's newspaper that staff were alerted to his presence. Arnold Garvey was reported to the Captain, given 'a firm dressing down' but let off with a caution. He later complained: "*I was made to look like a smuggler.*"

*****

The hunting season 2000/2001 started as usual. In December 2000, the Government introduced its first Hunting Bill. A month later, on January 17th 2001 during Prime Minister's Questions in the House of Commons, Prime Minister Tony Blair again repeated his opposition to hunting saying: "*I have made it quite clear, and my position has not changed. I am opposed to fox hunting for the reasons that I have given on many occasions.....I think that it is absolutely certain that the will of this place will be made very clear.*" [That does not suggest his opposition to hunting was the transitory, ill-considered, off-the-cuff remark he implied in his autobiography]. That hunting season that had started routinely ended abruptly in February 2001 because of the outbreak of foot and mouth disease amongst farm animals.

Violence from hunt supporters towards anti-hunt politicians increased. When Michael Meacher MP attended a live TV debate in the village hall at Moreton-in-the-Marsh on February 3rd he was pelted with eggs and flour. He had to leave the building under police escort. When Agriculture Minister Nick Brown arrived at Saxon Hall, Raunds, Wellingborough he was heckled and doused in pig urine by hunt supporters. In response Nick Brown was defiant: "*There is no amount of shouting or this sort of protest which will change my mind about hunting. People should not make their living out of cruelty*."

February 28th 2001 MPs voted, by a majority of 179, for an outright ban on hunting. The Hunting Bill cleared the House of Commons and went to the House of Lords. The CA had planned another march in London—Reclaim our Countryside Day—for March 18th but that was cancelled due to the outbreak of foot and mouth disease. The Guardian reported that up to half a million people had been expected to descend on London to express concerns about a raft of countryside measures, including plans to ban hunting. The Lords and the election cycle came to the rescue of hunting. On March 26th 2001 the Lords voted, by a majority of 249, against the ban. The Hunting Bill ran out of time when the General Election was called.

Election day, Thursday June 7th, 2001, saw Labour returned to power with a majority of 167. The Queen's Speech on June 20th included the following commitment: "*My Government will enable a free vote to take place on the future of hunting with dogs*." To boost campaigns for a ban the League produced an astonishing film, *Chaos in the Countryside—the secret face of hunting exposed* that revealed the violent reality lurking behind the glamorous façade of hunting. It contained film of fox, deer, mink and hare hunting, hare coursing, terrierwork and footage from inside a hunt kennels. The film also showed huntsmen, hunt supporters and hunt stewards causing mayhem and havoc as they harassed or attacked anti-hunt monitors, hunt saboteurs, journalists and the passing public.

As the noose tightened on the hunting world its apologists became ever more desperate and attention seeking. They even seized upon the horrific 9/11 attacks on Tuesday September 11th 2001 as an opportunity to promote their cause. Janet George commented on her website on September 13th: "*The horrors in America were of unprecedented scale and horror. But the scale is the only fundamental difference between Tuesday's atrocities and the regular behaviour of animal 'rights' extremists in this country and abroad.*"

The difference in scale was that in America nearly 3000 were killed and over 6000 injured and in the hunting fields of England a hunt supporter beating a conservationist just occasionally gets hit back. Dawn Preston from the HSA commented: "*I often think that there is nothing the pro-bloodsports lobby can do which will surprise me, but this comment sinks to an all time low. It is wholly inappropriate, and deeply offensive, to compare the actions of hunt saboteurs, using non-violent direct action against hunts, to that of those who took the lives of several thousand people last week. Certainly lives have also been lost in the fight to stop bloodsports, but perversely for George's argument, it is the lives of hunt saboteurs that have been lost—along with the lives of countless wild animals. If ever a more shining example of the self-absorbed world of the hunting fraternity can be found I will be surprised, a fact made even more horrific as George must truly know the power of her words—after all she was a Press Officer for the bastion of bloodsports itself in the past."*

Wednesday September 19th, the Scottish Parliament voted 84 to 34 in favour of a ban on fox hunting and hare coursing. Scott Barrie MSP spoke passionately during the debate saying: "*I do not want Scotland to become a haven for low-life fox baiters, high-life mounted hunters and frustrated stag hunters. I want to ban hunting. I ask my comrades on the Labour benches and in other parties to take a step forward today, not just for animal welfare, but also for morality and the reputation of our country.*" Commenting on the result Les Ward, Chairman of the SCAHD, said: "*This is a great day for Scotland's wildlife. For too long a small number of individuals have been free to bait and bully wild animals for sport.*"

Westminster politicians were determined to rid our countryside of the savagery of hunting. In October 2001 more than 200 MPs backed a House of Commons motion calling on the Government to honour its promises and make time for a vote on banning hunting.

December 17th 2001 brought some relief for hunters, but not for our wildlife, when hunting resumed after being banned for 10 months following the outbreak of foot and mouth disease. The last case of foot and mouth before that was confirmed on September 30th.

*****

February 13th 2002 was a momentous day for Scottish wildlife. The Scottish Parliament voted by 83 to 36 to ban hunting with hounds. The Protection of Wild Mammals (Scotland) Act 2002 made it illegal to chase or deliberately kill mammals with dogs. The Act came into effect on August 1st 2002.

Tony Blair, at Prime Minister's Questions, Wednesday February 27th 2002, confirmed there would be a vote on hunting. The next day Government Ministers set out a timetable for a hunting bill affecting England and Wales. On Monday March 18th 2002 the House of Commons were asked to choose from three options: a complete ban; the compromise of licensed hunting; and no change to hunting. The Commons voted for a complete ban by 386 to 175 votes. Tony Blair participated for the first time—and abstained. The next day the Lords rejected the complete ban by 331 to 74 votes and instead backed the 'middle way' option, licensed hunting, by 366 votes to 59.

March 21st brought the conclusion nearer when Rural Affairs Minister, Alun Michael, announced Government plans to resolve the situation. There would be a six-month consultation period to try to reach a compromise between the Commons and the Lords. A new Bill would be brought forward. The Government would facilitate the use of the Parliament Act to overcome objections in the House of Lords if necessary. The Government would allow MPs to amend any Bill put before them if it was not to their liking. The Government was committed to enabling Parliament to resolve the hunting issue during the life of that Parliament.

Aware of hunt supporters threatening mayhem and mischief Douglas Batchelor made clear the League's view: "*The pro-hunt lobby has threatened to take to the streets, to hijack all Government Bills in the Lords and to organise more fuel strikes. They are saying that they do not accept the will of democratically elected MPs. Who rules? The elected representatives of the people or those who believe it is fine to pursue and kill wild animals for sport? It is time Tony Blair got a grip, banned hunting and coursing and moved on to other key issues. None of us will forgive Blair for wasting a further two years and thousands of animals' lives before enacting the ban he has always promised. Just do it Tony! Ban hunting now!*" (*Wildlife Guardian*, Spring 2002)

Starting Monday September 9th 2002 the Department for Environment, Food and Rural Affairs (DEFRA) held public hearings on hunting with dogs at Portcullis House near Parliament. They were chaired by DEFRA Minister Alun Michael. I attended and gave evidence on Wednesday September 11th. Mike Hobday met me at Liverpool Street. He was concerned about my criminal record being used to discredit our side. The morning hearing was from 11:45 am to 12:45 pm and the afternoon session from 1:40 pm to 3:00 pm. We held a minute's silence at 1:46 pm in remembrance of the outrage the previous year. I noticed my erstwhile colleagues Jim Barrington and Miles Cooper attending for the hunting side. Peter Luff, a pro-hunt MP, generated guffaws of laughter when he welcomed me with, "*You are a man of conviction....*" (For extracts from transcript see Appendix)

Sunday September 22nd 2002 was another march day. The CA staged a huge 'Liberty and Livelihood' march in London to protest against any ban on hunting with dogs in England and Wales. It was well organised and hunt supporters travelled to it from all over the UK and abroad. The 'Liberty' march started from Hyde Park and the 'Livelihood' march from Mansion House. The CA claimed 407,791 attended. There were certainly a great many there and they caused a lot of hassle and inconvenience to Londoners. The march proved the immense wealth of the hunting lobby— with chartered trains and hired coaches bussing supporters in.

Once again Dave and Cee Wetton attended with their trusty 'Ban Bloodsports' banner. They joined conservationist colleagues Lynne Chamberlain, Robin Howard, Sue Roberts and others in the anti-hunt coral on the pavement outside the Treasury building opposite Parliament Square. Much verbal banter and gesturing was exchanged. March organisers claimed to have counted the attendance by the marchers passing through gates—but our observers saw that many nipped around the block and passed through several times.

In addition, hunters were undone by their own extravagant claims. Some ten years before, they had boasted in advertising that a million supported hunting on Boxing Day. Under pressure from the Advertising Standards Authority they retracted that claim. If their boast of a million supporters had been anything like true, then it became a fact that less than half those who watched hunting on Boxing Day could be bothered to support it in its hour of need. Furthermore, the traditional claim hunters made to politicians thinking of voting against hunting was that some six million participated in 'field sports'—and it would be a tactical error to anger them. If that were true, then about 1 in 15 of those turned out to march to protect such pastimes.

I spent the day of the march checking artificial earths in sites usually difficult to access. I also stopped off to photograph a well-attended horse show and gymkhana—proof that far from all equine enthusiasts supported hunting.

The CA staged one major rally (1997) and two massive marches (1998 and 2002) to support hunting wildlife with dogs. Never before, nor since, have so many given so much and marched so far, for so little reason. Hunters demanded the right to train their dogs to hunt and kill wild animals simply for fun. Back in 1992, on February 14th, during the debate over Kevin McNamara's Wild Mammals (Protection) Bill, Michael Colvin MP, Vice-Chairman of the BFSS had ridiculed the humane alternative drag-hunting: "*I have been looking for an analogy to a drag hunt. Someone I know likened it to kissing one's sister.*" That drew a retort from Labour's Elliot Morley MP, that induced laughter: "*I cannot comment on the Hon. Gentleman's sexual habits. Of course a drag hunt and a fox hunt are different. One of the differences is the lack of cruelty.*" The difference in outcome was obvious, but the hunting could be remarkably similar. When foxhounds were hunting a scent in a wood it took a real expert to tell if they were hunting fox, as trained to, rioting after deer or hare, or hunting the humane alternative.

People the world over have attended demonstrations and protest marches; nearly always to make the world a better or more caring place; to oppose cruelty or discrimination or to oppose war. Most march and protest for others. The CA protests drew people demanding advantages for themselves. They did not oppose cruelty and suffering; they rejoiced in it and demanded their right to inflict it on harmless and helpless animals. Otherwise respectable organisations embarrassed themselves in their rush to support the marchers. Shami Chakrabarti, as director of Liberty, sympathised with the CA. Whilst her organisation held no official position regarding hunting they clearly feared that banning people from being cruel to animals infringed their human rights. The rights of our nation to see wildlife free of pain and death and rights of rural dwellers to be free of hunt trespass and criminality were overlooked.

The 2002 'Liberty and Livelihood' march was soon eclipsed in size. The biggest demonstration in the UK took place the following year on February 16th 2003 when there was a huge march in London against the Iraq War. Police estimated numbers there at 750,000; the organisers claimed nearer 2 million. Tony Blair and his Government ignored them.

December 3rd 2002 the Rural Affairs Minister Alun Michael introduced a second Hunting Bill that would have banned deer hunting and hare coursing but allowed some fox, mink and hare hunting to continue under licence. The bill was passed by 368 votes to 155 on December 16th as police officers battled with pro-hunt protesters outside Westminster. Alun Michael expressed the hope that this compromise bill would avoid further lengthy battles between the House of Commons and the Lords. Ten days later Tony Blair indicated he would listen to Labour MPs calling for a complete ban and allow amendments to that effect. That same month Prince Charles was quoted in the *Daily Mirror* telling Tony Blair: "*If the Labour Government ever gets round to banning hunting I might as well leave this country and spend the rest of my life skiing.*"

*****

In February 2003 MPs amended the Bill to include the banning of hare hunting. June 26th 2003 Leader of the Commons Peter Hain warned MPs he had been advised that any amendments to the Bill—such as making it a complete ban—could mean it having to be sent to a standing committee and thereby delayed. Five days later, July 1st, an amendment from Labour MP Tony Banks (1943-2006), proposing a complete ban was passed by 362 votes to 154 after five hours of intense debate. Police officers soon weighed in with their opinion. Thursday July 3rd gave a hint of problems to come when Alastair McWhirter, Chief Constable of Suffolk, publicly stated his view that a complete ban on hunting could not be enforced.

July 10th 2003 seemed like the end for animal hunting as the Hunting Bill cleared the House of Commons. It was given a third reading by 317 votes to 145. Hunt supporters reacted angrily. The *Sunday Times* August 17th 2003 reported under the headline "*Hunt protesters plan tax boycott*" confidential documents prepared by the Countryside Alliance and leaked to the paper. These detailed plans by thousands of hunt supporters to boycott the payment of council tax, car licence tax and the BBC licence fee as part of a campaign of 'civil resistance' against the proposed ban on foxhunting. Senior figures in the CA boasted that only a few thousand supporters would be needed to boycott the payment of such taxes to cause chaos.

Other plans included an invasion of Chequers, the Prime Minister's country retreat in Buckinghamshire, with hundreds of horse-borne protesters and the disruption of milk supplies by blockading dairy centres. One strategy document, entitled Civil Resistance, argued the case for law-breaking on a massive scale: "*If it were to become apparent that the Parliament Act would be used then we would promise the government to make the ban unenforceable in the run-up to the next election.*"

On October 21st the Bill returned to the House of Lords. A cross-party group of peers threw out the plans for a complete ban and replaced them with a licensing regime for fox and stag hunting as well as hare coursing. Anti-hunting MPs then voted for the Bill to be re-written to become a complete ban on hunting with dogs and hare coursing in England and Wales. The following month the Bill ran out of time when the Lords opposed it.

To exert pressure on the Government pro-hunting campaigners created their Hunting Declaration. Some 40,000 people signed a pledge that if hunting was banned they would ignore the law, continue hunting as before and if necessary go to prison. The theory seemed to be that faced with the prospect of jails being packed with hunt supporters the politicians would give in to the hunters. This is the Hunting Declaration:

"In recent years a substantial number of MP's have demonstrated a cynical determination to ignore all reasoned, fair and objective advice concerning the proposed need for legislation relating to hunting with dogs. They have assiduously ignored the evidence of successive Government inquiries, and the findings and recommendations of independent research,

The process of objective debate leading to a democratic and balanced solution has been usurped by a vindictive and oppressive parliamentary majority representing a minority of the voting population. This Declaration is not a party-political protest, it is a protest by British people of all political parties on behalf of liberties that successive Governments have always promised to uphold. Our Prime Minister Tony Blair himself reaffirmed this in his speech to Congress (18 July 2003): "We are fighting for the inalienable right of human kind ... to be free. Free to be you, so long as being you does not impair the freedom of others. That's what we're fighting for. And that's a battle worth fighting."

It is a settled democratic principle that legislation should have the consent of law-abiding communities that are affected by it, and that it should be guided by natural justice. Those who hunt or support hunting would be the only people whose lives would be adversely affected by a ban on hunting. This Declaration clearly and unequivocally demonstrates that such a proposed law does not have their consent. Throughout history our citizens have put their personal freedom in the balance to resist oppressive and ill-considered laws. We intend to follow in this honourable tradition of civil disobedience - a tradition endorsed by law-abiding communities in both Britain and elsewhere. We believe that by publicly declaring our position now we are upholding true democratic principles and the spirit of tolerance.

Consequently, we the undersigned declare our intention to disobey, peacefully, any law purporting to ban hunting; any such law would be manifestly unjust. We do this with sadness, and recognising that our defiance inevitably threatens our freedoms and livelihoods. We believe that to date we have clearly demonstrated our respect for the law and its institutions. We take such action with the expectation and acceptance of any penalty that may follow, in the hope of persuading both the legislators and our fellow citizens of the injustice of such a ban. We feel it appropriate to put our personal freedoms at risk in this belief. Civil disobedience is being forced on us, and it is by this action that we demonstrate that the legislative process is being abused by those who would govern us. It is not we who are undermining the law, but the Government.

We call upon the Government to recognise that it must uphold and affirm the rights of law-abiding minorities if the rule of law and the sense of community are to endure. We ask those that govern us to reconsider introducing such ill-considered and subjective legislation, the consequence of which will be that law-abiding people are made, simply by following their traditional way of life, into criminals."

*****

The hunting and coursing season for 2003/2004 proceeded as usual in England and Wales. However, in Northern Ireland, Angela Smith MP, who was appointed Stormont Environment Minister, took decisive action to protect hares. BBC News reported Tuesday October 14th that Angela had refused permission for a hare coursing club to net hares for a coursing meeting, making her decision because the Irish hare was in danger. She said: "*It is low in numbers and the DoE has published a species action plan, which has among its objectives the doubling of the Irish hare population by 2010. Although I accept that the dogs are muzzled during coursing, there is evidence that deaths among the coursed hares can arise from causes other than being bitten. Anything that puts the lives and welfare of the Irish hare at risk is inconsistent with the policy objectives of the species action plan.*"

Douglas Batchelor welcomed the Minister's decision: "*Coursing hares for sport is cruel and unnecessary, and our campaign to end this barbaric practice has the full support of 74% of people across Northern Ireland.*" Angela also sought to stop hares being netted in the Republic of Ireland and exported to Northern Ireland for coursing.

[When Angela renewed the special preservation order in December 2004 it was challenged in court by the coursing clubs. BBC News Monday February 14th 2005 reported the Northern Ireland High Court had upheld the ban on netting hares for coursing. The court found that Angela was entitled to consider animal welfare as well as conservation issues in deciding to protect hares. The conservation orders were renewed annually, then in June 2010 the issue was finally resolved when the Northern Ireland Assembly voted to ban hare coursing. The legislation was part of the Wildlife and Natural Environment Act that came into effect on Wednesday August 17th 2011.]

November 2nd 2003 was momentous. Peter Hain MP said on Sky News: "*We will have to find a way of ensuring that a ban on cruelty to animals, which was what the House of Commons voted for overwhelmingly and what the people supported in two general elections, is implemented.*" Later that month during the debate over the Queen's Speech on November 26th 2003 Prime Minister Tony Blair said: "*We have said that we will resolve the issue during this Parliament, and so we will resolve the issue during this Parliament.*"

Ten months later, September 8th 2004, the Government announced plans to give MPs another free vote on the Hunting Bill by the end of the parliamentary session in November. The Bill, similar to the one originally proposed, would lead to an outright ban on hunting and coursing.

September 15th 2004 was a day when hunters showed their true colour as the Hunting Bill passed its third reading by 339 votes to 155. Tony Blair did not vote. Downing Street said that he had 'other engagements'. There were violent protests outside Parliament by between eight and ten thousand hunt supporters rallying in a demonstration organised by the CA. Hunt supporters surged towards Parliament and threw bottles, tin cans and fireworks at police lines. Police officers responded with batons. The *Daily Telegraph*, September 16th, described the police response in terms their 'field sports' loving readership could understand: "*For a moment, they resembled beaters driving birds towards guns.*" Some hunt supporters threw smoke canisters, one of which hit the *Telegraph* photographer, cutting his head badly.

Mike Hobday observed (*Guardian* September 15th) that the police behaved with remarkable restraint. He said: "*These appalling scenes show that the Countryside Alliance have no respect for the police, no respect for law and order and no respect for parliamentary democracy. The Countryside Alliance has been winding up their supporters all day with platform references, even while the rioting was going on, to war on the government and the chanting of death threats to Tony Blair.*"

Tim Bonner from the CA later admitted "*There were some very angry Welsh boys fired up and looking for a scrap.*" (*Daily Mail* April 17th 2009). Around 4:20 pm five prominent hunt supporters managed to evade security and invade the House of Commons chamber, causing Parliament to be suspended for 20 minutes. Another three hunt supporters were stopped by doorkeepers. All the men wore T-shirts bearing the slogan, "FCUK the bill". One of the doorkeepers, Danny Scanlon, later complained he was violently kicked by one protester.

The eight were Otis Ferry, Master of the South Shropshire Foxhounds; Luke Tomlinson, a professional polo player and friend of Prince William and Prince Harry; David Redvers, a horse breeder; Richard Wakeham, a surveyor; Nicholas Wood, a chef; John Holliday, Huntsman for the Ledbury Foxhounds; Robert Thame, a polo player; and Andrew Elliott, an auctioneer and former Whipper-in for the Ledbury Foxhounds. [After a four-day trial at Bow Street Magistrates court in May 2005 all eight were convicted of violating the Public Order Act. Each received an 18-month conditional discharge and was ordered to pay £350 costs.]

The BBC reported eleven hunters arrested outside Parliament for various offences including affray and using threatening words and behaviour. Hunt supporters were not used to meeting opponents who hit them back. Police officers defended themselves with batons. Some hunters ended up injured and bloodied as they were thwarted in their attempts to force their way through police lines defending Parliament. Sixteen members of the public and one police officer were injured, none seriously.

Simon Hart from the CA commented: "*The government has chosen the path of prejudice and spite - the reaction it unleashes will be entirely its own responsibility.*"

September 15th is Battle of Britain Day. That day the whole of the UK remembers the sacrifices made by young RAF pilots, the valiant 'Few', as they fought and died in the skies above southern England to defend Britain, its people, Parliament and democracy against the Nazi hordes from the Luftwaffe. There was never any doubt our Metropolitan Police officers would always defend our Parliament against hordes of hunt loving thugs. On that day, of all days, they would be particularly resolute.

Hunt supporters complained about their treatment by police. An investigation into the riot led to 17 officers being referred to the CPS for possible charges. Three officers faced trial; all were acquitted. The Independent Police Complaints Commission (IPCC) investigated. They took 1000 statements, logged 400 exhibits and 25,000 documents and in their 43-page report published in November 2006 endorsed the Metropolitan Police claims that the violence was provoked by elements in the crowd intent on breaking into Parliament. The report did not condemn the police concluding: *"The vast majority of police officers were clearly acting in a lawful manner, as they were trying to protect themselves, their colleagues, and also prevent the demonstrators from gaining access to Parliament."* The hunters involved, those who fought with police outside Parliament and pelted officers with missiles, and those who invaded Parliament, were revered as heroes throughout the hunting world.

Hunt supporters stepped up their protests against anti-hunting MPs. On Saturday September 25th, more than 100 protesters blockaded the Welsh home of Peter Hain MP, Leader of the House of Commons, to try and stop him travelling to the Labour conference in Brighton. There was more embarrassment for hunters the next day when the *Sunday Times* printed:
"Leaked pro-hunt letter belies claim foxes need culling.

Foxhunters secretly distributed a letter complaining about "a shortage of foxes" and berating landowners who did too little to encourage the animals to breed. The letter appears to undermine the argument that the animals need to be destroyed. Sent by the Masters of Foxhounds Association to masters and hunt chairmen it says "the safety of foxes and litters of cubs" ought to be supervised. The letter, circulated last March, has come to light following the leak of documents from the Countryside Alliance. It is referred to in an e-mail from Simon Hart, chief executive of the alliance, to Lord Daresbury the chairman of the foxhounds association. Hart warns the letter would be damaging if it were made public. "The notice refers in line one to a shortage of foxes," he wrote. "What for? For several years we have articulated a case for wildlife management. That management should be accounting for every rural interest not just hunting. I am concerned that nowhere in the letter do I see reference to the needs of farmers....only the interests of foxhunters. This would play badly in almost every sector outside hunting itself, and within too." Hart takes exception to the suggestion that hunt masters ought to put pressure on members to maintain fox populations: "This can only be interpreted by the outside world as suspicious—the artificial enhancement of a 'pest species' for purely sporting benefit. We would be ridiculed [if the remarks were published] in parliament and the media."

Some hunters claimed the letter was never sent, others that it was all a hoax. It now seems the letter was sent and strife over it was put down to an internal spat between the MFHA and the CA. The sentiments within

481

the Lord Daresbury letter provided yet more proof that it was at the very core of fox hunting that they should have plenty of foxes to hunt.

On November 12th 2004 Alun Michael urged peers to accept a compromise deal on licensed hunting that would avoid the use of the Parliament Act and an outright ban. November 18th brought the final showdown between the Commons and the Lords. The House of Lords rejected any ban so Speaker of the House of Commons, Michael Martin, invoked the Parliament Act. The Hunting Bill was passed into law and received Royal Assent.

The Commons had voted for an 18-month delay in implementing the ban, meaning that it would take effect in July 2006, but the Lords rejected that. The suspicion was they hoped to see the Government embarrassed by a campaign of civil disobedience in the run up to the May 2005 election. The Hunting Act came into force, with minimum delay, at midnight on February 18th 2005.

Tony Blair writing in *A Journey* attempted to explain his apparent support for hunting: "*During the course of our summer stay with the Strozzis, we visited the beautiful island of Elba. We went to lunch with some of their friends and there happened to be a woman who was mistress* [sic] *of a hunt near Oxford, I think. Instead of berating me, she took me calmly and persuasively through what they did, the jobs that were dependent on it, the social contribution of keeping the hunt and the social consequence of banning it, and did it with an effect that completely convinced me.*" He later observed that hunting was "*banned and not quite banned at the same time.*"

[The *Mail on Sunday* September 5th 2010 revealed the 'mistress' of the unnamed hunt was Chrissie Down, Master of the North Cotswold Foxhounds for five years from 1996 to 2001. Modestly Ms Down played down her role in convincing Tony Blair during their 1999 lunch date: "*I don't think he had a Eureka moment. I know he spoke to other hunting people. I think he felt trapped by his rash promise to ban it. And it is easier to admit he was wrong over that than over the Iraq War.*"]

Commenting on the success of the Act the LACS Vice-President, Tony Banks MP said: "*In all my time in the House of Commons this issue has been one of utmost significance to me. In years to come, I believe we will look back on this development in the protection of animals, and ask ourselves why it took so long after banning the horrors of bear baiting and cock fighting, to ban hunting with dogs.*" (*Wildlife Guardian*, Spring 2005). The front page of *The Independent*, February 18th 2005, was dominated by my photograph of hounds tussling over a dead fox taken whilst undercover at the Tetcott Foxhounds on October 5th 1982. The caption was: "*The thrill of the chase is over.*"

Future historians will surely be astonished hunters lost this battle in which they held so many advantages. It was not a struggle of rich against poor, or left against right but rather of kindness against cruelty. Sadly, in the real world—as opposed to Hollywood—kindness seldom triumphs. Hunters held all the advantages. They owned the land and had immense wealth and that bought influence. Ludicrous EU farm subsidies that lavishly rewarded land ownership rather than food production turned our countryside into a playground for those who delighted in killing wildlife.

The hunting side bathed in the support of Royalty, of the establishment and nearly all the media. It was easy for hunters to claim to be peaceful and law-abiding when they had everything they wanted—but even from that blessed position they were still aggressive and violent towards anyone who got in their way or threatened their dominance.

As soon as there was a chance of losing anything the hunters' peaceful façade evaporated. Their demonstrations became increasingly violent culminating when they fought with police who struggled to protect Parliament. Intellectually hunters proved shallow. They had brilliant spokesmen—such as my old adversary Ian Coghill—but he was held back because he was an ordinary guy living in a council house, rather than a chinless wonder with a double-barrelled name from a mansion. The best advocates for hunting came from outside—people like Jim Barrington and Janet George—but even they struggled in a world where class dominated.

After the ban, some hunt supporters lashed back in rage at the public. By their vindictiveness they confirmed their true nature. In 2004 London competed to hold the 2012 Olympics. One leader of the hunting world, the embittered gnome-like character Robin Page, set up an organisation to try and stop London being awarded the Olympics as some kind of punishment on the British public for daring to ban hunting. Kate Hoey MP, by then a passionate supporter of hunting, seized the opportunity to promote the dire outfit when she wrote in the *Daily Telegraph* December 13th 2004: *"A new organisation, independent of the Countryside Alliance, are about to be launched, called The Countryside Against The London Olympics – CALO. Led by Robin Page, chairman of the Countryside Restoration Trust and former presenter of the BBC's One Man And His Dog, it will be made up of a coalition of organisations already fighting what they term 'abuses' against the countryside.* **"Hunting is just the last straw,"** *Page says.* **"Urban Britain has not listened and has continued to interfere in things it does not understand so now the countryside will interfere with the town and try to stop the Olympics coming to London in 2012."'"**

So it was that Kate Hoey, an MP for the London constituency of Vauxhall from 1989, Minister of Sport from 1999 to 2001, publicised an attempt to stop London being awarded the supreme sporting event—the Olympics. It was no surprise when she was made Chairman of the Countryside Alliance in 2005. Despite the best efforts of Robin Page, Kate Hoey MP and their friends, on July 6th 2005 the International Olympic Committee awarded the games to London. The subsequent Olympic Games and Paralympic Games—real sports—were highly successful.

Hunt supporters also fought on in the courts. On December 23rd 2004 the CA launched a legal challenge against the use by the Government of the 1949 Parliament Act to pass the Hunting Act. In the new year, January 7th 2005, the LACS formally registered an interest in the case, seeking to defend the Hunting Act and ensure it came into effect as planned. The CA also challenged the Hunting Act on Human Rights grounds. The High Court heard the CA case over the use of the Parliament Act on January 25th 2005. Three days later the High Court judges rejected the challenge. The CA appealed against that judgement. On February 16th 2005 the CA lost its appeal in the High Court contesting the legality of the Hunting Act. Their lawyers sought an injunction delaying the implementation of the Hunting Act but that was denied. The CA was however granted leave to appeal to the House of Lords.

February 18th 2005 was memorable as the Hunting Act came into force. That made hare coursing and the hunting with dogs of wild mammals such as foxes, hares, deer and mink illegal in England and Wales. There were sadly many exemptions and loopholes that hunters fully exploited.

To the delight of the hunting fraternity and Prince Charles and in a mockery of the democratic process that gave him power, Prime Minister Tony Blair encouraged the police to ignore the Hunting Act. In *A Journey*, he admitted: "*When the law later came into force in 2004* [sic], *Hazel Blears was in the Home Office. She phoned me up and said, 'The police are asking do you want this policed vigorously so we can get some prosecutions under our belt?' After I replied, she said, 'I thought you might say that.'*" Tony Blair had bet Prince Charles that after he left office people would still be hunting. He certainly won that bet.

When I was young police officers advised me to shun direct action hunt sabotage. They said the way to campaign was through Parliament to change the law. They told me that if the law was changed to protect animals fully they would uphold that law, would be on my side and on the side of the compassionate majority. Wild animals are still waiting for the law enacted to protect them from cruelty to be upheld and enforced. Some police have tried to enforce the Hunting Act but too many have turned a blind eye to blatant flouting of the law by hunt supporters.

A few police officers seem to have made it their mission to help their friends in the hunts evade the law. Hunters have been advised to film themselves laying a trail at the start of every hunting day. That gives them proof of what they intended that day. Having taken that precaution some hunters then feel they can do as they like during the remainder of the day. In early 2007 there was startling evidence of a plan by the CA to sabotage anti-hunt videos. In a leaked email sent in early January and seen by the *Western Daily Press*, South West regional director Alison Hawes urged Countryside Alliance members, hunt staff and followers to turn the tables on monitors by pretending they have been threatened or attacked. She wrote: "*I have just been in conversation with one of the Police Wildlife Officers who has given me the following advice, which I think is very useful and I would recommend all hunts adopt this tactic....If you have the antis out filming you and they stick a camera in your face, advice is to say something along the lines of, "Will you stop using threatening language - please stop swearing at me... Now that you have turned the video on, I bet you won't repeat the foul language.*"

Other phrases to sabotage monitors' videos include: "*I will call the police if you threaten me once more - I will not put up with being called a *****...speak to me like that again and I will call the police. I am about to call the police as you have assaulted me.*"

In the email, Ms Hawes suggested these phrases should be said even if the monitors had done nothing wrong: "*By using one of these sentences (even though they have not been threatening) or similar it helps ruin their film as it does not look good if video evidence appears in court or is sent to the police, with a hunt supporter indicating they have been threatened, and the antis absolutely hate it.....I think it's excellent advice, particularly for hunt staff so please do pass it on amongst your hunt.*"

The LACS accused the CA of inciting the fabrication of evidence. Douglas Batchelor commented: "*It would appear that the Countryside Alliance is encouraging its supporters to deliberately fabricate evidence in order to mislead the police, the courts and the public. It is telling that it is doing this at a time when incidents of hunters assaulting monitors are being widely reported. It is disturbing that a serving police officer appears to be involved and I anticipate that a full investigation will be launched by the appropriate authorities....If hunts are acting within the law they have nothing to fear from being monitored, indeed one would have thought they would have welcomed it. That they are conspiring to fabricate evidence indicates they have something to hide.*" CA spokesman Tim Bonner said the advice originated in a shooting magazine and was not official Alliance policy (*Western Daily Press*, February 2007).

On November 22nd 2006, following an incident I filmed, PC Mark Bryant, the Suffolk officer responsible for enforcing the Hunting Act, visited me at home. He declared there was no chance of any prosecution based on my film but said he would warn the Master involved. He explained that all the Suffolk hunts had assured him they only hunted legally. He accepted that and told me that in consequence any film that appeared to show a hunt in Suffolk hunting illegally was only evidence of an accident—not illegal hunting. For those determined to protect wildlife it is easier (and better for the quarry) to stop illegal hunting than it is to prosecute in some later court case. This explains why conflict continues in the hunting fields.

Recent laws greatly restrict freedom to protest. You can protest so long as the government and those who abuse animals for profit or fun are happy with your protest. If you publish names and addresses of people who work in the animal abuse industry, then you become liable for whatever anyone sends them. If anyone sends anything malicious, you could be charged with conspiracy to blackmail. The Serious Organised Crime and Police Act 2005 has made protests against vivisection precarious. Dispersal powers under the Anti-social Behaviour, Crime and Policing Act 2014 have enabled police officers to protect hunters from anyone trying to uphold the Hunting Act. At one hunt in 2016, saboteurs presented police officers with video proof that the hunt were illegally hunting hares. The police issued those saboteurs with Section 35 dispersal orders, forcing them to leave the area, and allowed the hunters to carry on. We have a lot more work to do....

EPILOGUE

The Hunting Act (2004) must be strengthened by Parliament and properly enforced by our police. No-one should be above the law. People should help the police but whilst the public should be encouraged to watch over our wildlife—perhaps through a Countryside or Wildlife Watch to match Neighbourhood Watch—they should not be forced to enforce wildlife law.

Too often we see courageous hunt saboteurs and hunt monitors (particularly Associates of the group Protect Our Wild Animals) out in the fields facing aggression, criminal damage and violence from hunters as they observe and record hunting. Penny Little and Judy Gilbert are outstandingly successful hunt monitors—their video evidence helped secure the landmark 2012 conviction of the Heythrop Foxhounds for illegal hunting. The Heythrop Hunt Ltd, a Master and the Huntsman all pleaded guilty in a case brought at great expense by the RSPCA.

Hunt saboteurs, all volunteers, sometimes find themselves having to act, as necessary, to protect wildlife from illegal hunting. The public should not have to do the very jobs they pay our police so well to do. Furthermore, it is surely wrong that charities such as the RSPCA should feel obliged to take the considerable financial burden of prosecuting wildlife crimes where the CPS are unwilling to act.

The legal issues around hunting could all be resolved if only hunters looked closely at their own pastimes—saw the inherent cruelty—and took positive steps to walk away from it. However, as the National Trust found, proving the cruelty in the pastime deters few hunters.

Hunt followers should not flout the Hunting Act just because they can. Most hunt riders are only there for the thrill of a cross-country gallop. For them the pursuit of an artificial scent as in drag hunting is the answer.

Since August 1984—soon after I met Sue—I have campaigned entirely lawfully for better animal protection laws. I work closely with animal welfare and animal rights groups and the police to see the Hunting Act 2004 strengthened and enforced. I also strive with colleagues and other like-minded groups to extend the umbrella of animal protection legislation. Given my history I am exceptionally keen to help educate the next generation of campaigners to help them to avoid mistakes such as the ones I had made.

I offer some advice to young people entering the animal protection movement and eager to make an effective contribution. I have seen every phase of the struggle to protect animals—from collecting money and signing petition forms to Durham, Wayland and many other prisons—yet my most significant contributions to our cause were entirely lawful.

That was to work undercover and both see, and record for the world in turn to see, the reality of the cruel abuse of animals. This is campaigning work where individuals certainly can make a difference. We must strive to ensure that everyone obeys the law—and if anyone has to go to prison let it be the animal abusers—not the animal protectors.

We also need to change minds so that more view all life as valuable and to be cherished. Animals must no longer be seen as mere toys to be used, abused and destroyed on a whim. Life is precious. Every creature has a valuable role to play in our ecosystems.

We must never forget the many courageous people around the world who have given their lives to protect animals from cruelty. The memory of their sacrifice should inspire us all to do much more for the causes we know to be just. I particularly recall the following whose lives were taken by our opponents:-

James Piper, RSPCA Inspector: Died in 1838 after sustaining severe injuries tackling cockfighters at Hanworth, Middlesex.

William Sweet, LACS member: Murdered 6/1/1976 after an altercation with man shooting birds. Assailant was jailed for life but has long been released.

Fernando Pereira, Greenpeace photographer: Murdered 10/7/1985 by the French Secret Service when the vessel "Rainbow Warrior" was sunk by two explosions, Auckland Harbour, New Zealand.

Michael Hill, Hunt Saboteur: Killed 9/2/1991 protesting against hare hunting at the Cheshire Beagles.

Thomas Worby, Hunt Saboteur: Killed 3/4/1993 protesting against fox hunting at the Cambridgeshire Foxhounds.

Jill Phipps, Animal Rights Activist: Killed 1/2/1995 protesting against live exports of farm animals, Coventry Airport.

Paola Quartini, animal activist for LIPU (Italian League for Bird Protection - UK) from Genoa, Italy and **Elvio Fichera**, a volunteer for the Association of Abandoned Animals: Both were murdered 12/5/2010 whilst trying, with police, to serve a warrant on Renzo Castagnola for cruelty to animals. Renzo Castagnola shot them dead, then injured his wife, then killed himself.

Recent good news for UK wildlife has been the recovery of the otter. In 1983, when the original *Outfoxed* was published, otters faced imminent extinction. However, thanks to dedicated work by people like Philip Wayre (1921-2014) and his Otter Trust based in Earsham, Norfolk and the constant pressure against mink hunting by hunt saboteurs, otters have recovered and can be found in most rivers across the UK.

In conclusion, we have but one turn at life on this beautiful earth. To spend the entirety of it in misery at the whim of man, or to have it snuffed out prematurely, simply for fun, are crimes the full measure of which will one day be recognised.

*****

For information about the Animal Cruelty Investigation Group and the Animal Welfare Information Service please write to:
ACIG/AWIS, PO Box 8, Halesworth, Suffolk IP19 0JL.

You can visit their web site at: **www.acigawis.org.uk** To see some of the film clips referred to in this text and other relevant later video clips, taken by the ACIG and other groups, visit their YouTube channel at: **www.youtube.com/user/AWISACIG**

Bloodsports, with their overt gratuitous cruelty, have long caused great offence to decent people. Way back on December 16th 1929, the London *Evening Standard* printed this report:-

"*EXHAUSTED HIND LASSOED.*

How the quarry was caught with a rope at the end of a stag hunt near Dulverton, Exmoor, was described to-day.

The Tiverton Staghounds had hunted a hind from Haddon. When the hunt began the hind had a calf running beside it, but it left the calf sheltered in undergrowth.

Closely pursued, the hind was hunted in and out of the river Exe several times, and when exhausted it entered the river Barle, near Marsh Bridge. Because of the flooded state of the river the hounds and hunters could not reach it.

The hind was eventually caught by a hunter, who threw a rope over its head. The rope was drawn tight and the animal was pulled out of the water and killed."

Scores of letters were received by the *Evening Standard* commenting on this incident. Here are points from selected letters printed in the *Evening Standard* January 17th 1930:-

"*Never have I read of such cruelty, and it passes comprehension how such conduct is permitted in a Christian country.*" - J. BALFOUR, East Sheen, S.W.,

"*The humanitarian principles of the Labour Government might be usefully displayed by the complete abolition of blood sports.*" - L. H. BAXTER, N.

"*I am a West Countryman, but if this is the spirit now prevailing in the West Country, this will be the last occasion that I shall ever admit that I hail from this, apparently, degenerate part of England.*" - J. LEYLAND, West Croydon.

"*It makes me wonder how many clergy will raise a word of protest from their pulpits on a subject which is surely a disgrace to England or any civilised country professing Christianity.*" - H. R. WOOD, Ealing Common.

"*I wonder there was no one at the hunt enough of a sportsman and a man to cut the rope.*" -NORMAN B. SMITH, Conservative Club, S.W.

(Details from *Cruel Sports* February 1930)

It is shameful that it took nearly 75 years for Parliament to accede to the demands of our nation and ban such cruelty. That the ban is largely ignored and the cruelty continues to this day is beyond belief.

As for my position, I wanted to be the man to cut the rope, and encourage others to do likewise. Then I learned the hard way that if you do cut the rope you face the wrath of our judicial system—for causing criminal damage to the rope. So, I switched focus. Colleagues and I cannot for ever be cutting ropes; we had to make it illegal to treat wildlife that way, to ban the ropes. Having done that for hunting, we now work to see the law enforced and push forwards the boundaries of humane legislation elsewhere.

APPENDIX

(*News of the World* October 24th 1982)
FOUL TRICKS OF THE FOXHUNTERS

The man who quit in horror reveals all
By Paul Woodhouse

IN ALL my years of service with various packs of hounds I often saw foxes being treated cruelly. But the Derwent was undoubtedly the worst.

During hunts I worked as a whipper-in controlling the hounds, a job which meant I was always close to the kill. So I got first-hand experience of what happened to the fox. Sometimes it would go to ground—bolt down a hole to escape—and when that happened it was supposed to be dug up, killed humanely and its corpse fed to the dogs.

But during my time with the Derwent I saw all the normal, decent rules broken—like the time we went out "cubbing." Cubbing takes place in September and October before the hunt season starts in November.

Young hounds are taken out with more experienced ones to learn how to kill foxes. We met on a September day at Ebberston Dale, not far from the hunt's kennels at Snainton, near Scarborough.

The then joint master, Mr Roderick Ando, was in charge and on being told a fox had gone to ground he ordered it dug up. This was done by the hunt's terrierman, Mr Fred Jackson, a local farmer, and one of the other whips. Mr Ando then ordered them to let the fox go— but to make sure it would be easily caught. So the terrierman pulled out a pocket knife and cut one of the fox's feet.

It was then let loose, hounds were called and the fox was dead within 200 yards. That was the first of many times a knife was used to slit a fox's pad. Blood coming from the wound left more scent for the hounds and, of course, the animal was lamed.

Another time a fox went to ground at a place called Wydale. Only the master, a whip, the terrierman and myself were present. This time Mr Ando ordered that the fox was to be bolted into a net and as there were no members of the public about, it was to be given live to the hounds. This was done immediately.

I myself have thrown a live fox to hounds when ordered to do so by Mr Ando—but I hated doing it.

Haunted
The idea is that, before being torn to pieces, the fox might manage to bite two or three of the hounds and make them more aggressive in future. The self-disgust I felt after that terrible incident has haunted my mind ever since.

But that wasn't the only way the Derwent broke all the rules. To make sure the pack made a kill, rather than spend a cold wet day without one they would "drop" a "bagged" fox. The fox would have been caught previously and held captive for up to a week. It would then be released only 200 yards from the hounds.

It would be reeking of its own mess, cramped, terrified at being handled and totally disorientated. Its chances of escape were nil and it was always killed almost at once.

The Derwent used to place a bagged fox in a drain and the hounds would be taken across to it where of course they would set up the alarm.

When the fox bolted it would all look quite innocent to the public and there would be congratulations all round. But the trained eye could easily see what had really happened.

If the fox couldn't bolt the terriermen would entangle it in barbed wire wrapped around a long pole.

Dropping

He would then pull it out of the drain, drop it in front of the pack and leave it to its ghastly fate. The practice of "dropping" captive foxes is common, particularly when VIPs and distinguished guests are out with the pack. It has been done on each of the six packs I've worked for.

Because foxhunts like to have a kill to impress visiting dignitaries, titled people or members from other hunts, the master will tell the staff to have a fox ready for dropping on the day. When Prince Charles rode with the Derwent some years ago, a fox was dropped. He, of course, wouldn't have been aware of this and he probably went away saying he'd had a good day's sport.

Dropping is particularly cruel because the fox is a territorial animal, familiar only with its own home range. When released on strange ground it has no idea where the hiding places are and doesn't know which way to turn.

Sometimes it is soaked in strong-smelling liquid to make it even easier for the hounds to track. I've never seen a dropped fox survive longer than 20 minutes.

During my hunt service I was often asked three main questions: How do we train hounds? Do we breed foxes? And do they do much damage?

The answer to the first question is that hounds are very carefully bred and hunt foxes by instinct. They're also taken out while still young to hunt cubs along with older, more experienced dogs.

The terriers are given special extra training in killing and fighting foxes. This is done by digging up a young fox, which is then placed in a large box. A terrier pup is put in with it. Being a wild animal, the fox will instinctively fight off any aggressor. The terrier is faced with the choice between fighting back or retreating. If it fights back, it is taken out after a few minutes. If it retreats, it is pushed on to the fox to try to make it retaliate.

The terriers are also trained by putting them in cages with rats.

Kill

When they've learned to defend themselves by killing the rats they are then introduced to fox cubs.

Hunts don't breed foxes, either. But they often dig up cubs during the summer and put them in specially built artificial earths. That way they know where the cubs are when hunting starts the following season.

The hunts even feed the cubs throughout the summer months—proving, in my view, that arguments that foxhunting is a good form of pest control are nonsense.

All the hunts I've worked for had several artificial earths in their "country"—their hunting area. I've helped to build them, the last one being with the Derwent at a place called Scotswhin.

To the last question about damage, the answer is no. Of course foxes will kill poultry if you can't be bothered to shut them up securely. But they don't kill sheep or lambs. They may take away dead lambs or attack one which has been deserted and is sick. But they certainly do not cause havoc among healthy flocks.

An important part of any hunt's work is cub hunting. This has two purposes. The first is to train young foxhounds and the second is to familiarise foxcubs with their future opponents.

The night before a cub hunt I'd go out and block up all the fox earths to make sure the cubs would be above ground at daybreak. Other hiding places and escape routes such as badger setts and drains were also blocked.

Then it was my job to bring the young hounds to the selected location by 6 a.m. I've seen hunts take out as many as 100 hounds and kill up to 11 cubs in just three hours.

Most people who ride to hounds never see a fox or a kill, and don't know what really goes on. I think they could have a day's enjoyment in the countryside by following an artificial trail, a sport known as draghunting. If the drag is laid carefully, the hunt followers could have an even better day's riding by avoiding going across fields and damaging crops.

The Derwent hunt's a "country" measuring 25 by 12 miles. Half is arable land owned by four big landowners who are on the hunt committee, and so tolerate crop damage. Tenant farmers have no say because the owners always retain the sporting rights on their land. But the rest belongs to the Forestry Commission. It's shameful that the Government allows hunting on what is, after all, public land.

While I worked for other hunts, farmers and landowners often refused the pack permission to cross their fields. But although hounds can be stopped if the hunt staff are up with them, frequently the pack is two or three fields ahead. Then it's near-impossible to stop them if they're in full cry.

I've seen a lot of damage done by the hunts to fences, hedges, crops and gates. I was born into a hunting family and was "blooded" at the age of seven, but my three years with the Derwent were enough to make me want to get right out of the business.

In every hunt there are always one or two people, particularly the terrier-men, who get a sadistic pleasure from tormenting foxes. I regard such people with disgust and have vowed never again to have anything to do with them or the so-called "sport" of foxhunting.

Dog man Fred:
I never did it

HUNT terrierman Fred Jackson denied Paul Woodhouse's allegations. He said: "I know the rules of foxhunting — and I swear on my kids' lives that I've never done the things he said.

"It would be bloody unsporting."

Father-of-three Mr Jackson's denials came just six days before the start of the new hunting season. At his parents' remote farmhouse home in Troutsdale, near the Derwent hunt's kennels, he added: *"I've never thrown a live fox to hounds—I've always shot it first.*

Angry

"And I've certainly never cut a fox's pads to slow it up.

"I can't understand how Paul has turned on me like this. We were good friends."

Mr Jackson grew angry when asked if he had used a pole with barbed wire on to yank foxes out of hiding. And just before he ordered our two reporters off the land, his 73-year-old mother Lizzie snapped: *"Good God, how do you think I've brought my four boys up?*

"Fred would never do anything like that. It's a disgusting pack of lies."

The former Joint Master of the Derwent Hunt, Mr Roderick Ando said: *"I'm not interested in what Mr Woodhouse is alleging. I'm saying nothing.*

Any comment must come from the Master of Foxhounds Association, and as I'm no longer a Master of Foxhounds, I can't comment."

Mr Ando, of Fittleworth Road, Wisborough Green, West Sussex, resigned in March from the Derwent Hunt and now turns out with a local hunt, the Chiddingfold.

In readiness for the season's opening day next Saturday the sport's governing body, The Master of Foxhounds Association, have issued a new pamphlet stressing their regulations.

This "expressly forbids" the hunting of captive foxes and says there is a "firm rule" that foxes must be killed before being fed to hounds.

[Paul Woodhouse told us of his plans to find work outside hunting. It seems he found that difficult. He later changed his mind about some of what he revealed in his signed statement and returned to work in hunting. *Tag* the aged fox whose location Paul identified and was rescued by activists lived an idyllic life until passing away peacefully in his sleep. *Tag's* death was reported in *Cruel Sports* 15, Spring 1985.]

Frightened to death
New research reveals that the terror induced by hunting is itself traumatic enough to kill deer. Simon Denison reports
(*Weekend Telegraph* Saturday September 9th 1989 page IX)

Is it a cruel and unnecessary game? Or is it a useful contribution to animal-population control? As late summer ushers in the new hunting season, the old arguments for and against the use of packs of hounds for hunting have returned. But after decades of impasse, this year the arguments have set off in a new direction.

Red deer, which are hunted with hounds on Exmoor, are susceptible to a stress-related and potentially lethal condition known as myopathy, according to an article in the latest edition of *Deer*, the magazine of the pro-hunting British Deer Society. Its author, wildlife biologist Dr John Henshaw, a fellow of the Institute of Biology, explains that nothing is more effective at inducing the condition than chasing a deer over a long distance with a pack of dogs.

Deer differ in their susceptibility to the condition, but those it affects suffer muscle breakdown and eventual death, as the result of the apparent absence of an anti-self-destruct control mechanism that exists in other animals.

In other animals, including humans, fear triggers the release of adrenalin into the bloodstream which speeds up the metabolism and allows the muscles to work more vigorously. This in turn burns up body sugars rapidly, but only for a short period. Soon the release of lactic acid causes the muscles to begin to ache and the animal ceases to exert itself so strenuously. Deer, however, appear to be able to burn up their blood sugar to the point of fatal breakdown.

"*This introduces a whole new set of reasons for objecting to the sport,*" says John Hicks of the League Against Cruel Sports. "*Now we're not only worried about the deer that actually get caught by the hunt, but about all the other deer that get in the way as well.*"

Staghunting is, in theory, a method of culling deer that can be conducted with a high degree of finesse, and ought not to be open to this line of attack. Before each hunt, a particular stag is found and marked out for the chase, and is followed until it is caught. "*It's not just a question of loosing a pack of hounds and galloping after any deer that comes in your way,*" says Diana Scott, Joint Master of the Devon and Somerset Staghounds.

In practice, however, things do not always work out so neatly. Most hunts are written up by a hunt-member in the West Somerset Free Press, and the reports frequently speak of changing deer several times during a hunt, or of "*running a mixed herd*", which means chasing a complete herd until one stag breaks away and becomes a target.

Myopathy has been fully documented in New Zealand in recent years, where many deer have had to be captured from the wild to start up the country's deer-farming industry. But its first certain diagnosis in this country was in 1986, and was written up by R. M. Barlow, Professor of Pathology at the Royal Veterinary College.

Diana Scott, however, disputes the existence of the condition. *"If myopathy really exists,"* she asks, *"how come Exmoor is not littered with the bodies of dead deer after every hunt?"*

Dr Henshaw is not surprised by this state of affairs. *"Over the years I have myself found many carcases of deer which seem to have died in mysterious circumstances. And I have seen deer limping and staggering about after hunts have taken place. They may or may not have been cases of myopathy, but we couldn't diagnose it then, simply because we didn't know about the condition. . . it is thoroughly irresponsible of the hunting people to deny it.*

"It's not my role to be political. I am a scientist, and my job is just to report what I have seen. But of course I think it should be stopped."

From venery to veganism

By Lynn Sawyer (Printed in *Wildlife Guardian* Issue 29 Autumn 1994)

As the Criminal Justice and Public Order Bill worms its way into the statute book I am compelled to state my opposition to this draconian attack on civil liberties drawing on my past experiences and the conclusions I have eventually reached after years of deliberation.

I began hunting in 1982 at the age of fourteen and soon became addicted to the sport. At the age of sixteen I had become involved with information gathering activities and had joined the British Field Sports Society. As an undergraduate at Thames Polytechnic, I attended animal rights group meetings, read a lot of animal rights and 'anarchist' literature and provided BFSS Headquarters with any information I had gleaned from my excursions.

Meanwhile I was working on BFSS caravans at numerous shows, hunting with many different packs of hounds, helping at kennels and even at dig-outs of foxes on hunts. All in all, from 1984 to 1990, I was an active, perhaps even fanatical, hunt supporter who tended to be a bit sanctimonious with those in the hunting fraternity who I regarded as apathetic when it came to defending their sport. A combination of factors changed my views completely.

Unfortunately hunting, along with any practice that involves the killing or blatant commercial use of animals, remains a cruel activity despite any reform or code of conduct. Even more unfortunately, a small minority of people who hunt (*at all levels*) do not always act in a way that minimises the cruelty inflicted. The worst incident I can recall is whilst out with a neighbouring pack at a dig-out, a pregnant vixen was pulled out of her earth and shot in the head. However, although it was obvious to everyone present that she was still fully conscious, she was baited with terriers before being chucked in the back of a Land Rover to die. When I suggested that another bullet should be used to stop her pain, (she was groaning), I was told that to use a bullet would be 'a waste'. I managed to rationalise this incident along with a whole catalogue of 'mistakes', 'disasters' and 'botch' jobs each time, as a very unsavoury 'one-off'. Just like everyone else I became de-sensitised to any suffering caused by my activities in order to continue with those activities. The act of denial which enables the most decent, the most intelligent of individuals to engage in Orwellian double-think and commit the most abhorrent of atrocities in situations of war, torture, abuse and exploitation is certainly necessary in the hunting field as indeed it is when meat is served at the dining table. So the hunt follower showers affection on horses and dogs without batting an eyelid at the suffering of equally important pigs, foxes and deer.

As I grew older I found that I could tolerate this double standard less and less, mainly due to the fact that I was more involved with the sharp end of hunting than most, combined with what I had read and heard from the animal rights community.

In the field, non-violent saboteurs were a constant vocal reminder that hunting was perhaps not the humane, 'least cruel alternative' we all thought it was. Rather like the vegetarian who visibly reminds his omnivorous companions that they are eating dead animals, thus sending them on a guilt trip, so the sabs could make a hunting day seem less joyous simply by being present. The hunting status quo fed stories of paid sabs, sabs that were anti-establishment, sabs that were terrorists to their followers. Personally, whilst I did encounter the occasional aura of hostility, I usually found that the sabs chose to patiently lecture me on their philosophy rather than kick my head in as, according to pro-hunt propaganda, they were supposed to do. After a while I came to respect them as sincere and altruistic people with different opinions to my own. Many hunting folk did not like this at all and in 1990 I was *ordered* to discontinue any dialogue at all with the opposition. Faced with the option of either blindly obeying the autocracy of those who for some unknown reason regarded 'fraternising with the enemy' as heinous in the extreme or leaving the hunting fraternity altogether, I made the odd decision to declare myself neutral. This did not please anyone, least of all some members of the hunt. But neutrality gave me time (four years) to look at the situation objectively and the courage to change my way of life.

After a great deal of confusion combined with soul-searching and listening to the views of a wide range of people, I came to the conclusion that I could no longer condone the widespread, institutionalised human manipulation of non-humans. I became a dietary vegan, (with the intention of boycotting other animal derived things, wool etc. in the future) at the beginning of 1994 and then realised that the only thing which was holding me back from opposing hunting was my past allegiances and close friendships.

What has eventually made me realise that I have to reluctantly come down off a very uncomfortable fence is the past two years of unprecedented violence in the field, the introduction of hunt stewards and the Criminal Justice and Public Order Bill. At the beginning of the 1992/93 season I was astonished to read that it was deemed necessary for hunts to hire and/or train young men to 'deal with' sabs. As I had worked alone and been, usually, treated with courtesy in the field, I found it hard to believe that anyone could see the tactic of introducing fairly large numbers of 'the lads' into the field as somehow a constructive way of dealing with any violence.

'The lads' predictably antagonised an already volatile situation. Leading hunters directed their venom at 'the great unwashed', "*The field was swelled by a number of farmers on quadracycles. These were put to good effect rounding up a dirtier but less docile kind of beast*", (Horse and Hound 8th October 1992). The hunting press, after years of silence (with the exception of 'Hounds' magazine) suddenly erupted with articles condemning direct action against hunting, not all of them being too concerned with the truth either!

Then the saboteurs who had been 'escorted' from public rights of way as well as from private land did what they had always done when faced with unprovoked violence - they instigated mass hits on the hunts which had the stewards who seemed to be the most violent. Predictably, clashes ensued, people were hurt and violence increased to unprecedented levels. Even more predictably, the Home Secretary's response to this sorry state of affairs was not to look into how the use of stewards had raised the levels of assaults and counter-assaults, nor to question how hunts had been policed but to seek to crush the most vulnerable group in the equation, i.e. the sabs and others who oppose hunting. One terrifying implication for civil liberties is that one group have been deliberately singled out and legislated against because they happen to use direct action to save animal life. It is already illegal to thump someone or even to cause another person distress by swearing at them or threatening them. Legislation already exists to enable the police to arrest anyone on either side who wants to initiate violence and so not only is clause 52 of this Bill discriminatory, it is surplus to requirements. In addition, when the League Against Cruel Sports sought to amend the Bill so that anyone who suffers actual damage as the direct result of hunt trespass could prosecute via the criminal law rather than the rather more expensive civil law, the government was not interested.

We are now facing a situation whereby a road protester or hunt sab will face three months in prison and a £2,500 fine for doing nothing more than protesting on private property, or even on a public right of way whilst a hunt can literally run through someone's garden or farm causing much damage but with no recriminations. The police will now have powers to enforce exclusion zones around certain sites, they will be able to stop anyone they *think* might be opposed to hunting from going near the meet. In fact, the Government and the hunting fraternity have benefited mutually from the increased levels of violence. This 'coincidence' has enabled Mr Howard [the Home Secretary] to draft legislation against traditional Tory enemies, i.e. those opposed to the road programmes, those who attend raves, those who live alternative lives on the road, the squatters, the trade unionists etc. The Government was given a PR opportunity to legislate against them without too much difficulty, they were able to provide the public with a scapegoat - 'an enemy within' - and draw attention to the delusion that they were being tough on 'law and order'.

Finally, I cannot stand aside and allow the hunting fraternity to subjugate the animal rights movement in this manipulative way when I know that as some enlightened Masters of Hounds and sab groups have proved the way to eliminate violence is via dialogue and empathy. To crucify the civil liberties which our ancestors died for and which our children need to inherit is a national disgrace which has to be resisted before we enter a totalitarian regime.

Vivisection

Here is an eloquent statement of the case against vivisection:-

"Animal testing is a disaster

Thousands of people have been injured or killed by drugs that were found to be safe for other species

Jerome Burne (Guardian Thursday May 24, 2001)

What do you feel is more important - the life of your child or the life of a few rats? Such stark contrasts are common currency in the heavily polarised debate about experiments on animals. On the one side the misguided sentimentality of the animal rights campaigners, on the other side the tireless pursuit of human happiness and health by the researchers. But since those wide-eyed activists have put animals' rights somewhere on the election agenda, you may be interested to know that there is a totally hard-headed and rational case to be made for saying that animal experimentation has been a scientific and medical disaster. That far from saving lives, it has caused injury and death to thousands and that time and again it has led both researchers and legislators into a blind alley. But surely, you cry, we need animal experiments to discover how safe new drugs are before we give them to humans? Well, the combination of fenfluramine and dexfenfluramine, touted as the answer to a dieter's prayer a few years ago, was extensively tested on animals and found to be very safe. Unfortunately it caused heart valve abnormalities in humans. Or how about the arthritis drug Opren? Tests on monkeys found no problems but it killed 61 people before it was withdrawn. And as for having to choose between rats and your child, Cylert, given to children with attention deficit hyperactive disorder, was fine for animals but caused liver failure in 13 children.

The problem is not a new one, in fact it is blindingly obvious - animals are not the same as humans, so drugs that affect them in one way may well affect us differently.

Now this is usually presented as a solvable problem by researchers. We can get an idea of the mechanism from animals and then fine-tune with humans, they say, but it doesn't work like that. Species, even those that seem closely related, may function quite differently at a molecular level, and there is no way of predicting what the differences will be. Rats and mice, for instance, look pretty alike to us, but when it comes to something as basic as whether a chemical causes cancer or not, the results may be totally contradictory. Out of 392 chemicals tested for carcinogenic effects at the American National Institute of Environmental Health Sciences, 96 were positive in the rat and negative in the mouse or vice versa. So which of those are harmful to humans? The institute can't say. For 30 years they fed high doses of a range of new chemicals to animals to discover if they caused cancer or other damage. The results are recorded in blue books that take up 10 feet of shelving in the institute. But ask how many of the substances might produce tumours in humans at normal levels and no one knows. So what about the ones that didn't harm rodents, how many of them might harm humans? They don't know that either.

The lack of predictable differences between animal and human reactions is something that has bedevilled Aids research. Aids is a high profile disease with a lot of research money available, so it surely makes sense to ignore ethical objections and use chimpanzees. It is surely precisely because their genome is identical to ours, give or take a few percentage points, that they should yield more accurate results than rodents. Well, no, actually. Out of approximately 100 chimps infected with HIV over a 10-year period only two have become sick. Chimp vaccine trials have proved unreliable too because they don't show the antibody or cell-mediated response to HIV that humans do. Animal experimentation has played only a small role in developing drug treatments to the greatest plague of our time.

And the list could go on. There are drugs that have been held back because they caused dangerous reaction in animals, such as beta blockers and valium, but then turned out to be safe for humans. Legislation to halt the use of asbestos was held up for years because it didn't cause cancer in animals, while the carcinogen benzene continued to be used long after clinicians were worried because it didn't cause leukaemia in mice. All these examples, and many more, have been written up in the specialist journals but until last year they had been scattered. Then a man called Ray Greek, an American medical doctor who specialised in the highly technical field of anaesthesia collected them in a book called Sacred Cows and Golden Geese. He gave a talk in London about it last night. So was this scientific, rational contribution to the debate about animal experiments warmly welcomed, so medical research could be improved? Supporters of animal experiments are always calling for more public discussion and education.

Of course not. It was ignored.

Jerome Burne is editor of the monthly newsletter Medicine Today"

Extracts from the minutes of the Public Hearing on Hunting with Dogs at Portcullis House, Westminster on Wednesday September 11th 2002.
The morning session.

The Chairman was the Rt. Hon. Alun Michael MP

MR HUSKISSON: Good afternoon everyone. I am grateful for this opportunity to give first hand evidence about the pastime of hunting our wildlife with packs of dogs. I do so after some 31 years of close observation of this form of entertainment.

These amusements are both inherently cruel and entirely unnecessary. The cruelty exists at several levels. At its core is the choice of dogs that are bred, not for the speed that might produce a quick kill, but rather for the stamina that guarantees the lengthy chase that supporters seek.

In hare coursing, where the greyhounds are bred for speed, the fleeing hare is given a start. This ensures that supporters have the fun of watching the dogs work their hare.

There are specific cruelties associated with each pastime. In fox hunting there is the cruelty of digging out. The delayed death. It may take 30 minutes, an hour or longer. For the terrier enthusiasts, it is their sport. That it usually occurs out of sight of most hunt followers does not make it any less cruel, nor them any less responsible.

A dig-out often leads to an underground dog fight. In the damp and dark tunnel, the fox is fighting for his or her life. Evidence of the ferocity of the combat is proven by the injuries suffered by the terriers.

I have witnessed a dig-out that lasted nearly three hours. It was actually more like fox baiting as the fox battled with either one or both terriers. It was long after dark that it finished, long after the riders and car followers had left.

In fox hunting I have witnessed some outrageous cruelty. I have seen a fox, bleeding from terrier bites inflicted when it was dug out, bagged and then released for the dogs to hunt. To help them follow the scent, the huntsman when holding the fox, before it was dropped in the sack, bowed its head to its brush to make it soil itself with urine. That was at the Dulverton West Foxhounds.

I saw the Quorn Foxhounds hunt a fox cub to ground.

THE CHAIRMAN: Can I advise you please not to refer to specific organisations or individuals in giving your evidence?

MR HUSKISSON: Yes, Minister. It was eventually dug out and I saw the terrierman holding the fox. He could have killed it quickly but he did not. He released it; the hounds were summoned; the fox fled, was chased and killed. That all took place beside a hedge in open view of watching hunt followers.

In stag hunting, which is actually a misnomer as hinds are hunted as well, there is again the cruelty of the delayed death. The hunt, that can last all day, may end 25 miles from the start. Only a few hunt followers carry guns to put the exhausted and terrified quarry out of its misery.

I recall the end of one hunt. I saw the stag swimming in a small pool. There was one dog on his back and some 16 others baying close by. He was grabbed by his antlers and dragged to the bank. The supporters tried to stop the dogs from tearing at his flank. The sound of the baying dogs and whoops of glee from the watching crowd was deafening. There was no one with a gun nearby and the dense vegetation made access difficult.

The stag was dragged out and his head pressed into the mud to restrain him. We then waited. This was a terrified animal just waiting to die. It was pitiful. After some minutes, a chap with a pistol arrived and the stag was at last killed. The whipper-in then roused his dogs to a frenzy by banging the head of the lifeless stag onto the ground. Warm blood sprayed everywhere. The stag was beyond caring, but I mention it as an example of how these pastimes bring out the very worst in human nature.

To appreciate the cruelty in hare coursing, you just need to hear these harmless creatures screaming with pain and terror when caught. It is shocking. It ends when the picker-up reaches the scene and can release the hare and break her neck but sometimes in the tug of war with a live hare between two dogs one dog wins and runs off with the squealing hare. You try catching a coursing dog running with such a prize. I have seen it take several minutes.

There is also the cruelty inherent in the netting and transportation of hares to restock areas for coursing.

As for utility, let us consider first fox hunting. I think of all the artificial earths I have seen in England and Wales. I have seen 31 in the country of one hunt. In another hunt, I have seen three artificial earths in just a single wood that they hunt. The largest artificial earth complex that I have seen lies in an area hunted by a lakeland fell pack, right in the heart of the sheep rearing up there.

Artificial earths are built for foxes to breed in. In my experience, farmers are neither stupid nor the sort to be meekly put upon by outsiders. That they allow hunt supporters to build artificial earths confirms that they do not regard foxes as any real pest.

There is also the feeding of foxes by hunters. I have found hunted woods stinking with the putrid smell of rotting flesh from animals dumped as food for foxes. I have seen chicken, lambs, adult sheep, calves and even boxes of bacon rinds dumped. Fox hunting as fox control is a farce.

I recall the shameful sight of two fox cubs held captive in an artificial earth in a wood owned by a hunt in Yorkshire. They were held in what amounted to a stinking cesspit. They were being given food and water and were destined to be released to be hunted at a later date.

With the help of the RSPCA, they were removed and given the veterinary treatment they desperately needed.

Finally, there is the cruelty associated with hunt dogs running riot, an inevitable consequence of the pursuit of live quarry. I have seen hunt dogs chase just about every creature. They will of course hunt anything they are taught to. They could easily be trained to hunt something incapable of suffering. Some already are.

This is the crux of the matter. For as long as man contrives an interface between two species of animal with the purpose of killing one for entertainment, there will be cruelty. To replace the live animal quarry by a scented rag or by a willing human removes that cruelty.

Then later this exchange

MR LUFF: I expected not to agree with much of what Mr Huskisson said. You are a man of conviction -- no pun intended, I can assure you -- and yet I found in your evidence a great deal that I can agree with because many of the practices in the hunting field which you identify are ones which I think are unacceptable. You talk about giving deer an extra chance. If that is true, I find that unacceptable. You talk about the need to define breeding seasons properly and we do need to do that. You must hunt at the right time of the year. Climate changes change breeding seasons. Also, you talk about the nuisance the hunt can cause, disturbance, public safety orders, trespass and so on. I agree with all those points but surely we can deal with these issues by regulating so that those specific things should not be done and, when you agree that, you make hunting less cruel.

MR HUSKISSON: You are not that uncommon in being from the hunting side that agrees with me because in debates I have had hunting people come up to me and say afterwards, "If I had seen the sort of things you have seen, I would come on your side of the fence." I say, "It is a pity you have not. You will have to look a little bit harder because it is there. You just have to get off your horse and have a look."

There has been regulation within hunting for years and years. When the fox was put in a sack and tipped out, that was against the rules. When the fox was held alive and released, that was against the rules. The rules and regulations are there but they seem at times to be only there in the book, not in people's minds. That is the problem. As long as there is this interface for sport between man and animal, setting one animal on another, things get out of hand and they do.

People have said to me, "You seem to be remarkably unlucky" because it is almost like I can get my hand in a barrel of apples and come out with a rotten apple. I am the person who finds the rotten apples but how many rotten apples come out of the barrel before you start thinking: hang on, maybe the whole barrel is rotten. This is perhaps the problem: that there is a lot more to hunting than just the meet on the village green and the gallop over the fields.

AWIS letter writing campaign October/November 2004

Right from when I first worked as LACS Press Officer in April 1981 Richard Course, the Executive Director, impressed on me the value of writing letters to local papers as a campaigning weapon.

I wrote many over the years but in the autumn of 2004, with the hunting ban high on the political agenda, I made a maximum effort. I assembled a data base of nearly 470 addresses for local and regional papers and then used the resources of my AWIS to send out barrages of letters. Many of which were accompanied by suitable photographs.

My first letter, on October 4th, was about cub hunting:-

Dear Sir,

The long saga of the hunting debate would have ended sooner had the media been able to secure access to expose the cruelty behind the glamorous façade. An example now is cubhunting, the training of novice foxhounds to hunt foxcubs.

The leading hunting expert the late Duke of Beaufort highlighted the inherent cruelty in this pastime in his book '*Fox-Hunting*':-

"The object of cub-hunting is to educate both young hounds and fox-cubs.....it is not until he has been hunted that the fox draws fully on his resources of sagacity and cunning so that he is able to provide a really good run....It is essential that hounds should have their blood up and learn to be savage with their fox before he is killed."

If hounds being savage with fox cubs *before* killing them were televised, with multi-angle replays and slow motion as in the genuine sports of Rugby League or Cricket, blood sports would surely have been banned long ago.

The Burns Hunting Inquiry endeavoured to inform Parliament but even they were barred from seeing cubhunting. Their guided tours by the hunting fraternity lasted only from February to June 2000. With cubhunting staged from August until the end of October they missed observing the full measure of savagery. Nevertheless this Inquiry judged that foxhunting *"seriously compromises the welfare of the fox"*.

If only they, the media and public had seen what really happens!

Yours faithfully,

My second letter, sent October 12th, drew attention to the French origins of fox hunting:-

Dear Sir,

I see from the UKIP website that they are keen to declare support for hunting our wildlife with packs of dogs. If our Government has the wisdom to convert animal hunting to the humane alternative the Conservatives at their recent conference vowed to make time to repeal such legislation.

No surprise here your readers may think until one delves into the background of bloodsports. Aside from all the cruelty, mayhem and havoc inherent in hunting to support the pastime merely because apologists claim it to be part of our "tradition" is truly naïve. There is more to our true traditions than hunting scenes in pubs.

For all the polarity in the hunting debate both sides appear to agree that if Harold had won the battle of Hastings the pastime of tormenting wildlife with packs of hounds would never have arrived here. These games are a Norman French import, Euro-bloodsports if you like and it is surprising to see Eurosceptics rushing to support them.

Hunters are notoriously shy and keen to hide their cruelty but why hide their heritage? Why not wear the tricolour on their red coats? We have much to gain from our relationship with our continental neighbours but this cruelty is one import we could do without. Let's look beyond this odious pastime left here by a conqueror and value our true heritage, a cornerstone of which is surely revulsion for such bullying.

Yours faithfully,

Note for Editor: Claim that both sides agree that hunting is a foreign import is supported by the following quote from a 'country sports' book: "*It is an interesting thought that if Harold had won the battle of Hastings and no other Norman invasion had been successful, there would, most probably, be no hunting in the British Isles as we know it today. The Saxons and their kin did not use packs of hounds for hunting by scent; the hounds, the customs and the language of the chase came from France.*" From *Lurchers and Longdogs* by E.G. Walsh. The Boydell Press. 1984. Page 47, 2nd paragraph.

For my third letter sent October 18th I drew attention to the cruelty in stag hunting:-

Dear Sir,

Wherever cruelty is legalized in the UK we are all responsible so let us hope that our MPs will have the resolve to quickly end the pastime of hunting with dogs our native red deer in Devon and Somerset. We can manage wildlife without tormenting them in this cruel fashion that lasts hours. It brutalizes all involved particularly the youngsters encouraged to watch.

Government is guided on this issue by the Lord Burns Hunting Inquiry that was tasked with informing Parliament about the facts of hunting. They were specifically NOT asked to deliberate on whether hunting be banned, that was left to Parliament. The Inquiry team were given a guided tour of stag hunting by staghunters but never witnessed the worst cruelty.

They never saw a deer killed (some omission for an inquiry into deer killing) and missed the peculiar suffering inherent in Autumn stag hunting. The Inquiry visits were limited to February to June but Autumn stag hunting runs from August to the end of October. This timing imposes the cruelty of hunting stags throughout their rut, a "sport" worthy of the red card surely? Even with the little they did see the Burns team confirmed the barely startling fact that stag hunting seriously compromises the welfare of the deer. Having spent over 30 years exposing stag hunting and similar

pastimes I know that if they had just witnessed how the deer are killed they would have been far more forceful.
Yours faithfully,

My fourth letter, sent October 25th followed on from problems that Prince Harry had with the media:-

Dear Sir,
After Prince Harry has become the latest Royal to be hounded by the media pack might our Royal Princes now show some sympathy themselves for the quarry and refrain from hunting wildlife with hounds? They certainly should given that hunted animals suffer infinitely more. Also, whereas the media hunt Royalty for a living our Royals hunt animals for sheer fun. This fact is emphasized by the latest embarrassing leak from the hunting fraternity.
Earlier this year a secret circular letter from the Masters of Foxhounds Association complained of a shortage of foxes and berated landowners for doing too little to encourage foxes to breed. It described the need to supervise the safety of foxes and of litters of cubs. I don't recall foxhunters talking to the Burns Hunting Inquiry, or DEFRA in these terms.
This confirms that foxhunting is purely for pleasure. Moreover the first step in humane fox control is easy. Don't encourage them to breed. Without foxhunters raising the fox population artificially foxes will return to natural, wild levels and be healthier and cause minimal inconvenience.
Leaks like this have created a new bloodsport that arouses mirth not ire amongst animal welfarists. The "spy" chase within the bloodsports brigade is mole hunting. Given the severe embarrassment caused to those who swallowed the myth of foxhunting being "pest control" the attire for this hunt is doubtless red coats and faces to match.
Yours faithfully,

On November 1st I sent my fifth letter. It invited readers to consider the welfare of the hare:-

Dear Sir,
Whilst the hunting debate may appear complex it is in reality both simple and fundamental. At its core is how we view quarry such as the hare. Is the animal a mere toy for our amusement or a sentient being to be protected from unnecessary suffering?
Because most people, thankfully, oppose bullying it has always been difficult to recruit new hunters. In *The Art of Beagling*, his 1931 book, Captain Paget stressed that hunters should suppress any feelings of compassion:- *"In hunting, whether it be of fox or hare, every follower should identify himself with hounds' aims and give his entire sympathy to them. If he allows himself to sympathise with the hare, his pleasure in the chase will be neutralised and he might as well go home at once."*
Parliamentary problems for this pastime today come precisely because

505

most people DO sympathise with the hunted. With good reason as the Burns Hunting Inquiry confirmed that hare hunting *"seriously compromises the welfare of the hare"*. Hunting, unlike say punting, is far from being a harmless eccentricity.

Dynamic Government often legislates in the public interest to match changing times, e.g. car seat belts, ban on handguns, smoking in some public places, standing at football matches and protection for otters and badgers. When hare hunters are forced to switch to draghunting, the humane alternative, the only surprise surely is that reform has taken so long.

Yours faithfully,

For my sixth and last letter in that campaign I focussed on the savagery at the heart of hare coursing:-

Dear Sir,

We all have views about how our fellow creatures should be treated but it is in the nature of our democracy that the House of Commons decides the law. In the coming Hunting Bill debate I hope that due consideration is given to hare coursing, the nationwide pastime in which two dogs are unleashed against a lone hare.

MPs are guided by the Burns Hunting Inquiry set up NOT to decide whether hunting and hare coursing are cruel but rather to ascertain the facts to enable MPs to make up their minds. The Inquiry team looked at hare coursing and its humane alternative, drag coursing. Their findings deserve close study.

The postmortem reports on twelve of the many hares killed by coursing make grim reading. Five of the eight dead females were pregnant. One was described thus: *"This heavily pregnant female hare was in good condition. The large size of the foetuses and presence of milk in the mammary glands suggests she was close to giving birth."* Yet she was selected to run for her life and die, for sport.

Sadly some can read all that yet still love coursing hares but I suggest that for the vast majority to heap such torment on harmless creatures, just for fun, is no sport at all. Parliament has dithered far too long. Now surely elected MPs will reflect public opinion and force this cruel pastime to convert to the humane alternative.

Yours faithfully,

three in single wood 273
under construction 310
Art of Beagling, The 428, 505
Ashford Valley FH 248
Aston, Chris 136
Atherstone FH 350-353
Atkinson, Peter 14, 105,107, 160,
173-174, 219, 227
Auctioning Animal Flesh 147
Austin, Rebecca 254

B
Badger abuse
Builth Wells case (1990) 83-85
Four Oaks case (1988) 82
Marros case (1988) 81
Baily's Hunting Directory 301-
302, 306, 431, 436, 457-459
dangers of feeding foxes 306
Baker, Stanley (Coursing
Inspector) 158, 161
Ball, Christopher 357
Ball, Tony (Huntsman,
Cambridgeshire FH) 236, 356-
358
Balls, Bill (Coursing Inspector)
98, 102, 104, 160
Balls, John (Hare Coursing
Slip/Field Steward) 97, 175
Banks MP, Tony 234, 477, 482
Banwen Miners FH 293
Barfoot, Peter (Chairman New
Forest Buckhounds) 283
Barker, Capt. Fred (Master,
Quorn FH) 203
Barker, David (Deputy Clerk,
Bromley Magistrates) 52
Barrett-Jolley, Christopher 139
Barrie MSP, Scott 474
Barrington, Jim 8, 84, 86, 110,
158-159, 162, 174, 177-178, 200-
202, 205, 213, 216, 219, 222, 226,
228, 235, 238, 241-242, 248-250,
253-257, 277, 284-285, 296, 298,
305, 309, 319-320, 338, 341, 361-
364, 375, 377-378, 381, 389, 393,
437, 475, 483

changes his mind about fox
hunting 254-255
meeting with Lynn Sawyer 238
pretends to be a hunt supporter
177-178
resigns from the LACS 256
sacks two LACS staff 253
Barrington, Ursula 174, 219, 226,
257
Barter, Gwen 267-268
Batchelor, Douglas 268, 321,
327-329, 331, 381, 397, 475, 479,
485
Bateson, Professor Patrick 259,
386-388, 400
Beam and Da Silva 298-299
'Beauty and the Beast' campaign
234
Beeney, Tony (Huntsman,
Atherstone FH) 353
Beggs, John (Press Officer,
SEALL) 22, 28, 45
*Behavioural and Physiological
Effects of Culling Red Deer* 387
Bell, Paddy (Joint Hon. Sec.
Thurlow FH) 309, 410-416
Belvoir FH 260. 263, 334
Bennett, Jim (Joint Master,
Blencathra FH) 445
Bernard, Richard 77
Bettelheim, Eric 392
Bettinson, Rob 96-97, 99
Betts, Alan (Terrierman, Quorn
FH) 187-188, 190, 196-197, 199-
201, 204-205, 207
Betts, Henry 201
Bettws Hall Shooting Hatchery
348
Bicester with Whaddon Chase
FH 215, 228-229, 298, 305, 307,
339, 401, 404
Bidewell, Bruce 32, 35, 37, 39,
42, 55
Bingham, Bill 49
*Biohazard: The silent threat
from Biomedical Research and
the creation of AIDS* 49, 155

Hobson, Paul (RSPCA vet) 36
Hodges, Howard 219, 221-223, 228-229, 237, 243, 304-305, 437
Hoey MP, Kate 384, 391, 396, 483
Hogg MP, Douglas 396
Hole, Peter (Master, Colne Valley Beagles) 454
Holliday, John (Huntsman, Ledbury FH) 480
Home Office 29, 36, 38, 51, 112, 119, 121-124, 127-131, 353, 398, 460, 484
Home Secretary 46, 127-128, 130, 233, 397, 399, 497
Honey, Steve 241, 272
Honey, Val 241
Hope, Jonathan 327
Horan, Frankie 236, 261, 282-283, 292
Horse and Hound 90, 279, 290, 336-337, 384, 397, 448, 472
Horsebox stolen 246
Houghton of Sowerby, Lord 207
Hounds
  hound beaten by hunt staff 218
  hound killed on road 252
  killed on railway 285-287
  shot by kennelman 286-287
Hounds 303-304, 346-347, 447
House of Commons invaded by hunt supporters 480
Howard, Robin 475
Howarth MP, George 394, 398
HOWL 393, 437
HTV 222
Hudson, Pat 240
Hughes, Rob 321
Humane research funded 42
Humane Society of the United States (HSUS) 46, 112, 129
Hume, Mick 383
Humphrey, Gordon (Hon. Sec. Swaffham Coursing Club) 101-103, 105
Humphrey, Mervyn (Cockfighter) 267

Hunt disputes 349-350
Hunting Act (2004) 281, 337, 360, 372, 482-486
Hunting Declaration 477-479
Hunting Inquiry, Lord Burns 270, 279, 399-472
  bias in favour of hunting 400
  Coventry meeting 449-450
  findings 461-472
  Leeds meeting 454
  Oral examinations 449
  post mortem findings 469-472
  public hearings 475
  report published 461
  terms of reference 399-400
Hunting informants 108, 213, 281, 293-294, 299, 315, 335
Hunt monitoring 139, 234, 236, 265, 278, 363, 375-376
  hotline 250
  saves fox 259, 266
  saves hind 247-248
Hunt Monitors Conference 375
Hunt saboteurs 12-15, 86, 106-107, 109-110, 164, 166-168, 172, 216-217, 221, 223, 225-229, 231, 234-236, 238, 242-243, 251-252, 261-262, 264, 266, 268, 270, 282, 323, 328, 348, 350-361, 374, 389, 473-474
  grievously injured 14-15, 358-359
  killed at hunts 355-358
  save hare 268-269
Hunt seminar 175-177
Hunt stewards 228-232, 236, 238, 247, 359-362, 438, 473, 496
  costs 362
Hydestile Wildlife Hospital 135

I
Ibbott, John (Joint Master, Waveney Harriers) 427-430
ICI 22, 115
Illegal hare coursing 170, 247, 272-275, 278-280
Independent, The 207, 482